DOMESDAY BOOK

Essex

History from the Sources

DOMESDAY BOOK

A Survey of the Counties of England

LIBER DE WINTONIA

Compiled by direction of

KING WILLIAM I

Winchester
1086

DOMESDAY BOOK

general editor

JOHN MORRIS

32

Essex

edited by

Alexander Rumble

from a draft translation prepared by

Judy Plaister and Veronica Sankaran

PHILLIMORE
Chichester
1983

1983
Published by
PHILLIMORE & CO. LTD.
London and Chichester
Head Office: Shopwyke Hall,
Chichester, Sussex, England

ISBN 0 85033 483 7 (case)
ISBN 0 85033 484 5 (limp)

Printed in Great Britain by
Titus Wilson & Son Ltd.,
Kendal

ESSEX

Introduction

The Domesday Survey of Essex

Notes

Appendix

Index of Persons

Index of Places

Maps

Systems of Reference

Technical Terms

History from the Sources
General Editor: John Morris

The series aims to publish history written directly from the sources for all interested readers, both specialists and others. The first priority is to publish important texts which should be widely available, but are not.

DOMESDAY BOOK

The contents, with the folio on which each county begins, are:

1	Kent	I	1	20	Bedfordshire		209
2	Sussex		16	21	Northamptonshire		219
3	Surrey		30	22	Leicestershire		230
4	Hampshire		37	23	Warwickshire		238
5	Berkshire		56	24	Staffordshire		246
6	Wiltshire		64	25	Shropshire		252
7	Dorset		75	26	Cheshire		262
8	Somerset		86	27	Derbyshire		272
9	Devon		100	28	Nottinghamshire		280
10	Cornwall		120	29	Rutland		293
11	Middlesex		126	30	Yorkshire		298
12	Hertfordshire		132	31	Lincolnshire		336
13	Buckinghamshire		143		Claims, Yorkshire		373
14	Oxfordshire		154		Lincolnshire		375
15	Gloucestershire		162		Yorkshire, summary		379
16	Worcestershire		172				
17	Herefordshire		179	32	Essex	II	1
18	Cambridgeshire		189	33	Norfolk		109
19	Huntingdonshire		203	34	Suffolk		281

Supplementary volume (35) BOLDON BOOK

Domesday Book is termed *Liber de Wintonia* (The Book of Winchester) in column 332c

INTRODUCTION

The Domesday Survey

In 1066 Duke William of Normandy conquered England. He was crowned King, and most of the lands of the English nobility were soon granted to his followers. Domesday Book was compiled 20 years later. The Saxon Chronicle records that in 1085

> at Gloucester at midwinter ... the King had deep speech with his counsellors ... and sent men all over England to each shire ... to find out ... what or how much each landholder held ... in land and livestock, and what it was worth ... The returns were brought to him.[1]

William was thorough. One of his Counsellors reports that he also sent a second set of Commissioners 'to shires they did not know, where they were themselves unknown, to check their predecessors' survey, and report culprits to the King.'[2]

The information was collected at Winchester, corrected, abridged, chiefly by omission of livestock and the 1066 population, and fair-copied by one writer into a single volume, now known as Domesday Book Volume I, or DB. The task of abridgement and codification was not complete by the time work stopped at the death of King William. The remaining material, the commissioners' circuit returns for Norfolk, Suffolk and Essex, which there had not been time to reduce, was left unabridged, copied by several writers, in a second volume, smaller than the first, usually now referred to as Domesday Book Volume II or Little Domesday Book or LDB, which states that 'the Survey was made in 1086'. The surveys of Durham and Northumberland, and of several towns, including London, were not transcribed, and most of Cumberland and Westmorland, not yet in England, was not surveyed. The whole undertaking was completed at speed, in less than 12 months, though the fair-copying of the main volume may have taken a little longer. Both volumes are now preserved at the Public Record Office. Some versions of regional returns also survive. One of them, from Ely Abbey,[3] copies out the Commissioners' brief. They were to ask

> The name of the place. Who held it, before 1066, and now?
> How many *hides*?[4] How many ploughs, both those in lordship and the men's?
> How many villagers, cottagers and slaves, how many free men and Freemen?[5]
> How much woodland, meadow and pasture? How many mills and fishponds?
> How much has been added or taken away? What the total value was and is?
> How much each free man or Freeman had or has? All threefold, before 1066, when King William gave it, and now; and if more can be had than at present.

The Ely volume also describes the procedure. The Commissioners took evidence on oath 'from the Sheriff; from all the barons and their Frenchmen; and from the whole Hundred, the priests, the reeves and six villagers from each village'. It also names four Frenchmen and four Englishmen from each Hundred, who were sworn to verify the detail.

[1]Before he left England for the last time, late in 1086. [2]Robert Losinga, Bishop of Hereford 1079-1095 (see *E.H.R.* 22, 1907, 74). [3]*Inquisitio Eliensis*, first paragraph. [4]A land unit, reckoned as 120 acres. [5]*Quot Sochemani.*

The King wanted to know what he had, and who held it. The Commissioners therefore listed lands in dispute, for Domesday Book was not only a tax-assessment. To the King's grandson, Bishop Henry of Winchester, its purpose was that every 'man should know his right and not usurp another's'; and because it was the final authoritative register of rightful possession 'the natives called it Domesday Book, by analogy from the Day of Judgement'; that was why it was carefully arranged by Counties, and by landholders within Counties, 'numbered consecutively ... for easy reference'.[6]

Domesday Book describes Old English society under new management, in minute statistical detail. Foreign lords had taken over, but little else had yet changed. The chief landholders and those who held from them are named, and the rest of the population was counted. Most of them lived in villages, whose houses might be clustered together, or dispersed among their fields. Villages were grouped in administrative districts called Hundreds, which formed regions within Shires, or Counties, which survive today with minor boundary changes; the recent deformation of some ancient county identities is here disregarded, as are various short-lived modern changes. The local assemblies, though overshadowed by lords great and small, gave men a voice, which the Commissioners heeded. Very many holdings were described by the Norman term *manerium* (manor), greatly varied in size and structure, from tiny farmsteads to vast holdings; and many lords exercised their own jurisdiction and other rights, termed *soca*, whose meaning still eludes exact definition.

The Survey was unmatched in Europe for many centuries, the product of a sophisticated and experienced English administration, fully exploited by the Conqueror's commanding energy. But its unique assemblage of facts and figures has been hard to study, because the text has not been easily available, and abounds in technicalities. Investigation has therefore been chiefly confined to specialists; many questions cannot be tackled adequately without a cheap text and uniform translation available to a wider range of students, including local historians.

Previous Editions

The text has been printed once, in 1783, in an edition by Abraham Farley, probably of 1250 copies, at Government expense, said to have been £38,000; its preparation took 16 years. It was set in a specially designed type, here reproduced photographically, which was destroyed by fire in 1808. In 1811 and 1816 the Records Commissioners added an introduction, indices, and associated texts, edited by Sir Henry Ellis; and in 1861-1863 the Ordnance Survey issued zincograph facsimiles of the whole. Texts of individual counties have appeared since 1673, separate translations in the Victoria County Histories and elsewhere.

[6]*Dialogus de Scaccario* 1,16.

This Edition

Farley's text is used, because of its excellence, and because any worthy alternative would prove astronomically expensive. His text has been checked against the facsimile, and discrepancies observed have been verified against the manuscript, by the kindness of Miss Daphne Gifford of the Public Record Office. Farley's few errors are indicated in the notes.

The editor is responsible for the translation and lay-out. It aims at what the compiler would have written if his language had been modern English; though no translation can be exact, for even a simple word like 'free' nowadays means freedom from different restrictions. Bishop Henry emphasized that his grandfather preferred 'ordinary words'; the nearest ordinary modern English is therefore chosen whenever possible. Words that are now obsolete, or have changed their meaning, are avoided, but measurements have to be transliterated, since their extent is often unknown or arguable, and varied regionally. The terse inventory form of the original has been retained, as have the ambiguities of the Latin.

Modern English commands two main devices unknown to 11th century Latin, standardised punctuation and paragraphs; in the Latin, *ibi* ('there are') often does duty for a modern full stop, *et* ('and') for a comma or semi-colon. The entries normally answer the Commissioners' questions, arranged in five main groups, (i) the place and its holder, its hides, ploughs and lordship; (ii) people; (iii) resources; (iv) value; and (v) additional notes. The groups are usually given as separate paragraphs.

In both volumes of the MS, chapters were numbered 'for easy reference'. In the larger volume, sections within chapters are commonly marked, usually by initial capitals, often edged in red. In LDB (representing an earlier stage of the Inquiry's codification) sections are at first usually introduced by a paragraph mark, while red edging is reserved for chapter and Hundred headings; further on, however, the system of paragraphing the text becomes more haphazard and it is thus not always followed in the present translation. Owing to the less tabulated nature of the entries in LDB for Norfolk and Suffolk it is not possible to maintain throughout the translation of these two counties the sub-paragraphing that the late John Morris employed in the translation of other counties in the series. Maps, indices and an explanation of technical terms are also given. Later, it is hoped to publish analytical and explanatory volumes, and associated texts.

The editor is deeply indebted to the advice of many scholars, too numerous to name, and especially to the Public Record Office, and to the publisher's patience. The draft translations are the work of a team; they have been co-ordinated and corrected by the editor, and each has been checked by several people. It is therefore hoped that mistakes may be fewer than in versions published by single fallible individuals. But it would be Utopian to hope that the translation is altogether free from error; the editor would like to be informed of mistakes observed.

The maps are the work of Jim Hardy.

The preparation of this volume has been greatly assisted by a generous grant from the Leverhulme Trust Fund.

This support, originally given to the late Dr. J. R. Morris, has been kindly extended to his successors. At the time of Dr. Morris's death in June 1977, he had completed volumes 2, 3, 11, 12, 19, 23, 24. He had more or less finished the preparation of volumes 13, 14, 20, 28. These and subsequent volumes in the series were brought out under the supervision of John Dodgson and Alison Hawkins, who have endeavoured to follow, as far as possible, the editorial principles established by John Morris.

Conventions

★ refers to note on discrepancy between MS and Farley text

[ ] enclose words omitted in the MS

( ) enclose editorial explanation

Exsessa.

1 a

I . W. rex anglorum

★		Sca Trinitas de cantorbia.	XXV	Eudo dapifer
		Eps Londoniensis.	.XX.VI.	Rog de otburuilt.
		Feudu ejde episcopi.	XX.VII.	Hugo de montfort.
	V	Canonici Sci Pauli.	XX.VIII.	Hamo dapifer.
★	VI	Abbia de uuestmonastio.		Henric de ferrarijs. ★
	VII	Eps Dunelmensis.	XXX	Goisfrid de magnauilt.
	VIII.	Canonici de Waltham	XXX I	Comes de Ou.
	IX	Abbia de . . . ingis.	XXX .II.	Rob greno.
	X.	Abbia de eli.	XXX .III.	Rad baignard.
	XI	Abbia sci Edmundi.	XXX .IIII.	Ranulf piperell.
	XII	Canonici Sci Londoniensis Martini.	XXX V	Albic de uer
	XIII	Abbia de bello.	XXX .VI.	Petr ualoniensis.
	XIIII.	Scs Waleric.	XXX .VII.	Ranulf fr ilgeri
★	XV	Abbia S. Trinitatis de cadomo.	XXX .VIII.	Tihell brito.
	XVI	Abbia S. Stephani de eod.	XXX VIIII	Rog de ramis.
	XVII	Abbia Sci Audoeni.	XL	Johs fili Walerami.
	XVIII	Eps baiocensis.	.XLI.	Rob fili corbucionis. ★
★		Eps herefordensis.	XLII.	Galt diacon.
		Comes Eustachius.	XLIII	Rog bigot.
		Comes Alan.	XLIIII	Rob malet.
	XXII.	.W de uuarena.	XLV.	.W. de Scohies.
		Ricard fili comitis . G.	XLVI	Rog pictauensis.
★		Suen de Exsessa.	XLVII	Hugo de gurnai.

ESSEX

L [LIST OF LANDHOLDERS IN ESSEX] 1 a

1 William King of the English
[2] Holy Trinity, Canterbury
[3] The Bishop of London
[4] The same Bishop's Holding
5 The Canons of St. Paul's
6 Westminster Abbey
7 The Bishop of Durham
8 The Canons of Waltham
9 [Bark]ing Abbey
10 Ely Abbey
11 St. Edmund's Abbey
12 The Canons of St. Martin's, London
13 Battle Abbey
14 St. Valéry
15 Holy Trinity Abbey, Caen
16 St. Stephen's Abbey, also [Caen]
17 St. Ouen's Abbey
18 The Bishop of Bayeux
[19] The Bishop of Hereford
[20] Count Eustace
[21] Count Alan
22 William of Warenne
[23] Richard son of Count Gilbert
[24] Swein of Essex
25 Eudo the Steward
26 Roger of Auberville
27 Hugh de Montfort
28 Hamo the Steward
[29] Henry of Ferrers
30 Geoffrey de Mandeville
31 The Count of Eu
32 Robert Gernon
33 Ralph Baynard
34 Ranulf Peverel
35 Aubrey de Vere
36 Peter of Valognes
37 Ranulf brother of Ilger
38 Tihel the Breton
39 Roger of Raismes
40 John son of Waleran
41 Robert son of Corbucion
42 Walter the Deacon
43 Roger Bigot
44 Robert Malet
45 William of Écouis
46 Roger of Poitou
47 Hugh of Gournai

XLVIII .W. piperellꝰ.
XLIX Rađ de Limeseio.
.L. Rob̄ de todeneio.
.LI. Rađ de todeneio.
.LII. Walt̄ de doai.
.LIII. Matheuꝰ mauritaniensis.
.LIIII. Comitissa de Albamarla.
.LV. Judith comitissa.
.LVI. Frodo fr̄ abb̄is.
.LVII. Saisselinus.
.LVIII Gisleb̄ filiꝰ turoldi.
.LIX. Wills̄ Leuric.
.LX. Hugo de sc̄o q̄ntino.
.LXI. Edmundꝰ filiꝰ algoti
LXII. Roḡ Marescalcꝰ.
LXIII Adamꝰ filiꝰ durandi
LXIIII Goscelmꝰ Loremariꝰ.
LXV. Joh̄s nepos uualerami.
LXVI .W. diaconꝰ.
LXVII Galt̄ cocꝰ.
LXVIII Moduinꝰ.
LXIX. Ilbodo.
LXX. Haghebnꝰ.

LXXI Tedricꝰ point̄
.R. ds̄ salū dn̄as ★
LXXIII .G. filiꝰ Salomonis.
LXXIIII .W. f. costantini.
LXXV. An̄s cocus. ★
LXXVI Rob̄ . f. roscel
LXXVII. Rađ pinel
LXXVIII. Rob̄ . f. gob̄ti.
LXXVIIII Rainaldꝰ balistꝰ.
LXXX Gonduinꝰ
LXXXI. Otto auri fab̄
LXXXII. Gisleb̄ pb̄r
LXXXIII. Grimꝰ
LXXXIIII. Vlueua.
LXXXV. Eduuardꝰ.
LXXXVI. Tchillꝰ.
LXXXVII. Stanardꝰ
LXXXVIII. Goduinꝰ.
Liberi hōes regis. ★
Inuasiones.

48 William Peverel
49 Ralph of Limésy
50 Robert of Tosny
51 Ralph of Tosny
52 Walter of Douai
53 Matthew of Mortagne
54 The Countess of Aumâle
55 Countess Judith
56 Frodo the Abbot's brother
57 Sasselin
58 Gilbert son of Thorold
59 William Leofric
60 Hugh of St. Quentin
61 Edmund son of Algot
62 Roger Marshal
63 Adam son of Durand [Malzor]
64 Jocelyn Lorimer
65 John nephew of Waleran
66 William the Deacon
67 Walter Cook
68 Modwin
69 Ilbod
70 Hagebern
71 Theodoric Pointel
[72] Roger God-save-ladies
73 Gilbert son of Solomon
74 William son of Constantine
75 Ansger Cook
76 Robert son of Rozelin
77 Ralph Pinel
78 Robert son of Gobert
79 Reginald the Gunner
80 Gundwin
81 Otto the Goldsmith
82 Gilbert the priest
83 Grim [the Reeve]
84 Wulfeva [wife of Finn]
85 Edward [son of Swein]
86 Thorkell [the Reeve]
87 Stanhard
88 Godwin [the Deacon]
[89] The King's free men
[90] Annexations
[B Colchester]

1 b

.I EXSESSA. Terræ Regis. Hundret de berdestapla.

Benflet tenuit Harold tēpore regis Edduuardi pro uno mane
rio 7 ꝓ. VIII. hidis. M custodit hoc maneriū Ranulf fr ilgeri in
manu regis. Tc. XII. uillani. m̄. XXI. Sēp. VI. bor. Tc. III. serui. 7 m̄. III.
Tc. III. carrucæ in dn̄io: m̄. II. Tc. XI. carruce hominū m̄. V. 7 XXX.
acræ siluæ. Pastura. cxxx. ouib; Dimidiū molendinū. Tc appiatū
ē. VIII. lib. m̄ reddit. XII. s; tam̄ non ē appiatū n. VIII. lib. In hoc
manerio erat tc tēporis quidā lib homo de dimidia hid. qui m̄ effect ē
un de uillanis: 7 ē in supiori cōpoto. De hoc manerio data fuit cuidā
ecclæ de alio manerio: dimidia hida. tēpre regis. E. Postquā aut hoc
maneriū uenit in dn̄io regis: ablata fuit de eccla. 7 jac& iterū ī manerio;
In toto hoc hundret ht rex. XVIII. libos hōes tenentes. dimidiam
hidā 7 XLVIIII. acras. 7 pasturā. XX. ouib; Appiatū ē. X. sol.
In dn̄io supdicti manerij. ē. I. runcin. 7. I. asin. 7. XXX. porci. LXX. oues.

Dimidium Hundret de Witham.

Witham tenuit Harold tēpr reg. E. ꝓ. I. man. 7. ꝓ. V. hidis.
m̄ custodit hoc man. Petrus uicecomes in manu regis. Tc. II. car. in
dn̄io. m̄. III. Tc. XXI. uilli. m̄. XV. tc. IX. bor. m̄. X. Tc. VI. ser. m̄
. IX. Tc. XXIII. sochemani. 7 m̄ similit. Tc. XVIII. car hominū: M. VII.
7 hec pdicio fuit tēpr sueani. 7 baignardi uicecomitū. 7 p mortem
bestiarū. Silua. CL. porc. XXX. ac. pti. Pastura quæ tc reddebat
VI. den. m̄. XIIII. Sēp. I. molinū. Pdicti sochem. tenent. II. hid. 7. I.
uirg. hn̄tes. II. car. Tc int totū ual. X. lib. m̄. XX. sed uicecome[s]

2 a

int suas consuetudines 7 placita de dimidio hundret. recipit inde
XXXIIII. lib. 7. IIII. lib de gersuma. In dn̄io huj manerij recep Petrus
. IIII. 7. XXIIII. animalia. 7. CXXXVI. por. 7. CI. oues. Totū m̄ similit;

ESSEX

1 LANDS OF THE KING 1 b

Hundred of BARSTABLE

1 Harold held BENFLEET before 1066 as one manor, for 8 hides. Now Ranulf brother of Ilger has charge of this manor, in the King's hand.

Then 12 villagers, now 21; always 6 smallholders. Then 3 slaves, now 3.

Then 3 ploughs in lordship, now 2. Then 11 men's ploughs, now 5.

Woodland, 30 acres; pasture for 130 sheep; ½ mill.

Then it was assessed at £8; now it pays £12, but however it is only assessed at £8.

In this manor there was at that time a free man with ½ hide, who has now been made one of the villagers; he is in the above reckoning.

½ hide of this manor was given before 1066 to a church of another manor; but after this manor came into the King's lordship, it was taken from the church, and again lies in the (lands of the) manor.

In the whole of this Hundred the King has 18 free men, who hold ½ hide and 49 acres and pasture for 20 sheep. Assessment 10s.

In the lordship of the above manor 1 cob, 1 ass, 30 pigs, 70 sheep.

Half-Hundred of WITHAM

2 Harold held WITHAM before 1066 as 1 manor, for 5 hides. Now Peter the Sheriff has charge of this manor, in the King's hand. Then 2 ploughs in lordship, now 3.

Then 21 villagers, now 15; then 9 smallholders, now 10; then 6 slaves, now 9; then 23 Freemen, now the same. Then 18 men's ploughs, now 7; this loss was in the time of Sheriffs Swein and Baynard, and through the cattle plague.

Woodland, 150 pigs; meadow, 30 acres; pasture which then paid 6d, now 14d; always 1 mill.

The aforesaid Freemen, who have 2 ploughs, hold 2 hides and 1 virgate. Then, in total, value £10; now £20, but the Sheriff receives from it £34 between his customary dues and the pleas of 2 a
the Half-Hundred, and £4 in gifts.

In the lordship of this manor Peter acquired 4 ... , 24 cattle, 136 pigs and 101 sheep; now, wholly the same.

In hoc manerio adjacebant tēpr.r.e.xxxiiii.libi hōes.q̄ tc̄ reddebant.x. sol.de consuetudine.7.xi.đ; Ex ill ten& Ilbod.ii.de xlv.ac.7 ual .vi.sol.& reddt manerio suam consuetudinē. Tedric pointel.viii. de dimidia hid.7.xxii.ac.7.dim.reddentes consuet.7.ual.xx.sol. Ranulf piperell.x.de.ii.hid.7.xlv.ac.non reddentes consuetudin. 7 ual. xv.sol. Will fili grosse.v.de.i.hid.7 xv.ac.un tantū redd consuet.7 ual.iii.lib.7.xiii.sol. Rad baignard.vi.de dimid.hid 7.xxxv.ac.un redd consuetud.7 ual.xx.sol. Hamo dapifer.i. de dim hid.7 redd' cons' ual.xx.sol. Goscelm Loremari ht tr̄a uni 7 n̄ redd consuetudinē.scilic&.i.hid.quā calūpniant monachi scæ Adeldrede. de eli.7 hundret testatur eis de dimidia parte & de alia parte nich sciunt. Tc̄.ual.c.sol.m̄.lx.7 qdo Goscelm rec.c.sol. Int totū ual t.r.e.xiiii.lib.ii.sol.min m̄.xii.lib.7.ix.sol.

Dimidiu Hund de herlaua. Hadfeldā ten Harold.t.r.e. p.i.man.7.p.xx.hid.Tc̄.li.uillani.m̄.lx. Tc̄.xix.bor.m̄.xxx. Tc̄.xx.ser.m̄.xxii.Tc̄.ix.car in dnio.m̄.viii.7.iii.runc.7.xl. animalia.7 clxxxxv.por.7.cc.ou.vii.min. Tc̄.xl.car.hou m̄.xxxi.7.dim.hec pdicio tēpr ōmiū uicecomitū fuit 7 p mortem bestiarū. Silu.dccc.porc.cxx.ac.pti.Pastura que reddit.ix.multones

2 b

in manerio.7 xli.ac.de aratura. Ad ecclam huj manerij ptinebat .i.hid 7.xxx.ac.qđ Suen inde abstulit postquā pdidit uicecomitatū. & hec tr̄a reddebat consuetudinē huic manerio. Ptinebat & iā huic man .i.soc.de dim hid.t.r.e.q.G.de magna uilla inde abstulit.huic tr̄e adjac&.i.uill.de.i.ac.quā ten& Comes.E.7 ual.iiii.đ. Et.xxx.ac qs tenuit.i.fab.t.r.e. q̄ ppt Latrociniū infect fuit 7 ppósit reḡ addi dit illā tr̄a huic manerio; Et.xl.ac siluæ qs ten ppósit reḡ.E.7 Osmund angeuin de saisiuit ppositū regis 7 maneriū & de tr̄a 7 de silua.m̄.ten& Rob gernon. Dim hid quā ten.i.soc.t.r.e. Hoc &iā ten&.R.gernon.

In this manor before 1066 belonged 34 free men who then paid 10s as a customary due, and 11d. Ilbod holds 2 of them with 45 acres, value 6s; they pay their customary due to the manor. Theodoric Pointel (holds) 8, with ½ hide and 22½ acres, who pay the customary due; value 20s. Ranulf Peverel (holds) 10, with 2 hides and 45 acres, who do not pay the customary due; value 15s. William son of Gross (holds) 5, with 1 hide and 15 acres, 1 only pays the customary due; value £3 13s. Ralph Baynard (holds) 6, with ½ hide and 35 acres, 1 pays the customary due; value 20s. Hamo the Steward (holds) 1, with ½ hide, and he pays the customary due; value 20s. Jocelyn Lorimer has the land of one and does not pay the customary due, namely 1 hide which the monks of St. Etheldreda of Ely claim; the Hundred testifies for them for half [of it], but they know nothing of the other part; value then 100s, now 60s; when Jocelyn acquired it, 100s. In total, value before 1066 £14 less 2s; now £12 9s.

Half-Hundred of HARLOW

3 Harold held HATFIELD (Broad Oak) before 1066 as 1 manor, for 20 hides.

Then 51 villagers, now 60; then 19 smallholders, now 30; then 20 slaves, now 22.

Then 9 ploughs in lordship, now 8.

3 cobs, 40 cattle, 195 pigs and 200 sheep less 7.

Then 40 men's ploughs, now 31½; this loss was in the time of all of the sheriffs and through the cattle plague.

Woodland, 800 pigs; meadow, 120 acres; pasture which pays 9 wethers in the manor; 41 acres of ploughland. 2 b

To the church of this manor belonged 1 hide and 30 acres, which Swein took away after he lost the Sheriffdom; this land paid the customary due to this manor.

Before 1066, there also belonged to this manor 1 Freeman with ½ hide, whom G(eoffrey) de Mandeville took away; attached to this land is 1 villager with 1 acre which Count E(ustace) holds, value 4d.

Also 30 acres which a smith, who was put to death on account of robbery, held before 1066, and the King's reeve added that land to this manor; also 40 acres of woodland which King Edward's reeve held; of which land and woodland Osmund of Anjou dispossessed the King's reeve and the manor. Robert Gernon now holds it.

½ hide which 1 Freeman held before 1066; Robert Gernon also holds this.

P̄t hoc adjacebant huic manerio . t . r . e . III . bereuuitæ . Herefort . 7
Emuuella . 7 Hodesduna . jacentes in Herefort sira . quas ten& m̊ . Rađ
de Limeseio . Et . I . soc . de . XXX . ac . sep̄ ptinens huic manerio . 7 tc̄ . m̄ .
uał . XXXVI . lib . m̊ . LX . s; uicecomes inde recipit . LXXX . lib . 7 . c . soł
de gersuma . Et . III . berewitæ uał tc̄ . XII . lib . 7 . tr̄a sochemanorum .
XLV . soł . Silu . XL . porc . Postea recupauim dimid hid . quā tenuit
. I . soc haroldi . t . r . e . m̊ eā ten& Rađ de marcei . ad feudū hamonis
tc̄ uał . x . soł . m̊ . VII .

Hundret de beuentreu . Haueringas tenuit Harold
t . r . e . p . I . man . 7 . p . x . hiđ . Tc̄ XLI . uilł . m̊ . XL . Sep̄ . XLI . bor .
7 VI . ser . 7 . II . car in dn̄io . Tc̄ . XLI . car hom . m̊ . XL . Silu . D . porc .
. C . ac . p̄ti . m̊ . I . moł . 7 . II . runc . 7 . X . anim . 7 CLX . por . 7 . CC . 7
LXIX . ou . Huic manerio adjacebant . IIII . libi hoēs . de . IIII . hid . t . r . e .

3 a

reddentes consuetudinē . M̊ ten& Rob fili corbutionis . III . hid . 7 hug
de monteforti . q̊rtā hid . 7 n̄ reddider consuetudinē ex q̊ eas habuer . Et
adhuc idē Rob . ten& . IIII . hid . 7 . dim . q̊s tenebat . I . lib hō ad hoc man
t . r . e . Attinebat &iam . I . soc . de . XXX . ac . reddens consuetudinē .
7 m̊ ten& Johs fili galerami . & hoc man t . r . e . uał . XXXVI . lib . M̊ . XL .
& Petr uic inde recip̄ . LXXX . lib de . censu . 7 . X . lib de gersuma .
Huic maner ptinent . XX . ac . jacentes in Lochetuna q̊s tenuit . t . r . e .
p̄posit haroldi . m̊ ten& p̄posit regis . 7 uał . XL . đ . ★

Hunđ de dommawa . In Scelda . III . soc . de . XXXV . ac . 7 . uał
. III . soł . 7 . X . đ .

Hunđ de Witbrictesherna . In Lessenduna tenuit Aluuin
lib hō t . r . e . dim hid . 7 . XXX . ac . Post eā inuasit Tedric pointel .
7 . nc̄ h̄t rex . Sēp . dim car . 7 . uał . XV . soł . De eađ tra . ten& . I . uilł
. XXX . ac . ad Estolleiā . 7 . uał . V . soł . 7 . ali uilł . XV . ac . 7 . uał . III . soł . ★
Et . III . hōes tenent . dim . hid . 7 X . ac . 7 . dim . car . Tc̄ . uał . VIII . soł
m̊ . V . soł . 7 . IIII . đ .

Apart from this, 3 outliers were attached to this manor before 1066, HERTFORD, AMWELL and HODDESDON, which lie in Hertfordshire, (and) which Ralph of Limésy now holds.

Also 1 freeman with 30 acres who always belonged to this manor.

Value of the manor then £36; now £60, but the Sheriff receives £80 from it, and 100s in gifts. Also the value then of the 3 outliers £12, the Freemen's land 45s. Woodland, 40 pigs.

Later on we recovered ½ hide which 1 Freeman of Harold's held before 1066; now Ralph of Marcy holds it in Hamo's Holding.

Value then 10s; now 7[s].

Hundred of BECONTREE

4 Harold held HAVERING (atte-Bower) before 1066 as 1 manor, for 10 hides.

Then 41 villagers, now 40. Always 41 smallholders; 6 slaves; 2 ploughs in lordship. Then 41 men's ploughs, now 40. Woodland, 500 pigs; meadow, 100 acres; now 1 mill.

2 cobs, 10 cattle, 160 pigs and 269 sheep.

Attached to this manor before 1066 were 4 free men with 4 hides who paid the customary due. Now Robert son of Corbucion 3 a
holds 3 hides and Hugh de Montfort the fourth hide, and they have not paid the customary due since they have had them. And besides, Robert also holds 4½ hides which 1 free man held in this manor before 1066.

Also associated was 1 Freeman with 30 acres who paid the customary due; John son of Waleran now holds him.

Value of this manor before 1066 £36; now [£] 40; Peter the Sheriff receives from it £80 in dues and £10 in gifts.

To this manor belong 20 acres which lie in Loughton (and) which Harold's reeve held before 1066; now the King's reeve holds them. Value 40d.

Hundred of DUNMOW

5 In SHELLOW (Bowells) 3 Freemen with 35 acres. Value 3s 10d.

Hundred of 'WIBERTSHERNE'

6 In LATCHINGDON Alwin, a free man, held ½ hide and 30 acres before 1066. Later Theodoric Pointel annexed it. Now the King has it. Always ½ plough.

Value 15s.

Of this land, 1 villager holds 30 acres at 'STUDLY', value 5s; another villager (holds) 15 acres, value 3s. Also 3 men hold ½ hide and 10 acres and ½ plough; value then 8s; now 5s 4d.

In Lacenduna . I . lib hō Leuuin᷒ . xxx . ac̄ . t̄ . r̄ . ē
tc̄ dim̄ . car̄ . m̊ . n̄ . Tc̄ . uał . VIII . sol̄ . m̊ . v . 7 . IIII . đ . In Eađ . VIII . libi
hōes t̄ . r̄ . ē . m̊ . IIII . de . LII . ac̄ . Tc̄ . uał . VIII . sol̄ . m̊ IIII . sol̄ 7 . IIII . đ .
In Rodingis ten& Golstan᷒ soc̄ reg̅ Willi . I . hid̄ . 7 nq̄ inde seruitiū
ł consuet̄ . reddidit . & idō dedit uadē . In q̊ hida . ē . I . car̄ in dn̄io
7 . I . bor . 7 III . ser̄ . Silu̅ . x . por . x . ac̄ . p̄ti . Tc̄ uał . xx . sol̄ . m̊ . xxx .

3 b

Hunđ de Odelesforda Cestrefordā tenuit Comes Edgar᷒ . t̄ . r̄ . ē
p . I . M̄ . 7 . p . x . hid̄ . m̊ picot᷒ uicecomes in manu regis . Sēp . IIII . car̄ ī dn̄io.
Tc̄ . XVIII . car̄ hom̄ . P̄ 7 m̊ . XIIII . Sēp . XXIIII . uilli . 7 . XIII . bor . 7 . VI . ser̄.
Silu̅ . M̄ . porc̄ . xv . ac̄ p̄ti . sēp . II . mol̄ . Jac& huic manerio . I . hid̄ . 7 . đ
que ē in cantebruge sira . sēp . VII . uill̄ . 7 . III . bor . 7 . mol̄ . 7 . III . car̄
hom̄ . hoc totū uał . tc̄ XXIIII . lib P̄ 7 m̊ . xxx . In dn̄io huj᷒ manerii . II . r̄.
st̄ . 7 VII . an̄ . 7 . LXI . por . 7 . LXXXI . ou̅ . 7 LXXXVII . capræ . Huic man̄
adjacebat . t̄ . r̄ . ē . I . hid̄ . 7 . dim̄ . qđ ten& harduin᷒ de scalarijs . s; hunđ
nesc̄ q̊m̊ . Dim̄ hid̄ . erat de dn̄io in q̊ manebat . I . hō . 7 . Aliā hidā tene
bat . I . soc̄ . q̄ reddebat socā in manerio reg̅ Et picot᷒ ten& dim̄ hid̄
q ten̄ . I . soc̄ . t̄ . r̄ . ē . In his duab; hid̄ . II . car̄ . 7 uał . XL . sol̄.

Becangrā ten Horolf᷒ . t̄ . r̄ . ē . M̄ tascelin᷒ pb̄r in elemosina regis.
p . I . hid̄ . sēp . I . car̄ . 7 . II . bor . 7 . II . ser̄ . Silu̅ . XL . por . v . ac̄ . p̄ti . 7 . I . mol̄.
tc̄ 7 p᷒ uał . xx . sol̄ . m̊ . xxx . ★

7 In LATCHINGDON 1 free man, Leofwin, (held) 30 acres before 1066. Then ½ plough, now none.
Value then 8s; now 5[s] 4d.
In the same (Latchingdon) 8 free men before 1066, now 4, with 52 acres.
Value then 8s; now 4s 4d.

8 In (White) RODING Goldstan, a Freeman of King William's, holds 1 hide; he has never paid service or the customary due for it, and hence he has given a pledge. In this hide, 1 plough in lordship;
1 smallholder; 3 slaves.
Woodland, 10 pigs; meadow, 10 acres.
Value then 20s; now 30[s].

Hundred of UTTLESFORD 3 b

9 Earl 'Edgar' held (Great) CHESTERFORD before 1066 as 1 manor, for 10 hides. Now Picot the Sheriff (holds it), in the King's hand. Always 4 ploughs in lordship. Then 18 men's ploughs; later and now 14.
Always 24 villagers; 13 smallholders; 6 slaves.
Woodland, 1000 pigs; meadow, 15 acres; always 2 mills.
(In the lands of) this manor lie 1½ hides which are in Cambridgeshire.
Always 7 villagers; 3 smallholders; a mill; 3 men's ploughs.
Value of the whole then £24; later and now [£] 30.
In the lordship of this manor are 2 cobs, 7 cattle, 61 pigs, 81 sheep and 87 goats.
Attached to this manor before 1066 were 1½ hides which Hardwin of Scales holds, but the Hundred does not know how; ½ hide was of lordship (land) in which 1 man dwelt; 1 Freeman who paid suit in the King's manor held the other hide. Also Picot holds ½ hide which 1 Freeman held before 1066. In these 2 hides, 2 ploughs.
Value 40s.

10 Horwulf held BIRCHANGER before 1066. Now Tascelin the priest (holds it) in the King's alms, for 1 hide. Always 1 plough;
2 smallholders; 2 slaves.
Woodland, 40 pigs; meadow, 5 acres; 1 mill.
Value then and later 20s; now 30[s].

Hund de Hidingeforda.

Celdefordā tenuit Comes Algar t.r.e. p.i. man. 7.v. hid. 7.xxx. ac. post ea tenuit regina. M Otto aurifab ad censū in manu reg. Sep. iii. car in dnio. Tc. vi. car. hom. P 7 m. v. Tc 7 p. xiii. uilt. m. xii. sep. vi. bor. Tc. xii. ser. p 7 m. viii. Silu. c. por. xx. ac. ptj. i. mol. Tc uat xii. lib. Post 7 m. xxii. In dnio. iiii. runc. Tc lxv. an. m. lvi. 7. lii. ou. 7. cxviii. por. m. lxxx. 7. xl. cap. De hoc manerio dest .xxx. ac siluæ qs regina dedit. Ricardo filio comitis gislebti. Huic man jacebat dim hid de soca t.r.e. q ten& Galt fili guibtj.

4 a

Phincinghefeldā ten Idē Algar. t.r.e. 7 post regina M idē. Otto ad censū p. ii. hid. 7. dim. sep. iii. car in dnio. 7. v. car. hom. 7. x. uilt. 7. ix. bor. Tc. vi. ser. P. iiii. m. ii. Silu. lx. por. xvi. ac. pti. 7. i. mol. 7. xxv. an. 7. ii. runc. Tc. lxiii. por. m. lxi. 7. c. ou. Tc. uat. ix. lib. P 7 m. xviii.

Westrefeldā ten Idē Algar t.r.e. p. m. 7. p. ii. hid. xv. ac: min m Picot p totidē in manu regis. Tc. iiii. car. in dnio. P. ii. m. iii. Tc 7 p. xv. car hominū. m. x. Tc 7 p xxiiii. uilt. m. xxviii. Tc. vii. por. P. xv. M xxiiii. Tc. vii. ser. P. xiiii. M. vii. Tc silu. dccc. por. P 7 m. d. 7 xxiiii. ac. pti. Tc. 7 p. i. mol. m. ii. Tc. xvii. an. m. x. 7. c. ou. Tc. .c. por. m. xl. Tc. lxi. cap. m. xl. Huic man jacebant. t.r.e. vi. soc. m viii. tenentes. i. hid. 7. xiiii. ac. sep. ii. car. 7. i. bor. 7. v. ac. pti. Tc uat. xx. lib. P 7 m. xxviii. Huic man. adjac. t.r.e. xxx. ac. træ. qs ten. i. prb. in elemosina 7 reddebat soca. 7 viii. ac 7 dim ptinentes ad aliā ecclam. has. ii. tras ten& Gislebt fili garini. 7 uat. x. sol | Adptinebant ad huc huic. m. vii. ac. 7. d. qs m ten& comes Alam. Et. xlv. ac. de dnio qs ten& Suen ad feudū Ricardi. f. comitis. g. 7 uat. viii. sol. ★

Hundred of HINCKFORD

11 Earl Algar held SHALFORD before 1066 as 1 manor, for 5 hides and 30 acres. Later on the Queen held it. Now Otto the Goldsmith (holds it) as dues in the King's hand. Always 3 ploughs in lordship. Then 6 men's ploughs, later and now 5.

Then and later 13 villagers, now 12; always 6 smallholders. Then 12 slaves, later and now 8.

Woodland, 100 pigs; meadow, 20 acres; 1 mill.

Value then £12; later and now [£] 22.

In lordship 4 cobs; then 65 cattle, now 56; 52 sheep; then 118 pigs, now 80; 40 goats.

From this manor, 30 acres of woodland are missing which the Queen gave to Richard son of Count Gilbert.

(In the lands of) this manor lay ½ hide with jurisdiction before 1066, which Walter son of Gilbert holds.

12 (Earl) Algar also held FINCHINGFIELD before 1066. Later the Queen 4 a
(held it). Now Otto (the Goldsmith) also (holds it) as dues, for 2½ hides. Always 3 ploughs in lordship; 5 men's ploughs;

10 villagers; 9 smallholders. Then 6 slaves, later 4, now 2.

Woodland, 60 pigs; meadow, 16 acres; 1 mill.

25 cattle; 2 cobs; then 63 pigs, now 61; 100 sheep.

Value then £9; later and now [£] 18.

13 (Earl) Algar also held WETHERSFIELD before 1066 as a manor, for 2 hides less 15 acres. Now Picot (holds it) in the King's hand for as much. Then 4 ploughs in lordship, later 2, now 3. Then and later 15 men's ploughs, now 10.

Then and later 24 villagers, now 28; then 7 pigs, later 15, now 24; then 7 slaves, later 14, now 7.

Woodland, then 800 pigs, later and now 500; meadow, 24 acres; then and later 1 mill, now 2.

Then 17 cattle, now 10; 100 sheep; then 100 pigs, now 40; then 61 goats, now 40.

Attached to this manor before 1066 were 6 Freemen, now 8, who hold 1 hide and 14 acres. Always 2 ploughs; 1 smallholder.

Meadow, 5 acres.

Value then £20; later and now [£] 28.

Attached to this manor before 1066 were 30 acres of land which 1 priest held as alms and paid suit; and 8½ acres belonging to another church; these 2 lands Gilbert son of Warin holds. Value 10s.

There belonged to this manor 7½ acres, which Count Alan now holds.

Also 45 acres of the lordship which Swein holds as a holding of Richard son of Count G(ilbert). Value 8s.

In Isto hund hт rex . xviii . soc . tenent . xxvi . ac . 7 . dim . 7 nquā reddider consuetudinē pт seruiciū regis.

Hund de Witbrictesherna . Benflet ten Leuard lib hō . t . r . e p tedric pointel . p . i . hid . Sēp . i . bor . Tc . i . car . m nulla . Pastura xl . ouib Tc . i . piscina . m nulla . 7 . uat . xx . sol.

4 b

Steplam ten Aluric lib hō . t . r . e . p . i . hid . Tc . i . bor . m null . Tc . i . car . m . dim . Tc . uat . xx . sol . m . xvi . In Vluuinescherhā . iiii . libi hōes . de . i . hid . vi . ac . min . t . r . e . M n st ; Tc uat . xx . sol . m . x . hanc trā calumpniat . Tedric pointel p escangio . Franci hōes tenent . li . ac . 7 . n st in firma reg . Tc uat . viii . sol . m . v . hanc trā ten& famul reg 7 n reddit geldū . In Melduna . ii . libi hōes de . x . ac . Ex ill . hт Ranulf piperell . v . ac . 7 . hugo de monte forti . v . ac . Tc . uat . x . đ . m . xii . Duo libi hōes . ten . t . r . e . vi . ac . 7 . jacuer in hund reg 7 nc hт baignard.

In Hund de Rochesfort ten& sēp Grim pposit . x . ac . 7 . uat . xvi . đ.

Hund de Lassendene . Stanewegā ten harold . t . r . e p . i . m . 7 . p . v . hid . 7 . dim . M hт rex p totidē . Tc . xii . uill . P 7 . m . ix . tc . vi . bor . p 7 m . ix . Sēp . vi . ser . 7 . iii . car in dnio . Tc . xiii . car hom . P 7 m . ii . 7 . dim . sēp . i . mol . Silu . c . porc . xii . ac . pti . 7 . xx . an . 7 lix . por . 7 . cclx . ou . 7 . xi . runc . Est &iā . i . bereuuita de . ii . hid . 7 . dim 7 . xiii . ac . que uocat . Legra 7 jac& in isto manerio Sēp . vii . uill . 7 . ii . bor . 7 . iiii . ser . 7 . ii . car . in dnio . Tc . ii . car . hom P . 7 m . i . 7 . đ.

13a In this Hundred the King has 18 Freemen who hold 26½ acres and they have never paid the customary due apart from the King's service.

Hundred of 'WIBERTSHERNE'

14 Leofhard, a free man, held BENFLEET before 1066; later Theodoric Pointel (held it) for 1 hide.
Always 1 smallholder.
Then 1 plough, now none.
Pasture for 40 sheep; then 1 fishery, now none.
Value 20s.

15 Aelfric, a free man, held STEEPLE before 1066, for 1 hide. 4 b
Then 1 smallholder, now none.
Then 1 plough, now ½.
Value then 20s; now 16[s].

16 In *ULUUINESCHERHAM,* 4 free men with 1 hide less 6 acres before 1066. Now they are not there.
Value then 20s; now 10[s].
Theodoric Pointel claims this land by exchange.

16a (Certain) freemen hold 51 acres and are not in the King's revenue.
Value then 8s; now 5[s].
A servant of the King holds this land and does not pay tax.

17 In MALDON 2 free men with 10 acres; of these, Ranulf Peverel has 5 acres and Hugh de Montfort 5 acres.
Value then 10d; now 12[d].

17a 2 free men held 6 acres before 1066 and lay in the King's Hundred; now Baynard has them.

In the Hundred of ROCHFORD

18 Grim the reeve has always held 10 acres.
Value 16d.

Hundred of LEXDEN

19 Harold held STANWAY before 1066 as 1 manor, for 5½ hides. Now the King has it for as much.
Then 12 villagers, later and now 9; then 6 smallholders, later and now 9.
Always 6 slaves; 3 ploughs in lordship. Then 13 men's ploughs, later and now 2½.
Always 1 mill. Woodland, 100 pigs; meadow, 12 acres.
20 cattle, 59 pigs, 260 sheep and 11 cobs.
There is also 1 outlier of 2½ hides and 13 acres which is called LAYER and lies in (the lands of) this manor.
Always 7 villagers; 2 smallholders; 4 slaves;
2 ploughs in lordship. Then 2 men's ploughs, later and now 1½.

Adhuc ptin& . I . berewita que uocat Leffendena . de . IIII . hid . Tc. VI . uill . P 7 . m . V . Tc . X . bor . p 7 m . XII . Tc . IIII . ser . P 7 m . V . sep . II . car . in dnio . Tc . IIII . car hom p 7 m . III . Silu . C . porc . XVIII . ac . pti . m . II . mol Et . XVI . soc . de . II . hid . 7 . XXXVI . ac . sep . II . car 7 . dim . Tc ual totu . XXII . lib . M petr inde recip . XXXIII . lib . 7

5 a

. III . lib de gsuma . De hoc manerio tulit Reimund girald . I . uill . de dim hid . 7 reddebat consuetudine . Sep ibi e dim . car . 7 ual . X . sol . hanc tra tenuit Normann 7 reddidit consuet . Sed Raimund . abstulit . 7 . Rog similit . Et Rog pictau . accep . I . uillm tenente . I . ac . Et Ingelric abstulit . I . femina bricteua tenente . XVIII . ac . & reddebat unoqq anno huic maner . XXXII . nomos.

Hund de angre. Vlfelmestuna tenuit Herold . p man . 7 p . III . hid . 7 . XL . ac . M . Rex . W . Sep . IIII . uill . tc . II . bor . m . VI . Tc . int hoes . I . car . 7 m similit . Silu . LX . poc . IIII . ac . pti . Tc . ual . XX . sol . m . XL . Quida ho libe tenuit . XX . ac . t . r . e . tc . dim . car . m . nich . 7 . ual . III . Iste sep fuit dnic sed m e in manu uicecomitis ad firma regis.

Hund de cesfeworda. Phingheria ht rex . q ten Herold . t . r . e sep . I . car . in dnio . 7 VI . uill . 7 . VIII . bor hnt . II . car . I dnio . XXIIII . anim Silu . CC . porc . III . ac pti . Tc . uat . IIII . lib . m . XIIII . In Wochenduna ht . Rex . I . soc . de . XXV . ac . tc . uat . XXXII . d . m . LII .

Besides, there belongs 1 outlier which is called LEXDEN, of 4 hides.

Then 6 villagers, later and now 5; then 10 smallholders, later and now 12; then 4 slaves, later and now 5.

Always 2 ploughs in lordship. Then 4 men's ploughs, later and now 3.

Woodland, 100 pigs; meadow, 18 acres; now 2 mills.

Also 16 Freemen with 2 hides and 36 acres. Always 2½ ploughs.

Value of the whole, then £22. Now Peter receives from it £33, and £3 in gifts. 5 a

From this manor Raymond Gerald took 1 villager with ½ a hide and he paid a customary due. Always ½ plough there. Value 10s. Norman held this land and paid a customary due; but Raymond took it away and Roger likewise.

Also Roger of Poitou took 1 villager who held 1 acre.

Also Engelric took away 1 woman, Bricteva, who held 18 acres and paid 32 pennies each year to this manor.

Hundred of ONGAR

20 Harold held WOOLSTON (Hall) as a manor, for 3 hides and 40 acres. Now King William (holds it).

Always 4 villagers. Then 2 smallholders, now 6.

Then among the men 1 plough, now the same.

Woodland, 60 pigs; meadow, 4 acres.

Value then 20s; now 40[s].

A man held 20 acres freely before 1066. Then ½ plough, now nothing.

Value 3[s].

He was always in lordship but is now in the Sheriff's hand in the King's revenue.

Hundred of CHAFFORD

21 The King has FINGRITH (Hall), which Harold held before 1066.

Always 1 plough in lordship;

6 villagers and 8 smallholders have 2 ploughs.

In lordship 24 cattle. Woodland, 1000 pigs; meadow, 3 acres.

Value then £4; now [£] 14.

[Hundred of CHAFFORD]

21a In OCKENDON the King has 1 Freeman with 25 acres.

Value then 32d; now 52[d].

Gingā ten Friebt t.r.e.p.m.7 p.III.hid.7.dim.sēp.VI.uilt.
7.III.bor. Tc.II.ser.m.I.sēp.II.car in dnio.7.I.car hou.IIII.ac
pti; 7 LXXXVIII.por. App.in Phingheriā. Ciltendis ten.Her.P regina M uicec de
Surreia.p.I.hid.7.d.Tc.III.uilt.m.V.Tc.III.bor.M.IIII.I.ser.Tc.I.c.i dio.m.I.7.d. Tc. II c.hou.
p' 7 m. I. Silu'. c. por. past'. lx. ou'. tc. III. lib. m. IIII.
Hund de Celmeresfort. Writelam ten Herold p man.
7 p XVI. hid. t.r.e.M.rex.W.p.XIIII.hid. Tc.c.uilt.III.min
Post 7 m LXXIII. Tc.XXXVI.bor.P 7 m.LX. Tc.XXIIII.ser.p 7 m
XVIII.

5 b
Tc.XII.car in dnio.P 7 m.IX. Tc int hoes.LXIIII.car.P 7 m XLV.
tc.silu.M D por.m. M CC.LXXX.ac.pti. Tc.I.mol.m.II.sēp.IX.run.
7.V.pulli; 7 XL.an.7.CCCXVIII.ou.7.CLXXII.poc. Tc reddidit
hoc maneriū.X.noctes de firma.7.X.lib.m reddit.C.lib; ad pond.
7.C.sol.de gersuma. Ingelric poccupauit.II.hid.de tra ppositi
haroldi reddentis omnē consuet huic manerio.scil.XII.lib. postq
rex uenit in angliā; & m ten& comes.E.idō qd antecessor ej inde
fuit saisit.7 in tēpr haroldi fuit.I.porcari reddens consuet huic
manerio sedens.sup.I.uirg træ.7.XV.ac.s; Rob grino pq rex uenit
accepit eum de manerio.& fec foristariū de silua reg.7.I.hid dedit
Harold cuidā pro suo.s; hundret nescit si dedit libæ l in elemosina.
quā m ten&.R.epc Herefordensis.7 dim hid quā libe tenuit.I.soc.
reddens socā in manerio.7 tam cū tra sua poss& ire q uell&.hunc Comes.E.
adjunxit sue træ. In hoc man sēp.jacent.II.soc.de dim.hid.7.X.ac.
hntes sēp.dim.car.IIII.ac.pti. Appтiatū ē in Supdictis.C.lib.

[Hundred of CHELMSFORD]

22 Fridebert held MARGARETTING before 1066 as a manor, for 3½ hides.

Always 6 villagers; 3 smallholders. Then 2 slaves, now 1.

Always 2 ploughs in lordship; 1 men's plough.

Meadow, 4 acres. 88 pigs.

It is assessed in Fingrith (Hall).

[Hundred of CHAFFORD]

23 Harold held CHILDERDITCH. Later the Queen (held it). Now the Sheriff of Surrey (holds it) for 1½ hides.

Then 3 villagers, now 5; then 3 smallholders, now 4; 1 slave.

Then 1 plough in lordship, now 1½. Then 2 men's ploughs, later and now 1.

Woodland, 100 pigs; pasture, 60 sheep.

[Value] then £3; now [£] 4.

Hundred of CHELMSFORD

24 Harold held WRITTLE before 1066 as a manor, for 16 hides. Now King William (holds it) for 14 hides.

Then 100 villagers less 3, later and now 73; then 36 smallholders, later and now 60; then 24 slaves, later and now 18.

Then 12 ploughs in lordship, later and now 9. Then among the men 64 ploughs, later and now 45. 5 b

Woodland, then 1500 pigs, now 1200; meadow, 80 acres; then 1 mill, now 2.

Always 9 cobs, 5 foals, 40 cattle, 318 sheep and 172 pigs.

Then this manor paid 10 nights' provisions and £10; now it pays £100 by weight and 100s in gifts.

After the King came to England, Engelric misappropriated 2 hides of the land of Harold's reeve who paid all customary dues to this manor, namely £12; now Count E(ustace) holds it, since his predecessor was in possession of it.

In Harold's time there was 1 pigman who paid a customary due to this manor (and) who resided on 1 virgate of land and 15 acres, but, after the King came, Robert Gernon took him from the manor and made him a Forester of the King's woodland.

Harold gave 1 hide to a priest of his, but the Hundred does not know if he gave it free or in alms; now R(obert) Bishop of Hereford holds it.

Also ½ hide which 1 Freeman held freely, who paid suit in the manor although he could go whither he would with his land; Count Eustace added this man to his land.

In this manor, there have always been 2 Freemen with ½ hide and 10 acres who have always had ½ plough.

Meadow, 4 acres.

It is assessed in the above £100.

In Wiritela . ten& Idē epc . II . hid . 7 xx . ac . q̄rū . I . fuit t . r . e . in eccła
& alia in feudo reḡ . Sēp . III . uilł . 7 . I . p̄br . Tc . II . bor . m̄ . VIII . Tc . II . ser.
Sēp . I . car in dn̄io . 7 . II . car . hom . Silu . c . por . VIII . ac . p̄ti . 7 . uał . L . sol.
Dimidiū Hunđ de melduna . In Malduna h̄t rex . I . domū . 7 . past
ad . c . ou . 7 . I . soc de . XLIX . ac . hn̄s . I . bor . 7 . t . r . e . I . car . m̄ . dim . Tc uał
x . sol . m̄ . v . In Eađ h̄t rex . CLXXX . domos q̄s tenent burgenses . 7 .
. XVIII . mansuras uastatas . q̄z . xv . tenent . dim . hid . 7 . XXI . ac . 7 alij

6 a
hoēs n̄ tenent ampli q domos suas in burgo . 7 int eos h̄nt . XII . runc.
7 . CXL . an . 7 . CIII . por . 7 . CCCXXXVI . ou . De halla reḡ sēp exeunt . VI.
sol . 7 . VIII . đ . 7 de tr̄a Sueni . IIII . sol . 7 de . II . domib Eudonis . dap . XVI . đ
q̄s n̄ habuit rex pq uenit in hanc tr̄a . De p̄dicto sochemano habuit . Ra .
piperell . consuet . in uno q̄q anno p . III . sol . s; in tēpr . r . e . n̄ habuit ej
antec n tantū m̄ c̄mđoem . 7 tēpr . r . e . totū simul reddidit . XIII . lib.
7 . II . sol . 7 qdo petr rec . XXIIII . lib . m̄ . XVI . lib ad pond.
. H . de Tendering & . Brictricesceiā ten . Herold p . m̄ . 7 . p . x . hid. ★
m̄ . r . W . Sēp . XXIIII . uilł . Tc . x . bor . p . XI . m̄ . XVI . 7 . x . bor . n̄ tenentes
tr̄a . Tc . IIII . ser . m̄ . v . Tc . III . car . in dn̄io . P 7 m̄ . II . Tc . XVI . car . homin
post . 7 m̄ . XI . silu . c . por . m̄ . I . moł . Past . DC . ouib sēp . XVI . an . 7 . v . r.
7 . CLXVI . ou . 7 LXII . por . Tc int brictricesceiā 7 herchesteda reddider
. II . noct . de firma . 7 qn . p . rec . XXV . lib . m̄ . XXII . lib . S; ista bereuuit ★
jac& in Sudfolc . In dn̄io . IIII . an . 7 . v . porc.
Lalefordā ten Har . p . I . m̄ . 7 . p . x . hid . m̄ . rex W . p totidē . Sēp . xv.
uilł . 7 XXIIII . bor . Tc . VII . ser . m̄ . VI . sēp . IIII . car in dn̄io . Tc . int hōes
xx . car . 7 qdo baignard . tenuit . XVI . car . s; qn . P . rec . IX . 7 m̄ similit ★

In Writtle the Bishop also holds 2 hides and 20 acres of which 1 (hide) was in the (lands of the) Church before 1066 and the other was in the King's Holding.
Always 3 villagers; 1 priest. Then 2 smallholders, now 8; then 2 slaves.
Always 1 plough in lordship; 2 men's ploughs.
Woodland, 100 pigs; meadow, 8 acres.
Value 50s.

Half-Hundred of MALDON

25 In MALDON the King has 1 house and pasture for 100 sheep.
1 Freeman with 49 acres who has 1 smallholder. Before 1066, 1 plough; now ½.
Value then 10s; now 5[s].
In the same (Maldon) the King has 180 houses which burgesses hold and 18 derelict dwellings; 15 of them hold ½ hide and 21 acres, and the other men do not hold more than their houses in 6 a
the Borough; between them they have 12 cobs, 140 cattle, 103 pigs and 336 sheep.
From the King's hall have always come 6s 8d, and from Swein's land 4s; and from 2 of Eudo the Steward's houses 16d, which the King has not had since he came to this land.
From the aforesaid Freeman, Ranulf Peverel had a customary due each year for 3s; but before 1066 his predecessor had nothing except for patronage.
Before 1066 the whole together paid £13 2s; when Peter acquired it £24; now £16 by weight.

Hundred of TENDRING

26 Harold held BRIGHTLINGSEA as a manor, for 10 hides. Now King William (holds it).
Always 24 villagers. Then 10 smallholders, later 11, now 16; and 10 smallholders who do not hold land; then 4 slaves, now 5.
Then 3 ploughs in lordship, later and now 2. Then 16 men's ploughs, later and now 11.
Woodland, 100 pigs; now 1 mill; pasture for 600 sheep.
Always 16 cattle, 5 cobs, 166 sheep and 62 pigs.
Then Brightlingsea and Harkstead between them paid 2 nights' provisions; when P(eter) acquired (them) £25; now £22. However, the outlier lies in Suffolk.
In lordship 4 cattle and 5 pigs.

27 Harold held LAWFORD as 1 manor, for 10 hides. Now King William (holds it) for as much.
Always 15 villagers; 24 smallholders. Then 7 slaves, now 6.
Always 4 ploughs in lordship. Then among the men 20 ploughs; when Baynard held (it), 16 ploughs; but when Peter acquired (it), 9, and now the same.

Silua . xv . por . xii . ac . p̄ti . tc̄ . i . mol . m̄ . ii . past . ccc . ou . m̄ . i . salina. ★
Tc̄ reddidit . ii . noct de firma . 7 qn̄ baign . ten . xiiii . lib . m̄ . xi.
Huic manerio jacuer̄ . xvii . soc . t . r . e . de . i . hid . reddentes omnē consu.
7 pq rex uenit in hanc tr̄a . 7 Bain . fuit uicecomes: occupauit istā tr̄a
Tedric Pointel 7 qn̄ eā accep manebant in eā . xvii . soc . hntes . ix . car.

6 b
m̄ sr̄ in manu reg . 7 . xiii . hōes tenent hanc tr̄a . hn̄tes . iiii . car . Silu
xv . por . ii . ac 7 đ . p̄ti . Tc̄ . ual . iiii . lib 7 . qn tedric pointel ten . iiii . lib
m̄ . xl . sol . In dn̄io isti manerij . recep Petr . xxi . an . 7 . iiii . runc.
7 . xlv . porc . 7 . cc . ou . x . min . Huic manerio . ptinebat . t . r . e
. i . bereuuita . de . iiii . hid . qm inuasit Engelric . idē ten& comes . E.
Ptinebant adhuc . xxi . soc . tenentes . i . hid . 7 . ii . uirg . 7 . v . ac . qs ht
Rog de ramis p escangio: ut dicit . 7 inde uocat libatorē suanū.
Et . iiii . soc . fuer̄ t . r . e in isto manerio omnē consuet reddentes.
qs Ricard fili comitis gislebti inuasit tēpr̄ illo q Suen erat uicecomes.
tenentes dim . hid . 7 . xv . ac . que m̄ sr̄ in manu reg idō qđ null fuit
ex parte ej q dixiss& qm eos habuerit . Sep . i . car . 7 tēpr̄ . r . e . ual.
. xiii . sol . 7 hucusq habuit . R . istū censū . Waleram . inuasit . i . soc.
de . xxx . ac . tc̄ . i . car . m̄ . null . 7 ual . x . sol . 7 istū censū usq huc habuit
Wal . Hagebt ten& xxx . ac qs ten . i . soc 7 . inde reuocat libatorē
Suanū . Tc̄ . i . car . m̄ . dim . Tc̄ ual . v . sol . 7 . iiii . đ . m̄ . xxxii . đ.
Comes . E . ten& . i . hid . 7 . dim . 7 . xlv . ac . qđ inuasit Engelric . 7 . illā
tr̄a tenebant . viii . soc . Ep̄c baioc ten& dim hid . quā ten& Rađ
fili turoldi sub ipso . Ranulf fr̄ Ilgeri . ten& . xv . ac . Hugo de
monfort . xxx . ac . Rađ baignart dim hid . 7 . xxxv . ac . Eudo dap
xxxvii . ac . 7 . dim . Rog hō epi Londoniensis: . i . hid . 7 . xxx . ac.
Walt diacon . v . ac . Tota hec tr̄a reddebat consuetudinē omnē sup
dicto manerio . t . r . e.

Woodland, 15 pigs; meadow, 12 acres; then 1 mill, now 2; pasture, 300 sheep; now 1 salt-house.
Then it paid 2 nights' provisions; when Baynard held (it) £14; now [£] 11.

Attached to this manor before 1066 were 17 Freemen with 1 hide, who paid all customary dues; after the King came to this land and Baynard was Sheriff, Theodoric Pointel appropriated this land; when he acquired it, 17 Freemen dwelt there who had
9 ploughs, now they are in the King's hand. 13 men who have 4 6 b
ploughs hold this land.

Woodland, 15 pigs; meadow, 2½ acres.
Value then £4; when Theodoric Pointel held (it) £4; now 40s.

In this manor's lordship Peter acquired 21 cattle, 4 cobs, 45 pigs and 200 sheep less 10.

There belonged to this manor before 1066 1 outlier with 4 hides, which Engelric annexed. Count E(ustace) holds it.

There also belonged 21 Freemen, who held 1 hide, 2 virgates and 5 acres, whom Roger of Raismes has by exchange, as he states, and calls Swein as deliverer of them.

Also there were 4 Freemen in this manor before 1066 who paid all customary dues, whom Richard son of Count Gilbert annexed in the time when Swein was Sheriff, (and) who held ½ hide and 15 acres which are now in the King's hand, with the result that there was no one who might state on his behalf how he should hold them.

Always 1 plough.
Value before 1066, 13s and up to now R(ichard) has had these dues.

Waleran annexed 1 Freeman with 30 acres. Then 1 plough, now none. Value 10s and up to now Waleran has had these dues.

Hagebert holds 30 acres which 1 Freeman held and recalls Swein as its deliverer.

Then 1 plough, now ½.
Value then 5s 4d; now 32d.

Count E(ustace) holds 1½ hides and 45 acres, which Engelric annexed; 8 Freemen held that land. The Bishop of Bayeux holds ½ hide which Ralph son of Thorold holds under him. Ranulf brother of Ilger holds 15 acres; Hugh de Montfort 30 acres; Ralph Baynard ½ hide and 35 acres; Eudo the Steward 37½ acres; Roger, a man of the Bishop of London, 1 hide and 30 acres; Walter the deacon 5 acres.
The whole of this land paid all customary dues to the above manor before 1066.

Hund de Odelesfort. Neuport ten. Harold. t. r. e. p man.
7. p. viii. hid. 7 d. m rex. W. Tc. xviii. uill. P. xv. m xxvi. Tc.
viii. bor. p. vi. M. xiii. Tc. iiii. ser. p 7 m. ii. Tc. ii. car in dnio. p
7. m. i. Tc. 7 p int hoes. viii. car. m. x. Silu. c. por. xxiiii. ac. pti.
Sep. ii. mol. 7. x. an. 7. i. r. lxxix. porc. cii. ou. Tc reddebat
firmã de duab; noctib; Est adhuc. i. bereuuita que jac& in Cante
bruge sira 7 uocat. Scelfort. de. iii. hid. 7. xlvi. ac. Sep. viii. uill.
7. v. bor. 7. i. car. in dnio. 7. ii. car. hom. 7 xv. ac. pti. Tc. i. runc
m. n. sep. x. an. tc. lxxx. porc. m. l. Tc. lxxx. ou. m. lxxxvii.
Tc. xiii. capræ. m. xxiiii. Hec berewita erat in supdicta firma. t. r. e
m u reddit. xxv. lib. 7. xvi. sol. Rob grino ten&. ii. soc. de. ii. hid
7. dim. ptinentes huic manerio. 7 reddentes omne consuetudine
qs accepit cu Suen ess& uicecomes. & hund nescit q m eos habuerit
qa neq; breue neq; legat uenit ex parte regis in hund qd rex sibi
dediss& illã trã. Quidã cleric comitis. E. inuaserat xlii. ac. 7 teneb
illas ad feudu comitis. e. s; hund eas testat ad neuport. 7. ita m ht
rex. Cleric u judicat e esse in miscdia regis. 7 de omi cessu suo. 7
de corpore suo. In illa tra erat. tc. i. car. m nulla. i. ac pti. Silu
vi. por. 7. ual. vi. sol.

Richelingã ten. Har. p m. 7 p. viii. hid. m. rex. W. p totide
Tc. xiii. uill. p. xvi. m. xx. Tc 7 p. vi. bor. m. x. sep. iiii. ser.
7. ii. car. in dnio. Tc 7 p. viii. car. hom. m. x. Silu. xxx. porc.

7. iii. ac. pti. Tc. ual. viii. lib. m. xii. lib. 7. xvi. sol. in dnio. vii. an. 7
lxx. ou.

Hundred of UTTLESFORD 7 a

28 Harold held NEWPORT before 1066 as a manor, for 8½ hides. Now King William (holds it).

Then 18 villagers, later 15, now 26; then 8 smallholders, later 6, now 13; then 4 slaves, later and now 2.

Then 2 ploughs in lordship, later and now 1. Then and later among the men 8 ploughs, now 10.

Woodland, 100 pigs; meadow, 24 acres; always 2 mills. 10 cattle, 1 cob, 79 pigs, 102 sheep.

Then it paid (a revenue of) 2 nights' provisions.

There is besides 1 outlier which lies in Cambridgeshire and is called SHELFORD, with 3 hides and 46 acres.

Always 8 villagers; 5 smallholders; 1 plough in lordship; 2 men's ploughs.

Meadow, 15 acres. Then 1 cob, now none; always 10 cattle. Then 80 pigs, now 50; then 80 sheep, now 87; then 13 goats, now 24.

This outlier was in the above-mentioned revenue before 1066, but now it pays £25 16s. Robert Gernon holds 2 Freemen with 2½ hides who belong to this manor and who pay all customary dues, whom he received when Swein was Sheriff. The Hundred does not know how he should have them, because neither a writ nor a Commissioner came on the King's behalf to the Hundred (to say) that the King had given himself that land.

A cleric of Count E(ustace) had annexed 42 acres and held them in Count E(ustace)'s Holding, but the Hundred testifies that they (belong) to Newport, so the King now has them; the cleric is judged to be in the King's mercy regarding both all his property and his body.

In that land was then 1 plough, now none.

Meadow, 1 acre; woodland, 6 pigs.

Value 6s.

29 Harold held RICKLING as a manor, for 8 hides. Now King William (holds it) for as much.

Then 13 villagers, later 16, now 20; then and later 6 smallholders, now 10. Always 4 slaves; 2 ploughs in lordship.

Then and later 8 men's ploughs; now 10.

Woodland, 30 pigs; meadow, 3 acres. 7 b

Value then £8; now £12 16s.

In lordship 7 cattle and 70 sheep.

Dimidium Hund de Frosscewella.

Sanfort tenuit Edeua post. Rad comes. m. Godric dapifer in manu regis. p. m. 7 p. vii. hid. 7. xxx. ac. Tc. xxvi. uill. p. xiii. m. xvi. Tc. ix. bor. P. vi. m. v. sep. iiii. ser. 7. ii. car. in dnio. Tc int hoes. xxii. car. p. xv. m. xiiii. Silu. cl. por. xxx. ac. pti. sep. i. mol. Tc. ual. xx. lib. P. xxvi. m. xxx.

Hundret de Turestapla. Will rex. ht. iiii. salinas in isto hund. qs custodit uicecomes. 7. iii. hoes. de. x. ac. 7. ual. xx. d.

8 a

Terræ Scæ Trinitatis de cantorberia ad uictu monacoz .II.

Hund de Witham In Coghessala tenuit Sca trinitas. iii. uirg træ. t. r. e. 7 m. similit. Sep. ii. car. Tc. i. bor. m. viii. Tc. iii. ser. m. i. viii. ac. pti. i. mol. 7. ual. lx. sol. In dnio. iiii. r. iii. an. xx. ou. vii. por

Bochinges ten& sep. S. T. p. m. 7 p. iiii. hid. 7. d. 7. ii. car. i dnio. Tc. xxxv. car. hom. m. xxix. Tc. xix. uill. m. xviii. tc. xxv. bor. m. xliiii. Tc. iiii. ser. m. ii. Silu. ccc. por. Past. lx. ouib. xxii. ac. pti. 7. i. mol. 7 vi. an. 7. c. ou. 7 liiii. por. Huic manerio sep ptinent. ii. hid. in meresai. 7. i. car in dnio. 7. i. car hom. 7. ii. uill. 7. i. bor. pastura. l. ou. Tc int totu ual. xxiiii. lib. m. xxviii.

Stiesteda. tenuit sca. t. p. m. 7. p dim. hid. Tc. iiii. car. in dnio. m. iii. Tc. v. car. hom. m. vi. Tc. viii. uill. m. xiii. Tc. xi. bor m xxv. tc. vi. ser. m. iiii. Silu. dccc. por. xxvii. ac. pti. 7. i. mol. 7. iii. r. 7. xl. an. 7. cxx. ou. lxxvii. por. Tc ual. x. lib. m. xv.

Half-Hundred of FRESHWELL

30 Edeva held (Great) SAMPFORD; later Earl Ralph (held it). Now Godric the Steward (holds it) in the King's hand as a manor, for 7 hides and 30 acres.

Then 26 villagers, later 13, now 16; then 9 smallholders, later 6, now 5. Always 4 slaves; 2 ploughs in lordship. Then among the men 22 ploughs, later 15, now 14.

Woodland, 150 pigs; meadow, 30 acres; always 1 mill.

Value then £20; later [£] 26; now [£] 30.

Hundred of THURSTABLE

31 King William holds 4 salt-houses in the Hundred, which the Sheriff has charge of.

3 men with 10 acres.

Value 20d.

2 LANDS OF HOLY TRINITY, CANTERBURY, FOR THE MONKS' SUPPLIES 8 a

Hundred of WITHAM

1 In (Little) COGGESHALL, Holy Trinity held 3 virgates of land before 1066; now the same. Always 2 ploughs.

Then 1 smallholder, now 8; then 3 slaves, now 1.

Meadow, 8 acres; 1 mill.

Value 60s.

In lordship 4 cobs, 3 cattle, 20 sheep, 7 pigs.

[Hundred of HINCKFORD]

2 Holy Trinity has always held BOCKING as a manor, for 4½ hides. 2 ploughs in lordship. Then 35 men's ploughs, now 29.

Then 19 villagers, now 18; then 25 smallholders, now 44; then 4 slaves, now 2.

Woodland, 300 pigs; pasture for 60 sheep; meadow, 22 acres; 1 mill. 6 cattle, 100 sheep and 54 pigs.

To this manor have always belonged 2 hides in (West) MERSEA.

1 plough in lordship. 1 men's plough.

2 villagers; 1 smallholder.

Pasture, 50 sheep.

In total, value then £24; now [£] 28.

3 Holy Trinity held STISTED as a manor, for ½ hide. Then 4 ploughs in lordship, now 3. Then 5 men's ploughs, now 6.

Then 8 villagers, now 13; then 11 smallholders, now 25; then 6 slaves, now 4.

Woodland, 800 pigs; meadow, 27 acres; 1 mill. 3 cobs, 40 cattle, 120 sheep, 77 pigs.

Value then £10; now [£] 15.

Hund de Witbrictesherna. Lalinge ten. scā. T. p m. 7. p.
xiiii. hid. Tc. xiiii. uill. m. xxi. Tc. xvi. bor. m. xx. Tc. iii. ser. m. iiii.
Tc. ii. car. in dnio. m. iii. Tc. xvii. car. 7. dim. hom. m. xvi. 7. d.
sep. i. mol. Silu. dccc. por. 7. iii. r. 7. i. mul. 7 xvi. an. 7. lx. por. 7. cc.
ou. 7. xviii. cap. Tc. val. xii. lib. m. xvi.

Lachenduna ten. S. T. p. m. 7. ii. hid. 7. i. car. in dnio. m. ii. uilli. 7.
. i. ser. Pastura. xxx. ouib; . 7. vi. an. 7. lx. ou. 7. xvi. por. Tc. ual
xx. sol. m. xxv.

Niwelant. ten. S. T. p. m. 7. iii. hid. Tc. i. uill. m. iii. sep. ii. ser.

★

8 b

tc. ii. car. m. i. Tc. xxiiii. ou. 7. m similit. Tc ual. xx. sol. M. xl.

Hund de Rochefort. Mildentunā ten. S. T. p m. 7. ii. hid.
Sep. viii. uill. Tc. xiii. bor. m. xv. sep. i. ser. 7. ii. car in dnio. 7. vi.
car. hom. Silu. lx. por. 7. viii. an. 7. ii. r. 7. xxv. por. 7. cxxiiii.
ou. Tc. ual. c. sol. m. viii. lib.

Sudcercā. ten. S. T. p m. 7. p. iiii. hid. sep. xiiii. uill. 7. v. bor.
Tc. ii. ser. m. i. sep. ii. car. in dnio. 7. vi. car. hom. past. cc. ouib;
Silua. xl. por. 7. ii. pisc. 7. iiii. runc. 7. viii. an. 7. xiii. por. 7. cl.
ou. 7. xvi. cap. Tc. ual. c. sol. m. vii. lib.

Stanbruge tenuit Scā t. p. m. 7. i. hid. t. r. e. M Rad baignar.
de ecclia. sep. i. car. in dnio. Tc. iii. bor. m. vii. 7. i. ac. pti. Past.
cc. ouib; . 7. iiii. an. 7. x. por. 7. lviii. ou. Tc. ual. xxx. sol. m. xl.

9 a

EPS Londoniensis.
FEVDVM eiusdem epi.
CANONICI sci Pauli Londonie.
SCS PETRVS de West monasterio.
EPS DVNELMSIS.
CANONICI Sce CruciS De Waltham.

Hundred of 'WIBERTSHERNE'

Holy Trinity holds

4 LAWLING as a manor, for 14 hides.

Then 14 villagers, now 21; then 16 smallholders, now 20; then 3 slaves, now 4. Then 2 ploughs in lordship, now 3. Then 17½ men's ploughs, now 16½.

Always 1 mill. Woodland, 800 pigs. 3 cobs, 1 mule, 16 cattle, 60 pigs, 200 sheep and 18 goats.

Value then £12; now [£] 16.

5 LATCHINGDON as a manor, 2 hides. 1 plough in lordship.

Now 2 villagers; 1 slave.

Pasture for 30 sheep. 6 cattle, 60 sheep and 16 pigs.

Value then 20s; now 25[s].

6 ST. LAWRENCE as a manor, 3 hides.

Then 1 villager, now 3; always 2 slaves. Then 2 ploughs, now 1. 8 b

Then 24 sheep, now the same.

Value then 20s; now 40[s].

Hundred of ROCHFORD

7 MILTON as a manor, 2 hides.

Always 8 villagers. Then 13 smallholders, now 15. Always 1 slave; 2 ploughs in lordship; 6 men's ploughs.

Woodland, 60 pigs. 8 cattle, 2 cobs, 25 pigs and 124 sheep.

Value then 100s; now £8.

8 SOUTHCHURCH as a manor, for 4 hides.

Always 14 villagers; 5 smallholders. Then 2 slaves, now 1. Always 2 ploughs in lordship; 6 men's ploughs.

Pasture for 200 sheep; woodland, 40 pigs; 2 fisheries. 4 cobs, 8 cattle, 13 pigs, 150 sheep and 16 goats.

Value then 100s; now £7.

9 Holy Trinity held (Little) STAMBRIDGE as a manor; 1 hide before 1066. Now Ralph Baynard (holds it) from the Church. Always 1 plough in lordship.

Then 3 smallholders, now 7.

Meadow, 1 acre; pasture for 200 sheep. 4 cattle, 10 pigs and 58 sheep.

Value then 30s; now 40[s].

[3] *The Bishop of London* 9 a

[4] *The same Bishop's Holding*

[5] *The Canons of St. Paul's, London*

[6] *St. Peter, Westminster*

[7] *The Bishop of Durham*

[8] *The Canons of Waltham Holy Cross*

.III. Terra epi LondoniensiS. Hund de berdestapla. Legenduna
ten& epc qua tenuit Alftred queda femina. t. r. e. p. i. man. 7. ix. hid.
Tc. ii. car. in dnio. m. iii. Tc. vii. car hom. m. vi. Tc. viii. uill. m. iii.
m. xiiii. bor. Sep. vi. ser. Silu. c. por. Past. c. ou. Tc ual. ix. lib. m. x.
s; epc inderecip. xiiii. lib. De hoc manerio tenent Rad. 7 Will. de
epo. iii. hid. 7. lxxx. ac. 7. i. car in dnio. 7. ii. car. hom. 7 ual. c. sol. in
eod ptio. In dnio recep. Epc. c. ou. iii. min. 7. x. por.

Orseda ten& Eps. qua tenuit Will epc t. r. e. p. man. 7 xiii. hid.
s& comes Eustachi. i. ex illis ten& que n e de suis. c. mansionib;. Sep
. ii. car in dnio. Tc. xxxiiii. car hom. M. xxii. Tc. xxxiiii. uill. m
. xxii. Tc. vi. bor. m. xxxvi. Tc. iiii. ser. m. ii. Silu. m. 7 vi. anim.
7. cxv. ou. 7. xl. porc. Tc. ual. xxxv. lib. m. xxviii. De hoc eode
manerio tenent. Tidbald. Anschetill. Will. Gislebt. iiii. hid. 7. d.
7. xl. ac. 7 vi. car. 7 ual. viii. lib in eod ptio.

Ramesdana ten& Will. de epo. p. m. 7. iii. hid. Sep. i. car in dnio.
7. dim. car. hom. Tc. vi. bor. m. viii. 7. i. ser. Silu. c. por. m. i. mol.
Tc ual. lx. sol. m. xl.

Hundret de Witha. In Slamondesheia ten& Rog de epo
xv. ac. 7. ual. xxx. d.

Hund de beuentrev. Wenesteda tenuit Scs paul. m. Rad
fili brieu de epo. p. i. man. 7. i. hid. Tc. i. car. in dnio. m. i. 7. dim.
Sep. ii. car. hom. 7. iii. uill. Tc. vii. bor. m. viii. tc. ii. ser. m null.
Silu. ccc. por. m. i. mol. sep. i. salina. 7 ual. xl. sol. ★

3 LAND OF THE BISHOP OF LONDON 9 b

Hundred of BARSTABLE

1 The Bishop holds LAINDON which Aelfthryth, a woman, held before 1066 as a manor; 9 hides. Then 2 ploughs in lordship, now 3. Then 7 men's ploughs, now 6.

Then 8 villagers, now 3; now 14 smallholders; always 6 slaves.

Woodland, 100 pigs; pasture, 100 sheep.

Value then £9; now [£] 10, but the Bishop receives from it £14.

Of this manor, Ralph and William hold 3 hides and 80 acres from the Bishop. 1 plough in lordship. 2 men's ploughs.

Value 100s in the same assessment.

In lordship the Bishop acquired 100 sheep less 3 and 10 pigs.

2 The Bishop holds ORSETT which Bishop William held before 1066, as a manor; 13 hides. But Count Eustace holds 1 of these, which is not (part) of his 100 manors. Always 2 ploughs in lordship. Then 34 men's ploughs, now 22.

Then 34 villagers, now 22; then 6 smallholders, now 36; then 4 slaves, now 2.

Woodland, 1000 [pigs]. 6 cattle, 115 sheep and 40 pigs.

Value then £35, now [£] 28.

Of this same manor, Tidbald, Ansketel, William (and) Gilbert hold 4½ hides and 40 acres. 6 ploughs.

Value £8 in the same assessment.

3 William holds RAMSDEN (Belhus) from the Bishop as a manor; 3 hides. Always 1 plough in lordship; ½ men's plough.

Then 6 smallholders, now 8; 1 slave.

Woodland, 100 pigs; now 1 mill.

Value 60s; now 40[s].

Hundred of WITHAM

4 Roger holds 15 acres from the Bishop in SLAMPSEYS.
Value 30d.

Hundred of BECONTREE

5 St. Paul's held WANSTED. Now Ralph son of Brian (holds it) from the Bishop as 1 manor; 1 hide. Then 1 plough in lordship, now 1½. Always 2 men's ploughs;

3 villagers. Then 7 smallholders, now 8; then 2 slaves, now none.

Woodland, 300 pigs; now 1 mill; always 1 salt-house.

Value 40s.

Hund̄ de Wenſiſtreu. Legrā tenueȓ. II. libi hoēs. t. r. e

m̄. Rog̃ de ep̄o. ꝑ. III. hid. Sēp. I. car 7. đ. in dn̄io. 7. II. car hominv̄.

tc̄. v. uitti. m̄. IIII. Tc̄. IIII. bord. m̄. VI. Tc̄. III. ſer. m̄. IIII. Silua.

CL. por. 7. II. ac. p̄ti. tc̄ ual LXX. ſol. m̄. IIII. lib̄.

Legrā ten& Idē. R. de ep̄o. qđ tenuit. I. liba fem. t. r. e. ꝑ. III. hid.

Sēp. II carruc. in dn̄io. m̄. đ. car hom. M un uillan. Tc̄. Un.

bor. m̄. IIII. Tc̄. III. ſer. m̄. IIII. Silu. CL. por. m̄. I. mol. sēp. I. ſalina.

tc̄ ual LXX. ſol. m̄. IIII. lib̄. Hec duo maneria deratiocinauit Wep̄c

ad op ecctæ ſuæ poſt mortē reg̃. E. juſſu reg̃. Witti.

Hund̄ de hidinghafort. Raines ten. W. ep̄c. t. r. e. ꝑ. IIII.

hid. 7. XXX ac. Sēp. II. car. in dn̄io. Tc̄. v. car hom. m̄. IIII. Tc̄

XVI. uitt. m̄. x. Tc̄. IX. bor. m̄. VIII. Tc̄. IIII. ſer. m̄. III. Silua. CC. por

XVI. ac. p̄ti. m̄. I. mol. 7. x. an. XLV. ou. XXIIII. por. huic manerio

addite ſt̄. XV. ac. t. r. Witti. q̄s tenuit. I. lib̄ hō. t. r. e. ſic hund̄ teſtat.

Tūc ual. x. lib̄. m̄. XIIII. In hoc maneȓ ten& Rog̃ de ep̄o. III. uirg̃.

7. I. car. 7. II. ſer. 7 ual. L. ſol.

Hund̄ de Witbrictesherna In Sudmunſtrā. XXX. hid. q̄s tenent

epc̄ in dn̄io ~~XIIII. milites de ep̄o.~~ 7 t. r. e. XXII. uitt. m̄. XI. Tc̄. XXIII. bor. m̄. XXV.

Sēp. v. ſer. 7. III. car in dn̄io. Tc̄. XVIII. car hom. m̄. XI. Paſt. ꝺ. ou.

tc̄ ual. XXIIII. lib̄. m̄. XVI. In hoc manerio erant. t. r. e. XV. libi

hōes tenentes. XVIII. hid. 7. XXX. ac. m̄ ſt̄ XIIII. hōes q̄ tenent eas

de ep̄o. Tc̄. IIII. bor. m̄. XVI. Tc̄. IIII. ſer. m̄. VIII. Tc̄. XII. car. m̄. VII.

Hundred of WINSTREE 10 a

6 2 free men held LAYER (Marney) before 1066. Now Roger (holds it) from the Bishop, for 3 hides. Always 1½ ploughs in lordship; 2 men's ploughs.

Then 5 villagers, now 4; then 4 smallholders, now 6; then 3 slaves, now 4.

Woodland, 150 pigs; meadow, 2 acres.

Value then 70s; now £4.

7 Roger also holds from the Bishop LAYER (Marney), which 1 free woman held before 1066, for 3 hides. Always 2 ploughs in lordship. Now ½ men's plough.

Now 1 villager; then 1 smallholder, now 4; then 3 slaves, now 4.

Woodland, 150 pigs; now 1 mill; always 1 salt-house.

Value then 70s; now £4.

Bishop W(illiam) adjudged these 2 manors to the use of his Church after the death of King Edward, by King William's command.

Hundred of HINCKFORD

8 Bishop W(illiam) held RAYNE before 1066, for 4 hides and 30 acres. Always 2 ploughs in lordship. Then 5 men's ploughs, now 4.

Then 16 villagers, now 10; then 9 smallholders, now 8; then 4 slaves, now 3.

Woodland, 200 pigs; meadow, 16 acres; now 1 mill.

10 cattle, 45 sheep, 24 pigs.

To this manor were added 15 acres after 1066, which 1 free man held before 1066; so the Hundred testifies.

Value then £10; now [£] 14.

In this manor, Roger holds from the Bishop 3 virgates. 1 plough. 2 slaves.

Value 50s.

Hundred of 'WIBERTSHERNE'

9 In SOUTHMINSTER 30 hides which the Bishop holds in lordship.

Before 1066, 22 villagers, now 11; then 23 smallholders, now 25. Always 5 slaves; 3 ploughs in lordship. Then 18 men's ploughs, now 11.

Pasture, 1000 sheep.

Value then £24; now [£] 16.

In this manor were 15 free men before 1066 who held 18 hides and 30 acres. Now there are 14 men who hold them from the Bishop.

Then 4 smallholders, now 16; then 4 slaves, now 8. Then 12 ploughs, now 7.

paſtura . ccc . ou̇ . Tc̄ ual . xii . lib̄ . m̄ . viii . In dn̄io huȷ̇ manerij . st̄ xi . an̄ . 7 . dcc . ou̇ . iiii . min̄ . 7 . xx . por . Hanc tr̄a tulit Gnut rex . s;

10 b

Will epc̄ recuperauit t̄ . r . Willi . Copefordā ten& ep̄c in dn̄io . p . i . hid̄ . 7 dim̄ . 7 . xviii . ac̄ . Tc̄ . xvi . bor . m̄ . xiiii . Tc̄ . v . ser . m̄ . iii . Sep̄ . ii . car̄ in dn̄io . Tc̄ . vii . car̄ . hom̄ . m̄ . v . Silu̇ . c . porc̄ . xvi . ac̄ . prat̄ . 7 . vi . an̄ . 7 . xii . por . 7 . xxxvii . ou̇ . Sep̄ ual . viii . lib̄ . Huic manerio ptinebant . t̄ . r̄ . ē . . xii . soc̄ . m̄ . x . tenentes . i . hid̄ . 7 . ii . ac̄ . 7 . dim̄ . 7 n̄ potant recede ſicuti hund testat̄ . Tc̄ . int̄ eos . ii . car̄ . m̄ . i . 7 d̄ . Apptiatū ē in ſupiori ptio . De hac tr̄a ten& Roḡ de ep̄o . xxv . ac̄ . 7 . d̄ . car̄ 7 . ual . xv . sol . In hoc maner̄ . fuere . xvii . ac̄ . q̄s ten̄ Ep̄c . t̄ . r̄ . ē . ſed m̄ ten& Rob̄ gnon de dono reḡ . Adhuc ten& . Rob̄ . i . uirg t̄ræ quā tenuit epc̄ . & q̄dā lib̄ hō tenuit illā ita qd̄ poss& ire q̄ uell& s; soca remanebat in manerio.

Hund de Ceſſeorda . Wareleiā tenuit Guert . p m̄ . 7 . iiii . hid̄ . xv . ac̄ . min̄ . m̄ Humfrid̄ de ep̄o . sep̄ . v . uill . 7 . ii . bor . m̄ . ii . ser̄ . Tc̄ . iii . car̄ in dn̄io . m̄ . ii . sep̄ . iii . car̄ hom̄ Silua . dcc . por . past . c . ou̇ . tc̄ 7 p̄ ual . vi . lib̄ . m̄ . vii . de hoc manerio ten& taſcelin̄ pr̄ . xv . ac̄ . hoc man̄ . dedit Will rex Willo ep̄o pq̄ mare tranſiuit . q̄ in antiq̄ tēpr̄ fuit de eccla sc̄i pauli.

Celmeresfort tenuit Will epc̄ t̄ . r̄ . ē . m̄ epc̄ in dn̄io . p . m̄ . 7 viii . hid̄ . tc̄ . v . uill . m̄ . iiii . Tc̄ . ii . car̄ . in dn̄io . m̄ . iii . Tc̄ . int̄ hōes . v . car̄ . m̄ . i . silu̇ . ccc . porc̄ . xxx . ac̄ . p̄ti . sep̄ . i . mol . 7 . ii . an̄ . 7 . xxvii . por . 7 . c . ou̇ . 7 . ual . viii . lib̄ .

Pasture, 300 sheep.
Value then £12; now [£] 8.
In the lordship of this manor are 11 cattle, 700 sheep less 4 and 20 pigs.
King Canute took this land; but Bishop William recovered it after 1066. 10 b

[Hundred of LEXDEN]

10 The Bishop holds COPFORD in lordship, for 1½ hides and 18 acres.
Then 16 smallholders, now 14; then 5 slaves, now 3. Always 2 ploughs in lordship. Then 7 men's ploughs, now 5.
Woodland, 100 pigs; meadow, 16 acres. 6 cattle, 12 pigs and 37 sheep.
Value always £8.
To this manor belonged 12 Freemen before 1066; now 10, who hold 1 hide and 2½ acres and they cannot withdraw; so the Hundred testifies. Then among them 2 ploughs, now 1½.
It is assessed in the above assessment.
Of this land, Roger holds from the Bishop 25 acres. ½ plough.
Value 15s.
In this manor were 17 acres which the Bishop held before 1066, but now Robert Gernon holds (them) by the King's gift. Robert also holds 1 virgate of land which the Bishop held, and a free man held it on condition that he could go whither he would, but the jurisdiction stayed in the manor.

Hundred of CHAFFORD

11 Gyrth held (Little) WARLEY as a manor; 4 hides less 15 acres. Now Humphrey (holds it) from the Bishop.
Always 5 villagers; 2 smallholders. Now 2 slaves. Then 3 ploughs in lordship, now 2. Always 3 men's ploughs.
Woodland, 700 pigs; pasture, 100 sheep.
Value then and later £6; now [£] 7.
Of this manor, Tascelin the priest holds 15 acres.
King William, after he crossed the sea, gave this manor to Bishop William because in former times it was (in the lands) of St. Paul's Church.

[Hundred of CHELMSFORD]

12 Bishop William held CHELMSFORD before 1066. Now the Bishop (holds it) in lordship as a manor; 8 hides.
Then 5 villagers, now 4. Then 2 ploughs in lordship, now 3. Then among the men 5 ploughs, now 1.
Woodland, 300 pigs; meadow, 30 acres; always 1 mill. 2 cattle, 27 pigs and 100 sheep.
Value £8.

Hund de Tureſtapla. Wicham ten& epc̄ in dn̄io qđ tenuit
Wilł epc̄. t. r. e. p. m. 7. III. hid. Tc̄. VII. uiłł. m̄. v. tc̄. I. bor. m̄. IIII. Sēp
. IIII. ſer. 7. II. car in dn̄io. Tc̄. IIII. car hom. m̄. II. 7. dim. ſilu. xxx. por.
xxxI. ac. p̄ti. Sēp. I. moł. 7. VI. an. 7. L. ou. x. por. xx. cap̄. 7 uał. VI. lib.

11 a
In eađ. I. lib hō de. v. ac. 7 ual. XII. đ.
Hund de tenderinga. Cice. ten& epc in dn̄io. p. m. 7. VII.
hid. 7. t. r. e. XVIII. uiłł. m̄. IX. sēp. v. bor. tc̄. III. car in dn̄io. m̄. I. tc̄ iť ★
hōes. IX. car. m̄. v. IIII. ac. p̄ti. paſtura. cc. ouib; 7. VI. an. CL. ou 7 XVI. 7
xxx. porc. Tc̄ uał. XVIII. lib. m̄. XII.
Clachintuna sēp in epopatu fuit. p m. 7. xx. hid. Tc̄. L. uiłł. m̄. XLV.
Tc̄. xx. bor. m̄. L. Tc̄. XIII. ſer. m̄. VII. Tc̄. IIII. car. in dn̄io. m̄. III. tc̄. inť
hōes. L. car. m̄. xx. Silu. cccc. porc. xx. ac. p̄ti sēp. I. piſc. m̄. I. molin.
past. c. ou. 7. I. runc. 7. VII. an. 7. xxx. por. 7. XLI. ou. Tc̄. uał. XL. lib. m̄
XXVI. De hoc eođ manerio. tenent. v. milites. IIII. hid. 7. VI. car. 7
. II. uiłł. 7. XLV. bor. 7. III. ſer. hntes. III. car. 7 uał. VIII. lib. 7. II. ſoł. in eođ
p̄tio. In Coleceſtra ħt epc. XIIII. domos. 7. IIII. ac. n̄ reddentes conſuet.
p̄t Scotū: n epo In Eađ ten& hugo de epo. II. hid. 7. I. ac. 7 reddit 9ſuet. Sēp. II. car
in dn̄io. 7. I. car hom. 7. II. uiłł. 7. XI. bor. 7. I. ſer. VI. ac 7. đ. p̄t. M. I. moł. Tc̄ 7 p uał. XL. ſoł. m̄. L.

Hundred of THURSTABLE

13 The Bishop holds in lordship WICKHAM (Bishops), which Bishop William held before 1066 as a manor; 3 hides.

Then 7 villagers, now 5; then 1 smallholder, now 4.

Always 4 slaves; 2 ploughs in lordship. Then 4 men's ploughs, now 2½.

Woodland, 30 pigs; meadow, 31 acres; always 1 mill.

6 cattle, 50 sheep, 10 pigs and 20 goats.

Value £6.

In the same (Wickham) 1 free man with 5 acres. 11 a

Value 12d.

Hundred of TENDRING

14 The Bishop holds in lordship ST. OSYTH as a manor; 7 hides.

Before 1066, 18 villagers, now 9; always 5 smallholders.

Then 3 ploughs in lordship, now ... Then among the men 9 ploughs, now 5.

Meadow, 4 acres; pasture for 200 sheep. 6 cattle, 150 sheep and 16, and 30 pigs.

Value then £18; now [£] 12.

15 CLACTON was always in the (lands of the) Bishopric as a manor; 20 hides.

Then 50 villagers, now 45; then 20 smallholders, now 50; then 13 slaves, now 7. Then 4 ploughs in lordship, now 3. Then among the men 50 ploughs, now 20.

Woodland, 400 pigs; meadow, 20 acres; always 1 fishery; now 1 mill; pasture, 100 sheep. 1 cob, 7 cattle, 30 pigs and 41 sheep.

Value then £40; now [£] 26.

Of this same manor, 5 men-at-arms hold 4 hides. 6 ploughs.

2 villagers, 45 smallholders and 3 slaves who have 3 ploughs.

Value £8 2s in the same assessment.

In COLCHESTER

16 The Bishop has 14 houses and 4 acres which, apart from the levy, pay customary dues only to the Bishop.

In the same (Colchester) Hugh holds from the Bishop 2 hides and 1 acre and pays a customary due. Always 2 ploughs in lordship; 1 men's plough;

2 villagers; 11 smallholders; 1 slave.

Meadow, 6½ acres; now 1 mill.

Value then and later 40s; now 50[s].

Hund de Ceffeorda. Wocheduna tenuit Aluric.t.r.e.
p.m.7.III.hid.7.XL.ac.M ten& Hugo de epo.Tc.VI.uill.m.VIII.
Tc.v.bor.m.xv.Tc.VI.ser.m.IIII.Sep.III.car.in dnio.7.IIII.car
hom.Silu.D.por.xx.ac.pti.7.IIII.pulli.CXLIIII.ou.xx.animal
Tc 7 p ual.IIII.lib.m.VI.

Toteham ten& Will fili brien de epo.qd tenuit Eduuolt p m.
7.dim hid.7 xxx.ac.m.I.uill.Sep.VI.bor.7.II.ser.7.I.car.in dnio.
Silu LX.por.IIII.ac pti.7.I.piscator.past.XL.ou.7.I.salina.m.IIII.
an.7.IIII.por.LX.ou.Sep.ual.xxx.sol.

11 b

Toteham ten& Will balt de epo.qd tenuit.Aluric.p.m.7.dim hid
7 xxx.ac.m.III.bor.sep.I.car.7.I.sal.7.II.ac.pti.Silu.xxx.por.Sep.
ual.xxx.sol.

Elesforda tenuit Eduuold.p.m.7.II.hid.træ.m Humfrid de epo.
sep.II.uill.Tc.II.bor.m.VI.tc.III.ser.m.II.tc.II.car.in dnio m nulla.
Sep.I.car.hom.Tc ual.XL.sol.m.xx.

Tenderinge ten& Rog de epo.qd tenuit Aluuard p.I.hid.7.XLV.ac.
t.r.e.sep.v.bor.Tc.IIII.ser.m.III.Sep.II.car in dnio.7.III.ac.pti.past.
.L.ouib; Tc.III.runc.m.IIII.m.III.an.Tc.VI.por.m.XVI.Tc XXXVI.
ou.m LXVI.Sep ual.xxx.sol.

Hundret de berdestapla. Turrucca ten& Anschetill de epo
q tenuit Vluuin lib ho sub rege.E.p.I.m.7.II.hid.7.II.ac.Sep.II.car
in dnio.Tc.I.bor.m.VI.Tc.VI.ser.m.I.Silu.L.por.Past.L.ou.Tc.I.piscin

4 THE HOLDING OF THE BISHOP OF LONDON

Hundred of CHAFFORD

1 Aelfric held CRANHAM before 1066 as a manor; 3 hides and 40 acres. Now Hugh holds it from the Bishop.

Then 6 villagers, now 8; then 5 smallholders, now 15; then 6 slaves, now 4. Always 3 ploughs in lordship; 4 men's ploughs.

Woodland, 500 pigs; meadow, 20 acres. 4 foals, 144 sheep, 20 cattle.

Value then and later £4; now [£] 6.

[Hundred of THURSTABLE]

2 William son of Brian holds TOTHAM from the Bishop, which Edwold held as a manor; ½ hide and 30 acres.

Now 1 villager. Always 6 smallholders; 2 slaves; 1 plough in lordship.

Woodland, 60 pigs; meadow, 4 acres; 1 fisherman; pasture, 40 sheep; 1 salt-house. Now 4 cattle, 4 pigs, 60 sheep.

Value always 30s.

3 William Bold holds TOTHAM from the Bishop, which Aelfric held 11 b
as a manor; ½ hide and 30 acres.

Now 3 smallholders. Always 1 plough.

1 salt-house; meadow, 2 acres; woodland, 30 pigs.

Value always 30s.

[Hundred of TENDRING]

4 Edwold held ALRESFORD as a manor; 2 hides of land. Now Humphrey (holds it) from the Bishop.

Always 2 villagers. Then 2 smallholders, now 6; then 3 slaves, now 2. Then 2 ploughs in lordship, now none. Always 1 men's plough.

Value then 40s; now 20[s].

5 Roger holds TENDRING from the Bishop, which Alfward held for 1 hide and 45 acres before 1066.

Always 5 smallholders. Then 4 slaves, now 3. Always 2 ploughs in lordship.

Meadow, 3 acres; pasture for 50 sheep. Then 3 cobs, now 4; now 3 cattle; then 6 pigs, now 16; then 36 sheep, now 66.

Value always 30s.

Hundred of BARSTABLE

6 Ansketel holds (Little) THURROCK from the Bishop which Wulfwin, a free man, held under King Edward as 1 manor; 2 hides and 2 acres. Always 2 ploughs in lordship.

Then 1 smallholder, now 6; then 6 slaves, now 1.

Woodland, 50 pigs; pasture, 50 sheep; then 1 fishery,

m̄.n̄.Tc̄.IIII.an.m̄.v.m̄.II.runc.7.II.pulli.Tc̄.XII.por.m̄ XVI.Tc̄
LXXX.ou.m̄.CXX.7 VIII.Sēp.uał.XXX.sol.7.IIII.đ.

Wellā tenent.Rađ.7 Torold de ēpo qđ tenuit Idē Vluuin.t.r.e.p.m.
7.p.I.hid.7.XXX.ac.Sēp.I.car.Tc̄.I.uilł.m̄.n̄.Sēp.II.bor.Silu.XL.por.
7 uał.XX.sol.

Burghestedā ten& Galt̄ de ēpo.q tenuit.Goduin.t.r.e.p.m̄.7 p
.III.hid.Sēp.II.car in dn̄io.7.I.car hom.7.II.uilł.Tc̄.I.bor.m̄.VI.Tc̄
.IIII.ser.m̄.I.Silu.LX.por.7 aliæ.XXX.ac.calūpniant̄ de tēpr̄.r.e.
m̄.II.pulli.7.IIII.an.Tc̄.V.por.m̄.XXIIII.Tc̄.L.ou.m̄ LXXXVIII.
7.XLIIII.cap.Tc̄ uał LX.sol.m̄.L.

Currincham ten& Wilł.de ēpo qđ tenuit Sigar lib hō.p.I.m̄.7.IIII.

12 a

hid.7.X.ac.M.III.hid.7,đ.7.X.ac.dimidia hida ē inde ablata quā ten&
ēpc baioc.Tc̄.III.car in dı̄o.M.II.7 dim.Sēp.IIII.car.hom.Tc̄.III.uilł.m̄.II.
Tc̄.VII.bor.m̄.XXV.Tc̄.V.ser.m̄.III.Silu.CCC.por.Past.CCCC.ou.Sēp.I.mol.
Tc̄.II.runc:m̄ n̄.Tc̄.III.an.m̄.VI.Tc̄.VIII.por.m̄.X.Tc̄.CCCC.ou.m̄.D.
7 XXI.cap.Tc̄ uał.VII.lib.m̄.VII.7 VI.sol.

Hornindunā ten&.Idē de ēpo.q ten Goduin lib hō.p.I.m̄.7.I.hid
7.dim.Sēp.I.car.in dn̄io.7.IIII.bor.7.I.ser.Silū.X.por.VIII pars.I.pisc.
Sēp uał.XX.sol.De hoc manerio ablata ē dim hid.q ten& ēpc baiocensis.

Celde uuellā ten& Hugolin de ēpo.qđ ten Aluric teign reḡ.E.p.m̄.
7.II.hid.Sēp.II.car.in dn̄io.7.I.car 7 đ.hom.Tc̄.I.pb̄r.7 III.bor.m̄.I.
pb̄r.7 VII.bor.Sēp.IIII.ser.past.C.ouib;.Tc̄.I.pisc.m̄.n̄.II.runc.X.
an.LXXXI.ou.Tc̄ 7 p uał:XL:sol.m̄.XXX.

now none.
Then 4 cattle, now 5; now 2 cobs and 2 foals; then 12 pigs, now 16; then 80 sheep, now 128.
Value always 30s 4d.

7 Ralph and Thorold hold WELL (Farm) from the Bishop, which Wulfwin also held before 1066 as a manor, for 1 hide and 30 acres. Always 1 plough.
Then 1 villager, now none; always 2 smallholders.
Woodland, 40 pigs.
Value 20s.

8 Walter holds (Little) BURSTEAD from the Bishop, which Godwin held before 1066 as a manor, for 3 hides. Always 2 ploughs in lordship; 1 men's plough.
2 villagers. Then 1 smallholder, now 6; then 4 slaves, now 1.
Woodland, 60 pigs; another 30 acres are claimed, from before 1066. Now 2 foals and 4 cattle; then 5 pigs, now 24; then 50 sheep, now 88; 44 goats.
Value then 60s; now 50[s].

9 William holds CORRINGHAM from the Bishop which Sigar, a free man, held as 1 manor; 4 hides and 10 acres. Now 3½ hides and 12 a
10 acres. ½ hide, which the Bishop of Bayeux holds, was taken from it. Then 3 ploughs in lordship, now 2½. Always 4 men's ploughs.
Then 3 villagers, now 2; then 7 smallholders, now 25; then 5 slaves, now 3.
Woodland, 300 pigs; pasture, 400 sheep; always 1 mill. Then 2 cobs, now none; then 3 cattle, now 6; then 8 pigs, now 10; then 400 sheep, now 500; 21 goats.
Value then £7; now [£] 7 6s.

10 He also holds HORNDON (-on-the-Hill) from the Bishop which Godwin, a free man, held as 1 manor; 1½ hides. Always 1 plough in lordship;
4 smallholders; 1 slave.
Woodland, 10 pigs; the eighth part of 1 fishery.
Value always 20s.
From this manor, ½ hide has been taken away which the Bishop of Bayeux holds.

11 Hugolin holds CHADWELL from the Bishop which Aelfric, a thane of King Edward's, held as a manor; 2 hides.
Always 2 ploughs in lordship; 1½ men's ploughs.
Then 1 priest and 3 smallholders, now 1 priest and 7 smallholders; always 4 slaves.
Pasture for 100 sheep; then 1 fishery, now none. 2 cobs, 10 cattle, 81 sheep.
Value then and later 40s; now 30[s].

Ramesdanā ten& Will de epo qđ tenuit Godric . p . i . m . 7 . i . hid . 7 x. ac . Sep . i . car in dnio . 7 . iiii . bor . Silu . xxv . por; . viii . por . l . ou . xii . cap. vat . xx . sol.

Leiendunā ten& Rađ de epo . qđ tenuit Vlmar p . m . 7 . dim . hid . t . r . e Tc . i . ser . m . n . 7 uat . vi . sol.

Hund de Witham . Bractedā ten& Hugolin de epo . q ten . Aluric lib hō . p . m . 7 . p . i . hid . Sep . ii . car in dnio . Tc . ii . car hom . m nulla. Tc . iiii . uill . m null . Tc . iii . bor . m . viii . 7 . i . pbr . Tc . iiii . ser . m . ii . Silu xl . por . i . mol . i . runc . iiii . an . xiii . por . cxxx . ou . Sep . uat . lx . sol.

Hobruge . ten& . Rađ . fili brien . q tenuit Aluuin lib hō . p . i . m. 7 . dim hid; Sep . i . car in dnio . 7 . i . car hom . 7 . i . uill . 7 . x . bor . Tc . ii . ser . m null . Silu . c . por . xii . ac pti . xvi . an . c . ou . xx . cap . xiiii . porc.

7 uat . xl . sol.

12 b

Dimidium Hund de herlaua . In Halinghebia ten Edeua . xxx . ac. t . r . e . Sep . dim . car . 7 . ii . ac pti . 7 uat . v . sol.

Hund de Witbrictesherna . Vleham ten& hugo de epo qđ ten Goder lib hō . t . r . e . p . m . 7 . p . ii . hid . 7 . xx . ac . Tc . iii . uill . m null . Tc. . iii . bor . m . i . Tc . iiii . ser . m . ii . Sep . ii . car in dnio . Tc . i . car hom . m null past . xxx . ou . iii . runc . cxl . ou . Tc 7 p uat . lx . sol . m . xl.

Mildemet ten& Rađ fili brien de epo qđ tenuit Aluuin lib hō t . r . e p . m . 7 dim . hid . 7 . xiiii . ac . Tc . ii . uill . m . null . Sep . iii . bor . Tc . i . ser . m . ii. Sep . i . car . Silu . xx . por . viii . ac . pti . vat . xx . sol.

12 William holds RAMSDEN (Belhus) from the Bishop, which Godric held as 1 manor; 1 hide and 10 acres. Always 1 plough in lordship;
4 smallholders.
Woodland, 25 pigs. 8 pigs, 50 sheep, 12 goats.
Value 20s.

13 Ralph holds LAINDON from the Bishop, which Wulfmer held as a manor; ½ hide before 1066.
Then 1 slave, now none.
Value 6s.

Hundred of WITHAM

14 Hugolin holds (Little) BRAXTED from the Bishop which Aelfric, a free man, held as a manor, for 1 hide. Always 2 ploughs in lordship. Then 2 men's ploughs; now none.
Then 4 villagers, now none; then 3 smallholders, now 8, and 1 priest; then 4 slaves, now 2.
Woodland, 40 pigs; 1 mill. 1 cob, 4 cattle, 13 pigs, 130 sheep.
Value always 60s.

15 Ralph son of Brian holds HOWBRIDGE which Alwin, a free man, held as 1 manor; ½ hide. Always 1 plough in lordship; 1 men's plough;
1 villager; 10 smallholders. Then 2 slaves, now none.
Woodland, 100 pigs; meadow, 12 acres. 16 cattle, 100 sheep, 20 goats, 14 pigs.
Value 40s.

Half-Hundred of HARLOW 12 b

16 Edeva held 30 acres in HALLINGBURY before 1066. Always ½ plough.
Meadow, 2 acres.
Value 5s.

Hundred of 'WIBERTSHERNE'

17 Hugh holds ULEHAM ('s Farm) from the Bishop which Godhere, a free man, held before 1066 as a manor, for 2 hides and 20 acres.
Then 3 villagers, now none; then 3 smallholders, now 1; then 4 slaves, now 2. Always 2 ploughs in lordship. Then 1 men's plough, now none.
Pasture, 30 sheep. 3 cobs, 140 sheep.
Value then and later 60s; now 40[s].

18 Ralph son of Brian holds BASSETTS from the Bishop which Alwin, a free man, held before 1066 as a manor; ½ hide and 14 acres.
Then 2 villagers, now none; always 3 smallholders. Then 1 slave, now 2. Always 1 plough.
Woodland, 20 pigs; meadow, 8 acres.
Value 20s.

.V. TERRA CANONICOꝶ SCI PAVLI IN EXSESSA.

Hund de bdestapla. Leam. tenuit Edeua. libe. t. r. e. p. m. 7 dim hid. 7. xxx. ac. Tc. II. car in dnio. 7. II. car hom. m nulla. Tc. II. uill m. VI. Tc. VI. bor. m. V. tc. II. ser. m. III. Silu. xxv. por. Past. c. ouib; I. an. I. porc. VII. ou. Tc. ual. XL. sol. m. xx. hec tra calupniata e ad op regiS.

Hund de Waltham. Cinghefort tenuit Scs paul. t. r. e. p. I. m. 7 p. VI. hid. Sep. II. car in dnio. Tc. III. car hom. m. IIII. Tc. VII. uill. m. VIII. Tc. III. bor m. VI. sep. IIII. ser. Silu. D. por. L. ac. pti. 7. II. pisc. IX. an. II. runc. XXVII. por. c. ou. Tc ual. IIII. lib. m. c. sol. De hoc ma nerio abstulit petr de ualonijs. I. hid. 7. VIII. ac. pti. que ptinebant manerio. t. r. e. 7 silua ad. L. por. Val. x. sol. De eod manerio tulit Goisfrid de magna uilla. x. ac. pti.

Hund de hidingaforda. Belcham ten. Scs paul. t. r. e. p. m. 7. v. hid.

13 a

Sep. II. car in dnio. 7. XII. car hom. XXIIII. uill. x. bor. v. ser. Silu. LX. po. xxx. ac. pti. IX. an. II. runc. XL. por. c. ou. v. cap. Sep. ual. XVI. lib.

Wicham. ten. S. P. t. r. e. p. m. 7. III. hid. I. uirg min. Tc. I. car i dio m. II. Tc. IIII. car hom. m. III. Tc. VI. uill. m. v. Tc. IIII. bor. m. x. Tc. I. ser. m. III. Silu. cc. porc. x. ac. pti. II. runc. IIII. an. XXIII. por. L. ou. XXIIII. cap. II. uasa apu. Tc ual. XL. sol. m. IIII. lib.

5 LAND OF THE CANONS OF ST. PAUL'S IN ESSEX

Hundred of BARSTABLE

1 Edeva held LEE (Chapel) freely before 1066 as a manor; ½ hide and 30 acres. Then 2 ploughs in lordship and 2 men's ploughs, now none.

Then 2 villagers, now 6; then 6 smallholders, now 5; then 2 slaves, now 3.

Woodland, 25 pigs; pasture for 100 sheep. 1 (head of) cattle, 1 pig, 7 sheep.

Value then 40s; now 20[s].

This land was claimed for the King's use.

Hundred of WALTHAM

2 St. Paul's held CHINGFORD before 1066 as 1 manor, for 6 hides. Always 2 ploughs in lordship. Then 3 men's ploughs, now 4.

Then 7 villagers, now 8; then 3 smallholders, now 6; always 4 slaves.

Woodland, 500 pigs; meadow, 50 acres; 2 fisheries. 9 cattle, 2 cobs, 27 pigs, 100 sheep.

Value then £4; now 100s.

From this manor, Peter of Valognes took away 1 hide and 8 acres of meadow which belonged to the manor before 1066, and woodland for 50 pigs. Value 10s.

From the same manor, Geoffrey de Mandeville took 10 acres of meadow.

Hundred of HINCKFORD

3 St. Paul's held BELCHAMP (St. Paul's) before 1066 as a manor; 5 hides. Always 2 ploughs in lordship; 12 men's ploughs; 13 a

24 villagers; 10 smallholders; 5 slaves.

Woodland, 60 pigs; meadow, 30 acres. 9 cattle, 2 cobs, 40 pigs, 100 sheep, 5 goats.

Value always £16.

4 St. Paul's held WICKHAM (St. Paul's) before 1066 as a manor; 3 hides less 1 virgate. Then 1 plough in lordship, now 2. Then 4 men's ploughs, now 3.

Then 6 villagers, now 5; then 4 smallholders, now 10; then 1 slave, now 3.

Woodland, 200 pigs; meadow, 10 acres. 2 cobs, 4 cattle, 23 pigs, 50 sheep, 24 goats, 2 beehives.

Value then 40s; now £4.

Hund̄ de Witbrictesherna Tillingham ten̄ . S̄ . P̄ . p m̄ . 7 xx . hid̄ .
7 . vi . ac̄ . Sēp . xx . uilt̄ . 7 . viii . bor 7 . iiii . ser̄ . Tc̄ . iii . car̄ . in dn̄io . m̄ . iiii .
Sēp . x . car̄ . hom̄ . Past̄ . cccc . ou̇ . m̄ . i . mol̄ . 7 . i . pisc̄ . xv . an̄ . xxx . por .
cccxl . ou̇ . P̄t hanc tr̄a datæ suer̄ ecclæ . x . ac̄ . quæ jacent huic man̄ .
Tc̄ totū uat . x . lib̄ m̄ . xv .

Hund̄ de Angra Nortunā tenuit Godid . quedā femina . t̄ . r̄ . ē
p . dim̄ . hid̄ . m̄ . S̄ . P̄ . Sēp . i . car̄ . 7 . ii . bor . Silu̇ . xl . por . iiii . ac̄ . p̄ti . i . r̄ . v . an̄ .
vat . xx . sol̄ . Hanc tr̄a dedit Godid sc̄o paulo p̄q rex uenit in angliā
s; non ostendit̄ breuē neq; concessum regis.

Nasestocā tenuer̄ . ii . libi hōes . Houard . 7 Vlsi . p . ii . man̄ . 7 p . v . hid̄
. xx . ac̄ . min̄ . m̄ . ht̄ sc̄s paul̄ p totidē . p̄q rex uenit in hanc tr̄a . 7
dicit̄ se habuisse ex dono reḡ . Sēp . xii . uilt̄ . 7 . xi . bor Tc̄ . iiii . ser̄ . m̄ . ii .
sēp . iiii . car̄ in dn̄io . 7 . iiii . car̄ hom̄ . Silu̇ . dc . por . xliiii . ac̄ . p̄ti . Sēp
xiii . an̄ . ii . runc̄ . cxvi . ou̇ . xxiiii . por . xxiiii . cap̄ . iiii . uasa apum .
Sēp . uat . x . lib̄ .

Aliam nessetocham . tenuit Turstin̄ ruff p . m̄ . 7 . p . i . hid̄ . 7 . xl . ac̄ .
m̄ sc̄s paul̄ inuasit . 7 . ē cū alia tr̄a . 7 ten& p tantundē . Tc̄ . i . bor .
m̄ . ii . Sēp . ii . car̄ Silu̇ . c . por . Sēp . uat . xxx . sol̄ . In ead̄ uilt̄

13 b
tenuerunt . vii . libi hōes . ii . hid̄ . q̄s ten& Sc̄s paul̄ similit̄ . 7 . m̄ in ista
tr̄a . xii . hōes . M̊ . iii . bor . Sēp . iiii . car̄ . Silu̇ . ccx . por . vii . ac̄ . p̄ti . Sēp vat
xl . sol̄ . In Nassestoca ten& . i . p̄br . dim̄ . hid̄ . 7 . xx . ac̄ . s; hund̄ fert
testimoniū qd̄ ē sc̄i pauli . Sēp . ii . bor . Tc̄ . i . car̄ . m̄ . dim̄ . Sēp uat . x . sol̄ .
m̄ ē in manu reḡ

Hundred of 'WIBERTSHERNE'

5 St. Paul's holds TILLINGHAM as a manor; 20 hides and 6 acres.

Always 20 villagers; 8 smallholders; 4 slaves. Then 3 ploughs in lordship, now 4. Always 10 men's ploughs.

Pasture, 400 sheep; now 1 mill; 1 fishery. 15 cattle, 30 pigs, 340 sheep.

Apart from this land, 10 acres which lie in (the lands of) this manor were given to the Church.

Total value then £10; now [£] 15.

Hundred of ONGAR

6 Godith, a woman, held NORTON (Mandeville) before 1066, for ½ hide. Now St. Paul's (holds it). Always 1 plough;

2 smallholders.

Woodland, 40 pigs; meadow, 4 acres. 1 cob, 5 cattle.

Value 20s.

Godith gave this land to St. Paul's after the King came to England; but (St. Paul's) shows neither a writ nor the King's assent.

7 2 free men, Howard and Wulfsi, held NAVESTOCK as 2 manors, for 5 hides less 20 acres. Now St. Paul's has it for as much, after the King came to this land. They state they had it by the King's gift.

Always 12 villagers; 11 smallholders. Then 4 slaves, now 2. Always 4 ploughs in lordship; 4 men's ploughs.

Woodland, 600 pigs; meadow, 44 acres. Always 13 cattle, 2 cobs, 116 sheep, 24 pigs, 24 goats, 4 beehives.

Value always £10.

8 Thurstan the Red held the other NAVESTOCK as a manor, for 1 hide and 40 acres. Now St. Paul's has annexed it and it is with the other land and it holds it for as much.

Then 1 smallholder, now 2. Always 2 ploughs.

Woodland, 100 pigs.

Value always 30s.

In the same village 7 free men held 2 hides, which St. Paul's 13 b
holds likewise.

Now in this land 12 men; now 3 smallholders. Always 4 ploughs.

Woodland, 210 pigs; meadow, 7 acres.

Value always 40s.

In Navestock 1 priest holds ½ hide and 20 acres; but the Hundred bears witness that it is of St. Paul's.

Always 2 smallholders. Then 1 plough, now ½.

Value always 10s.

Now it is in the King's hand.

Hund de . Celmeresforda . Runewellā ten& sēp . sc̄s paul' . p . viii . hid' . Sēp . viii . uill . 7 . viii . bor . Tc̄ . ii . ser' . m̄ . i . Tc̄ . iii . car' 7 . dim' in dn̄io . 7 m̄ similit' . Tc̄ . int' hōes . ii . car' . 7 . dim' . Silu' . cc . por . ii . runc' . i . an' . viii . por . c . ou' . Sēp uat . viii . lib.

Hund de Turestapla . Tidwoldituna ten& sēp . sc̄s . P . p viii . hid' . 7 p . i . man' . s; Rad baignard ten& dimid' . hid' 7 hundret nescit q̄m eā habuerit ; Sēp . xvi . uill . 7 . iiii . bor . 7 . iiii . ser' . Tc̄ . ii . ca' in dn̄io . m̄ . i . 7 . d . Tc̄ . viii . car' hom' . m̄ . iii . Silu' . lx . por . xxx . ac' p̄ti . past' . clx . ou' . sēp . i . mol . 7 . i . sal . i . runc' . viii . an' . xii . por . cl . ou' . iii . uasa . apū . Sēp . uat . viii . lib.

Hund de tendringa . Ælduluesnasā ten& sēp sc̄s paul' p . man' 7 . p xxvii . hid' . Tc̄ lxxxvi . uill . m̄ lxiii . Tc̄ . xl . bor . m̄ . l . Sēp . vi . ser' . 7 vi . car' in dn̄io . Tc̄ int' hōes . lx . car' . m̄ . xxx . Silu' . ccc . por . ix . ac' p̄ti . m̄ . ii . mol Tc̄ . iii . sal . m̄ . ii . Past' . ccc . ou' . xxii . an' . xxx . porc' . cc . ou' . iiii . uasa apū . Tc̄ uat . xxvi . lib . m̄ . xxx . 7 . i . marc' argenti.

Hund de Rochefort . Berlingā ten& sēp . Sc̄s paul' . p . i . man' . 7 . p . ii . hid' . 7 . dim' . xv . ac' min' . Tc̄ . ii . uill . m̄ . n̄ . Tc̄ . v . bor . m̄ . ix . Sēp . i . ser' . 7 . i . car' in dn̄io . 7 . ii . car' hom' . Past' . xl . ou' . ii . runc' . ii . an' . iiii . por . clx . ou' . Tc̄ uat . iiii . lib . 7 . x . sol . m̄ . vi . lib . In Ead tenuit . i . lib hō

14 a

dim' hid' . 7 . x . ac' . t' . r' . e' . m̄ sc̄s . P . Sēp . i . car' . 7 uat . xx . sol . hanc trā occu pauer' canonici p'q rex uenit in angliā ;

Hundred of CHELMSFORD

9 St. Paul's has always held RUNWELL for 8 hides.

Always 8 villagers; 8 smallholders. Then 2 slaves, now 1. Then 3½ ploughs in lordship, now the same. Then among the men 2½ ploughs.

Woodland, 200 pigs. 2 cobs, 1 (head of) cattle, 8 pigs, 100 sheep.

Value always £8.

Hundred of THURSTABLE

10 St. Paul's has always held HEYBRIDGE for 8 hides, as 1 manor; but Ralph Baynard holds ½ hide and the Hundred does not know how he should have it.

Always 16 villagers; 4 smallholders; 4 slaves. Then 2 ploughs in lordship, now 1½. Then 8 men's ploughs, now 3.

Woodland, 60 pigs; meadow, 30 acres; pasture, 160 sheep; always 1 mill; 1 salt-house. 1 cob, 8 cattle, 12 pigs, 150 sheep, 3 beehives.

Value always £8.

Hundred of TENDRING

11 St. Paul's has always held THE NAZE as a manor, for 27 hides.

Then 86 villagers, now 63; then 40 smallholders, now 50. Always 6 slaves; 6 ploughs in lordship. Then among the men 60 ploughs, now 30.

Woodland, 300 pigs; meadow, 9 acres; now 2 mills; then 3 salt-houses, now 2; pasture, 300 sheep. 22 cattle, 30 pigs, 200 sheep, 4 beehives.

Value then £26; now [£] 30 and 1 mark of silver.

Hundred of ROCHFORD

12 St. Paul's has always held BARLING as 1 manor, for 2½ hides less 15 acres.

Then 2 villagers, now none; then 5 smallholders, now 9. Always 1 slave; 1 plough in lordship; 2 men's ploughs.

Pasture, 40 sheep. 2 cobs, 2 cattle, 4 pigs, 160 sheep.

Value then £4 10s; now £6.

In the same (Barling) 1 free man held ½ hide and 10 acres 14 a
before 1066. Now St. Paul's (holds it). Always 1 plough. Value 20s.

The Canons appropriated this land after the King came to England.

TERRA sci petri de Westmonasterio. Hund de bdestapla. .VI.

In Benflet ht Scs Petrus. VII. hid. 7. XXX. ac. que jacebant in eccla scæ mariæ t. r. e. s; rex. W. dedit ecclam cu tra sco petro. de Westmonasterio jn q tra st. II. car. in dnio. 7. V. car hom; sep. XV. uill. Tc. VII. bor. m XII. Pastur. CC. ou. m. dim. mol. Tc uat. IIII. lib. m. VI. Octaua hid de ead eccla scæ mariæ. dedit Ingelric sco martino. 7 adhuc ibi e ut consu lat testat sine jussu regis. ★ .L. ou. III. porc. ★

In Phantuna. IIII. hid. 7 XXX. ac. Sep. I. car in dnio. Tc. IIII. car hom. M. I. Tc. VI. uill. m. I. tc. IIII. ser. Tc. I. bor m. IX. 7 in ead uill posst adhuc fieri. II. car in dnio; XXX. ac silue uastæ. II. runc. XXX. ou. Tc uat. LX. sol. m. VI. lib.

In Bura ht. S. P. L. ac. qs ten&. I. anglic de eo. sep. I. uill. 7. uat. L. d.

Phantuna tenuit Alestan stric. t. r. e. p. m. 7. I. hid. Tc. I. car. m. n. Sep. I. bor. Tc. 7 p uat. XX. sol. m. X. hec tra calupniata e ad op reg qd p falsu breue uenerit ad ecclam. In dnio. II. runc. XXX. ou;

Hund de Witham. In Chelleuedana. t. r. e. V. hid. qs ten& scs pet. Sep. II. car. in dnio. Tc. VIII. car. hom. m. IIII. Tc. XX. uill m. XVIII. Tc. III. bor. m. VII. Sep. III. ser. Silu. L. porc. 7. XXV. ac pti. I. mol. Tc. uat. C. sol. m. VIII. lib. 7 abbas ht inde. XII. lib; In dnio. II. runc. VI. an. XXXV. por. XXXV. ou.

6 LAND OF ST. PETER'S, WESTMINSTER

Hundred of BARSTABLE

1 In (South) BENFLEET, St. Peter's has 7 hides and 30 acres, which lay in (the lands of) St. Mary's Church before 1066; but King William gave the church with the land to St. Peter's, Westminster, on which land there are 2 ploughs in lordship and 5 men's ploughs.
Always 15 villagers. Then 7 smallholders, now 12.
Pasture, 200 sheep; now ½ mill. 50 sheep, 3 pigs.
Value then £4; now [£] 6.
Engelric gave the eighth hide of the same Church of St. Mary to St. Martin's, and it is still there, as the County testifies, without the King's command.

2 In FANTON (Hall), 4 hides and 30 acres. Always 1 plough in lordship. Then 4 men's ploughs, now 1.
Then 6 villagers, now 1; then 4 slaves; then 1 smallholder, now 9.
In the same village, 2 ploughs in lordship still possible.
30 acres of waste woodland. 2 cobs, 30 sheep.
Value then 60s; now £6.

3 In BOWERS (Gifford) St. Peter's has 50 acres, which 1 Englishman holds from it.
Always 1 villager.
Value 50d.

4 Alstan Stric held FANTON (Hall) before 1066 as a manor; 1 hide. Then 1 plough, now none.
Always 1 smallholder.
Value then and later 20s; now 10[s].
This land was claimed for the King's use because it had come to the Church by a false writ.
In lordship 2 cobs, 30 sheep.

Hundred of WITHAM

5 In KELVEDON before 1066, 5 hides, which St. Peter's holds. Always 2 ploughs in lordship. Then 8 men's ploughs, now 4.
Then 20 villagers, now 18; then 3 smallholders, now 7; always 3 slaves.
Woodland, 50 pigs; meadow, 25 acres; 1 mill.
Value then 100s; now £8. The Abbot has from it £12.
In lordship 2 cobs, 6 cattle, 35 pigs, 35 sheep.

Hund de Beuentreu. Hanc. tenuit Scs Petr. t. r. e. p. m. ★
7. II. hid. Sep. I. car. Tc. III. bor. m. v. Silu. VIII. por. Tc ual. xx. sol. M
LX. In Leituna ten&. Rad baignard. de abbe. I. hid. quā tenuit
Tosti. t. r. e. Tc. I. car. m. dim. m. v. bor. xx. ac. pti. I. mol. Tc. ual.
xxx. sol. m. XL.
Hund de Lexendena. Pheringas. tenuit Harold. t. r. e. p.
IIII. hid. 7. xxx. ac. M ten&. S. P. Tc. XXXIIII. uill. m. XXVII.
Tc. x. bor. m. XXIIII. Sep. XI. ser. 7. IIII. car. in dnio. Tc. xv. carr.
hom. m. x. Silu. D. porc. xx. ac pti. III. mol. 7 XII. sochemani
q n potant recede manentes in duab; hid. 7. dim. pt istā supdictā
trā. Sep sub ipsis. VI. bor. 7. II. car. 7. dim. Silu. xx. por. XII. ac pti.
7. II. dom in cole castro. que jacent huic manerio; In dnio. v. runc.
XVI. an. LX. por. LXXXIIII. ou. Tc ual. XXII. lib. 7. x. sol. M. XXXIIII.
lib. 7. x. sol. Rog de ramis ten& LXXXV ac. de abbe. 7 reddit uno
qq; anno p suo seruitio ad abbm. x. sol. Malger hō archiepi inuasit
sup regē. I. libm hoem q erat de manerio sci petri. t. r. e. tenentem
dimid uirg. 7 nc ē in manu reg; Sep. dim. car. 7. ual. v. sol.
Hund de Angra. Keluendunā tenuit Ailric. t. r. e. p. m.
7. II. hid. m. S. P. Sep. I. uill. Tc. v. bor. m. x. Sep. II. ser. 7. II. car i dnio.
7. I. car. hom. Silu. cc. por. XVI. ac. pti. m. I. mol. Tc. ual. XL. sol,
m. LX. Hic supdict Ailric abiit in nauale pliū cont Willm regē
7 qn rediit cecidet in infirmitate. tc dedit sco petro istud maneriū ★
sed null hominū ex comitatu scit hoc n un. 7 huc usq; tenuit
scs petr tali m hoc man. 7 neq; breuē neq; famulū reg ex parte

15 a

habuerunt postquā rex uenit in istā trā.

Hundred of BECONTREE 14 b

6 St. Peter's held (East) HAM before 1066 as a manor; 2 hides. Always 1 plough.
Then 3 smallholders, now 5.
Woodland, 8 pigs.
Value then 20s; now 60[s].

7 In LEYTON Ralph Baynard holds from the Abbot 1 hide, which Tosti held before 1066. Then 1 plough, now ½.
Now 5 smallholders.
Meadow, 20 acres; 1 mill.
Value then 30s; now 40[s].

Hundred of LEXDEN

8 Harold held FEERING before 1066, for 4 hides and 30 acres. Now St. Peter's holds (it).
Then 34 villagers, now 27; then 10 smallholders, now 24. Always 11 slaves; 4 ploughs in lordship. Then 15 men's ploughs, now 10.
Woodland, 500 pigs; meadow, 20 acres; 3 mills.
12 Freemen who could not withdraw (and) who live on 2½ hides apart from the above-mentioned land. Under these, always 6 smallholders; 2½ ploughs.
Woodland, 20 pigs; meadow, 12 acres; 2 houses in Colchester which lie in (the lands of) this manor.
In lordship 5 cobs, 16 cattle, 60 pigs, 84 sheep.
Value then £22 10s; now £34 10s.
Roger of Raismes holds 85 acres from the Abbot and pays 10s every year for his service to the Abbot. Mauger, a man of the Archbishop, annexed 1 free man in the King's despite, who was of the manor of St. Peter's before 1066 (and) who held ½ virgate. Now he is in the King's hand. Always ½ plough.
Value 5s.

Hundred of ONGAR

9 Alric held KELVEDON (Hatch) before 1066 as a manor; 2 hides. Now St. Peter's (holds it).
Always 1 villager. Then 5 smallholders, now 10. Always 2 slaves; 2 ploughs in lordship; 1 men's plough.
Woodland, 200 pigs; meadow, 16 acres; now 1 mill.
Value then 40s; now 60[s].
This above-mentioned Alric went away to a naval battle against King William and when he returned he fell ill; then he gave this manor to St. Peter's but only one man from the County knows this. St. Peter's has held this manor in this way up to now and they have had neither a writ nor a servant of the King on (his) behalf after the King came to this land. 15 a

In Wochenduna ten& Witt camerari9 de abbe . i . hid . 7 . i . car . in dnio. 7 . i . car hom . iiii . uill . val . xl . sol.

Hund de Cefeorda Wochenduna ten Harold . p . m . 7 . ii . hid. xl . ac . min9 . t . r . e . m ten& S . P . Tc . viii . uill . m . vii . Tc . v . bor . m . viii. Sep . iiii . ser . 7 . ii . car . in dnio . Tc . vi . car . hom . m . iiii . Silu . ccc . por. . i . runc . vi . an . xxx . por . cx . ou . Tc ual . iiii . lib . m . x . hec tra est p escangio pq9 rex transfretauit.

Wemtuna ten& . sep . S . P . p . m . 7 . ii . hid . 7 . dim . Tc . iii . uill . m . ii. Tc . iii . bor . m . i . Tc . ii . ser . m . null9 . Tc . i . car in dnio . m . dim . Tc . i. car . hom . m . dim . i . runc . i . uac . iiii . por . lx . ou . Tc . ual . xl . sol . m lx . Vn9 lib ho misit in sco petro . dim . hid . s; Rob inuesiat9 ho Rob grenonis . pocupauit . 7 reddit p annu . xx . d. ★

Geddesduna ten . S . P . p . i . hid . Sep . i . uill . 7 . i . bor . Tc . dim . car . m . i . Sep . ual . xx . sol.

Hund de Celmeresfort . Molesham ten& Sep scs Petr9. p . v . hid . xxx . ac . min9 . Tc . viii . uill . m . iii . Tc . iiii . bor . m . xxi. M . ii . ser . Sep . iii . car . in dnio . 7 . iiii . car . hom . Silu . cccc . por. xxx . ac . pti . i . mol . i . runc . ii . uac . xxxvi . por . c . ou . Tc . ual . ix . lib . m . xii.

Hund de Rochefort . Pachesham ten& scs P . p . m . 7 . p . i . hid . 7 . dim . Tc . ii . bor . m . xi . Tc . iiii . ser . Tc . ii . car in dnio . m . i. Sep . i . car hom . past . xx . ou . i . runc . iiii . an . c . ou . Tc . ual. . iiii . lib m . vi . Hanc tra dedit . i . teign9 . ecclæ . qn iuit ad bellu i Eurewic cu haroldo.

[Hundred of CHAFFORD]

10 In (North) OCKENDON, William the Chamberlain holds 1 hide from the Abbot. 1 plough in lordship. 1 men's plough.
4 villagers.
Value 40s.

Hundred of CHAFFORD

11 Harold held (North) OCKENDON as a manor; 2 hides less 40 acres before 1066. Now St. Peter's holds (it).
Then 8 villagers, now 7; then 5 smallholders, now 8.
Always 4 slaves; 2 ploughs in lordship. Then 6 men's ploughs, now 4.
Woodland, 300 pigs. 1 cob, 6 cattle, 30 pigs, 110 sheep.
Value then £4; now [£] 10.
This land was (acquired) by exchange after the King crossed the sea.

12 St. Peter's has always held WENNINGTON as a manor; 2½ hides.
Then 3 villagers, now 2; then 3 smallholders, now 1; then 2 slaves, now none. Then 1 plough in lordship, now ½.
Then 1 men's plough, now ½.
1 cob, 1 cow, 4 pigs, 60 sheep.
Value then 40s; now 60[s].
A free man disposed of ½ hide to St. Peter's, but Robert the Perverted, a man of Robert Gernon's, misappropriated (it) and pays 20d a year.

13 St. Peter's holds *GEDDESDUNA* for 1 hide.
Always 1 villager; 1 smallholder. Then ½ plough, now 1.
Value always 20s.

Hundred of CHELMSFORD

14 St. Peter's has always held MOULSHAM (Lodge) for 5 hides less 30 acres.
Then 8 villagers, now 3; then 4 smallholders, now 21; now 2 slaves. Always 3 ploughs in lordship; 4 men's ploughs.
Woodland, 400 pigs; meadow, 30 acres; 1 mill. 1 cob, 2 cows, 36 pigs, 100 sheep.
Value then £9; now [£] 12.

Hundred of ROCHFORD

15 St. Peter's holds PAGLESHAM as a manor, for 1½ hides.
Then 2 smallholders, now 11; then 4 slaves. Then 2 ploughs in lordship, now 1. Always 1 men's plough.
Pasture, 20 sheep. 1 cob, 4 cattle, 100 sheep.
Value then £4; now [£] 6.
1 thane gave this land to the Church when he went to battle in York(shire) with Harold.

15 b

.VII. TERRÆ EPI DVNELMENSIS IN EXSESSA.

Dimidium Hundret de Walthā. Walham tenuit Harold t.r.e.
pro uno Man. 7. XL. hid. Sēp. LXXX. uilt. 7. XXIIII. bor. Tc. VI. ser. m VII.
Tc. VII. car in dnio. m. VI. Sēp. XXXVII. car hom. Silu. II. 7 CC. por.
LXXX. ac. pti. II. runc. XX. an. LXXX. ou. XII. cap. XL. por. Pastura
ē ibi que ual. XVIII. sol. Tc. I. mol. m. III. v. piscinæ. 7 tc. XX. censarij.
m. XXXVI. 7. I. car pot in manerio. restaurari. Huic Man adjacent.
.II. soc. tenentes. VI. hid. t.r.e. m. v. 7 medietatē sextæ hid ht Sca crux.
7 altam partē tulit Wilt de War. 7. IIII. soc de. II. hid. 7 dim uirg.
7. adhuc ptinebat. huic man. I. hid. XV. ac. min qm inde tulit
idē Wilt. Et Ranulf fr ilgeri. XXX. ac. træ. 7. IIII. pti.
Oms illi soc q ibi m st hnt. VII. hid. 7. XV. ac. 7 habebant. t.r.e. in
coz dnio. IIII. car. m. IIII. 7. đ. 7 sēp. I. uilt. Tc. VI. bor. m. VIII. Tc. II.
ser. m null. Silu. CLXXX. II. por. XVI. ac. 7. dim. pti. 7. IIII. ac. pasturæ.
De hoc toto. 7 de manerio habebat Har. t.r.e. XXXVI. lib. 7 hões epi
appțiant. LXIII. lib. 7. V. sol. 7. IIII. đ. M ů ut alij hões de hund testant:
ual. C. lib. 7 Londoniæ. st. XII. dom ptinentes Manerio. quæ reddt
XX. sol. 7 una. porta qm rex dedit ~~suo~~ antecessori ēpi. que &iā redd.
XX. sol.

.VIII. TERRÆ Canonicoz scē Crucis de Waltham Hundret de
Walthā. Epingam. ten& sēp. sca crux. p. m. 7. II. hid. 7. XV. ac; Sēp
. I. car 7. dim in dnio. 7. II. bor. 7. II. ser. Silu. L. por. III. ac. pti. X. an.

16 a
. I. runc. XX. por. XX. ou. VIII. cap. 7 ual. XV. sol.
Nasingā sēp ten& Scā crux. p. V. hid. Tc. I. car in dnio. m. I. 7 dim. Tc. I.
car hom. m. I. 7. đ. Sēp. V. uilt. m. II. bor. Tc. II. ser. m null. Silu. L. por.
. XIII. ac. pti. dim pisc. I. r. IIII. an. X. por. XV. ou. Tc. ual. XL. sol. m LX.

7 LANDS OF THE BISHOP OF DURHAM IN ESSEX 15 b

Half-Hundred of WALTHAM

1 Harold held WALTHAM (Holy Cross) before 1066 as one manor; 40 hides.

Always 80 villagers; 24 smallholders. Then 6 slaves, now 7. Then 7 ploughs in lordship, now 6. Always 37 men's ploughs.

Woodland, 202 pigs; meadow, 80 acres. 2 cobs, 20 cattle, 80 sheep, 12 goats, 40 pigs. Pasture is there which is worth 18s; then 1 mill, now 3; 5 fisheries; then 20 tributaries, now 36; 1 plough can be restored in the manor.

To this manor belong 2 Freemen who held 6 hides before 1066, now 5. Holy Cross has half of the sixth hide. William of Warenne took the other part. 4 Freemen with 2 hides and ½ virgate. 1 hide less 15 acres still belongs to this manor, which the same William took from it. Ranulf brother of Ilger (holds) 30 acres of land and 4 (acres) of pasture.

All the Freemen who are there now have 7 hides and 15 acres. Before 1066 they had in their lordship 4 ploughs; now 4½.

Always 1 villager. Then 6 smallholders, now 8; then 2 slaves, now none.

Woodland, 182 pigs; meadow, 16½ acres; pasture, 4 acres.

From the whole of this and from the manor, Harold had £36 before 1066. The Bishop's men are assessed at £63 5s 4d. But now, as the other men of the Hundred testify, value £100.

In London there are 12 houses which belong to the manor (and) which pay 20s, and a gate which the King gave to the Bishop's predecessor and which also pays 20s.

8 LANDS OF THE CANONS OF WALTHAM HOLY CROSS

Hundred of WALTHAM

1 Holy Cross has always held EPPING as a manor; 2 hides and 15 acres. Always 1½ ploughs in lordship;

2 smallholders; 2 slaves.

Woodland, 50 pigs; meadow, 3 acres. 10 cattle, 1 cob, 20 pigs, 20 sheep, 8 goats. 16 a

Value 15s.

2 Holy Cross has always held NAZEING for 5 hides. Then 1 plough in lordship, now 1½. Then 1 men's plough, now 1½.

Always 5 villagers. Now 2 smallholders; then 2 slaves, now none.

Woodland, 50 pigs; meadow, 13 acres; ½ fishery. 1 cob, 4 cattle, 10 pigs, 15 sheep.

Value then 40s; now 60[s].

Hundret de beuentreu. Wdefort ten& sep̄ sc̄a crux. t. r. e.
.v. hid. Sep̄. II. car. in dn̄io. Tc̄. XIII. car hom. m̄. VII. Sep̄. XIII. uilt. Silu. D. porc xxvi. ac pti
Tc̄. IIII. bor. m̄. VII. Tc̄. IIII. ser. m̄ null. Tc̄. I. an. m̄. VI. c. ou. L. por. tc̄. I. mol. m̄. n̄;
XL. cap. Sep̄ ual. c. sol.

Lochintunā ten& sep̄. sc̄a crux. p. m̄ 7. IIII. hid. 7. XX. ac. Tc̄. II. car
in dn̄io. m̄. I. Sep̄. I. car hom. 7. II. uilt. Tc̄. II. bor. m̄. v. Silu. c. por. v. ac. pt.
. I. car pot restaurari. v. an. v. ou. 7 ual. XL. sol.

Lochintunā ten& Sc̄a cr. p m̄. 7. II. hid. 7. dim. Sep̄. I. car in dn̄io.
tc̄. II. bor. m̄. IIII. Silu. XL. por. IIII. ac. pti. IX. an. x. por. XX. ou. val. XX. sol.

Hund de Angra. Passefeldā ten& sep̄. S. cr. p. m̄. 7 p. II. hid. XXX.
ac. min. Tc̄. VI. uilt. m̄. v. m̄. IIII. bor. Tc̄. VII. ser. m̄. III. Tc̄. II. car ī dn̄io
m̄. III. Tc̄. III. car. hom. m̄. II. Silu. dcc. porc. VIII. ac. pti. Tc̄. III. an.
m̄. VI. Tc̄. XX. por. m̄. XXX. L. ou. Tc̄. XVI. cap. m̄. XXXVI. M. I. runc.
Sep̄ ual. VI. lib.

Aluertunā ten& sep̄. S. cr. p. m̄. 7. IIII. hid. 7. dim. 7. x. ac. Tc̄. VII.
uilt. m̄. IX. Tc̄. II. bor. m̄. VI. Tc̄. v. ser. m̄. III. Sep̄. II. car in dn̄io. Tc̄
. III. car hom. m̄. II. Silu. cccc. por. xv. ac. pti. II. an. VIII. ou. x. por
xv. cap. Sep̄ ual. IIII. lib.

Tippedanā ten& sep̄ sc̄. cr. p m̄. 7. III. hid. 7. XL. ac. Sep̄. IIII. uilt. 7
VII. bor. Tc̄. IIII. ser. m̄ null. Tc̄. II. car. in dn̄io. m̄. I. tc̄. II. car hom m̄. I.

Hundred of BECONTREE

3 Holy Cross has always held WOODFORD, 5 hides before 1066. Always 2 ploughs in lordship. Then 13 men's ploughs, now 7.

Always 13 villagers. Then 4 smallholders, now 7; then 4 slaves, now none.

Woodland, 500 pigs; meadow, 26 acres; then 1 mill, now none.

Then 1 (head of) cattle, now 6; 100 sheep, 50 pigs, 40 goats.

Value always 100s.

4 Holy Cross has always held LOUGHTON as a manor; 4 hides and 20 acres. Then 2 ploughs in lordship, now 1. Always 1 men's plough; 2 villagers. Then 2 smallholders, now 5.

Woodland, 100 pigs; meadow, 5 acres; 1 plough could be restored. 5 cattle, 5 sheep.

Value 40s.

5 Holy Cross holds LOUGHTON as a manor; 2½ hides. Always 1 plough in lordship.

Then 2 smallholders, now 4.

Woodland, 40 pigs; meadow, 4 acres. 9 cattle, 10 pigs, 20 sheep.

Value 20s.

Hundred of ONGAR

6 Holy Cross has always held PASLOW (Hall) as a manor, for 2 hides less 30 acres.

Then 6 villagers, now 5; now 4 smallholders; then 7 slaves, now 3. Then 2 ploughs in lordship, now 3. Then 3 men's ploughs, now 2.

Woodland, 700 pigs; meadow, 8 acres. Then 3 cattle, now 6; then 20 pigs, now 30; 50 sheep; then 16 goats, now 36; now 1 cob.

Value always £6.

7 Holy Cross has always held ALDERTON (Hall) as a manor; 4½ hides and 10 acres.

Then 7 villagers, now 9; then 2 smallholders, now 6; then 5 slaves, now 3. Always 2 ploughs in lordship. Then 3 men's ploughs, now 2.

Woodland, 400 pigs; meadow, 15 acres. 2 cattle, 8 sheep, 10 pigs, 15 goats.

Value always £4.

8 Holy Cross has always held DEBDEN (Green) as a manor; 3 hides and 40 acres.

Always 4 villagers; 7 smallholders. Then 4 slaves, now none. Then 2 ploughs in lordship, now 1. Then 2 men's ploughs, now 1.

Silū . ccc . por . vi . ac̄ . p̄ti . ii . an̄ . viii .. por . ix . ou̇ . Sēp uał . xl . sol . ⸿ Q̇dam lib hō tenuit . xl . ac̄ . quē inuasit eccła . p̄q rex uenit in hanc trā . 7 ten& adhuc . Tc̄ . i . car̄ . m̄ nulla . 7 qn̄ recep̄ dim̄ . iiii . ac̄ . p̄ti . Tc̄ uał . vi . sol 7 . viii . đ . m̊ . v . sol . 7 . iiii . đ.

⸿ Hunđ de Cesseorda. Wełda ten& sēp̱ . sc̄ . cr̄ . ꝑ uno maner̄ . 7 . t̄ . r̄ . ē ꝑ . ii . hid̄ . m̊ . ꝑ . i . 7 dim̄ . Goisfrid̄ de magna uilla ħt aliā dim̄ . s; hunđ nescit qre habeat . 7 . G . dicit se habē ꝑ escangio . Sēp̱ . x . uilł . 7 . vi . bor . 7 . iii . ser̄ . 7 . ii . car̄ in dn̄io . Tc̄ . vi . car̄ hom̄ . m̄ . iiii . Silū . cc . por . i . ac̄ 7 . đ . p̄ti . m̊ . iiii . an̄ . Tc̄ . x . por . m̊ . xxv . Tc̄ xxv . ou̇ . m̊ . lxv . 7 Vał vi . lib In ho manerio jacuit . i . soc̄ . q̇ tenuit . i . carr̄ . trǣ . s; m̄ ħt Rob̄ gnon . ex dono reḡ ut ipse dic̄.

⸿ Vpmonstrā ten& sc̄ . c̄ . ꝑ . ii . hid̄ . 7 . dim̄ . 7 . xl . ac̄ . Tc̄ . viii . uilł . m̄ vi . Tc̄ . ii . bor . m̊ . iiii . Tc̄ . iiii . ser̄ . m̄ . iii . Sēp̱ . ii . car̄ in dn̄io . 7 . iiii . car̄ hōū Silū . ccc . por . vi . ac̄ p̄ti . ii . an̄ . Tc̄ . xx . ou̇ . m̊ . l . Tc̄ . xi . por . m̊ xxx . Sēp̱ uał . iiii . lib . huic manerio jac& . i . soc̄ . de . xxx . ac̄ . 7 dim̄ . car̄ . 7 uał . xx . đ.

⸿ Walcfarā ten& sēp̱ ecła . ꝑ . iiii . hid̄ . xl . ac̄ min̄ . Tc̄ . iiii . bor . m̊ . x . Tc̄ . vi . ser̄ . m̊ . iii . Sēp̱ . ii . car̄ in dn̄io . 7 . i . car̄ . hom̄ Silū . xxx . por . xviii . ac̄ . p̄ti . M̊ . i . runc̄ . Sēp̱ . v . an̄ . v . por . xl . ou̇ . ii . uasa apū . Vał . xl . sol.

Woodland, 300 pigs; meadow, 6 acres. 2 cattle, 8 pigs, 9 sheep. 16 b
Value always 40s.

A free man held 40 acres, which the Church annexed after the King came to this land and still holds. Then 1 plough, now none; when acquired, ½.

Meadow, 4 acres.
Value then 6s 8d; now 5s 4d.

Hundred of CHAFFORD

9 Holy Cross has always held (South) WEALD as one manor; before 1066, for 2 hides, now for 1½. Geoffrey de Mandeville has the other ½ (hide); but the Hundred does not know why he has it. Geoffrey states he had it by exchange.

Always 10 villagers; 6 smallholders; 3 slaves; 2 ploughs in lordship. Then 6 men's ploughs, now 4.

Woodland, 200 pigs; meadow, 1½ acres. Now 4 cattle; then 10 pigs, now 25; then 25 sheep, now 65.

Value £6.

In this manor belongs 1 Freeman who held 1 carucate of land; but now Robert Gernon has it by the King's gift, as he himself states.

10 Holy Cross holds UPMINSTER for 2½ hides and 40 acres.

Then 8 villagers, now 6; then 2 smallholders, now 4; then 4 slaves, now 3. Always 2 ploughs in lordship; 4 men's ploughs.

Woodland, 300 pigs; meadow, 6 acres. 2 cattle; then 20 sheep, now 50; then 11 pigs, now 30.

Value always £4.

To this manor belongs 1 Freeman with 30 acres and ½ plough. Value 20d.

[Hundred of CHELMSFORD]

11 The Church has always held WALTER (Hall) for 4 hides less 40 acres.

Then 4 smallholders, now 10; then 6 slaves, now 3. Always 2 ploughs in lordship; 1 men's plough.

Woodland, 30 pigs; meadow, 18 acres. Now 1 cob; always 5 cattle, 5 pigs, 40 sheep, 2 beehives.

Value 40s.

17 a

SCA . MARIA De berchinges. In Exsessa.
SCA Aldreda de eli.
SCS ETmund
SCS MArtin Londonie.
SCS Martin de Bello.
SCS Walerie.
SCA TrinitaS Decadomo.
SCS Stephan de cadomo.
SCS Audoen.
EPS Baiocensis.

17 b

.IX. TERRA SCE MARIE DE BERCHINGIS.

Hund de berdestapla . Mucinga . ten& Sca maria p . VII . hid ; 7 . XXX . ac.
inde abstulit Turold de Rouecestra . 7 jacent ad feudu epi baiocensiS.
7 t . r . e . I . car in dnio . m . II . Sep . IX . car uillis . 7 . XII . uill . Tc . XIIII . bor . m
XXV . Tc . IIII . ser . m . null . Silu . CCC . por . Pastura . CCC . ou . XL . ac . pti.
M . I . mol . I . Piscina . X . an . II . runc . XVIII . por . CCL . ou . Sep uat . X . lib.
Bulgeuen . ten& S . M . p . VII . hid . Tc . I . car in dnio m . II . Tc . VII . car hou
m . X . Tc . X . uill . m . XVI . Tc . V . bor . m . XVI . III . ser . Silu . D . porc . VIII . an.
XV . por . I . runc . LXXX . ou . Tc uat . VIII . lib . m . X . De hac tra tulit Rauen
gari . XXIIII . ac . In Fantuna . XL . ac . tre ten& . I . uills . sep . dim . car . 7 uat
XL . d . De Supdicto manerio scilic& de Muchinga . ten& Will . dim . hid
7 . XXX . ac . 7 . III . bor . 7 . uat . XVIII . sol in supdicto ptio ejde manerii.

[9] *St. Mary, Barking. In Essex* 17 a
[10] *St. Etheldreda, Ely*
[11] *St. Edmund*
[12] *St. Martin, London*
[13] *St. Martin, Battle*
[14] *St. Valéry*
[15] *Holy Trinity, Caen*
[16] *St. Stephen, Caen*
[17] *St. Ouen*
[18] *The Bishop of Bayeux*

9 LAND OF ST. MARY'S, BARKING 17 b

Hundred of BARSTABLE

1 St. Mary's holds MUCKING for 7 hides. Thorold of Rochester took 30 acres away from there and they lie in the Bishop of Bayeux's Holding. Before 1066, 1 plough in lordship, now 2. Always 9 villagers' ploughs;
12 villagers. Then 14 smallholders, now 25; then 4 slaves, now none.
Woodland, 300 pigs; pasture, 300 sheep; meadow, 40 acres; now 1 mill; 1 fishery. 10 cattle, 2 cobs, 18 pigs, 250 sheep.
Value always £10.

2 St. Mary's holds BULPHAN for 7 hides. Then 1 plough in lordship, now 2. Then 7 men's ploughs, now 10.
Then 10 villagers, now 16; then 5 smallholders, now 16; 3 slaves.
Woodland, 500 pigs. 8 cattle, 15 pigs, 1 cob, 80 sheep.
Value then £8; now [£] 10.
Of this land, Ravengar took 24 acres.

3 In FANTON (Hall) 1 villager holds 40 acres of land. Always ½ plough. Value 40d.

4 William holds ½ hide and 30 acres of the above-mentioned manor, namely MUCKING.
3 smallholders.
Value 18s in the above-mentioned assessment of the same manor.

In hoc hund st̃ . vi . libi hões tenentes . ii . hid . 7 . l . ac . Sep̃ . ii . car . Tc̃ . iii .
bor . m̃ . vi . Tc̃ . i . ser . m̃ . ñ . Tc̃ silu . c . por . M . lv . xiii . pars uni piscinæ . Totũ
ual xxx . sol . Isti hões libe exstiterunt ad berchingũ s; rex m̃ ex ipsis
pot facere qđ sibi placuerit . De silu huis tr̃æ ht̃ Rob grinon . l . porc.
Et de supdicta tr̃a ten& Goduin cudhen . iii . uirg̃ . 7 ual . x . sol.

Dimidiũ Hund de herlaua . In Perenduna ten& sep̃ . scã mar . dim
hid . dim . car . i . bor . silu . x . por . v . ac . p̃ti . Val . x . sol.

Hund de beuentreu . Berchingas ten& sep̃ sc̃a . m . p xxx . hid.
Tc̃ . iiii . car in dñio . m̃ . iii . 7 . iiii . poss& fieri . Tc̃ . lxx . car hom . m̃ lxviii.
Tc̃ . c . uilt . m̃ . cxl . Tc̃ . l . bor M . lxxxx Tc̃ . x . ser . m̃ . vi . Silu . m . porc.
. c . ac . p̃ti . ii . mol . i . pisc . ii . runc . xxxiiii . an . cl . por . cxiiii . oues.
xxiiii . cap̃ . x . uasa apũ . In Londonia . xxviii . dom quæ reddt . . .

18 a

xiii . sol . 7 . viii . đ . 7 dim ecctia quæ t . r . e . reddebat vi . sol . 7 . viii . đ . 7
m̃ ñ reddit . Hoc maneriũ ual t . r . e . lxxx . lib . 7 m̃ similit ut dicunt
anglici . s; franci app̃tiant . c . lib . Huic manerio p̃tinebant t . r . e.
xxiiii . ac . qs inde tulit Goscelin . Loremari . 7 . iii . milit . ten . ii . hid . 7 . iii . car

Hund de Wensistreu . Wicghebg̃a ten& sep̃ . sc̃a maria p . xi . hid (7 . iii . uilt . 7 . x . bor . 7 ual xlv sol ĩ eod p̃tio.)
7 . dim . 7 . xiii . ac . Tc̃ . ii . car 7 đ . in dñio . m̃ . ii . Tc̃ . x . car hom . m̃ . ix . Tc̃
ix . uilt . m̃ . x . Tc̃ . xxiiii . bor . m̃ xxxiii . Sep̃ . viii . ser . Silu . c . por . Past
. c . ou . quæ redđ . xvi . đ . vi . sal . Tc̃ . xii . an . 7 m̃ simil . ii . runc . xiiii.
por . ccxxx . ou . Tc̃ ual . xii . lib . m̃ . x . Huic man . p̃tinent . iii . dom
in colecastro.

5 In this Hundred are 6 free men who hold 2 hides and 50 acres.
Always 2 ploughs.
Then 3 smallholders, now 6; then 1 slave, now none.
Then woodland, 100 pigs, now 55; the thirteenth part of 1 fishery.
Total value 30s.
These men existed freely at Barking; but the King might now do with them as he pleases.
Of the woodland of this land, Robert Gernon has 50 pigs.
Of the above land, Godwin Woodhen holds 3 virgates; value 10s.

Half-Hundred of HARLOW

6 St. Mary's has always held ½ hide in PARNDON.
½ plough.
1 smallholder.
Woodland, 10 pigs; meadow, 5 acres.
Value 10s.

Hundred of BECONTREE

7 St. Mary's has always held BARKING for 30 hides. Then 4 ploughs in lordship, now 3; 4 possible. Then 70 men's ploughs, now 68.
Then 100 villagers, now 140; then 50 smallholders, now 90; then 10 slaves, now 6.
Woodland, 1000 pigs; meadow, 100 acres; 2 mills; 1 fishery.
2 cobs, 34 cattle, 150 pigs, 114 sheep, 24 goats, 10 beehives.
In London 28 houses which pay 13s 8d and ½ church which 18 a
paid 6s 8d before 1066 and now does not pay.
The value of this manor before 1066 was £80; now the same, as the Englishmen state, but the Frenchmen assess it at £100.
To this manor before 1066 belonged 24 acres which Jocelyn Lorimer took away from it.
3 men-at-arms hold 2 hides and 3 ploughs.
3 villagers and 10 smallholders.
Value 45s in the same assessment.

Hundred of WINSTREE

8 St. Mary's has always held WIGBOROUGH for 11½ hides and 13 acres. Then 2½ ploughs in lordship, now 2. Then 10 men's ploughs, now 9.
Then 9 villagers, now 10; then 24 smallholders, now 33; always 8 slaves.
Woodland, 100 pigs; pasture, 100 sheep, which pays 16d; 6 salt-houses. Then 12 cattle, now the same; 2 cobs, 14 pigs, 230 sheep.
Value then £12; now [£] 10.
To this manor belong 3 houses in Colchester.

Hund de Cessorda. Wareleiā ten& sēp sc̄a maria . p . iii . hid sēp . ix . uitt . Tc̄ . viii . bor . m̄ . x . Tc̄ . iii . ser . m̄ . v . sēp . ii . car . in dnio . Tc . viii . car hom . m̄ . vi . silu . cc . por . past . c . ou . viii . an . xi . porc . cl . ou . i . uas ap . sēp uat . vii . lib . In Stiforda ht S . M . xl . ac . Tc̄ . i . uitt . M . ii . 7 . ii . bor . i . ac p̄ti . Tc̄ . i . car . m̄ . dim . 7 uat . iii . sot . Fuere &iā ad hanc trā xxx . ac . qs ht Witt de war p escangio ut ipse dicit. Sunt adhuc . aliæ . xxx . ac . 7 . ii . ac . 7 dim p̄ti . 7 uat . iii . sot

Hund de celmeresfort . Ingā ten& sēp sc . M . p . iii . hid . 7 . dim . 7 . x . ac . sēp . ii . uitt . Tc̄ . vi . bor . m̄ . vii . sēp . i . ser . 7 . i . car . in dnio . Tc̄ . i . car 7 d . hom . m̄ . i . silu . d . por . 7 . i . soc de . xxx . ac . i . runc . ix . an . ix . an . xx . porc . xvi . ou . Tc̄ uat . lxx . sot . m̄ lx .

Festinges ten& sc . M . p . i . uirg 7 . dim . Tc̄ . iii . bor . m̄ . iiii . Tc̄ . i . ser . m̄ null . sēp . i . car . silu . cc . por . iiii . an . xxxvii . ou . x . cap . Tc̄ uat . viii . sot . m̄ . x .

18 b

Hund de Rochefort . Hocheleiā ten& sēp . S . M . p M . 7 . vii . hid 7 . dim . Tc̄ xxiiii . uitt . m̄ . xxvii . sēp . xii . bor . Tc̄ . iii . ser . m̄ . null . Sēp . ii . car in dnio . 7 . xv . car hom . past . cc . ou . i . mot . ii . runc . viii . an . cli . ou . xxvi . por . Sēp uat . x . lib . De hoc man ten& Witt de bursigni de eccta . iii . uirg . 7 . i . car . 7 uat . xxi . sot . in eod . p̄tio .

Hundred of CHAFFORD

9 St. Mary's has always held (Great) WARLEY for 3 hides.
Always 9 villagers. Then 8 smallholders, now 10; then 3 slaves, now 5. Always 2 ploughs in lordship. Then 8 men's ploughs, now 6.
Woodland, 200 pigs; pasture, 100 sheep. 8 cattle, 11 pigs, 150 sheep, 1 beehive.
Value always £7.

10 In STIFFORD St. Mary's has 40 acres.
Then 1 villager, now 2. 2 smallholders.
Meadow, 1 acre. Then 1 plough, now ½.
Value 3s.
There were also 30 acres (belonging) to this land which William of Warenne has by exchange, as he himself states.
There are besides another 30 acres.
Meadow, 2½ acres.
Value 3s.

Hundred of CHELMSFORD

11 St. Mary's has always held INGATESTONE for 3½ hides and 10 acres.
Always 2 villagers. Then 6 smallholders, now 7. Always 1 slave; 1 plough in lordship. Then 1½ men's ploughs, now 1.
Woodland, 500 pigs; 1 Freeman with 30 acres. 1 cob, 9 cattle, 9 cattle, 20 pigs, 16 sheep.
Value then 70s; now 60[s].

12 St. Mary's holds FRISTLING for 1½ virgates.
Then 3 smallholders, now 4; then 1 slave, now none. Always 1 plough.
Woodland, 200 pigs. 4 cattle, 37 sheep, 10 goats.
Value then 8s; now 10[s].

Hundred of ROCHFORD 18 b

13 St. Mary's has always held HOCKLEY as a manor; 7½ hides.
Then 24 villagers, now 27; always 12 smallholders; then 3 slaves, now none. Always 2 ploughs in lordship; 15 men's ploughs.
Pasture, 200 sheep; 1 mill. 2 cobs, 8 cattle, 151 sheep, 26 pigs.
Value always £10.
Of this manor, William of Boursigny holds 3 virgates from the Church. 1 plough.
Value 21s in the same assessment.

Hund de Turestapla. Tolesbiam ten& sep. S. Æ. p. m. 7. VIII. hid. Tc. XI. uill. m. XII. Tc XIIII. bor. M. XVI. Tc. V. ser. m. VII. Sep. II. car in dnio. Tc. VIII. car. hom. m. VII. silu. D. porc. Past. CCCC. ou. m. I. mol. 7. I. piscina. 7. II. sal. II. runc. X. an. XXVIII. por. CCC. ou. Sep. ual. X. lib. Ranulf piperell. ten&. I. hid. qm tenuit Siuuard. de abb. 7 ipse uult facere tale seruitiu qle suus antecessor fecit. s; abbatissa non uult. qa erat de uictu ecclæ. Odo ho suani accepit X. ac. quæ fuer de eccla. 7 hund hoc testat. s; inde uocat dnm suu ad tutore. Sep ualent. XVI. d.

.X. TERRE Sce Adeldredæ de eli. Hund de dommauua.
Brocchesheuot ten& sep Sca. A. p. m. 7. III. hid. sep. II. car i dnio 7. IIII. car hom. XVI. uilli. Tc. II. bor. m. V. V. ser. Silu. CCL. por. XXX. ac. pti. Tc 7 m. XVI. an. II. runc. LXX. ou. II. uasa apu. Tc ual. X. lib. m. VIII. De hoc manerio ablatæ sunt IX. ac tre. t. r. Willi. qs ten& Eudo dapifer. 7 adhuc II. car træ de dominio quas ten&. Ide Eudo. 7 ual. IIII. lib. ★

19 a

Rodinges ten& sep. sca. A. 7 t. r. e. p. III. hid. 7. XLV. ac. m. p. II. hid. 7. XLV. ac. 7 tcia hida de dnio tulit Will de uuarenna. quæ ibi jacebat t. r. e; Sep. VIII. uill. 7. I. pbr. II. bor. IIII. ser. Tc. III. car in dnio. m. II. Sep IIII. car hom. Silu. C. por. XX. ac. pti. II. runc. IX. an. XVVIII. porc. XV. ou. 7 tres soc attinent huic manerio. 7. XI. bor. 7. III. ser. Tc ual. IIII. li. m. VI;

Ratendunā tenuit Sca. A. t. r. e. p. I. m. 7. p. XX. hid. M. ten& p XVI. hid. 7. dim. Sep XXVI. uill. 7 VI. bor. Tc. VII. ser. m. VI. Sep. III. car in dnio. 7. XII. car hom. Silu. CCC. porc. IX. an. XLI. porc. CLX. ou. 7. IIII.

Hundred of THURSTABLE

14 St. Mary's has always held TOLLESBURY as a manor; 8 hides.
Then 11 villagers, now 12; then 14 smallholders, now 16; then 5 slaves, now 7. Always 2 ploughs in lordship. Then 8 men's ploughs, now 7.
Woodland, 500 pigs; pasture, 400 sheep; now 1 mill; 1 fishery; 2 salt-houses. 2 cobs, 10 cattle, 28 pigs, 300 sheep.
Value always £10.

Ranulf Peverel holds 1 hide which Siward held from the Abbey. He himself wants to perform such service as his predecessor performed; but the Abbess did not want (it so), because it was for the Church's supplies.

Odo, a man of Swein's, received 10 acres which were the Church's. The Hundred testifies to this but he vouches his lord as guarantor for it.
Value always 16d.

10 LANDS OF ST. ETHELDREDA'S, ELY

Hundred of DUNMOW

1 St. Etheldreda's has always held BROXTED as a manor; 3 hides. Always 2 ploughs in lordship; 4 men's ploughs.
16 villagers; then 2 smallholders, now 5; 5 slaves.
Woodland, 250 pigs; meadow, 30 acres. Then and now 16 cattle, 2 cobs, 70 sheep, 2 beehives.
Value then £10; now [£] 8.

From this manor, 9 acres of land were taken away after 1066, which Eudo the Steward holds. Also 2 carucates of land from the lordship which Eudo also holds.
Value £4.

2 St. Etheldreda's has always held (Aythorp) RODING; before 1066 19 a
for 3 hides and 45 acres, now for 2 hides and 45 acres. William of Warenne took the third hide from the lordship which lay there before 1066.
Always 8 villagers; 1 priest; 2 smallholders; 4 slaves. Then 3 ploughs in lordship, now 2. Always 4 men's ploughs.
Woodland, 100 pigs; meadow, 20 acres. 2 cobs, 9 cattle, 23 pigs, 15 sheep.
3 Freemen belong to this manor; 11 smallholders; 3 slaves.
Value then £4; now [£] 6.

[Hundred of CHELMSFORD]

3 St. Etheldreda's held RETTENDON before 1066 as 1 manor, for 20 hides. Now it holds (it) for 16½ hides.
Always 26 villagers; 6 smallholders. Then 7 slaves, now 6. Always 3 ploughs in lordship; 12 men's ploughs.
Woodland, 300 pigs. 9 cattle, 41 pigs, 164 sheep.

Tc̄ ual . xvii . lib̄ . m̄ . xx . 7 . i . hid 7 . xxx . ac . ten& Siuuard de sc̄a . A.
M̊ ten& Ranulf piperell de rege . s; hunđ testat de abbatia.
7 . ii . hid . 7 . xxx . ac . q̃ tenuit ecc̄lia 7 Leuesun de ea . t . r . e . M̊ ten& ★
eudo de abb̄e . q̃ antecessor ej tenuit eā . s; hunđ testat . qđ non
poterat uenđe eā sine licentia abb̄is.

Dimidium Hunđ de Frossewella . Cadenhov ten& sep̄ . sc̄a.
A . p . i . m̄ . 7 . ii . hid . Tc̄ . viii . uill . m̄ . xii . Tc̄ . iiii . bor . m̄ . xiii . Tc̄ . iiii .
ser . m̄ . ii . Sep̄ . ii . car . in dn̄io . Tc̄ . iii . car . hom . m̄ . iiii . Silu . c . porc.
vi . ac . p̄ti . Tc̄ . i . mol . m̄ . null . i . runc . iiii . an . xvi . por . xxxvi . oues
viii . cap . Tc̄ ual . vi . lib̄ . m̄ . x.

Hunđ de udelesfort Litelbyriā ten& sep̄ . S . A . p . i . maner.
7 . xxv . hid . Sep̄ . xxxix . uill . 7 . xix . bor . vii . ser . Tc̄ . v . car in
dn̄io . m̄ . iiii . Tc̄ . xvii . car . hom . m̄ . xv . Silu . clx . por . lv . ac . p̄ti.
sep̄ . iiii . mol . ii . runc . xxxii . porc . lxxx . ou . iii . uasa apum.
Val . xx . lib̄ . Est &iā . i . bereuuita que vocat Strathala quā ★
tenuer . ii . hoes . Wills . Eluui . p . v . hid . 7 n̄ poterant receđe

19 b

a tr̃a sine licentia abb̄is . m̄ ten& hugo sub abb̄e . Tc̄ . vii . uill . m̄ . vi.
Tc̄ . iiii . bor . m̄ . vii . Sep̄ . vi . ser . 7 . iii . car . in dn̄io . Tc̄ . iiii . car . hom . M̊ . v.
silu . x . por . xii . ac . p̄ti . i . mol . Tc̄ . ual . vii . lib̄ . m̄ . viii . In dn̄io . vii . an . c . ou.
xxii . porc . ii . uasa apū.
Est adhuc . i . bereuuita que uocat . hamdena quā Eluui p đ . hid . 7 ★
xv . ac . Tc̄ . ii . car . in dn̄io . m̄ . i . Tc̄ . iiii . ser . m̄ null . Tc̄ . lv . ou . 7 m̄;
Tc̄ . ual . lx . sol . m̄ . xxx . De hoc maner accepit Will cardon : hō . G. ★
de magna uill . xxiiii . ac . siluæ . qn̄ Suan erat uicecomes . ut hundret
testatur

Value then £17; now [£] 20.

Siward holds 1 hide and 30 acres from St. Etheldreda's. Now Ranulf Peverel holds (it) from the King; but the Hundred testifies that (it is) the Abbey's.

2 hides and 30 acres, which the Church held and Leofson from it before 1066. Eudo now holds from the Abbot, because his predecessor held it; but the Hundred testifies that he could not sell it without the Abbot's permission.

Half-Hundred of FRESHWELL

4 St. Etheldreda's has always held HADSTOCK as 1 manor; 2 hides.

Then 8 villagers, now 12; then 4 smallholders, now 13; then 4 slaves, now 2. Always 2 ploughs in lordship. Then 3 men's ploughs, now 4.

Woodland, 100 pigs; meadow, 6 acres; then 1 mill, now none. 1 cob, 4 cattle, 16 pigs, 36 sheep, 8 goats.

Value then £6; now [£] 10.

Hundred of UTTLESFORD

5 St. Etheldreda's has always held LITTLEBURY as 1 manor; 25 hides.

Always 39 villagers; 19 smallholders; 7 slaves. Then 5 ploughs in lordship, now 4. Then 17 men's ploughs, now 15.

Woodland, 160 pigs; meadow, 55 acres; always 4 mills. 2 cobs, 32 pigs, 80 sheep, 3 beehives.

Value £20.

There is also 1 outlier which is called STRETHALL, which 2 men, William (and) Alwin, held for 5 hides; they could not withdraw
from the land without the Abbot's permission. Now Hugh holds 19 b
(it) under the Abbot.

Then 7 villagers, now 6; then 4 smallholders, now 7. Always 6 slaves; 3 ploughs in lordship. Then 4 men's ploughs, now 5.

Woodland, 10 pigs; meadow, 12 acres; 1 mill.

Value then £7; now [£] 8.

In lordship 7 cattle, 100 sheep, 22 pigs, 2 beehives.

There is also 1 outlier which is called HEYDON, which Alwin [held] for ½ hide and 15 acres. Then 2 ploughs in lordship, now 1.

Then 4 slaves, now none.

Then and now 55 sheep.

Value then 60s; now 30[s].

From this manor, William Cardon, a man of G(eoffrey) de Mandeville's, wrongfully received 24 acres of woodland when Swein was Sheriff, as the Hundred testifies.

.XI. ꟾTerra Sci Edmundi. Hund de Witham.

Breddinchou ten& Witt fili grosse de abbe. p. I. hid. 7. xv. ac. Tc. II.
car in dnio. m. I. Sep. I. car. hom. IIII. uitt. III. bor. m. I. mol. Silu. L. por.
.xx. ac. pti. II. runc. VI. an. XII. por. v. cap. Val. L. sol.

ꟾDimidiu Hund de Herlaua Herlaua ten& sep. scs. E. p. I.
Man. 7. I. hid. 7. d. Sep. II. car. in dnio. 7. VI. car hom. 7. XII. uitt. XV. bor.
7. IIII. ser. Silu. CL. por. XXX. ac. pti. I. molin. IIII. runc. XXV. an.
. III. pulli. L. porc. LX. ou. v. uasa apu. Huic manerio addite sunt.
. III. hid. t. r. Witti. qs tenebant. v. libi hoes. t. r. e. In qb; st sep. VI. car
in dnio VIII. bor. IIII. ser. Silu. C. por. XIIII. ac. pti. Sep. ual. maner.
VIII. lib. 7. III. hid. ual. tc. LXX. sol. m. IIII. lib.

ꟾLattuna ten& scs. E. p. man. 7. p. IIII. hid. 7. d. qd tenuit Turgot
. I. lib ho. t. r. e. Sep. II. car in dnio. 7. I. car. hom. IIII. uitt. Tc. IIII

20 a

bor. m. v. sep. IIII. ser. silu. CC. por. XXXV. ac. pti. IIII. an. L. por. XXX. ou. XXV
cap. Sep. ual. VI. lib.

ꟾHund de hidinghefort. In Alfelmestuna ten&. S. E. dim. hid. I. car
in dnio. Tc. I. ser. M. III. bor. II. ac. pti. Tc. ual. x. sol. M. XX.

ꟾHund de Laxefelda In Colu ten&. S. E. XXXVI. ac. Tc. III. bor.
m. IIII. Sep. dim. car. silu. XL. por. III. ac. pti. Val. XX. sol.

ꟾHund de Angra. Staplefort ten& sep. S. E. p. III. hid. 7. dim.
7. VI. ac. 7. dim. Tc. VIII. uitt. m. IX. Sep. v. bor. 7. II. ser. 7. I. car. in
dnio. Tc. IIII. car. hom. m. III. Silu. CCL. por. XII. ac. pti. XX. an. I. r.

11 LAND OF ST. EDMUND'S

Hundred of WITHAM

1 William son of Gross holds BENTON (Hall) from the Abbot for 1 hide and 15 acres. Then 2 ploughs in lordship, now 1. Always 1 men's plough.

4 villagers and 3 smallholders.

Now 1 mill; woodland, 50 pigs; meadow, 20 acres. 2 cobs, 6 cattle, 12 pigs, 5 goats.

Value 50s.

Half-Hundred of HARLOW

2 St. Edmund's has always held HARLOW as 1 manor; 1½ hides. Always 2 ploughs in lordship; 6 men's ploughs;

12 villagers; 15 smallholders; 4 slaves.

Woodland, 150 pigs; meadow, 30 acres; 1 mill. 4 cobs, 25 cattle, 3 foals, 50 pigs, 60 sheep, 5 beehives.

To this manor were added 3 hides after 1066, which 5 free men held before 1066. In them have always been 6 ploughs in lordship.

8 smallholders and 4 slaves.

Woodland, 100 pigs; meadow, 14 acres.

Value of the manor always £8. Value of the 3 hides then 70s; now £4.

3 St. Edmund's holds LATTON as a manor, for 4½ hides which 1 free man, Thorgot, held before 1066. Always 2 ploughs in lordship; 1 men's plough.

4 villagers; then 4 smallholders, now 5; always 4 slaves. 20 a

Woodland, 200 pigs; meadow, 35 acres. 4 cattle, 50 pigs, 30 sheep, 25 goats.

Value always £6.

Hundred of HINCKFORD

4 In ALPHAMSTONE St. Edmund's holds ½ hide. 1 plough in lordship.

Then 1 slave; now 3 smallholders.

Meadow, 2 acres.

Value then 10s; now 20[s].

Hundred of LEXDEN

5 In COLNE St. Edmund's holds 36 acres.

Then 3 smallholders, now 4. Always ½ plough.

Woodland, 40 pigs; meadow, 3 acres.

Value 20s.

Hundred of ONGAR

6 St. Edmund's has always held STAPLEFORD (Abbotts) for 3½ hides and 6½ acres.

Then 8 villagers, now 9. Always 5 smallholders; 2 slaves; 1 plough in lordship. Then 4 men's ploughs, now 3.

Woodland, 250 pigs; meadow, 12 acres. 20 cattle, 1 cob,

XLVIII . oves . XLIII . por . III . pulli . 7 . II . libi hões in focã manerij . de XXXVI . ac . 7 . dim . I . car . silu . XL . por . II . ac pti . Tc uat . XLV . sol . m . L.

Hund de Celmeresfort . Waltham ten& Albt de abbe . qđ tenuit Stanhard . t . r . e . p . I . Man . 7 . II . hid . XV . ac . min . 7 . scs . E . de. dono regis . Sep . I . uilt 7 . VII . bor . 7 . II . ser . 7 . II . car . in dnio . 7 . I . car hom . Silu . XXX . por . VII . ac . pti . I . an . L . ou . II . por . X . cap . Tc uat XL sol. M . LX.

Hund de tendringa Wrabenasã ten& sep . scs . E . p . I . Man . 7 p . V . hid Sep . VI . uilt . VIII . bor . VI . ser . Tc . III . car . in dnio . m . II . Tc . VI . ca hom . m . V . 7 . dim . I . ac . pti . m . I . mol . 7 . I . sal . II . pulli . XXX . porc. CC . ou . V . uasa ap . Vat . VI . lib.

★

20 b

.XII. TERRA Sci martini Londoniæ . Estrã tenuit Ailmar . I . teinn regis . E . 7 consul Eustachi dedit sco martino . p . I . M . 7 . IIII . hid . 7 . L . ac. Tc . III . car . in dnio . m . II . Sep . VIII . car . hom . VIII . uilt . Tc . XVI . bor . m. XXI . Tc . VIII . ser . m . III . Silu . LX . por . XX . ac . pti . M . I . mol . Tc . uat . VIII. lib . m . X . Huic manerio attinebat . I . bereuuita de dim . hid . 7 XX . ac . t . r . e . s; consul . E . eã sibi retinuit . 7 jac& in hund de cel meresfort.

XIII. TERRA Sci Martini de bello . Hund de bdestapla . Atahov tenuit Goti lib hõ . t . r . e . p . I . Man . 7 . III . hid . XX . ac . min . sep . II . car in dnio . 7 . III . car hom . Tc . I . uilt . m . II . Tc . X . bor . m . XV . IIII . ser. silu . M . porc . Tc . I . pisc . m n . Tc . II . runc . m . III . Tc . IIII . an . m XIX. . C . ou . Tc . LX . porc . m . C . VIII . min . IIII . uasa apũ . 7 . III . soc . de . I. hid . 7 . XXX . ac . sep . I . car . 7 . XV . ac . libæ træ . Tc . uat . C . sol . m . VI. lib . 7 . illæ . XV . ac . uat . XXX . đ.

48 sheep, 43 pigs, 3 foals.
2 free men in the jurisdiction of the manor with 36½ acres.
1 plough. Woodland, 40 pigs; meadow, 2 acres.
Value then 45s; now 50[s].

Hundred of CHELMSFORD

7 Albert holds (Little) WALTHAM from the Abbot, which Stanhard held before 1066 as 1 manor, 2 hides less 15 acres. St. Edmund's (holds) by the King's gift.
Always 1 villager; 7 smallholders; 2 slaves; 2 ploughs in lordship; 1 men's plough.
Woodland, 30 pigs; meadow, 7 acres. 1 (head of) cattle, 50 sheep, 2 pigs, 10 goats.
Value then 40s; now 60[s].

Hundred of TENDRING

8 St. Edmund's has always held WRABNESS as 1 manor, for 5 hides.
Always 6 villagers; 8 smallholders; 6 slaves. Then 3 ploughs in lordship, now 2. Then 6 men's ploughs, now 5½.
Meadow, 1 acre; now 1 mill and 1 salt-house. 2 foals, 30 pigs, 200 sheep, 5 beehives.
Value £6.

12 LAND OF ST. MARTIN'S, LONDON 20 b

[Hundred of DUNMOW]

1 Aelmer, 1 thane of King Edward's, held (Good) EASTER. Count Eustace gave (it) to St. Martin's as 1 manor, 4 hides and 50 acres. Then 3 ploughs in lordship, now 2. Always 8 men's ploughs.
8 villagers; then 16 smallholders, now 21; then 8 slaves, now 3.
Woodland, 60 pigs; meadow, 20 acres; now 1 mill.
Value then £8; now [£] 10.
To this manor belonged 1 outlier with ½ hide and 20 acres before 1066, but Count Eustace kept it for himself.
It lies in the Hundred of CHELMSFORD.

13 LAND OF ST. MARTIN'S, BATTLE

Hundred of BARSTABLE

1 Goti, a free man, held HUTTON before 1066 as 1 manor, 3 hides less 20 acres. Always 2 ploughs in lordship; 3 men's ploughs.
Then 1 villager, now 2; then 10 smallholders, now 15; 4 slaves.
Woodland, 1000 pigs; then 1 fishery, now none. Then 2 cobs, now 3; then 4 cattle, now 19; 100 sheep; then 60 pigs, now 100 less 8; 4 beehives.
3 Freemen with 1 hide and 30 acres. Always 1 plough. 15 acres of free land.
Value then 100s; now £6. Value of the 15 acres 30d.

Hund de hidingforda. Hersā tenuit Orgar lib hō. t. r. e. p. Ma.
7. p. i. hid. Sēp. ii. car. in dnio. 7. i. car hom. Tc 7. p. v. uilt. m. iii.
Tc. i. bor. m. iii. Tc. iii. ser. m. ii. xiii. ac. pti. viii. an. x. por. Tc.
xxx ou. m. xxv. iii. uasa apū. Vat. xl. sot.

XIIII. TERRA SCI Walerici. Hund de herLAVA.
Metcingā tenuit Godric. i. lib hō. t. r. e. p. xl. ac. Tc. i. car
m. nulla. Vat. x. sot. 7. viii. d.
Lindeselā tenuit Horolf. i. lib hō. t. r. e. p. i. m. 7. p. i. hid.

21 a
m Scs Wat. Sēp. ii. car in dnio. 7. iii. car hom. Tc. viii. uilt. m. ix.
Tc. iiii. bor. m. xv. Tc. iiii. ser. m null. Silu. l. por. vi. ac. pti.
. iiii. an. xl. por. xxviii. ou. v. uasa apū. Tc. 7 p uat. c. sot. ★
M. vi. lib.
Hund de Vdelesfort. Tacheleiā ten&. Scs
Wat. qd tenuit Turchill lib hō. t. r. e. p. dim. hid.
Sēp. ii. car in dnio. 7. iii. car hom. viii. uilt. Tc. 7. p. iii.
bor. m. v. Sēp. ii. ser. Tc 7 p silu. M. por. m. dc. xxiiii. ac. pti. Tc.
7 p. i. mot. m. d. iii. runc. iiii. an. xxx. por. xxviii. ou. l. cap. v. uas
apu. Tc 7 p uat. vi. lib. m. vii.
Bilichangrā tenuit Ide Turchill. p. ii. hid. 7. p. i. Man. Tc. 7. p.
. ii. car in dnio. m. i. Sēp. ii. car hom. i. uilt. v. bor. Tc. ii. ser. Tc silu.
. c. por. M. l. vi. ac. pti. i. mot. ii. runc. vi. an. xxviii. por. xxxvi.
cap. Tc 7 p. uat. lx. sot. m. l.

Hundred of HINCKFORD

2 Ordgar, a free man, held HORSEHAM (Hall) before 1066 as a manor, for 1 hide. Always 2 ploughs in lordship; 1 men's plough.

Then and later 5 villagers, now 3; then 1 smallholder, now 3; then 3 slaves, now 2.

Meadow, 13 acres. 8 cattle, 10 pigs; then 33 sheep, now 25; 3 beehives.

Value 40s.

14 LAND OF ST. VALERY'S

Hundred of HARLOW

1 1 free man, Godric, held MATCHING before 1066 for 40 acres. Then 1 plough, now none.

Value 10s 8d.

[Hundred of DUNMOW]

2 1 free man, Horwulf, held LINDSELL before 1066 as 1 manor, for 1 hide. Now St. Valéry's (holds it). Always 2 ploughs in 21 a
lordship; 3 men's ploughs.

Then 8 villagers, now 9; then 4 smallholders, now 15; then 4 slaves, now none.

Woodland, 50 pigs; meadow, 6 acres. 4 cattle, 40 pigs, 28 sheep, 5 beehives.

Value then and later 100s; now £6.

Hundred of UTTLESFORD

3 St. Valéry's holds TAKELEY which Thorkell, a free man, held before 1066, for ½ hide. Always 2 ploughs in lordship; 3 men's ploughs.

8 villagers; then and later 3 smallholders, now 5; always 2 slaves.

Woodland then and later, 1000 pigs, now 600; meadow, 24 acres; then and later 1 mill, now ½. 3 cobs, 4 cattle, 30 pigs, 28 sheep, 50 goats, 5 beehives.

Value then and later £6; now [£] 7.

4 Thorkell also held BIRCHANGER for 2 hides, as 1 manor. Then and later 2 ploughs in lordship, now 1. Always 2 men's ploughs.

1 villager, 5 smallholders; then 2 slaves.

Woodland, then 100 pigs, now 50; meadow, 6 acres; 1 mill. 2 cobs, 6 cattle, 28 pigs, 36 goats.

Value then and later 60s; now 50[s].

Widitunā tenuit Idē Turchill᷒. ꝓ.m̄.7.IIII.hid.7.đ.Tc̄.7.p᷒.III.
car.in dn̄io.M.II.Sēp.VI.car.hom.Tc̄.7.p᷒.VIII.uilt.M.XI.XX.ou.
VI.ser.silu.X.por.XII.ac.p̄ti.V.an.XXIIII.por.L.ou.Sēp ual.
VII.lib. huic tr̄æ.jacent.II.hid.q̄s sēp.tenent.IIII.soc.7.ual.XXX.sol.

Hund de Witbricteſherna. Effeceſtrā tenuit Turchill᷒.
lib hō.t.r.e.ꝓ.I.hid.7.dim.7.XX.ac.Tc̄.II.bor.m̄.III.sēp.II.ser.
7.I.car.past.CCC.ou.I.pisc.III.an.XX.porc.CCXVI.ou.Tc̄ ual
XL.sol.M.LXX. In Ead.III.libi hōes.de.I.hid.7.đ.I.car.Val.XX.sol.

Daneſeiā ten Idē.ꝓ.II.hid.7 đ.IIII.uilt.Tc̄.I.bor.m̄.VIII.sēp.IIII.ser.
.II.ca.i dio.7 II.ca.hom.Past.CC.ou.Tc̄.IIII.lib.m̄.C.sol.In Ead uilt

21 b
tenent.IIII.libi hōes.L.ac.7 ual.V.sol.

.XV. Terra sc̄e trinitatis de Cadomo. Hund de hidingfort
Phenſtedā tenuit.Comes Algar᷒.t.r.e.ꝓ.V.hid.m̄ ten& sc̄a trin.
ꝓ.IIII.hid.Sēp.III.car in dn̄io.7.XVI.car hom.Tc̄.XXII.uilt.Post
7.m̄.XX.Tc̄ 7 p᷒ XXIII.bor.m̄.XXXIII.sēp.XI.ser.Silu.DC.porc.
XXXVI.ac.p̄ti.II.mol.XXI.an.CC.porc.LVIII.ou.XXX.cap.I.runc.
Huic manerio jacebant.t.r.e.LV.ac.q̄s tenebant.III.soc.m̄.IIII.
tc̄.II.car.m̄.III.M.II.bor.Silu.XXX.por.XII.ac.p̄ti.Tc̄ ual.XX.
lib.Post.XXX.m̄.XXXII.Quinta hida n̄ ē huic manerio.rex
enī Witt dedit Rogo ds̄ saluæt dn̄as.III.uirḡ.7 Giſlebto filio Sa
lomonis.IIII.

5 Thorkell also held WIDDINGTON as a manor, 4½ hides. Then and later 3 ploughs in lordship, now 2. Always 6 men's ploughs.
Then and later 8 villagers, now 11; 20 sheep; 6 slaves.
Woodland, 10 pigs; meadow, 12 acres. 5 cattle, 24 pigs, 50 sheep.
Value always £7.
To this land belong 2 hides which 4 Freemen have always held.
Value 33s.

Hundred of 'WIBERTSHERNE'

6 Thorkell, a free man, held ST. PETER'S CHAPEL before 1066 for 1½ hides and 20 acres.
Then 2 smallholders, now 3. Always 2 slaves; 1 plough.
Pasture, 300 sheep; 1 fishery. 3 cattle, 20 pigs, 216 sheep.
Value then 40s; now 70[s].
In the same (Bradwell) 3 free men with 1½ hides. 1 plough.
Value 20s.

7 He also held DENGIE for 2½ hides.
4 villagers; then 1 smallholder, now 8. Always 4 slaves; 2 ploughs in lordship; 2 men's ploughs.
Pasture, 200 sheep.
[Value] then £4; now 100s.
In the same village 4 free men hold 50 acres. 21 b
Value 5s.

15 LAND OF HOLY TRINITY, CAEN

Hundred of HINCKFORD

1 Earl Algar held FELSTED before 1066 for 5 hides. Now Holy Trinity holds (it) for 4 hides. Always 3 ploughs in lordship; 16 men's ploughs.
Then 22 villagers, later and now 20; then and later 23 smallholders, now 33; always 11 slaves.
Woodland, 600 pigs; meadow, 36 acres; 2 mills. 21 cattle, 200 pigs, 58 sheep, 30 goats, 1 cob.
To this manor belonged 55 acres before 1066 which 3 Freemen held, now 4.
Then 2 ploughs, now 3.
Now 2 smallholders.
Woodland, 30 pigs; meadow, 12 acres.
Value then £20; later [£]30; now [£]32.
The fifth hide is not in this manor; for King William gave 3 virgates to Roger God-Save-Ladies and the fourth to Gilbert son of Solomon.

Hund de Celmeresforda. Baduuen. tenuit Comes. Algar
p.i. Man. 7 p. viii. hid. m. Sca. Trin. p tantundē. Sep. xvi. uill. Tc
viii. bor. m. xv. sep. vi. ser. 7. iii. car in dnio. Tc. viii. car hom.
m. xii. Silu. cccc. porc. xlv. ac. pti. i. mol. i. runc. 7. i. pull. 7
xiiii. an. c. porc. iiii. min. xxxviii. ou. xiii. cap. 7. iii. soch.
q̄ n̄ potant recede. de. i. uirḡ. 7. xx. ac. 7. d. Tc reddidit. viii. noct.

22 a
de firma. m. xvii. lib.

TERRA Sci Stephani de cadomo. Hund de hidinghfort; .XVI.
Penfeldā tenuit. i. liba fem. t. r. e. p. i. hid. 7. iii. uirg. t. r. e. Tc
. iiii. car. in dnio. m. iii. Tc. ii. car. hom. qn recep nulla. m. dimid.
Tc. iiii. uill. m null. Sep. viii. bor. Tc. viii. ser. m. vii. Silu. cc. por.
xii. ac. pti. ii. runc. xii. an. clxv. ou. xxxvii. porc. Tc ual. x. lib.
Post. c. sol. m. x. lib.

Tra sci Audoeni. Hund de Wensistreu. Meresaiam tenuit .XVII.
Scs Audoen. t. r. e. p. xx. hid. Tc. iiii. car in dnio. m. vi. Sep. xvi. car
hom. xxxvi. uill. lxii. bor. Tc. x. ser. m. iii. xi. runc. 7. ii. pulli. xvi.
an. xxxiiii. porc. ccc. ou. Huic manerio adjac& dim hid. q̄ sep. ten&
. i. pbr. 7. val. x. sol. 7. silu. cc. por. Past. ccc. ou. Tc. i. pisc. Tc ual
xxvi. lib. m. xxii. Est &iā in Colecestra. i. dom. quæ ptinuit huic trǣ.
s; Waleram eā abstulit; Et in Hund de Wensistreu | viii. sochm
regis tenentes. cvii. ac. 7 ual. x. sol de his ht scs Audoen. ii. partes.
Et. ii. soc. tulit Ingelric. de. dim hid. 7. xxx. ac. m ht eos comes. E.
Et. ii. soc q̄ st̄ additi ad Legrā maneriū regis in alio hund. & de tota
hac soca ht scs. Audoen. duas partes. 7. rex. tciā. Et sep. ii. partes
de forisfacturis de hundret

Hundred of CHELMSFORD

2 Earl Algar held (Great) BADDOW as 1 manor, for 8 hides. Now Holy Trinity (holds it) for as much.

Always 16 villagers. Then 8 smallholders, now 15. Always 6 slaves; 3 ploughs in lordship. Then 8 men's ploughs, now 12.

Woodland, 400 pigs; meadow, 45 acres; 1 mill. 1 cob, 1 foal, 14 cattle, 100 pigs less 4, 38 sheep, 13 goats.

3 Freemen, who cannot withdraw, with 1 virgate and 20½ acres.

Then it paid 8 nights' provisions; now £17. 22 a

16 LAND OF ST. STEPHEN'S, CAEN

Hundred of HINCKFORD

1 1 free woman held PANFIELD before 1066, for 1 hide and 3 virgates before 1066. Then 4 ploughs in lordship, now 3. Then 2 men's ploughs, when acquired none, now ½.

Then 4 villagers, now none; always 8 smallholders; then 8 slaves, now 7.

Woodland, 200 pigs; meadow, 12 acres. 2 cobs, 12 cattle, 165 sheep, 37 pigs.

Value then £10; later 100s; now £10.

17 LAND OF ST. OUEN'S

Hundred of WINSTREE

1 St. Ouen's held (West) MERSEA before 1066 for 20 hides. Then 4 ploughs in lordship, now 6. Always 16 men's ploughs.

36 villagers, 62 smallholders. Then 10 slaves, now 3.

11 cobs, 2 foals, 16 cattle, 34 pigs, 300 sheep.

To this manor is attached ½ hide which 1 priest has always held; value 10s.

Woodland, 200 pigs; pasture, 300 sheep; then 1 fishery.

Value then £26; now [£] 22.

There is also 1 house in Colchester which belonged to this land; but Waleran took it away.

2 Also in Winstree Hundred 8 King's Freemen who hold 107 acres. Value 10s; of these, St. Ouen's has two parts.

Engelric took 2 Freemen with ½ hide and 30 acres. Count E(ustace) has them now. Also 2 Freemen who have been added to the King's manor at Layer in another Hundred. Of all this jurisdiction St. Ouen's has two parts and the King (has) the third part; and always two parts of the forfeitures of the Hundred.

XVIII. TERRE EPI Baiocensis in Exsessa Hundret de

Berdestapla. Phenge ten& . fili turoldi de epo qđ tenuer . II . libi hões p . v . hid . 7 . dim . Sep . II . car in dnio 7 . IIII . car hom . VI . uilt . IX . bor . I . ser . dimidia hid siluæ . Past . cxx . ou . I . piscina . m . I . mol . II . runc . IIII . an . IIII . porc . Tc . LXVII . ou . M . CCLXX . De hac tra tenebat . I . lib hõ . xxx . ac . quæ . t . r . Willi addite st ad pdicta tra . 7 nescit qm . Tc uat . c . sol . m . VIII . lib .

Burghesteda ten& Epc in dnio qđ tenuit Ingar teinn . t . r . e . p . I . Man . 7 . x . hid . Sep . III . car in dnio . Tc . XII . car hom . m . XI . Tc . XX . uilt . m . XXII . Tc . v . bor . m . x . Dim hid . siluæ past . CL . ou . II . runc . XI . an . c^VI porc . CCXVIIII . ou . Vat . xx . lib . Huic manerio additi sunt . t . r . Willi . XXVIII . libi hões . tenentes . XXVIII . hid . 7 . v . ac . in quib; erant . tc . XVI . car . m . XIII . v . hid . siluæ . XXIII . ac pti . Pastura . CCL . ou . LIIII . bor . IIII . ser . hoc additamtu uat . tc . xx . lib . M XVI .

Dantuna ten& epc in dnio qđ tenuit . I . pbr lib hõ . t . r . e . p . VII . hid . 7 . XL . ac . Tc . IIII . car . in dnio . m . II . sep . IIII . car hom . Tc . VII . uilt m . II . 7 . VI . bor . Tc . v . ser . m . II . II . runc . II . an . XV . por . XXXIIII . ou . Tc uat . XII . lib . m . VII .

Berdestestapla ten& fili Turoldi . de epo . qđ tenuit . I . lib hõ . p . v . hid . 7 dim . 7 . XXX . ac . [7 . xxx . ac siluæ . past . c . o .] Sep . III . car . in dnio . 7 . II . hom . VI . uilt . XI . bor . Tc uat . IIII . lib . m . c . sol . [tc .] In dnio . II . runc . v . anim . XVIII por . XXXVI . ou . M . I . runc . IX . an . XXIIII . porc . LXXX . ou ;

18 LANDS OF THE BISHOP OF BAYEUX IN ESSEX 22 b

Hundred of BARSTABLE

1 Thorold's son holds VANGE from the Bishop. 2 free men held it for 5½ hides. Always 2 ploughs in lordship; 4 men's ploughs.
6 villagers; 9 smallholders; 1 slave.
Woodland, ½ hide; pasture, 120 sheep; 1 fishery; now 1 mill.
2 cobs, 4 cattle, 4 pigs; then 67 sheep, now 270.
Of this land, 1 free man held 30 acres which were added to the aforesaid land after 1066; it is not known how.
Value then 100s; now £8.

2 The Bishop holds (Great) BURSTEAD in lordship. Ingvar, a thane, held it before 1066 as 1 manor, 10 hides. Always 3 ploughs in lordship. Then 12 men's ploughs, now 11.
Then 20 villagers, now 22; then 5 smallholders, now 10.
Woodland, ½ hide; pasture, 150 sheep. 2 cobs, 11 cattle, 106 pigs, 219 sheep.
Value £20.
28 free men were added to this manor after 1066; they hold 28 hides and 5 acres. On these there were then 16 ploughs, now 13.
Woodland, 5 hides; meadow, 23 acres; pasture, 250 sheep.
54 smallholders, 4 slaves.
Value of this addition then £20; now [£] 16.

3 The Bishop holds DUNTON in lordship. 1 priest, a free man, held it before 1066 for 7 hides and 40 acres. Then 4 ploughs in lordship, now 2. Always 4 men's ploughs.
Then 7 villagers, now 2; 6 smallholders; then 5 slaves, now 2.
2 cobs, 2 cattle, 15 pigs, 34 sheep.
Value then £12; now [£] 7.

4 Thorold's son holds BARSTABLE (Hall) from the Bishop. 1 free man held it for 5½ hides and 30 acres.
Woodland, 30 acres; pasture, 100 sheep.
Always 3 ploughs in lordship; 2 men's [ploughs].
6 villagers, 11 smallholders.
Value then £4; now 100s.
In lordship then 2 cobs, 5 cattle, 18 pigs, 36 sheep; now 1 cob, 9 cattle, 24 pigs, 80 sheep.

Ingā ten& fili⁹ Turoldi de ep̄o . qđ tenuit . I . lib hō . t . r . e . p . II . hid.
Sēp . I . car in dn̄io . 7 . I . car hom . I . uilł . Tc̄ . I . bor . m̄ . V . III . ser . I . hid . 7 . đ

(siluæ)

23 a

. III . runc . VIII . an . Tc̄ . XXX . por . m̄ . LVIII . Tc̄ . XL . ou . m̄ . LXXVI . Tc̄
XXXII . cap . m̄ . XIIII . Tc̄ uał . LX . sol . m̄ LXX . huic manerio additi
st̄ VII . libi hoes . de . V . III . hid . t . r . Willi . Sēp . V . car . I . hid . 7 . đ . siluæ.
XI . bor . IIII . ac . p̄ti . Tc̄ . uał . IIII . lib . m̄ . XL . sol.

Ramesdanā tenent . II . milit . de ep̄o . qđ tenuer̄ . II . libi hoēs . p . III.
hid . & sic anglici dicunt Rauengari⁹ abstulit . trā ab uno illoꝝ
7 Rob fili⁹ Wimarc altam trā ab alto . m̄ ū nesciunt q̄m uenerit
ad epm . Tc̄ . habuer̄ . II . car . m̄ ibi nulla ē . Tc̄ . V . bor . m̄ . VII . dim
hid siluæ . Pastura . C . ou . Tc̄ uał . III . lib . m̄ . IIII.

In Wateleia . 7 . in Wincfort . tenent . Pointel . 7 Osbn̄⁹ . II . hid . quas
tenuer̄ . II . libi hoēs . t . r . e Tc̄ . II . car . m̄ . I . IIII . bor . I . hid . Siluæ . XXV.
ac . p̄ti . Past . XL . ou . Tc̄ . uał . XL . sol . m̄ . XXX . Et istā trā abstulit eis
Rauengari⁹ . 7 m̄ nesciunt angli q̄m uenerit in manu epi

Wicfort ten& fili⁹ turoldi . de ep̄o . qđ tenuer̄ . V . libi hoēs . t . r . e.
p . II . hid . 7 . XLVIII . ac . sēp . II . car . V . bor . II . ser . Silu . XXX . porc . Vał
XL . sol . Wicfort ten& Teher⁹ de ep̄o . qđ tenuit . Godric⁹ . I . lib hō
. t . r . e . p . I . hid . Sēp . I . car . Tc̄ . I . bor . m̄ . II . Silu . XXX . por . VIII . ac.
p̄ti Vał . XX . sol.

Hasinghebroc ten& fili⁹ turoldi . qđ tenuer̄ . XVI . libi . hoēs . t . r . e
p . XII . hid . 7 . XIII . ac . 7 . dim . Tc̄ . XI . car . m̄ . VII . m̄ . XIIII . bor
XX . soc . Silu . CC . por . XVI . ac . p̄ti . Past . CCCC . ou . Vał . X . lib.

5 Thorold's son holds INGRAVE from the Bishop. 1 free man held it before 1066 for 2 hides. Always 1 plough in lordship; 1 men's plough.
1 villager. Then 1 smallholder, now 5; 3 slaves.
Woodland, 1½ hides. 3 cobs; 8 cattle; then 30 pigs, now 58; then 40 sheep, now 76; then 32 goats, now 14. 23 a
Value then 60s; now 70[s].
7 free men with 3 hides have been added to this manor after 1066. Always 5 ploughs.
Woodland, 1½ hides. 11 smallholders. Meadow, 4 acres.
Value then £4; now 40s.

6 2 men-at-arms hold RAMSDEN (Cray) from the Bishop, which 2 free men held for 3 hides. So the English state, Ravengar took the land away from one of them and Robert son of Wymarc took the other land away from the other one; but now they do not know how it has come to the Bishop. Then they had 2 ploughs, now there is none there.
Then 5 smallholders, now 7.
Woodland, ½ hide; pasture, 100 sheep.
Value then £3; now [£] 4.

7 In WHEATLEY and in WICKFORD Pointel and Osbern hold 2 hides which 2 free men held before 1066. Then 2 ploughs, now 1.
4 smallholders.
Woodland, 1 hide; meadow, 25 acres; pasture, 40 sheep.
Value then 40s; now 30[s].
Ravengar took this land away from them; now the English do not know how it came into the Bishop's hand.

8 Thorold's son holds WICKFORD from the Bishop, which 5 free men held before 1066, for 2 hides and 48 acres. Always 2 ploughs.
5 smallholders, 2 slaves.
Woodland, 30 pigs.
Value 40s.

9 Teher holds WICKFORD from the Bishop, which 1 free man, Godric, held before 1066, for 1 hide. Always 1 plough.
Then 1 smallholder, now 2.
Woodland, 30 pigs; meadow, 8 acres.
Value 20s.

10 Thorold's son holds HASSENBROOK (Hall), which 16 free men held before 1066, for 12 hides and 13½ acres. Then 11 ploughs, now 7.
Now 14 smallholders, 20 Freemen.
Woodland, 200 pigs; meadow, 16 acres; pasture, 400 sheep.
Value £10.

Celdewellā ten&. Idē de epo qđ tenuit Eduuolt pposit regis. E. p. I. hid. 7. dim. Sēp. I. car. 7. đ. in dnio. dim. car hom. Tc. VI. bor. m̄. VII. Tc. II. ser. m̄. I. Qdā soc. de. XXX. ac. Silu. LXXX. por. Past. C. ou.

23 b

Tc. I. pisc. m̄ n̄ s; poť fieri. De hac tra fuer t. r. e. XXX. ac. ad aliā trā Tc uał. XL. soł. m̄ totū simul. XXX. soł. In Torinduna ht epc. XX. ac. qs ten. I. lib hō. t. r. e. Vał. XXX. đ.

Hunđ de Witham. In Hafelda. XV. ac. qs tenuit. I. soc. Tc uał. III. soł. m̄. IIII.

Hunđ de Rochefort. Stanbruge ten& Suen de epo. qm ten Osuuard. t. r. e. p. III. hid. 7. dim. 7. XXX. ac. Tc. VII. uilł. m̄. null. Tc. VI. bor. m̄. X. Tc. III. ser. m̄ null. Sēp. II. car. in dnio. Tc. III. car homin. m̄. IIII. Past. CCC. ou. I. mol. M. I. runc. Tc. IIII. am. M. II. Tc. XV. por. m̄. XXV. Tc. C. ou. m̄ LVIII. Sēp. uał. VI. lib.

Bacheneiā ten. Rauengari. m̄ epc. in dnio. p. dim. hid. Tc. I. ser. m̄. I. bor. Sēp. I. car in dnio. Pastur. XXX. ou. Tc uał. XX. soł. m̄. XXX. In ptio de his. XXX. soł st adhuc. XXX. ac. 7. I. bor. 7. dim. car.

Berlingā ten& epc in dnio qđ tenuit. I. lib hō. p. dim. hid. Sēp. I. bor. Tc. I. car. m̄. nulla. sed poť fieri. Vał. X. soł.

Sobiam ten& epc in dīo. qđ tenuit. I. lib hō p. I. hid. 7. XXX. ac. Sep. II. uilł. Tc. II. bor. m̄. III. Tc. I. car. in dnio. m̄. II. bou. Sēp. I. car hou. Past. XL. ou. Tc uał. XL. soł. m̄. LV.

11 He also holds CHADWELL from the Bishop, which Edwold, King Edward's reeve, held for 1½ hides. Always 1½ ploughs in lordship; ½ men's plough.
Then 6 smallholders, now 7; then 2 slaves, now 1. A Freeman with 30 acres.
Woodland, 80 pigs; pasture, 100 sheep; then 1 fishery, now none, but (1) possible. 23 b
Before 1066, 30 acres of this land (belonged) to another land.
Value then 40s; now altogether 30s.

12 In HORNDON the Bishop has 20 acres, which 1 free man held before 1066.
Value 30d.

Hundred of WITHAM

13 In HATFIELD (Peverel) 15 acres, which 1 Freeman held.
Value then 3s; now 4[s].

Hundred of ROCHFORD

14 Swein holds (Great) STAMBRIDGE from the Bishop, which Osward held before 1066, for 3½ hides and 30 acres.
Then 7 villagers, now none; then 5 smallholders, now 10; then 3 slaves, now none. Always 2 ploughs in lordship. Then 3 men's ploughs, now 4.
Pasture, 300 sheep; 1 mill. Now 1 cob; then 4 cattle, now 2; then 15 pigs, now 25; then 100 sheep, now 58.
Value always £6.

15 Ravengar held BECKNEY. Now the Bishop (holds it) in lordship for ½ hide.
Then 1 slave; now 1 smallholder. Always 1 plough in lordship.
Pasture, 30 sheep.
Value then 20s; now 30[s]. In the same assessment of these 30s are a further 30 acres and
1 smallholder; ½ plough.

16 The Bishop holds BARLING in lordship, which 1 free man held, for ½ hide.
Always 1 smallholder. Then 1 plough, now none, but (1) possible.
Value 10s.

17 The Bishop holds SHOEBURY in lordship, which 1 free man held, for 1 hide and 30 acres.
Always 2 villagers. Then 2 smallholders, now 3. Then 1 plough in lordship, now 2 oxen. Always 1 men's plough.
Pasture, 40 sheep.
Value then 40s; now 55[s].

Hund de Witbrictesherna Cricchesciã ten& Suen de epo qd tenuit Edric lib ho . t . r . e . p . I . m . 7 . p . I . hid . Tc . II . bor . m . III . sep . II . ser . 7 . I . car . in dnio . silu . xx . porc . Past . xx . ou . Tc . IIII . an . 7 m ; simil . Tc 7 p uał . XIII . sol m . XXX .

Cricchesciam ten& . Pointel de epo . qd tenuit Leuric . t . r . e . p . d . hid . Tc . dim . car . m . n . Tc . uał . x . sol . m . v .

24 a

Hund de Wensistrev . Samantunã ten& Rad fili turoldi de epo . qd tenuer . II . libi hoes . p . dim . hid . 7 xxx^v . ac . Sep . dim . car . M . II . bor . Tc uał . XVI . sol . m . XV .

Hund de Hidincfort . Nepstedã ten& Vxor albici de epo qd tenuer . VIII . libi hoes . t . r . e . p . XXII . ac . 7 . d . Sep . I . car . silu . XX . porc . VI . ac . pti . Sep . uał . XXX . sol . In Hoc hundret ten& Tiheli de herion XXII . libos hoes . de . II . hid . 7 . XIII . ac . 7 . dim . sep . v . car . Tc 7 p . I . bor . m . IX . sep . I . ser . silu . IIII . porc . XXXI . ac . pti . Tc 7 p uał . LX . sol m . IIII . lib .

Hund de Witbrictesherna . Danesciã ten& . I . mil episcopi . qd tenuit Siric . t . r . e . p . II . hid . 7 . dim . Sep . II . uilł . m . VI . bor . Sep . III . ser 7 . II . car . in dnio . 7 . I . car . hom . Past . CLX . ou . Tc uał . IIII . lib . m . c . sol in dnio . CL . ou . I . runc . XIII . por . Ad hoc maneriũ erant t . r . e . II . libi homines . de XLVII . ac . qs occupau Idẽ miles epi . Sep . uał . IIII . sol .

Hundred of 'WIBERTSHERNE'

18 Swein holds CREEKSEA from the Bishop, which Edric, a free man, held before 1066, as 1 manor, for 1 hide.
Then 2 smallholders, now 3. Always 2 slaves; 1 plough in lordship.
Woodland, 20 pigs; pasture, 20 sheep. Then 4 cattle, now the same.
Value then and later 23s; now 30[s].

19 Pointel holds CREEKSEA from the Bishop, which Leofric held before 1066, for ½ hide. Then ½ plough, now none.
Value then 10s; now 5[s].

Hundred of WINSTREE 24 a

20 Ralph son of Thorold holds SAMPSON'S (Farm) from the Bishop, which 2 free men held for ½ hide and 35 acres. Always ½ plough.
Now 2 smallholders.
Value then 16s; now 15[s].

Hundred of HINCKFORD

21 Aubrey's wife holds 'NAPSTED' from the Bishop, which 8 free men held before 1066, for 22½ acres. Always 1 plough.
Woodland, 20 pigs; meadow, 6 acres.
Value always 30s.

21a In this Hundred Tihel of Helléan holds 22 free men with 2 hides and 13½ acres. Always 5 ploughs.
Then and later 1 smallholder, now 9; always 1 slave.
Woodland, 4 pigs; meadow, 31 acres.
Value then and later 60s; now £4.

Hundred of 'WIBERTSHERNE'

22 1 man-at-arms of the Bishop's holds DENGIE, which Siric held before 1066, for 2½ hides.
Always 2 villagers. Now 6 smallholders. Always 3 slaves; 2 ploughs in lordship; 1 men's plough.
Pasture, 160 sheep.
Value then £4; now 100s.
In lordship 150 sheep, 1 cob, 13 pigs.
In this manor before 1066 were 2 free men with 47 acres, whom the Bishop's man-at-arms also appropriated.
Value always 4s.

Hacslet ten& . I . mil epi . qđ tenuit Aluuard lib hō
. p . II . hid . 7 . xxx . ac . Tc . IIII . bor . m̄ . x . Sep . I . car . Past.
. cc 7 LX . ou . I . pisc . Ecclia ten& XL . ac . Tc uat . LX . sol . m̄.
. IIII . lib . 7 . XI . sol . In hac uilla erat . I . lib hō de . xxx . ac . 7 udlagau
m̄ hōes sueni acceperunt trā 7 adhuc tenent.

Hunđ de Lassendene. Aldeham tenuit Leueua p . I . hid . v.
ac min . t . r . e . M ten& vxor albici de epo . Tc . I . uill . m̄ null . Sep
. IIII . ser . 7 . II . car in dnio . Silu . XII . por . III . ac . pti . I . runc . VI . an . Tc 7 post
uat . xxx . sol . m̄ . LX.

Hunđ de Angra. Kelendunā ten& nepos herbti de epo qđ tenuit
Algar lib hō p . dim . hid . 7 . xx . ac . Sep . IIII . bor . 7 . I . car . Silu . LX . por

24 b

VII . ac . 7 . dim pti . I . an . v . porc . XLVII . ou . Vat . xx . sol.

Hunđ de Cessеorda. Vpmunstrā ten& Malger de epo qđ tenuit Vluuin
p . I . hid . 7 dim . Tc . II . bor . 7 m̄ similit . Sep . I . car . Tc uat . xx . sol . m̄ xxx.

Aluithcleam ten& Idē Malger . qđ tenuit Eduuard un lib homo . p . I . hid . 7 xxx . ac.
Sep . VI . bor . 7 . I . car in dnio . 7 . I . car hominū . Tc uat . xx . sol . m̄ . xxx.

Turocham ten& Hugo de epo . qđ tenuit Aluuard lib hō p . I . hid . 7 . XL . ac . Sep
. II . bor . Tc . II . car . m̄ . I . silu . x . porc . VIII . ac . pti . Pastur . L . ou . Tc . uat . xxx . sol.
m̄ XL . Tc . I . runc . Tc . I . an . m̄ . II . Tc . XXV . por . m̄ . IX . Tc . L . ou . m̄ XLVIII.

23 1 man-at-arms of the Bishop's holds BRADWELL QUAY, which Alfward, a free man, held for 2 hides and 30 acres.
Then 4 smallholders, now 10. Always 1 plough.
Pasture, 260 sheep; 1 fishery. The church holds 40 acres.
Value then 60s; now £4 11s.
In this village there was 1 free man with 30 acres and he was outlawed; now Swein's men have received the land and still hold (it).

Hundred of LEXDEN

24 Leofeva held ALDHAM for 1 hide less 5 acres before 1066. Now Aubrey's wife holds (it) from the Bishop.
Then 1 villager, now none. Always 4 slaves; 2 ploughs in lordship.
Woodland, 12 pigs; meadow, 3 acres. 1 cob, 6 cattle.
Value then and later 30s; now 60s.

Hundred of ONGAR

25 Herbert's nephew holds KELVEDON (Hatch) from the Bishop, which Algar, a free man, held for ½ hide and 20 acres.
Always 4 smallholders; 1 plough.
Woodland, 60 pigs; meadow, 7½ acres. 1 (head of) cattle, 24 b
5 pigs, 47 sheep.
Value 20s.

Hundred of CHAFFORD

26 Mauger holds UPMINSTER from the Bishop, which Wulfwin held for 1½ hides.
Then 2 smallholders, now the same. Always 1 plough.
Value then 20s; now 30[s].

27 Mauger also holds AVELEY, which Edward, a free man, held for 1 hide and 40 acres.
Always 6 smallholders; 1 plough in lordship; 1 men's plough.
Value then 20s; now 30[s].

28 Hugh holds THURROCK from the Bishop, which Alfward, a free man, held for 1 hide and 40 acres.
Always 2 smallholders. Then 2 ploughs, now 1.
Woodland, 10 pigs; meadow, 8 acres; pasture, 50 sheep.
Value then 30s; now 40[s].
Then 1 cob; then 1 (head of) cattle, now 2; then 25 pigs, now 9; then 50 sheep, now 48.

Turochā ten& Anschetill⁹. de ep̄o . qđ tenuit Mannic⁹ lib hō . t . r . e . p̄ . II . hid . 7 . dim . 7 . XL . ac . M̊ . II . uilł . Tc̄ . III . bor . m̊ . VIII . Tc̄ . VI . ser . m̊ null⁹ . Sēp . I . car in dn̄io. 7 . I . car hominū . VIII . ac . p̄ti . Tc̄ uał . III . lib . m̊ . IIII.

Reneham ten& Hugo de epo . qđ tenuit Alsi⁹ lib hō p̄ . Man . 7 p̄ . IIII . hid t . r . e . Sēp . VIII . uilł . Tc̄ . III . bor . m̊ . v . Tc̄ . IIII . ser . m̊ null⁹ . Tc̄ . III . car . in dn̄io 7 . qn̄ recep . II . m̊ nulla . Tc̄ . 7 . p̄ . III . car hom . m̊ . II . Tc̄ . 7 p̄ uał VI . lib . m̊ . XL . sol . In Turoc tenuit Vluuin⁹ . dimid . hid . M̊ . hugo de ep̄o Tc̄ . I . car . m̊ n̄ . Silu . v . por . VIII . ac . p̄ti . Past . L . ou . Vał . XX . sol. ★

Estinfort tenuit Aluric⁹ . lib hō p̄ . I . hid . 7 . XXX . ac . m̊ ten& Idē hugo . sēp . I . bor . 7 . I . car . v . ac . p̄ti . Vał . XXX . sol. ★
De hac t̄ra sī XV . ac . in Soca Willi piperelli . de turoc . sicut comitat⁹ testat̄ . Ad ecclīa huj⁹ manerij jacent . XXX . ac . qs uicini de der̄ in elemosina.

Craohv . ten& hugo de ep̄o qđ tenuit Aluuin⁹ lib hō p̄ . M . 7 p̄ . I . hid . 7 . đ . Sēp . I . uilł . 7 . I . bor . Tc̄ . I . car . M̊ . dim . Silu . c . porc . I . ac . 7 . dim . p̄ti . Tc̄ 7 post uał . L . sol . m̊ . XX . In Estinfort . tenuit Gislebt⁹ hō ep̄i baioc.

25 a

. I . hid . 7 . dim . qđ ten& fili turoldi de ep̄o . Sēp . III . uilł . 7 . IIII . bor . 7 . II . car in dn̄o. Vał . XXX . sol Hoc testatur hund qđ hec hid jacuit t . r . e . in Turroc maner Willi piperelli . exceptis . X . ac.

Limpwellā ten& Hugo de ~~comite~~ ep̄o qđ tenuit Edric⁹ lib hō . p̄ . I . Man . 7 dim hid . Tc̄ . I . bor . m̊ . II . Tc̄ . I . car . m̊ . dim . Silu . XX . porc . Pastura XX . ou. Tc̄ uał . X . sol . m̊ . XX.

29 Ansketel holds THURROCK from the Bishop, which Manning, a free man, held before 1066, for 2½ hides and 40 acres.
Now 2 villagers; then 3 smallholders, now 8; then 6 slaves, now none. Always 1 plough in lordship; 1 men's plough.
Meadow, 8 acres.
Value then £3; now [£] 4.

30 Hugh holds RAINHAM from the Bishop, which Alfsi, a free man, held as a manor, for 4 hides before 1066.
Always 8 villagers. Then 3 smallholders, now 5; then 4 slaves, now none. Then 3 ploughs in lordship, when acquired 2, now none. Then and later 3 men's ploughs, now 2.
Value then and later £6; now 40s.

31 Wulfwin held ½ hide in THURROCK. Now Hugh (holds it) from the Bishop. Then 1 plough, now none.
Woodland, 5 pigs; meadow, 8 acres; pasture, 50 sheep.
Value 20s.

32 Aelfric, a free man, held STIFFORD for 1 hide and 30 acres. Now Hugh also holds it.
Always 1 smallholder; 1 plough.
Meadow, 5 acres.
Value 30s.
Of this land, 15 acres are in William Peverel's jurisdiction of (Grays) Thurrock, as the County testifies. 30 acres, which neighbours gave in alms, lie in (the lands of) this manor's church.

33 Hugh holds CRANHAM from the Bishop, which Alwin, a free man, held as a manor, for 1½ hides.
Always 1 villager; 1 smallholder. Then 1 plough, now ½.
Woodland, 100 pigs; meadow, 1½ acres.
Value then and later 50s; now 20[s].

34 In STIFFORD Gilbert, a man of the Bishop of Bayeux's, held 1½ 25 a
hides, which Thorold's son holds from the Bishop.
Always 3 villagers; 4 smallholders; 2 ploughs in lordship.
Value 30s.
This Hundred testifies that these hides lay in (the lands of Grays) Thurrock, William Peverel's manor, before 1066, apart from 10 acres.

35 Hugh holds *LIMPWELLA* from the Bishop, which Edric, a free man, held as 1 manor; ½ hide.
Then 1 smallholder, now 2. Then 1 plough, now ½.
Woodland, 20 pigs; pasture, 20 sheep.
Value then 10s; now 20[s].

Hund de Celmeresfort. Haneghefeldā tenuit Friebt p. i. Man. 7 p. ix. hid. t. r. e. m̄ ten& Rad fili Turoldi de epo. Sēp. iii. uitt. Tc̄. ii. bor. m̄. v. Tc̄. iiii. ser. m̄. viii. Tc̄. ii. car in dn̄io. m̄. iii. Sēp. ii. car. hom. Silu. lx. por. iii. runc. xvi. an. xxxii. por. Tc̄. cxvii. ou. m̄. dcccx. Tc̄ ual. c. sol. m̄. vii. lib. In ead tenuer xxiii. libi hoes xiiii. hid. q possent recede sine licentia dn̄i ipsi mansiois Hos ten& Epc̄. s; comitat nescit q m̄ eos habuerit. Sēp. i. uitt. 7. xviii. bor. 7. viii. ser. Tc̄. xi. car. m̄. x. Silu. cl. por. Tc̄ ual. viii. lib. m̄. vii. lib. 7. . ii. sol. has hid. p̄occupau turold de Rouecestra. 7 abbatia de eli calump niat. ii. hid. 7. iii. uirg: qs tenebant. ii. hoēs. 7 hund testat. qd ipsi tenebant libe trā suā. 7 tantū m̄ erant cōmdati abbi de eli.

Berewic tenuit Oin dac. lib hō. t. r. e. M Turold de epo. p. vi. hid. 7. xxxvii. 7. a. ac. Tc̄. iiii. uitt. m̄. vi. Tc̄. iiii. bor. m̄. vi. Tc̄. iii. ser. m̄. v. Sēp. iii. car in dn̄io 7. ii. car hom. Silu. c. porc. iii. ac. p̄ti. Tc̄. iii. runc. m̄. v. 7. x. pulli | Tc̄. iiii. an. m̄. xviii. Tc̄. xvi. porc m̄. lxi. Tc̄. lx. ou. m̄. cxxvi. Tc̄ ual. iiii. lib. m̄. vi.

Laghenbiam. tenuit Turchill p. m. t. r. e. p. ii. hid. 7. dim. 7. vi. ac. M . R. p tantundē. de epo. Tc̄. ii. uitt. m̄. i. Sēp. v. bor 7. ii. ser. 7. i. car in dn̄io. 7. i. car. hom. Silu. c. porc. xvii. ac. pti. Tc̄. iii. runc. m̄. i. Tc̄. v. an. m̄. ix. Tc̄. xix. por. m̄. xl. Tc̄. xlv. ou. M. cx. Tc̄ 7 p ual. xl. sol. m̄. lx.

25 b

Walfarā. tenuit. Anunt dac. t. r. e. p. iii. 7. p. i. hid. 7. dim. m̄. R. de epo. Sēp. ii. bor. 7. i. ser. 7. i. car. Silu. lx. porc. xv. ac. p̄ti. i. runc. Tc̄. v. an. m̄. iiii. Tc̄. xv. ou. m̄. l. Tc̄. xi. por. m̄. xvii. i. cap. Tc̄ ual. xx. sol. m̄. xxx.

Hundred of CHELMSFORD

36 Fridebert held (South) HANNINGFIELD as 1 manor, for 9 hides before 1066. Now Ralph son of Thorold holds (it) from the Bishop.

Always 3 villagers. Then 2 smallholders, now 5; then 4 slaves, now 8. Then 2 ploughs in lordship, now 3. Always 2 men's ploughs.

Woodland, 60 pigs. 3 cobs, 16 cattle, 32 pigs; then 117 sheep, now 810.

Value then 100s; now £7.

In the same (Hanningfield), 23 free men, who could withdraw without the lord of the place's permission, held 14 hides. The Bishop holds these, but the County does not know how he has them.

Always 1 villager; 18 smallholders; 8 slaves. Then 11 ploughs, now 10.

Woodland, 150 pigs.

Value then £8; now £7 2s.

Thorold of Rochester misappropriated these hides. Ely Abbey claims 2 hides and 3 virgates, which 2 men held; the Hundred testifies that they held their land freely and were nevertheless under the Abbot of Ely's patronage.

37 Odin the Dane, a free man, held *BEREWIC* before 1066. Now Thorold (holds it) from the Bishop for 6½ hides and 37 acres.

Then 4 villagers, now 6; then 4 smallholders, now 6; then 3 slaves, now 5. Always 3 ploughs in lordship; 2 men's ploughs.

Woodland, 100 pigs; meadow, 3 acres. Then 3 cobs, now 5 and 10 foals; then 4 cattle, now 18; then 16 pigs, now 61; then 60 sheep, now 126.

Value then £4; now [£] 6.

38 Thorkell held LAWN (Hall) as a manor before 1066, for 2½ hides and 6 acres. Now R(alph holds it) from the Bishop for as much.

Then 2 villagers, now 1. Always 5 smallholders; 2 slaves; 1 plough in lordship; 1 men's plough.

Woodland, 100 pigs; meadow, 17 acres. Then 3 cobs, now 1; then 5 cattle, now 9; then 19 pigs, now 40; then 45 sheep, now 110.

Value then and later 40s; now 60[s].

39 Anand the Dane held WALTER (Hall) before 1066 as a manor, for 25 b
1½ hides. Now R(alph holds it) from the Bishop.

Always 2 smallholders; 1 slave; 1 plough.

Woodland, 60 pigs; meadow, 15 acres. 1 cob; then 5 cattle, now 4; then 15 sheep, now 50; then 11 pigs, now 17; 1 goat.

Value then 20s; now 30[s].

Pacingas tenuit Segar p. ω.7.p.II.hid.7.xxx.ac.t.r.e.m.R.de epo.Tc
.I.uill.m.III.Sep.IIII.bor.7.I.ser.7.I.car.in dio.7.I.car.hom.Silu.xv.porc.
VIII.ac.pti.I.mol.Tc.III.runc.m.IIII.Tc.II.an.m.IIII.Tc.XI.ou.m.XXIII.
Val.XL sol. M

Melesham tenuit Godric p m.7.p.II.hid.7.dim.7 xxx.ac.M.R.de epo.
Tc.I.uill.m.II.Tc.I.bor.m.VI.Tc.IIII.ser.m.III.Sep.II.car.in dnio.Tc.I.car
7.dim.hom.m.I.silu.LX.porc.x.ac.pti.Sep.I.mol.Tc.III.runc.7.I.pull.
m.II.runc.7.IIII.pull.Tc.IX.an.m.XXVIII.Tc.XLVII.ou.m.CXL.Tc ual
.L.sol.m.IIII.lib.

Alia Molesham tenuit Vlmar lib ho.p.ω.7.p.I.hid.7.XL.ac.M.R.
de epo.Tc.I.bor.Sep.II.ser.7.I.car.Silu.XL.porc.x.ac.pti.Val.xx.sol.

Hund de Tendringe. Torinduna tenuit Adstan p.uno maner.
7.p.IIII.hid.M.Rad.de epo p tantunde.7 hanc tra inuasit Turoldus
de ruuecestra.Sep.III.uill.7.IX.bor.7.V.ser.Tc.II.car.in dnio.m.I.7.d.
s; tcia potest esse.Tc int hoes.II.car 7.dim.m.I.7.dim.Silu.c.porc.
.I.ac.pti.Past.c.ou.M.I.mol.I.sal.Sep.ual.IIII.lib.
Quidam lib homo tenuit in Eilesforda dim hida.que inuasit Torold sic
alia tra.7.qn recepit.dim.car.m nulla.s; pot esse.7 hund nescit qm
ht hanc tra.7 qa neq; Legat neq; ali ho uenit ex parte sua q derationass&
hanc.tra.ido e in manu regis cu alia.Tc 7 p ual.x.sol.m.V.7.IIII.d.

Hund de Turestapla. Toleshunta tenuit Oslac lib ho p.I.hid.M.epc

26 a

p tantunde.Tc.II.bor.m.III.m.I.ser.Tc.I.car.m.dim.Silu.xxx.porc.
past.LX.ou.Tc ual xx.sol.Post 7.m.xxx.

40 Saegar held PATCHING (Hall) as a manor, for 2 hides and 30 acres before 1066. Now R(alph holds it) from the Bishop.
Then 1 villager, now 3. Always 4 smallholders; 1 slave; 1 plough in lordship; 1 men's plough.
Woodland, 15 pigs; meadow 8 acres; 1 mill. Then 3 cobs, now 4; then 2 cattle, now 4; then 11 sheep, now 23.
Value 40s.

41 Godric held MOULSHAM (Hall) as a manor, for 2½ hides and 30 acres. Now R(alph holds it) from the Bishop.
Then 1 villager, now 2; then 1 smallholder, now 6; then 4 slaves, now 3. Always 2 ploughs in lordship. Then 1½ men's ploughs, now 1.
Woodland, 60 pigs; meadow, 10 acres; always 1 mill. Then 3 cobs and 1 foal, now 2 cobs and 4 foals; then 9 cattle, now 28; then 47 sheep, now 140.
Value then 50s; now £4.

42 Wulfmer, a free man, held the other MOULSHAM (Hall) as a manor for 1 hide and 40 acres. Now R(alph holds it) from the Bishop.
Then 1 smallholder. Always 2 slaves; 1 plough.
Woodland, 40 pigs; meadow, 10 acres.
Value 20s.

Hundred of TENDRING

43 Aethelstan held THORRINGTON as 1 manor, for 4 hides. Now Ralph (holds it) from the Bishop for as much. Thorold of Rochester annexed this land.
Always 3 villagers; 9 smallholders; 5 slaves. Then 2 ploughs in lordship, now 1½; but 3 possible. Then among the men 2½ ploughs, now 1½.
Woodland, 100 pigs; meadow, 1 acre; pasture, 100 sheep; now 1 mill; 1 salt-house.
Value always £4.

44 A free man held ½ hide in ALRESFORD, whom Thorold annexed, like the other land. When acquired, ½ plough, now none; but (1) possible. The Hundred does not know how he has this land and because neither a Commissioner nor another man came on his behalf to adjudge this land, it is now in the King's hand with the other (land).
Value then and later 10s; now 5s 4d.

Hundred of THURSTABLE

45 Oslac, a free man, held TOLLESHUNT for 1 hide. Now the Bishop (holds it) for as much. 26 a
Then 2 smallholders, now 3; now 1 slave. Then 1 plough, now ½.
Woodland, 30 pigs; pasture, 60 sheep.
Value then 20s; later and now 30[s].

Terra Epi Herefordensis. In Writa. ten& Epc. II. hid. 7. XX. ac. qru una fuit in eccla t. r. e. 7 alia feudo haroldi. Sep. III. uill. 7. I. pbr. Tc. II. bor. m. VIII. Tc. II. ser m null. sep. I. car in dnio. 7. II. car hom. silu. C. porc. VIII. ac. pti. Val. L. sol. XIX.

TERRE Comitis Eustachij In Exsessa. Hund de berdestapla. .XX.
Phobinge tenuit Brictmar un teinn regis Eaduuardi p. V. hid. 7. p uno man. m ten& comes. E. in dnio. Sep. IIII. car in dnio. 7. V. carruc. hominu. Tc. VIII. uill m. III. Tc. VIII. bor. m. XXII. Tc. XII. ser. m. VI. Silu. DCC. porc. Past. DCC. ouib;. dim piscina. XXXI. porc. DCC. ou. 7 XVII. Ex hac tra tulit Turold. XXX. ac. quæ st ad feudu epi baiocensis. Pt hoc addidit Ingelric huic manerio. XXII. libos hoes tenentes. XV. hid. 7. dimid. 7. XV. ac. 7. dim. In q tra. st sep. XII. car. 7. XX. bord. 7. III. ser. Silu. L. porc. X. ac. pti. Past. CCCC. ou. Tcia pars uni piscinæ. 7 posst addi. III. car. 7. dim. Tc ual. maneriu. XX. lib. 7 tra. sochemanoz. XII. lib. M int totu. XXXVI. lib.

Horninduna ten& Garner de comite qd tenuit Vluric lib ho. p. uno manerio. 7. p. II. hid. 7. L. ac. Sep. II. car. in dnio. Tc. II. uill. m null. Tc. VII.

26 b

bord. m. XII. Tc. II. ser. m. III. XII. ac. pti. Past. LX. ou. II. uac. X. por. CX. ou. Pt hoc XV. ac. ad elemosina ecclæ. Tc ual. LX. sol. m. L.

Scenefelda ten& Rog de comite qd tenuit Bodd. I. lib ho. t. r. e. p. I. Man. 7 p. II. hid. Tc. II. carrc. in dnio. m. I. m dim. car hom Tc. I. bor. m. VI. Tc. II. ser m null. Silu. XL. porc. II. animalia. XX. porc. XV. cap. Val. LX. sol.

19 LAND OF THE BISHOP OF HEREFORD

[Hundred of CHELMSFORD]

1 In WRITTLE the Bishop holds 2 hides and 20 acres of which 1 (hide) was in the (lands of the) Church before 1066 and the other (was) in Harold's Holding.

Always 3 villagers; 1 priest. Then 2 smallholders, now 8; then 2 slaves, now none. Always 1 plough in lordship; 2 men's ploughs.

Woodland, 100 pigs; meadow, 8 acres.

Value 50s.

20 LANDS OF COUNT EUSTACE IN ESSEX

Hundred of BARSTABLE

1 Brictmer, a thane of King Edward's, held FOBBING for 5 hides, as one manor. Now Count Eustace holds it in lordship. Always 4 ploughs in lordship; 5 men's ploughs.

Then 8 villagers, now 3; then 8 smallholders, now 22; then 12 slaves, now 6.

Woodland, 700 pigs; pasture, 700 sheep; ½ fishery. 31 pigs, 717 sheep.

From this land, Thorold took 30 acres which are in the Bishop of Bayeux's Holding. Besides this, Engelric added to this manor 22 free men who hold 15½ hides and 15½ acres. In this land have always been 12 ploughs;

20 smallholders; 3 slaves.

Woodland, 50 pigs; meadow, 10 acres; pasture, 400 sheep; the third part of 1 fishery. 3½ ploughs could be added.

Value then of the manor £20, of the Freemen's land £12; now £36 in total.

2 Warner holds HORNDON (-on-the-Hill) from the Count which Wulfric, a free man, held as one manor, for 2 hides and 50 acres. Always 2 ploughs in lordship.

Then 2 villagers, now none; then 7 smallholders, now 12; then 26 b
2 slaves, now 3.

Meadow, 12 acres; pasture, 60 sheep. 2 cows, 10 pigs, 110 sheep.

Besides this, 15 acres in the church's alms.

Value then 60s; now 50[s].

3 Roger holds SHENFIELD from the Count which 1 free man, Budd, held before 1066 as 1 manor, for 2 hides. Then 2 ploughs in lordship, now 1. Now ½ men's plough.

Then 1 smallholder, now 6; then 2 slaves, now none.

Woodland, 40 pigs. 2 cattle, 20 pigs, 15 goats.

Value 60s.

Dorsedā ten& Comes qđ tenuit Epc̄ Londoniensis . t . r . e . ꝓ . I . hid . quā tene
bat InGelric de eccła . Sēp . I . car in dn̄io . 7 . I . pb̄r . ħt ibi . I . carc . Vał . xx . sol.
hec hid n̄ jac& ad suos . c . man.

Grauesandā Tenuit Harold . 7 Ingelric de eo . ꝓ . man . 7 . ꝓ . I . hid . Sēp . I . car.
Tc̄ . I . uilł . m̊ . II . Tc̄ . uał . x . sol . m̊ . xx . 7 hec hid n̄ adjac& suis . c . manerijs.

Hunđ de Witham. Nutleam Ten& Aluric teinn . ꝓ . uno manerio.
de comite qđ tenuit Harold . t . r . e . Tc̄ 7 post . III . car in dn̄io . m̊ . II.
Tc̄ 7 post v . car hom . m̊ . III . Tc̄ 7 post . x . uilłi . m̊ . VI . Tc̄ . III . bor . Post.
7 m̊ . XVI . Tc̄ IX . ser . m̊ . IIII . Tc̄ silu . cc . por . M̊ . c . xxx . ac . p̄ti . past . c . ou.
m̊ . II . mol . v . uacas . XIIII . porc . c . ou . VII . cap̄ . III . eq̄s . De hoc manerio
tulit Rađ de marci . xxx . ac . 7 . jacent in feudo filij . hamonis . Sēp uał.
. x . lib.

Coghesħalā ten& Comes in dn̄io qđ tenuit Colo . lib hō . t . r . e . ꝓ uno
manerio . 7 ꝓ . III . hid . 7 . dim . 7 . XXXIII . ac . Sēp . III . car in dn̄io . 7 . qn̄ eam
recepit . I . carrc . Tc̄ . XVI . car hominū : post 7 m̊ . XIIII . Tc̄ . XI . uilł . Post
7 . m̊ . IX . Tc̄ . XXII . bor . m̊ . XXXI . M̊ . IIII . ser . Tc̄ . silu . dc . porc . m̊ . d.
XXXVIII . ac . p̄ti . Tantū pasturæ que uał . x . đ . Sēp . I . mol . I . runc.
xv . porc . IIII . cap̄ . IIII . uasa apū . huic manerio ꝑtinent . XI . sochem̄
7 . I . pb̄r . 7 . I . porcari . 7 . I . mercennari . huic tr̄e . additæ sť . XXXVIII.
ac.

27 a

qs . I . lib hō ten& de rege . Tc̄ uał hoc manerium . x . lib . M̊ . XIIII.
s; tam̄ reddit . xx . lib . 7 sup̄dictæ XXXVIII . ac . uał . x . sol.

Ruenhalē . ten& Comes in dn̄io qđ tenuit Edeua regina t . r . e
ꝓ . uno manerio . 7 . ꝓ . II . hid . 7 . dim . Tc̄ . III . car in dn̄io . M̊ . II . Tc̄ . VIII.
car . hom . m̊ . VI . Tc̄ . XII . uilł . m̊ . XIII . Tc̄ . VIII . bor . m̊ . XIIII . Sēp . VI . ser.

4 The Count holds ORSETT which the Bishop of London held before 1066 for 1 hide, which Engelric held from the Church.
Always 1 plough in lordship.
1 priest has 1 plough there.
Value 20s.
This hide does not lie in his 100 manors.

5 Harold held 'GRAVESEND' and Engelric from him as a manor, for 1 hide. Always 1 plough.
Then 1 villager, now 2.
Value then 10s; now 20[s].
This hide does not lie in his 100 manors.

Hundred of WITHAM

6 Aelfric, a thane, holds (White) NOTLEY as one manor from the Count, which Harold held before 1066. Then and later 3 ploughs in lordship, now 2. Then and later 5 men's ploughs, now 3.
Then and later 10 villagers, now 6; then 3 smallholders, later and now 16; then 9 slaves, now 4.
Woodland, then 200 pigs, now 100; meadow, 30 acres; pasture, 100 sheep; now 2 mills. 5 cows, 14 pigs, 100 sheep, 7 goats, 3 horses.
From this manor Ralph of Marcy took 30 acres; they lie in the Holding of Hamo's son.
Value always £10.

7 The Count holds COGGESHALL in lordship, which Cola, a free man, held before 1066 as one manor, for 3½ hides and 33 acres. Always 3 ploughs in lordship. When acquired, 1 plough. Then 16 men's ploughs, later and now 14.
Then 11 villagers, later and now 9; then 22 smallholders, now 31; now 4 slaves.
Woodland, then 600 pigs, now 500; meadow, 38 acres; pasture to the value of 10d; always 1 mill. 1 cob, 15 pigs, 4 goats, 4 beehives.
To this manor belong 11 Freemen, 1 priest, 1 pigman and 1 hired man.
To this land have been added 38 acres, which 1 free man holds 27 a
from the King.
Value of this manor then £10; now [£] 14, but however it pays £20.
Value of the above 38 acres 10s.

8 The Count holds RIVENHALL in lordship, which Queen Edith held before 1066 as one manor, for 2½ hides. Then 3 ploughs in lordship, now 2. Then 8 men's ploughs, now 6.
Then 12 villagers, now 13; then 8 smallholders, now 14; always 6 slaves.

Tc̄ . silu . cccc . porc . m̄ . ccc . 7 . dim . xxx . ac . p̄ti . Pastura de q̄ accipi
unt . iii . sol . Tc̄ . i . mol . m̄ . dim . i . soc . de . xv . ac . i . burgensis de colē
castro . 7 medietatē molini . abstulit Ricard de Sacheuilla . i . runc.
vi . an . xl . porc . viii . cap̄ . ii . uasa apū . Tc̄ . ual . ix . lib . M . xii . s; tn̄
reddit . xx . lib.
Ruenhalā ten& comes in dn̄io . qđ tenuit harold p . i . maner . 7 . p . i .
hid . 7 . xv . ac . Tc̄ . ii . car . in dn̄io . m̄ . i . Sēp . i . car . hom . Tc̄ . ii . uill . m̄ . v .
Tc̄ . i . bor . m̄ . ii . Tc̄ . v . ser . m̄ . iiii . & xxi . ac . 7 . đ . p̄ti . Past . de . vi . đ .
. x . porc . xxvii . ou . Tc̄ uał . lx . sol . m̄ . xxx.
Blundeshalā ten& Comes in dn̄io . qđ tenuit . i . liba femina . t . r . e
p . i . Man . 7 . dim . hid . Sēp . i . car in dn̄io . 7 . i . bor . vi . ac . p̄ti . Tc̄ . ual
xx . sol . m̄ . x.
Witham ten& Ricard de comite qđ tenuit harold p . li . ac . Sēp . i . car .
7 . i . borđ . ii . ac . 7 . dim . p̄ti . Val . xx . sol.
Hunđ de herlaua . Perendunā ten& Junain de comite qđ tenuit
Vlf teinn reg t . r . e . p uno manerio . 7 . p . iii . hid . 7 . dim . Sēp . ii . car
in dn̄io . 7 . ii . car . hom . Tc̄ . iiii . uill . m̄ . iii . Tc̄ . iiii . bor . m̄ . v . Sēp . ii .
ser . Silu . cc . porc . xiiii . ac . p̄ti . Val . iiii . lib.
Lattunā ten& Adelolf . de comite qđ tenuit Ernulf lib hō . t . r . e

27 b
p uno manerio . 7 . p . i . hid . 7 . dim . 7 . xxx . ac . ii . car in dn̄io . tc̄ . m̄ . i . Sēp . i .
uillanus . 7 . ii . bor . Tc̄ . iiii . ser . m̄ . ii . Silu . ccc . porc . xxxv . ac . p̄ti . 7 . i . pbr q̄
ten& dim . hidā ad unā ecctiam . Tc̄ uał . l . sol . m̄ lx.
Herlauā ten& Goisfrid de comite qđ tenuit Brictnar lib hō . t . r . e .
7 dim hid . Sēp . dim . car . Silu . xl . porc . iii . ac . p̄ti . Val . xi . sol. ★

Woodland, then 400 pigs, now 300 and a half; meadow, 30 acres; pasture, from which 3s are received; then 1 mill. now ½. 1 Freeman with 15 acres. 1 burgess of Colchester. Richard of Sackville took away ½ mill. 1 cob, 6 cattle, 40 pigs, 8 goats, 2 beehives.
Value then £9; now [£] 12, but however it pays £20.

9 The Count holds RIVENHALL in lordship, which Harold held as 1 manor, for 1 hide and 15 acres. Then 2 ploughs in lordship, now 1.
Always 1 men's plough.
Then 2 villagers, now 5; then 1 smallholder, now 2; then 5 slaves, now 4.
Meadow, 21½ acres; pasture at 6d. 10 pigs, 27 sheep.
Value then 60s; now 30[s].

10 The Count holds BLUNT'S HALL in lordship, which 1 free woman held before 1066 as 1 manor; ½ hide. Always 1 plough in lordship;
1 smallholder.
Meadow, 6 acres.
Value then 20s; now 10[s].

11 Richard holds WITHAM from the Count, which Harold held for 51 acres. Always 1 plough;
1 smallholder.
Meadow, 2½ acres.
Value 20s.

Hundred of HARLOW

12 Iwain holds (Great) PARNDON from the Count, which Ulf, a King's thane, held before 1066 as one manor, for 3½ hides. Always 2 ploughs in lordship; 2 men's ploughs.
Then 4 villagers, now 3; then 4 smallholders, now 5; always 2 slaves.
Woodland, 200 pigs; meadow, 14 acres.
Value £4.

13 Adelulf holds LATTON from the Count, which Ernulf, a free man, held before 1066 as one manor, for 1½ hides and 30 acres. 27 b
2 ploughs in lordship then, now 1.
Always 1 villager; 2 smallholders. Then 4 slaves, now 2.
Woodland, 300 pigs; meadow, 35 acres. 1 priest who holds ½ hide at a church.
Value then 50s; now 60[s].

14 Geoffrey holds HARLOW from the Count, which Brictmer, a free man, held before 1066; ½ hide. Always ½ plough.
Woodland, 40 pigs; meadow, 3 acres.
Value 11s.

Hunđ. de Dommauua. Dommauuā ten& Adelolf⁹ de merc de comite
qđ tenuit Edmar⁹. I. lib̄ hō. t. r. e. ꝑ. uno manerio. 7. ꝑ. II. hid. 7. xxx.
ac. Tc̄. III. car. in dn̄io. m̄. II. Tc̄. I. car. hom. m̄. III. Tc̄. III. uilt. m̄. XIII.
m̄. IX. bor. Tc̄. X. ser. m̄. IIII. Silu. ccc. porc. XXXVI. ac. pti. 7. una carr
pot̄. restaurari. XII. an. L. por. c. ou. I. runc. IIII. uasa apū. Val. VIII.
lib̄.

Hunđ de Witbrictesherna. Eltenai. ten& Comes in dn̄io. qđ tenuit
Ingelric⁹. t. r. e. ꝑ uno manerio. 7. ꝑ. II. hid. Tc̄. I. ser. m̄. II. bor. sep̄. I. car̄
in dn̄io. Pastur. L. ou. Val. xxx. sol.
Purlai tenuit Edeua t. r. e. ꝑ. uno man. 7. ꝑ. I. hid. 7. xxx. ac. s; non
fuit de feudo Ingelrici. 7. nc̄ ht̄ Eustachi⁹. Tc̄. ual. XVI. sol. 7. VIII. đ.
m̄. XXIII. sol. Tc̄. I. bi. manser̄. II. hoēs. m̄. I. pbr.

Hunđ de Dommauua. Plesinchov ten& Bernard⁹ de comite.
qđ tenuit. I. lib̄ hō. t. r. e. ꝑ. dim. hid. Sep̄. dim. car. Tc̄. II. bor. m̄. I. ser.
Silu. xx. pocc. V. ac. pti. Val. X. sol.

Hunđ de Wensistrev. Langhou tenuit Ingelric⁹. t. r. e. ꝑ uno
manerio. 7. ꝑ. VII. hid. M̊ ten& Comes in dn̄io. Tc̄. V. car̄ in ★
dn̄io. Post. IIII. M̊. III. Tc̄ 7 p⁹. I. car. 7. dim. hominū. m̄. II. Tc̄
V. uilt. m̄. IX. Sep̄. VII. bor. Tc̄. XII. ser. m̄. VIII. Silu. cc. por.

28 a
. I. ac. pti. Pastura. ð. ou. I. mol. I. sal. II. an. ccc. ou. XIII. porc. 7. III. runc.
huic manerio addidit Ingelric⁹. t. r. Willi. II. hid. q̄s tenuit. I. lib̄ homo
t. r. e. 7. dim. hid quā tenuer̄. III. libi hoēs. t. r. e. In his hid. 7 dim. st̄ sep̄. II.
car. M̊. IIII. bor. Past. c. ou. Tc̄. totū simul. ual. XVII. lib̄. 7 m̄. XVII. 7. V. sol
7. qn̄ recep̄ similit̄.

Hundred of DUNMOW

15 Adelulf of Marck holds DUNMOW from the Count, which 1 free man, Edmer, held before 1066 as one manor, for 2 hides and 30 acres. Then 3 ploughs in lordship, now 2. Then 1 men's plough, now 3.

Then 3 villagers, now 13; now 9 smallholders; then 10 slaves, now 4.

Woodland, 300 pigs; meadow, 36 acres; 1 plough could be restored. 12 cattle, 50 pigs, 100 sheep, 1 cob, 4 beehives.

Value £8.

Hundred of 'WIBERTSHERNE'

16 The Count holds ILTNEY (Farm) in lordship, which Engelric held before 1066 as one manor, for 2 hides.

Then 1 slave; now 2 smallholders. Always 1 plough in lordship.

Pasture, 50 sheep.

Value 30s.

17 Edeva held PURLEIGH before 1066 as one manor, for 1 hide and 30 acres. But it was not of Engelric's Holding. Now Eustace has it. Value then 16s 8d; now 23s.

Then 2 men dwelt there, now 1 priest.

Hundred of DUNMOW

18 Bernard holds 'PLESINGHO' from the Count, which 1 free man held before 1066 for ½ hide. Always ½ plough.

Then 2 smallholders; now 1 slave.

Woodland, 20 pigs; meadow, 5 acres.

Value 10s.

Hundred of WINSTREE

19 Engelric held LANGENHOE before 1066 as one manor, for 7 hides. Now the Count holds it in lordship. Then 5 ploughs in lordship, later 4, now 3. Then and later 1½ men's ploughs, now 2.

Then 5 villagers, now 9; always 7 smallholders; then 12 slaves, now 8.

Woodland, 200 pigs; meadow, 1 acre; pasture, 500 sheep; 1 mill; 28 a
1 salt-house. 2 cattle, 300 sheep, 13 pigs and 3 cobs.

To this manor after 1066 Engelric added 2 hides which 1 free man held before 1066, and ½ hide which 3 free men held before 1066. On these hides and the half have always been 2 ploughs.

Now 4 smallholders.

Pasture, 100 sheep.

Value altogether then £17; now [£]17 5s; when acquired the same.

Edburghetunā ten& Rad de marci. qđ tenuit Siuuard. lib hō. t. r. e.
ꝑ uno manerio. 7. ꝑ. I. hid. 7. dim. 7. I. uirḡ. Sēp. I. car in dñio. Tc̄. dim. car.
hom. 7 m̄ similit. Tc̄. IIII. bor. m̄. III. Tc̄. I. ser. m̄ null. silu. c. porc. IIII. ac
p̄ti. IIII. an. c. ou. xxx. porc. II. runc. Val. LX. sol.
Legrā tenuit. I. lib hō. Alric. t. r. e. ꝑ. II. hid. 7. dim. 7. I. uirḡ. Tc̄. I. car. 7. đ.
in dñio. m̄. II. Tc̄. I. bor. m̄. III. Tc̄. II. ser. m̄. I. Silu. XL. porc. m̄. I. mol. Tc̄.
. I. runc. m̄. II. Tc̄. III. an. m̄. v. xxxvIII. ou. m̄. CXLVI. VI. uasa apū. Tc̄
ual. IIII. lib. m̄. III.
Hund de Odelesforda. Sortegrauā tenuit. I. lib hō. t. r. e. m̄ ten&
Adelolf de comite. ꝑ uno Man. 7. ꝑ. I. hid. 7. xxx. ac. Tc̄. 7. p. I. car. in dñio.
m̄. II. Tc̄. 7. p. I. uill. m̄ null. Tc̄. 7 p. I. bor. m̄. III. Tc̄. I. ser. m̄ n̄. IX. ac. p̄ti. III.
an. II. runc. XI. por. LXXXX. ou. Val. XL. sol. hanc trā occupauit Ingelric.
tēpore regis Willi;
Hund de Hidincforda. Rideuuellā tenuit. t. r. e. I. lib hō. nōe Godu
in. ꝑ. uno man. 7. ꝑ. II. hid. 7. III. uirḡ. Tc̄. v. car. in dñio. post. 7. m̄. IIII.
XIIII. uilli. XIIII. ser. III. bord. Silu. LXXX. por. XXXVI. ac. p̄ti. XXII. an
XLIIII. porc. CII. ou. XXX. cap. 7. II. runc. Huic manerio adjacent sēp. XIIII.
soc. de LXVII. ac. 7. dim. hn̄tes. I. car. 7. dim. VI. ac. p̄ti. Tc̄ totū ual XVIII.
lib. Post 7 m̄. XXIIII. hoc ten& Comes in dñio;

28 b

Sortegrauā ten& Adelolf de comite qđ tenuit. I. lib hō. t. r. e. ꝑ uno
Man. 7. ꝑ. I. hid. 7. XXX. ac. Tc̄. I. car. in dñio. m̄ nulla. Sēp. I. uill. 7. I. bor.
7. I. ac. p̄ti. Tc̄ 7 p ual. XXX. sol. M̄. XXXIII.

20 Ralph of Marcy holds ABBERTON which Siward, a free man, held before 1066 as one manor, for 1½ hides and 1 virgate. Always 1 plough in lordship. Then ½ men's plough, now the same.
Then 4 smallholders, now 3; then 1 slave, now none.
Woodland, 100 pigs; meadow 4 acres. 4 cattle, 100 sheep, 30 pigs, 2 cobs.
Value 60s.

21 1 free man, Alric, held LAYER (de la Haye) before 1066 for 2½ hides and 1 virgate. Then 1½ ploughs in lordship, now 2.
Then 1 smallholder, now 3; then 2 slaves, now 1.
Woodland, 40 pigs; now 1 mill. Then 1 cob, now 2; then 3 cattle, now 5; then 38 sheep, now 146; 6 beehives.
Value then £4; now [£] 3.

Hundred of UTTLESFORD

22 1 free man held SHORTGROVE before 1066. Now Adelulf holds (it) from the Count as one manor, for 1 hide and 30 acres. Then and later 1 plough in lordship, now 2.
Then and later 1 villager, now none; then and later 1 smallholder, now 3; then 1 slave, now none.
Meadow, 9 acres. 3 cattle, 2 cobs, 11 pigs, 90 sheep.
Value 40s.
Engelric appropriated this land after 1066.

Hundred of HINCKFORD

23 1 free man, Godwin by name, held RIDGEWELL before 1066 as one manor, for 2 hides and 3 virgates. Then 5 ploughs in lordship, later and now 4.
14 villagers; 14 slaves; 3 smallholders.
Woodland, 80 pigs; meadow, 36 acres. 22 cattle, 44 pigs, 102 sheep, 30 goats and 2 cobs.
To this manor have always been attached 14 Freemen with 67½ acres, who have 1½ ploughs.
Meadow, 6 acres.
Value of the whole then £18; later and now [£] 24.
The Count holds it in lordship.

[Hundred of UTTLESFORD] 28 b

24 Adelulf holds SHORTGROVE from the Count, which 1 free man held before 1066 as one manor, for 1 hide and 30 acres. Then 1 plough in lordship, now none.
Always 1 villager; 1 smallholder.
Meadow, 1 acre.
Value then and later 30s; now 33[s].

Clare tenuit Ledmar̃.i.lib hō.t.r.e.p.i.hid.7.dim.7.xxxv.ac.
Tc̄.v.car in dnio P̄ 7 m̄.iii.Sēp.ii.car hominū.Tc̄.vii.uill.Post 7.m̄
.iiii.Post 7.m̄.xii.bord.Tc̄.x.ser.Post 7.m̄.iiii.xxvii.ac.p̄ti.i.mol.
.iii.runc.viii.an.xl.porc.ccxxxix.ou.Huic manerio adjac& sēper
.i.bereuuita.que uocat.geldeham de.ii.hid.7.xviii.ac.Tc̄.iii.car
in dnio.Post.7.m̄.ii.Sēp.ii.car hom.Tc̄.viii.uill.Post 7.m̄.vi.Post
7.m̄.viii.bor.viii.ser.tc̄.Post 7 m̄.vi.xviii.ac.p̄ti.Adhuc adjac&
huic manerio.vii.soc.de xxxv.ac.træ.hn̄tes.i.car.Tc̄ ual.xviii.
lib hoc maner̃.Post 7 m̄.xxii.Huic &iā manerio addidit Ingelric.
.i.libum hōem.t.r.Willi.7 habebat.xv.ac.7.i.car.7.ual.x.sol.hoc
maneriū ten& Comes in dnio.

Belcham tenuit Ledmar.lib hō.t.r.e.p.i.hid.7 xlv.ac.m̄ ten&
Vlmar de comite.Sēp.ii.car.in dnio.7.ii.car houm.7.iiii.uill.
Tc̄.7 p̄.iiii.bor.m̄.v.Tc̄.7 p̄.iiii.ser.m̄.ii.Silu.xx.porc.viii.ac p̄ti.
huic manerio jacent.v.sochem.q̄z.ii.occupauit Ingelric tēpore
regis Willi.q̄ tc̄ erant libi hōes.7 hn̄t.xxxv.ac.træ.In dnio.ix.
anim.ii.runc.xx.porc.c.ou.Tc̄.ual.xl.sol.Post 7 m̄.iiii.lib.

Bummestedā ten& Adelolf de Merc de comite.qd tenuit.i.lib
hō.t.r.e.p.ɱ.7.p.dim.hid.Tc̄.iii.car.in dnio.Post 7.m̄.ii.
Sēp.ii.car hom.vii.uill.xi.bord.iiii.ser.xv.ac.p̄ti.i.runc.
huic maner' addidit Engelric'.i.libm homē iii.ac'.7.dim'.
.iii.anim.Tc̄ ual.iiii.lib.Post 7 m̄.c.sol.

★

29 a

Belcham ten& Bernard de comite qd ~~tenuit~~ qd tenuit Etnod lib hō
t.r.e.p.dim hid.7.x.ac.Sēp.i.car.in dnio.M.ii.bor.ii.ser.iiii.ac.p̄ti.
.i.sochem de.xx.ac.i.runc.iiii.uac.Tc̄.xiiii.porc.m̄ null.Sēp.l.ou.
Val.xxx.sol.

[Hundred of HINCKFORD]

25 1 free man, Ledmer, held CLARET (Hall) before 1066 for 1½ hides and 35 acres. Then 5 ploughs in lordship, later and now 3. Always 2 men's ploughs.

Then 7 villagers, later and now 4; later and now 12 smallholders; then 10 slaves, later and now 4.

Meadow, 27 acres; 1 mill. 3 cobs, 8 cattle, 40 pigs, 239 sheep.

To this manor has always been attached 1 outlier, which is called (Little) YELDHAM, with 2 hides and 18 acres. Then 3 ploughs in lordship, later and now 2. Always 2 men's ploughs.

Then 8 villagers, later and now 6; later and now 8 smallholders; then 8 slaves, later and now 6.

Meadow, 18 acres.

Besides, attached to this manor are 7 Freemen with 35 acres of land, who have 1 plough.

Value of this manor then £18; later and now [£] 22.

To this manor Engelric also added 1 free man after 1066; he had 15 acres. 1 plough. Value 10s.

The Count holds this manor in lordship.

26 Ledmer, a free man, held BELCHAMP (Otten) before 1066 for 1 hide and 45 acres. Now Wulfmer holds (it) from the Count. Always 2 ploughs in lordship; 2 men's ploughs;

4 villagers. Then and later 4 smallholders, now 5; then and later 4 slaves, now 2.

Woodland, 20 pigs; meadow, 8 acres.

Attached to this manor are 5 Freemen, 2 of whom Engelric appropriated after 1066. They were then free men; they have 35 acres of land.

In lordship 9 cattle, 2 cobs, 20 pigs, 100 sheep.

Value then 40s; later and now £4.

27 Adelulf of Marck holds (Steeple) BUMPSTEAD from the Count, which 1 free man held before 1066 as 1 manor, for ½ hide. Then 3 ploughs in lordship, later and now 2. Always 2 men's ploughs;

7 villagers; 11 smallholders; 4 slaves.

Meadow, 15 acres. 1 cob, 3 cattle.

To this manor Engelric added 1 free man (with) 3½ acres.

Value then £4; later and now 100s.

28 Bernard holds BELCHAMP from the Count which Ednoth, a free 29 a
man, held before 1066 for ½ hide and 10 acres. Always 1 plough in lordship.

Now 2 smallholders; 2 slaves.

Meadow, 4 acres. 1 Freeman with 20 acres. 1 cob, 4 cows; then 14 pigs, now none; always 50 sheep.

Value 30s.

⸿ Vueſtunā ten& ~~ten&~~ Adelolfus de comite qđ tenuit . i . lib hō . t . r . e . p .
xxx . ac . sēp . i . car . 7 . iiii . ac p̄ti Tc . ual . xx . sol . m̄ . xxv .
⸿ Phincingefeldā ten& Wido de comite qđ tenuit Normannus . t . r . e .
p . Man . 7 . p . dim hid . 7 . x . ac . Sēp . i . car in dn̄io . 7 . i . bor . 7 . i . ser . Silua
xx . porc . ix . ac . p̄ti . iii . an . xx . i . minus . Tc ual . xx . sol . m̄ . xl .
⸿ Phincinghefeldā tenuit Vluricus lib hō . t . r . e . M . Idē Wido de
comite p . xxxvii . ac . Sēp . i . car . Tc . i . ser . m̄ . ii . bor . Tc . silu . xx . porc .
m̄ . v . iiii . ac . p̄ti . i . mol . ual . xvi . sol .
⸿ Smedetunā ten& Ranerus de comite qđ . tenuit . i . liba femina . t . r . e .
p uno manerio . 7 . p . iii . hid . Tc . iiii . car . in dn̄io Post . 7 . m̄ . ii . Tc . 7 postea
. i . car . 7 . dim . hom . m̄ . i . Tc . 7 . postea . iiii . uill . m̄ . iii . Sēp . xiiii . bor . 7
. ii . ser . Silu . xx . porc . xx . ac . p̄ti . Tc ual . vii . lib . m̄ . viii . Hec
maneria tenuit Ingelricus
⸿ Topesfeldā ten& Bernardus de comite qđ tenuit . i . lib hō . p . xv . ac .
t . r . e . Sēp . i . car in dn̄io . 7 . i . uill . 7 . i . bor . Tc . i . ser . m̄ nullus . Silua .
. x . porc . vi . ac . p̄ti . Val . xx . sol .
⸿ Hund de Witbrictesherna . Meldunā ten& Scs Martinus
Londoniæ de comite . qđ tenuit . i . lib . hō . t . r . e . p . i . hid . 7 . dim . 7 . xxx . ac .
postea tenuit Ingelricus . Sēp . vi . bor . 7 . ii . ser . 7 . ii . car . Silu . xxx . porc .
Paſtura . c . ou . ~~Tc ual . iiii . lib . M . c . sol .~~ In dn̄io . ii . uac . xiiii .
. porc .

29 b

. c . ou . Tc ual . iiii . lib . m̄ . c . sol . In Ead . i . lib hō tenuit . xxx . ac . t . r . e . quē
occupauit Ingelricus . m̄ ten& Scs Martinus de comite . 7 aliū libum hominē .
de . xxx . ac . Iſtos hōes posuit Ingelricus ad suā hallā . In t̄ra eorum ē sēp . i .
car . 7 . ual . xx . sol .

29 Adelulf holds WESTON (Hall) from the Count, which 1 free man held before 1066 for 30 acres. Always 1 plough.
Meadow, 4 acres.
Value then 20s; now 25[s].

30 Guy holds FINCHINGFIELD from the Count, which Norman held before 1066 as a manor, for ½ hide and 10 acres. Always 1 plough in lordship;
1 smallholder; 1 slave.
Woodland, 20 pigs; meadow, 9 acres. 3 cattle, 20 ... less 1.
Value then 20s; now 40[s].

31 Wulfric, a free man, held FINCHINGFIELD before 1066. Now Guy also (holds it) from the Count for 37 acres. Always 1 plough.
Then 1 slave; now 2 smallholders.
Woodland, then 20 pigs, now 5; meadow, 4 acres; 1 mill.
Value 16s.

32 Rainer holds SMEETHAM (Hall) from the Count, which 1 free woman held before 1066 as one manor, for 3 hides. Then 4 ploughs in lordship, later and now 2. Then and later 1½ men's ploughs, now 1.
Then and later 4 villagers, now 3. Always 14 smallholders; 2 slaves.
Woodland, 20 pigs; meadow, 20 acres.
Value then £7; now [£] 8.
Engelric held these manors.

33 Bernard holds TOPPESFIELD from the Count, which 1 free man held for 15 acres before 1066. Always 1 plough in lordship;
1 villager; 1 smallholder. Then 1 slave, now none.
Woodland, 10 pigs; meadow, 6 acres.
Value 20s.

Hundred of 'WIBERTSHERNE'

34 St. Martin's, London, holds MALDON from the Count, which 1 free man held before 1066 for 1½ hides and 30 acres. Later on Engelric held it.
Always 6 smallholders; 2 slaves; 2 ploughs.
Woodland, 30 pigs; pasture, 100 sheep.
In lordship 2 cows, 14 pigs, 100 sheep. 29 b
Value then £4; now 100s.

In the same (Maldon) 1 free man held 30 acres before 1066, which Engelric appropriated. Now St. Martin's holds it from the Count and another free man with 30 acres. Engelric placed these men in his hall. On their land, has always been 1 plough. Value 20s.

Vleham ten& Rob. de comite qd tenuit. I. lib hō. t. r. e. Post Ingelric. p. I. hid. Tc. ual. VIII. sol. 7. IIII. d. m. XIIII. sol.

Hund de Lassendena. Teiam tenuit. I. lib homo. t. r. e. p. III. hid 7. dim. m comes. E. Tc. VI. uilli. m. II. Tc. XVI. bor. m. XXXV. Tc. IX. ser. m. X. Tc. IIII. car in dnio. m. II. Tc. int hoes. VI. car. m. IIII. Silu. CLX. porc. XX. ac. pti. III. runc. VII. an. LXVIII. porc. LXXX. ou. XXXIIII. cap. huic manerio jac& una biuuita. de. I. hid. 7. dim. X. ac. min. Sep. I. bor. 7. II. ser. Tc. II. car. in dnio. m. I. silu. XXIIII. porc. 7. XVII. soc. tenentes. II. hid. 7. V. ac. in isto manerio. m tenent illā trā XVI. soc. Sep. sub ipsis VI. bor. Tc. II. ser. m null. Tc. int eos. VI. car. m. IIII. Silu. XXX. porc. XII. ac. pti. sep. I. mol. 7. isti soc. n potant recede ab hoc manerio. 7. ad huc jac& huic manerio. I. dom in colecestra. Tc ual hoc maneriū. XVI. lib. 7 qn recep similit. m ual. XXII. lib. candidas.

In Ead tenuer. V. libi hoēs LX. ac. 7 XXVIII. ac. q n erant de isto man. qs m ht comes. qa antec suus saisit fuit. 7 ptiū isti tre e in supdicto ptio. Bocchestedā tenuit Aluric. p. IIII. hid. 7. dim. m. Comes. in dnio. Sep. V. uill. 7. XVIII. bor. Tc. II. ser. m. null. Tc. II. car. in dnio. m similit. Sep. VI. car. hom. Silu. CCC. porc. VIII. ac. pti. Tc. I. mol. m null. 7. I. soc. q n potuit recede. tenens dim. hid. Tc. dim. car. m nulla. II. ac. pti. XIII. an. XXXV. porc. 7. CXL. ou. 7 XXV. cap. 7. II. runc.

30 a

Tc. 7 p ual. VIII. lib. M. XII. blanc.

Dunulanda tenuit Edric p. man. 7. p. I. hid. 7. dim. m. ten& Comes i dnio. Sep. X. bor. Tc. IIII. ser. m. I. Tc. II. car in dnio. m. I. Tc. II. car. hom. m. I.

35 Robert holds ULEHAM ('s Farm) from the Count, which 1 free man held before 1066. Later Engelric (held it) for 1 hide.
Value then 8s 4d; now 14s.

Hundred of LEXDEN

36 1 free man held TEY before 1066 for 3½ hides. Now Count Eustace (holds it).
Then 6 villagers, now 2; then 16 smallholders, now 35; then 9 slaves, now 10. Then 4 ploughs in lordship, now 2. Then among the men 6 ploughs, now 4.
Woodland, 160 pigs; meadow, 20 acres. 3 cobs, 7 cattle, 68 pigs, 80 sheep, 34 goats.
Attached to this manor is one outlier of 1½ hides less 10 acres.
Always 1 smallholder; 2 slaves. Then 2 ploughs in lordship, now 1.
Woodland, 24 pigs.
In this manor, 17 Freemen who held 2 hides and 5 acres; now 16 Freemen hold this land.
Always 6 smallholders under them. Then 2 slaves, now none. Then among them 6 ploughs, now 4.
Woodland, 30 pigs; meadow, 12 acres; always 1 mill.
These Freemen could not withdraw from this manor.
Also attached to this manor is 1 house in Colchester.
Value of this manor then £16; when acquired, the same; value now £22 blanched.
In the same (Tey) 5 free men, who were not part of this manor, held 60 acres and 28 acres, whom the Count now has, because his predecessor was in possession. The assessment of this land is in the above assessment.

37 Aelfric held BOXTED for 4½ hides. Now the Count (holds it) in lordship.
Always 5 villagers; 18 smallholders. Then 2 slaves, now none. Then 2 ploughs in lordship, now the same. Always 6 men's ploughs.
Woodland, 300 pigs; meadow, 8 acres; then 1 mill, now none.
1 Freeman, who could not withdraw, who holds ½ hide. Then ½ plough, now none.
Meadow, 2 acres. 13 cattle, 35 pigs, 140 sheep, 25 goats and 2 cobs.
Value then and later £8; now [£] 12 blanched. 30 a

38 Edric held (East) DONYLAND as a manor, for 1½ hides. Now the Count holds it in lordship.
Always 10 smallholders. Then 4 slaves, now 1. Then 2 ploughs in lordship, now 1. Then 2 men's ploughs, now 1.

Silu . c . porc . vi . ac . p̄ti . Pastura . c . ou . Tc̄ 7 p̄ ual . xl . sol . m̄ . iii . lib . In dn̄io lxxx . oues . In Ead tenuit . i . lib hō dim hid . quā m̄ ten& Comes sed Ingelric eam habuit . 7 hund nescit q̄m eam habuerit . Val . v . sol.

Bricceiā ten& Hugo de comite qd tenuit Edric . p . uno manerio. 7 . p . iii . hid . 7 post tenuit Ingelric . Tc̄ . xiii . uill . m̄ . vi . Tc̄ . v . bor. m̄ . xvii . Tc̄ . vi . ser . m̄ . iiii . Tc̄ . iii . car . in dn̄io . m̄ . ii . 7 . đ . Tc̄ . viii . car hōū m̄ . vi . Silu . c . por . xvi . ac . p̄ti . 7 . ii . dom in colecastro . que jacent huic manerio . 7 . i . soc . q n̄ potat recede . de . xiii . ac . Sēp ħt . dim . car. In dn̄io . Tc̄ . i . runc . m̄ . iii . Tc̄ . xx . an . m̄ . x . Tc̄ . xxxv . por . m̄ . xxxiiii. Tc̄ . cxl . ou . m̄ . cxx . Tc̄ . xl . cap . m̄ . xx . Tc̄ . 7 p̄ ual . vi . lib . m̄ . c . sol.

Estorp ten& Idē de comite . qd tenuit . Edric lib hō . t . r . e . p . m̄. 7 . p . i . hid . 7 . xxv . ac . Tc̄ . ii . bor . m̄ . viii . Tc̄ . iiii . ser . m̄ . ii . Tc̄ . ii . car in dn̄io . m̄ . i . Tc̄ . int hōes . i . car . m̄ . iii . Silu . xxx . por . vi . ac . p̄ti . Tc̄ . i . runc . 7 . xvi . an . 7 . xv . porc . 7 . xxx . ou . M̊ . x . por . 7 . i . runc . Tc̄ ual. xl . sol . m̄ . xxx.

Colū tenet . Rob de comite qd tenuit Aluric biga . p . i . uirḡ . 7 . x . ac. t . r . e . Tc̄ . i . bor . m̄ . iii . Sēp . ii . car in dn̄io . m̄ . int hōes . i . car . Tc̄ . v. ser . m̄ . iii . xiii . ac . p̄ti . silu . xl . porc . Tc̄ . ual . xxx . sol . m̄ . xl . Hic Aluric libe tenuit istā trā . sed Ingelric . habuit eā pq rex uenit . 7 hund nescit q̄m.

Dunilandā ten& Idē qd tenuit Godric de colæ castro . p . xxv . ac.
. Val . xii . đ.

Woodland, 100 pigs; meadow, 6 acres; pasture, 100 sheep.
Value then and later 40s; now £3.

In lordship 80 sheep.

In the same (Donyland) 1 free man held ½ hide which the Count now holds but Engelric had it and the Hundred does not know how he should have it.
Value 5s.

39 Hugh holds (Great) BIRCH from the Count, which Edric held as one manor, for 3 hides. Later Engelric held it.

Then 13 villagers, now 6; then 5 smallholders, now 17; then 6 slaves, now 4. Then 3 ploughs in lordship, now 2½. Then 8 men's ploughs, now 6.

Woodland, 100 pigs; meadow, 16 acres. 2 houses in Colchester which lie (in the lands of) this manor. 1 Freeman who could not withdraw, with 13 acres; he has always had ½ plough. In lordship then 1 cob, now 3; then 20 cattle, now 10; then 35 pigs, now 34; then 140 sheep, now 120; then 40 goats, now 20.

Value then and later £6; now 100s.

40 He also holds EASTHORPE from the Count which Edric, a free man, held before 1066 as a manor, for 1 hide and 25 acres.

Then 2 smallholders, now 8; then 4 slaves, now 2. Then 2 ploughs in lordship, now 1. Then among the men 1 plough, now 3.

Woodland, 30 pigs; meadow, 6 acres. Then 1 cob, 16 cattle, 15 pigs, 30 sheep; now 10 pigs, 1 cob.

Value then 40s; now 30[s].

41 Robert holds COLNE from the Count, which Aelfric Big held for 1 virgate and 10 acres before 1066.

Then 1 smallholder, now 3. Always 2 ploughs in lordship. Now among the men 1 plough. Then 5 slaves, now 3.

Meadow, 13 acres; woodland, 40 pigs.

Value then 30s; now 40[s].

This Aelfric held this land freely but Engelric had it after the King came and the Hundred does not know how.

42 He also holds (East) DONYLAND, which Godric of Colchester held for 25 acres.
Value 12d.

30 b

Hund de Angra. Stanfort tenuit Leuuin. t. r. e. 7 post. Ingelric p. uno manerio. 7. p. IX. hid. M ten& Comes in dnio. p tantūdē. Sēp. XXIIII. uill. Tc. II. bor. m. XVII. Tc. XXII. ser. m. XVI. Tc. X. car. in dnio. 7. qn recep. VII. m. V. Sēp. XV. car. hom. Silu. CCCC. porc. L. ac. pti. ★
Sēp. I. mol. IIII. runc. XL. an. XI. porc. CCXXXIII. ou. Tc ual. XXIIII. lib 7. qn recep. similit. M. XL. lib. blancas.

In Ead tenuit qdā lib hō. XL. ac. s; Ingelric accep eū adjungens isti træ. Sēp. ibi ē dim. car. silua. XX. porc. Sēp. ual. v. sol. ~~v. sol.~~ Et brictuuin. tenuit XX. ac. qs ingelric adjunxit suæ træ. 7. adptiatū ē in supdictis lib.

Paruā Stanfort ten Pat Alurici. t. r. e. p. uno manerio. 7. p. I. hid. 7 LXXX. ac. M ten& Comes. E. p tantū de feudo ingelrici. Tc. III. uill. 7. qn recep. V. M. similit. Sēp. III. ser. Tc. II. car. in dnio. m null. Sēp. I. car. hōū. Silu. C. porc. VI. ac. pti. VI. an. CCXIII. ou. Val. XL. sol.

De hoc manerio ten& Aluric. dim hid. de comite. 7 ual. X. sol. in eod ptio.

Lagafarā tenuit Leuuin t. r. e. p. I. hid. 7. XL. ac. 7 Aluuin tenuit aliā partē illi manerij. p. I. hid. 7. XL. ac. p. Man. s; Ingelric adjunxit suo Man. m ten& Comes. E. in dnio. Sēp. VII. uill. 7. X. bor. 7. XV. ser. 7. V. car. 7. dim. in dnio. 7. V. car. hom. Silu. CC. por. XXXVII. ac. 7. dim. pti. II. an. XI. porc. LXXX. ou. III. runc. Tc 7 p ual. XVI. lib. m. XX. candidas.

De hoc manerio ten& Rad LXXX. ac. 7. I. uill. 7. III. bor. 7. I. car. 7. ual XX. sol. in eod ptio.

In Ead tenuit qdā. lib hō. XL. ac. qs adjunx Ingelric isti træ. M. ten& Rad de comite. 7 ē in eod ptio. 7 ual. X. sol.

Angrā tenuit Ailida p. I. hid. 7. p uno Man. M comes in dnio. Sēp

31 a

VIII. uill. 7. VIII. bor 7. III. ser. 7. II. car in dnio. 7. III. car hominum

Hundred of ONGAR 30 b

43 Leofwin, and later Engelric, held STANFORD (Rivers) before 1066 as one manor, for 9 hides. Now the Count holds it in lordship for as much.

Always 24 villagers. Then 2 smallholders, now 17; then 22 slaves, now 16. Then 10 ploughs in lordship, when acquired 7, now 5. Always 15 men's ploughs.

Woodland, 400 pigs; meadow, 50 acres. Always 1 mill. 4 cobs, 40 cattle, 11 pigs and 233 sheep.

Value then £24; when acquired, the same; now £40 blanched.

In the same (Stanford) a free man held 40 acres, but Engelric acquired him, adding him to this land. Always ½ plough there.

Woodland, 20 pigs.

Value always 5s.

Also Brictwin held 20 acres, which Engelric added to his land. It is assessed in the above pounds.

44 Aelfric's father held STANFORD (Rivers) before 1066 as one manor, for 1 hide and 80 acres. Now Count Eustace holds it (as) of Engelric's Holding for as much.

Then 3 villagers, when acquired 5, now the same. Always 3 slaves. Then 2 ploughs in lordship, now none. Always 1 men's plough.

Woodland, 100 pigs; meadow, 6 acres. 6 cattle, 213 sheep.

Value 40s.

Of this manor, Aelfric holds ½ hide from the Count. Value 10s in the same assessment.

45 Leofwin held LAVER before 1066 for 1 hide and 40 acres. Alwin held another part of that manor for 1 hide and 40 acres as a manor. But Engelric added them to his manor. Now Count Eustace holds them in lordship.

Always 7 villagers, 10 smallholders and 15 slaves; 5½ ploughs in lordship; 5 men's ploughs.

Woodland, 200 pigs; meadow, 37½ acres. 2 cattle, 11 pigs, 80 sheep, 3 cobs.

Value then and later £16; now [£] 20 blanched.

Of this manor Ralph holds 80 acres.

1 villager, 3 smallholders. 1 plough.

Value 20s in the same assessment.

In the same (Laver) a free man held 40 acres which Engelric added to this land. Now Ralph holds (them) from the Count and he is in the same assessment.

Value 10s.

46 Aethelgyth held (Chipping) ONGAR for 1 hide, as one manor. Now the Count (holds it) in lordship.

Always 8 villagers, 8 smallholders, 3 slaves; 2 ploughs in lordship; 3 men's ploughs. 31 a

Silu . ·ɱ· . porc . xxviii . ac . pti . ii . runc . x . an . xxxvi . porc . cxii . ou.
Tc ual . c . sol . m . viii . lib.
In Ead . tenuit . i . lib ho . dim . hid . que fuit de hoc manerio . m ten&
Rad baignard.
Laghefara ten& Ricard de comite qd tenuit brictmar p . xl.
ac . 7 . p uno Maner . Sep . i . ser . 7 . i . car . vi . ac . pti . Val . x . sol.
Lamburna ten& Dauid de Comite qd tenuit Lefsi . p uno Man.
7 p . ii hid . 7 . lxxx . ac . Sep . i . uill . Tc . x . bor . m . xii . Sep . i . ser . 7 . ii.
car . in dnio . 7 . i . car . hom . Silu . c . porc . xx . ac . pti . Tc ual xl . sol . m . lx.
In dnio . ix . an . 7 . lxxx . ou.
Fifhida . ten& Ricard . de comite qd tenuit Brictmar . p . xl . ac . t . r . e.
7 p uno maner . Sep . iii . ser . 7 . i . car . in dnio . Silu . xxiiii . porc . xx . ac
pti . Tc . ual . x . sol . m . xx . Qda lib ten . x . ac . s; Ing . iuasit . sep . iii . ser . silu . xxiiii . por.
Fifhida ten& Junan de comite qd tenuit Aluuin . t . r . e . p . uno . ɱ . [iiii . ac' p'ti . tc ual . v . sol . m . x.]
7 . p . lxxx . ac . Sep . i . uill . Tc . iiii . bor . m . vi . Sep . ii . ser . 7 . i . car . in dio.
7 . i . car . hom . Silu . l . porc . x . ac . pti . Tc ual . xxx . sol . m . xl.
Hund de Celmeresfort. Neuuelanda ten& . Malger de com.
qd tenuit Harold . t . r . e . p uno Man 7 . p . iii . hid . Sep . xv . uill.
7 . vii . bor . 7 . ii . ser . 7 . ii . car . in dnio . ii . car . hom . Silu . c . porc . xx.
ac . pti . Tc . ual . c . sol . m . vii . lib . Ingelr iuas hoc ɱ . 7 hund testat q jacuit
in Wiretela . t' . r' . e' . 7 m ten& Comes . E.

Woodland, 1000 pigs; meadow, 28 acres. 2 cobs, 10 cattle, 36 pigs, 112 sheep.
Value then 100s; now £8.
In the same (Ongar) 1 free man held ½ hide which was this manor's. Now Ralph Baynard holds it.

47 Richard holds LAVER from the Count, which Brictmer held for 40 acres, as one manor.
Always 1 slave; 1 plough.
Meadow, 6 acres.
Value 10s.

48 David holds LAMBOURNE from the Count, which Leofsi held as one manor, for 2 hides and 80 acres.
Always 1 villager. Then 10 smallholders, now 12. Always 1 slave; 2 ploughs in lordship; 1 men's plough.
Woodland, 100 pigs; meadow, 20 acres.
Value then 40s; now 60[s].
In lordship 9 cattle and 80 sheep.

49 Richard holds FYFIELD from the Count, which Brictmer held for 40 acres before 1066, as one manor.
Always 3 slaves; 1 plough in lordship.
Woodland, 24 pigs; meadow, 20 acres.
Value then 10s; now 20[s].
A free [man] held 10 acres, but Engelric annexed (him). Always 3 slaves.
Woodland, 24 pigs; meadow, 4 acres.
Value then 5s; now 10[s].

50 Iwain holds FYFIELD from the Count, which Alwin held before 1066 as one manor, for 80 acres.
Always 1 villager. Then 4 smallholders, now 6. Always 2 slaves; 1 plough in lordship; 1 men's plough.
Woodland, 50 pigs; meadow, 10 acres.
Value then 30s; now 40[s].

Hundred of CHELMSFORD

51 Mauger holds NEWLAND (Hall) from the Count, which Harold held before 1066 as one manor, for 3 hides.
Always 15 villagers, 7 smallholders, 2 slaves; 2 ploughs in lordship; 2 men's ploughs.
Woodland, 100 pigs; meadow, 20 acres.
Value then 100s; now £7.
Engelric annexed this manor and the Hundred testifies that it lay in (the lands of) Writtle before 1066. Now Count Eustace holds it.

Baduuen tenuit Leuuin ꝓ. v. hid. t. r. e. M ten& Lābt de com̄. ꝓ tantund. Hanc &iā trā inuasit Ingelric. post q rex aduenit. Tc 7 p. III. uill. m null. Tc 7 p. IIII. bor. m. VIII. Tc 7 p. VI. ser. m. III.

31 b

Sep. III. car. in dn̄io. Tc. 7 p. I. car hom. m. null. Silu. c. porc. XXIIII. ac. p̄ti. I. runc. XV. an. L. porc. CXXXV. ou. Tc 7 p uat. c. sol. m. VI. lib.

Runewella ten& Ide Lābt de comite. qd ten. Lefstan. t. r. e. ꝓ. M. 7. ꝓ. I. hid. 7 hoc inuasit Ingelric. Tc. II. bor. m. III. Sep. I. car. Silu. L. porc. II. ac. p̄ti. XIII. an. XX. porc. XXXVI. ou. Val. XX. sol.

Runeuuella ten& Adelolf de comite qd tenuit Edeua t. r. e. ꝓ. uno Man. 7. ꝓ. IIII. hid. 7 hoc inuasit Ingelric. Tc. IIII. bor. m. v. Tc. II. ser. m. I. Tc. 7. p. dim. car in dn̄io. m. II. 7. dim. Sep. dim. car hominū. Silu. LXXX. porc. Tc. 7 p. uat. c. sol. m. VI. lib.

Waltham ten& Lābt de comite q tenuit Lefstan. t. r. e. ꝓ. uno. M. 7. ꝓ. II. hid. 7. I. uirḡ. 7 hanc inuasit. ingelric. Tc. 7 p. IIII. bor. m. VII. Tc. II. ser. m. I. Tc. 7 p. II. car. in dn̄io. m. I. 7. d. Sep. dim. car. hom. Silu. x. porc. XII. ac. p̄ti. I. runc. VIII. an. c. ou. Tc 7 p uat. L. sol m. LX.

Borham ten& Ide Lambt de comite. qd tenuer. XIIII. libi hoēs ꝓ. VIII. hid. 7. XXIII. ac. 7 hoc inuasit Ingelric post q rex uenit in hanc trā. Tc. sub ipsis. IIII. bor. m. VIII. Sep. III. ser. 7. II. car. in dn̄io. Tc. int hoēs. XIII. car; qn̄ recep. 7. m. II. Silu. x. porc. LIIII. ac. p̄ti. m. I. mol. I. runc. XV. an. CXXXII. ou. Tc. uat. XII. lib. 7. qn̄ rec. VI. lib. m. VIII.

52 Leofwin held (Little) BADDOW for 5 hides before 1066. Now Lambert holds it from the Count for as much. This land also Engelric annexed after the King arrived.

Then and later 3 villagers, now none; then and later 4 smallholders, now 8; then and later 6 slaves, now 3. Always 3 ploughs in lordship. Then and later 1 men's plough, now none. 31 b

Woodland, 100 pigs; meadow, 24 acres. 1 cob, 15 cattle, 50 pigs, 135 sheep.

Value then and later 100s; now £6.

53 Lambert also holds RUNWELL from the Count, which Leofstan held before 1066 as a manor, for 1 hide. Engelric annexed this.

Then 2 smallholders, now 3. Always 1 plough.

Woodland, 50 pigs; meadow, 2 acres. 13 cattle, 20 pigs, 36 sheep.

Value 20s.

54 Adelulf holds RUNWELL from the Count, which Edeva held before 1066 as one manor, for 4 hides. Engelric annexed this.

Then 4 smallholders, now 5; then 2 slaves, now 1. Then and later ½ plough in lordship, now 2½. Always ½ men's plough.

Woodland, 80 pigs.

Value then and later 100s; now £6.

55 Lambert holds (Little) WALTHAM from the Count, which Leofstan held before 1066 as one manor, for 2 hides and 1 virgate. Engelric annexed this.

Then and later 4 smallholders, now 7. Then 2 slaves, now 1. Then and later 2 ploughs in lordship, now 1½. Always ½ men's plough.

Woodland, 10 pigs; meadow, 12 acres. 1 cob, 8 cattle, 100 sheep.

Value then and later 50s; now 60[s].

56 Lambert also holds BOREHAM from the Count, which 14 free men held for 8 hides and 23 acres. Engelric annexed this after the King came to this land.

Then 4 smallholders under them, now 8. Always 3 slaves; 2 ploughs in lordship. Then among the men 13 ploughs, when acquired and now 2.

Woodland, 10 pigs; meadow, 54 acres. Now 1 mill. 1 cob, 15 cattle, 132 sheep.

Value then £12; when acquired £6; now [£] 8.

In Ead ten&. I. lib hō. v. ac. 7 uat. x. đ.
Ranulf piperell calumpniat dim. hid. 7. XVIII. ac. que jacent
ad ecctiam huj manerij 7 dim ecctiam. 7 Ingelric n̄ fuit saisit.
s; comes. E. dedit cuidā suo militi unde reuocat eā ad defensorē. ★

32 a
7. XXX. ac. que reddebant p annū. XII. đ. antecessori Ranulfi piperelli.
u hund testat.
Hund de Turestapla. Toleshuntā ten& Adelolf de comite. qđ
tenuit Torbn p uno manerio. 7 p. VIII. hid. 7. đ. Tc. v. uilt. m̄. III. Tc. XVI.
bor. m̄. XIIII. tc. VIII. ser. m̄. IIII. Tc. IIII. car. in dn̄io. m̄. III. Tc. IIII. car
hom. m̄. II. Silu. LX. porc. Past. ccc. ou. Tc. XII. salinæ. m̄. v. II. runc.
XVI. an. XL. porc. cccc. ou. Tc. 7 p uat. x. lib. m̄. c. sot.
In Ead. tenuer. III. libi hoēs. dim. hid. 7. I. ac. 7 uat. x. sot.
Goldhangram ten& Idē Adelolf de comite. qđ tenuit Elric.
p. I. hid. 7. XV. ac. m̄. IIII. bor. Tc. II. ser. m̄ null. Sēp. I. car. in dn̄io. m̄
dim. car. hom. Silu. XL. por. III. ac. 7. dim. pti. Past. L. ou. Tc uat. XX. sot
. m̄. XXX.
Toleshunta. ten. comes in dn̄io. qđ tenuit Almar p. II. hid. 7. v. ac.
Tc. III. bor. m̄. v. Sēp. II. ser. 7. I. car. in dn̄io. 7. I. car. hom. Silu. c. porc.
past. CLX. ou. L. ou. Tc. uat. XL. sot. 7 qn̄ recep. XV. sot. m̄. XX.
Toleshuntā ten& Scs Martin de comite qđ tenuit Vluric. lib
hō. p uno Manerio. 7. p. I. hid. 7. XXXV. ac. Sēp. II. bor. 7. I. car. Silu. XXX.
porc. I. animat. Vat. XXX. sot.
In Blacham tenuer. IIII. libi hoēs. dim. hid. 7 potant eā uendē. M
ten& Comes. E. Sēp. I. car. Vat. x. sot. 7. qn̄ rec. x. sot. m̄. VII. sot.

In the same (Boreham) 1 free man holds 5 acres.
Value 10d.
Ranulf Peverel claims ½ hide and 18 acres which lie (in the lands of) the church of this manor and ½ church. Engelric was not in possession. But Count Eustace gave it to one of his men-at-arms who calls him as his defender.
30 acres which paid 12d a year to Ranulf Peverel's predecessor, 32 a
as the Hundred testifies.

Hundred of THURSTABLE

57 Adelulf holds TOLLESHUNT from the Count, which Thorbern held as one manor, for 8½ hides.
Then 5 villagers, now 3; then 16 smallholders, now 14; then 8 slaves, now 4. Then 4 ploughs in lordship, now 3. Then 4 men's ploughs, now 2.
Woodland, 60 pigs; pasture, 300 sheep; then 12 salt-houses, now 5. 2 cobs, 16 cattle, 40 pigs, 400 sheep.
Value then and later £10; now 100s.
In the same (Tolleshunt) 3 free men held ½ hide and 1 acre.
Value 10s.

58 Adelulf also holds GOLDHANGER from the Count, which Alric held for 1 hide and 15 acres.
Now 4 smallholders; then 2 slaves, now none. Always 1 plough in lordship. Now ½ men's plough.
Woodland, 40 pigs; meadow, 3½ acres; pasture, 50 sheep.
Value then 20s; now 30[s].

59 The Count holds TOLLESHUNT in lordship, which Aelmer held for 2 hides and 5 acres.
Then 3 smallholders, now 5. Always 2 slaves; 1 plough in lordship; 1 men's plough.
Woodland, 100 pigs; pasture, 160 sheep. 50 sheep.
Value then 40s; when acquired 15s; now 20[s].

60 St. Martin's holds TOLLESHUNT from the Count which Wulfric, a free man, held as one manor for 1 hide and 35 acres.
Always 2 smallholders; 1 plough.
Woodland, 30 pigs. 1 (head of) cattle.
Value 30s.

61 4 free men held ½ hide in 'BLATCHAMS' and could sell it. Now Count Eustace holds it. Always 1 plough.
Value 10s; when acquired 10s; now 7s.

Tolesbiā ten& Almfrid⁹ de comite qđ tenuit Gudmund⁹ lib
lib hō . p uno manerio . 7 . p . III . hid . t . r . e . 7 hoc ē de feudo ingelrici.
Tc . IIII . bor . M . III . Tc . IIII . ser . m . II . Tc . in dnio . III . car . m . II.
Sep . dim . car hom . Past . c . ou . I . sal . Tc ual . IIII . lib . P⁹ 7 m . III.

32 b

Hund de Tenderinga. Citā ten&. Comes in dnio . qđ ten
Eduuard⁹ p uno man . 7 . p . III . hid . 7 . XL . ac . t . r . e . Post Ingelric⁹ . Tc.
IX . uilt . Post 7 m . VII . m . II . bor . Tc . VIII . ser . P⁹ 7 m . II . Tc . in dnio . I . car.
7 . qn recep . nichil . m . I . Tc . VI . car hominū Post 7 m . III . Silu . CCCC.
porc . VI . ac . pti . I . uac . XI . ou . Tc . ual . XII . lib . 7 . qn recep . XL . sol.
m . X . lib . Huic manerio jac& . I . bereuuita que uocat . Fratinga.
de . XL . ac . m . dim . car . Apptiatū ē supi⁹ . 7 Ad Burnā . XXX . ac.
Tc . I . car . m . dim . Val . XX . sol . 7 In Froruuica . L . ac . 7 Sep . III . bor
7 . I . ser . 7 . I . ac . 7 . đ . pti . m . I . car . Silu . XII . porc . Val . X . sol.

Tendringā tenuit Freuuin . t . r . e . p . uno maner . 7 . p . đ . hid . M
ten& Comes in dnio . p tantudē . Sep . I . uilt . 7 . II . bor . 7 . II . ser . Tc . II.
car . in dnio . Post 7 m . I . Sep . I . car . houm . Silu . XXX . porc . II . ac . pti.
Tc . II . runc . m . IIII . Tc . IIII . an . m . VII . Sep . XX . porc . Tc . XL . ou . m . C.
Tc . XIIII . cap . m . XX . Tc . ual . XL . sol . m . LX.

Elesfordam ten& Hato de comite qđ tenuit Eduuard⁹ . p uno
manerio . 7 . p . II . hid . 7 . L . ac . Tc . IIII . bor . m . VII . Tc . VI ser . m . II . Tc . in dīo
. II . car . 7 . qn recep . null . M . dim . Tc . I . car . hominū . m . dim . Silu . C . por.
. III . ac . pti . Past . XX . ou . Val . LX . sol.

62 Amalfrid holds TOLLESBURY from the Count which Guthmund, a free man, held as one manor for 3 hides before 1066. This is (part) of Engelric's Holding.

Then 4 smallholders, now 3; then 4 slaves, now 2. Then 3 ploughs in lordship, now 2. Always ½ men's plough.

Pasture, 100 sheep; 1 salt-house.

Value then £4; later and now [£] 3.

Hundred of TENDRING 32 b

63 The Count holds ST. OSYTH in lordship, which Edward held as one manor, for 3 hides and 40 acres before 1066. Later Engelric (held it).

Then 9 villagers, later and now 7; now 2 smallholders; then 8 slaves, later and now 2. Then 1 plough in lordship, when acquired nothing, now 1. Then 6 men's ploughs, later and now 3.

Woodland, 400 pigs; meadow, 6 acres. 1 cow, 11 sheep.

Value then £12; when acquired 40s; now £10.

1 outlier, which is called FRATING, lies in (the lands of) this manor, with 40 acres. Now ½ plough. It is assessed above.

At *BURNA* 30 acres. Then 1 plough, now ½.

Value 20s.

In FROWICK (Hall) 50 acres.

Always 3 smallholders; 1 slave.

Meadow, 1½ acres; now 1 plough; woodland, 12 pigs.

Value 10s.

64 Frewin held TENDRING before 1066 as one manor, for ½ hide. Now the Count holds it in lordship for as much.

Always 1 villager; 2 smallholders; 2 slaves. Then 2 ploughs in lordship, later and now 1. Always 1 men's plough.

Woodland, 30 pigs; meadow, 2 acres. Then 2 cobs, now 4; then 4 cattle, now 7; always 20 pigs; then 40 sheep, now 100; then 14 goats, now 20.

Value then 40s; now 60[s].

65 Hato holds ALRESFORD from the Count, which Edward held as one manor, for 2 hides and 50 acres.

Then 4 smallholders, now 7; then 6 slaves, now 2. Then 2 ploughs in lordship, when acquired none, now ½. Then 1 men's plough, now ½.

Woodland, 100 pigs; meadow, 3 acres; pasture, 20 sheep.

Value 60s.

Frietunā ten& Rađ de marci . de comite . qđ tenuit Harold ꝑ . I .
maner . 7 . ꝑ . III . hid . t . r . e . post tenuit Ingelric . Tc̄ . VI . uilł . m̊ . IIII .
Tc̄ . III . bor . m̊ null . tc̄ . II . ser . m̊ . I . Sēp . I . car . in dn̄io . Tc̄ . II . car . houm .
m̊ . dim . Past . LX . ou . II . an . VII . por . XX . ou . Tc̄ uał . LX . soł . m̊ . IIII .
lib̄ . 7 . x . soł .
Birichou ten& Rob̄ de comite . qđ tenuit Ingelric de sc̄o Paulo

33 a
Londoniæ . ꝑ uno manerio 7 ꝑ . III . hid . Tc̄ . VI . bor . M̊ VIII . Tc̄ . II . ser . M̊ . I .
Tc̄ . in dn̄io . II . car . m̊ nulla . Tc̄ . int̄ hoēs . I . car . m̊ . II . Silu . x . por . Past .
. c . ou . Tc̄ . II . runc . m̊ null . Tc̄ . VIII . an . m̊ nulla . Tc̄ . XIII . ou . m̊ nulł .
Tc̄ . VI . porc . m̊ null . Tc̄ uał . LX . soł . M̊ . IIII . lib̄ . 7 . VII . soł .
Hoilandam ten& Adelolf de comite qđ tenuit Lestan ꝑ uno
Manerio . 7 . ꝑ . IIII . hid . t . r . e . postea tenuit Ingelric . Tc̄ . XI . uilł . m̊ .
VIII . Sēp . v . bor . Tc̄ . II . ser . m̊ . I . Tc̄ . II . car . in dn̄io . m̊ . I . Tc̄ . int̄ hoēs . VI .
car . m̊ . II . Silu . L . porc . Past . c . ouib; . XIII . porc . XIIII . ou . Tc̄ uał . VI .
lib̄ . m̊ . IIII .
Lelefordā ten& Idē de comite . qđ . tenuit Aluric lib̄ hō . t . r . e . Post
Ingelric . ꝑ . M̄ . 7 . ꝑ . II . hid . Tc̄ . IIII . uilł . m̊ . I . Tc̄ . VII . bor . m̊ . x . Tc̄ . IIII .
ser . m̊ . v . Tc̄ . in dn̄io . II . car . m̊ . I . Tc̄ . int̄ homines . IIII . car . m̊ . II .
Silu . x . por . VI . ac . p̊ti . Past . cc . ou . IIII . animał . LXXX . ou . I . r
VIII . porc . Sēp . uał . x . lib̄ . In Eađ . tenuer̄ . III . soc . dim . hid . 7 .
XXX . ac . q̄s inuasit Ingelric . 7 . m̊ ten& eos comes . E . 7 . Idē ade
lolf de eo . Tc̄ . int̄ eos . II . car . m̊ . I . II . ac . p̊ti . Vał . xx . soł
Tendringe ten& b̄nard de comite qđ . tenuit . Ætnod . ꝑ . Man .
7 . ꝑ . I . hid . XV . ac . min . 7 hoc ē de feudo Ingelrici . Tc̄ . VIII . uilł .
m̊ . VI . m̊ . VI . bor . Tc̄ . VI . ser . m̊ . I . Sēp . II . car . in dn̄io . 7 . III . car
hominū . Silu . cc . porc . II ac . p̊ti . Sēp . uał . IIII . lib̄ .

66 Ralph of Marcy holds FRINTON from the Count, which Harold held as 1 manor, for 3 hides before 1066. Later Engelric held it.

Then 6 villagers, now 4; then 3 smallholders, now none; then 2 slaves, now 1. Always 1 plough in lordship. Then 2 men's ploughs, now ½.

Pasture, 60 sheep. 2 cattle, 7 pigs, 20 sheep.

Value then 60s; now £4 10s.

67 Robert holds BIRCH HALL from the Count, which Engelric held from St. Paul's, London, as one manor for 3 hides. 33 a

Then 6 smallholders, now 8; then 2 slaves, now 1. Then 2 ploughs in lordship, now none. Then among the men 1 plough, now 2.

Woodland, 10 pigs; pasture, 100 sheep. Then 2 cobs, now none; then 8 cattle, now none; then 13 sheep, now none; then 6 pigs, now none.

Value then 60s; now £4 7s.

68 Adelulf holds (Little) HOLLAND from the Count, which Leofstan held as one manor, for 4 hides before 1066. Later on Engelric held it.

Then 11 villagers, now 8; always 5 smallholders; then 2 slaves, now 1. Then 2 ploughs in lordship, now 1. Then among the men 6 ploughs, now 2.

Woodland, 50 pigs; pasture, 100 sheep. 13 pigs, 14 sheep.

Value then £6; now [£] 4.

69 He also holds LAWFORD from the Count, which Aelfric, a free man, held before 1066. Later Engelric (held it) as a manor, for 2 hides.

Then 4 villagers, now 1; then 7 smallholders, now 10; then 4 slaves, now 1. Then 2 ploughs in lordship, now 1. Then among the men 4 ploughs, now 2.

Woodland, 10 pigs; meadow, 6 acres; pasture, 200 sheep. 4 cattle, 80 sheep, 1 cob, 8 pigs.

Value always £10.

In the same (Lawford) 3 Freemen held ½ hide and 30 acres, which Engelric annexed. Now Count Eustace holds them and Adelulf also from him. Then among them 2 ploughs, now 1.

Meadow, 2 acres.

Value 20s.

70 Bernard holds TENDRING from the Count, which Ednoth held as a manor, for 1 hide less 15 acres. This is (part) of Engelric's Holding.

Then 8 villagers, now 6; now 6 smallholders; then 6 slaves, now 1. Always 2 ploughs in lordship; 3 men's ploughs.

Woodland, 200 pigs; meadow, 2 acres.

Value always £4.

Hund. de Vdelesfort. Cristeshalã tenuit Inguar. p uno manerio. 7. p. vi. hid. t. r. e. m ten& comes. E. in dñio de feudo Ingelrici. Sẽp. xxxii. uilt. Tc. vi. bor. m. xiii.

33 b

Sẽp. vi. ser. 7. iii. car. in dñio. 7. xvi. car. hominũ. Silu. cc. por. 7 viii. ac. pti. i. runc. xl. porc. cl. ou. xxiiii. cap. iiii. uasa. apũ. Sẽp. ual. xv. lib. Huic manerio ptinent. ii. soc. de. viii. ac. 7. i. soc. de. viii. ac. quẽ occupaũ Ingelric. t. r. Willi. In istis. viii. ac. st. iii. bor. 7. ual. xvi. d. Huic manerio attinebat. i. soc. de. iii. uirg. t. r. e. quẽ m. ten& Will cardun ad feudũ. G. de magna uilla. 7. reddebat. p. annũ. ii. d.

Cishellã ten& Wido de comite. qd tenuit Si~~uuard~~ red. lib hõ. t. r. e. p. m. 7. p. vi. hid. 7. xxx. ac. Tc. v. uilt. m. vi. Tc. iii. bor. m. v. Sẽp. vi. ser. 7. iii. car. in dñio. 7. v. car. hom. 7. viii. ac. pti. xxiiii. porc. ccl. ou. Tc. 7 p. ual. c. sol. 7. m. vi. lib. ★

Cishellã tenuit. Godric lib hõ. t. r. e. m. ten&. Idẽ Wido de comite p. uno manerio. 7. p. ii. hid. 7. dim. Val. lx. sol. In Eadẽ tenuit. i. lib hõ. dim hid. quã occupauit Ingelric. t. r. Willi. 7 m ten& Enselm de comite. In illa tra st sẽp. ii. bor. 7. i. car. 7. ii. ac. pti. Val. x. sol.

Elmdunã ten& Rog de Sumeri de comite. qd tenuit. Almar. lib hõ. t. r. e. 7 Ingelric occupaũ hoc maneriũ t. r. Willi. Sẽp ibi st. xiiii. hid. 7. xxvi. uilt. 7. xv. bor. Tc. xii. ser. m null. Tc. vi. car. in dñio. 7. qñ recep. iii. m. iiii. Sẽp. x. car. hominũ. Silu. ccl. porc. vii. ac. pti. xx. porc. cc. ou. 7. lxxxviii. ou. Tc ual xvi. lib. 7 qñ recep. M. xx. lib.

Hundred of UTTLESFORD

71 Ingvar held CHRISHALL as one manor, for 6 hides before 1066. Now Count Eustace holds it in lordship (as) of Engelric's Holding.

Always 32 villagers. Then 6 smallholders, now 13. Always 6 slaves; 3 ploughs in lordship; 16 men's ploughs. 33 b

Woodland, 200 pigs; meadow, 8 acres. 1 cob, 40 pigs, 150 sheep, 24 goats, 4 beehives.

Value always £15.

To this manor belong 2 Freemen with 8 acres, and 1 Freeman with 8 acres whom Engelric appropriated after 1066.

On these 8 acres are 3 smallholders.

Value 16d.

To this manor was attached 1 Freeman with 3 virgates before 1066, whom William Cardon holds for G(eoffrey) de Mandeville's Holding.

He paid 2d a year.

72 Guy holds CHISHILL from the Count, which Sired, a free man, held before 1066 as a manor for 6 hides and 30 acres.

Then 5 villagers, now 6; then 3 smallholders, now 5. Always 6 slaves; 3 ploughs in lordship; 5 men's ploughs.

Meadow, 8 acres. 24 pigs, 250 sheep.

Value then and later 100s; now £6.

73 Godric, a free man, held CHISHILL before 1066. Now Guy also holds it from the Count as one manor, for 2½ hides.

Value 60s.

In the same (Chishill) 1 free man held ½ hide which Engelric appropriated after 1066. Now Anselm holds it from the Count.

On that land have always been 2 smallholders; 1 plough.

Meadow, 2 acres.

Value 10s.

74 Roger of Sommery holds ELMDON from the Count, which Aelmer, a free man, held before 1066. Engelric appropriated this manor after 1066. There have always been 14 hides there;

26 villagers; 15 smallholders. Then 12 slaves, now none. Then 6 ploughs in lordship, when acquired 3, now 4. Always 10 men's ploughs.

Woodland, 250 pigs; meadow, 7 acres. 20 pigs, 200 sheep and 88 sheep.

Value then and when acquired £16; now £20.

⌈Leam tenuit. Bričtulf. lib hō. t. r. e. p. manerio. 7. p. II. hid

34 a
7 dim. Postea. tenuit Ingelric. m. Idē Rog de comite. Sēp.
v. uilt. Tc. I. bor. P 7 m. VIII. Tc. IIII. ser. M null. Tc. III. car. in
dnio. P 7 m. II. Tc. IIII. car. hom. 7. qn rec. III. 7. m similit. Silu.
. L. porc. Tc. 7. p ual. IIII. lib. m. c. sol.
⌈Crauuelæam. ten&. Idē de comite. qd tenuit Lefsi lib hō. t. r. e. p XXX. ac.
7 Ingelric. occupauit. t. r. Willi. Sēp. II. bor. Tc. I. ser. Sēp. I. car. II. ac.
pti. Val. x. sol.
⌈Hund de Frosseuuella. dimidiū; Benedisc. tenuit Ledmar
pbr. t. r. e. p. M. 7. p. IIII. hid. 7. dim. Post tenuit Ingelric. m. ten&
comes in dnio. Sēp. VIII. uilt. 7. III. bor. 7. VIII. ser. 7. IIII. car in
dnio. Tc. int hoēs. IIII. car. Post 7 m. III. Silu. c. por. VIII. ac. pti.
XXVIII. por. c. 7 XII. ou. 7. I. soc. tenuit. I. ac. 7. I. pertic. quē in
uasit Ingelric. M ten& comes. Tc ual. totū. XI. lib. m. XII.
⌈Neuuham tenuit. Alsi. p. I. hid. t. r. e. Post ten. Ingelric. m. ten&
comes in dnio. Tc. VI. uilt. m. IX. Tc. II. bor. P 7. m. VII. Sēp. VI.
ser. 7. III. car. in dnio, Tc. IIII. car. hominū. P 7 m. III. Silu. XX.
porc. V. ac. pti. XIIII. porc. LVI. ou. I. runc. Huic manerio fuer.
v. soc. tenentes. dim. hid. 7. XXXV. ac. remanentes. cū soca. Tc.
. III. car. P 7. m. II. V. ac. pti. Tc. ual. XI. lib. m. XII.
⌈Birdefeldā. ten& Adolof. de comite. qd tenuit. Normann. t. r. e.
p. II. hid. 7. I. uirg. post ea. tenuit Ingelric. 7 inuasit eū. Sēp
VI. uilt. Tc. 7 p. I. bor. m. XII. Sēp. IIII. ser. 7. III. car. in dnio. 7. II.
car. hom. Silu. CC. porc. XLIX. ac. pti. V. an. XXV. porc. II. uasa. ap.

34 b
XXX. cap. I. runc. Sēp. I. mol. m. I. piscina. Tc. ual. VIII. lib. m
x. lib.

75 Brictwulf, a free man, held (Elmdon) LEE before 1066 as a manor, for 2½ hides. Later on Engelric held it. Now Roger also (holds it) 34 a
from the Count.

Always 5 villagers. Then 1 smallholder, later and now 8; then 4 slaves, now none. Then 3 ploughs in lordship, later and now 2. Then 4 men's ploughs, when acquired 3, now the same.

Woodland, 50 pigs.

Value then and later £4; now 100s.

76 He also holds CRAWLEYBURY from the Count, which Leofsi, a free man, held before 1066 for 30 acres. Engelric appropriated it after 1066.

Always 2 smallholders. Then 1 slave. Always 1 plough.

Meadow, 2 acres.

Value 10s.

Half-Hundred of FRESHWELL

77 Ledmer the priest held BENDYSH (Hall) before 1066 as a manor, for 4½ hides. Later Engelric held it. Now the Count holds it in lordship.

Always 8 villagers, 3 smallholders, 8 slaves; 4 ploughs in lordship. Then among the men 4 ploughs, later and now 3.

Woodland, 100 pigs; meadow, 8 acres. 28 pigs, 112 sheep.

1 Freeman held 1 acre and 1 perch, whom Engelric annexed. Now the Count holds it.

Value of the whole then £11; now [£] 12.

78 Alfsi held NEWNHAM (Hall) for 1 hide before 1066. Later Engelric held it. Now the Count holds it in lordship.

Then 6 villagers, now 9; then 2 smallholders, later and now 7. Always 6 slaves; 3 ploughs in lordship. Then 4 men's ploughs, later and now 3.

Woodland, 20 pigs; meadow, 5 acres. 14 pigs, 56 sheep, 1 cob.

(Belonging) to this manor were 5 Freemen who hold ½ hide and 35 acres (and) who remain with the jurisdiction. Then 3 ploughs, later and now 2.

Meadow, 5 acres.

Value then £11; now [£] 12.

79 Adelulf holds (Little) BARDFIELD from the Count, which Norman held before 1066 for 2 hides and 1 virgate. Later on Engelric held it and annexed him.

Always 6 villagers. Then and later 1 smallholder, now 12. Always 4 slaves; 3 ploughs in lordship; 2 men's ploughs.

Woodland, 200 pigs; meadow, 49 acres. 5 cattle, 25 pigs,
2 beehives, 30 goats, 1 cob. Always 1 mill. Now 1 fishpond. 34 b

Value then £8; now £10.

⁊ Hund de Rochefort. Scopelandã. tenuit. I. lib hõ. t. r. e.
p. v. hid. Post tenuit Ingelric. m. comes. E. in dnio. Sep. v. uilt. 7
. II. soc. 7. dns eoz habebat socã 7. sacã. Sep. IX. bord. 7. II. car. in dnio.
7. v. car. hom. Silu. XL. porc. Past. CCCC. ou. II. an. LIIII. ou. XIIII.
porc. XIII. cap. III. runc. Tc ual. VI. lib. m. x. In ead tenuit. I. lib hõ
dim. hid. 7. XXX. ac. qd occupauit Ingelric. Sep. I. car. 7. III. bor 7 hoc est
apptiatũ in x. lib.

35 a ⁊ TERRA COMITIS ALANI. XXI

⁊ Hund de Herlaua. Eppingam tenuit
Wisgarus lib homo tẽpore regis. E. p uno maner.
7 p. I. hid. 7. dim. 7 dim uirg. Semp. I. car in dnio.
7. dim. car hom. 7. II. uilt. 7. II. bor. Silu. c. porc. VIII. ac.
pti. Tc ual. xx. sol. m. xxx. hoc. M. ten& Osbn. de Comite.

⁊ Hund de Dommauua. Vlinghehalam ten& Herueus
de comite qd tenuit Edeua t. r. e. p uno. M. 7 p. I. hid. 7. I.
uirg. 7. dim. Sep. III. car in dnio. 7. I. car 7. dim hominũ.
7. IIII. uilt. 7. VIII. bord. 7. IIII. ser. Silu. CCL. porc. XII. ac
pti. Tc uat LX. sol. m. c.

⁊ Canefeldã ten& Albic deuer de comite qd tenuit
Edeua t. r. e. p. I. hid. 7. XXX. ac. Sep. I. car. in dnio.
7. I. car. hom. Tc. III. uilt. m. I. Tc. v. bord. m. x. Silu.
. c. porc. XLVIII. ac. pti. int ptũ 7 maresc. Sep ual. LX. sol.

⁊ Hund de Hidinghafort. Phincingefeldam ten&
Herueus de Comite qd ten. III. libi hões. t. r. e. p. II. hid.
7. dim. sub Edeua. Sep. v. car. in dnio. 7 VII. car hoũ
7. III. uilt. 7. L. bord. v. ser. Silu. CLX. porc. XVI. ac. pti.
Tc ual. c. sol. m. VIII. lib.

Hundred of ROCHFORD

80 1 free man held SHOPLAND before 1066 for 5 hides. Later Engelric held it. Now Count Eustace (holds it) in lordship.

Always 5 villagers; 2 Freemen, their lord had full jurisdiction. Always 9 smallholders; 2 ploughs in lordship; 5 men's ploughs.

Woodland, 40 pigs; pasture, 400 sheep. 2 cattle, 54 sheep, 14 pigs, 13 goats, 3 cobs.

Value then £6; now [£] 10.

In the same (Shopland) 1 free man held ½ hide and 30 acres, which Engelric appropriated. Always 1 plough;

3 smallholders.

This is assessed in the £10.

21 LAND OF COUNT ALAN 35 a

Hundred of HARLOW

1 Withgar, a free man, held EPPING before 1066 as one manor, for 1½ hides and ½ virgate. Always 1 plough in lordship; ½ men's plough;

2 villagers; 2 smallholders.

Woodland, 100 pigs; meadow, 8 acres.

Value then 20s; now 30[s].

Osbern holds this manor from the Count.

Hundred of DUNMOW

2 Hervey holds WILLINGALE (Spain) from the Count, which Edeva held before 1066 as one manor, for 1 hide and 1½ virgates. Always 3 ploughs in lordship; 1½ men's ploughs;

4 villagers; 8 smallholders; 4 slaves.

Woodland, 250 pigs; meadow, 12 acres.

Value then 60s; now 100[s].

3 Aubrey de Vere holds (Great) CANFIELD from the Count, which Edeva held before 1066 for 1 hide and 30 acres. Always 1 plough in lordship; 1 men's plough.

Then 3 villagers, now 1; then 5 smallholders, now 10.

Woodland, 100 pigs; meadow, 48 acres among meadow and marsh.

Value always 60s.

Hundred of HINCKFORD

4 Hervey holds FINCHINGFIELD from the Count, which 3 free men held before 1066 for 2½ hides under Edeva. Always 5 ploughs in lordship; 7 men's ploughs;

3 villagers; 50 smallholders; 5 slaves.

Woodland, 160 pigs; meadow, 16 acres.

Value then 100s; now £8.

In Bumesteda ten& . I . mil . VII . ac . 7 . dim . qd tenuit
. I . soc . sub Edeua . t . r . e . 7 . I . ac . 7 . dim . pti . Tc ual . II . sol.
M . III . In Gerham . XLII . ac . qs tenuit . I . lib ho . t . r . e.

35 b
Sep . I . car . 7 . III . bor . Tc . II . ser . m . I . Silu . XV . porc . V . ac.
pti . m . I . mol . Tc uat . XX . sol . m . XXV.
In Phincingefelda . ten& Comes in dnio . XXXVIII . ac . 7 dim.
qs tenuer . II . soc . 7 . I . lib ho . t . r . e . Sep . dim . car . 7 . II . bord
. II . ac . pti . Val . V . sol.
Hund de Angra Roinges ten& Albic de uer de com.
qd tenuit Leuuin 7 Etsi p . m . t . r . e . 7 . p . I . hid . 7 . dim.
Sep . II . uill . 7 . XIII . bord . 7 . III . car . in dnio . 7 . I . car hominu
Silu . CC . porc . L . ac . pti Tc ual . IIII . lib . p . 7 m . C . sol.
Hund de Tendringa . Benetlea ten& Herueus de ispa-
nia de comite q tenuit Eluuin p . XLII . ac . 7 . dim . libe han tra
tenuit Comes . R . Sep . III . uill . 7 . dim . car . 7 . I . ac pti . Silu.
VI . porc . Val . III . sol . Iste Ide tenuit dim hid . Sep . IIII . uill.
7 . I . car . Silu . VI . porc . dim . ac . pti . Val . X . sol.
Hund de Udelesforda Monehala ten& Ide . H . de com.
qd ten . Siuuard . p . I . hid . Sep . II . uill . Tc . I . ser . m . null.
m . I . bord . Sep . dim . car . VII . ac . pti . 7 . II . part mol . val.
XX . sol.

5 In (Steeple) BUMPSTEAD 1 man-at-arms holds 7½ acres, which 1 Freeman held under Edeva before 1066.
Meadow, 1½ acres.
Value then 2s; now 3[s].

6 In YELDHAM 42 acres which 1 free man held before 1066. Always 1 plough; 35 b
3 smallholders. Then 2 slaves, now 1.
Woodland, 15 pigs; meadow, 5 acres; now 1 mill.
Value then 20s; now 25[s].

7 In FINCHINGFIELD the Count holds 38½ acres in lordship, which 2 Freemen and 1 free man held before 1066. Always ½ plough;
2 smallholders.
Meadow, 2 acres.
Value 5s.

Hundred of ONGAR

8 Aubrey de Vere holds (Beauchamp) RODING from the Count, which Leofwin and Edsi held as a manor before 1066, for 1½ hides.
Always 2 villagers; 13 smallholders; 3 ploughs in lordship; 1 men's plough.
Woodland, 200 pigs; meadow, 50 acres.
Value then £4; later and now 100s.

Hundred of TENDRING

9 Hervey of 'Spain' holds (Little) BENTLEY from the Count, which Alwin held freely for 42½ acres. Earl R(alph) held this land.
Always 3 villagers; ½ plough.
Meadow, 1 acre; woodland, 6 pigs.
Value 3s.
This same man also held ½ hide.
Always 4 villagers; 1 plough.
Woodland, 6 pigs; meadow, ½ acre.
Value 10s.

Hundred of UTTLESFORD

10 Hervey also holds EMANUEL (Wood) from the Count, which Siward held for 1 hide.
Always 2 villagers. Then 1 slave, now none; now 1 smallholder. Always ½ plough.
Meadow, 7 acres; 2 parts of a mill.
Value 20s.

Dim Hund de Frossenuella. In Rodā ten& Idē xxx. ac. qđ tenuit Edeua Sēp. dim. car. Silu. viii. porc. ii. ac. 7 dim. pti. Tc. uat. v. sol. m. x. In Stauintuna tenuit Edeua . v. ac. qđ ten& Herueu. vat. ii. sol

36 a

Terra Witti de Warenna in Exsessa. Hund de bdestapla. .XXII.

Vpham tenuit Edeua quedā femina t. r. e. p dim hid. 7. xxx. ac. m ten& Witt in dnio. vat. x. sol.

Tilibiam ten& Ranulf de Witto qđ tenuit Sueting lib hō. t. r. e. p. xxx. ac. sēp. i. bor. Past. xl. ou. i. ac. pti. Tc. uat. vii. sol. m. xiiii.

Dim Hund de herlaua Ouesham ten& Ricard. de. W. qđ tenuit Holefest. lib hō. t. r. e. p uno manerio. 7. p. i. hid. 7. iii. uirg. Tc. ii. car in dnio. m. i. Tc. iii. car. 7. dim houm. m. v. Tc. vi. uitt. m. x. Sēp. . iii. bor. Tc. iii. ser. m. i. Silu. l. porc. x. ac. pti. Qn recepit. v. anim. 7. i. uitul. 7. xl. porc. xl. ou. M. vi. an. 7. l. porc. xc. ou. iii. uasa apū. Huic manerio addita. i. uirg. t. r. Witti. quā tenuit Vluric. lib hō. t. r. e. Tc. dim. car. m. nulla. sēp. i. bor. Silu. x. porc. ii. ac. pti. tc uat. iiii. sol. m. vi. 7 maneriū uat. tc. vi lib. m. vii.

Cuicā ten& Idē Ricard de Witto. qđ tenuit Alnuin godtuna. t. r. e. p. iii. hid. Sēp. ii. car. in dnio. Tc. iii. car. 7. dim. hominū. m. iii. Tc. vii. uitt. m. vi. m. vi. bord. tc. v. ser. m. ii. xx. ac. pti. Sēp. i. mol. Tc. xlvii. ou. m. lii. 7. ii. pulli. Vat. c. sol

Half-Hundred of FRESHWELL

11 He also holds 30 acres in ROTH(END), which Edeva held. Always ½ plough.
Woodland, 8 pigs; meadow, 2½ acres.
Value then 5s; now 10[s].

12 In STEVINGTON (End) Edeva held 5 acres, which Hervey holds.
Value 2s.

22 LAND OF WILLIAM OF WARENNE IN ESSEX 36 a

Hundred of BARSTABLE

1 Edeva, a woman, held *UPHAM* before 1066 for ½ hide and 30 acres. Now William holds it in lordship.
Value 10s.

2 Ranulf holds TILBURY from William, which Sweeting, a free man, held before 1066 for 30 acres.
Always 1 smallholder.
Pasture, 40 sheep; meadow, 1 acre.
Value then 7s; now 14[s].

Half-Hundred of HARLOW

3 Richard holds HOUSHAM (Hall) from William, which Holdfast, a free man, held before 1066 as one manor for 1 hide and 3 virgates. Then 2 ploughs in lordship, now 1. Then 3½ men's ploughs, now 5.
Then 6 villagers, now 10. Always 3 smallholders. Then 3 slaves, now 1.
Woodland, 50 pigs; meadow, 10 acres. When acquired 5 cattle, 1 calf, 40 pigs, 40 sheep; now 6 cattle, 50 pigs, 90 sheep, 3 beehives.
To this manor was added 1 virgate after 1066 which Wulfric, a free man, held before 1066. Then ½ plough, now none.
Always 1 smallholder.
Woodland, 10 pigs; meadow, 2 acres.
Value then 4s; now 6[s].
Value of the manor then £6; now [£] 7.

4 Richard also holds QUICK(SBURY Farm) from William, which Alwin Gotton held before 1066 for 3 hides. Always 2 ploughs in lordship. Then 3½ men's ploughs, now 3.
Then 7 villagers, now 6; now 6 smallholders; then 5 slaves, now 2.
Meadow, 20 acres. Always 1 mill. Then 47 sheep, now 52; 2 foals.
Value 100s.

Hund de Dommauua. Estanes tenuit Duua. liba femina t.r.e. p. man. 7. p. II. hid. m. Will in dnio. Sep. II. car in dnio tc. IIII. car. hominu. m. II. Sep. IIII. uill. Tc. III. bor. m. VIII. Tc III. ser. m. II. Silua tc. ad. cc. porc. m. CL. LII. ac. pti. Tc. I. r. 7. VII. an. 7. LX. porc. 7. LX. ou. M. I. r. XXIII. an. XX. por. LXX. ou. IIII. uasa apu. Val. c. sol.

36 b

Canefelda tenuerunt. II. libi hoes. t. r. e. p. II. hid. VIII. ac. min. m. Will in dnio Tc. IIII. car. in dnio m. II. Tc. VIII. car. hou m. VI. Tc. I. pbr. 7. VII uill. m. I. pbr. 7. VII. uill. Tc. III. bor. m. XVII. Sep. II. ser. M. I. mol. Tc. silu. CLX. porc. m. CXX. LXX. ac. pti. Tc. I. runc. 7. VIII. an. 7. C. porc. 7. CC. ou. M. I. runc. XV. an. L. porc. LXX. ou. IX. cap. Tc ual. VIII. lib. m. IX.

Rodinges ten&. W. de uuateuill. de Willo. qd tenuit Abbas de eli. t. r. e. p uno manerio. 7. p. II. hid. 7. dim. Sep. III. car. in dnio. 7. III. car. hom. &. I. pbr. 7. VIII. uill. Tc. XII. bor. m. XI. Sep. VII. ser. Silu. CCC. porc. XLII. ac. pti. Sep. III. runc. VIII. an. 7. CXX. ou. m. VII. porc. Tc ual. X. lib. 7. qn rec. XII. m. XVIII.

Rodinges ten& Galt de Willo. qd tenuit. liba femina. t. r. e p. uno maner. 7. p. II. hid. 7. dim. 7 M st. III. hid. 7. dim; Tc. III. car. in dnio. m. II. 7 qn rec. III. Sep. I. car. hom. Tc. III. uill. M. I. pbr. 7. IIII. uill. Tc. IIII. bor. m. XIII. Tc. IIII. ser. m. II. Silu. L. por. XXX. ac. pti. m. IIII. an. 7. XL. porc. LXXX. ou. 7. III; I. uas. ap. Val. VIII. lib. Et illa hid. que huic manerio addita e. adjacebat. t. r. e. abbatiæ de eli ut hund testat.

Dommauua ten& Guibt de. W. qd tenuit comes Algar. t. r. e. p. dim. hid. Sep. dim. car. in dnio. m. III. bor tc. III. ser. m null. Silu. XL. porc. VII. ac. pti. Tc. X. porc. XXX. ou. M. IX. an. XXX. porc. LXXX. ou. XII. cap. VIII. uasa. ap. Tc ual. XX. sol. 7 qndo rec. XXX. sol. M ual XXXV. sol.

Hundred of DUNMOW

5 Dove, a free woman, held (Great) EASTON before 1066 as a manor, for 2 hides. Now William (holds it) in lordship. Always 2 ploughs in lordship. Then 4 men's ploughs, now 2.

Always 4 villagers. Then 3 smallholders, now 8; then 3 slaves, now 2.

Woodland, then for 200 pigs, now 150; meadow, 52 acres. Then 1 cob, 7 cattle, 60 pigs, 60 sheep; now 1 cob, 23 cattle, 20 pigs, 70 sheep, 4 beehives.

Value 100s.

6 2 free men held (Little) CANFIELD before 1066 for 2 hides less 8 36 b
acres. Now William (holds it) in lordship. Then 4 ploughs in lordship, now 2. Then 8 men's ploughs, now 6.

Then 1 priest and 9 villagers, now 1 priest and 7 villagers; then 3 smallholders, now 17; always 2 slaves.

Now 1 mill; woodland, then 160 pigs, now 120; meadow, 70 acres. Then 1 cob, 8 cattle, 100 pigs, 200 sheep; now 1 cob, 15 cattle, 50 pigs, 70 sheep, 9 goats.

Value then £8; now [£] 9.

7 W(illiam) of Vatteville holds (High) RODING from William, which the Abbot of Ely held before 1066 as one manor, for 2½ hides. Always 3 ploughs in lordship; 3 men's ploughs;

1 priest, 8 villagers. Then 12 smallholders, now 11; always 7 slaves.

Woodland, 300 pigs; meadow, 42 acres. Always 3 cobs, 8 cattle, 120 sheep; now 7 pigs.

Value then £10; when acquired [£] 12; now [£] 18.

8 Walter holds (Leaden) RODING from William, which a free woman held before 1066 as one manor, for 2½ hides. Now there are 3½ hides. Then 3 ploughs in lordship, now 2; when acquired 3. Always 1 men's plough.

Then 3 villagers, now 1 priest and 4 villagers; then 4 smallholders, now 13; then 4 slaves, now 2.

Woodland, 50 pigs; meadow, 30 acres. Now 4 cattle, 40 pigs, 83 sheep, 1 beehive.

Value £8.

The hide which was added to this manor lay in (the lands of) Ely Abbey before 1066, as the Hundred testifies.

9 Wulfbert holds DUNMOW from William, which Earl Algar held before 1066 for ½ hide. Always ½ plough in lordship.

Now 3 smallholders; then 3 slaves, now none.

Woodland, 40 pigs; meadow, 7 acres. Then 10 pigs, 30 sheep; now 9 cattle, 30 pigs, 80 sheep, 12 goats, 8 beehives.

Value then 20s; when acquired 30s. Value now 35s.

37 a

Dim Hund de Clauelinga. Pachen hov. ten& Simond.
de Willo qd ten. I. lib ho. p. m. 7. p. I. hid. 7 xxx. ac. t. r. e. Sep.
. I. car in dnio. 7. I. car hom. Tc 7 p. III. uilt. m. II. Tc. 7 p. III. bor. m. VII.
VII. ac. pti. I. runc. tc. 7. IX. por. M. I. runc. IX. por. XL. ou. Tc ual
XX. sol. m. XXV.

Hund de Hidingforda. In Haltesteda. ten& Wilt de gar.
. II. hid. IIII. ac. min. qs tenuer. XXX. libi hoes. t. r. e. In q tra st
sep. X. car in dnio. 7. III. car. hom. 7. VIII. uilt. 7. XXIII. bor. 7. VI. ser.
Silu. CXL. porc. XLVI. ac. pti. II. mol. Tc. VI. an. XL. ou. XII. porc. m.
XIIII. an. XXXVI. ou. XX. porc. II. runc. II. uasa. ap. Tc. 7 p.
ual. X. lib. m. XIII. lib. 7. XVII. sol. 7. IIII. d. De hac tra ten&
Ricard. XXXIIII. ac. 7. ual. X. sol. in eod ptio.

In Bumesteda. ten& Gulbt. III. hid. 7. XVIII. ac. qs tenuer
. XII. libi hoes. t. r. e. In illa tra st sep. IX. car. 7. III. uilt. 7. XVIII.
bord. 7. V. ser. Silu. XX. porc. XL. ac. pti. Tc. I. runc. XL. ou. XXX
porc. M. I. runc. XVI. an. C. porc. C. ou. IIII. uasa. ap. Tc. 7 p ual
. X. lib. m. XII.

In Polheia. ten& Wilt. III. hid. 7. dim. 7. XIII. ac. Ex hac tra. ten&
Ricard. XXV. ac. 7. Gladiou. III. uirg. Tota hanc tra tenuer
XXIII. hoes. t. r. e. Tc. habebant. X. car. Post. 7. m. st. ibi. VIII.
car. m. VI. bor. Tc. VII. ser. m ~~null~~. V. M. I. mol Tc. silu. LX.
porc. M. XL. XXX. ac. pti. VIII. an. XX. porc. XX. ou. m. XII.
an. XXX. porc. LX. ou. II. uasa ap. Tc ual. X. lib. m. XIIII. lib

37 b

7. XVI. sol. Istas tras reclamat Wilt p escangio.

Half-Hundred of CLAVERING 37 a

10 Simond holds PEYTON (Hall) from William, which 1 free man held as a manor for 1 hide and 30 acres before 1066. Always 1 plough in lordship; 1 men's plough.

Then and later 3 villagers, now 2; then and later 3 smallholders, now 7.

Meadow, 7 acres. 1 cob then and 9 pigs; now 1 cob, 9 pigs, 40 sheep.

Value then 20s; now 25[s].

Hundred of HINCKFORD

11 In HALSTEAD William of Warenne holds 2 hides less 4 acres, which 30 free men held before 1066. In this land there have always been 10 ploughs in lordship; 3 men's ploughs;

8 villagers; 23 smallholders; 6 slaves.

Woodland, 140 pigs; meadow, 46 acres; 2 mills. Then 6 cattle, 40 sheep, 12 pigs; now 14 cattle, 36 sheep, 20 pigs, 2 cobs, 2 beehives.

Value then and later £10; now £13 17s 4d.

Richard holds 34 acres of this land.

Value 10s in the same assessment.

12 In (Steeple) BUMPSTEAD Wulfbert holds 3 hides and 18 acres, which 12 free men held before 1066. In this land have always been 9 ploughs;

3 villagers; 18 smallholders; 5 slaves.

Woodland, 20 pigs; meadow, 40 acres. Then 1 cob, 40 sheep, 30 pigs; now 1 cob, 16 cattle, 100 pigs, 100 sheep, 4 beehives.

Value then and later £10; now [£] 12.

13 In HUNT'S HALL William holds 3½ hides and 13 acres. Of this land Richard holds 25 acres and Gladiou 3 virgates. 23 men held all this land before 1066. Then they had 10 ploughs, later and now there are 8 ploughs.

Now 6 smallholders; then 7 slaves, now 5.

Now 1 mill; woodland, then 60 pigs, now 40; meadow, 30 acres. [Then] 8 cattle, 20 pigs, 20 sheep; now 12 cattle, 30 pigs, 60 sheep, 2 beehives.

Value then £10; now £14 16s. 37 b

William claims these lands by exchange.

Hund̄ de Ceffeurda. Kelitunā tenuer̄. III. libi hões ꝓ. IIII. hid.
t. r. e. M ten& Witt. ꝓ tantundē ꝓ escangio. ut dicit. 7 Wlbt
de illo. Tc̄. I. uiłł. m̄. VII. m̄. I. bor. Tc̄. III. ser. m̄. I. Tc̄. int̄ totū. III. car
m̄. I. 7. dim. Silu. c. porc. VIII. ac. p̄ti. Tc̄. II. an. 7. XV. porc. XX. ou.
m̄. II. an. XV. por. L. ou. Tc̄. uał. sol. 7. qn̄ rec. XXX. m̄. c. sol. III. sol
min. Hť &iam. Ranulf. dim. hid. quam tenuit Vluuin lib hõ. t. r. e.
Tc̄. I. car. m̄. dim. Vał. VI. sol.

Hund̄ de celmeresfort Haningefeldā tenuer̄. III. libi. hões. ꝓ
. III. Man. 7. ꝓ. IIII. hid. 7. XXVII. ac. m̄. Witt ꝓ tantundē. ꝓ suo escan
gio. 7 Vlbt de eo. Sēp. III. bor. 7. II. ser. Tc̄. III. car. in dn̄io. m̄. IIII.
Silu. XL. por. II. ac. p̄ti. Past. c. ou. Tc̄. II. runc. 7. XII. an. LX ou. XL.
por. m̄. II. runc. XXX. an. c. ou. XV. porc. Tc̄. uał. LX. sol. m̄.
. IIII. lib.

Haningefeldā ten& Ranulf de uuiłło. qđ tenuit Godric scipri.
t. r. e. ꝓ uno manerio. 7. ꝓ. II. hid. XXX. ac. min. Tc̄. II. ser. m̄ nułł.
Sēp. I. car. III. ac. p̄ti. Tc̄. uał. XXX. sol. m̄. XL.

Borham ten& Witt in dn̄io. qđ tenuit Anschill ꝓ. M̄. 7. ꝓ. dim.
hid. Sēp. I. bor. Tc̄. I. ser. m̄. null. Tc̄. I. car. m̄. dim. V. ac. p̄ti. Silua
XX. por. Vał. X. sol.

Belestedam ten& Ricard de Wiłło. qđ tenuit Godric poinc
ꝓ. M̄. 7. ꝓ. I. hid. X. ac. min. Tc̄. II. ser. m̄. I. Tc̄. II. car in dn̄io. M. I.
VI. ac. p̄ti. Silu. XX porc. Vał. XL sol.

Hundred of CHAFFORD

14 3 free men held KENNINGTONS for 4 hides before 1066. Now William holds them for as much by exchange, as he states, and Wulfbert from him.

Then 1 villager, now 7; now 1 smallholder; then 3 slaves, now 1. Then in total 3 ploughs, now 1½.

Woodland, 100 pigs; meadow, 8 acres. Then 2 cattle, 15 pigs, 20 sheep; now 2 cattle, 15 pigs, 50 sheep.

Value then ... s; when acquired 30[s]; now 100s less 3s.

Also Ranulf has ½ hide which Wulfwin, a free man, held before 1066. Then 1 plough, now ½.

Value 6s.

Hundred of CHELMSFORD

15 3 free men held (West) HANNINGFIELD as 3 manors, for 4 hides and 27 acres. Now William (holds it) for as much by his exchange, and Wulfbert from him.

Always 3 smallholders; 2 slaves. Then 3 ploughs in lordship, now 4.

Woodland, 40 pigs; meadow, 2 acres; pasture, 100 sheep. Then 2 cobs, 12 cattle, 60 sheep, 40 pigs; now 2 cobs, 30 cattle, 100 sheep, 15 pigs.

Value then 60s; now £4.

16 Ranulf holds (West) HANNINGFIELD from William, which Godric Skipper held before 1066 as one manor, for 2 hides less 30 acres.

Then 2 slaves, now none. Always 1 plough.

Meadow, 3 acres.

Value then 30s; now 40[s].

17 William holds BOREHAM in lordship, which Ansketel held as a manor, for ½ hide.

Always 1 smallholder. Then 1 slave, now none. Then 1 plough, now ½.

Meadow, 5 acres; woodland, 20 pigs.

Value 10s.

18 Richard holds BELSTEAD (Hall) from William, which Godric Poinc held as a manor, for 1 hide less 10 acres.

Then 2 slaves, now 1. Then 2 ploughs in lordship, now 1.

Meadow, 6 acres; woodland, 20 pigs.

Value 40s.

Hund de Vdelesfort. Wendenā ten& Ricard. de Willo. qđ ten.
Vlmar ꝑ.m̄. 7. ꝑ. I. hid. 7. dim. 7. xxx. ac. 7 hoc ē ꝑ escangio. Sēp. II.
uill. 7. VII. bor. Tc. 7. p. I. car. in dnio. m̄. I. 7. dim. Sēp. I. car. 7. dim. hoūm
XVI. ac. pti. Tc. XVII. por. m̄ null. Sēp. L. ou. Tc. ual. XL. sol. m̄. LX.
Einesuurdam ten& Idē. R. qđ tenuit Vlmar. ꝑ. ↄ. 7. ꝑ. II. hid. 7. dim.
Tc. IIII. uill. m̄. III. Tc. bor. m̄. VIII. Tc. II. ser. Tc. I. car. 7. dim. in dio.
7 qn̄ rec. nich. m̄. I. car. 7. dim. Sēp. I. car. 7. dim. hominū. x. ac. pti.
Tc nichil recep. M. XXXII. porc. LII. ou. II. an. III. uas. ap. Tc. ual
XL. sol. m̄. LX. In Cishella tenuer. VIII. libi. hoēs. I. hid. 7. XLV. ac.
m̄ ht. Will de uuar. ꝑ escangio. 7 Idē. R. de eo. Tc. III. car. m̄. II.
7 qn̄ recep. nichil. II. ac. pti. Val. XXX. sol.
Hund de. Rochefort. Ī Pachesham ten& Will de gar. I. hid. in
dnio. qđ tenuit. I. lib hō. t. r. e. Sēp. I. car. in dnio. Tc. IIII. ser. m̄
. III. Past. c. ou. Val. XX. sol.
In Plubga. ten& Ranulf de W. XXX. ac. qđ. ten. I. lib. hō. t. r. e
Tc dim. car. m̄. I. Tc. V. sol. m̄. X. has tras reclamat. pro escangio
de normannia.
Hund de Lexsendena. In Forham tenuit. Aluric XXV. ac.
libe. M Will ꝑ eod escangio. Sēp dim. car. I. ac. 7. dim. pti. Tc
ual. X. sol. m̄. VI. sol. 7. VIII. đ. hec tra ē de socna regis.

Hundred of UTTLESFORD 38 a

19 Richard holds WENDENS (Ambo) from William, which Wulfmer held as a manor, for 1½ hides and 30 acres. This is by exchange.
Always 2 villagers; 7 smallholders. Then and later 1 plough in lordship, now 1½. Always 1½ men's ploughs.
Meadow, 16 acres. Then 17 pigs, now none; always 50 sheep.
Value then 40s; now 60[s].

20 Richard also holds CHARDWELL, which Wulfmer held as a manor, for 2½ hides.
Then 4 villagers, now 3; then ... smallholders, now 8; then 2 slaves. Then 1½ ploughs in lordship; when acquired, nothing; now 1½ ploughs. Always 1½ men's ploughs.
Meadow, 10 acres. Then (when) acquired nothing; now 32 pigs, 52 sheep, 2 cattle, 3 beehives.
Value then 40s; now 60[s].

21 In (Great) CHISHILL 8 free men held 1 hide and 45 acres. Now William of Warenne has it by exchange and Richard also from him. Then 3 ploughs, now 2; when acquired, nothing.
Meadow, 2 acres.
Value 30s.

Hundred of ROCHFORD

22 In PAGLESHAM William of Warenne holds 1 hide in lordship, which 1 free man held before 1066. Always 1 plough in lordship.
Then 4 slaves, now 3.
Pasture, 100 sheep.
Value 20s.

23 In PLUMBEROW Ranulf holds 30 acres from William, which 1 free man held before 1066. Then ½ plough, now 1.
[Value] then 5s; now 10[s].
He claims these lands by exchange in Normandy.

Hundred of LEXDEN

24 In FORDHAM Aelfric held 25 acres freely. Now William (holds them) by the same exchange. Always ½ plough.
Meadow, 1½ acres.
Value then 10s; now 6s 8d.
This land is of the King's jurisdiction.

38 b

.XXIII. TRA Ricardi filij comitis Gislebti. Hundret de
Herlaua. Wallã ten& Ricard in dñio. Qđ tenuit Toti.i.lib hõ.t.r.e
p.uno maner.7.p.i.hid.Tc.ii.car.in dñio.m.i.Sep.i.car.hom.Tc.ii.
bor.m.vi.Tc.ii.ser.m null.Silu.c.porc.xxiiii.ac.apti.Tc.uat.
xxx.sol.m.xl.
Hund.de Dommauua. Tachestedã tenuit Wisgar.t.r.e.m.R.
in dñio.p.uno manerio.7.p.ix.hid.7.dim.Tc.viii.car.in dñio.m.vii.
Tc.xxxiiii.car.hom.M.xviii.Tc.lv.uilt.m.lii.Sep.xxiiii.bor.
7.xvi.ser.Tc silu.M.porc.m.dccc.cxx.ac.pti.Tc.i.mol.m.ii.
Adhuc posst restaurari.xvi.car.Sep.iiii.runc.7.xxxvi.an.
cxxviii.porc.Tc.cc.ou.m.cccxx.Tc.x.uasa.ap.m.xvi.Tc.
uat.xxx.lib.7 qñ recep.similit.M uat.l.lib.ut dic franci.7.an ★
glici.S; Ricard dedit cuidã anglico.ad.Censũ.p.lx.lib.s; uno qq;
anno deficiunt illi ad min.x.lib. Huic manerio adjacent sep.
.iii.soc.de.ii.hid.7.xv.ac.qs ten& Garner de.R.Tc.iiii.car.m.
.iii.7.dim.Tc.x.uilt.m.ii.Tc.ii.bor.m.x.Tc.iiii.ser.m.null.
Silu.l.porc.xxxiiii.ac.pti.Vat.vi.lib.7 de hac tra tenuit.i.
soc.regis.t.r.e.vii.ac.7.dim.que st addite huic manerio t.r.Witt.
7.ñ reddiđunt consuetudinẽ regis.

Dommauua tenuit Wisgar.t.r.e.p uno manerio.7.p.ii.hid.7
xxx.ac.Sep.ii.car.in dñio.7.ii.car.hom.7.v.uilt.Tc.iiii.bord.
m.vii.Sep.iiii.ser.Tc silu.d.porc.m.ccc.xv.ac.pti.Sep.i.mol.
Tc.7 p uat.lx.sol.m.c.7 istã trã calũpniat.uitat.i.miles.quã ut

39 a

testat.tenuit.i.lib.hõ.t.r.e. In Isto manerio ten& sep.i.pbr.dim.
hid.in elemosina.7 sep.dim.car.7.ii.bor.hoc.M.ten& Ernald.

23 LAND OF RICHARD SON OF COUNT GILBERT 38 b

Hundred of HARLOW

1 Richard holds WALL(BURY) in lordship which Toti, 1 free man, held before 1066 as one manor, for 1 hide. Then 2 ploughs in lordship, now 1. Always 1 men's plough.

Then 2 smallholders, now 6; then 2 slaves, now none.

Woodland, 100 pigs; meadow, 24 acres.

Value then 30s; now 40[s].

Hundred of DUNMOW

2 Withgar held THAXTED before 1066. Now Richard (holds it) in lordship as one manor, for 9½ hides. Then 8 ploughs in lordship, now 7. Then 34 men's ploughs, now 18.

Then 55 villagers, now 52. Always 24 smallholders; 16 slaves.

Woodland, then 1000 pigs, now 800; meadow, 120 acres; then 1 mill, now 2. 16 ploughs can still be restored. Always 4 cobs, 36 cattle, 128 pigs; then 200 sheep, now 320; then 10 beehives, now 16.

Value then £30; when acquired, the same. Value now £50, as the French and English say; but Richard gave it to an Englishman for £60 for the dues; but each year they are deficient in at least £10.

In (the lands of) this manor have always been 3 Freemen with 2 hides and 15 acres, whom Warner holds from Richard. Then 4 ploughs, now 3½.

Then 10 villagers, now 2; then 2 smallholders, now 10; then 4 slaves, now none.

Woodland, 50 pigs; meadow, 34 acres.

Value £6.

Of this land, 1 Freeman held 7½ acres before 1066 which were added to this manor after 1066. They have not paid the King's customary dues.

3 Withgar held (Great) DUNMOW before 1066 as one manor, for 2 hides and 30 acres. Always 2 ploughs in lordship; 2 men's ploughs;

5 villagers. Then 4 smallholders, now 7; always 4 slaves.

Woodland, then 500 pigs, now 300; meadow, 15 acres; always 1 mill.

Value then and later 60s; now 100[s].

Vitalis, 1 man-at-arms, lays claim to this land which, as he 39 a
testifies, 1 free man held before 1066. In that manor 1 priest has always held ½ hide in alms. Always ½ plough;

2 smallholders.

Arnold holds this manor.

Hund de Hidincforda. Ghestingetorp ten&. W. peccatū de. R. qd tenuit Ledmar pbr. t. r. e. p. dim. hid. Sēp. III. car. in dnio. 7. III. car. hom. 7. VIII. uilt. m. IX. bor. Sēp. VI. ser. Silu. XX. porc. XX. ac. p̄ti. Tc. I. mol. m. null. Huic tre sēp jac&. I. soc. de. XV. ac. 7. ht. dim. car. 7. II. bor. 7. I. ac. p̄ti. Tc. ual. c. sol. M. VII. lib.

Phincinghefeldā tenuer. II. soc. t. r. e. p. XLVIII. ac. m. ten& Elinant de. R. Sēp. I. car. 7. dim. Tc. 7 p. IIII. bor. m. VII. Silu. VI. porc. 7 VI. ac. 7. dim. p̄ti. Tc. I. runc. 7. m null. Tc. X. an. m. VIII. Tc. XX. por. m. XXVI. Tc. c. ou. M. CXXVII. Tc. ual. X. sol. m. XXX.

Penfeldā ten& Rob de. R. qd tenuit Wisgar. t. r. e. p uno man. 7. p. I. hid. 7. dim. 7. XXX. ac. Tc. IIII. car. in dnio. Post 7. m. II. Sēp. V. car. hominū. Tc. 7 p. X. uilt. m. VIII. Tc. 7 p. VIII. bord. m. XV. Tc 7 p. VIII. ser. m. VII. Silu. CXX. porc. XIII. ac. p̄ti. 7. II. car. posst restaurari. Tc 7 p ual. VIII. lib. m. X.

In Geldham ten& Goismer. I. hid. 7. V. ac. qd tenuer. VIII. soc. t. r. e. sub uuisgaro Sēp. III. car. 7. dim. in dnio. 7. dim. car. hom. Tc. 7 p. V. bor. m. VIII. Tc. 7. p. V. ser. m. II. Silu. XX. porc. XXIII. ac. p̄ti. Tc. I. mol. Tc 7 p ual. LX. sol. m. c. sol.

In Wicam ten& Ernald. dim. hid. 7. X. ac. de. R. qd tenuer. II. soc. sub Wisgaro. t. r. e. sēp. II. car. in dnio. Tc. 7 p. V. bor. m X. Tc 7 p. I. ser. m. null. Tc. silu. XL. porc. m. XX. X. ac. p̄ti.

39 b

Tc. 7 p. ual. XXX. sol. m. XL.

Hundred of HINCKFORD

4 W(illiam) Peche holds GESTINGTHORPE from Richard, which Ledmer the priest held before 1066 for ½ hide. Always 3 ploughs in lordship; 3 men's ploughs;

8 villagers. Now 9 smallholders; always 6 slaves.

Woodland, 20 pigs; meadow, 20 acres; then 1 mill, now none.

1 Freeman with 15 acres has always lain in (the lands of) this manor and has ½ plough.

2 smallholders.

Meadow, 1 acre.

Value then 100s; now £7.

5 2 Freemen held FINCHINGFIELD before 1066 for 48 acres. Now Elinant holds it from Richard. Always 1½ ploughs.

Then and later 4 smallholders, now 7.

Woodland, 6 pigs; meadow, 6½ acres. Then 1 cob, now none; then 10 cattle, now 8; then 20 pigs, now 26; then 100 sheep, now 127.

Value then 10s; now 30[s].

6 Robert holds PANFIELD from Richard, which Withgar held before 1066 as one manor, for 1½ hides and 30 acres. Then 4 ploughs in lordship, later and now 2. Always 5 men's ploughs.

Then and later 10 villagers, now 8; then and later 8 smallholders, now 15; then and later 8 slaves, now 7.

Woodland, 120 pigs; meadow, 13 acres. 2 ploughs can be restored.

Value then and later £8; now [£] 10.

7 In (Great) YELDHAM Goismer holds 1 hide and 5 acres, which 8 Freemen held before 1066 under Withgar. Always 3½ ploughs in lordship; ½ men's plough.

Then and later 5 smallholders, now 8; then and later 5 slaves, now 2.

Woodland, 20 pigs; meadow, 23 acres; then 1 mill.

Value then and later 60s; now 100s.

8 In WICKHAM (St. Paul's) Arnold holds ½ hide and 10 acres from Richard, which 2 Freemen held under Withgar before 1066. Always 2 ploughs in lordship.

Then and later 5 smallholders, now 10; then and later 1 slave, now none.

Woodland, then 40 pigs, now 20; meadow, 10 acres.

Value then and later 30s; now 40[s]. 39 b

In Fincinghefelda ten& Idē Ernald
xxxviii . ac . qđ tenueř . ii . soc . sub Wisgaro . t . r . e . Sep . i . car.
m . iii . bor . 7 . i . ser . 7 . iiii . ac . 7 . dim . pti. Val : x . sol.
In Bineslea . ten& Wielard . i . hid qđ tenuit . i . soc . sub Wisgaro.
sep . i . car . in dnio . 7 . dim . car . hom . 7 . ii . uill . Tc . 7 . p . xvi . bor . m.
vii . Tc . ii . ser . m . null . Silu . xx . porc . iiii . ac . pti . Tc . ual . xx . sol.
P 7 m xl. In Alreforda . tenent . ii . milit . xxxvi . ac . qs
tenueř . iii . soc . sub Wisg . Sep . ii . car . 7 . iiii . bor . Silu . xii . ix . ac . pti.
xxx . ou . Tc . ual . xl . sol . Post 7 . m . lx.

Ad Asce . ten& Ricard in dnio . dim . hid . 7 . xl . ac . qđ . tenueř . ii.
soc . t . r . e . sub Wisgaro . Sep . i . car . Tc . 7 . p . ii . bor . m . vi . ix . ac.
pti . m . i . mol . Tc . ual . xx . sol . P 7 m . xxxv.

Ad Fincingefeldā tenent . ii . Milit . de . R . xxxvi . ac . qđ tenueř
. iii . soc . sub Wisg . t . r . e . Sep . ii . car . 7 . iiii bor . Tc . iii . ser . P 7 . m . ii. ★
Silu . x . porc . vii . ac . pti . Tc . 7 p ual . xl . sol . m . lxv.

In Bulenemera ten& Mascerel . dim . hid . 7 . xxx . ac . qđ tenuit.
. i . soc . sub Wisg . Sep . ii . car . m . i . bor . Silu . v . porc . ii . ac . pti . 7
ual . xxii . sol . 7 . ii . đ.

Ad Weninchou ten& Germund . xxxii . ac . 7 . dim . qđ tenueř
. iii . soc . sub Wisg . Sep . ii . car . 7 . v . bor . 7 . iii . ser . Silu xxx . porc.
viii . ac . pti . Tc . v . an . m . viii . Modo . iiii . porc . Tc . xx . ou . m . lxxx.
7 . iii ; M . xxxii . cap . Tc 7 p Val . xxx . sol . m . l.

In buro . ht . R . in dnio . xiii . soc . de . xxxv . ac . Sep . iiii . car.

40 a

Tc . ix . bor . m . xvi . Tc . i . ser . m . null . Silu . xx . porc . xi . ac . pti.

9 In FINCHINGFIELD Arnold also holds 38 acres, which 2 Freemen held under Withgar before 1066. Always 1 plough.
Now 3 smallholders; 1 slave.
Meadow, 4½ acres.
Value 10s.

10 In 'BINSLEY' Widelard holds 1 hide, which 1 Freeman held under Withgar. Always 1 plough in lordship; ½ men's plough;
2 villagers. Then and later 16 smallholders, now 7; then 2 slaves, now none.
Woodland, 20 pigs; meadow, 4 acres.
Value then 20s; later and now 40[s].

11 In ALDERFORD 2 men-at-arms hold 36 acres, which 3 Freemen held under Withgar. Always 2 ploughs;
4 smallholders.
Woodland, 12 [pigs]; meadow, 9 acres. 30 sheep.
Value then 40s; later and now 60[s].

12 At ASHEN Richard holds ½ hide and 40 acres in lordship, which 2 Freemen held before 1066 under Withgar. Always 1 plough.
Then and later 2 smallholders, now 6.
Meadow, 9 acres; now 1 mill.
Value then 20s; later and now 35[s].

13 At FINCHINGFIELD 2 men-at-arms hold 36 acres from Richard, which 3 Freemen held under Withgar before 1066. Always 2 ploughs;
4 smallholders. Then 3 slaves; later and now 2.
Woodland, 10 pigs; meadow, 7 acres.
Value then and later 40s; now 65[s].

14 In BULMER Mascerel holds ½ hide and 30 acres, which 1 Freeman held under Withgar. Always 2 ploughs.
Now 1 smallholder.
Woodland, 5 pigs; meadow, 2 acres.
Value 22s 2d.

15 At HOWE Germund holds 32½ acres, which 3 Freemen held under Withgar. Always 2 ploughs;
5 smallholders; 3 slaves.
Woodland, 30 pigs; meadow, 8 acres. Then 5 cattle, now 8; now 4 pigs; then 20 sheep, now 83; now 32 goats.
Value then and later 30s; now 50[s].

16 In BURES Richard has in lordship 13 Freemen with 35 acres. Always 4 ploughs.
Then 9 smallholders, now 16; then 1 slave, now none. 40 a
Woodland, 20 pigs; meadow, 11 acres.

In Focſearde.xix.ſoc̄.de.i.hid̄.7.dim̄.7.xv.ac̄.Sēp.v.car̄.7.
x.bor.7.i.ſer̄.xxii.ac̄.pti.7 In Pebenhers.xviii.ſoc̄.de dim̄ hid̄.
7.xii.ac̄.Sēp.iii.car̄.7.iii.bord̄.7.iii.ac̄.pti.
In Alfelmeſtuna.i.hid̄.v.ac̄.min̄.tenent sēp.xv.ſoc̄.7.hnt.ii.car̄.
7.iii.bord̄.Silu̇.v.porc̄.iiii.ac̄.pti.
In Mildeltuna.xiii.ſoc̄.de.i.hid̄.7.dim̄.7.xxx.ac̄.Sēp.iii.car̄.7.viii.
bor.Silu̇.viii.porc̄.xiii.ac̄.pti.
In Bumeſteda.iii.ſoc̄.q̄ tenent sēp.xxv.ac̄.Sēp.i.car̄.7.ii.bor.
7.vi.ac̄.pti. In Phincinghefelda.xi.ſoc̄.de.dim̄ hid.Sēp.i.car̄.7.iii.ac̄.pti.
In Celueſtuna.v.ſoc̄.de dim̄.hid̄.v.ac̄.min̄.sēp.i.car̄.ii.ac̄.pti.
In Tumeſteda xviii.ſoc̄.de dim̄ hid̄.7.xv.ac̄.sēp.ii.car̄.7.vii.bor.
Silu̇.viii.porc̄.iii.ac̄.pti. In Cheneboltuna xv.ſoc̄.dim̄.hid̄.7 v.
ac̄.Sēp.i.car̄.7.dim̄.iii.bord̄.iiii.ac̄.pti.
In Halſteda tenent.xxii.ſoc̄.dim̄.hid̄.7.xi.ac̄.Sēp.v.car̄.7.i.
uilt.xv.bor.ii.ſer̄.Silu̇.l.porc̄.xix.ac̄.pti.i.mot.
In Sudbia.v.burgenſes.tenentes.ii.ac̄. Iſti cū omnib; ſupdictis.
reddt.xv.lib.7.vi.ſol.7.vi.đ.7 totū ē in dn̄io Ricardi.

17 In FOXEARTH 19 Freemen with 1½ hides and 15 acres. Always 5 ploughs;
10 smallholders; 1 slave.
Meadow, 22 acres.

18 In PEBMARSH 18 Freemen with ½ hide and 12 acres. Always 3 ploughs;
3 smallholders.
Meadow, 3 acres.

19 In ALPHAMSTONE 15 Freemen have always held 1 hide less 5 acres and have 2 ploughs.
3 smallholders.
Woodland, 5 pigs; meadow, 4 acres.

20 In MIDDLETON 13 Freemen with 1½ hides and·30 acres. Always 3 ploughs;
8 smallholders.
Woodland, 8 pigs; meadow, 13 acres.

21 In (Steeple) BUMPSTEAD 3 Freemen who have always held 25 acres. Always 1 plough;
2 smallholders.
Meadow, 6 acres.

22 In FINCHINGFIELD 11 Freemen with ½ hide. Always 1 plough.
Meadow, 3 acres.

23 In COUPALS FARM 5 Freemen with ½ hide less 5 acres. Always 1 plough.
Meadow, 2 acres.

24 In TWINSTEAD 18 Freemen with ½ hide and 15 acres. Always 2 ploughs;
7 smallholders.
Woodland, 8 pigs; meadow, 3 acres.

25 In *CHENEBOLTUNA* 15 Freemen. ½ hide and 5 acres. Always 1½ ploughs;
3 smallholders.
Meadow, 4 acres.

26 In HALSTEAD 22 Freemen hold ½ hide and 11 acres. Always 5 ploughs;
1 villager; 15 smallholders; 2 slaves.
Woodland, 50 pigs; meadow, 19 acres; 1 mill.

27 In SUDBURY 5 burgesses who hold 2 acres.
They with all the above pay £15 6s 6d. The whole is in Richard's lordship.

In Boituna tenuit Colsege. lib hō. t. r. e. dim. hid. 7. x. ac. Sēp. II. car. in dnio. Tc. III. car. hom. P 7 m. II. Sēp. I. uill. Tc. VII. bor. P 7 m. VIII. Tc. 7 p. IIII. ser. m. II. Silu. XXX. porc. VIII. ac. pti. Tc 7 ual XL. sol. P 7 m. IIII. lib. Huic manerio addite st t. r. Willi. XLV. ac. quæ jacebant ad uuestrefeldā. maneriū regis. Tc. dim. car. m nulla.

40 b

Tc 7 p. I. bor. m. II. Silu. x. porc. II. ac. pti. Val. VIII. sol. In Bura tenuit Leueua. liba femina XL. ac. Sēp. I. car. 7. dim. hom. 7. I. uill. Tc. 7 p. II. bor. m. III. Sēp. II. ser Silu. XX. porc. V. ac. pti. Val. XXX. sol. Hanc trā scil boitunā. 7. buro. ht Ricard p escangio ut dicē sui hoēs.

Roinges tenuit Coleman. t. r. e. p. III. uirg. m. R. p tantundē in dnio. 7. iste fuit ita lib. qd poss& ire q uell& cū soca. 7. sacna. s; tm fuit homo. Wisgari antecessoris Ricardi. Sēp. I. uill. 7. II. bor. Tc. IIII. ser. m. I. Sēp. II. car. in dnio. 7. dim. car. hom. Silu. CC. porc. XX. ac. pti. Tc. ual. LX. sol. Post. XL. M. IIII. lib.

Hund de tendringe. Menetleam tenuit Wisgar p. I. hid. 7 p. I. man. M ten& Rog de Ricardo. Sēp. III. uill. 7. IIII. bord. Tc. I. ser. m null. Sēp. I. car. in dnio. 7. I. car. hom. Silu. C. porc. III. ac. pti. Tc ual. XL. sol. m. L.

Brumleā tenuit Aluuin libe. p. uno man. 7. p. dim. hid. 7 erat cō mdat Wisgaro potens trā suā uende. Modo ten&. R. sub. Ricardo. Sēp. I. uill. m. II. bor. Tc. in dnio. I. car. m null. Silu. c. porc. II. ac. pti. m. XI. oues. Val. XL. sol.

28 In BOYTON (Hall) Colsege, a free man, held ½ hide and 10 acres before 1066. Always 2 ploughs in lordship. Then 3 men's ploughs, later and now 2.
Always 1 villager. Then 7 smallholders, later and now 8; then and later 4 slaves, now 2.
Woodland, 30 pigs; meadow, 8 acres.
Value then 40s; later and now £4.
To this manor 45 acres were added after 1066 which lie in (the lands of) the King's manor of Wethersfield. Then ½ plough, now none.
Then and later 1 smallholder, now 2. 40 b
Woodland, 10 pigs; meadow, 2 acres.
Value 8s.

29 In BURES Leofeva, a free woman, held 40 acres. Always 1½ men's ploughs;
1 villager. Then and later 2 smallholders, now 3; always 2 slaves.
Woodland, 20 pigs; meadow, 5 acres.
Value 30s.
Richard has this land, namely Boyton (Hall) and Bures, by exchange, as his men state.

[Hundred of ONGAR]

30 Colman held ('Morrell') RODING before 1066 for 3 virgates. Now Richard (holds it) for as much in lordship. That man was so free that he could go whither he would with full jurisdiction, although he was the man of Withgar, Richard's predecessor.
Always 1 villager; 2 smallholders. Then 4 slaves, now 1.
Always 2 ploughs in lordship; ½ men's plough.
Woodland, 200 pigs; meadow, 20 acres.
Value then 60s; later 40[s] ; now £4.

Hundred of TENDRING

31 Withgar held (Little) BENTLEY for 1 hide, as 1 manor. Now Roger holds it from Richard.
Always 3 villagers; 4 smallholders. Then 1 slave, now none.
Always 1 plough in lordship; 1 men's plough.
Woodland, 100 pigs; meadow, 3 acres.
Value then 40s; now 50[s].

32 Alwin held (Little) BROMLEY freely as one manor, for ½ hide. He was under the patronage of Withgar (and) able to sell his land. Now R(oger) holds it under Richard.
Always 1 villager. Now 2 smallholders. Then 1 plough in lordship, now none.
Woodland, 100 pigs; meadow, 2 acres. Now 11 sheep.
Value 40s.

Alefordā ten. Algar. p. xxxvii. ac. t. r. e. m̄ ten& Idē sub. R.
7. hoc ē de socha regis. de laleforda. ut hund testar. Tc̄. i. car. m̄.
nulla. Past. xl. ou. Tc̄. ual. x. sol. m̄. vi.

Hund de Laxedana. In tēpr̄ reg Eduuardi fuer. v. soc.
q̄s tenuit Wisgar. Vluuin 7. ii. sorores ej in colun ~~tenentes~~

41 a

tenentes lxiiii. ac. 7 Leuric. tenens. xxx. ac. in ead uilla. 7. isti n̄
poterant recede a soca Wisgari. Sēp. sub ipsis. ii. bor. 7. i. car. Silu. xii.
porc. ix. ac. p̄ti. sēp. i. mol. Val. xx sol. In Sordehā tenuit Vlmar sub Wisgaro. xl. ac. ★
& ten& sub. R. 7 n̄ potat recede de soca tc̄. iii. bor. m̄. vi. dim. car. silu. x. por. iii. ac p̄ti. val. x. sol.
In bcolta tenuit Lefcild. xxxi. ac. 7. dim. Mo ten& Goding sub. R.
Tc̄. ii. bor. m̄. vi. m̄. i. ser. Sēp. dim. car. Silu. xvi. porc. iii. ac. p̄ti.
Tc̄. i. mol. m̄. null. Val. x. sol.

In Witesuuorda. tenuit Algar sub Wisgaro. xii. ac. 7. dim. qui
n̄ potat. recede de. soca. m̄. i. bor. 7. i. ac. p̄ti. Val. iii. sol.

Laingaham ten& Walt̄ tirelde. R. qd tenuit Phin. dac. p. ii. hid.
7. dim. 7 p uno manerio. Tc̄. xxii. uill. m̄. xvii. Tc̄. ix. bor. m̄. xxvii.
Tc̄. iiii. ser. m̄ null. Sēp. i. car. in dn̄io. Tc̄. xi. car. hominū. m̄. vii.
Silu. M. porc. xl. ac. p̄ti. Tc̄. i. mol. m̄. ii. Tc̄. vi. runc. m̄. null.
Sēp. xxii. an. Tc̄. xlvi. porc. M lxxx. Tc̄. liiii. ou. m̄. cc. Tc̄. lxii.
cap. m̄. lxxx. Tc̄. iii. uasa ap. m̄. n̄. Tc̄ ual. xii. lib. m̄. xv.

33 Algar held ALRESFORD for 37 acres before 1066. Now he also holds it under Richard. This is in the King's jurisdiction of Lawford, as the Hundred testifies. Then 1 plough, now none.
Pasture, 40 sheep.
Value then 10s; now 6[s].

Hundred of LEXDEN

34 Before 1066 there were 5 Freemen whom Withgar held. Wulfwin and 2 of his sisters who hold 64 acres in COLNE and Leofric who 41 a
holds 30 acres in the same village. They could not withdraw from Withgar's jurisdiction.
Under them always 2 smallholders; 1 plough.
Woodland, 12 pigs; meadow, 9 acres; always 1 mill.
Value 20s.

35 In FORDHAM Wulfmer held 40 acres under Withgar and holds under R(ichard). He could not withdraw from the jurisdiction.
Then 3 smallholders, now 6. ½ plough.
Woodland, 10 pigs; meadow, 3 acres.
Value 10s.

36 In (West) BERGHOLT Leofcild held 31½ acres. Now Goding holds it under Richard.
Then 2 smallholders, now 6; now 1 slave. Always ½ plough.
Woodland, 16 pigs; meadow, 3 acres; then 1 mill, now none.
Value 10s.

37 In *WITESUUORDA* Algar, who could not withdraw from the jurisdiction, held 12½ acres under Withgar.
Now 1 smallholder.
Meadow, 1 acre.
Value 3s.

38 Walter Tirel holds LANGHAM from Richard, which Finn the Dane held for 2½ hides, as one manor.
Then 22 villagers, now 17; then 9 smallholders, now 27; then 4 slaves, now none. Always 1 plough in lordship. Then 11 men's ploughs, now 7.
Woodland, 1000 pigs; meadow, 40 acres; then 1 mill, now 2. Then 6 cobs, now none; always 22 cattle; then 46 pigs. now 80; then 54 sheep, now 200; then 62 goats, now 80; then 3 beehives, now none.
Value then £12; now [£] 15.

Dim. Hund de Frosseuuella. Birdefeldā tenuit Wisgar p
uno man. 7. p. IIII. hid. M ten& Ricard in dnio. Tc. XXIIII. uill.
m. XX. Tc 7 p. VII. bor. m. XXII. Sep. VIII. ser. Sep. IIII. car. in dnio.
Tc 7 p XXI. car. M. IX. Silu. DCCC. porc. XXXII. ac. pti. Sep. II.
mol. Tc. IIII. runc. M. V. Tc. XXVIII. an. M. XLI. Tc. LX. porc.
M. CVII. Tc. C. ou. m. CC. Sep. ual. XVI. lib.

Sanfordā tenuit Wisgar p. uno man. 7. p. V. hid. M. ten&.
Ricard in dnio. Tc. XXIII. uill. m. XIIII. Tc. II. bor. m. XVIII.
Tc. VI. ser. m. IIII. Sep. III. car. in dnio. Tc. XXI. car hou. m. X.

41 b

Silu. LX. porc. XXII. ac. pti. Tc. I. mol. m null. Tc ual. XII. lib. m. XVII.
Qn Ricard recep hoc. M. tc inuenit. ibi. III. runc. m. II. Tc. XIX. an. m
IX. Tc. L. porc. m. XXX. Tc. C. ou. m. LXXX. 7 VIII; Tc. III. uasa ap. m. I.
De hoc manerio 7 de supdictis. V. hid. tenent. II. franci. I. hid. 7. dimidiā.
7. IX. bord. 7. II. car. 7. XVI. ac. pti. Apptiatū ē supi.

Hamstedā tenuit Wisg. p. I. M. 7. p. IIII. hid. XXX. ac. min. t. r. e. m.
Rob de uuateuill de. R. Sep. XXII. uill. Tc. VI. bor. m. X. Tc. VIII. ser. m. VII.
Tc. in dio. IIII. car. m. III. Tc. XIIII. car. m. X. Silu. CC. porc. XV. ac. pti. Tc
ual. XII. lib. m. XVI.

In bdefelda ten& Wielard. I. hid. qm tenuer. II. seruientes Wisgari 7
tc n reddebant consuetudinē. t gelt regi. nec potant abire sine jussu
dni. sui. sic hund testat. Sep. I. car. in dnio. Val. XX. sol.

Hund de Rochefort. Berreuuerā tenuit Phin dac. I. hid. 7. dim.
m. R. in dnio. Sep. III. bord. 7. III. ser. 7. II. car. Silu. XXX. porc. Tc. ual
XL. sol. m. IIII. lib.

Half-Hundred of FRESHWELL

39 Withgar held (Great) BARDFIELD as one manor, for 4 hides. Now Richard holds it in lordship.

Then 24 villagers, now 20; then and later 7 smallholders, now 22; always 8 slaves. Always 4 ploughs in lordship. Then and later 21 [men's] ploughs, now 9.

Woodland, 800 pigs; meadow, 32 acres; always 2 mills. Then 4 cobs, now 5; then 28 cattle, now 41; then 60 pigs, now 107; then 100 sheep, now 200.

Value always £16.

40 Withgar held (Little) SAMPFORD as one manor, for 5 hides. Now Richard holds it in lordship.

Then 23 villagers, now 14; then 2 smallholders, now 18; then 6 slaves, now 4. Always 3 ploughs in lordship. Then 21 men's ploughs, now 10.

Woodland, 60 pigs; meadow, 22 acres; then 1 mill, now none. 41 b

Value then £12; now [£] 17.

When Richard acquired this manor, he then found there 3 cobs, now 2; then 19 cattle, now 9; then 50 pigs, now 30; then 100 sheep, now 88; then 3 beehives, now 1.

Of this manor and of the above 5 hides, 2 Frenchmen hold 1½ hides.

9 smallholders. 2 ploughs.

Meadow, 16 acres.

It is assessed above.

41 Withgar held HEMPSTEAD as 1 manor, for 4 hides less 30 acres before 1066. Now Robert of Vatteville (holds it) from Richard.

Always 22 villagers. Then 6 smallholders, now 10; then 8 slaves, now 7. Then 4 ploughs in lordship, now 3. Then 14 [men's] ploughs, now 10.

Woodland, 200 pigs; meadow, 15 acres.

Value then £12; now [£] 16.

42 In BARDFIELD Widelard holds 1 hide, which 2 servants of Withgar held. Then they did not pay customary dues or tax to the King and could not go away without their lord's order; so the Hundred testifies. Always 1 plough in lordship.

Value 20s.

Hundred of ROCHFORD

43 Finn the Dane held BARROW (Hall). 1½ hides. Now Richard (holds it) in lordship.

Always 3 smallholders; 3 slaves; 2 ploughs.

Woodland, 30 pigs.

Value then 40s; now £4.

TERRA SVENI De Exsessa. Hund de bdestapla .XXIIII.

Tornindunam tenuit Aluuin teinn reg. E. t. r. e. 7 Rex Witt dedit Robto. M. ten& Suen. 7 Siric de illo. p uno manerio. 7. p. v. hid. 7. xv. ac. Sep. II. car in dnio. 7. III. car. hom. 7. III. uitt. Tc. VII. bor. m. x. Tc. IIII. ser. m. I. II. hid. siluæ. 7. II. soc. de. L. ac. hntes sep. dim. car. In hoc manerio recep. Suen. I. runc. VIII. an. XX. por. LX. ou. m. IIII. an. XII. porc. L. ou. Val. c. sol.

Langenduna ten&. Walt de Sueno. qd tenuit Alric teinn reg. e. p. M. 7. p. v. hid. Sep. II. car. in dnio. 7. III. car. hom. 7. v. uitt. Tc. IIII. ser. m. IIII. 7. I. hid. siluæ. Past. c. ou. Tc. v. an. 7. x. porc. LX. ou. m. x. porc. XLII. ou. Tc ual. c. sol. m. VI. lib.

Tilibiam tenent. II. franci de Sueno. scil Osbn. 7. Rad. qd tenuit Aluric pbr lib hō t. r. e. p uno manerio. 7 p. II. hid. Sep. II. car in dnio. 7. IIII. car hominum. 7. I. uitt. 7. XI. bor. 7. II. ser. 7. IIII. hid siluæ. Past. CCC. ou. 7. I. pisc. Tc. I. runc. 7. LX. ou. M. I. runc. 7. XII. pulli. 7. XXXI. an. IX. porc. 7. CCLX. ou. Tc ual. VIII. lib m. c. sol

Ciltedic. ten& Osbn de. S. qd tenuit Aluuen liba femina. t. r. e. 7 nescit q m uenerit ad Robtum filium Wicmarc. Sep. I. bi ē. I. hid. 7. XL. ac. Sep. I. car. in dnio. Tc. dim. car. hom. m nich. Tc. I. uitt m nuil. Tc. I. bord. m. IIII. Tc. II. ser. m. I. Silu. c. porc. Past. c. ou. Tc. I. animal. m. x. an. Val. XL. sol.

24 LAND OF SWEIN OF ESSEX 42 a

Hundred of BARSTABLE

1 Alwin, a thane of King Edward's, held (West) HORNDON before 1066. King William gave it to Robert. Now Swein holds it, and Siric from him, as one manor for 5 hides and 15 acres. Always 2 ploughs in lordship; 3 men's ploughs;

3 villagers. Then 7 smallholders, now 10; then 4 slaves, now 1.

Woodland, 2 hides. 2 Freemen with 50 acres who have always had ½ plough.

In this manor Swein acquired 1 cob, 8 cattle, 20 pigs, 60 sheep; now 4 cattle, 12 pigs, 50 sheep.

Value 100s.

2 Walter holds LANGDON from Swein which Alric, a thane of King Edward's, held as a manor for 5 hides. Always 2 ploughs in lordship; 3 men's ploughs;

5 villagers. Then 4 slaves, now 4.

Woodland, 1 hide; pasture, 100 sheep. Then 5 cattle, 10 pigs, 60 sheep; now 10 pigs, 42 sheep.

Value then 100s; now £6.

3 2 Frenchmen, namely Osbern and Ralph, hold (West) TILBURY from Swein, which Aelfric the priest, a free man, held before 1066 as one manor for 2 hides. Always 2 ploughs in lordship; 4 men's ploughs;

1 villager; 11 smallholders; 2 slaves.

Woodland, 4 hides; pasture, 300 sheep; 1 fishery. Then 1 cob, 60 sheep; now 1 cob, 12 foals, 31 cattle, 9 pigs and 260 sheep.

Value then £8; now 100s.

[Hundred of CHAFFORD]

4 Osbern holds CHILDERDITCH from Swein which Alwen, a free woman, held before 1066 and it is not known how it came to Robert son of Wymarc. Always 1 hide there and 40 acres. Always 1 plough in lordship. Then ½ men's plough, now nothing.

Then 1 villager, now none; then 1 smallholder, now 4; then 2 slaves, now 1.

Woodland, 100 pigs; pasture, 100 sheep. Then 1 (head of) cattle, now 10 cattle.

Value 40s.

Hornindunā tenuit Aluric pbr lib hō.t.r.e. p uno Man. 7. p .II. hid. 7. XXX. ac. Sēp. I. car. in dn̄io. 7. dim. car houm. 7. XI. bor

42 b
7. III. ser. De hac tr̄a dedit Aluric pbr cuidā eccle dim. hid. 7. XXX. ac. sed Suen abstulit de ecl̄ia Sēp. I. runc. 7. II. an. Val. XXX. sol. Hoc maner ten& Pagan de Sueno.

Hasingebroc ten& Turold de. S. qđ tenuit Lefstan lib hō. t. r. e. p. I. hid. 7. XXX. ac. Sēp. I. car. in dn̄io. Tc. II. bor. m̄. III. Tc. II. ser m̄ null. VI. ac. p̄ti. Tc. X. ou. m̄. XIII. 7. V. porc. Val. XX. sol.

Belesdunam ten& Idē Turold de. S. qđ tenuit Idē Lefstan. t. r. e p. I. hid. 7. p. m̄. 7. XV. ac. Sēp. I. car. Tc. III. bor. m̄. I. Sēp. II. ser. Past. .C. ou. Tc. II. runc. 7. VII. porc. 7. XV. ou. M̊. I. runc. 7. I. uac. 7. I. por. 7 LXXXXV. ou. Tc ual. XX. sol. M̊. XXV.

Berlesduna ten&. W. qđ tenuit God& q̄dā lib hō. t. r. e. p. m̄. 7 p. .III. hid. Tc. III. car. in dn̄io. m̄. II. 7. dim. Tc. I. car. hom. m̄. I. 7. dim. Tc. II. uilt. m̄. I. Tc. IIII. borđ. m̄. III. Tc. IIII. ser. m̄ null. Silua XL. porc. Past. C. ou. Tc. I. runc. 7. XVII. ou. M̊. V. an. 7. XVI. porc. 7. XXXIX. ou. Val. LX. sol.

Wicfort tenet Turchill qđ tenuit Leftan libe. p. m̄. 7. p. dim. hid. 7. XXXV. ac. Sēp. I. car. 7. I. borđ. Tc. I. ser. m̄ null. XXX. ac. siluæ. .III. ac. p̄ti. Tc. II. runc. 7. XVI. an. 7. III. porc. 7. C. ou. m̄. III. runc. 7 VIII. an. 7. XI. porc. 7. LX. ou. P̄t hanc tr̄a tenuit bricteua liba femina dim hid. 7. XV. ac. q̄m Suen addidit p̄dicte træ. in q erat tc. I. car. m̄. n̄. Sēp. II. borđ. 7. I. uilt. XX. ac. siluæ. Addidit &iam .III. libos hōes. de XLV. ac. in qb; erat. tc. I. car. m̄. dim. Addidit &iam. I. libm hom. de. IX. ac. Tc ual totū. t. r. e. LX. sol. m̄. L.

[Hundred of BARSTABLE]

5 Aelfric the priest, a free man, held HORNDON (-on-the-Hill) as one manor, for 2 hides and 30 acres. Always 1 plough in lordship; ½ men's plough;

11 smallholders; 3 slaves. 42 b

Of this land, Aelfric the priest gave ½ hide and 30 acres to a church, but Swein took it away from the church.

Always 1 cob; 2 cattle.

Value 30s.

Payne holds this manor from Swein.

6 Thorold holds HASSENBROOK (Hall) from Swein, which Leofstan, a free man, held before 1066 for 1 hide and 30 acres. Always 1 plough in lordship.

Then 2 smallholders, now 3; then 2 slaves, now none.

Meadow, 6 acres. Then 10 cattle, now 13 and 5 pigs.

Value 20s.

7 Thorold also holds BASILDON from Swein, which Leofstan also held before 1066 as a manor for 1 hide and 15 acres. Always 1 plough.

Then 3 smallholders, now 1; always 2 slaves.

Pasture, 100 sheep. Then 2 cobs, 7 pigs, 15 sheep; now 1 cob, 1 cow, 1 pig and 95 sheep.

Value then 20s; now 25[s].

8 W. holds BASILDON, which Godith, a free man, held before 1066 as a manor for 3 hides. Then 3 ploughs in lordship, now 2½. Then 1 men's plough, now 1½.

Then 2 villagers, now 1; then 4 smallholders, now 3; then 4 slaves, now none.

Woodland, 40 pigs; pasture, 100 sheep. Then 1 cob, 17 sheep; now 5 cattle, 16 pigs and 39 sheep.

Value 60s.

9 Thorkell holds WICKFORD, which Leofstan held freely as a manor for ½ hide and 35 acres. Always 1 plough;

1 smallholder. Then 1 slave, now none.

Woodland, 30 acres; meadow, 3 acres. Then 2 cobs, 16 cattle, 3 pigs and 100 sheep; now 3 cobs, 8 cattle, 11 pigs and 60 sheep.

Besides this land, Bricteva, a free woman, held ½ hide and 15 acres which Swein added to the above-mentioned land, in which there was then 1 plough, now none.

Always 2 smallholders; 1 villager.

Woodland, 20 acres.

He also added 3 free men with 45 acres, in which there was then 1 plough, now ½. He also added 1 free man with 9 acres.

Value of the whole then, before 1066, 60s; now 50[s].

Wicfort ten& Suen in dnio . qđ tenuit Goduin teinnus reg.

43 a

p uno man . 7 . p . x . hid . Sep . II . car in dnio . Tc . VI . car . hom . m . IIII. Sep . VII . uilt . Tc . II . bor . m . XII . Tc . VI . ser . m . null . Tc . XII . hid . siluæ m . VI . ac . Tc . I . runc . 7 . XII . ou . 7 . XVII . cap . 7 . II . uasa ap . m . I . uac . 7 XX . ou . 7 . II . pult . 7 . IIJ . uasa ap . Tc uat . XVI . lib . m . IX. ★

Wicfort ten& Wilt filius Odonis qđ tenuit Dot lib ho . t . r . E . p . ϖ . 7 . đ. hid . 7 . XLV . ac . Sep . I . car in dnio . 7 . I . bor . Silu . X . porc . Vat . X . sot. ★

Wicfort ten& Mainardus . qđ tenuit . t . r . e . Godric . p . XXX . ac . Vat. . V . sot.

Benflet ten& Suen in dnio qđ tenuit Aluuin . lib ho . t . r . e . p ϖ . 7 . p . II . hid . Tc . III . car in dnio . m . I . 7 . I . car poss& restaurari. m . V . bord . 7 . II . ser . Past . CCL . ou . Vat . XL . sot. ★

Wateleam ten& Galt de Sueno . qđ tenuit Edric . t . r . e . p . ϖ . 7 p . dim hid . Sep . I . car . m . I . bord 7 XV . ac . pasturæ ; Vat . X . sot.

Wateleam ten& Suen in dnio . qđ tenuit Leuecilt . t . r . e . tegn reg. . p . I . Man . 7 . p . V . hid . Tc . II . car . 7 . I . car . hom . 7 . m simit . Tc . I . uilt . m null . Tc . X . bor . M XI . dim hid silue uastatæ . Past . C . ou . Tc . I . pisc. m . II . Tc . III . runc . 7 . V . an . 7 . XX . porc . 7 . C . ou . m . I . runc . 7 . I . pull. 7 . VII . an . 7 . LXX . ou . Tc . uat . LX . sot . m . IIII . lib.

Thunresleam ten& S . in dnio . qđ tenuit Godric tegn reg . t . r . e. p uno Man . 7 . p . V . hid . 7 . XV . ac . Sep . II . car . in dnio . 7 . II . car hou. 7 . V . uilt . 7 . V . bord . Tc . IIII . ser . m . II . Past . CC . ou . Silu . L . porc. Tc . II . runc . 7 . VII . an . 7 . XVI . porc . 7 . CC . ou . 7 . II . uasa ap . M . III. runc . 7 . I . runc . XIIII . an . XXXVI . porc . CC . ou . II . uasa ap . Tc uat . CII sot . M . C . sot.

10 Swein holds WICKFORD in lordship which Godwin, a King's thane, held as one manor for 10 hides. Always 2 ploughs in lordship. 43 a
Then 6 men's ploughs, now 4.
Always 7 villagers. Then 2 smallholders, now 12; then 6 slaves, now none.
Woodland, then 12 hides, now 6 acres. Then 1 cob, 12 sheep, 17 goats, 2 beehives; now 1 cow, 20 sheep, 2 foals, 3 beehives.
Value then £16; now [£] 9.

11 William son of Odo holds WICKFORD which Dot, a free man, held before 1066 as a manor. ½ hide and 45 acres. Always 1 plough in lordship;
1 smallholder.
Woodland, 10 pigs.
Value 10s.

12 Maynard holds WICKFORD, which Godric held before 1066 for 30 acres.
Value 5s.

13 Swein holds (South) BENFLEET in lordship which Alwin, a free man, held before 1066 as a manor, for 2 hides. Then 3 ploughs in lordship, now 1; 1 plough can be restored.
Now 5 smallholders; 2 slaves.
Pasture, 250 sheep.
Value 40s.

14 Walter holds WHEATLEY from Swein, which Edric held before 1066 as a manor, for ½ hide. Always 1 plough.
Now 1 smallholder.
Pasture, 15 acres.
Value 10s.

15 Swein holds WHEATLEY in lordship, which Leofcild, a King's thane, held before 1066 as 1 manor for 5 hides. Then 2 ploughs and 1 men's plough; now the same.
Then 1 villager, now none; then 10 smallholders, now 11.
Woodland, ½ hide, laid waste; pasture, 100 sheep; then 1 fishery, now 2. Then 3 cobs, 5 cattle, 20 pigs and 100 sheep; now 1 cob, 1 foal, 7 cattle and 70 sheep.
Value then 60s; now £4.

16 Swein holds THUNDERSLEY in lordship, which Godric, a King's thane, held before 1066 as one manor for 5 hides and 15 acres.
Always 2 ploughs in lordship; 2 men's ploughs;
5 villagers; 5 smallholders. Then 4 slaves, now 2.
Pasture, 200 sheep; woodland, 50 pigs. Then 2 cobs, 7 cattle, 16 pigs, 200 sheep and 2 beehives; now 3 cobs and 1 cob, 14 cattle, 36 pigs, 200 sheep, 2 beehives.
Value then 102s; now 100s.

Hund de Rochefort. Rageneiã. ten& Suen in dn̄io p̄. uno Man. 7 p. v. hid. Tc̄. II. car in dn̄io. m̄. III. Sep̄. x. car. hom. Tc̄. XXI. uilt. m̄. VI. Tc̄. VI. bord. m̄. xv. Sep̄. II. ser. x. ac. p̄ti. Silu. XL. porc. m̄ . I. parc. 7 VI. arpenni uineæ. 7 reddit. xx. modios uini si bene procedit. Tc̄. IIII. runc. 7. XIII. an. XXV. porc. CV. ou. m̄. v. runc. 7. II. pulli. 7. XX. an. 7 XI. porc. 7 LXXX. ou. 7. XI. cap. Tc̄ ual. x. lib. m̄ p̄t uinum tantundē. 7 in hoc manerio fecit Suen suū castellū. De hoc manerio tenent. IIII. franci. II. hid. 7. IIII. car. 7. IIII. bord. 7 ual. LX. sol in eod̄ p̄tio.

Ragheleiam ten&. S. in dn̄io qd̄ tenuit. I. lib hō. t. r. e. p. Man. 7 p. . II. hid. 7. dim. Sep̄. II. car in dn̄io. tc̄. III. uilt. m̄. II. Tc̄. v. bor. m̄. VI. hntes tc̄. II. car 7 dim. m̄ dim tantū. Tc̄. I. runc. 7. II. an. 7. xv. ou. m̄. II. runc. IX. an. IX. por. xx. ou. Tc̄ 7 p̄ ual. XXX. sol. m̄. XL.

Hocheleiam tenent. II. franci de Sueno. Godebold. I. hid. 7 Odo . XXX. ac. 7 hoc Man tenuit. I. lib hō. t. r. e. Sep̄. II. car. 7. dim. in dn̄io. Tc̄. III. bord. m̄. v. Tc̄. v. ser. m̄. III. Past. c. ou Sep̄. I. mol. Tc̄. v. an. 7. x. porc. 7. c. ou. 7. VII. cap. M. I. runc. 7. XIII. an. 7 XXII. porc. 7. c. ou. 7. IIII. uasa ap. Tc̄ ual. XXX. sol. P 7 m̄. XL.

Estuudā. ten& Suen in dn̄io. qd̄ tenuit Pat̄ suus. t. r. e. p uno Man. 7 p. III. hid 7. dim. Sep̄. III. uilt. 7. II. car. in dn̄io. Tc̄. VIII. car hom. m̄. v. Tc̄. XXI. bor. m̄. XXX. Sep̄. II. ser. IIII. ac. p̄ti. Tc̄ silu . L. porc. m̄. XXX. m̄. I. mol Past. CCC. ou. Tc̄. II. runc. 7. VI. an. . XXX. porc. CCC. ou. m̄. II. runc. 7. II. pult. 7. XXXIII. an. XL. porc. CXXXVI. ou. Tc̄ ual. VI. lib. m̄. x. De hoc manerio

ten& Goisfrid. dim hid. 7. I. bor. 7. I. car. 7 ual XX. sol. in eod̄ p̄tio.

Hundred of ROCHFORD 43 b

17 Swein holds RAYLEIGH in lordship as one manor, for 5 hides. Then 2 ploughs in lordship, now 3. Always 10 men's ploughs.
Then 21 villagers, now 6; then 6 smallholders, now 15; always 2 slaves.
Meadow, 10 acres; woodland, 40 pigs; now 1 park; 6 *arpents* of vines and it pays 20 measures of wine if it does well. Then 4 cobs, 13 cattle, 25 pigs, 105 sheep; now 5 cobs, 2 foals, 20 cattle, 11 pigs, 80 sheep and 11 goats.
Value then £10; now, apart from the wine, as much.
In this manor Swein made his castle.
Of this manor, 4 Frenchmen hold 2 hides. 4 ploughs.
4 smallholders.
Value 60s in the same assessment.

18 Swein holds RAYLEIGH in lordship, which 1 free man held before 1066 as a manor, for 2½ hides. Always 2 ploughs in lordship.
Then 3 villagers, now 2; then 5 smallholders, now 6, who then had 2½ ploughs and now have only ½.
Then 1 cob, 2 cattle and 15 sheep; now 2 cobs, 9 cattle, 9 pigs, 20 sheep.
Value then and later 30s; now 40[s].

19 2 Frenchmen hold HOCKLEY from Swein, Godbold (holds) 1 hide and Odo 30 acres. 1 free man held this manor before 1066. Always 2½ ploughs in lordship.
Then 3 smallholders, now 5; then 5 slaves, now 3.
Pasture, 100 sheep; always 1 mill. Then 5 cattle, 10 pigs, 100 sheep and 7 goats; now 1 cob, 13 cattle, 22 pigs, 100 sheep and 4 beehives.
Value then 30s; later and now 40[s].

20 Swein holds EASTWOOD in lordship, which his father held before 1066 as one manor, for 3½ hides.
Always 3 villagers; 2 ploughs in lordship. Then 8 men's ploughs, now 5. Then 21 smallholders, now 30; always 2 slaves.
Meadow, 4 acres; woodland, then 50 pigs, now 30; now 1 mill; pasture, 300 sheep. Then 2 cobs, 6 cattle, 30 pigs, 300 sheep; now 2 cobs, 2 foals, 33 cattle, 40 pigs, 136 sheep.
Value then £6; now [£] 10.
Of this manor, Geoffrey holds ½ hide. 44 a
1 smallholder. 1 plough.
Value 20s in the same assessment.

Wachelingam ten&. S. in dn̄io p. I. Man. 7. p. v. hid. 7 dim. Sēp. . II. uill. 7. XVIII. bord. 7. II. car in dn̄io. 7 tcia poss& fieri. Tc. III. . car hom. m. v. Silu. XL. porc. Past. CCC. ou. Tc. IIII. runc. IX. an. XXXVIII. porc. CXV. ou. M. IIII. runc. II. an. CX. ou. XXVII. porc. Tc ual. IX. lib. m. x. De hoc man. tenent Garner 7. W. I. hidam. 7. II. car. 7 ual. XXX. sol. in eod ptio.

Pritteuuellā. ten&. S. in dn̄io. p. VII. hid. 7. dim. Tc. VII. uill. m. IIII. Tc. XIIII. bord. m. XXIII. Tc. II. car. in dn̄io m. III. Tc. VII. car. hou m. IX. Past. XII. porc. Past. CC. ou. Tc. II. runc. VIII. an. XXX. porc. . C. ou. M. I. runc. III. pull. XIII. an. LXV. porc. CC. ou. IIII. min. . LXVI. cap. IX. uasa ap. De hac tr̄a ten&. I. lib hō. I. uirg quā potat uende. s; soca jacuit in hoc manerio. 7 ad eccliam huj manerij. apposuer. II. hōes. XXX. ac. de alia tr̄a. Sēp ual. XII. lib. De hoc Man ten& Grapinel dim. hidā. 7. II. bord. 7. I. car. 7. ual. X. sol in eod ptio.

Essobiam tenuit. R. fili uuimarcæ post mortē reg. E. m. Suen in dn̄io. p uno Man. 7. p. v. hid. Sēp. IX. uill. Tc. IIII. bor. m. VI. Sēp. II. car. in dn̄io. 7. VIII. car. hom. III. ac. pti. Silu. XX. porc. Tc. II. runc. IIII. an. XII. porc. C. ou. m. II. runc. XVI. porc. LXIIII. ou. Tc. 7 p ual. VI. lib. m. X.

Carendunā ten&. S. in dn̄io. p. VI. hid. 7. dim. 7. XXX. ac. Tc. XXII. uill. m. XVI. Tc. II. bord. m. VIII. Tc. III. ser. m. I. Tc. II. car i dn̄io m. III. 7 qrta pot fieri. Tc. X. car. hom. M. VI. Past. DC. ou. Tc. . III. runc. X. an. XXIIII. porc. CCCXXXVI. ou. m. III. runc. 7. V. an. ★

44 b

. XX. porc. CCC. XLII. ou. Tc. ual. XII. lib. m. XIII. In hoc manerio ht Hugo de monteforti. I. hid. 7. ual. XX. sol. De hoc man. tenent . II. franci. Girold. I. hid. 7. ihos. XXX. ac. 7. III. bord. 7. I. car. 7 ual. XL. sol. in eod ptio. Ht &iā. S. I. hid. 7. IIII. bord. 7. I. car. qd tenuit. I. lib hō t. r. e. cū socā. Val. XX. sol.

21 Swein holds (Great) WAKERING in lordship as 1 manor, for 5½ hides.

Always 2 villagers; 18 smallholders; 2 ploughs in lordship, 3 possible. Then 3 men's ploughs, now 5.

Woodland, 40 pigs; pasture, 300 sheep. Then 4 cobs, 9 cattle, 38 pigs, 115 sheep; now 4 cobs, 2 cattle, 110 sheep, 27 pigs.

Value then £9; now [£] 10.

Of this manor, Warner and W. hold 1 hide. 2 ploughs.

Value 30s in the same assessment.

22 Swein holds PRITTLEWELL in lordship for 7½ hides.

Then 7 villagers, now 4; then 14 smallholders, now 23. Then 2 ploughs in lordship, now 3. Then 7 men's ploughs, now 9.

Pasture, 12 pigs; pasture, 200 sheep. Then 2 cobs, 8 cattle, 30 pigs, 100 sheep; now 1 cob, 3 foals, 13 cattle, 65 pigs, 200 sheep less 4, 66 goats, 9 beehives.

Of this land, 1 free man holds 1 virgate which he could sell; but the jurisdiction lay in (the lands of) this manor. To (the lands of) this manor's church 2 men added 30 acres of another land.

Value always £12.

Of this manor, Grapinel holds ½ hide.

2 smallholders. 1 plough.

Value 10s in the same assessment.

23 Robert son of Wymarc held SHOEBURY after the death of King Edward. Now Swein (holds it) in lordship as one manor, for 5 hides.

Always 9 villagers. Then 4 smallholders, now 6. Always 2 ploughs in lordship; 8 men's ploughs.

Meadow, 3 acres; woodland, 20 pigs. Then 2 cobs, 4 cattle, 12 pigs, 100 sheep; now 2 cobs, 16 pigs, 64 sheep.

Value then and later £6; now [£] 10.

24 Swein holds CANEWDON in lordship for 6½ hides and 30 acres.

Then 22 villagers, now 16; then 2 smallholders, now 8; then 3 slaves, now 1. Then 2 ploughs in lordship, now 3; 4 possible. Then 10 men's ploughs, now 6.

Pasture, 600 sheep. Then 3 cobs, 10 cattle, 24 pigs, 336 sheep; now 3 cobs, 5 cattle, 20 pigs, 342 sheep. 44 b

Value then £12; now [£] 13.

In this manor Hugh de Montfort has 1 hide.

Value 20s.

2 Freemen hold (parts) of this manor, Gerald 1 hide and John 30 acres.

3 smallholders. 1 plough.

Value 40s in the same assessment.

Swein also has 1 hide, 4 smallholders and 1 plough, which 1 free man held before 1066 with the jurisdiction.

Value 20s.

Torpeiam ten& Odo de . S . qđ tenuit Godric . tegn reḡ . E . 7 Rob fili uuimarce habuit p morte reḡ . E . p uno Man . 7 . p . I . hid . 7 . xxx . ac . Tc . I . uilt . m . II . Tc . IIII . bor . m . VI . tc . IIII . ser . m . I . Sep . II . car in dnio . 7 . I . car hom . Past . c . ou . Tc . I . runc . 7 . VII . an . XVIIII . porc . LX VIII . ou . m . VI . an . XXXIIII . porc . CLX . ou . II . uasa ap . Tc ual . XL . sol . P 7 m . LX .

Rochefort ten& Alured de . S . qđ ten . I . lib ho . t . r . e . p . M . 7 p . II . hid . 7 . dim . Sep . V . uilt . Tc . IIII . bor . m . XII . Tc . II . ser . m . III tc . II . car in dnio . m . III . Tc . III . car . hom . m . IIII . 7 . I . lib ho ten& . XXX . ac . 7 adhuc jacent huic man . II . ac pti . Silu . XX . porc . I . mot . Tc . I . runc . 7 . VIII . porc . 7 . XI . ou . m . III . runc . 7 . II . pult . 7 . X . an . 7 . XXI . porc . 7 . CLX . ou . 7 XXIII . ou . Tc ualuit . c . sol . m . VII . lib .

Stanbruge ten& Wiard de . S . qđ tenuit . I . lib ho . t . r . e . p . uno man . 7 . p . I . hid . 7 . dim 7 . VII . ac . 7 . dim . Sep . II . bord . 7 . I . ser . 7 . dim . car . tc . m . I . Past . c . ou . Tc ual . X . sol . m . XXV .

Essobiam . ten& Galt de . S . qđ tenuit . I . lib ho . t . r . e . p . I . Man . 7 . p . IIII . hid . Sep . IIII . uilt . Tc . VI . bor . m . VIII . Tc . II . ser . m . null . Tc . II . car . in dnio . m . III . Sep . II . car hominu . Silu . XII . porc . Quarta hida ex h ten& . I . lib ho Past . c . ou .

45 a

Tc . I . runc . 7 . II . an . 7 . XL . ou . m . I . runc . 7 . VI . an . I . porc . CXV . ou . tc 7 p ual . VI . lib . m VIII .

Wacheringa ten& . S . qđ tenuit . I . lib ho . t . r . e . p . Man . 7 p . II . hid . 7 hoc tenuit Rob fili uuimarcæ p morte reḡ Eduuardi . Tc . I . bor . 7 . XV . ser . m . X . bor . Sep . II . car in dnio . 7 . I . car hom . Past . CCC . ou . Tc . II . an . 7 . C . ou . m . I . runc . 7 . II . an . CXV . ou . I . uas ap . Tc . ual . III . lib P 7 m . IIII . De hoc eod Man . Ten& Rob . I . hid . 7 . Godric . dim . 7 ual . XL . sol in eod . ptio .

25 Odo holds (LITTLE)THORPE from Swein which Godric, a thane of King Edward's, held, and (which) Robert son of Wymarc had after the death of King Edward as one manor, for 1 hide and 30 acres.
Then 1 villager, now 2; then 4 smallholders, now 6; then 4 slaves, now 1. Always 2 ploughs in lordship; 1 men's plough.
Pasture, 100 sheep. Then 1 cob, 7 cattle, 19 pigs, 68 sheep; now 6 cattle, 34 pigs, 160 sheep, 2 beehives.
Value then 40s; later and now 60[s].

26 Alfred holds ROCHFORD from Swein, which 1 free man held before 1066 as a manor, for 2½ hides.
Always 5 villagers. Then 4 smallholders, now 12; then 2 slaves, now 3. Then 2 ploughs in lordship, now 3. Then 3 men's ploughs, now 4.
1 free man holds 30 acres and they also lie in (the lands of) this manor.
Meadow, 2 acres; woodland, 20 pigs; 1 mill. Then 1 cob, 8 pigs and 11 sheep; now 3 cobs, 2 foals, 10 cattle, 21 pigs, 160 sheep and 23 sheep.
Value then 100s; now £7.

27 Wicard holds (Great) STAMBRIDGE from Swein, which 1 free man held before 1066 as one manor, for 1½ hides and 7½ acres.
Always 2 smallholders; 1 slave. ½ plough then, now 1.
Pasture, 100 sheep.
Value then 10s; now 25[s].

28 Walter holds SHOEBURY from Swein, which 1 free man held before 1066 as 1 manor, for 4 hides.
Always 4 villagers. Then 6 smallholders, now 8; then 2 slaves, now none. Then 2 ploughs in lordship, now 3. Always 2 men's ploughs. Woodland, 12 pigs.
1 free man holds the fourth of these hides.
Pasture, 100 sheep. Then 1 cob, 2 cattle, 40 sheep; now 1 cob, 45 a
6 cattle, 1 pig, 115 sheep.
Value then and later £6; now [£] 8.

29 Swein holds (Little) WAKERING, which 1 free man held before 1066 as a manor, for 2 hides. Robert son of Wymarc held this after the death of King Edward.
Then 1 smallholder, 15 slaves; now 10 smallholders. Always 2 ploughs in lordship; 1 men's plough.
Pasture, 300 sheep. Then 2 cattle and 100 sheep; now 1 cob, 2 cattle, 115 sheep, 1 beehive.
Value then £3; later and now [£] 4.
Of this manor, Robert holds 1 hide and Godric ½.
Value 40s in the same assessment.

Suttunã ten& Afcelin̄ de . S . qđ tenuer̄ . II . libi . hões . t . r . e . p . ϖ.
7 . p . I . hid . 7 . dim . 7 . xxx . ac . m̄ . VIII . bord . Tc̄ . IIII . fer . m̄ null.
Sep̄ . II . car in dn̄io 7 . dim . car hom . Past . ccc . ou . Tc̄ . II . runc.
. & . L . porc . cc . ou . m̄ . VII . an . CLX . ou . Tc̄ 7 p uat . LX . fol . m̄ . IIII . lib. ★

Plumbgã ten& Ide . A . de . S . qđ tenuit Rob fili Wimarcæ . p . ϖ . 7 . p
. I . hid . Tc̄ . I . bord . 7 . I . fer . m̄ . VIII . bor . Tc̄ . I . car 7 dim in dn̄io . m̄ . I.
dim . car . hom . Silu . xxx . porc . Past . c . ou . m̄ . I . mol . Tc̄ . I . runc.
. VII . an . xxx . porc . c . ou . XL . cap . m̄ . II . runc . 7 . I . pull . III . an.
xx . porc . c . ou . XXIII . cap . Tc̄ uat . xx . fol . m̄ . XL.

Putefeiam ten& ide . Afc . de . S . qđ tenuit . I . lib hõ . t . r . e . p . ϖ.
7 . LII . ac . 7 . dim . Sep̄ . II . bor . 7 . I . car . Past . xxx . ou . m̄ . I . mol.
Tc̄ . I . runc . 7 . I . pull . 7 . I . an . 7 . III . porc . 7 . LXXX . ou . m̄ fimilit.
Tc̄ 7 p uat . xx . fol . m̄ . xxx.

Hacheleiã ten& Pagan de . S . p . I . ϖ . 7 . p . I . hid . Sep̄ . XII . bord.
7 . I . car . in dn̄io . Tc̄ . II . car . hom . m̄ . I . Silu . xxx . porc . Past.
. cc . ou . M̊ . I . mol . Tc̄ . II . runc . 7 . II . an . 7 . XII . porc . 7 . CLX . ou.
7 . xxx . cap . m̄ . IIII . runc . x . an . XXIIII . porc . ccc . ou . LIII . cap.

45 b

VI . uafa ap . Tc̄ uat . III . lib . m̄ . IIII.

Putefeiam ten& . johs de . S . qd tenuit . I . lib hõ t . r . e . p . ϖ . 7 . p . I . hid
7 . dim . 7 . xxx . ac . Sep̄ . VIII . bor . Past . L . ou . Tc̄ . I . runc . 7 . VIII . porc.
7 . xxv . ou . m̄ . XI . porc . LXXXVI . ou . Vat . XL . fol.

Suttunã ten& Aluid quedã anglica de . S . qđ tenuit Rob fili uuim.
p morte reḡ . E . p uno Man . 7 . p . I . hid . 7 . xv . ac . Sep̄ . III . bord . Tc̄ . II . fer.
m̄ null . Sep̄ . I . car in dn̄io . Tc̄ . II . runc . 7 . x . an . 7 . XI . porc . 7 . c . ou.
m̄ . x . an . x . porc . LXIII . ou . Vat . xxx . fol.

30 Ascelin holds SUTTON from Swein, which 2 free men held before 1066 as a manor, for 1½ hides and 30 acres.

Now 8 smallholders; then 4 slaves, now none. Always 2 ploughs in lordship; ½ men's plough.

Pasture, 300 sheep. Then 2 cobs, 50 pigs, 200 sheep; now 7 cattle, 160 sheep.

Value then and later 60s; now £4.

31 A(scelin) also holds PLUMBEROW from Swein, which Robert son of Wymarc held as a manor, for 1 hide.

Then 1 smallholder and 1 slave; now 8 smallholders. Then 1½ ploughs in lordship, now 1. ½ men's plough.

Woodland, 30 pigs; pasture, 100 sheep; now 1 mill. Then 1 cob, 7 cattle, 30 pigs, 100 sheep, 40 goats; now 2 cobs, 1 foal, 3 cattle, 20 pigs, 100 sheep, 23 goats.

Value then 20s; now 40[s].

32 Ascelin also holds PUDSEY (Hall) from Swein, which 1 free man held before 1066 as a manor, for 52½ acres.

Always 2 smallholders; 1 plough.

Pasture, 30 sheep; now 1 mill. Then 1 cob, 1 foal, 1 (head of) cattle, 3 pigs and 80 sheep; now the same.

Value then and later 20s; now 30[s].

33 Payne holds HOCKLEY from Swein as 1 manor, for 1 hide.

Always 12 smallholders; 1 plough in lordship. Then 2 men's ploughs, now 1.

Woodland, 30 pigs; pasture, 200 sheep; now 1 mill. Then 2 cobs, 2 cattle, 12 pigs, 160 sheep and 30 goats; now 4 cobs,
10 cattle, 24 pigs, 300 sheep, 53 goats, 6 beehives. 45 b

Value then £3; now [£] 4.

34 John holds PUDSEY (Hall) from Swein, which 1 free man held before 1066 as a manor, for 1½ hides and 30 acres.

Always 8 smallholders.

Pasture, 50 sheep. Then 1 cob, 8 pigs, 25 sheep; now 11 pigs, 86 sheep.

Value 40s.

35 Alfith, an Englishwoman, holds SUTTON from Swein, which Robert son of Wymarc held after the death of King Edward as one manor, for 1 hide and 15 acres.

Always 3 smallholders. Then 2 slaves, now none. Always 1 plough in lordship.

Then 2 cobs, 10 cattle, 11 pigs and 100 sheep; now 10 cattle, 10 pigs, 63 sheep.

Value 30s.

Puteseiam ten& Almar de . S . qd ten . i . soc . Robti . p . m . 7 . p dim. hid . 7 . xv . ac . Sep . iii . bord . 7 . i . car in dnio . Past . l . ou . Tc . i . runc. 7 . viii . porc . 7 . xxv . ou . m . xi . porc . 7 . lxxxvi . ou . Val . xxx . sol.

Puteseiam ten& Hugo de . S . qd tenuit . i . lib . ho . t . r . e . 7 . Rob habebat soca . p . m . 7 . xxxviii . ac . Tc . i . uill . m . ii . Sep . dim . car . Past . xxx . ou. Tc . i . runc . 7 . ii . an . 7 . x . porc . lxxv . ou . m . i . runc . 7 . i . uac . 7 . c . xiiii . ou . Val . x . sol.

In Nesenduna ten& Rog dim . hid . de . S . qd tenuit . Rob . Sep . i . bor Past . xl . ou . Tc . i . car . m . dim . 7 . tota pot . fieri . Val . x . sol.

In Suttuna ten& . Rog . dimid hid . qd tenuit . Rob . t . r . e . Sep . i . car . Past . xl . ou . Val . xx . sol.

In Hacheuuella ten& Godefrid . xv . ac . 7 . dim . car . 7 . i . bord . Val x . sol.

In Nestuda ten& Rob . xxx . ac . de . S . 7 . v . bord . Tc . dim . car . m . i . Tc ual . x . sol . m . xx . 7 In hoc pdicto hund ht Suen . de placitis. . c . sol.

Hund de Witbrictesherna . Altenai ten& Rad de Sueno.

46 a

qd tenuit Lestan libe p Man . 7 . p dim hid . 7 . xl . ac . Sep . i. uill . 7 . i . bord . Tc . ii . ser . m . i . Sep . i . car in dnio . 7 . dim . car hou Past . l . ou . Tc . v . anim . 7 . xl . ou . m . v . an . 7 . lx . ou . 7 . xxvi . porc. 7 . ii . runc . Tc 7 p ual . xx . sol . m . xxvi.

Hainctuna ten& Garner de . S . qd tenuit Godric libe . t . r . e. p . m . 7 p dim . hid . 7 . xxxvii . ac . tc . iii . bor . m . ii . Sep . i . car. v . ac . pti . Tc . nichil . m . iii . an . iiii . porc . xi . cap . Val . xx . sol. hoc . m . habuit . R . fili uuimarcæ . p aduentu reg Willi.

36 Aelmer holds PUDSEY (Hall) from Swein, which a Freeman of Robert's held as a manor, for ½ hide and 15 acres.
Always 3 smallholders; 1 plough in lordship.
Pasture, 50 sheep. Then 1 cob, 8 pigs and 25 sheep; now 11 pigs and 86 sheep.
Value 30s.

37 Hugh holds PUDSEY (Hall) from Swein, which 1 free man held before 1066, and Robert had the jurisdiction, as a manor for 38 acres.
Then 1 villager, now 2. Always ½ plough.
Pasture, 30 sheep. Then 1 cob, 2 cattle, 10 pigs, 75 sheep; now 1 cob, 1 cow and 114 sheep.
Value 10s.

38 In ASHINGDON Roger holds ½ hide from Swein, which Robert held.
Always 1 smallholder.
Pasture, 40 sheep. Then 1 plough, now ½; a whole one possible.
Value 10s.

39 In SUTTON Roger holds ½ hide which Robert held before 1066.
Always 1 plough.
Pasture, 40 sheep.
Value 20s.

40 In HAWKWELL Godfrey holds 15 acres. ½ plough.
1 smallholder.
Value 10s.

41 In EASTWOOD Robert holds 30 acres from Swein.
5 smallholders. Then ½ plough, now 1.
Value then 10s; now 20[s].

41a In this said Hundred Swein has 100s from pleas.

Hundred of 'WIBERTSHERNE'

42 Ralph holds ILTNEY (Farm) from Swein, which Leofstan held freely as a manor, for 1½ hides and 40 acres. 46 a
Always 1 villager; 1 smallholder. Then 2 slaves, now 1.
Always 1 plough in lordship; ½ men's plough.
Pasture, 50 sheep. Then 5 cattle, 40 sheep; now 5 cattle, 60 sheep, 26 pigs and 2 cobs.
Value then and later 20s; now 26[s].

43 Warner holds ASHELDHAM from Swein, which Godric held freely before 1066 as a manor, for ½ hide and 37 acres.
Then 3 smallholders, now 2. Always 1 plough.
Meadow, 5 acres. Then nothing; now 3 cattle, 4 pigs, 11 goats.
Value 20s.

Robert son of Wymarc had this manor after the arrival of King William.

Hunđ de Witham Ruuuenhalā ten& Clarenbaldꝰ de . S.
qđ tenuit Leſtanꝰ lib̄ hō . ꝓ . xxx . ac . t . r . e . Sēꝑ . i . car in dn̄io . 7 . đ
car . hom . Tc̄ . v . borđ . m̊ . vi . Sēꝑ . ii . ſer . x . ac . p̊ti . Paſt . de . iiii . ſol.
7 . i . ſoc . de . v . ac . tc̄ . ii . an . 7 . ii . runc . 7 . xv . ou . m̊ . ii . an . ii . runc.
. c . ou . vi . porc . viii . cap̄ . ii . uaſa ap . Tc̄ . ual xl . ſol . m̊ . xxx.

Nuthleam ten& Godeboldꝰ . dim . hid . 7 . xxx . ac . qđ tenuit
Achiꝰ lib̄ hō . t . r . e . ꝓ uno man . Tc̄ . ii . car . in dn̄io . m̊ . i . Tc̄ . ii.
car . hom . m̊ . i . Tc̄ . iiii . uilł . m̊ . ii . Tc̄ . iiii . borđ . m̊ . v . Tc̄ . ii . ſer.
m̊ . nullꝰ . Tc̄ . ſilu . xl . porc . m̊ . xxx . x . ac . p̊ti . Tc̄ . i . runc . 7 . ii . uac.
m̊ . ii . runc . 7 viii . an . xxx . porc . xi . ou . x . uaſa . ap . Tc̄ ual . xl . ſol.
m̊ . lx.

Hunđ de Herlaua . Halingebiam ten& Galt̄ . de . S . qđ ten
Godricꝰ lib̄ hō . ꝓ uno man . 7 . ꝓ . ii . hid . 7 . dim . Sēꝑ . ii . car . in dn̄io.
Tc̄ . iii . car . hom . m̊ . iiii . Tc̄ . viii . uilł . m̊ . x . m̊ . xvii . borđ . Sēꝑ
. iiii . ſer . Tc̄ ſilu . cl . porc . m̊ . c . xxx . ac . p̊ti . m̊ dim . mol.
Tc̄ . ii . runc . 7 . vi . an . 7 . xxiiii . porc . xxx . ou . xxx . cap . m̊ . ii.
pulł . 7 . vii . an . 7 . xiii . porc . l . ou . xxxii . cap . vii . uaſa . apū.

46 b
Tc̄ ual . c . ſol . m̊ . vi . lib̄.

Hunđ de Dommauua . Willingehalam ten& Garnerꝰ de
. Sueno qđ tenuit . i . lib̄ hō t . r . e . ꝓ . xx . ac . Tc̄ . ual . iiii . ſol . m̊ viii.

Dommauuā . ten& Edmarꝰ de . S . qđ tenuit . i . lib̄ hō . t . r . e . ꝓ
xxxvii . ac . 7 illæ . vii . ac . sť additæ p̄ aduentū regꝰ Willi . quæ
fuer cujdā aliꝰ libi hōis . Tc̄ . dim . car . m̊ . i . Tc̄ . ii . bor . m̊ . iii . Sēꝑ
. i . ſer . Silu . xxx . porc . v . ac . p̊ti . m̊ . i . mol . Tc̄ . iiii . an . ix . porc.
xi . ou . v . cap . m̊ . v . anim . viii . porc . xiii . oues . vii . cap.
Tc̄ ual . x . ſol . m̊ . xx.

Hundred of WITHAM

44 Clarenbold holds RIVENHALL from Swein, which Leofstan, a free man, held for 30 acres before 1066. Always 1 plough in lordship; ½ men's plough.

Then 5 smallholders, now 6; always 2 slaves.

Meadow, 10 acres; pasture at 4s; 1 Freeman with 5 acres.

Then 2 cattle, 2 cobs, 15 sheep; now 2 cattle, 2 cobs, 100 sheep, 6 pigs, 8 goats, 2 beehives.

Value then 40s; now 30[s].

45 Godbold holds NOTLEY, ½ hide and 30 acres, which Aki, a free man, held before 1066 as one manor. Then 2 ploughs in lordship, now 1. Then 2 men's ploughs, now 1.

Then 4 villagers, now 2; then 4 smallholders, now 5; then 2 slaves, now none.

Woodland, then 40 pigs, now 30; meadow, 10 acres. Then 1 cob, 2 cows; now 2 cobs, 8 cattle, 30 pigs, 11 sheep, 10 beehives.

Value then 40s; now 60[s].

Hundred of HARLOW

46 Walter holds (Little) HALLINGBURY from Swein which Godric, a free man, held as one manor for 2½ hides. Always 2 ploughs in lordship. Then 3 men's ploughs, now 4.

Then 8 villagers, now 10; now 17 smallholders; always 4 slaves.

Woodland, then 150 pigs, now 100; meadow, 30 acres; now ½ mill. Then 2 cobs, 6 cattle, 24 pigs, 30 sheep, 30 goats; now 2 foals, 7 cattle, 13 pigs, 50 sheep, 32 goats, 7 beehives.

Value then 100s; now £6. 46 b

Hundred of DUNMOW

47 Warner holds WILLINGALE from Swein, which 1 free man held before 1066 for 20 acres.

Value then 4s; now 8[s].

48 Edmer holds DUNMOW from Swein, which 1 free man held before 1066, for 37 acres, and the 7 acres were added after the arrival of King William (and) were those of another free man. Then ½ plough, now 1.

Then 2 smallholders, now 3; always 1 slave.

Woodland, 30 pigs; meadow, 5 acres; now 1 mill. Then 4 cattle, 9 pigs, 11 sheep, 5 goats; now 5 cattle, 8 pigs, 13 sheep, 7 goats.

Value then 10s; now 20[s].

Hunđ de Wenſiſtreu Mereſai ten& Suen̄ in dn̄io qđ ten̄
Rob̄ fili uuimarcæ . t . r . e . p . ɱ . 7 . p . vi . hid . Sēp . ii . car . in dn̄io.
Tc̄ . viii . car . m̊ . vi . Tc̄ . ix . uill . m̊ . viii . Tc̄ . xii . bor . m̊ . xiiii.
Tc̄ . iii . ſer . m̊ null . Tc̄ ſilu . xl . porc . v . ac . p̊ti . iiii . piſcinæ.
Tc̄ . i . runc . ix . an . xxv . porc . cvii . ou . m̊ . iii . runc . xii . an.
. x . porc . c . ou . i . uas . ap . Val . x . lib.
Peltendunā ten& . Odo de Sueno qđ tenuit . i . lib . hō . t . r . e . p ɱ.
7 . p . dim . hid . Sēp . dim . car . Val . x . sol.
Edburgetunā ten& Idē . p . xv . ac . qs tenuit . i . lib hō . t . r . e.
Tc̄ . i . lib homo . m̊ . i . borđ . v . ac . p̊ti . Val . v . sol
Dimidium Hunđ de clauelinga ē sueni . 7 placita de
eođ hunđ reddt̄ ſibi p annū . xxv . sol.
Dimidiū Hunđ de Clauelinga Clauelinga ten&
Suen in dn̄io . qđ tenuit Rob̄ fili uuimarcæ . t . r . e . p uno . Man.
7 . p . xv . hid . Tc̄ . 7 p . iiii . car in dn̄io . m̊ . v . Sēp . xxv . car hoū.
7 . xvii . uill . Tc̄ 7 p . ix . borđ . m̊ . xxxvii . Tc̄ 7 p . viii . ſer . m̊ xii.

47 a

Tc̄ ſilu . dccc . porc . m̊ . dc . xxxv . ac . p̊ti . Tc̄ . i . mol . 7 . i . car.
pot reſtaurari in hoc man . Tc̄ . iii . runc . 7 . xxv . an . l . porc . xl . ou
xv . cap . xii . uaſa apū . m̊ . ii . runc . 7 . i . pull xiiii . an . xxi . porc.
. xc . ou . xxiii . cap . v . uaſa ap . Tc̄ ual . xx . lib . m̊ . xxx.
Berdane tenuit Godman . i . ſoc . Robti . t . r . e . m̊ ten& Alured.
de . S . p . ɱ . 7 . p . ii . hid . Sēp . i . car . in dn̄io . 7 . ii . car . hom . 7 . iiii . uill.
7 . v . borđ . Tc̄ 7 p . iiii . ſer . m̊ null . Silu . x . porc . ii . ac . p̊ti . Tc̄
. xiiii . porc . 7 . xxv . ou . M . iii . runc . 7 . ii . pull . 7 . xiii . an . 7 . xxi . porc.
. cxxii . ou . viii . cap . i . uas . ap . Tc̄ ual . xxx . sol . m̊ . xl.
Hunđ de Wibrictesherna . Haintunā ten& Rađ de . S.
p . ɱ . 7 p . dim hid . 7 . xxxvii . ac . qđ tenuit . i . lib hō . t . r . e . Sēp . i . car.

Hundred of WINSTREE

49 Swein holds (East) MERSEA in lordship, which Robert son of Wymarc held before 1066 as a manor, for 6 hides. Always 2 ploughs in lordship. Then 8 [men's] ploughs, now 6.
Then 9 villagers, now 8; then 12 smallholders, now 14; then 3 slaves, now none.
Woodland, then 40 pigs; meadow, 5 acres; 4 fisheries. Then 1 cob, 9 cattle, 25 pigs, 107 sheep; now 3 cobs, 12 cattle, 10 pigs, 100 sheep, 1 beehive.
Value £10.

50 Odo holds PELDON from Swein, which 1 free man held before 1066 as a manor, for ½ hide. Always ½ plough.
Value 10s.

51 He also holds ABBERTON for 15 acres, which 1 free man held before 1066.
Then 1 free man; now 1 smallholder.
Meadow, 5 acres.
Value 5s.

52 The Half-Hundred of CLAVERING is Swein's. The pleas of this Hundred pay him 25s a year.

Half-Hundred of CLAVERING

53 Swein holds CLAVERING in lordship, which Robert son of Wymarc held before 1066 as one manor, for 15 hides. Then and later 4 ploughs in lordship, now 5. Always 25 men's ploughs;
17 villagers. Then and later 9 smallholders, now 37; then and later 8 slaves, now 12.
Woodland, then 800 pigs, now 600; meadow, 35 acres; then 47 a
1 mill; 1 plough can be restored in this manor. Then 3 cobs, 25 cattle, 50 pigs, 40 sheep, 15 goats, 12 beehives; now 2 cobs, 1 foal, 14 cattle, 21 pigs, 90 sheep, 23 goats, 5 beehives.
Value then £20; now [£] 30.

54 Godman, a Freeman of Robert's, held BERDEN before 1066. Now Alfred holds it from Swein as a manor, for 2 hides. Always 1 plough in lordship; 2 men's ploughs.
4 villagers; 5 smallholders. Then and later 4 slaves, now none.
Woodland, 10 pigs; meadow, 2 acres. Then 14 pigs and 25 sheep; now 3 cobs, 2 foals, 13 cattle, 21 pigs, 122 sheep, 8 goats, 1 beehive.
Value then 30s; now 40[s].

Hundred of 'WIBERTSHERNE'

55 Ralph holds ASHELDHAM from Swein as a manor, for ½ hide and 37 acres, which 1 free man held before 1066. Always 1 plough.

Tc . III . bor . m . II . v . ac . pti . Val . xx . sol . Hanc tra habuit Rob filius uuimarce ꝓ aduentu reg Willi.

De Supdicto manerio scilic& de Clauelinga tenet Ansgot . dim . h. 7 . xxx . ac . de Sueno . 7 Wicard . III . uirg . 7 Rob dim . hid . 7 . xv . ac. 7 Rad . xv . ac . 7 int totu . XIIII . bord . 7 . III . car . 7 . dim . 7 totu ual . IIII . lib in eod ptio.

Hund de Lexendena . Eiland tenuit . R . ꝓ uno . Man . 7 . ꝓ . v. hid . 7 . dim . m ten& . S . in dnio . Sep . XVIII . uill . Tc . XXXIII . bor . m. . XLII . Sep . VII . ser . 7 . II . car . in dnio . 7 . x . car . hom . Silu . dc . porc. XXIIII . ac . pti . Sep . I . mol . Tc . ual . x . lib . m . XII . De hoc maner. ten& Godebold de Sueno . I . hid . 7 . dim . 7 . xxx . ac . 7 . II . uill. 7 . VIII . bord . 7 . II . car . in dnio . 7 . II . car . hom . 7 Val LX . sol in eod ptio . Adhuc ten& Idem . XXXVII . libos hoes . manentes . in . III . hid træ . qs habuit . Rob . t . r . e . 7 Suen postea . Tc . int eos . IIII.

47 b

m . v . m . I . mol . Silu . LX . porc . XIIII . ac . pti Tc ual . IIII . lib . m . c . sol . 7 qda lib homo erat comdat Robto tenuit . VII . ac. 7 . dim . 7 potat ire q uell& . 7 illa tra ht Suen . Val . v . sol.

Hund de Celmeresforda . Borham ten& . Osbt . de . S . qd ten. Turchill ꝓ uno Man . 7 . ꝓ . I . hid . Sep . I . bord . m . I . ser . Tc . I . car . m null . VIII . ac pti . Val . xx . sol.

Hund de Angra Staplefort ten& Siric . de Sueno . qd ten. Godric . ꝓ uno man . 7 . ꝓ . v . hid . 7 de his . v . hid . dedit suis . x . libis hominib; libe . IIII . hid . 7 . I . retinuit in dnio . 7 pq rex aduenit :

Then 3 smallholders, now 2.
Meadow, 5 acres.
Value 20s.
Robert son of Wymarc had this land after the arrival of King William.

[Half-Hundred of CLAVERING]

56 Of the above manor, namely CLAVERING, Ansgot holds ½ hide and 30 acres from Swein, Wicard 3 virgates, Robert ½ hide and 15 acres, and Ralph 15 acres.
In total 14 smallholders; 3½ ploughs.
Value of the whole £4 in the same assessment.

Hundred of LEXDEN

57 R(obert) held NAYLAND as one manor, for 5½ hides. Now Swein holds it in lordship.
Always 18 villagers. Then 33 smallholders, now 42. Always 7 slaves; 2 ploughs in lordship; 10 men's ploughs.
Woodland, 600 pigs; meadow, 24 acres; always 1 mill.
Value then £10; now [£] 12.
Of this manor, Godbold holds from Swein 1½ hides and 30 acres.
2 villagers; 8 smallholders. 2 ploughs in lordship. 2 men's ploughs.
Value 60s in the same assessment.
He also holds 37 free men who dwell on 3 hides of land, whom Robert had before 1066, and Swein later on.
Then among them 4 [ploughs], now 5. 47 b
Now 1 mill; woodland, 60 pigs; meadow, 14 acres.
Value then £4; now 100s.
A free man was under the patronage of Robert. He held 7½ acres and could go whither he would. Swein has that land.
Value 5s.

Hundred of CHELMSFORD

58 Osbert holds BOREHAM from Swein, which Thorkell held as one manor, for 1 hide.
Always 1 smallholder. Now 1 slave. Then 1 plough, now none.
Meadow, 8 acres.
Value 20s.

Hundred of ONGAR

59 Siric holds STAPLEFORD (Tawney) from Swein, which Godric held as one manor, for 5 hides. Of these 5 hides, he freely gave 4 hides to his 10 free men and kept one in lordship. After the King came,

dono reg̃ tenuit Rob̃ . I . hidᵗ . 7 Suen⁹ fili⁹ ej⁹ adjunxit . IIII . hidᵗ . cũ
iſta . poſt mortẽ patris ſui . Tc̃ in . I . hida . null⁹ bordari⁹ erat . 7 tc̃
in . IIII . hidᵗ . VI . bordᵗ . m̊ . II . uill̃ . 7 XVIII . bordᵗ . Siluᵗ . CCC . porcᵗ . XX .
acᵗ . p̃ti . Sep̃ . I . mol̃ . Tc̃ . ual̃ . VIII . lib̃ . m̊ . X . Tc̃ . in dñio . I . uacᵗ . 7
. XIII . ouᵗ . m̊ . VIII . anᵗ . 7 . XVII . porcᵗ . CXVIII . ouᵗ . II . uaſa . apũ.

Teidanam ten& Rob̃ de . S . qd̃ tenuit . Godric⁹ . ꝓ uno manᵗ . 7 . ꝓ .
III . hidᵗ . 7 . LXXX . acᵗ . 7 . S . ten& hoc Manᵗ de dono regis . Willi qd̃ dedit
patri . ſuo . Robto . Tc̃ . V . uill̃ . m̊ . I . Tc̃ . III . bordᵗ . m̊ . XVII . Tc̃ . IIII . ſer̃ .
m̊ . null⁹ . Tc̃ . in dñio . II . carᵗ . m̊ . III . Tc̃ . int̃ hoẽs . IIII . carᵗ . m̊ . III .
Siluᵗ . D . porcᵗ . XXVIII . acᵗ . p̃ti . Tc̃ . I . runcᵗ . 7 . XII . anᵗ . LX . por . C . ou.
m̊ . III . runcᵗ . III . pull̃ . XIII . anᵗ . XXXIX . porcᵗ . CXLVIII . ouᵗ . Tc̃ . ual̃ .
VI . lib̃ . 7 qñ recᵗ ſimil̃ . m̊ ual̃ . IX .

Hund̃ de Ceſſeurda . Warleiã tenuit Godric⁹ lib̃e . ꝓ uno Manᵗ .
7 . ꝓ . II . hidᵗ . tᵗ . rᵗ . eᵗ . m̊ . S . ſimil̃ in ſuo dñio . Tc̃ . II . uill̃ . m̊ . III . Tc̃ . II .
bordᵗ . m̊ . VIII . Tc̃ . III . ſerᵗ . m̊ . I . Sep̃ . II . carᵗ . in dñio . Tc̃ . int̃ hoẽs . I . car.
m̊ . II . 7 . dimᵗ . Siluᵗ . CL . porcᵗ . III . acᵗ . p̃ti . Tc̃ . II . runcᵗ . 7 . VII . anᵗ . 7 . XVII . porc. ★

48 a

Tc̃ ual̃ . IIII . lib̃ . 7 . qñ recᵗ . ſimilit̃ . m̊ . VI . lib̃ . ★

Helitunã ten& Leuuin⁹ de . S . qd̃ tenuit Vſtanᵗ . lib̃e . ꝓ . Ⓜ . 7 . ꝓ . I .
hidᵗ . tᵗ . rᵗ . eᵗ . Tc̃ . III . bordᵗ . m̊ . IIII . 7 . I . carᵗ . I . uacᵗ . 7 . II . anᵗ . XVI . porc.
. XXX . ouᵗ . Val̃ . XX . ſol̃ .

Dimᵗ Hund̃ de Melduna . In Melduna tenuit . Rob̃ . dimᵗ .
hidᵗ . m̊ ten& . S . 7 . Guner⁹ de . eo . 7 . in hac t̃ra hab& rex . IIII . ſol̃ de
conſuetudine . 7 facit adjutorium cum alijs burgenſibꝫ . inuenire
caballũ in exercitu . 7 ad nauẽ faciendã . c&as uero conſuetudines . ht̃
Suen⁹ . Sep̃ . I . bor . 7 . I . carᵗ . 7 . ual̃ . XX . ſol̃ .

Robert held 1 hide as a gift of the King; Swein, his son, joined 4 hides with that one after his father's death.

Then on 1 hide there were no smallholders, then on 4 hides 6 smallholders; now 2 villagers and 18 smallholders.

Woodland, 300 pigs; meadow, 20 acres; always 1 mill.

Value then £8; now [£] 10.

Then in lordship 1 cow and 13 sheep; now 8 cattle, 17 pigs, 118 sheep, 2 beehives.

60 Robert holds THEYDON (Mount) from Swein, which Godric held as one manor, for 3 hides and 80 acres. Swein holds this manor as a gift of King William, which he gave to his father, Robert.

Then 5 villagers, now 1; then 3 smallholders, now 17; then 4 slaves, now none. Then 2 ploughs in lordship, now 3. Then among the men 4 ploughs, now 3.

Woodland, 500 pigs; meadow, 28 acres. Then 1 cob, 12 cattle, 60 pigs, 100 sheep; now 3 cobs, 3 foals, 13 cattle, 39 pigs, 148 sheep.

Value then £6; when acquired, the same. Value now [£] 9.

Hundred of CHAFFORD

61 Godric held WARLEY freely as one manor, for 2 hides before 1066. Now Swein (holds it) likewise in his lordship.

Then 2 villagers, now 3; then 2 smallholders, now 8; then 3 slaves, now 1. Always 2 ploughs in lordship. Then among the men 1 plough, now 2½.

Woodland, 150 pigs; meadow, 3 acres. Then 3 cobs, 7 cattle and 17 pigs.

Value then £4; when acquired, the same; now £6. 48 a

62 Leofstan holds KENNINGTONS from Swein, which Wulfstan held freely as a manor, for 1 hide before 1066.

Then 3 smallholders, now 4. 1 plough.

1 cow, 2 cattle, 16 pigs, 30 sheep.

Value 20s.

Half-Hundred of MALDON

63 Robert held ½ hide in MALDON. Now Swein holds it and Gunner from him. In this land the King has 3s from customary dues; and he aids the other burgesses to find a horse on campaign and to make a ship. But Swein has the other dues.

Always 1 smallholder; 1 plough.

Value 20s.

Hund de Tendringe. Almestedā tenuit Rob fili uuimarc.
m Suen. 7 Siric de eo. p uno Man. 7. p. VIII. hid. Tc. XIIII. uilt
m. XIII. Tc. XXXI. bord. m. XXXVI. Tc. VI. ser. m. I. Tc. in dnio.
. III. car. m. IIII. Tc. XIX. car hom. m. XVIII. Silu. D. porc.
XXII. ac. pti. Past. LX. ou. Sēp. I. mol. 7. I. sal. Tc. III. runc.
7. XVIII. an. 7 XXX. porc. CL. ou. XL. cap. V. uasa ap. m. V.
runc. X. an. XXXII. porc. CXC. ou. LXXX. cap. II. uasa apū.
Tc ual. IX. lib. m. X.

Fuletunā ten& Odard. de. S. qd tenuit Bricsi. p. I. hid.
X. ac. min. 7. p. uno Man. Hanc trā tenuit Iste libe. & qndo
rex uenit in hanc trā: utlagauit. 7. R. accep. trā suam. pea
habuit. S. Sēp. ibi. ē. I. bord. 7. I. ser. 7. I. car. 7. II. ac. pti. past.
. C. ou. Tc. nichil rec. m. VI. an. 7. X. porc. 7. XX. ou. 7. II.
uasa apū. Tc. ual. X. sol. m. XX.

Hund de Turestapla. Toleshuntā ten& Odo. de Sueno
qd tenuit Brun p. Man. 7. p. I. hid. 7. dim. 7. XL. ac. s; Rob habuit

48 b

pquam rex uenit in hanc trā. 7 m ht. S. M. ibi. st. IIII. bord ★
Tc. II. ser. m. I. Silu. XII. porc. Past. XX. ou. Tc. II. an. 7. I. runc. 7
. XX. ou. m. XII. an. II. runc. XII. porc. LXXX. ou. Tc ual. XX. sol.
m. XXV.

Totham tenuit Gunner. t. r. e. 7 adhuc ten& sub Sueno. p. XXX.
ac. Sēp. III. bord. Tc. dim. car. m simil. Silu. XX. porc. Past. LX. ou.
val. X. sol.

Hundred of TENDRING

64 Robert son of Wymarc held ELMSTEAD. Now Swein (holds it) and Siric from him as one manor, for 8 hides.

Then 14 smallholders, now 13; then 31 smallholders, now 36; then 6 slaves, now 1. Then 3 ploughs in lordship, now 4. Then 19 men's ploughs, now 18.

Woodland, 500 pigs; meadow, 22 acres; pasture, 60 sheep. Always 1 mill; 1 salt-house. Then 3 cobs, 18 cattle, 30 pigs, 150 sheep, 40 goats, 5 beehives; now 5 cobs, 10 cattle, 32 pigs, 190 sheep, 80 goats, 2 beehives.

Value then £9; now [£] 10.

65 Odard holds FOULTON from Swein, which Brictsi held for 1 hide less 10 acres, as one manor. He held this land freely and when the King came to this land, he was outlawed and Robert received his land; later on Swein had (it).

Always 1 smallholder there; 1 slave; 1 plough.

Meadow, 2 acres; pasture, 100 sheep. Then he acquired nothing; now 6 cattle, 10 pigs, 20 sheep and 2 beehives.

Value then 10s; now 20[s].

Hundred of THURSTABLE

66 Odo holds TOLLESHUNT from Swein, which Brown held as a manor, for 1½ hides and 40 acres. But Robert had it after the King came 48 b
to this land and now Swein has it.

Now 4 smallholders there; then 2 slaves, now 1.

Woodland, 12 pigs; pasture, 20 sheep. Then 2 cattle, 1 cob and 20 sheep; now 12 cattle, 2 cobs, 12 pigs, 80 sheep.

Value then 20s; now 25[s].

67 Gunner held (Little) TOTHAM before 1066 and still holds it under Swein for 30 acres.

Always 3 smallholders. Then ½ plough, now the same.

Woodland, 20 pigs; pasture, 60 sheep.

Value 10s.

TERRA EudoniS dapiferi. .XXV.

Hund de Witham Brachestedam ten& Ricard de. E.
qd tenuit tegn reg. p uno man. 7. p. II. hid. xv. ac. min. Sep. II.
car in dnio. 7. III. car. houm. Tc. v. uill. m. vI. Tc. IIII. bord. m. vI.
Tc. II. ser. m null. Silua. ccc. porc. xxx. ac. pti. m dim mol.
.I. soc. de. IIII. ac. Tc. II. runc. 7. XIIII. an. XL. porc. LXXX. ou. m. I.
runc. vI. an. XLVI. porc. cx. ou. IIII. uasa apu. Val. vIII. lib.

Dim Hund de Herlaua. Herlaua ten& Turgis de. Eudone
qd tenuit Goduin lib homo. t. r. e. p. m. 7. p. I. hid. 7. III. uirg. Tc.
.II. car in dnio. m. I. Tc. I. car hom. m nulla. Tc. III. uill. m. null.
m. II. bord. Tc. II. ser. m. I. Silu. L. porc. x. ac. pti. Tc. I. an. 7
xxx. ou. m. xvIII. an. IIII. runc. xvIIII. porc. LXXV. II. uasa ap.
De hac tra st. L. ac. que fuer additæ. t. r. Willi. 7 eas addidit Lefsi huic
træ. Sep ual. XL. sol.

Hund de dommauua. Rodinges ten& turgisus de Eudone
qd tenuit Samar lib ho. t. r. e. p. I. hid. 7. dim. 7. XLV. ac. Sep. II. car
in dnio. Tc. II. car. hom. m. I. Tc. IX. uill. m. III. tc. I. bord. m
.III. Tc. III. ser. m. I. Silu. c. porc. XIX. ac. pti. Tc. I. runc. m.
.vII. Tc. x. an. m. xxv. Tc. vI. porc. m LXXXIX. Tc. L. ou. m. ccxxv.
m. Lv. cap. 7. vIII. uasa ap. Tc ual. c. sol. m. vI. lib. Hoc Man. calupniat abb de eli.

Lindeseles ten& Eudo in dnio. qd tenuit Vlmar lib ho. t. r. e. |teste hund.
p uno Man. 7 p. I. hid. Sep. II. car. in dnio. 7. III. car. hom. IX. uill.
7. I. pbr. Tc. I. bord. m. IX. Tc. IIII. ser. m. I. Silu. xxx. porc.
vI. ac. pti. m. I. mol. Tc. I. runc. 7. v. an. 7. LX. porc. M. I. runc. 7

49 b

Tc ual. c. sol. m. vI. lib Et hoc manerium tale erat qn recep.

25 LAND OF EUDO THE STEWARD 49 a

Hundred of WITHAM

1 Richard holds (Great) BRAXTED from Eudo, which a King's thane held as one manor, for 2 hides less 15 acres. Always 2 ploughs in lordship; 3 men's ploughs.

Then 5 villagers, now 6; then 4 smallholders, now 6; then 2 slaves, now none.

Woodland, 300 pigs; meadow, 30 acres; now ½ mill; 1 Freeman with 4 acres. Then 2 cobs, 14 cattle, 40 pigs, 80 sheep; now 1 cob, 6 cattle, 46 pigs, 110 sheep, 4 beehives.

Value £8.

Half-Hundred of HARLOW

2 Thorgils holds HARLOW from Eudo which Godwin, a free man, held before 1066 as a manor, for 1 hide and 3 virgates. Then 2 ploughs in lordship, now 1. Then 1 men's plough, now none.

Then 3 villagers, now none; now 2 smallholders; then 2 slaves, now 1.

Woodland, 50 pigs; meadow, 10 acres. Then 1 (head of) cattle and 30 sheep; now 18 cattle, 4 cobs, 19 pigs, 75 [sheep], 2 beehives.

Of this land, there are 50 acres which were added after 1066 and Leofsi added them to this land.

Value always 40s.

Hundred of DUNMOW

3 Thorgils holds ('Morrell') RODING from Eudo which Saemer, a free man, held before 1066 for 1½ hides and 45 acres. Always 2 ploughs in lordship. Then 2 men's ploughs, now 1.

Then 9 villagers, now 3; then 1 smallholder, now 3; then 3 slaves, now 1.

Woodland, 100 pigs; meadow, 19 acres. Then 1 cob, now 7; then 10 cattle, now 25; then 6 pigs, now 89; then 50 sheep, now 225; now 55 goats and 8 beehives.

Value then 100s; now £6.

The Abbot of Ely lays claim to this manor as the Hundred testifies.

4 Eudo holds LINDSELL in lordship which Wulfmer, a free man, held before 1066 as one manor, for 1 hide. Always 2 ploughs in lordship; 3 men's ploughs;

9 villagers; 1 priest. Then 1 smallholder, now 9; then 4 slaves, now 1.

Woodland, 30 pigs; meadow, 6 acres; now 1 mill. Then 1 cob, 5 cattle, 60 pigs; now 1 cob, ...

Value then 100s; now £6. And this manor was worth that much when acquired. 49 b

⸿ Hunđ de Witbrictesherna Mundunā tenuit Goduin teinn
reḡ . ꝓ uno man . 7 ꝓ . x . hid . M ten& Eudo in dn̄io . Tc̄ . x . uitt . m̄ . xv.
Tc̄ . viii . bord . m̄ . xiiii . Tc̄ . ix . ser . m̄ . vii . 7 . ii . franci hōes hn̄tes . dim . hid.
quā occupauit Lisois . q̄a un illoꝝ utllagauit . In hoc manerio . sт̄ . iiii.
car . in dn̄io . Tc̄ . viii . car . hom . m̄ . x . 7 . ii . arpenni uineæ . Silu . xxiiii.
porc . Past . cc . ou Tc̄ . iiii . runc . 7 . viii . an . xl . porc . ccl . m̄ . iiii . runc.
7 . xv . an . 7 lxv . porc . cccliiii . ou . iiii . uasa ap . Tc̄ . ual . x . lib.
m̄ . xvii : 7 fuit ad firmā ꝓ . xxx . lib sub ipso eudone | huic manerio adjacent . xxx . ac . Tc̄ . ualebant . xxx . đ.
m̄ . xxxvi . Adjacent adhuc . xx . ac . de Wringehala . q̄s ten& . i . soc.
Tc̄ . ual . xx . đ . m̄ . iii . sol.

⸿ Lalinge ten& Ricard de . E . qđ tenuit Vluric cassa ꝓ . m̄ . 7 . ꝓ . iii
hid . t . r . e . 7 dim ; Tc̄ . iiii . ser . m̄ . iii . m̄ . i . borđ . Tc̄ . ii . car in dn̄io . m̄
. i . Tc̄ . i . runc . m̄ n̄ . Tc̄ . lxxxvii . ou . m̄ . lxiii . Tc̄ . ual . lx . sol . qn̄ rec.
. xl . sol . m̄ . iiii . lib.

Steplam ten& Idē . R . de . E . qđ tenuit Normann . t . r . e . ꝓ . m̄ . 7 . pro
. iii . hid . 7 . xxxv . ac . Sēp . i . bord . 7 . ii . ser . 7 . ii . car . Silu . x . porc . Tc̄ . vi.
anim . m̄ . xxvii . Sēp . i . runc . 7 . xv . porc . Tc̄ . cxx . ou . m̄ . clx . Val
. iiii . lib.

⸿ Donā ten& Idē . R . de . E . qđ tenuit Modinc . t . r . e . ꝓ . m̄ . 7 . ꝓ . ii.
hid . 7 . xx . ac . Sēp . ii . bord . 7 . ii . ser . 7 . i . car . Pastura . c . ou . Tc̄ . i . runc.
m̄ . iii . m̄ . iii . an . Tc̄ . cxx . ou . m̄ . clx . i . min . Val . lx . sol.

⸿ Landunā ten& Idē . R . de . E . qđ tenuerunt . iiii . libi hōes . t . r . e.
ꝓ . dim hid . 7 . xx . ac . Sēp . dim . car . Val . x . sol . ⸿ Acletā ten& Idē
de . E . qđ ten . Modinc ꝓ . m̄ . 7 ꝓ . i . 7 dim . 7 . x . ac . Sēp . i . borđ . 7 . i . car.

50 a

pastura . c . ouibꝫ Sēp . ii . animal . 7 . lxxx . ou . 7 . ix . porc . Tc̄ 7 post ual . xl.
sol . m̄ . l.

Hundred of 'WIBERTSHERNE'

5 Godwin, a King's thane, held MUNDON as one manor, for 10 hides. Now Eudo holds it in lordship.

Then 10 villagers, now 15; then 8 smallholders, now 14; then 9 slaves, now 7. 2 freemen who have ½ hide which Lisois appropriated because one of them was outlawed. In this manor are 4 ploughs in lordship. Then 8 men's ploughs, now 10.

2 *arpents* of vines; woodland, 24 pigs; pasture, 200 sheep. Then 4 cobs, 8 cattle, 40 pigs, 250 [sheep] ; now 4 cobs, 15 cattle, 65 pigs, 354 sheep, 4 beehives.

Value then £10; now [£] 17. It was at a revenue under Eudo himself for £19.

30 acres are attached to this manor.

Value then 30d; now 36[d].

A further 20 acres of *Wringehala* are attached, which 1 Freeman holds.

Value then 20d; now 3s.

6 Richard holds LAWLING from Eudo, which Wulfric Cave held as a manor, for 3½ hides before 1066.

Then 4 slaves, now 3; now 1 smallholder. Then 2 ploughs in lordship, now 1.

Then 1 cob, now none; then 87 sheep, now 63.

Value then 60s; when acquired, 40s; now £4.

7 Richard also holds STEEPLE from Eudo, which Norman held before 1066 as a manor, for 3 hides and 35 acres.

Always 1 smallholder; 2 slaves; 2 ploughs.

Woodland, 10 pigs. Then 6 cattle, now 27. Always 1 cob; 15 pigs. Then 120 sheep, now 160.

Value £4.

8 Richard also holds DOWN (Hall) from Eudo, which Moding held before 1066 as a manor, for 2 hides and 20 acres.

Always 2 smallholders; 2 slaves; 1 plough.

Pasture, 100 sheep. Then 1 cob, now 3; now 3 cattle; then 120 sheep, now 160 less 1.

Value 60s.

9 Richard also holds *LANDUNA* from Eudo, which 4 free men held before 1066 for ½ hide and 20 acres. Always ½ plough.

Value 10s.

10 He also holds *ACLETA* from Eudo, which Moding held as a manor, for 1½ [hides] and 10 acres.

Always 1 smallholder; 1 plough.

Pasture, 100 sheep. Always 2 cattle, 80 sheep and 9 pigs. 50 a

Value then and later 40s; now 50[s].

Hund de Rochefort. Hechuuellā ten& Pirot de. Eudone qđ ten Vlmer. t. r. e. p Man. 7. p. III. hid. 7. dim. xv. ac. min. Tc. XI. uitti. m̄ VIII. Sēp. v. bord. Tc. II. ser. m̄. III. Sēp. II. car. in dn̄io. Tc. VI. car. hominū. m̄ v. IIII. ac. pti. Silu. x. porc. Tc. II. runc. 7. v. an. CII. ou. xx. porc. m̄. XVI. an. CVI. ou. xx. porc. II. uasa apū. Tc 7 p uat. VI. lib. m̄. VII.

In Supdicto hund de dōmauua ten&. Ricard de Eudone. I. Man de. IX. ac. qđ uocat. Brochesheuot. qđ tenuer. II. sochem. t. r. e. de abbe de eli. Tc. III. car in dnio. m̄. II. 7. dim. M. I. car hom. 7. II. uilt. Tc. III. bor m̄. v. Tc. III. ser. m̄. I. Silu. c. porc. VI. ac. pti. Tc. I. runc. 7. III. an. 7. XVI. porc. m̄. v. an. XXXIII. porc. Tc 7 p uat. LX. sol. m̄. IIII. lib.

Scelgā ten& Eudo in dn̄io qđ tenuit Vlmar lib hō. t. r. e. p. ω. 7. p. dim hida. Sēp. dim car in dn̄io. m̄. II. bord. Silu. XVI. porc. IIII. ac. pti. Vat sēp. x. sol.

Dommauuā ten&. Rađ de. E. qđ tenuit. I. lib hō. t. r. e. p Man. 7. p. XXXVII. ac. 7 dim. Sēp. dim. car in dn̄io. 7. dim. car. hom. 7. II. uilt. m̄. II. bor. Tc. I. ser. m̄ null. Silu. xv. porc. IIII. ac. pti. Tc 7 p uat. x. sol m̄. xx. 7 in eađ uilla alie. xxx. VII. ac. 7 dim. qs tenuit ali lib hō. in qbꝫ idē ē qđ in alijs. 7. tantundē ualent.

Hund de Vdelesfort. Tacheleiam ten&. E. in dn̄io qđ tenuit Vlmar lib hō. t. r. e. p. Man. 7. p. I. hid. 7. xv. ac. Sēp. II. car in dn̄io. 7. II. car hom. Tc. III. uilt. m̄. v. 7. I. pbr. Tc. III. bor. p 7. m̄. x. Sēp. II. ser. Tc silu. ω. porc. Post 7 m̄. DC. XVI. ac. pti. Tc. I. runc. 7. XIIII. anim. xxx. porc. xxx. cap. LXXX. ou. m̄. II. runc xx. an. XLIII. porc CIII. ou

50 b

XL. cap. Tc 7 post uat. VIII. lib. m̄ x.

Hundred of ROCHFORD

11 Pirot holds HAWKWELL from Eudo, which Wulfmer held before 1066 as a manor, for 3½ hides less 15 acres.

Then 11 villagers, now 8; always 5 smallholders. Then 2 slaves, now 3. Always 2 ploughs in lordship. Then 6 men's ploughs, now 5.

Meadow, 4 acres; woodland, 10 pigs. Then 2 cobs, 5 cattle, 102 sheep, 20 pigs; now 16 cattle, 106 sheep, 20 pigs, 2 beehives.

Value then and later £6; now [£] 7.

In the above Hundred of DUNMOW

12 Richard holds from Eudo 1 manor with 9 acres which is called BROXTED, which 2 Freemen held before 1066 from the Abbot of Ely. Then 3 ploughs in lordship, now 2½. Now 1 men's plough;

2 villagers. Then 3 smallholders, now 5; then 3 slaves, now 1.

Woodland, 100 pigs; meadow, 6 acres. Then 1 cob, 3 cattle, 16 pigs; now 5 cattle, 33 pigs.

Value then and later 60s; now £4.

13 Eudo holds SHELLOW (Bowells) in lordship which Wulfmer, a free man, held before 1066 as a manor, for ½ hide. Always ½ plough in lordship.

Now 2 smallholders.

Woodland, 16 pigs; meadow, 4 acres.

Value always 10s.

14 Ralph holds DUNMOW from Eudo, which 1 free man held before 1066 as a manor, for 37½ acres. Always ½ plough in lordship; ½ men's plough;

2 villagers. Now 2 smallholders; then 1 slave, now none.

Woodland, 15 pigs; meadow, 4 acres.

Value then and later 10s; now 20[s].

In the same village another 37½ acres which another free man held and on which there is the same as on the others.

Value as much.

Hundred of UTTLESFORD

15 Eudo holds TAKELEY in lordship which Wulfmer, a free man, held before 1066 as a manor, for 1 hide and 15 acres. Always 2 ploughs in lordship; 2 men's ploughs.

Then 3 villagers, now 5 and 1 priest; then 3 smallholders, later and now 10; always 2 slaves.

Woodland, then 1000 pigs, later and now 600; meadow, 16 acres. Then 1 cob, 14 cattle, 30 pigs, 30 goats, 80 sheep; now 2 cobs, 20 cattle, 43 pigs, 103 sheep, 40 goats. 50 b

Value then and later £8; now [£] 10.

Hund de Clauelinga. Plicedanā ten& Ricard de. E. qd tenuer. II. libi hões. t. r. e. p. Man. 7. p. v. hid. xx. ac. min. Tc. IIII. car. in dnio. Post 7 m. II. Tc. 7 post. I. car. hom. m. III. Tc 7. p. II. uill. m. VI. tc 7 post. II. bord. m. XVI. tc 7 p. II. ser. m null. Silu. xx. porc. xx. ac. pti. Tc. II. runc. m null. tc. II. anim. M. LXVI. porc. Tc. ccc. ou. m. cc. VI. uasa ap. Tc. 7 p uat. c. sol. m. VIII. lib. de hac tra calumpniat. G. de magna uilla. II. hid. xx. ac. min. 7. hund testat ei.

Hund de Laxendena. Bucchestedā ten& Artur de. E. qd ten Grim. p. ꝯ. 7. p. I. hid. Tc. I. uill. m null. Tc. II. bord. m. IX. Sep. I. car in dnio. tc. II. car. hom. m. I. Silu. XLII. porc. II. ac. pti. Tc. VI. anim. m. IIII. Tc. xxx. ou. m. LXIIII. Tc. x. porc. m. XIII. m. XIII. cap. 7. I. uas. ap. Tc uat. xx. sol. m. XL. 7 qdā lib tenuit. v. ac. m ten& Idē Artur de. E. Sep. dim. car. vat. v. sol.

Hund de Angra. Taindenā ten&. Eudo in dnio qd tenuit Vlmar p. I. hid. 7. XL. ac. t. r. e. Tc. IIII. uill. m. VI. tc. II. bor. m. IIII. tc. IIII. ser. m. I. Sep. II. car in dnio. 7. II. car. hom. Silu. cccc. porc. . v. ac. pti. Sep. II. runc. Tc. VIII. an. m. XIII. Tc. xxxv. porc. m. LXVI. tc. LXXXVII. ou. m. c. 7. xv. cap. Tc. II. uasa ap. m. VI. Tc 7 p uat. XL. sol. m. IIII. lib. 7. I. soc tenuit. VI. ac. q potat uendē suā tra s; soca remanebat in manerio. Vat. XII. d

Roinges ten&. E. in dnio. qd tenuit Vlmar p. ꝯ. 7. p. III. hid. t. r. e. Sep. VII. uill. m. II. bord. Sep. IIII. ser. 7. II. car. in dnio. 7 III. car. hou.

Hundred of CLAVERING

16 Richard holds PLEDGDON (Hall) from Eudo, which 2 free men held before 1066 as a manor, for 5 hides less 20 acres. Then 4 ploughs in lordship, later and now 2. Then and later 1 men's plough, now 3.

Then and later 2 villagers, now 6; then and later 2 smallholders, now 16; then and later 2 slaves, now none.

Woodland, 20 pigs; meadow, 20 acres. Then 2 cobs, now none; then 2 cattle; now 66 pigs; then 300 sheep, now 200; 6 beehives.

Value then and later 100s; now £8.

Of this land, G(eoffrey) de Mandeville lays claim to 2 hides less 20 acres. The Hundred testifies to it.

Hundred of LEXDEN

17 Arthur holds BOXTED from Eudo, which Grim held as a manor, for 1 hide.

Then 1 villager, now none; then 2 smallholders, now 9. Always 1 plough in lordship. Then 2 men's ploughs, now 1.

Woodland, 42 pigs; meadow, 2 acres. Then 6 cattle, now 4; then 30 sheep, now 64; then 10 pigs, now 13; now 13 goats and 1 beehive.

Value then 20s; now 40[s].

A free man held 5 acres; now Arthur also holds (them) from Eudo. Always ½ plough.

Value 5s.

Hundred of ONGAR

18 Eudo holds THEYDON (Garnon) in lordship, which Wulfmer held for 1 hide and 40 acres before 1066.

Then 4 villagers, now 6; then 2 smallholders, now 4; then 4 slaves, now 1. Always 2 ploughs in lordship; 2 men's ploughs.

Woodland, 400 pigs; meadow, 5 acres. Always 2 cobs. Then 8 cattle, now 13; then 35 pigs, now 66; then 87 sheep, now 100; 15 goats; then 2 beehives, now 6.

Value then and later 40s; now £4.

1 Freeman, who could sell his land, held 6 acres; but the jurisdiction remained in the manor.

Value 12d.

19 Eudo holds (Abbess) RODING in lordship, which Wulfmer held as a manor, for 3 hides before 1066.

Always 7 villagers. Now 2 smallholders. Always 4 slaves; 2 ploughs in lordship; 3 men's ploughs.

Silū . xx . porc̄ . xx . ac̄ . p̄ti . Tc̄ . i . runc̄ . m̊ . iii . tc̄ . x . an̄ . m̊ . xiiii .
Tc̄ . xl . porc̄ . m̊ . lx . Tc̄ . c . ou̇ . m̊ . cxxxi . 7 . i . sochem̄ . qui poss&

51 a
uendere tr̄am suam . s; soca remanebat in manerio tenens dim̄ uirḡ.
7 . viii . ac̄ . 7 . dim̄ . Tc̄ . 7 p̄ . i . car̄ . m̊ dim̄ . Sep̄ . i . ser̄ . Tc̄ . 7 . post ual totum
. viii . lib̄ . m̊ . xii .

Hund de Celmeresfort . Ratenduna ten& . Ricard̄ . de . E . qđ
tenuit Leuesun̄ p . Man̄ . t̄ . r̄ . ē . 7 . p . ii . hid̄ . 7 . xxx . ac̄ . 7 istā trā calumpni
at̄ . Æcclia de Eli . 7 Hund fert testimoniū . Sep̄ . iiii . bord . 7 . ii . ser̄ . 7 . i . car̄
in dn̄io . 7 . i . car̄ . hom̄ . Tc̄ . ii . runc̄ . m̊ . iiii . Tc̄ . iiii . an . m̊ . vii . Tc̄ . x . porc̄.
M̊ xxxiii . Tc̄ . lxxx . ou̇ . m̊ . c . iii . min̄ . Tc̄ ual . xl . sol . m̊ . lxx .

Legā ten& . Ricard̄ de . E . qđ tenuit . Edric̄ p . Man̄ . 7 . p . ii . hid̄ . Sep̄ . iii .
uill . Tc̄ . ii . bord̄ . m̊ . ix . Tc̄ . vii . ser̄ . m̊ . ii . Tc̄ . in dn̄io . ii . car̄ . m̊ . i . 7 . dim̄ . Silū
dccc . porc̄ . xvi . ac̄ . p̄ti . m̊ . i . mol . Tc̄ . iii . runc̄ . m̊ . i . Tc̄ . x . an̄ . m̊ . ix . tc̄
xl . porc̄ . m̊ . xxxv . Tc̄ . l . ou̇ . m̊ lxiii . 7 . xi . cap̄ . Tc̄ ual . lx . sol . m̊ . iiii . lib̄.

Hund de Tendringa Wileiam tenuit Goduin̄ p . Man̄ . 7 . p . iii . hid̄.
7 . xxxviii . ac̄ . m̊ ten& . E . in dn̄io . Tc̄ . xiii . uill . m̊ . xi . Tc̄ . iiii . bord̄.
m̊ . ix . Tc̄ . viii . ser . m̊ . iiii . Silū . cc . porc̄ . vi . ac̄ . p̄ti . Past̄ . c . ou̇ . 7 . ii .
soc̄ . tenuer̄ . ii . hid̄ . 7 . xlv . ac̄ . qui adjacebant huic manerio . Sep̄ . v . bord̄.
7 . ii . car̄ . Silū . xxx . porc̄ . iii . ac̄ . p̄ti . Past̄ . lx . ou̇ . Tc̄ in dn̄io . xv . an̄.
m̊ . xvi . Tc̄ . lx . porc̄ . m̊ . xxx . Sep̄ . ccxl . ou̇ . Tc̄ . v . uasa ap̄ . m̊ . ii .
Tc̄ ual . totū simul . viii . lib̄ . m̊ . xix . lib̄ . 7 . i . unciā auri.

Woodland, 20 pigs; meadow, 20 acres. Then 1 cob, now 3; then 10 cattle, now 14; then 40 pigs, now 60; then 100 sheep, now 131.

1 Freeman, who holds ½ virgate and 8½ acres (and) who could sell his land; but the jurisdiction remained in the manor. 51 a

Then and later 1 plough, now ½.

Always 1 slave.

Value of the whole then and later £8; now [£] 12.

Hundred of CHELMSFORD

20 Richard holds RETTENDON from Eudo, which Leofson held as a manor before 1066, for 2 hides and 30 acres. The Church of Ely lays claim to this land and the Hundred bears witness.

Always 4 smallholders; 2 slaves; 1 plough in lordship; 1 men's plough.

Then 2 cobs, now 4; then 4 cattle, now 7; then 10 pigs, now 33; then 80 sheep, now 100 less 3.

Value then 40s; now 70[s].

21 Richard holds LEIGHS from Eudo, which Edric held as a manor, for 2 hides.

Always 3 villagers. Then 2 smallholders, now 9; then 7 slaves, now 2. Then 2 ploughs in lordship, now 1½.

Woodland, 800 pigs; meadow, 16 acres; now 1 mill. Then 3 cobs, now 1; then 10 cattle, now 9; then 40 pigs, now 35; then 50 sheep, now 63; 11 goats.

Value then 60s; now £4.

Hundred of TENDRING

22 Godwin held WEELEY as a manor, for 3 hides and 38 acres. Now Eudo holds it in lordship.

Then 13 villagers, now 11; then 4 smallholders, now 9; then 8 slaves, now 4.

Woodland, 200 pigs; meadow, 6 acres; pasture, 100 sheep.

2 Freemen held 2 hides and 45 acres which were attached to this manor.

Always 5 smallholders; 2 ploughs.

Woodland, 30 pigs; meadow, 3 acres; pasture, 60 sheep. Then in lordship 15 cattle, now 16; then 60 pigs, now 30; always 240 sheep. Then 5 beehives, now 2.

Value then of the whole altogether £8; now £19 and 1 ounce of gold.

Hund de Vdelesfort. Kuenadanam ten& Ricard. de . E . qd
tenuit Aldred . p . Man . 7 . p . ii . hid . Tc . vi . uill . p 7 m . iii . m . iiii . bord.
Sep . iii . ser . 7 . ii . car . in dnio . 7 . iii . car int hoes tc . m . ii . Silu . xl . porc.
. vi . ac . pti . Tc . runc . m . v . Tc . vi . an . m . ix . Tc . xxxii . porc . m . l.
Tc . lxxx . ou . m . cc . m . xliiii . cap . Tc . iiii . uasa ap . m . xvii Tc ual

51 b
viii . lib . m . vi.
Dim Hund de Froffeuuella . In Redeuuintra ten& Ricard
. xv . ac . qd tenuit Aluric uuand . Sep . i . uill . 7 . i . bor . 7 . i . ser . 7 . i . car.
. v . ac . pti . Tc . v . anim . m . viii . m . ii . runc . Tc . v . ou . 7 . iii . porc . m
null . Tc ual . x . sol . m . xxx.
Hund de Rochefort . ~~Hacuuella ten& . E . in dnio .~~ qd tenuit ★
Vlmar . lib ho . p . ω . 7 . ~~p . iii . hid . 7 . dim .~~ xv . ac . min . t . r . e . Tc . xi . uill.
m . viii . Sep . v . bord . Tc . ii . ser . m . iii . Sep . ii . car . in dnio . Tc . vi . car.
houm m . v . iiii . ac . pti . Silu . x . porc . Tc . ii . runc . m . vi . Tc . v . anim.
m . xvi . Tc . cii . ou . m . cvi . Sep . xx . porc . m . ii . uasa apu . Tc
ual . vi . lib . m . vii.
Hund de Vdelesforda . Archesdana ten& . E . in dnio . q
tenuit Aluric uuants . p . Man . 7 . p . ii . hid . xv . ac . min . Sep . ii . uill.
7 . vii . bord . 7 . ii . ser . Tc . 7 p . ii . car . in dnio . m . i . Sep . ii . car . hom.
Silu . xx . porc . x . ac . pti . Val . c . sol.

Hundred of UTTLESFORD

23 Richard holds QUENDON from Eudo, which Aldred held as a manor, for 2 hides.

Then 6 villagers, later and now 3; now 4 smallholders. Always 3 slaves; 2 ploughs in lordship. Then among the men 3 ploughs, now 2.

Woodland, 40 pigs; meadow, 6 acres. Then ... cobs, now 5; then 6 cattle, now 9; then 32 pigs, now 50; then 80 sheep, now 200; now 44 goats; then 4 beehives, now 17.

Value then £8; now [£] 6. 51 b

Half-Hundred of FRESHWELL

24 In RADWINTER Richard holds 15 acres which Aelfric Wand held.

Always 1 villager; 1 smallholder; 1 slave; 1 plough.

Meadow, 5 acres. Then 5 cattle, now 8; now 2 cobs; then 5 sheep and 3 pigs, now none.

Value then 10s; now 30[s].

Hundred of ROCHFORD

25 Eudo holds HAWKWELL in lordship which Wulfmer, a free man, held as a manor, for 3½ hides less 15 acres before 1066.

Then 11 villagers, now 8; always 5 smallholders. Then 2 slaves, now 3. Always 2 ploughs in lordship. Then 6 men's ploughs, now 5.

Meadow, 4 acres; woodland, 10 pigs. Then 2 cobs, now 6; then 5 cattle, now 16; then 102 sheep, now 106; always 20 pigs; now 2 beehives.

Value then £6; now [£] 7.

Hundred of UTTLESFORD

26 Eudo holds ARKESDEN in lordship, which Aelfric Wand held as a manor, for 2 hides less 15 acres.

Always 2 villagers; 7 smallholders; 2 slaves. Then and later 2 ploughs in lordship, now 1. Always 2 men's ploughs.

Woodland, 20 pigs; meadow, 10 acres.

Value 100s.

TERRA Rogeri de Otburuilla Hund de herlaua .XXVI.

Halingebiam tenuer̄ . II . libi hões . t . r . e . ꝓ . Man . 7 . ꝓ . III . hid . 7 .
xxxviii . ac . Tc̄ . vi . car . in dn̄io . m̄ . iii . Tc̄ . x . car . 7 . dim . hōu
m̄ . ii . 7 . dim . Tc̄ . xviii . uill . m̄ . viii . Tc̄ . iiii . bord . m̄ . v . Tc̄ . i . ser
m̄ null . Silu . ðc . porc . xxv . ac . p̄ti . Past . de . xxviii . đ . i . mol .
7 . ix . carr . posst̄ restaurari . 7 unū maneriū ex istis ualebat
. t . r . e . viii . lib . 7 . qn̄ recep . c . sol . m̄ . iiii . lib . 7 aliud ual . tc̄ . lx .
sol . m̄ . xl . In dn̄io recep . Rog . i . runc . 7 . iii . an . 7 . xxx . ou . 7 .
xl . porc . m̄ . i . runc . 7 . viii . an . 7 lxxx . porc . 7 . cxx . ou . 7 . iii . uasa
apū.

Hund de Dommauua . Rodinges tenuit Turchill . lib
hō . t . r . e . ꝓ . M . 7 . ꝓ . ii . hid . Tc̄ . in dn̄io . m̄ . i . 7 . dim . Tc̄ : iii . uill .
m̄ . i . p̄r . 7 . ii . uill . Tc̄ . ii . bord . m̄ . v . Tc̄ . iiii . ser . m̄ . iii . hn̄tes . i . car .
Silu . xxx . porc . xxiiii . ac . p̄ti . Tc̄ . ual . vi . lib . m̄ . c . sol . & qn̄
recep . n̄ inuenit n̄ solā trā . 7 . i . carrucā.

Hund de Vdelesfort . Archesdanā tenuit Leuuin libe
. ꝓ . Man . 7 . ꝓ . i . hid . 7 Rog in suo escangio . Tc̄ . ii . uill . P 7 m̄ . i .
Sēp . iii . bord . Tc̄ . i . car . in dn̄io . Qn̄ rec nulla . m̄ . i . Tc̄ . 7 . p̄ . i . car
hominū . m̄ nulla . vii . ac . p̄ti . Silu . x . porc . Tc̄ . i . an . 7 . xix . ou .
m̄ . i . pull . xiiii . porc . lxxxx . ou . Tc̄ . ual . xl . sol . m̄ . l .

In Ead uilla tenuit Vlfo . i . hid . libæ . t . r . e . 7 . Rog ꝓ escangio.
Tc̄ . ii . uill . P 7 m̄ . i . Sēp . iii . bord . Tc̄ . i . car in dn̄io . 7 qn̄ rec
nulla . m̄ . i . Tc̄ . 7 p̄ . i . car . hom . m̄ null . vii . ac . p̄ti . Silu . x . porc .
Tc̄ . ual . xl . sol . m̄ . l .

Cishellam tenuit Edric ꝓ Man . 7 . ꝓ . iii . hid . 7 . dim . Tc̄ . viii . uill .
p 7 m̄ . vi . Sēp . ii . bord . Tc̄ . ii . ser . m̄ . i . Tc̄ . 7 . p̄ . ii . car in dn̄io . m̄ . i .
tc̄ 7 p̄ . iii . car hom . m̄ . ii . Silu . xl . porc . vi . ac . p̄ti . Tc̄ . i . runc . 7 . ii . porc .
7 . ccxiii . ou . M . ii . runc . 7 . i . anim . xxxii . porc . cc . ou . Sēp ual
. iiii . lib .

26 LAND OF ROGER OF AUBERVILLE 52 a

Hundred of HARLOW

1 2 free men held (Great) HALLINGBURY before 1066 as a manor, for 3 hides and 38 acres. Then 6 ploughs in lordship, now 3. Then 10½ men's ploughs, now 2½.

Then 18 villagers, now 8; then 4 smallholders, now 5; then 1 slave, now none.

Woodland, 600 pigs; meadow, 25 acres; pasture at 28d; 1 mill. 9 ploughs can be restored.

Value of one of these manors before 1066 £8; when acquired 100s; now £4. Value of the other then 60s; now 40[s].

In lordship Roger acquired 1 cob, 3 cattle, 30 sheep and 40 pigs; now 1 cob, 8 cattle, 80 pigs, 120 sheep and 3 beehives.

Hundred of DUNMOW

2 Thorkell, a free man, held RODING before 1066 as a manor, for 2 hides. Then ... [ploughs] in lordship, now 1½.

Then 3 villagers, now 1 priest and 2 villagers; then 2 smallholders, now 5; then 4 slaves, now 3; who have 1 plough.

Woodland, 30 pigs; meadow, 24 acres.

Value then £6; later and now 100s; when acquired, he found only the land and 1 plough.

Hundred of UTTLESFORD

3 Leofwin held ARKESDEN freely as a manor, for 1 hide. Roger (holds it) by his exchange.

Then 2 villagers, later and now 1; always 3 smallholders. Then 1 plough in lordship, when acquired none, now 1. Then and later 1 men's plough, now none.

Meadow, 7 acres; woodland, 10 pigs. Then 1 (head of) cattle and 19 sheep; now 1 foal, 14 pigs, 90 sheep.

Value then 40s; now 50[s].

4 In the same village Wulfa held 1 hide freely before 1066. Roger (holds it) by exchange.

Then 2 villagers, later and now 1; always 3 smallholders. Then 1 plough in lordship, when acquired none, now 1. Then and later 1 men's plough, now none.

Meadow, 7 acres; woodland, 10 pigs.

Value then 40s; now 50[s].

5 Edric held CHISHILL as a manor, for 3½ hides. 52 b

Then 8 villagers, later and now 6; always 2 smallholders. Then 2 slaves, now 1. Then and later 2 ploughs in lordship, now 1. Then and later 3 men's ploughs, now 2.

Woodland, 40 pigs; meadow, 6 acres. Then 1 cob, 2 pigs and 213 sheep; now 2 cobs, 1 (head of) cattle, 32 pigs, 200 sheep.

Value always £4.

.XXVII. TERRA HVGoniS de monteforti. Hundret de Berdestapla. Ramesdanam ten& Osbnus de Hugone qđ tenuer .III. libi hões. t. r. e. p Man. 7. p. II. hid. 7. XL. ac. Sēp. I. car. in dnio. Tc dim. car hom. m. I. Tc. III. borđ. m. V. Tc. I. ser. m. n. Silu. LX. porc. .III. ac. p̄ti. Tc. II. an. 7. III. porc. 7. LX. ou. M. I. runc. 7. II. anim. 7. IX. porc. 7 LXX. ou. Val. XL. sol. In Eađ uilla sr. XXX. ac. q ptinent ad ecctiam. 7 Val. XXX. đ.

Hunđ de Witham Chelleuadanā ten& Wills fili grossæ. de hugone. qđ tenuit Gudmund. tegn regis p. Man. 7. p. III. hid. 7. dim. Sēp. II. car in dnio. Tc. IIII. car hom. m. I. Sēp. IX. uilt. 7. III. ser. 7. V. bord. Silu. L. porc. XXV. ac. p̄ti. I. mol. Tc. I. runc. 7. IIII. an. 7. VII. porc. 7. XL. ou. m. II. runc. CXL. ou. Tc uat. VI. lib. m. VII.

Hunđ de Beuentrev. Leintunā ten& Hugo in dnio qđ tenuit

53 a

Alsi. t. r. e. p Man. 7 p. III. hid. 7. XXX. ac. Tc. II. car. in dnio. m. I. Tc .I. car hom. m. I. 7. dim. Tc. VI. uilt. m. I. pbr. 7. I. uills. Tc. IIII. bord. m. III. Tc. II. ser. m. null. Silu. CL. porc. XXX. ac. p̄ti. Tc LX. ou. m. .IIII. porc. 7. LX. ou. Tc uat. XXX. sol. m. XL. 7 una istarū hidarū reddebat. t. r. e. consuetudinē ad Hauelingas manerium regis. 7 m n reddit.

Hunđ de Witbrictesherna Purlai ten& Hugo in dnio qđ tenuit Gudmund lib hō. t. r. e. p Man. 7. p. IIII. hid. Sēp. V. uitti. Tc. VI. bord. m. VII. Tc. VI. ser. m. V. Sēp. II. car in dnio. Tc. III. car hom. m. II. 7. tcia pot fieri. Silu. DCC. porc. Sēp. III. runc. 7. XVI. an. Tc. CCC. ou. m. CCCVI. Tc. XXX. porc. m. XXXV. Tc uat. VIII. lib Post 7 m. VII.

27 LAND OF HUGH DE MONTFORT

Hundred of BARSTABLE

1 Osbern holds RAMSDEN from Hugh, which 3 free men held before 1066 as a manor, for 2 hides and 40 acres. Always 1 plough in lordship. Then ½ men's plough, now 1.

Then 3 smallholders, now 5; then 1 slave, now none.

Woodland, 60 pigs; meadow, 3 acres. Then 2 cattle, 3 pigs and 60 sheep; now 1 cob, 2 cattle, 9 pigs and 70 sheep.

Value 40s.

In the same village are 30 acres which belong to the church.

Value 30d.

Hundred of WITHAM

2 William son of Gross holds KELVEDON from Hugh, which Guthmund, a King's thane, held as a manor for 3½ hides. Always 2 ploughs in lordship. Then 4 men's ploughs, now 1.

Always 9 villagers; 3 slaves; 5 smallholders.

Woodland, 50 pigs; meadow, 25 acres; 1 mill. Then 1 cob, 4 cattle, 7 pigs and 40 sheep; now 2 cobs, 140 sheep.

Value then £6; now [£] 7.

Hundred of BECONTREE

3 Hugh holds LEYTON in lordship, which Alfsi held before 1066 as a 53 a
manor, for 3 hides and 30 acres. Then 2 ploughs in lordship, now 1. Then 1 men's plough, now 1½.

Then 6 villagers, now 1 priest and 1 villager; then 4 smallholders, now 3; then 2 slaves, now none.

Woodland, 150 pigs; meadow, 30 acres. Then 60 sheep; now 4 pigs and 60 sheep.

Value then 30s; now 40[s].

One of those hides paid a customary due to the King's manor of Havering (-atte-Bower) before 1066; now it does not pay.

Hundred of 'WIBERTSHERNE'

4 Hugh holds PURLEIGH in lordship which Guthmund, a free man, held before 1066 as a manor, for 4 hides.

Always 5 villagers. Then 6 smallholders, now 7; then 6 slaves, now 5. Always 2 ploughs in lordship. Then 3 men's ploughs, now 2; 3 possible.

Woodland, 700 pigs. Always 3 cobs; 16 cattle. Then 300 sheep, now 306; then 30 pigs, now 35.

Value then £8; later and now [£] 7.

Lachentunam tenuit Gudmundꝰ ꝑ Man̄. 7 ꝑ. III. hid̄. 7. dim̄. 7. xx. ac̄.
Sēp. II. uilli. Tc̄. II. bord̄. m̄. IIII. tc̄. v. ser̄. m̄. IIII. Sēp. II. car̄ in dn̄io.
7. dim̄. car̄. hominū. Pastura. cc. ou̇. Silu̇. c. porc̄. Tc̄ ual. vii. lib.
Post 7 m̄. c. sol. De hoc eod̄ manerio ten&. Hunfridꝰ. II. hid̄. de hugone
7 Vlmarꝰ. I. hid̄. 7 ual. LX. sol in eod̄ ꝑtio.

In Purlai tenuer̄. x. libi hoēs. vii. hid̄. q̄s recep̄ hugo ꝑ. II. man̄.
s; hund̄ hoc nescit. Tc̄ erant in hac t̄ra. IIII. bord̄. m̄. VIII. Tc̄. I. ser̄
m̄ nullꝰ. Tc̄. VIII. car̄. m̄. VI. Silu̇. xv. porc̄. Past̄. c. ou̇. Tc̄ 7 pꝰ ual
. VI. lib. m̄. c. sol.

Adhuc ten& Hugo in purlai. I. Man̄. de. I. hid̄. 7. dim̄. 7. VIII. ac̄. 7. dim̄.
qd̄ tenuer̄. III. libi hoēs. t. r. e. cū soca. Sēp. I. car̄. 7. dim̄. Pastura
XL. ou̇. Sēp ual. xx. sol. Hoc totū sup̄dictū ualebat. xxx. lib. qn̄
recep̄.

53 b

Halesdunam ten& Hugo in dn̄io. qd̄ tenuit Aluuinꝰ teinnꝰ. t. r. e.
ꝑ Man̄. 7. ꝑ. II. hid̄. Tc̄. I. bord̄. 7. I. uills. m̄ similit̄. Sēp. I. ser̄. 7. I. car̄.
in dn̄io. Past̄. XL. ou̇ Tc̄ ual. xxx. sol. qn̄ rec̄. xx. sol. m̄. xxx.

Estoleiam ten&. H. in dn̄io. qd̄ tenuit sēp. II. uill. Tc̄. II. bord̄. 7 m̄ ★
similit̄. 7. I. car̄ 7. dim̄. 7 m̄ similit̄. Val. xxx. sol.

Hund̄ de Wensistreu Legrā. ten& Hugo. in dn̄io qd̄ tenuit
Liuuinꝰ lib hō. t. r. e. ꝑ. Man̄. 7. ꝑ. I. hid̄. 7. dim̄. 7. XVIII. ac̄. Sēp
. I. car̄ 7 dim̄ in dn̄io. M dim̄. car̄ hom̄. m̄. III. bord̄. Tc̄. III. ser̄. m̄
nullꝰ. Sēp. III. uac̄. Tc̄. xx. ou̇. m̄. LX. m̄. XIIII. porc̄. 7. I. runc.
7. VII. cap̄. Tc̄. ual. L. sol. 7 qn̄ rec̄. xx. sol. m̄. XL. sol.

5 Guthmund held LATCHINGDON as a manor, for 3½ hides and 20 acres.

Always 2 villagers. Then 2 smallholders, now 4; then 5 slaves, now 4. Always 2 ploughs in lordship; ½ men's plough.

Pasture, 200 sheep; woodland, 100 pigs.

Value then £7; later and now 100s.

Of this same manor, Humphrey holds 2 hides from Hugh and Wulfmer (holds) 1 hide.

Value 60s in the same assessment.

6 In PURLEIGH 10 free men held 7 hides which Hugh acquired as 2 manors; but the Hundred does not know this.

Then there were on this land 4 smallholders, now 8; then 1 slave, now none. Then 8 ploughs, now 6.

Woodland, 15 pigs; pasture, 100 sheep.

Value then and later £6; now 100s.

7 Hugh holds a further 1 manor in PURLEIGH with 1½ hides and 8½ acres, which 3 free men held before 1066 with the jurisdiction. Always 1½ ploughs.

Pasture, 40 sheep.

Value always 20s.

Value of the whole of the above when acquired £30.

8 Hugh holds *HALESDUNA* in lordship which Alwin, a thane, held 53 b
before 1066 as a manor, for 2 hides.

Then 1 smallholder, 1 villager; now the same. Always 1 slave; 1 plough in lordship.

Pasture, 40 sheep.

Value then 30s; when acquired 20s; now 30[s].

[Hundred of CHELMSFORD]

9 Hugh holds 'STUDLY' in lordship which 2 villagers have always held.

Then 2 smallholders, now the same. [Then] 1½ ploughs, now the same.

Value 30s.

Hundred of WINSTREE

10 Hugh holds LAYER in lordship which Leofing, a free man, held before 1066 as a manor, for 1½ hides and 18 acres. Always 1½ ploughs in lordship. Now ½ men's plough.

Now 3 smallholders; then 3 slaves, now none.

Always 3 cows. Then 20 sheep, now 60; now 14 pigs, 1 cob and 7 goats.

Value then 50s; when acquired 20s; now 40s.

Hund de hidingaforda. Raines ten& Alcher' de hugone qđ tenuit Gudmund. p. Man. 7. p. II. hid. xx. ac. min. Sep. III. car. in dñio. Tc. 7 p. VII. car. hom. m. II. 7. dim. tc. 7 p. XVIII. uilt. m. v. Tc. 7 p. VI. bor. m. VII. Tc. 7 p. VI. ser. m. IIII. Silu. CL. porc. XVI. ac. pti. sep. I. mot. 7. I. runc. Tc. XVIII. an. m. XVII. Sep. LXX. ou. 7. x. cap. Tc. 7 p uat. VI. lib. m. VII.

Hund de Witbrictesherna. Effecestre ten& Vlmar de. hug qđ tenuit Ingulf lib hō. t. r. e. p. Man. 7. p. I. hid. 7. dim. Sep. II. bord. Tc. I. ser. m null. I. car. in dñio. 7. dim. hom. Past. cc. oūs. Val. xxx sol. ★

Hund de Laxendena Mercheshalam ten& Nigell de hugone qđ tenuit Gudmund t. r. e. p uno maner. 7. p dim hid. 7. XIII. ac. Sep. II. uilt. Tc. VII. bord. m. VIII. Sep. v. ser. Tc. II. car. in dñio m. I. 7. dim. Sep. I. car. 7 dim hom. Silu. cc. porc. I. ac. pti. Sep

54 a

. I. runc. Tc. II. anim. m. x. Tc. xxx. ou. m. LXXX. Sep. XII. porc. m. III. uasa apū. Tc uat. XL. sol. m LX.

Hund de Celmeresfort. Bedenestedā ten&. Rob de hug qđ tenuit Gudmund t. r. e. p. Man. 7. p. IIII. hid. Tc. I. uilt. m null. Tc. IX. bord. m. x. Tc. 7. p. VI. ser. m. I. Tc. 7. p. II. car. in dñio. m. I. Sep. I. car hom. v. ac. pti. Tc. III. runc. m. null. Tc xxv. an. m. I. uac. Tc. c. porc. m. XIIII. Tc. c. 7. VIII. ou. m. XXIIII. tc. LX. cap. m. nulla. Tc uat. VIII. lib. 7 qn rec. similit. m. IIII. lib. 7. v. libi hōes tenuer. I. hid. 7. dim. 7. XXIII. ac. qs ten& Idē Rob de Hugone. Sep. v. bord. 7. II. car. 7. dim. Silu. XL. porc. IIII. ac. pti. Sep uat. L. sol. hoc maneriū calumpniant monachi de eli qđ fuit in abbia in dñio t. r. e. 7 hoc testat hund.

Hundred of HINCKFORD

11 Alchere holds RAYNE from Hugh, which Guthmund held as a manor, for 2 hides less 20 acres. Always 3 ploughs in lordship. Then and later 7 men's ploughs, now 2½.

Then and later 18 villagers, now 5; then and later 6 smallholders, now 7; then and later 6 slaves, now 4.

Woodland, 150 pigs; meadow, 16 acres. Always 1 mill; 1 cob. Then 18 cattle, now 17. Always 70 sheep; 10 goats.

Value then and later £6; now [£] 7.

Hundred of 'WIBERTSHERNE'

12 Wulfmer holds ST. PETER'S CHAPEL from Hugh which Ingulf, a free man, held before 1066 as a manor, for 1½ hides.

Always 2 smallholders. Then 1 slave, now none. 1 plough in lordship; ½ men's (plough).

Pasture, 200 sheep.

Value 30s.

Hundred of LEXDEN

13 Nigel holds MARKSHALL from Hugh, which Guthmund held before 1066 as one manor, for ½ hide and 13 acres.

Always 2 villagers. Then 7 smallholders, now 8; always 5 slaves. Then 2 ploughs in lordship, now 1½. Always 1½ men's ploughs.

Woodland, 200 pigs; meadow, 1 acre. Always 1 cob. Then 2 54 a
cattle, now 10; then 30 sheep, now 80. Always 12 pigs. Now 3 beehives.

Value then 40s; now 60[s].

Hundred of CHELMSFORD

14 Robert holds 'BENSTED' from Hugh, which Guthmund held before 1066 as a manor, for 4 hides.

Then 1 villager, now none; then 9 smallholders, now 10; then and later 6 slaves, now 1. Then and later 2 ploughs in lordship, now 1. Always 1 men's plough.

Meadow, 5 acres. Then 3 cobs, now none; then 25 cattle, now 1 cow; then 100 pigs, now 14; then 108 sheep, now 24; then 60 goats, now none.

Value then £8; when acquired the same; now £4.

5 free men held 1½ hides and 23 acres which Robert also holds from Hugh.

Always 5 smallholders; 2½ ploughs.

Woodland, 40 pigs; meadow, 4 acres.

Value always 50s.

The monks of Ely lay claim to this manor which was in lordship in the (lands of the) Abbey before 1066. The Hundred testifies to this.

Hund de Tendringa . Wica tenuit Edeua Regina . t . r . e .
p Man . 7 p . i . hid . m ten& Rog de hug . Sep . ii . uill . Tc . ii . bord . m . viii .
Tc . ii . ser . m null . Sep . i . car . Silu . x . porc . iii . ac . pti . Val . x . sol .
hanc tra ten& Rog 7 hund nescit qm . 7 regina habuit socam.

Hund de Turestapla . Totham ten& hugo fili Malgi de
hugone . qd tenuit Cola . Post Ricard . p Man . 7 . ii . hid . 7 . xxxii .
ac . Tc . iiii . bord . m . iii . Tc . iiii . ser . m . v . Tc . ii . car . in dnio
m . i . Silu . xx . porc . Past . c . ou . iii . ac . pti . Tc . i . sal . m . iii . Tc
. iii . runc . m . ii . Tc . xvi . porc . m . xx . Tc . xlviii . cap . m lxxxxiii .
m . xviii . cap . Tc ual . xl . sol . 7 . qn rec . x . sol . m ual . xl . sol

Goldhangra . ten& Ide de hug . qd tenuit Leuuin post hagra ★
p . Man . 7 p . i . hid . 7 . xv . ac . Sep . i . uill . 7 . vi . bord . 7 . iiii . ser .

54 b

Tc . i . car . m . dim . Silu . lx . porc . vii . ac . pti . Past . lx . ou . Tc . dim
salina . m . i . 7 dim . Tc . ual . xxx . sol . 7 . qn rec . x . sol . m . ual . xx . sol .
7 . ix . libi hoes . manser in dim hid . 7 . un ho tegn tenuit . xxx . ac . 7 . ii .
alij libi hoes . tenuer . x . ac . Tc . i . car . m . dim . Tc ual . xxvi . sol
7 . viii . d . m . viii . sol . Quida miles hugonis de monte forti . noe hugo
fili Malgeri accepit xv . ac . de uno franco teigno . 7 misit cu sua tra . 7
n habuit libatore . sic hund testat . 7 ita e in manu regis.

Toleshunta ten& Humfrid . de hugone qd tenuit Vlsi . t . r . e .
p Man . 7 . p dim hid . 7 . xxx . ac . Sep . ii . bord . 7 . i . car . Silu . xxx . porc .
. ii . ac . 7 . dim . pti . Val . xx . sol .

XXVIII. TERRA Hamonis dapiferi . Hundret de berdestapla
Ateleiam ten& Serlo de hamone qd tenuit Goti de heroldo . t . r . e
p . Man . 7 . p . i . hid . Sep . i . car . 7 . i . bord . 7 . i . ser . Val . xx . sol .

Hundred of TENDRING

15 Queen Edith held WIX before 1066 as a manor, for 1 hide. Now Roger holds it from Hugh.

Always 2 villagers. Then 2 smallholders, now 8; then 2 slaves, now none. Always 1 plough.

Woodland, 10 pigs; meadow, 3 acres.

Value 10s.

Roger holds this land and the Hundred does not know how. The Queen had the jurisdiction.

Hundred of THURSTABLE

16 Hugh son of Mauger holds (Little) TOTHAM from Hugh, which Cola (and) later Richard held as a manor, 2 hides and 32 acres.

Then 4 smallholders, now 3; then 4 slaves, now 5. Then 2 ploughs in lordship, now 1.

Woodland, 20 pigs; pasture, 100 sheep; meadow, 3 acres; then 1 salt-house, now 3. Then 3 cobs, now 2; then 16 pigs, now 20; then 48 goats, now 93; now 18 goats.

Value then 40s; when acquired 10s; value now 40s.

17 He also holds GOLDHANGER from Hugh, which Leofwin (and) later Hager held as a manor, for 1 hide and 15 acres.

Always 1 villager; 6 smallholders; 4 slaves. Then 1 plough, now ½. 54 b

Woodland, 60 pigs; meadow, 7 acres; pasture, 60 sheep; then ½ salt-house, now 1½.

Value then 30s; when acquired 10s; value now 20s.

9 free men dwelt on ½ hide. One man, a thane, held 30 acres and 2 other free men held 10 acres. Then 1 plough, now ½. Value then 26s 8d; now 8s.

One of Hugh de Montfort's men-at-arms, Hugh son of Mauger by name, acquired 15 acres from 1 free thane and put it with his own land. He did not have a deliverer, so the Hundred testifies; therefore it is in the King's hand.

18 Humphrey holds TOLLESHUNT (D'Arcy) from Hugh, which Wulfsi held before 1066 as a manor, for ½ hide and 30 acres.

Always 2 smallholders; 1 plough.

Woodland, 30 pigs; meadow, 2½ acres.

Value 20s.

28 LAND OF HAMO THE STEWARD

Hundred of BARSTABLE

1 Serlo holds *ATELEIA* from Hamo, which Goti held from Harold before 1066 as a manor, for 1 hide. Always 1 plough;

1 smallholder; 1 slave.

Value 20s.

Hund de Witham. Falcheburnā ten& Rad de hamone qđ tenuit Turbn.t.r.e.p.Man.7.p.I.hid.7.dim.7.VII.ac.7.dim. Sēp.II.car.in dn̄io.m̄.VIII.bord.Tc̄.VI.ser.m̄.III.V.ac.pti.Tc̄.I. mol.m̄ non.Val.L.sol.

55 a

Nutleam ten& Rad de.H.qđ tenuit Alestan lib hō p Man. 7.p dim hid.7.XXX.ac.Sēp.I.car.m̄.I.bor.Tc̄.II.ser.m̄.I.I.ac 7 đ pti.Val.XXX.sol. In Ead ten& Idē.XXX.ac.qs tenuit Aluric .t.r.e.Sēp dim.car.7 ual.V.sol.

Raines ten& Idē.R.de h.qđ tenuit Goding p.Man.7 p dim hid. Sēp.I.car.7.I.bord.7.II.ac.pti.Val.XX.sol.

Braccheſtedam ten& Gudmund.p.Man.7.p.I.hid.7.XXXV.ac. qđ tenuit Turbn.t.r.e.Tc̄.II.car.in dn̄io.m̄.I.Tc̄.I.car hōū m̄ nulla.Tc̄.III.uilt.m̄.I.Tc̄.IIII.bord.m̄.VI.Tc̄.IIII.ser.m̄.II. Tc̄.silu.C.porc.m̄ LXXX.XV.ac.pti.Tc̄.XX.ou.m̄.L.Tc̄.XVI. porc.m̄.XI.Tc̄ ual.C.sol.7 qn̄ eā rec.IIII.lib.m̄.LX.sol.

Hund de herlaua. Siricesleam ten&.Rad.de hamone qđ tenuit Herold ad maneriū de hatfelde.t.r.e.p.dim.hid. Tc̄.I.car.in dn̄io.m̄.dim.Tc̄.I.ser.m̄.I.uilt.Silu.XX.porc. .III.ac.7 dim.pti.Tc̄.ual.X.sol.m̄.VII.

Hund de Dōmauua. Dommauuā ten& Serlo de hamone qđ tenuit.I.lib hō.t.r.e.p.XXX.ac.7.VII.ac 7.dim.st addite.t.r.Willi. Sēp.dim.car.in dn̄io.7.II.bord.Silu.XL.porc.IIII.ac.pti. Val.XVI.sol.

Hundred of WITHAM

2 Ralph holds FAULKBOURNE from Hamo, which Thorbern held before 1066 as a manor, for 1½ hides and 7½ acres. Always 2 ploughs in lordship.

Now 8 smallholders; then 6 slaves, now 3.

Meadow, 5 acres; then 1 mill, now none.

Value 50s.

3 Ralph holds NOTLEY from Hamo which Alstan, a free man, held as a manor, for ½ hide and 30 acres. Always 1 plough. 55 a

Now 1 smallholder; then 2 slaves, now 1.

Meadow, 1½ acres.

Value 30s.

In the same (Notley) he also holds 30 acres which Aelfric held before 1066. Always ½ plough.

Value 5s.

[Hundred of HINCKFORD]

4 R(alph) also holds RAYNE from Hamo, which Goding held as a manor, for ½ hide. Always 1 plough;

1 smallholder.

Meadow, 2 acres.

Value 20s.

[Hundred of WITHAM]

5 Guthmund holds (Great) BRAXTED as a manor, for 1 hide and 35 acres, which Thorbern held before 1066. Then 2 ploughs in lordship, now 1. Then 1 men's plough, now none.

Then 3 villagers, now 1; then 4 smallholders, now 6; then 4 slaves, now 2.

Woodland, then 100 pigs, now 80; meadow, 15 acres. Then 20 sheep, now 50; then 16 pigs, now 11.

Value then 100s; when he acquired it £4; now 60s.

Hundred of HARLOW

6 Ralph holds RYES from Hamo, which Harold held with the manor of Hatfield (Broad Oak) before 1066 for ½ hide. Then 1 plough in lordship, now ½.

Then 1 slave; now 1 villager.

Woodland, 20 pigs; meadow, 3½ acres.

Value then 10s; now 7[s].

Hundred of DUNMOW

7 Serlo holds DUNMOW from Hamo, which 1 free man held before 1066 for 30 acres. 7½ acres were added after 1066. Always ½ plough in lordship;

2 smallholders.

Woodland, 40 pigs; meadow, 4 acres.

Value 16s.

Rodinges ten& Serlo de . H . qd tenuit Widi de Heroldo. t . r . e . p Man . 7 . p . I . hid . 7 . dim . m . I . hid . 7 . xv . ac . Sep . II . car in dnio . 7 . I . car . hom . Tc . IIII . uill . m . III . Tc . II . bord . m . xI. Tc . II . ser . m . I . Silu . c . porc . xvI . ac . pti . Tc uat . IIII . lib . 7 qn rec . xL . sol . m . c . sol . Ex hac tra ten& Eudo dapifer . xLv . ac

55 b

qs calumpniat Hamo.

Hundret de Wensistrev . Wighebgam ten& Vital de. hamone qd tenuit Goti lib ho . t . r . e . p . Man . 7 . p . vII . hid . træ. 7 una siluæ . Sep . II . car in dnio . Tc . II . car . hom . m . I . Sep . III . uill. 7 . I . bord . Tc . vI . ser . m . IIII . past . cc . ou . Tc . x . anim . m . xIIII. Tc . Lx . ou . m . cc Lx . Sep . vI . runc 7 . x . porc . Sep uat . vII. lib . De hac tra tulit Bernard . supdicta hida siluæ . 7 ten& ad feudu baignardi 7 Engelric tulit dim hid . træ . qua ten& Comes . Eust.

Hund de Clauelinga . In Pherneham ten& Serlo dim . hid de hamone qd tenuit lib ho . t . r . e . Val . x . sol.

Hund de hidingfort . In Scanburne 7 In Topesfelde ten& Hamo . I . hid . in dnio . p Man . qd tenuit Goti . t . r . e . Tc . 7 p . IIII. car . in dnio . m . III . Sep . III . car . hom . xIIII . uill . 7 . x . bord . 7. vI . ser . Silu . xL . porc . xv . ac . pti . Sep . III . runc . Tc . xxIIII. an . m . xIII . Tc . xL . porc . m . xx . Tc . cxx . ou . m . c . IIII . uasa apu . Et . xv . soc sep adjacent huic manerio . tenentes dim. hid . x . ac . min . 7 hnt . III . car . 7 . xII . ac . pti . 7 . v . bord . I . arpen. uineæ . hec tra fuit in . II . manerijs . t . r . e . Tc uat . Stanburna . c . sol . Post 7 m . vI . lib . 7 Topesfelda ualebat . tc . vII . lib . Post 7 m . vIII . lib . De hoc man tenent . v . milit . LvIII . ac . 7 uat . xx . sol i eod ptio.

8 Serlo holds RODING from Hamo, which Withi held from Harold before 1066 as a manor, for 1½ hides. Now 1 hide and 15 acres. Always 2 ploughs in lordship; 1 men's plough.

Then 4 villagers, now 3; then 2 smallholders, now 11; then 2 slaves, now 1.

Woodland, 100 pigs; meadow, 16 acres.

Value then £4; when acquired 40s; now 100s.

Of this land, Eudo the Steward holds 45 acres which Hamo claims. 55 b

Hundred of WINSTREE

9 Vitalis holds (Little) WIGBOROUGH from Hamo which Goti, a free man, held before 1066 as a manor for 7 hides of land and 1 (hide) of woodland. Always 2 ploughs in lordship. Then 2 men's ploughs, now 1.

Always 3 villagers; 1 smallholder. Then 6 slaves, now 4.

Pasture, 200 sheep. Then 10 cattle, now 14; then 60 sheep, now 260. Always 6 cobs; 10 pigs.

Value always £7.

From this land Bernard took the above hide of woodland and holds it in Baynard's Holding. Engelric took ½ hide of land which Count Eustace holds.

Hundred of CLAVERING

10 In FARNHAM Serlo holds ½ hide from Hamo, which a free man held before 1066.

Value 10s.

Hundred of HINCKFORD

11 In STAMBOURNE and in TOPPESFIELD Hamo holds 1 hide in lordship as a manor, which Goti held before 1066. Then and later 4 ploughs in lordship, now 3. Always 3 men's ploughs;

14 villagers; 10 smallholders; 6 slaves.

Woodland, 40 pigs; meadow, 15 acres. Always 3 cobs. Then 24 cattle, now 13; then 40 pigs, now 20; then 120 sheep, now 100; 4 beehives.

15 Freemen have always belonged to this manor, who hold ½ hide less 10 acres and have 3 ploughs.

Meadow, 12 acres.

5 smallholders.

1 *arpent* of vines.

This land was in 2 manors before 1066.

Value then of Stambourne 100s; later and now £6.

Value then of Toppesfield £7; later and now £8.

Of this manor, 5 men-at-arms hold 58 acres.

Value 20s in the same assessment.

Hunđ de Witbrictesherna Carseiam ten& Ricard de hamone qđ tenuit Turbn lib hō . t . r . e . p . Man . 7 . p . IIII . hid . 7 . XL . ac . Tc . II . uilt . m . III . Sēp . IIII . ser . 7 . II . car in dnio . 7 . I . car hom . Past . LX . ou . Tc ual . LX . sol . m . IIII . lib.

56 a

Hunđ de Angra . Gernestedam ten& Hamo in dnio qđ tenuit Gotild p Man . 7 p . II . hid . t . r . e . Sēp . X . uilt . Tc . IIII . bord . m . IX . Tc VI . ser . m . IIII . Tc . III . car . in dnio . 7 . qn rec . II . m . I . Tc 7 p . V . car 7 . dim hom . m . III . 7 . dim . Silu . CCCC . porc . XVI . ac . pti . m . I . mol . Tc . II . runc . m . I . Tc . IIII . anim . m . III . Tc . XXX . porc . m . XIIII . m . XL . cap . 7 . XX . ou . Tc . ual . IIII . lib . 7 . qn rec . XL . sol . m ual . C . sol . de hoc maner ten& Serlo . XL . ac . 7 ual . X . sol . in eođ ptio . In Eađ tenuer . III . libi hōes . dim . hid . 7 . XLV . ac . Tc . sub ipsis . X . bord . m . XVI . Tc . III . ser . m . II . Sēp . III . car . 7 . dim . Silu . CXX . porc . XIX . ac . pti . Tc . ual . XXXV . sol . m LX . De hac tra ten& Rađ dim hid . 7 . V . ac . 7 ual . XL . sol . in eođ ptio .

Astocam ten& Idē de ham . qđ tenuit Gotil . p Man . 7 . p LXXX . ac . t . r . e Tc . II . bord . m . V . Tc . I . car . m nulla . s; pot ibi esse . Silu . L . porc . II . ac . pti . tc ual . XII . sol . 7 qn rec . VIII . sol . m . XV .

Kalendunam ten& Rađ de hamone qđ tenuit Leueua . p . I . hid . 7 XLV . ac . 7 p uno man . 7 hamo dicit se habe istā tram in suo feudo . Tc . II . uilt . m . I . tc . II . bord . m . VII . tc . II . ser . m . I . tc . in dnio . II . car m . I . 7 . dim . Tc . int hōes . I . car . m . dim . Silu . XX . porc . XVII . ac . pti . Tc ual . XXX . sol . 7 . qn rec . XX . m . XXXV . sol .

Hundred of 'WIBERTSHERNE'

12 Richard holds NORTHEY ISLAND from Hamo which Thorbern, a free man, held before 1066 as a manor, for 4 hides and 40 acres.

Then 2 villagers, now 3. Always 4 slaves; 2 ploughs in lordship; 1 men's plough.

Pasture, 60 sheep.

Value then 60s; now £4.

Hundred of ONGAR 56 a

13 Hamo holds GREENSTED in lordship, which Gotild held as a manor, for 2 hides before 1066.

Always 10 villagers. Then 4 smallholders, now 9; then 6 slaves, now 4. Then 3 ploughs in lordship, when acquired 2, now 1. Then and later 5½ men's ploughs, now 3½.

Woodland, 400 pigs; meadow, 16 acres; now 1 mill. Then 2 cobs, now 1; then 4 cattle, now 3; then 30 pigs, now 14; now 40 goats; 20 sheep.

Value then £4; when acquired 40s; value now 100s.

Of this manor, Serlo holds 40 acres.

Value 10s in the same assessment.

In the same (Greensted) 3 free men held ½ hide and 45 acres.

Then 10 smallholders under them, now 16; then 3 slaves, now 2. Always 3½ ploughs.

Woodland, 120 pigs; meadow, 19 acres.

Value then 35s; now 60[s].

Of this land, Ralph holds ½ hide and 5 acres.

Value 40s in the same assessment.

14 He also holds NAVESTOCK from Hamo, which Gotild held as a manor, for 80 acres before 1066.

Then 2 smallholders, now 5. Then 1 plough; now none, but it could be there.

Woodland, 50 pigs; meadow, 2 acres.

Value then 12s; when acquired, 8s; now 15[s].

15 Ralph holds KELVEDON (Hatch) from Hamo, which Leofeva held for 1 hide and 45 acres as one manor. Hamo states that he has this land in his Holding.

Then 2 villagers, now 1; then 2 smallholders, now 7; then 2 slaves, now 1. Then 2 ploughs in lordship, now 1½. Then among the men 1 plough, now ½.

Woodland, 20 pigs; meadow, 17 acres.

Value then 30s; when acquired 20[s]; now 35s.

Nortunā ten& Wimund. de ham. qđ tenuit Gotil. ꝑ. Maner.
7 ꝑ. I. hid. 7. dim. 7. xv. ac. Tc. IIII. uill. m̊. vi. Sēp. IIII. bord. 7. IIII.
ser. Tc. II. car. in dnio. m̊. I. Tc. int hoēs. I. car. m̊. I. 7. dim. Silu.
. cc. porc. x. ac. pti. Sēp. II. an. m̊. I. runc. 7. XL. ou. 7. xx. cap.
tc. xvi. porc. m̊. xxvi. Tc 7 p uat. XL. sol. m̊. IIII. lib.
Hund de Turestapla. Toteham ten& Ricard de hamone

56 b
qđ tenuit Turbt. ꝑ uno man. 7. ꝑ. v. hid. t. r. e. Tc. x. uill. m̊. IX. Sēp. XVI.
borđ. Tc. XII. ser. m̊. XIII. Tc. IIII. car. in dnio. m̊. III. Sēp. v. car. hominū.
Silu. c. porc. xvi. ac. pti. II. salinæ. Sēp. xx. an. 7. XL. porc. Tc. v. runc.
m̊. II. Tc. c. ou. m̊. CL. Sēp. XL. cap. Tc 7 p uat. c. sol. m̊. vi. lib.
In Eađ tenuer. VIII. libi hoēs. I. hid. 7. dim. qđ ten& Idē Ricard. Sēp. II.
car. III. ac. pti. Val. xx. sol.
Vueseiam ten& Idē qđ tenuit Turb. t. r. e. ꝑ Man. 7 ꝑ. IIII. hid. Tc. I. bord.
m̊ null. Sēp. III. ser. I. pisc. Past. LX. ou. Val. LX. sol.

.XXIX. TERRA HENRICI de Ferrerijs Hund de Dōmauua
Tileteiam ten& Henric in dnio qđ tenuit. Doding. t. r. e. ꝑ Man. 7 ꝑ dim.
hid. Sēp. II. car. in dnio. 7. I. car hoū. Sēp. III. uill. Tc. II. bor. m̊. vi. tc.
. III. ser. 7 m̊ simil. xxx. ac. pti. xx. ac. de maresc. m̊. XL. animalia. Tc uat
. c. sol. m̊. VII. lib.
Hund de Hidingaforda. Stibingā ten&. H. in dnio qđ tenuit
Siuuard ꝑ Man. 7. ꝑ. II. hid. 7. xxx. ac. Tc. 7 p. II. car in dnio. m̊. III. Tc
int hoēs. IIII. car. m̊. vi. 7. dim. Tc. vi. uilli. m̊. VIII. Tc. XVI. bord. m̊. XXXIII.

16 Wimund holds NORTON (Mandeville) from Hamo, which Gotild held as a manor, for 1½ hides and 15 acres.
Then 4 villagers, now 6. Always 4 smallholders; 4 slaves.
Then 2 ploughs in lordship, now 1. Then among the men 1 plough, now 1½.
Woodland, 200 pigs; meadow, 10 acres. Always 2 cattle.
Now 1 cob, 40 sheep and 20 goats. Then 16 pigs, now 26.
Value then and later 40s; now £4.

Hundred of THURSTABLE

17 Richard holds (Great) TOTHAM from Hamo, which Thorbert held 56 b
as one manor, for 5 hides before 1066.
Then 10 villagers, now 9; always 16 smallholders. Then 12 slaves, now 13. Then 4 ploughs in lordship, now 3. Always 5 men's ploughs.
Woodland, 100 pigs; meadow, 16 acres; 2 salt-houses. Always 20 cattle; 40 pigs. Then 5 cobs, now 2; then 100 sheep, now 150; always 40 goats.
Value then and later 100s; now £6.
In the same (Totham) 8 free men held 1½ hides which Richard also holds. Always 2 ploughs.
Meadow, 3 acres.
Value 20s.

18 He also holds OSEA (Island), which Thorbert held before 1066 as a manor, for 4 hides.
Then 1 smallholder, now none; always 3 slaves.
1 fishery; pasture, 60 sheep.
Value 60s.

29 LAND OF HENRY OF FERRERS

Hundred of DUNMOW

1 Henry holds TILTY in lordship, which Doding held before 1066 as a manor, for ½ hide. Always 2 ploughs in lordship; 1 men's plough.
Always 3 villagers. Then 2 smallholders, now 6; then 3 slaves, now the same.
Meadow, 30 acres; marsh, 20 acres. Now 40 cattle.
Value then 100s; now £7.

Hundred of HINCKFORD

2 Henry holds STEBBING in lordship, which Siward held as a manor, for 2 hides and 30 acres. Then and later 2 ploughs in lordship, now 3. Then among the men 4 ploughs, now 6½.
Then 6 villagers, now 8; then 16 smallholders, now 33;

57 a

Tc̄.ii.ser.m̄.i.Silu.cl.porc̄.ix.ac.p̄ti.tc̄.Qn̄ rec.dim mol.m̄.n̄.Sep ē.ibi .i.pbr.Tc̄.vii.anim.7.xl.ou.7 lx.porc.7.i.runc.m̄.xviii.anim. 7.cxl.ou.7.lxxx.porc.7.i.runc.Tc̄.ual.x.lib.m̄.xii.7 in tēpr reḡ .ē.fuit totū similit̄ 7 tantū ualuit qn̄ recep. ★

Hund de Witbrictesherna Steplam ten&.H.in dn̄io qd tenuit Bondi lib hō.t.r.e.p Man.7 p.iii.hid.7.dim.Sep.ii.bord.Tc̄.iiii.ser.m̄.iii.Sep.i. car in dn̄io.7.dim.car.hom.Tc̄.c.ou.m̄.cxxx. Val sep.lx.sol.

Hund de Celmeresfort Vdeham ten&.H.in dn̄io qd tenuit Bondi p uno man.7.p.xiiii.hid Sep.xxiiii.uilt.Tc̄.viii.bord.m̄.xxxi. Tc̄.vi.ser.m̄.iiii.Sep.iii.car in dn̄io.7.xvi.car.hom.Silu.dccc.porc. m̄.i.mol.Tc̄ rec.xx.anim.7.xiii.runc.7.ccc.ou.7.lx.porc.m̄.xxviii. anim.7.xv.runc.7.ccc.ou.7.c.porc.7.xxxv.cap.Tc̄ ual.xx.lib.m̄ xxviii.

Cingam ten& dapifer Henrici de eo qd tenuit Bondi p Man.7.p.v. hidis.7.dim.Tc̄.vi.uilt.m̄.iiii.Tc̄.viii.bord.m̄.xii.tc̄.iiii.ser.m̄.iii. Sep.ii.car.in dn̄io.7.iiii.car.hom.Silu.d.porc.Past.c.ou.Tc̄.xx. anim.7.l.porc.7 lx.ou.m̄.vii.an.7.c.ou.7.xl.porc.Sep ual.vii. lib.

57 b

.XXX. TERRA Goisfridi de Magna uilla. Hund de Laxendena.

Teiam ten&.G.in dn̄io qd tenuit Vluric.t.r.e.p Man.7.p.i.hid.7.d. 7.xx.ac.Tc̄.xi.bord.m̄.xv.Sep.iiii.ser.7.ii.car in dn̄io.Tc̄.int̄ hōes .iii.car.m̄.ii.7.dim.Silu.c.porc.xx.ac.p̄ti.Tc̄.rec.G.ccl.ou.7.viii. anim.7.vi.uit.7.ii.runc.xxviii.porc.ii.uasa apū.m̄ lxvii.ou.7.viii. anim.7.vi.uit.7.ii.runc.7.xxi.porc.In Ead tenuer̄.xx.soc.i.hid.7.d. 7.xxxi.ac.M̄ tenent.xxx.soc.illā trā.7 n̄ potant recede ab illo manerio.Sep hn̄t.iii.car.vi.ac.p̄ti.Tc̄ 7 qn̄ rec ual.vii.lib.m̄.x.

then 2 slaves, now 1. 57 a

Woodland, 550 pigs; meadow, 9 acres; then, when acquired ½ mill, now none. 1 priest has always been there. Then 7 cattle, 40 sheep, 60 pigs and 1 cob; now 18 cattle, 140 sheep, 80 pigs and 1 cob.

Value then £10; now £12. Before 1066 and when acquired it was all the same and the value was as much.

Hundred of 'WIBERTSHERNE'

3 Henry holds STEEPLE in lordship which Bondi, a free man, held before 1066 as a manor, for 3½ hides.

Always 2 smallholders. Then 4 slaves, now 3. Always 1 plough in lordship; ½ men's plough.

Then 100 sheep, now 130.

Value always 60s.

Hundred of CHELMSFORD

4 Henry holds WOODHAM (Ferrers) in lordship, which Bondi held as one manor, for 14 hides.

Always 24 villagers. Then 8 smallholders, now 31; then 6 slaves, now 4. Always 3 ploughs in lordship; 16 men's ploughs.

Woodland, 800 pigs; now 1 mill. Then he acquired 20 cattle, 13 cobs, 300 sheep and 60 pigs; now 28 cattle, 15 cobs, 300 sheep, 100 pigs and 35 goats.

Value then £20; now [£] 28.

5 Henry's steward holds BUTTSBURY from him, which Bondi held as a manor, for 5½ hides.

Then 6 villagers, now 4; then 8 smallholders, now 12; then 4 slaves, now 3. Always 2 ploughs in lordship; 4 men's ploughs.

Woodland, 500 pigs; pasture, 100 sheep. Then 20 cattle, 50 pigs and 60 sheep; now 7 cattle, 100 sheep and 40 pigs.

Value always £7.

30 LAND OF GEOFFREY DE MANDEVILLE 57 b

Hundred of LEXDEN

1 Geoffrey holds (Marks) TEY in lordship, which Wulfric held before 1066 as a manor, for 1½ hides and 20 acres.

Then 11 smallholders, now 15. Always 4 slaves; 2 ploughs in lordship. Then among the men 3 ploughs, now 2½.

Woodland, 100 pigs; meadow, 20 acres. Then Geoffrey acquired 250 sheep, 8 cattle, 6 calves, 2 cobs, 28 pigs, 2 beehives; now 67 sheep, 8 cattle, 6 calves, 2 cobs and 21 pigs.

In the same (Tey) 20 Freemen held 1½ hides and 31 acres.

Now 30 Freemen hold that land. They could not withdraw from that manor. They have always had 3 ploughs.

Meadow, 6 acres.

Value then and when acquired £7; now [£] 10.

7 ibi fuer̄ . III . lib̄i . hōes tenentes . XII . ac . s; n̄ fuer̄ de illo man qđ . G . h̄t s; ipse reuocat lib̄atorē . Sēp . ibi . ē . I . car . 7 ual . XL . sol.

Hunđ de Hangra. Senleiam ten& Rainald . de Goisfrido qđ tenuit Leuedai ꝓ . Man . 7 ꝓ LXXX . ac . 7 . n̄ fuit de feudo angari . s; tantū fuit hō suus . Tc̄ . IIII . uilł . m̄ . V . m̄ . V . bord . Tc̄ . II . ser . m̄ . III . Tc̄ . 7 p̄ . II . car . in dn̄io . m̄ . I . Tc̄ . int̄ hōes . I . car . m̄ . II . Silu . CL . porc . XX . ac . p̄ti. Tc̄ 7 p̄ ual . LX . sol . m̄ . IIII . lib̄.

Roinges ten& Goisfrid martel . de . G . qđ tenuit Leuild ꝓ . M . 7 ꝓ . III . uirḡ . Sēp . I . uilł . 7 . II . bord Tc̄ . I . ser . m̄ null . Sēp . I . car . in dn̄io. 7 . dim . car hom . Silu . XL . porc . XV . ac . p̄ti . Tc̄ 7 p̄ ual . XXX . sol . m̄ . XL. 7 hec t̄ra q̄m m̄ ten& . G . fuit in abb̄ia de b̄chingis sicuti hund testat̄. s; ille q̄ tenuit hanc t̄rā fuit tantū m̄ hō antecessoris Goisfridi . 7 . n̄ potuit istā t̄rā mittere in aliq̄ loco n̄ in abb̄ia.

Hunđ de Cesseorda. Wochadunā ten& Turold de . G . qđ ten Freb̄t lib̄e tainn . ꝓ uno manerio . 7 . ꝓ . X . hid . 7 dim . 7 . XX . ac.

58 a

7 Goisfrid h̄t ꝓ escangio ut dicit . Sēp . III . uilli . XXXIIII . bord . Tc̄ . III . ser m̄ null . Tc̄ . in dn̄io . II . car . m̄ . III . Tc̄ . int̄ hōes . VII . car . m̄ . VIII . Silu . CL . porc . VIII . ac . p̄ti . Past . c . ou . m̄ . I . mol . Tc̄ . V . anim . 7 . XVIII . ou . m̄ . XVIII . an. 7 . I . runc . XXXV . porc . CCXX . ou . I . uas apū . Tc̄ 7 q̄n rec ual . VII . lib̄ . m̄ ual . XVI . lib̄. In hac t̄ra s̄t . XIII . soc . q̄ lib̄e tenent VIII . hid . 7 . dim . 7 . XX . ac. 7 . h̄nt . XII . bord . 7 jacent ad hanc firmā . de XVI . lib̄ . 7 adhuc s̄t . XL . ac. 7 . IIII . bor.

There were 3 free men who held 12 acres but they were not of the manor which Geoffrey has; but he himself calls the deliverer. 1 plough has always been there.
Value 40s.

Hundred of ONGAR

2 Reginald holds SHELLEY from Geoffrey, which Leofday held as a manor, for 80 acres. It was not (part) of Asgar's Holding; he was only his man.
Then 4 villagers, now 5; now 5 smallholders; then 2 slaves, now 3. Then and later 2 ploughs in lordship, now 1. Then among the men 1 plough, now 2.
Woodland, 150 pigs; meadow, 20 acres.
Value then and later 60s; now £4.

3 Geoffrey Martel holds (Abbess) RODING from Geoffrey, which Leofhild held as a manor, for 3 virgates.
Always 1 villager; 2 smallholders. Then 1 slave, now none. Always 1 plough in lordship; ½ men's plough.
Woodland, 40 pigs; meadow, 15 acres.
Value then and later 30s; now 40[s].
This land which Geoffrey now holds was in (the lands of) Barking Abbey, as the Hundred testifies. He who held this land was only the man of Geoffrey's predecessor; he could not dispose of that land to any place except the Abbey.

Hundred of CHAFFORD

4 Thorold holds OCKENDON from Geoffrey which Fridebert, a thane, held freely as one manor, for 10½ hides and 20 acres.
Geoffrey has it by exchange, as he states. 58 a
Always 3 villagers; 34 smallholders. Then 3 slaves, now none. Then 2 ploughs in lordship, now 3. Then among the men 7 ploughs, now 8.
Woodland, 150 pigs; meadow, 8 acres; pasture, 100 sheep; now 1 mill. Then 5 cattle and 18 sheep; now 18 cattle, 1 cob, 35 pigs, 220 sheep, 1 beehive.
Value then and when acquired £7; value now £16.
On this land are 13 Freemen who hold 8½ hides and 20 acres freely and have 12 smallholders. They belong to this revenue of £16.
There are also 40 acres and 4 smallholders.

Hund de Celmeresfort Waldham ten& . G . in dn̄io qđ tenuit Ansgar ꝑ Man̄ . 7 . ꝑ . VIII . hid . t . r . e . Sēp . LXXII . uitti . 7 XXVIII . bor . Tc̄ . XIIII . ser . m̄ . XIII . Tc̄ . VI . car . in dn̄io . m̄ . V . Tc̄ . int̄ hōes . XLII . car m̄ . XXXVI . Silua . ↀCC . porc . XLIIII . ac . p̄ti . Sēp . II . mot . m̄ . X . arpenni uineæ . Tc̄ . V . runc . XII . uac . L . porc . LXXX . cap . m̄ . III . runc . XI . uac . LX . porc . CXXXII . ou . VII . cap . XX . uasa apū . Tc̄ ual . L . lib . m̄ . LX. ★
De hoc manerio ten& Hubt . I . uirg . 7 . dim . car . 7 ual . V . sol ī eođ p̄tio 7 Walt̄ . I . uirg . 7 . dim . car . 7 ual . V . sol . in eođ . p̄tio . Turchill . I . uirg . 7 . II . borđ . 7 . dim . car . 7 val . V . sol . in eođ . p̄tio . 7 Galt̄ . XXX . ac . 7 . Turchill . XXX . ac . 7 Hubt . XXX . ac.

In Waltham tenuit Vluuin . libæ . cū soca . I . hid . 7 . L . ac . m̄ ten& . Rog . de . G . ꝑ Man . 7 ꝑ tantundē . Sēp . III . uitti . tc̄ IIII bor . m̄ . VI . Tc̄ . in dn̄io . II . car . m̄ . I . 7 dim . Sēp . I . car hom . 7 . I . ser . VII . ac . p̄ti . 7 . I . mol . Tc̄ ual . XL . sol . m̄ . LX.

Cetham tenuit Eduuard ꝑ man . 7 ꝑ . II . hid . & XXX . ac . m̄ ten& Galt̄ de Goisfrido . ꝑ tantundē . Sēp . II . uitt . Tc̄ . II . bor . m̄ . V . Sēp VI . ser . 7 . II . car . in dn̄io . 7 . I . car . hom . Silu . C . porc . VI . ac . p̄ti.

58 b

Tc̄ 7 post ual . XL . sol . m̄ LX.

Pacinges . ten . Idē . E . t . r . e . ꝑ man . 7 . ꝑ . II . hid . m̄ . ten& Galt̄ de G. Sēp . I . ser . 7 . I . car . Silu . XXX . porc . IX . ac . p̄ti . Val . XX . sol.

Brumfeldam tenuit . Saulf . p . ↀ . 7 ꝑ . IIII . hid . m̄ . Idē . Walt̄ de . G. Sēp . IX . uitt . Tc̄ . IIII . borđ . Tc̄ . V . ser . m̄ . IIII . Sēp . II . car . in dn̄io . 7 . IIII . car . hom . silu . L . porc . XIIII . ac . p̄ti . Sēp . I . mol . Tc̄ 7 . p ual . C . sol . m̄ . VI . lib.

Hundred of CHELMSFORD

5 Geoffrey holds (Great) WALTHAM in lordship, which Asgar held as a manor, for 8 hides before 1066.

Always 72 villagers; 28 smallholders. Then 14 slaves, now 13. Then 6 ploughs in lordship, now 5. Then among the men 42 ploughs, now 36.

Woodland, 1200 pigs; meadow, 44 acres; always 2 mills; now 10 *arpents* of vines. Then 5 cobs, 12 cows, 50 pigs, 80 goats; now 3 cobs, 11 cows, 60 pigs, 132 sheep, 7 goats, 20 beehives.

Value then £50; now [£] 60.

Of this manor Hubert holds 1 virgate. ½ plough.

Value 5s in the same assessment.

Walter (holds) 1 virgate. ½ plough.

Value 5s in the same assessment.

Thorkell (holds) 1 virgate.

2 smallholders. ½ plough.

Value 5s in the same assessment.

Walter (holds) 30 acres, Thorkell 30 acres and Hubert 30 acres.

6 In (Great) WALTHAM Wulfwin held 1 hide and 50 acres freely with the jurisdiction. Now Roger holds it from Geoffrey as a manor, for as much.

Always 3 villagers. Then 4 smallholders, now 6. Then 2 ploughs in lordship, now 1½. Always 1 men's plough; 1 slave.

Meadow, 7 acres; 1 mill.

Value then 40s; now 60[s].

7 Edward held CHATHAM as a manor, for 2 hides and 30 acres. Now Walter holds it from Geoffrey for as much.

Always 2 villagers. Then 2 smallholders, now 5. Always 6 slaves; 2 ploughs in lordship; 1 men's plough.

Woodland, 100 pigs; meadow, 6 acres.

Value then and later 40s; now 60[s]. 58 b

8 Edward also held PATCHING (Hall) before 1066 as a manor, for 2 hides. Now Walter holds it from Geoffrey.

Always 1 slave; 1 plough.

Woodland, 30 pigs; meadow, 9 acres.

Value 20s.

9 Saewulf held BROOMFIELD as a manor, for 4½ hides. Now Walter also (holds it) from Geoffrey.

Always 9 villagers. Then 4 smallholders; then 5 slaves, now 4. Always 2 ploughs in lordship; 4 men's ploughs.

Woodland, 50 pigs; meadow, 14 acres; always 1 mill.

Value then and later 100s; now £6.

Cingehalam tenuer̃ . III . libi hões . t . r . e . p . I . hid . 7 . XV . ac . m̃
Ricard . de . G . p Man . 7 p tant . Tc̃ . II . bor . m̃ . X . m̃ . III . uilt . sep̃ . III .
ser . Tc̃ . 7 p . II . car . hom dñio . m̃ . I . M . int hões . I . car . Silu . X . porc. ★
XV . ac . p̃ti . Tc̃ . ual . XXX . sot . m̃ . XLV.

Cingehalam tenuit Goduin diacon t . r . e p Man . 7 p . I . hid . 7 . đ
. V . ac . min . m̃ ten& Ric gernet . p Man . 7 p tant . Sep̃ . I . uilt . Tc̃ . I. ★
bor . m̃ . III . Tc̃ . III . ser . m̃ . II . Sep̃ . I . car in dñio . Tc̃ . int hões . I . car . m̃ . dim.
Silu . XII . porc . XVI . ac . p̃ti . Tc̃ ual . XXX . sot . m̃ . XL.

In Eađ uilla tenuit Vluuin . XLV . ac . t . r . e . m̃ ten& . Rađ de . G.
p Man . 7 p tant . Sep̃ . III . bord . 7 . I . car . 7 . III . ac . p̃ti . Vat . X . sot.
In Eađ ten& Lefsun de . G . I . uirg . qđ tenuit Idẽ . t . r . e . Sep̃ . I . car.
. V . ac . p̃ti . Vat . V . sot . 7 Leuric tenuit 7 ten& . XXX . ac . de . G . Tc̃ . dim
car . m̃ nult . VII . ac . p̃ti . vat . III . sot . 7 Leuuin tenuit 7 ten& . XV . ac.
7 . II . ac . p̃ti . Vat . XXX . đ . 7 Alestan ten& sep̃ . X . ac . 7 . III . ac . p̃ti . vat
. II . sot.

In Maſſebirig tenuit 7 . ten& Eduin . XLV . ac . sub . G . Sep̃ . III . bor.
Tc̃ . dim . car . m̃ nult . Vat . X . sot.

59 a

Danengebiam tenuit Arling p . Man . 7 p . II . hid . 7 . dim . m̃ . Witts de
. G . p tant . Sep̃ . I . uilt . Tc̃ . III . bord . m̃ . IX . Tc̃ . IIII . ser . m̃ . I . Sep̃ . I . car ĩ dñio.
7 . I . car . hom . Silu . C . porc . XVI . ac . p̃ti . Tc̃ ual . XXX . sot . m̃ . XL.

10 3 free men held CHIGNALL before 1066 for 1 hide and 15 acres. Now Richard (holds it) from Geoffrey as a manor, for as much.
Then 2 smallholders, now 10; now 3 villagers; always 3 slaves. Then and later 2 ploughs in lordship, now 1. Now among the men 1 plough.
Woodland, 10 pigs; meadow, 15 acres.
Value then 30s; now 45[s].

11 Godwin the deacon held CHIGNALL before 1066 as a manor, for 1½ hides less 5 acres. Now Richard Garnet holds it as a manor, for as much.
Always 1 villager. Then 1 smallholder, now 3; then 3 slaves, now 2. Always 1 plough in lordship. Then among the men 1 plough, now ½.
Woodland, 12 pigs; meadow, 16 acres.
Value then 30s; now 40[s].

12 In the same village Wulfwin held 45 acres before 1066. Now Ralph holds them from Geoffrey as a manor, for as much.
Always 3 smallholders; 1 plough.
Meadow, 3 acres.
Value 10s.
In the same (Chignall) Leofson holds 1 virgate from Geoffrey which he also held before 1066. Always 1 plough.
Meadow, 5 acres.
Value 5s.
Leofric held and holds 30 acres from Geoffrey. Then ½ plough, now none. Meadow, 7 acres.
Value 3s.
Leofwin held and holds 15 acres.
Meadow, 2 acres.
Value 30d.
Alstan has always held 10 acres.
Meadow, 3 acres.
Value 2s.

[Hundred of DUNMOW]

13 In MASHBURY Edwin held and holds 45 acres under Geoffrey.
Always 3 smallholders. Then ½ plough, now none.
Value 10s.

[Hundred of CHELMSFORD] 59 a

14 Erling held DANBURY as a manor, for 2½ hides. Now William (holds it) from Geoffrey for as much.
Always 1 villager. Then 3 smallholders, now 9; then 4 slaves, now 1. Always 1 plough in lordship; 1 men's plough.
Woodland, 100 pigs; meadow, 16 acres.
Value then 30s; now 40[s].

In Cingehala ten . Sauin pbr . xv . ac . m̄ . Ricard de . G . Tc̄ . dim . car m̄ . nich . val . v . sol . In Ead uill . tenuit Etsin . xv . ac . m̄ . Idē . R . ii . ac. pti . val . iii . sol . Isti supdicti fuer libi ita qd ipsi possent uende trā cū soca 7 saca q uellent ut hund testat.

Legram tenuit Ansgar p Man . 7 . p . ii . hid . 7 dim . 7 xv . ac . m̄ . W . de . G: p tant . Tc̄ . iiii . uill . m̄ . ii . Tc̄ . viii . bord . m̄ . xii . Tc̄ . iii . ser . m̄ . iiii . Tc̄ . ii . car . in dn̄io . m̄ . iii . Sēp . ii . car . hom . Silu . xl . porc . vi . ac . pti . Sēp . i . mol . M . x . an . x . porc . c . ou . Tc̄ 7 p ual . iiii . lib . m̄ . iiii . lib 7 . x . sol . Istud qq; maner t . r . e . dedit Esgar Haroldo . 7 herold itū dedit cuidā suo huscarlo . nōe scalpino . 7 iste Scalpin dedit uxori suæ in dote . uidentib; iib; hōib; scil Rogo marescalco 7 qdā anglico. 7 hoc testat . hund . qd audier recognoscere scalpino . 7 pq rex uenit in hanc trā tenuit ipse . donec iuit ubi mortuus fuit in ebroica. in utlagaria.

Keuentunā tenuit Toli p Man . 7 p . ii . hid . 7 . i . uirg . m̄ Osbt de . G. in suo escangio ut dicit . Sēp . i . uill . Tc̄ . vi . bord . m̄ . iiii . Sēp . iii . ser. 7 . ii . car . in dn̄io . tc̄ . int hōes . i . car . m̄ . dim . xviii . ac . pti . Sēp . i . mol . Tc̄ . ii . uac . xiii . ou . xii . porc . m̄ . viii . anim . xxxii . ou . xx . porc . xiiii . cap . ii . runc . v . uasa . ap . Tc̄ ual . xl . sol . m̄ . lx.

Hund de Tendringa . Mosam tenuit Leuesun p Man . 7 p . iiii . hid . m̄ . Goisfrid in dn̄io . Sēp . xiiii . uill . m̄ . xiii . bord.

59 b

Tc̄ . xiii . ser . 7 . qn̄ rec . xi . m̄ . iii . Tc̄ 7 p . iiii . car in dn̄io m̄ . ii . Tc̄ 7 p vi . car hom . m̄ . iiii . Silu . cl . porc . vi . ac 7 dim pti . Tc̄ . i . mol . m̄ null. past . cl . ou . iii . salinæ . 7 hoc maner . dedit Rex . G . qn̄ remansit Londoniæ.

15 In CHIGNALL Saewin the priest held 15 acres. Now Richard (holds them) from Geoffrey. Then ½ plough, now nothing.
Value 5s.
In the same village Edsi held 15 acres. Now Richard also (holds them).
Meadow, 2 acres.
Value 3s.
These above-mentioned people were free to the extent that they themselves could sell the land with full jurisdiction whither they would, as the Hundred testifies.

16 Asgar held (Great and Little) LEIGHS as a manor, for 2½ hides and 15 acres. Now W. (holds it) from Geoffrey for as much.
Then 4 villagers, now 2; then 8 smallholders, now 12; then 3 slaves, now 4. Then 2 ploughs in lordship, now 3. Always 2 men's ploughs.
Woodland, 40 pigs; meadow, 6 acres; always 1 mill. Now 10 cattle, 10 pigs, 100 sheep.
Value then and later £4; now £4 10s.
And Asgar gave this manor to Harold and Harold in turn gave it to one of his Guards, Scalpi by name. This Scalpi gave it to his wife in dowry in the sight of two men, namely Roger the Marshal and an Englishman. The Hundred testifies to this, that they heard (them) acknowledge Scalpi. After the King came to this land, he himself held it until he went to where he died in outlawry in York(shire).

17 Toli held CUTON (Hall) as a manor, for 2 hides and 1 virgate. Now Osbert (holds it) from Geoffrey by his exchange, as he states.
Always 1 villager. Then 6 smallholders, now 4. Always 3 slaves; 2 ploughs in lordship. Then among the men 1 plough, now ½.
Meadow, 18 acres; always 1 mill. Then 2 cows, 13 sheep, 12 pigs; now 8 cattle, 32 sheep, 20 pigs, 14 goats, 2 cobs, 5 beehives.
Value then 40s; now 60[s].

Hundred of TENDRING

18 Leofson held MOZE as a manor, for 4 hides. Now Geoffrey (holds it) in lordship.
Always 14 villagers. Now 13 smallholders; then 13 slaves, when 59 b
acquired 11, now 3. Then and later 4 ploughs in lordship, now 2. Then and later 6 men's ploughs, now 4.
Woodland, 150 pigs; meadow, 6½ acres; then 1 mill, now none; pasture, 150 sheep; 3 salt-houses.
The King gave this manor to Geoffrey when he stayed at London.

Tc̄.II.runc.7.IX.anim.CLXXX.ou.XIIII.porc.m̄.II.runc.XIIII.an.
XV.porc.CLX.ou.L.cap.III.uasa apū.Tc̄ uał.VIII.lib.7 qn̄ recepit
simił.m̄.uał.IX.lib.

Frientunam ten& Renelm de.G.qđ tenuit Leuesun p Man.7.p.
.III.hid.7 Tc̄.7 p.III.uilł.m̄.I.Tc̄.7 p.IIII.ser.m̄.III.Sēp.II.car in dn̄io.
7.tc̄.II.car hom.7 qn̄ rec.I.7 dim.m̄.dim tantū.III.ac.7 dim pti.
Past.L.ou.Tc̄.XLIX.ou.m̄.II.runc.7.IIII.porc.7.XL.ou.Tc̄ 7 post
uał.VII.lib.m̄.IIII.

Erleiam ten& Wilł de.G.qđ tenuer.II.libi hoes fr̄es.Bund 7 Alric.
s; non poŧant receđe.sine licentia illi Algari.p.II.hid.7 p.II.Man.
Sēp.V.uilł.7.VIII.bord.Tc̄.I.ser.m̄ null.Sēp.II.car in dn̄io.Tc̄.7 p.
.V.car.hom.m̄.IIII.Silu.C.porc.XII.ac.pti.Past.L.ou.Tc̄ 7 p uał
.IIII.lib.m̄.XL.sol.

In Hund de Berdestapla.erant.VI.libi hoes.t.r.e.qs.G.in
uasit sup regē.Willm.tenentes.XII.hid.tr̄æ.qs tenent.V.milites de eo.
Sēp.IX.car.7.dim.Tc̄.I.uilł m̄ null.tc̄.X.bord.m̄.XXXVI.tc̄.XIIII.
ser.m̄.VII.Tc̄.silu.C.porc.m̄.L.Past.CCC.ou.X.ac.pti.I.piscina.
De his.XII.hid.tulit Rauengari.XII.ac.tr̄æ.7 apposuit suo feudo.
7 Suen inde tulit.XXX.ac.7 posuit in Tilibia suo manerio.Tc̄ totū
simul uał.VII.lib.7 m̄ simiłr.

Hund de Witham.Nutleam ten& Galt de.G.

60 a

qđ tenuit Esgar p.man.7 p.I.hid.7.dim.7.XLV.ac.Sēp.II.car.in dn̄io.7.
.IIII.car hom.Sēp.X.uilł.7.V.bord.7.IIII.ser.Silu.C.porc.m̄.I.mol.7.II.
libi hoes de.XL.ac.7 de eis clamat regē ad uuarant.Tc̄.VI.anim.7.I.runc.
7.XII.porc.LX.ou.m̄.VIII.an.XVI.porc.C.ou.I.runc.Tc̄.uał.C.sol.m̄
.VI.lib.

Then 2 cobs, 9 cattle, 180 sheep, 14 pigs; now 2 cobs, 14 cattle, 15 pigs, 160 sheep, 50 goats, 3 beehives.
Value then £8; when acquired, the same. Value now £9.

19 Rainalm holds FRINTON from Geoffrey, which Leofson held as a manor, for 3½ hides.
Then and later 3 villagers, now 1; then and later 4 slaves, now 3. Always 2 ploughs in lordship. Then 2 men's ploughs; when acquired 1½; now only ½.
Meadow, 3½ acres; pasture, 50 sheep. Then 49 sheep; now 2 cobs, 4 pigs and 40 sheep.
Value then and later £7; now [£] 4.

20 William holds ARDLEIGH from Geoffrey which 2 free men, the brothers Bondi and Alric, held for 2 hides as 2 manors; but they could not withdraw without the permission of a certain Algar.
Always 5 villagers; 8 smallholders. Then 1 slave, now none. Always 2 ploughs in lordship. Then and later 5 men's ploughs, now 4.
Woodland, 100 pigs; meadow, 12 acres; pasture, 50 sheep.
Value then and later £4; now 40s.

In the Hundred of BARSTABLE
21 6 free men were there before 1066 whom Geoffrey annexed from King William. They held 12 hides of land which 5 men-at-arms hold from him. Always 9½ ploughs.
Then 1 villager, now none; then 10 smallholders, now 36; then 14 slaves, now 7.
Woodland, then 100 pigs, now 50; pasture, 300 sheep; meadow, 10 acres; 1 fishery.
Of these 12 hides, Ravengar took 12 acres of land and placed them in his Holding, and Swein took 30 acres from there and placed them in his manor of (West) Tilbury.
Value of the whole altogether then £7; now the same.

Hundred of WITHAM
22 Walter holds (Black) NOTLEY from Geoffrey, which Asgar held as a manor, for 1½ hides and 45 acres. Always 2 ploughs in lordship; 4 men's ploughs. 60 a
Always 10 villagers; 5 smallholders; 4 slaves.
Woodland, 100 pigs; now 1 mill. 2 free men with 40 acres and he claims the King as a warrantor for them. Then 6 cattle, 1 cob, 12 pigs, 60 sheep; now 8 cattle, 16 pigs, 100 sheep, 1 cob.
Value then 100s; now £6.

¶ Retleiam ten& Galt de . G . qđ tenuit Esgar . t . r . e . p . Man . 7 . p . I . hid. Sep . I . car . in dnio . 7 . dim . car hom . m . III . bord . Tc . III . ser . m . I . Silu . x . porc. . IIII . ac . pti . 7 . xxx . ac adjacebant t . r . e . huic træ . ex qbz . G . de magn uill . ht . xx . ac . 7 Ricard fili comitis . Gislebti . x . ac . s; hund testat totā recte esse ad tra Gosfridi . Totū simul . ual . xxx . sol.

¶ Hund de herlaua . Halingebiam ten& Martel . de . G . qđ ten. Esgar . t . r . e . p . Man . 7 . p . I . hid . Tc . II . car . in dnio . m . I . tc . I . pbr . 7 . I. . uill . de . xx . ac . que attinebant ad ecclam s; m n st ad ecclam . m . IIII. bord . tc . III . ser . m . II . Silu . c . porc . xx . ac . pti . m . dim . mol . Seper ual . XL . sol.

¶ Matcingā tenuit Esgar p Man . 7 p . XL . ac . qđ ten& . G . in dnio. Sep . I . car . tc . I . ser . m . n . Silu . x . porc . III . ac . pti . Val . x . sol.

¶ Hallingebiam ten& hugo de . G . qđ tenuit Godid liba femina . t . r . e . p Man . 7 p dim . hid . VIII . ac min . Tc . dim . car . m . nulla . Tc. . II . uill . m . null . v . ac . pti . Val . v . sol.

¶ Hund de Dommauua . Estram tenuit Esgar . t . r . e. p Man . 7 p . II . hid . m ten& . G . in dnio Sep . IIII . car in dnio . 7. . XII . car hom . Tc . XLVI . uill . m . XLVII . Tc . XIIII . bor . m . XXXIII. Sep . IX . ser . Silu . DC . porc . XXX . ac . pti . 7 . v . car pot fieri in dnio.

60 b

tc . III . runc . 7 . VII . anim . 7 . LX . porc . 7 . LX . ou . XXX . cap . x . uasa apū.
m . III . runc . 7 . VII . uac . XXVII . porc . L . ou . & . IIII . cap . XVII . uasa apū.
Tc 7 p ual . xx . lib . m . xxx.
Huic manerio adjacent semp . VI . soc . de . I . hid . 7 dim . tc . II . car . m . I.

23 Walter holds RIDLEY (Hall) from Geoffrey, which Asgar held before 1066 as a manor, for 1 hide. Always 1 plough in lordship; ½ men's plough.

Now 3 smallholders; then 3 slaves, now 1.

Woodland, 10 pigs; meadow, 4 acres.

30 acres belonged to this land before 1066, of which Geoffrey de Mandeville has 20 acres and Richard son of Count Gilbert (has) 10 acres; but the Hundred testifies that it is all rightly appurtenant to Geoffrey's land.

Value of the whole altogether 30s.

Hundred of HARLOW

24 Martel holds (Little) HALLINGBURY from Geoffrey, which Asgar held before 1066 as a manor, for 1 hide. Then 2 ploughs in lordship, now 1.

Then 1 priest and 1 villager with 20 acres which belonged to the church; but now they are not appurtenant to the church. Now 4 smallholders; then 3 slaves, now 2.

Woodland, 100 pigs; meadow, 20 acres; now ½ mill.

Value always 40s.

25 Asgar held MATCHING as a manor for 40 acres. Geoffrey holds it in lordship. Always 1 plough.

Then 1 slave, now none.

Woodland, 10 pigs; meadow, 3 acres.

Value 10s.

26 Hugh holds HALLINGBURY from Geoffrey which Godith, a free woman, held before 1066 as a manor, for ½ hide less 8 acres. Then ½ plough; now none.

Then 2 villagers; now none.

Meadow, 5 acres.

Value 5s.

Hundred of DUNMOW

27 Asgar held (High) EASTER before 1066 as a manor, for 2 hides. Now Geoffrey holds it in lordship. Always 4 ploughs in lordship; 12 men's ploughs.

Then 46 villagers, now 47; then 14 smallholders, now 33; always 9 slaves.

Woodland, 600 pigs; meadow, 30 acres; 5 ploughs possible in lordship. Then 3 cobs, 7 cattle, 60 pigs, 60 sheep, 30 goats, 60 b
10 beehives; now 3 cobs, 7 cows, 27 pigs, 50 sheep, 4 goats, 17 beehives.

Value then and later £20; now [£] 30.

Attached to this manor have always been 6 Freemen with 1½ hides. Then 2 ploughs, now 1.

m̃ . III . bord . VIII . ac . p̃ti . Tc̃ uat . XX . sol . m̃ . XXX. ⸋ Adjacent &iam huic
manerio . II . hid . 7 . I . uirḡ . q̃s tenuer̄ . II . soc . t . r . e . In q̃b; st̄ sēp . IIII . car
in dn̄io . 7 . I . car 7 dim . hom . Tc̃ . VIII . uitt . m̃ . VII . Tc̃ . VI . bord . m̃ . VII .
Sēp . III . ser . Silu . LX . porc . XXIIII . ac . p̃ti . Tc̃ 7 p̃ uat . c . sol . m̃ . X . lib.
hoc tenent . IIII . milit de . Gosfrido . 7 adhuc jacent illi manerio . dim.
hid . que p̃tinebat ad eccliam manerij . t . r . e . 7 eam m̃ ten& Gutbt de . G.
Sēp . I . car . tc̃ . I . bord . m̃ . III . 7 . I . ser . Silu . XX . porc . V . ac . p̃ti . Tc̃ uat . XX.
sol . m̃ . XXX . 7 hoc sup̃dictū maneriū calumpniat abbas de eli . 7 hund
testat q̃d fuit in abbia . t . r . e . s; Ansgar tenuit hoc maneriū eo die
q̃ Eaduuard rex . uiu 7 mortuus fuit.

⸋ Niuuetunā ten& Hugo de bneris de . G . q̃d tenuit Vluric
cauuā t . r . e . p̃ . Man . 7 p̃ . II . hid . 7 . I . uirg . Tc̃ . II . car in dn̄io . m̃ . I . 7 . dim.
Sēp . I . car hom . 7 . V . uitti . Tc̃ . I . bord . m̃ . V . sēp . II . ser . Silu . CLX . porc.
. XII . ac . p̃ti . Tc̃ . uat . LX . sol . 7 q̃n rec . XL . sol . m̃ . IIII . lib.

⸋ Bernestunā ten& Idē q̃d tenuit Vluuin t . r . e . p̃ . Man . 7 . p̃ . II.
hid . 7 . XXX . ac . Sēp . II . car in dn̄io . 7 . III . car . hom . Tc̃ . VI . uitt . m̃ . VII.
tc̃ . V . bord . m̃ . VII . Sēp . II . ser . Silu . CC . porc . XX . ac . p̃ti . Tc̃ uat . IIII . lib
m̃ . c . sol . 7 q̃n rec simit.

⸋ Rodinges ten& Idē . q̃d tenuit Vluric . t . r . e . p̃ Man . 7 p̃ . II . hid.
7 . dim . Sēp . II . car in dn̄io . 7 . I . car 7 dim . hom . Sēp . IIII . uitti . 7 . III . bord.

61 a

7 . IIII . ser . Silu . c . porc . XXVII . ac . p̃ti . Sēp . I . mol . Tc̃ . 7 p̃ uat . c . sol . m̃.
VII . lib . 7 hec . III . maneria p̃cep rex . p̃ Robtū de Oilleio . ut hugo te-
ner& de . G . de magna uitt . si ipse . G . poss& ea deratiocinari ad suū feudū.
7 anteq̃ . G . de rationar& ea p̃tinere suo feudo . Hugo ea tenuit de.
Goisfrido.

Now 3 smallholders.
Meadow, 8 acres.
Value then 20s; now 30[s].
Also attached to this manor, 2 hides and 1 virgate which 2 Freemen held before 1066. On them have always been 4 ploughs in lordship and 1½ men's ploughs.
Then 8 villagers, now 7; then 6 smallholders, now 7; always 3 slaves.
Woodland, 60 pigs; meadow, 24 acres.
Value then and later 100s; now £10.
3 men-at-arms hold this from Geoffrey.
Also attached to this manor is ½ hide which belonged to the church of the manor before 1066. Now Gutbert holds it from Geoffrey. Always 1 plough.
Then 1 smallholder, now 3; 1 slave.
Woodland, 20 pigs; meadow, 5 acres.
Value then 20s; now 30[s].
The Abbot of Ely lays claim to the above-mentioned manor and the Hundred testifies that it was in (the lands of) the Abbey before 1066; but Asgar held this manor in 1066.

28 Hugh of Bernières holds NEWTON (Hall) from Geoffrey, which Wulfric Cave held before 1066 as a manor, for 2 hides and 1 virgate. Then 2 ploughs in lordship, now 1½. Always 1 men's plough;
5 villagers. Then 1 smallholder, now 5; always 2 slaves.
Woodland, 160 pigs; meadow, 12 acres.
Value then 60s; when acquired 40s; now £4.

29 He also holds BARNSTON, which Wulfwin held before 1066 as a manor, for 2 hides and 30 acres. Always 2 ploughs in lordship; 3 men's ploughs.
Then 6 villagers, now 7; then 5 smallholders, now 7; always 2 slaves.
Woodland, 200 pigs; meadow, 20 acres.
Value then £4; now 100s; when acquired, the same.

30 He also holds (Berners) RODING, which Wulfric held before 1066 as a manor, for 2½ hides. Always 2 ploughs in lordship; 1½ men's ploughs.
Always 4 villagers; 3 smallholders; 4 slaves. 61 a
Woodland, 100 pigs; meadow, 27 acres; always 1 mill.
Value then and later 100s; now £7.
The King commanded through Robert d'Oilly that Hugh should hold these 3 manors from Geoffrey de Mandeville if Geoffrey himself could prove that they (belonged) to his Holding; and before Geoffrey proved that they belonged to his Holding, Hugh held them from Geoffrey.

Alferestunam ten& Martell' de . G . qđ tenuit Ansgar' . t . r . e . p uno man . 7 p . IIII . hid . 7 . x . ac . Sep . III . car in dnio . 7 . II . car . hom. tc . XI . uilli . m . VII . Tc . VI . bord . m . XXIIII . Tc . VI . ser . m . IIII . Silua tc . CCCC . porc . m . CCCL . XXXVI . ac . pti . Sep . I . mol . Tc . 7 p' uat . VII . lib. m . x . lib.

Domauua . ten& Ide de . G . qđ tenuit . Ide . Ansgar' . t . r . e . p . Man. 7 p . I . hid . 7 . dim . Sep . II . car in dnio . 7 . II . car hom . Tc . XIII . uill . m . v. Tc . VII . bord . m . VI . Tc . I . ser . m . III . Silu . CC . porc . XXVI . ac . pti . Tc uat . c . sol . m . VII . lib.

Scelgam ten& . Lambt' de . G . qđ tenuit . A . t . r . e . p . Man . 7 . p . I . hid. 7 dim . Sep . II . car in dnio . Tc . II . uill . m . I . Tc . v . bord . m . VIII . Tc . II . ser . m . I. Silu . CL . porc . x . ac . pti . III . anim . III . porc . XXV . ou . m . I . uasa ap . Tc 7 p' uat . XL . sol . m . LX.

Scelga ten& . G . in dnio qđ tenuit Vluric' lib ho de haroldo . t . r . e. p . Man . 7 p . II . hid . Sep . II . car in dnio . Tc . I . car hom . m . dim . Tc . II. uill . m . I . Tc . II . bord . m . IIII . tc . IIII . ser . m . VI . Silu . CL . porc . XII . ac pti. 7 adhuc . I . car poss& fieri . Tc uat . IIII . lib m . c . sol . Huic tre adjac& dim hid tre qm sep ten& . I . soc . Tc . I . car in dnio . m . dim . Sep . I . bord. 7 . I . ac . 7 dim . pti . 7 . đ . car pot restaurari . Vat . x . sol.

61 b

Rodinges ten& . Martell' de . G . qđ tenuit Ansgar' p Man . 7 p . II . hid . t . r . e. Sep . II . car in dnio . tc . III . car hom . m . II . 7 . tcia potest restaurari . Tc. . VI . uill . m . VIII . Tc . I . bor . m . v . Tc . I . ser . m null' . Silu . XX . porc . XX . ac. pti . Tc 7 p' uat . c . sol . m . VI . lib.

31 Martel holds BIGODS from Geoffrey, which Asgar held before 1066 as one manor, for 4 hides and 10 acres. Always 3 ploughs in lordship; 2 men's ploughs.

Then 11 villagers, now 7; then 6 smallholders, now 24; then 6 slaves, now 4.

Woodland, then 400 pigs, now 350; meadow, 36 acres; always 1 mill.

Value then and later £7; now £10.

32 He also holds (Little) DUNMOW from Geoffrey, which Asgar also held before 1066 as a manor, for 1½ hides. Always 2 ploughs in lordship; 2 men's ploughs.

Then 13 villagers, now 5; then 7 smallholders, now 6; then 1 slave, now 3.

Woodland, 200 pigs; meadow, 26 acres.

Value then 100s; now £7.

33 Lambert holds SHELLOW (Bowells) from Geoffrey, which A(sgar) held before 1066 as a manor, for 1½ hides. Always 2 ploughs in lordship.

Then 2 villagers, now 1; then 5 smallholders, now 8; then 2 slaves, now 1.

Woodland, 150 pigs; meadow, 10 acres. 3 cattle, 3 pigs, 25 sheep. Now 1 beehive.

Value then and later 40s; now 60[s].

34 Geoffrey holds SHELLOW (Bowells) in lordship which Wulfric, a free man, held from Harold before 1066 as a manor, for 2 hides. Always 2 ploughs in lordship. Then 1 men's plough, now ½.

Then 2 villagers, now 1; then 2 smallholders, now 4; then 4 slaves, now 6.

Woodland, 150 pigs; meadow, 12 acres; 1 more plough possible.

Value then £4; now 100s.

Attached to this land is ½ hide of land which 1 Freeman has always held. Then 1 plough in lordship, now ½.

Always 1 smallholder.

Meadow, 1½ acres; ½ plough can be restored.

Value 10s.

35 Martel holds (White) RODING from Geoffrey, which Asgar held as 61 b
a manor, for 2 hides before 1066. Always 2 ploughs in lordship. Then 3 men's ploughs, now 2; a third could be restored.

Then 6 villagers, now 8; then 1 smallholder, now 5; then 1 slave, now none.

Woodland, 20 pigs; meadow, 20 acres.

Value then and later 100s; now £6.

Dommauua teñ& Wills ꝑ Man 7 ꝑ dim. hid. & xv. ac. qđ tenuit. Idē . A. t. r. e. Sēp. i. car. in dñio. Tc. iiii. uill. m̃. i. 7. iiii. bor. Silu. l. porc. xvi. ac. p̃ti. Tc 7 p uał. xx. sol. m̃. lx.

Estanes teñ& Ricard de. G. qđ tenuit. i. lib hō. t. r. e. ꝑ. Man. 7. ꝑ dim hid. Sēp. i. car in dñio. Tc. i. ser. m̃. i. bord. xii. ac. p̃ti. Tc. 7 p uał . x. sol. m̃. xxx.

Chenefeldam ten&. Ricard. de. G. qđ tenuit. A. t. r. e. ꝑ. Man. 7. ꝑ. đ hid. 7. xvi. ac. Tc. ii. car. in dñio. m̃. i. m̃. i. car hom. m̃. ii. uill. Tc. viii. bord. m̃. iiii. Silu. xxx. porc. xvi. ac. p̃ti. Tc uał. xl. sol. 7. qñ rec simil. m̃. lx.

Roinges ten& Rainalm de. G. qđ ten. A. t. r. e. ꝑ. man. 7 ꝑ. ii. hid. . x. ac min. Sēp. ii. car in dñio. m̃. viii. bord. sēp. ii. ser. Silu. xx. por. xxxii. ac. p̃ti. Tc 7 p uał lx. sol. m̃. c. 7 adhuc poss& restaurari . i. car. Huic t̃re addite st̃. x. ac. qs tenuit. i. lib hō. t. r. e. 7 m̃ eas tot hund testat de dñio reg Willi.

Rodinges ten& Wills. qđ tenuit. i. lib hō. t. r. e. ꝑ. Man. 7. ꝑ. i. hid. 7. iii. uirg. hec t̃ra dimidia reddebat socā Ansgaro. 7 altā pars erat liba quā rex dedit. G. ut sui hoēs dict. Tc. i. car 7. dim. in dñio. m̃. i. m̃. i. car. hom. Sēp. iiii. uill. m̃. ii. bord. Tc. ii. ser m̃ null nec qñ recep. Silu. xxx. porc. xvi. ac. p̃ti. Tc 7 p uał

62 a

xl. sol. m̃. iiii. lib.

Scelgā ten& Wills. de. G. qđ tenuit. i. lib hō ꝑ xxxv. ac. t. r. e. Silua xx. porc. iiii. ac p̃ti. Tc. uał. v. sol. m̃. x. hec t̃ra jacuit ad Rodinges maneriū Eudonis dapiferi. t. r. e. 7 abbas de eli calumpniat teste hundrēt 7 t̃rā 7 maneriū de Rodingis.

36 William holds DUNMOW as a manor, for ½ hide and 15 acres. Asgar also held it before 1066. Always 1 plough in lordship.
Then 4 villagers, now 1; 4 smallholders.
Woodland, 50 pigs; meadow, 16 acres.
Value then and later 20s; now 60[s].

37 Richard holds EASTON from Geoffrey, which 1 free man held before 1066 as a manor, for ½ hide. Always 1 plough in lordship.
Then 1 slave; now 1 smallholder.
Meadow, 12 acres.
Value then and later 10s; now 30[s].

38 Richard holds (Little) CANFIELD from Geoffrey, which A(sgar) held before 1066 as a manor, for ½ hide and 16 acres. Then 2 ploughs in lordship, now 1. Now 1 men's plough.
Now 2 villagers; then 8 smallholders, now 4.
Woodland, 30 pigs; meadow, 16 acres.
Value then 40s; when acquired, the same; now 60[s].

39 Rainalm holds RODING from Geoffrey, which A(sgar) held before 1066 as a manor, for 2 hides less 10 acres. Always 2 ploughs in lordship.
Now 8 smallholders; always 2 slaves.
Woodland, 20 pigs; meadow, 32 acres.
Value then and later 60s; now 100[s]. 1 more plough could be restored.
To this land have been added 10 acres which 1 free man held before 1066. Now the whole Hundred testifies that they are part of King William's lordship.

40 William holds RODING, which 1 free man held before 1066 as a manor, for 1 hide and 3 virgates. Half this land paid suit to Asgar, the other part was free; the King gave it to Geoffrey, as his men state. Then 1½ ploughs in lordship, now 1. Now 1 men's plough.
Always 4 villagers. Now 2 smallholders; then 2 slaves, now none, nor when acquired.
Woodland, 30 pigs; meadow, 16 acres.
Value then and later 40s; now £4. 62 a

41 William holds SHELLOW (Bowells) from Geoffrey, which 1 free man held for 35 acres before 1066.
Woodland, 20 pigs; meadow, 4 acres.
Value then 5s; now 10[s].
This land lay in Eudo the Steward's manor of ('Morrell') Roding before 1066. The Abbot of Ely lays claim to both the land and the manor of ('Morrell') Roding, with the Hundred as witness.

In Dommauua ten&. G. in dn̄io. xxx. ac. q̄s tenuit. I. soc angari
Sēp. dim. car. Tc̄. I. bor. m̄. III. Silu. x. porc. IIII. ac. p̄ti. Tc̄ uat
VII. sot. m̄. x.

Rodinges ten& Martell qđ tenuit Ansg. t. r. e. 7 Leuid
quedā femina sub ansgaro. p. dim. hid. IIII. ac. p̄ti. Tc̄. uat. x. sot
m̄. XII.

Hunđ de Witbrictesherna Fenne ten& Hugo. de. G. qđ
tenuit Friebn lib homo. t. r. e. p Man. 7 p. IIII. hid. t. r. e. Sēp.
. IIII. uilt. Tc̄. II. bor. m̄. VII. Tc̄. II. ser. m̄ null. Sēp. II. car in
dn̄io. Tc̄. I. car hom. m̄. dim. Silu. XL. porc. Past. xxx. ou.
Sēp uat. LX. sot. hr̄ &iā Idē Hugo. I. hid. quam tenuit lib homo.
Vat. xx. sot. 7. xxx. VII. ac. ht Idē q̄s tenuit. I. lib. hō. Tc̄. dim. car
m̄. nulla. Vat. v. sot.

Hunđ de Vdelesforda. Waledanā ten&. G. in dn̄io. qđ ten
Ansgar. t. r. e. p Man. 7 p XVIIII. hid. 7. dim. Tc̄ 7 p VIII. car
in dn̄io. m̄. x. Sēp XXII. car hom. Tc̄ 7 p. LXVI. uilt. m̄ XLVI.
Tc̄ 7 p XVII. borđ. m̄. XL. Tc̄ 7 p. XVI. ser. m̄. xx. Tc̄ 7 p silua
. M. porc. m̄. DCCC. 7. LXXX. ac. p̄ti. Sēp. I. mot. huic manerio
adjacebant. t. r. e. XIII. soc. m̄. XIIII. tenentes. VI. hid. &. dimiđ hid

62 b

Tc̄ 7 post. VIII. car 7 dim. m̄. VIII. Tc̄ 7 p. x. bord. m̄. XIIII. Tc̄ 7 p silu.
. L. porc. m̄. xxx. xx. ac p̄ti. tc̄ia pars molini. Tc̄. VI. runc. XI... im.
. CC. ou. CX. porc. XL. cap. IIII. uasa apū. m̄. IX. runc. x. an. CCXLIII. ou.
. C. porc. xx. cap. xxx. uasa apū. Tc̄ 7 p uat. XXXVI. lib. m̄ uat. L. lib.

De hoc manerio ten&. Odo. I. hid. 7. I. uirg. 7 Renald. I. hid. XII. ac.
min. 7. II. car. 7. XIII. bord. 7 uat. L. sot in eođ p̄tio.

42 In DUNMOW Geoffrey holds 30 acres in lordship, which 1 Freeman of Asgar's held. Always ½ plough.
Then 1 smallholder, now 3.
Woodland, 10 pigs; meadow, 4 acres.
Value then 7s; now 10[s].

43 Martel holds (White) RODING, which Asgar held before 1066. Leofith, a woman, (held it) under Asgar for ½ hide.
Meadow, 4 acres.
Value then 10s; now 12[s].

Hundred of 'WIBERTSHERNE'

44 Hugh holds STOW MARIES from Geoffrey which Fridebern, a free man, held before 1066 as a manor, for 4 hides before 1066.
Always 4 villagers. Then 2 smallholders, now 7; then 2 slaves, now none. Always 2 ploughs in lordship. Then 1 men's plough, now ½.
Woodland, 40 pigs; pasture, 30 sheep.
Value always 60s.
Hugh also has 1 hide which a free man held.
Value 20s.
He also has 37 acres which 1 free man held. Then ½ plough, now none.
Value 5s.

Hundred of UTTLESFORD

45 Geoffrey holds (Saffron) WALDEN in lordship, which Asgar held before 1066 as a manor, for 19½ hides. Then and later 8 ploughs in lordship, now 10. Always 22 men's ploughs.
Then and later 66 villagers, now 46; then and later 17 smallholders, now 40; then and later 16 slaves, now 20.
Woodland, then and later 1000 pigs, now 800; meadow, 80 acres; always 1 mill.
Attached to this manor before 1066 were 13 Freemen, now 14, who hold 6½ hides. Then and later 8½ ploughs, now 8. 62 b
Then and later 10 smallholders, now 14.
Woodland, then and later 50 pigs, now 30; meadow, 20 acres; the third part of a mill. Then 6 cobs, 11 cattle, 200 sheep, 110 pigs, 40 goats, 4 beehives; now 9 cobs, 10 cattle, 243 sheep, 100 pigs, 20 goats, 30 beehives.
Value then and later £36; value now £50.
Of this manor, Odo holds 1 hide and 1 virgate and Reginald (holds) 1 hide less 12 acres. 2 ploughs.
13 smallholders.
Value 50s in the same assessment.

Cishellam ten& Will cardon de . G . qđ tenuit Vlfeih . lib hō . t . r . e.
p Man . 7 p . II . hid . 7 . dim . Tc . III . car in dnio . p 7 m . II . Tc 7 p . III . car
hom . m nulla . Tc 7 p . IX . uill . m null . Sep . VI . bord . Tc . 7 p . VI . ser.
m . I . silu . XXX . porc . VI . ac . pti . Tc . cc . ou . 7 . x . porc . m . ccxx . ou.
xxx . porc . LXVI . cap . III . an . Tc 7 p ual . VI . lib . m . c . sol.
In Ead uilla ten& Idē . III . hid . 7 XVII . ac . qs tenuer . v . libi hoēs
t . r . e Tc . v . car . 7 qn rec . II . m null . m . I . uill . 7 . III . bord . IIII . ac.
pti . Tc 7 p ual . c . sol . m . XL . Istas tras reclamat . G . p escangio.

In Munehala . ten& . qda anglic . de . G . III . uirg . qs tenuit lib hō
t . r . e . 7 . tepr reg uuilli . effect ē homo Goisfridi sponte sua . 7 dict
hōes Goisfridi . qđ p ea rex concessit Goisfrido p escangio . s; neq; ipse
homo nec hundret testimonium Goisfrido phibent . In illa tra erat
tc . I . car . m . dim . Sep . III . bord . VII ac . pti . Val . x . sol.

Blichangram ten& Germund de . G . qđ ten . I . soc . Ansgari p . dim.
hid . t . r . e . Sep . I . car in dnio . 7 . III . bord . Tc 7 p silu . XL . porc . m . XXX.
Tc . ual . XX . sol . m . x.

Hund de Clauelinga In Plicedana ten& Ricard soc Angari
. I . hid 7 . XX . ac . t . r . e . Tc . I . car . m null . Sep . III . bord . Silu . x . porc.

63 a
. x . ac . pti . Sep ual . XXI . sol.

46 William Cardon holds (Great) CHISHILL from Geoffrey which Wulfheah, a free man, held before 1066 as a manor, for 2½ hides. Then 3 ploughs in lordship, later and now 2. Then and later 3 men's ploughs, now none.

Then and later 9 villagers, now none; always 6 smallholders. Then and later 6 slaves, now 1.

Woodland, 30 pigs; meadow, 6 acres. Then 200 sheep and 10 pigs; now 220 sheep, 30 pigs, 66 goats, 3 cattle.

Value then and later £6; now 100s.

In the same village he also holds 3 hides and 17 acres which 5 free men held before 1066. Then 5 ploughs, when acquired 2, now none.

Now 1 villager; 3 smallholders.

Meadow, 4 acres.

Value then and later 100s; now 40[s].

Geoffrey claims back these lands by exchange.

47 In EMANUEL (Wood) an Englishman holds 3 virgates from Geoffrey, which a free man held before 1066. After 1066 he was made Geoffrey's man of his own accord. Geoffrey's men state that afterwards the King granted (it) to Geoffrey by exchange; but neither the man himself nor the Hundred bears witness for Geoffrey. On that land there was then 1 plough, now ½.

Always 3 smallholders.

Meadow, 7 acres.

Value 10s.

48 Germund holds BIRCHANGER from Geoffrey, which 1 Freeman of Asgar's held for ½ hide before 1066. Always 1 plough in lordship; 3 smallholders.

Woodland, then and later 40 pigs, now 30.

Value then 20s; now 10[s].

Hundred of CLAVERING

49 In PLEDGDON (Hall) Richard holds. A Freeman of Asgar's ... ; 1 hide and 20 acres before 1066. Then 1 plough, now none.

Always 3 smallholders.

Woodland, 10 pigs; meadow, 10 acres. 63 a

Value always 21s.

Hund de Witbrictesherna Phennã ten& hugo de uerli qđ tenuit Friebn p Man. 7. p. III. hid. Sep. II. uilt. Tc. II. borđ. m. VII. Tc. II. ser. m null. Sep. II. car in dnio. Tc. I. car hom. m. dim. Silu. XL. porc. Past. .xxx. ou. Tc. v. porc. xxx. ou. 7. m. LXX. porc. Vat. LX. sot. In Ead ten& Idē XXXVII. ac. Tc. dim. car. m. nult. Vat. v. sot. ★

Wenesuuic tenuit Ansgar. t. r. e. p. Man. 7. p. v. hid. 7 XL. ac. qđ tenent Godefrid 7 Eurard de. G. sep. II. uilt. Tc. IIII. bor. m. VII. Sep. III. ser. 7. II. car. in dnio. Tc. II. car hom. m. I. 7. dim. vat. IIII. lib. In Ead .VI. libi hoes tenuer. I. hid. 7. XL. ac. qđ tenent Idē. Tc uat. xx. sot. m. x.

TRA Comitis de. Ov. Turruc ten& Comes in dnio qđ tenuit Herold. p. man. 7. p. XIII. hid. Tc. XII. uilt. m. XVII. Tc. XVI. bor. m. XLV. Tc. XVI. ser. m. VIII. Tc. VI. car in dnio. m. v. Tc. x. car hom. m. XIII. Silu. .cc. porc. XL. ac. pti. Past. D. ou. Tc. I. pisc. m. II. Sep. v. uac. III. runc XVI. porc. DL. ou. Tc uat. XII. lib. m. XXX. 7. VII. dom st Londoniæ que jacent huic manerio 7. in hac firma. .XXXI.

63 b

.XXXII. TERRE Robti grenonis. Hundret de bdestapla.

Ramesdanam ten& Rob in dnio qđ tenuer. III. libi hoes. t. r. e. p. Man. 7 p. III. hid. 7. dim. 7. XXX. ac. Sep. II. car in dnio. 7. I. car hom. Tc. III. uilt. m. II. Tc. III. borđ. m. XIII. Tc. III. ser. m. IIII.

Hundred of 'WIBERTSHERNE'

50 Hugh of Verly holds STOW MARIES, which Fridebern held as a manor, for 3 hides.

Always 2 villagers. Then 2 smallholders, now 7; then 2 slaves, now none. Always 2 ploughs in lordship. Then 1 men's plough, now ½.

Woodland, 40 pigs; pasture, 30 sheep. Then 5 pigs, 30 sheep; now 70 pigs.

Value 60s.

In the same (Stow Maries) he also holds 37 acres. Then ½ plough, now none.

Value 5s.

51 Asgar held *WENESUUIC* before 1066 as a manor, for 5 hides and 40 acres. Godfrey and Evrard hold it from Geoffrey.

Always 2 villagers. Then 4 smallholders, now 7. Always 3 slaves; 2 ploughs in lordship. Then 2 men's ploughs, now 1½.

Value £4.

In the same (*Wenesuuic*) 6 free men held 1 hide and 40 acres which they also hold.

Value then 20s; now 10[s].

31 LAND OF THE COUNT OF EU

[Hundred of CHAFFORD]

1 The Count holds (West) THURROCK in lordship, which Harold held as a manor, for 13 hides.

Then 12 villagers, now 17; then 16 smallholders, now 45; then 16 slaves, now 8. Then 6 ploughs in lordship, now 5. Then 10 men's ploughs, now 13.

Woodland, 200 pigs; meadow, 40 acres; pasture, 500 sheep; then 1 fishery, now 2. Always 5 cows, 3 cobs, 16 pigs, 550 sheep.

Value then £12; now [£] 30.

There are 7 houses in London which lie in (the lands of) this manor and in this revenue.

32 LANDS OF ROBERT GERNON 63 b

Hundred of BARSTABLE

1 Robert holds RAMSDEN in lordship, which 3 free men held before 1066 as a manor, for 3½ hides and 30 acres. Always 2 ploughs in lordship; 1 men's plough.

Then 3 villagers, now 2; then 3 smallholders, now 13; then 3 slaves, now 4.

Silua . LXXXX . porc . Tc̄ . I . runc . ṁ . II . Tc̄ . II . an . ṁ . x . Sēp . LX . ou .
7 . XL . porc . ṁ . II . uasa apū . Vat . L . sol.

Ramesdunā ten& Anschetill de . Robto . qd tenuit Aluric libe . p.
Man . 7 p . II . hid . Sēp . I . car in dnio . 7 . dim . car hom . Tc̄ . II . uill . ṁ . I.
Sēp . VI . bord . tc̄ . II . ser . ṁ . null . Silu XL . porc . Sēp . I . runc . Tc̄ . VII . porc.
ṁ . XX . ṁ . VI . an . Tc̄ . XX . ou . ṁ . LXXX . II . uasa apū . vat . XXX . sol.

Hund de Witham . Witham ten& Hugo de . R . qd tenuit Burcard
lib hō . t . r . e . p uno Man . 7 p . IIII . hid . Tc̄ . IIII . car in dnio . ṁ . II . ṁ . II . car
hom . 7 . II . uill . 7 . VI . bord . Tc̄ . VI . ser . ṁ . III . VI . ac . pti . I . mol . Tc̄ . I.
runc . 7 . II . anim . 7 . LXXX . ou . 7 . XII . porc . ṁ . I . runc . 7 . IIII . anim.
7 . C . ou . 7 . XX . porc . 7 . III . uasa apū . Sep uat . IIII . lib.

Hobruge ten& Ricard de . R . qd tenuit Brictmar . t . r . e . p M.
7 p . II . hid . 7 dim . Sēp . II . car in dnio . 7 . I . car hom . 7 . II . uill . 7 . VI.
bord . Tc̄ . VI . ser . ṁ null . Silu . XL . porc . XI . ac . pti . I . mol . Tc̄ . II . an.
ṁ . IIII . Tc̄ . I . runc . ṁ null . Tc̄ . XII . porc . ṁ . XL . Tc̄ . XXX . ou . ṁ.
LIIII . ṁ . XXIIII . cap . Vat . XL . sol.

Riuuehalā . ten& Ascelin . de . R . qd tenuit Alestan lib hō . t . r . e.
p Man . 7 p . dim . hid . Sēp . I . car in dnio . Tc̄ . I . bord . ṁ . VIII . Tc̄ . I.
ser . ṁ null . Silu . X . porc . VIII . ac . pti . ṁ . VIII . porc . Vat . XX . sol

64 a

Hund de herlaua . Matcingam ten& Hugo de . Rob . qd ten
Aluric cild lib homo t . r . e . p Man . 7 p . I . hid . Sēp . I . car . in dnio . tc̄ . dim.
car . hom . ṁ nulla . Tc̄ . I . uill . ṁ . null . Tc̄ . I . bord . ṁ . IIII . Tc̄ . III . ser . ṁ
null . Silu . XL . porc . VIII . ac . pti . Tc̄ . I . runc . 7 . VIII . porc . ṁ . XVI . porc
7 . XII . ou . 7 . VIII . cap . 7 . IIII . anim . Tc̄ . uat . XX . sol . ṁ . XXX.

Woodland, 90 pigs. Then 1 cob, now 2; then 2 cattle, now 10. Always 60 sheep; 40 pigs. Now 2 beehives.
Value 50s.

2 Ansketel holds RAMSDEN from Robert, which Aelfric held freely as a manor, for 2 hides. Always 1 plough in lordship; ½ men's plough.
Then 2 villagers, now 1; always 6 smallholders. Then 2 slaves, now none.
Woodland, 40 pigs. Always 1 cob. Then 7 pigs, now 20; now 6 cattle; then 20 sheep, now 80; 2 beehives.
Value 30s.

Hundred of WITHAM

3 Hugh holds WITHAM from Robert which Burghard, a free man, held before 1066 as one manor, for 4 hides. Then 4 ploughs in lordship, now 2. Now 2 men's ploughs;
2 villagers; 6 smallholders. Then 6 slaves, now 3.
Meadow, 6 acres; 1 mill. Then 1 cob, 2 cattle, 80 sheep and 12 pigs; now 1 cob, 4 cattle, 100 sheep, 20 pigs and 3 beehives.
Value always £4.

4 Richard holds HOWBRIDGE from Robert, which Brictmer held before 1066 as a manor, for 2½ hides. Always 2 ploughs in lordship; 1 men's plough;
2 villagers; 6 smallholders. Then 6 slaves, now none.
Woodland, 40 pigs; meadow, 11 acres; 1 mill. Then 2 cattle, now 4; then 1 cob, now none; then 12 pigs, now 40; then 30 sheep, now 54; now 24 goats.
Value 40s.

5 Ascelin holds RIVENHALL from Robert which Alstan, a free man, held before 1066 as a manor, for ½ hide. Always 1 plough in lordship.
Then 1 smallholder, now 8; then 1 slave, now none.
Woodland, 10 pigs; meadow, 8 acres. Now 8 pigs.
Value 20s.

Hundred of HARLOW 64 a

6 Hugh holds MATCHING from Robert which Young Aelfric, a free man, held before 1066 as a manor, for 1 hide. Always 1 plough in lordship. Then ½ men's plough, now none.
Then 1 villager, now none; then 1 smallholder, now 4; then 3 slaves, now none.
Woodland, 40 pigs; meadow, 8 acres. Then 1 cob and 8 pigs; now 16 pigs, 12 sheep, 8 goats and 4 cattle.
Value then 20s; now 30[s].

Hund de Waltham Cingefort ten& Orgar teinn de. Rob
qd tenuit. i. lib hō. t. r. e. [p man'. 7. v. hid.] 7 reddit. x. den. de Soca ad uualtham Tc. ii.
car in dnio. m. i. Tc. iii. car hom. m. ii. Sep. vii. uill. 7. vi. bord. 7. iiii.
ser. Silu. d. porc. l. ac. pti. Sep. i. mol. 7. iiii. piscinæ. 7 adhuc posst
restaurari. ii. car. una in dnio. 7 alia uillis. Tc. xi. anim. m. null.
tc. xxx. porc. m. xxi. Sep ual. lxx. sol.

Hund de beuentreu. Hame. ten& Rob in dnio. qd tenuit
Alestan lib hō. t. r. e. p Man. 7 p. viii. hid. 7. xxx. ac. 7 hoc maneriu
Will rex Ranulfo piperello. 7 Rob grenoni. Tc. v. car in dnio. m
. iiii. tc. viii. car hom. m xii. tc. xxxii. uill. m. xlviii. Tc. xvi.
bord. m. lxxx. i. min. Sep. iii. ser. Silu. c. porc. lx. ac. pti. ix. mol tc.
m. viii. Tc. ual. xvi. lib. 7 qn recepunt. xii. lib. m ual. xxiiii. lib.
7 de hoc manerio ht. R. piperell medietate. 7 in dnio Robti rec.
. R. i. runc. 7 m. similit ibi e. Tc. i. uac. m. ix. anim. Tc. vi. ou.
m. xii. Tc. v. porc. m. xi. de hoc manerio tenet Osbn de Robto
xxx. ac. 7. d. car. 7 ual. x. sol. in eod. ptio.

Hame ten& Rob in dnio qd tenuit Leured lib hō. t. r. e. p. Man.
7 p. vii. hid. Sep. iii. car in dnio. Tc. vii. car hom. m. xiii. Tc
xxxiiii. uill. m. xxxviii. Tc. iii. bord. m. xxvi. Tc. xix. ser

64 b

m. iii. Silu. dcc. porc. l. ac. pti. Tc. viii. anim. m. xv. Tc. xx. porc. m
xxxiiii. m. cc. ou. xx. min. m. iiii. runc. 7. iii. uasa ap. 7 huic træ
addite st. iii. uirg. t. r. Willi. qs ten Eduin. lib hōr. t. r. e. Tc. i. car
m. dim. m. ii. bord. Silu. x. porc. ix. ac. pti. 7 hoc man ual t. r. e. x.
lib. 7 qn rec. vii. lib. m. xviii. lib. 7 huic maner adjacent. xxx.
ac. qs ten. i. soc. De hoc man. ten& Ilger. xl. ac. 7. ii. bord. 7. i. car.
7 ual. xv. sol. in eod ptio.

Hundred of WALTHAM

7 Ordgar, a thane of Robert's, holds CHINGFORD which 1 free man held before 1066 as a manor, for 5 hides. He pays 10d of suit to Waltham (Holy Cross). Then 2 ploughs in lordship, now 1. Then 3 men's ploughs, now 2.

Always 7 villagers; 6 smallholders; 4 slaves.

Woodland, 500 pigs; meadow, 50 acres. Always 1 mill; 4 fisheries. 2 more ploughs can be restored, 1 in lordship, the other for the villagers. Then 11 cattle, now none; then 30 pigs, now 21.

Value always 70s.

Hundred of BECONTREE

8 Robert holds (West) HAM in lordship which Alstan, a free man, held before 1066 as a manor, for 8 hides and 30 acres. King William [gave] this manor to Ranulf Peverel and Robert Gernon. Then 5 ploughs in lordship, now 4. Then 8 men's ploughs, now 12.

Then 32 villagers, now 48; then 16 smallholders, now 80 less 1; always 3 slaves.

Woodland, 100 pigs; meadow, 60 acres; then 9 mills, now 8.

Value then £16; when acquired £12. Value now £24.

Ranulf Peverel has half of this manor. And in Robert's lordship, R(obert) acquired 1 cob, now the same is there; then 1 cow, now 9 cattle; then 6 sheep, now 12; then 5 pigs, now 11.

Of this manor, Osbern holds 30 acres from Robert. ½ plough.

Value 10s in the same assessment.

9 Robert holds (East) HAM in lordship which Leofred, a free man, held before 1066 as a manor, for 7 hides. Always 3 ploughs in lordship. Then 7 men's ploughs, now 13.

Then 34 villagers, now 38; then 3 smallholders, now 26; then 19 slaves, now 3. 64 b

Woodland, 700 pigs; meadow, 50 acres. Then 8 cattle, now 15; then 20 pigs, now 34; now 200 sheep less 20; now 4 cobs; 3 beehives.

3 virgates were added to this land after 1066 which Edwin, a free priest, held before 1066. Then 1 plough, now ½.

Now 2 smallholders.

Woodland, 10 pigs; meadow, 9 acres.

Value of this manor before 1066 £10; when acquired £7; now £18.

30 acres are attached to this manor which 1 Freeman holds.

Of this manor, Ilger holds 40 acres.

2 smallholders. 1 plough.

Value 15s in the same assessment.

In Leituna ten& Rob . in dnio . dim . hid . qm tenuit . i . lib ho . t . r . e.
Sep . dim . car . 7 . ii . bord . v . ac . pti . val . v . sol.

In Lochetuna ten& . W . corbun . de . R . xliiii . ac . qd ten . i . lib ho.
t . r . e . Sep . dim . car . m . ii . bord . Silu . xx . porc . i . ac . pti . val . x . sol.

Hund de Witbrictesherna . Purlai . ten& Ricard de . R . qd
tenuit Algar lib ho . p . Man . 7 p . ii . hid . 7 . xv . ac . Tc . i . ser . m . i . bord.
Sep . i . car . Tc . ual . x . sol . 7 qn rec . xx . m . xxx . In dnio st m.
xxxiiii . ou . 7 nichil recep.

Witham ten& Anschetill de . R . qd tenuit Lestan lib ho . t . r . e . p
Man . 7 p . i . hid . 7 . dim . Tc . ii . uill . m . null . tc . iiii . bord . m . viii.
Sep . i . ser . 7 . ii . car in dnio . Tc . i . car 7 dim hom . m . i . Silu . cl . porc.
Tc . ii . uac . m . viii . anim . Tc . c . ou . m . cxl . Tc . xvi . porc . m . xx.
sep . i . runc . Tc . ual . xl . sol . 7 qn rec . xxx . m . ual . iiii . lib.

Hund de Wensistreu . Lega ten& Rob de uerli de Robto.
qd tenuit Gotre lib ho . t . r . e . p . Man . 7 p . iiii . hid . 7 . dim . Tc . iii.
car . in dnio . m . ii . Sep . iii . car . hom . Tc . vii . uill . m . v . Tc . v.
bord . m . xii . Tc . vii . ser . m . iii . Silu . c . porc . m . i . mol.

65 a

Tc . i . runc . m . viii . Tc . clx . ou . m . lxxx . tc . xx . porc . m null.
Sep ual . iiii . lib.

Salcota ten& Ide . R . de eod . qd tenuit . i . lib ho . t . r . e . p . Man . 7.
p . i . hid . 7 . dim . Sep . i . car in dnio . Tc . iiii . bord . m . iii . Sep . i . ser . Tc . nich.
m . ii . runc . xx . porc . lxxx . ou . ii . anim . Tc . ual . xxvi . sol . m . xxx.

10 In LEYTON Robert holds ½ hide in lordship, which 1 free man held before 1066. Always ½ plough;
2 smallholders.
Meadow, 5 acres.
Value 5s.

11 In LOUGHTON W. Corbun holds 44 acres from Robert, which 1 free man held before 1066. Always ½ plough.
Now 2 smallholders.
Woodland, 20 pigs; meadow, 1 acre.
Value 10s.

Hundred of 'WIBERTSHERNE'

12 Richard holds PURLEIGH from Robert which Algar, a free man, held as a manor, for 2 hides and 15 acres.
Then 1 slave, now 1 smallholder. Always 1 plough.
Value then 10s; when acquired 20[s]; now 30[s].
34 sheep are now in lordship; he acquired nothing.

13 Ansketel holds (Great) WHITMANS from Robert which Leofstan, a free man, held before 1066 as a manor, for 1½ hides.
Then 2 villagers, now none; then 4 smallholders, now 8. Always 1 slave; 2 ploughs in lordship. Then 1½ men's ploughs, now 1.
Woodland, 150 pigs. Then 2 cows, now 8 cattle; then 100 sheep, now 140; then 16 pigs, now 20; always 1 cob.
Value then 40s; when acquired 30[s]. Value now £4.

Hundred of WINSTREE

14 Robert of Verly holds *LEGA* from Robert which Gotre, a free man, held before 1066 as a manor, for 4½ hides. Then 3 ploughs in lordship, now 2. Always 3 men's ploughs.
Then 7 villagers, now 5; then 5 smallholders, now 12; then 7 slaves, now 3.
Woodland, 100 pigs; now 1 mill. Then 1 cob, now 8; then 65 a
160 sheep, now 80; then 20 pigs, now none.
Value always £4.

15 Robert also holds VIRLEY from him, which 1 free man held before 1066 as a manor, for 1½ hides. Always 1 plough in lordship.
Then 4 smallholders, now 3; always 1 slave.
Then nothing; now 2 cobs, 20 pigs, 80 sheep, 2 cattle.
Value then 26s; now 30[s].

⸿ Hund de Wdelesforda. Stanestedam ten& Rob in dnio. qd tenuit lib ho. t. r. e. p. Man. 7 p. vi. hid. Tc. iiii. car. in dnio. Post. ii. m. iii. Sep. x. car hom. 7. xi. uill. 7. i. pbr. Tc. 7 p. iiii. bord. m. xviii. tc. viii. ser. Post. iiii. m. iii. Silu. ∞. porc. xx. ac. pti. Sep. i. mol. Tc. viii. an. m. xvi. Tc. cxl. ou. m. cxx. Tc. xx. porc. m. lx. xl. cap. tc. m. xxiiii. m. ii. runc. 7. v. asini. Huic man. adjac&. i. bereuuita quæ uocat magghedana. de. i. hid. Sep. i. car. in dnio. 7. ii. bord. Silu. x. porc. Tc 7 p uat. viii. lib. m. xi.

⸿ Tacheleiam ten&. R. in dnio. qd. tenuit. i. lib ho. t. r. e. p. Man. 7. p. iii. hid. 7. xv. ac. Sep. ii. car. in dnio. 7. iii. car hom. 7. iii. uill. m. viii. bord. Tc. 7 p. iii. ser. m. ii. Silu. cc. porc. xx. ac pti. Tc. ii. runc. m. i. Tc. xii. an. m. iii. Tc. xvi. ou. m. x. Tc. xx. porc. m xxxviii. Sep uat. c. sol. Petr ten& de. R. d. hid. 7. i. b. val. xii. sol.

⸿ Wendenã ten& Hugo de. R. qd ten. i. lib ho. t. r. e. p Man. 7 p. vii. hid. vi. ac. min. Sep. iii. car in dnio. Tc. iiii. car hom. 7 qn rec. m. v. Tc 7 p. viii. uill. m. ix. m. v. bord. tc. 7 p vi. ser. m. v. xxiiii. ac. pti. Tc. 7 p. i. mol. m. ii. Tc. v. ou. 7. vii. porc. m. iii. pulli. 7. xxx. porc. 7 lxvii. ou. Tc 7 p uat. vii. lib. m. viii.

⸿ Dim Hund de Claueling. Benedfeldã ten&. R. in dnio

65 b

qd tenuit. lib homo. t. r. e. p Man. 7 p. v. hid. Sep. iii. car in dnio. Tc. vii. car. hominũ. Post. vi. m. iiii. Tc. x. uill. Post 7 m. ix. tc. 7 p. ii. bord. m. xi. Tc. 7 p. vii. ser. m. iiii. Silu. cc. porc. xvi. ac. pti. i. mol. Tc. ii. runc. m. iii. Tc. i. an. m. xiiii. Tc. lxxx. ou. m. xxx. Tc. l. porc. m. xl. Tc 7 post uat. c. sol. m. vii. lib. Huic tre adjac& sep. i. soc. de. xxx. ac.

Hundred of UTTLESFORD

16 Robert holds STANSTED (Mountfitchet) in lordship, which a free man held before 1066 as a manor, for 6 hides. Then 4 ploughs in lordship, later 2, now 3. Always 10 men's ploughs;

11 villagers; 1 priest. Then and later 4 smallholders, now 18; then 8 slaves, later 4, now 3.

Woodland, 1000 pigs; meadow, 20 acres; always 1 mill. Then 8 cattle, now 16; then 140 sheep, now 120; then 20 pigs, now 60; then 40 goats, now 24; now 2 cobs and 5 asses.

Attached to this manor is 1 outlier which is called MANUDEN with 1 hide. Always 1 plough in lordship;

2 smallholders.

Woodland, 10 pigs.

Value then and later £8; now [£] 11.

17 Robert holds TAKELEY in lordship, which 1 free man held before 1066 as a manor, for 3 hides and 15 acres. Always 2 ploughs in lordship; 3 men's ploughs;

3 villagers. Now 8 smallholders; then and later 3 slaves, now 2.

Woodland, 200 pigs; meadow, 20 acres. Then 2 cobs, now 1; then 12 cattle, now 3; then 16 sheep, now 10; then 20 pigs, now 38.

Value always 100s.

Peter holds ½ hide from Robert.

1 smallholder.

Value 12d.

18 Hugh holds WENDENS (Ambo) from Robert, which 1 free man held before 1066 as a manor, for 7 hides less 6 acres. Always 3 ploughs in lordship. Then 4 men's ploughs, and when acquired; now 5.

Then and later 8 villagers, now 9; now 5 smallholders; then and later 6 slaves, now 5.

Meadow, 24 acres; then and later 1 mill, now 2. Then 5 sheep and 7 pigs; now 3 foals, 30 pigs and 67 sheep.

Value then and later £7; now [£] 8.

Half-Hundred of CLAVERING

19 Robert holds BENTFIELD (Bury) in lordship, which a free man held 65 b
before 1066 as a manor, for 5 hides. Always 3 ploughs in lordship. Then 7 men's ploughs, later 6, now 4.

Then 10 villagers, later and now 9; then and later 2 smallholders, now 11; then and later 7 slaves, now 4.

Woodland, 200 pigs; meadow, 16 acres; 1 mill. Then 2 cobs, now 3; then 1 (head of) cattle, now 14; then 80 sheep, now 30; then 50 pigs, now 40.

Value then and later 100s; now £7.

To this land has always been attached 1 Freeman with 30 acres.

In Bolituna ten& Rob in dnio . I . hid 7 dim' . xv . ac . Tc . I . car 7 . dim. Post 7 m . I . Sep . II . bord . Tc . x . porc . 7 . xxvIII . ou . m . I . anim . 7 . II . porc . 7 . IIII . ou . Sep . ual . xxv . sol . In hoc manerio ten&. Rob . de . R . dim . hid . 7 . dim . car . 7 . ual . x . sol . in eod ptio.

Phernham ten& Rob in dnio . qd tenuit . I . lib ho . t . r . e . p . Man. 7 p . II . hid . Sep . II . car . in dnio . 7 . II . car . hom . Tc 7 p . II . uill . m . I. Sep . vIII . bord . Tc 7 p . vIII . ser . m . I . Tc 7 post silu . cc . por . m . CL. . x . ac pti . Tc . IIII . runc . m . II . Tc . xv . anim . m . null . Tc . xL . por. m . xvII . Tc . Lx . ou . m . xxx . m . xxxIx . cap . 7 . III . uasa apu. Tc ual . xL . sol . m . L.

Menghedana . tenuer . IIII . libi hoes . t . r . e . p . Man . 7 p . IIII . hid m tenent . IIII . milit . de . R . Sep . III . car . 7 . II . uill . 7 . v . bord. 7 . I . ser . Silu . xxx . porc . xIII . ac . pti . Tc . vIII . anim . 7 Lxxx . ou. 7 . xx . cap . 7 . xx . porc . m . v . an . 7 . xxxIII . porc . 7 . I . pull . 7 . xLIIII. ou . 7 . vIII . cap . Tc ual . L . sol . m . Lx.

Hund de hidingforda . Mapledesteda ten& Ilger de . R . qd tenuit Vluuin lib ho . t . r . e . p . Man . 7 . p dim hid . Sep . II . car in dnio. 7 . III . car . hom . 7 . v . uilli . tc . 7 p . II . bord . m . vI . Tc 7 p . IIII . ser . m . II.

66 a

Tc silua . c . porc . m . Lx . xxvI . ac . pti . Tc . I . runc . 7 . vIII . anim . 7 . x . porc. 7 . xx . ou . 7 . xx . cap . m . I . runc . 7 . xIIII . anim . 7 . xvIII . porc . 7 . Lxxx. ou . 7 . xxIII . cap . 7 . II . uasa apu . Val . Lx . sol.

20 In BOLLINGTON (Hall) Robert holds 1½ hides and 15 acres in lordship. Then 1½ ploughs, later and now 1.
Always 2 smallholders.
Then 10 pigs and 28 sheep; now 1 (head of) cattle, 2 pigs and 4 sheep.
Value always 25s.
In this manor Robert holds ½ hide from R(obert). ½ plough.
Value 10s in the same assessment.

21 Robert holds FARNHAM in lordship, which 1 free man held before 1066 as a manor, for 2 hides. Always 2 ploughs in lordship; 2 men's ploughs.
Then and later 2 villagers, now 1; always 8 smallholders. Then and later 8 slaves, now 1.
Woodland, then and later 200 pigs, now 150; meadow, 10 acres. Then 4 cobs, now 2; then 15 cattle, now none; then 40 pigs, now 17; then 60 sheep, now 30; now 39 goats; 3 beehives.
Value then 40s; now 50[s].

22 4 free men held MANUDEN before 1066 as a manor, for 4 hides. Now 4 men-at-arms hold (it) from Robert. Always 3 ploughs;
2 villagers; 5 smallholders; 1 slave.
Woodland, 30 pigs; meadow, 13 acres. Then 8 cattle, 80 sheep, 20 goats and 20 pigs; now 5 cattle, 33 pigs, 1 foal, 44 sheep and 8 goats.
Value then 50s; now 60[s].

Hundred of HINCKFORD

23 Ilger holds (Great) MAPLESTEAD from Robert which Wulfwin, a free man, held before 1066 as a manor, for ½ hide. Always 2 ploughs in lordship; 3 men's ploughs;
5 villagers. Then and later 2 smallholders, now 6; then and later 4 slaves, now 2.
Woodland, then 100 pigs, now 60; meadow, 26 acres. Then 66 a
1 cob, 8 cattle, 10 pigs, 20 sheep and 20 goats; now 1 cob, 14 cattle, 18 pigs, 80 sheep, 23 goats and 2 beehives.
Value 60s.

Hund de Laxedana. Widemondefort ten& Ilger de. R. qđ tenuit Goduin p Man. 7 p. I. hid. 7. dim. 7. x. ac. Tc. III. uitti m. IIII. Tc. II. borđ. m. VIII. Sep. IIII. ser. Tc. III. car in dnio. m. IIII. Sep. II. car hom. Silu. c. porc. XVI. ac. pti. m. I. mol. I. pisc. Tc. I. runc. m. VI. Tc. v. anim. m. XXXIII. Tc. XL. porc. m. LX. tc. VI. ou. m. CC. tc. XV. cap. m, XLVII. m. VII. uasa apu. Tc uat. IIII. lib. m. VI. 7 XVIIII. soc. t. r. e tenentes. II. hid. 7. dim. VI. ac. min. qs. R. ht in suo escangio sic dicit. qs tenet Ide Ilger. de eo. 7 hnt. VIII. bor. Sep. II. car. IIII. ac. pti. Silu. XVI. porc. Sep uat. XL. sol. 7 isti sochemani sic comitat testat. non potant remouere ab illo man. 7. I. uittm abstulit Reimund girald de q fuit Robt saisit. 7 adhuc ht Rog pictauensis.

Wiunhov ten& Nigell de. R. qđ tenuit Aluric p Man. 7 p. v. hid xv. ac. min. Sep. v. uitt. tc. VI. borđ. m. XX. tc. I. ser. m. II. Sep. II. car in dnio. tc. int hoes. III. car. m. II. Silu. c. porc. XII. ac. pti. Past. LX. ou. m. I. mol. Tc. VIII. anim. m. X. tc. I. runc. m. II. tc. LX. ou. m. LXXXVII. tc. XXX. cap. m. XX. Tc. XX. porc. m XXIIII. Sep uat. XL. sol. 7. I. lib ho. tenuit. XX. ac. qs ten& Rob de dono reg 7. Nigell de eo. Sep. dim. car. vat. III. sol. 7 ali lib tenuit. XX. ac. qs ht custos hundret vat. III. sol; Ide Nigell ten&.

Briciam ten& Rob de. R. qđ tenuit Vluuin p. Man. 7. p. II. hid.

66 b

. IIII. ac. 7 dim min. Sep. XII. borđ. tc. VI. ser. m. v. Sep. II. car. in dnio. 7. II. car hom. Silu. XL. porc. XII. ac. pti. Sep. I. mot. Tc. II. anim. m. VII. Tunc XXXVIII. ou. m LXXX. m. XXXIII. cap. Tc. v. porc. m. XXXIII. m. II. runc. Sep uat. LX. sol.

Hundred of LEXDEN

24 Ilger holds WORMINGFORD from Robert, which Godwin held as a manor, for 1½ hides and 10 acres.

Then 3 villagers, now 4; then 2 smallholders, now 8; always 4 slaves. Then 3 ploughs in lordship, now 4. Always 2 men's ploughs.

Woodland, 100 pigs; meadow, 16 acres; now 1 mill; 1 fishery. Then 1 cob, now 6; then 5 cattle, now 33; then 40 pigs, now 60; then 6 sheep, now 200; then 15 goats, now 47; now 7 beehives.

Value then £4; now [£] 6.

19 Freemen who held 2½ hides less 6 acres before 1066 (and) whom Robert has in exchange, so he states. Ilger also holds them from him.

They have 8 smallholders. Always 2 ploughs.

Meadow, 4 acres; woodland, 16 pigs.

Value always 40s.

These Freemen, so the County testifies, could not move away from this manor.

Raymond Gerald took away 1 villager of whom Robert was in possession. Roger of Poitou still has (him).

25 Nigel holds WIVENHOE from Robert, which Aelfric held as a manor, for 5 hides less 15 acres.

Always 5 villagers. Then 6 smallholders, now 20; then 1 slave, now 2. Always 2 ploughs in lordship. Then among the men 3 ploughs, now 2.

Woodland, 100 pigs; meadow, 12 acres; pasture, 60 sheep; now 1 mill. Then 8 cattle, now 10; then 1 cob, now 2; then 60 sheep, now 87; then 30 goats, now 20; then 20 pigs, now 24.

Value always 40s.

1 free man held 20 acres which Robert holds by the King's gift. Nigel (holds them) from him. Always ½ plough.

Value 3s.

Another free (man) held 20 acres which the Hundred-reeve has.

Value 3s.

Nigel also holds (them).

26 Robert holds (Little) BIRCH from Robert, which Wulfwin held as a manor, for 2 hides less 4½ acres. 66 b

Always 12 smallholders. Then 6 slaves, now 5. Always 2 ploughs in lordship; 2 men's ploughs.

Woodland, 40 pigs; meadow, 12 acres; always 1 mill. Then 2 cattle, now 7; then 38 sheep, now 80; now 33 goats; then 5 pigs, now 33; now 2 cobs.

Value always 60s.

Hund de Angra. Stapleforđam ten&.R. in dnio. qđ tenuer.v.
libi hões ꝑ.II.hid.7.dim.7.VI.ac.7 dim.Tc.VIII.borđ.m.XIIII.Tc.int
eos.v.car.m.IIII.Silu.cc.porc.XXI.ac.pti.Tc 7 p uat.L.sol.m.LX.
De hoc manerio ten& Nigell.I.hid.7.dim.7.III.uill.7.VI.borđ.7.II.car.
7 uat.XXVIII.sol.in eođ ptio.

Hund de Cesseorda. Renaham ten& Rob de.R.qđ tenuit Aluard.
ꝑ.Man.7.ꝑ.III.hid.7.dim.Tc.IIII.uill.m.v.Tc.7.p.VI.borđ.m.IIII.
Tc.II.ser.m null.Sep.II.car in dnio Tc.int hões.II.car 7 dim.m.I.
Tc.III.runc.7.XIIII.anim.7.VI.porc.7.c.ou.m.IIII.runc.7.XI.
anim.7 XXIIII.porc.7.LXXX.ou.7.XII.uasa.apu.Tc,uat.VI.lib.
7 qn rec.m.uat.IIII.lib.7.I.hid tenuit.I.lib ho.qui post ea forisfec.
eam.qa furat e.7 fuit in manu regis.s; rob lasciuus inuasit ut hunđ.
test.Tc.I.car.Post 7 m nulla.Sep uat.xx.sol.hoc ten& Ide Rob de.R.

Waldam ten& Rađ.de.R.qđ tenuit Sprot.ꝑ Man.7 ꝑ.I.hid.m.I.
uill.7.VI.borđ.7.I.car.Silu XL.porc.Vat.xx.sol. hanc tra ht.R.
sic dicit ꝑ escangio.ꝑ hubtu de portu.7 numq reddidit geltu 7 neq;
ultimum

Hund de Celmeresforda. Inga ten& Rob in dnio qđ tenuit
Siuuard ꝑ man.7.ꝑ.III.hid.t.r.e.Sep.I.uill.Tc.III.borđ.m.IX.
Tc.I.ser.m.III.Sep.I.car in dnio.Tc.dim.car hom.m.I.Silua

67 a

.CCCC.porc.Tc.v.anim.m.IIII.Tc.XXVIII.ou.m.XXVI.Tc.XII.porc.
m.XVII.Tc uat.XXX.sol.m.XX.

Hundred of ONGAR

27 Robert holds STAPLEFORD (Abbotts) in lordship, which 5 free men held, for 2½ hides and 6½ acres.

Then 8 smallholders, now 14. Then among them 5 ploughs, now 4.

Woodland, 200 pigs; meadow, 21 acres.

Value then and later 50s; now 60[s].

Of this manor, Nigel holds 1½ hides.

3 villagers; 6 smallholders. 2 ploughs.

Value 28s in the same assessment.

Hundred of CHAFFORD

28 Robert holds RAINHAM from Robert, which Alfward held as a manor, for 3½ hides.

Then 4 villagers, now 5; then and later 6 smallholders, now 4; then 2 slaves, now none. Always 2 ploughs in lordship. Then among the men 2½ ploughs, now 1.

Then 3 cobs, 14 cattle, 6 pigs and 100 sheep; now 4 cobs, 11 cattle, 24 pigs, 80 sheep and 12 beehives.

Value then £6, and when acquired. Value now £4.

1 free man held 1 hide. He later forfeited it because he had stolen and was in the King's hand. But Robert the Lascivious annexed it as the Hundred testifies. Then 1 plough, later and now none.

Value always 20s.

Robert also holds this from Robert.

29 Ralph holds (South) WEALD from Robert, which Sprot held as a manor, for 1 hide.

Now 1 villager; 6 smallholders; 1 plough.

Woodland, 40 pigs.

Value 20s.

Robert has this land, so he says, by exchange through Hubert of Port. It has never paid tax and did not (pay) the last one.

Hundred of CHELMSFORD

30 Robert holds FRYERNING in lordship, which Siward held as a manor, for 3 hides before 1066.

Always 1 villager. Then 3 smallholders, now 9; then 1 slave, now 3. Always 1 plough in lordship. Then ½ men's plough, now 1.

Woodland, 400 pigs. Then 5 cattle, now 4; then 28 sheep, now 26; then 12 pigs, now 17. 67 a

Value then 30s; now 20[s].

Ingā tenuit Eduin⁹ grut ꝑ Man̄ . 7 . ꝑ . i . hid . 7 . xxxiii . ac̄ . m̄ ten& Ilger⁹
de . Robto . Sēp . i . bord . 7 . i . car . Silu . xl . porc . ii , ac . p̄ti . Val . xx . sol . hanc
trā habuit . R . in Suo escangio.

Cinguehellam ten& Anschetill⁹ de . R . qđ tenuit Doth . ꝑ Man̄ . 7
ꝑ . ii . hid . Sēp . i . uill . 7 . ii . bord . 7 . ii . car in dn̄io . 7 . i . car hom . Silu . xxx .
porc . xx . ac . p̄ti . Sēp . i . runc . 7 . vi . anim . 7 . xii . ou . 7 . xiiii . porc . Tc̄ uał
xl . sol . m̄ . iiii . lib

Springinghefeldā ten& Corp . de . R . qđ tenuit Godric⁹ ꝑ Man̄ . 7 ꝑ .
. ii . hid . 7 . xl . ac . Sēp . iiii . uill . 7 . vii . bord . 7 . ii . car . in dn̄io . 7 . i . car
hom . Silu . xxx . porc . xx . ac . p̄ti . i . pisc . Tc̄ . i . runc . m̄ . x . Tc̄ . v . anim .
m̄ . xxx . Tc̄ . iiii . ou . m̄ . c . Tc̄ . xiii . porc . m̄ . xl . Tc̄ . uał . xl . sol . m̄ lx.

Ingā ten& Will de . R . qđ tenuer̄ . Selua 7 Topi⁹ ꝑ . Man̄ . 7 ꝑ . ii . hid . 7 . đ .
7 . xxxi . ac . 7 . Rob ħt in escangio . Sēp . i . uill . 7 . xiiii . bord . 7 . i . car . 7 . đ
in dn̄io . 7 . i . car . 7 . dim . hom . Silu . c . porc . iiii . ac . p̄ti . Tc̄ . x . anim .
m̄ . similit̄ Tc̄ . i . runc . m̄ . v . Sēp . xx . ou . Tc̄ . xxx . porc . m̄ . xvi .
m̄ . ii . uasa apū . Sēp . uał . iiii . lib . 7 . xxx . ac . ten . borda m̄ . R . Sēp .
dim . car . 7 . ii . ac 7 đ . p̄ti . vał . x . sol .

Pacingas ten& Picot . qđ tenuit borda ꝑ Man̄ . 7 ꝑ . ii . hid . 7 . dim .
t . r . e . Tc̄ . i . uill . m̄ null⁹ . m̄ . vi . bord . Tc̄ . iiii . ser . m̄ null⁹ . Tc̄ . ii . car
in dn̄io m̄ . i . Sēp . dim . car hom . Silu . l . porc . x . ac . p̄ti . Tc̄ . iiii . an .
7 . xx . porc . 7 xx . ou . m̄ nichil Sēp uał . xl . sol . Istā trā ħt . R .
in Escangio .

31 Edwin Groat held FRYERNING as a manor, for 1 hide and 33 acres. Now Ilger holds (it) from Robert.
Always 1 smallholder; 1 plough.
Woodland, 40 pigs; meadow, 2 acres.
Value 20s.
Robert had this land in exchange.

32 Ansketel holds CHIGNALL from Robert, which Dot held as a manor, for 2 hides.
Always 1 villager; 2 smallholders; 2 ploughs in lordship; 1 men's plough.
Woodland, 30 pigs; meadow, 20 acres. Always 1 cob, 6 cattle, 12 sheep and 14 pigs.
Value then 40s; now £4.

33 Corp holds SPRINGFIELD from Robert, which Godric held as a manor, for 2 hides and 40 acres.
Always 4 villagers; 7 smallholders; 2 ploughs in lordship; 1 men's plough.
Woodland, 30 pigs; meadow, 20 acres; 1 fishery. Then 1 cob, now 10; then 5 cattle, now 30; then 4 sheep, now 100; then 13 pigs, now 40.
Value then 40s; now 60[s].

34 William holds FRYERNING from Robert, which Selva and Topi held as a manor, for 2½ hides and 31 acres. Robert has (it) in exchange.
Always 1 villager; 14 smallholders; 1½ ploughs in lordship; 1½ men's ploughs.
Woodland, 100 pigs; meadow, 4 acres. Then 10 cattle, now the same; then 1 cob, now 5; always 20 sheep. Then 30 pigs, now 16; now 2 beehives.
Value always £4.
Borda held 30 acres, now Robert (holds them). Always ½ plough.
Meadow, 2½ acres.
Value 10s.

35 Picot holds PATCHING (Hall), which Borda held as a manor, for 2½ hides before 1066.
Then 1 villager, now none; now 6 smallholders; then 4 slaves, now none. Then 2 ploughs in lordship, now 1. Always ½ men's plough.
Woodland, 50 pigs; meadow, 10 acres. Then 4 cattle, 20 pigs and 20 sheep; now nothing.
Value always 40s.
Robert has this land in exchange.

De feudo. Richeham ten& Asso de. R. qđ ten. Goduin.

67 b

ꝑ Man. 7 ꝑ. I. hid. 7. dim. Tc. I. uill. 7. I. ser. m. II. bord. Sep. I. car. 7. đ. in dnio. 7. x. ac. pti. Sep. I. mol. Sep. ual. xxx. sol.

In Toleshunta ten& Rob de uli. XL. ac. quæ jacent in hoc hund. 7 appptiate st in manerio.

Hund de Tendringa Accleiam ten&. R. in dnio. qđ tenuit Aluric cap ꝑ manerio. 7 ꝑ. x. hid. t. r. e. Tc. 7. p. XII. uill. m. XI. Tc. 7 p xx. bord. m. xxx. tc. 7 p. x. ser. m. v. Sep. III. car in dnio. Tc. int hoes. x. car. m. IX. Silu. c. porc. VIII. ac. pti. m. I. mol. II. salinæ. Past. xx. ou. Tc. x. runc. m. IIII. tc. x. anim. m. v. Sep. cc. ou. xx. min. tc. xx. porc. m. xv. Tc. ual. XI. lib. 7. qn rec. M ual. XVI. lib. De hoc manerio ten&. Rad. II. hid. 7. x. ac. 7. XIII. bord. 7. I. car. 7. ual. xxx. sol. in eod ptio. 7 tra cujda libi hois ten&. Rob. quæ uocat Tendringa qm ten& Galt de eo. ꝑ Man. 7 ꝑ. I. hid. xv. ac. min. Tc. v. uill. m. II. Tc. III. bord. m. VII. Tc. III. ser. m null. Sep. I. car. in dnio. tc. int hoes. III. car. m. II. Silu. xx. porc. I. ac. pti. Tc. II. runc. m. IIII. tc. II. anim. m. x. tc. xx. porc. m. XXVII. tc. XLIX. ou. m. LX. tc. XXIIII. cap. m. XXXVII. m. III. uasa apu Tc ual. xx. sol m. xxx. hoc recepit. R. in suo escangio.

Dicheleiam ten& Nigell de. R. qđ tenuit Alestan. ꝑ man. 7 ꝑ. I. hid. 7. XXXVII. ac. 7. dim. Sep. VIII. bord. tc. I. ser. m null. Tc. in dnio. II. car. m. I. 7. dim. Sep. II. car. hom. Silu. x. porc. II. ac. pti. tc. VII. anim. m. VIII. tc. I. runc. m. IIII. tc. XXXVII. ou. m. LI. tc. VII. porc. m. xv. Sep. xx. cap. Val. xx. sol.

36 From the Holding, Azo holds CULVERT'S FARM from Robert, which Godwin held as a manor, for 1½ hides. 67 b
Then 1 villager; 1 slave. Now 2 smallholders. Always 1½ ploughs in lordship.
Meadow, 10 acres; always 1 mill.
Value always 30s.

37 In TOLLESHUNT (D'Arcy) Robert of Verly holds 40 acres which lie in (the lands of) this Hundred. They are assessed in the manor.

Hundred of TENDRING

38 Robert holds (Great) OAKLEY in lordship, which Aelfric Kemp held as a manor, for 10 hides before 1066.
Then and later 12 villagers, now 11; then and later 20 smallholders, now 30. Then and later 10 slaves, now 5. Always 3 ploughs in lordship. Then among the men 10 ploughs, now 9.
Woodland, 100 pigs; meadow, 8 acres; now 1 mill; 2 salt-houses; pasture, 20 sheep. Then 10 cobs, now 4; then 10 cattle, now 5; always 200 sheep less 20. Then 20 pigs, now 15.
Value then, and when acquired, £11. Value now £16.
Of this manor, Ralph holds 2 hides and 10 acres.
13 smallholders. 1 plough.
Value 30s in the same assessment.

38a Robert holds the land of a free man, which is called TENDRING. Walter holds it from him as a manor, for 1 hide less 15 acres.
Then 5 villagers, now 2; then 3 smallholders, now 7; then 3 slaves, now none. Always 1 plough in lordship. Then among the men 3 ploughs, now 2.
Woodland, 20 pigs; meadow, 1 acre. Then 2 cobs, now 4; then 2 cattle, now 10; then 20 pigs, now 27; then 49 sheep, now 60; then 24 goats, now 37; now 3 beehives.
Value then 20s; now 30[s].
Robert acquired this in exchange.

39 Nigel holds 'DICKLEY from Robert, which Alstan held as a manor, for 1 hide and 37½ acres.
Always 8 smallholders. Then 1 slave, now none. Then 2 ploughs in lordship, now 1½. Always 2 men's ploughs.
Woodland, 10 pigs; meadow, 2 acres. Then 7 cattle, now 8; then 1 cob, now 4; then 37 sheep, now 51; then 7 pigs, now 15; always 20 goats.
Value 20s.

Erleiam ten& Wilt de . R . qđ ten . Scapi . p Man . 7 p dim . hiđ.

68 a

7 . xxx . ac . 7 . jac& cuidam manerio in Sudfolc . ſ; in iſto hund ptin&
Tc . i . uill . m null . Sep . i . ſer . tc . in dnio . ii . car . qndo rec . i . m nulla.
tc . ii . borđ . m . null . i . ac . pti . Tc . ual . xl . ſol . 7 . qn rec . xx . m . v.

Hund de Vdelesfort Widintunā ten& . Rob de . R . qđ ten
Ingulf . p Man . 7 p . iii . hid . 7 . i . uirg . 7 Rob ht in eſcangio ut dic.
Tc . v . uill . m . iiii . tc . iii . bor . m . v . Sep . v . ſer . 7 . ii . car . in dnio.
Tc . iiii . car . hom . m . ii . x . ac . pti . Tc . iii . ou . m . lxv . Tc . xxiiii.
porc . m . xlix . Tc ual . lx . ſol . m . iiii . lib.

Scortegrauā ten& Idē . R . qđ tenuit Vluuin 7 Grichell . p . Man.
7 . p . ii . hiđ . 7 Rob ht in Eſcangio . Tc . 7 p . vi . ſer . m . iii . Tc . in dnio
. iii . car . Poſt 7 m . ii . xii . ac . pti . Tc . i . mol . m null . Tc . iii . runc . m
null . tc . iii . uac . m . null . Sep . c . ou . Tc . lx . porc . m null . Tc . xxiii.
uaſa apū . m . xi . Tc ual . iiii . lib . 7 qn rec . l . ſol . m . lx.

Archeſdanam ten& Picot de . R . qđ tenuit Grichell p Man . 7 p . i . hiđ.
. viii . ac . min . 7 . Rob . ht p eſcangio . m . iiii . borđ . Sep . ii . ſer . 7 . i . car.
. vi . ac . pti . m . ii . anim . Sep . xii . porc . 7 . xxxii . ou . m . ii . uaſa apū
vat . xx . ſol.

Elſenham ten& Petr de . R . qđ ten . Leftan p Man . 7 . p . i . hiđ . 7 . R.
ht in eſcangio . Tc . iiii . uill . P 7 m . iii . Tc . 7 p . iii . bor . m . vi . Tc . iiii.
ſer . m null . tc . 7 p . ii . car . in dnio . m . i . Tc . 7 p . ii . car hom . m . iii.
Silu . c . porc . xx . ac . pti . Sep . i . runc . Tc . vii . anim . m . i . uitul . Tc
xvi . ou . m null . tc . viii . porc . m . xviii . Tc . xx . cap . m . null . Sep.
ual . xl . ſol.

40 William holds ARDLEIGH from Robert, which Scalpi held as a manor, for ½ hide and 30 acres. It lies in (the lands of) a manor 68 a
in Suffolk; but it belongs in this Hundred.

Then 1 villager, now none; always 1 slave. Then 2 ploughs in lordship, when acquired 1, now none. Then 2 smallholders, now none.

Meadow, 1 acre.

Value then 40s; when acquired 20[s]; now 5[s].

Hundred of UTTLESFORD

41 Robert holds WIDDINGTON from Robert, which Ingulf held as a manor, for 3 hides and 1 virgate. Robert has (it) in exchange as he states.

Then 5 villagers, now 4; then 3 smallholders, now 5. Always 5 slaves; 2 ploughs in lordship. Then 4 men's ploughs, now 2.

Meadow, 10 acres. Then 3 sheep, now 65; then 24 pigs, now 49.

Value then 60s; now £4.

42 Robert also holds SHORTGROVE which Wulfwin and Grimkel held as a manor, for 2 hides. Robert has (it) in exchange.

Then and later 6 slaves, now 3. Then 3 ploughs in lordship, later and now 2.

Meadow, 12 acres; then 1 mill, now none. Then 3 cobs, now none; then 3 cows, now none; always 100 sheep. Then 60 pigs, now none; then 23 beehives, now 11.

Value then £4; when acquired 50s; now 60[s].

43 Picot holds ARKESDEN from Robert, which Grimkel held as a manor, for 1 hide less 8 acres. Robert has (it) by exchange.

Now 4 smallholders. Always 2 slaves; 1 plough.

Meadow, 6 acres. Now 2 cattle. Always 12 pigs; 32 sheep. Now 2 beehives.

Value 20s.

44 Peter holds ELSENHAM from Robert, which Leofstan held as a manor, for 1 hide. Robert has (it) in exchange.

Then 4 villagers, later and now 3; then and later 3 smallholders, now 6; then 4 slaves, now none. Then and later 2 ploughs in lordship, now 1. Then and later 2 men's ploughs, now 3.

Woodland, 100 pigs; meadow, 20 acres. Always 1 cob. Then 7 cattle, now 1 calf; then 16 sheep, now none; then 8 pigs, now 18; then 20 goats, now none.

Value always 40s.

Hund de Turestapla. Toleshuntā ten&. Rob. de uerli de. R.

68 b

qđ tenuit Gotra ꝓ Man. 7. ꝓ. v. hid. 7. dim. Tc. IIII. uill. m. VII. tc, VI.
bord. m. XIIII. tc. III. ser. m. v. Sep. II. car. in dnio. 7. II. car hom. Silu.
. cc. porc. I. ac. pti. Past. XL. ou. I. sal. Tc. III. runc. m. null. Tc. XIIII. an.
m null. Tc. XL. porc. m. XX. Tc. C. ou. m. LX. Tc. XXX. cap. m. XX. m
. VIII. uasa apū. Tc 7 p uat. IIII. lib. m. C. sol. 7. II. libi hões tenuert
XXX. ac. Tc. I. car. m null. Sep uat. X. sol. 7 hanc trā dicit se habe
in suo escangio.

XXXIII Terra. Radulfi baignardi. Hund de Witham.

Vltingam. ten& Girard de. Radulfo baignardo. qđ tenuit Hacon t. r. e
ꝓ Man. 7 ꝓ. I. hid. 7. XL. ac. Sep. IIII. car in dnio. Tc. III. car. hom. m.
. I. 7 dim. Tc. VII. uill. m. IIII. m. XII. bord. tc. VI. ser. m null. Silu
. C. porc. XX. ac. pti. sep. II. mol. 7. v. ac tre addite st t. r. Willi. 7
st de sua consuetudine. Tc. v. runc. XX. an. VII. porc. LXX. ou.
m. IIII. runc. IX. an. XXIIII. porc. XXXV. ou. II. uasa Tc uat. IIII.
lib. 7 qn rec. m. uat. C. sol.

In Langefort ten& Goisfrid. v. libos hões de. R. de. III. uirg. trae.

69 a

7. I. ac. q reddebant regi. XV. đ. de consuetudine t. r. e. Sep. hnt. I. car. 7. đ.
7. I. bor. III. ac. Tc. uat. X. sol. m. XX.

Hundred of THURSTABLE

45 Robert of Verly holds TOLLESHUNT (D'Arcy) from Robert, which Gotre held as a manor, for 5½ hides. 68 b

Then 4 villagers, now 7; then 6 smallholders, now 14; then 3 slaves, now 5. Always 2 ploughs in lordship; 2 men's ploughs.

Woodland, 200 pigs; meadow, 1 acre; pasture, 40 sheep; 1 salt-house. Then 3 cobs, now none; then 14 cattle, now none; then 40 pigs, now 20; then 100 sheep, now 60; then 30 goats, now 20; now 8 beehives.

Value then and later £4; now 100s.

2 free men held 30 acres. Then 1 plough, now none.

Value always 10s.

He states that he has this land in exchange.

33 LAND OF RALPH BAYNARD

Hundred of WITHAM

1 Gerard holds ULTING from Ralph Baynard, which Hakon held before 1066 as a manor, for 1 hide and 40 acres. Always 4 ploughs in lordship. Then 3 men's ploughs, now 1½.

Then 7 villagers, now 4; now 12 smallholders; then 6 slaves, now none.

Woodland, 100 pigs; meadow, 20 acres; always 2 mills.

5 acres of land were added after 1066 and are part of the customary due.

Then 5 cobs, 20 cattle, 7 pigs, 70 sheep; now 4 cobs, 9 cattle, 24 pigs, 35 sheep, 2 [bee] hives.

Value then, and when acquired, £4. Value now 100s.

[Hundred of THURSTABLE]

2 In LANGFORD Geoffrey holds 5 free men from Ralph with 3 virgates of land and 1 acre, who paid the King 15d of the 69 a
customary due before 1066. They have always had 1½ ploughs;

1 smallholder.

3 acres.

Value then 10s; now 20[s].

Hund de Witbrictesherna. Nortunā ten& . R . in dn̄io . qđ tenuit Vluric . lib hō . t . r . e . p Man . 7 p . VIII . hid . Sēp . v . uilt . 7 . XI . borđ . tc̄ . II . ser . m̄ . null . Tc̄ . II . car . in dn̄io . m̄ . III . Tc̄ . IIII . car . hom . m̄ . III . Ex his hid . st̄ . II . siluæ . Past . XL . ou . m̄ . I . mol . Tc̄ . IIII . runc . 7 . XV . anim . XX . porc . CL . ou . m̄ . VI . runc . VIII . anim . XX . porc . 7 . LX . ou . Tc̄ ual . VI . lib . m̄ . VII . Hr̄ &iam . R . p Maner . III . hid . 7 . XLV . ac . qs sēp tenent . VI . libi hōes . Tc̄ . V . car . m̄ . III . Tc̄ ual . XL . sol . m̄ . XXX . hoc libatū ē p escangio . De hoc man . ten& Walicher . dim hid . 7 ual x . sol . ī eođ ptio.

Wdeham ten& Pointell de . R . qđ tenuit Leueua p man . 7 . p . VII . hid . Tc̄ . XII . uilt . m̄ . VI . Sēp . IIII . borđ . Tc̄ . VI . ser . m̄ . IIII . Sēp . III . car in dn̄io . Tc̄ . IIII . car hom . m̄ . I . XXIIII . ac . p̄ti . Silu . D . porc . Tc̄ . I . mol m̄ . II . Tc̄ . II . an . 7 . VII . porc . XXXVII . ou . m̄ . VIII . anim . XXI . porc . VI . asini . CXXX . ou . XIII . uasa apū . Tc̄ ual . VIII . lib . 7 . qn̄ rec . XL . sol . m̄ ual . VII . lib.

Curlai ten& Idē de eođ . qđ ten Grim t . r . e . p man . 7 p . I . hid . Tc̄ . II . uilt . m̄ . IIII . Sēp . IX . borđ . Tc̄ . IIII . ser . m̄ null . Sēp . II . car . in dn̄io . 7 . I . car hom . XXII . ac . p̄ti . Silu . XL . porc . Tc̄ . I . mol . m̄ . null . Tc̄ 7 post ual . XL . sol . m̄ . IIII . lib . Hr̄ &iam Godric . de . R . dim . hid . qm ht p escangio . ut dicit s; hund nescit . Sēp dim . car . val . x . sol.

Hund de Dommauua . Dōmauuā ten& . R . in dn̄io qđ tenuit Ailid q̄dā femina libæ . p man . 7 p . IIII . hid . 7 . dim . Sēp . III . car ī dn̄io . tc̄ . VII . car hom . m̄ . VI . Sēp . XV . uilt . 7 . I . pbr . Tc̄ . XII . borđ . m̄ . XVI .

Hundred of 'WIBERTSHERNE'

3 Ralph holds (Cold) NORTON in lordship which Wulfric, a free man, held before 1066 as a manor, for 8 hides.

Always 5 villagers; 11 smallholders. Then 2 slaves, now none. Then 2 ploughs in lordship, now 3. Then 4 men's ploughs, now 3.

2 of these hides are of woodland. Pasture, 40 sheep; now 1 mill. Then 4 cobs, 15 cattle, 20 pigs, 150 sheep; now 6 cobs, 8 cattle, 20 pigs and 60 sheep.

Value then £6; now [£] 7.

Ralph also has as a manor 3 hides and 45 acres which 6 free men have always held. Then 5 ploughs, now 3.

Value then 40s; now 30[s].

This was handed over by exchange.

Of this manor, Walchere holds ½ hide.

Value 10s in the same assessment.

4 Pointel holds WOODHAM (Walter), which Leofeva held as a manor, for 7 hides.

Then 12 villagers, now 6; always 4 smallholders. Then 6 slaves, now 4. Always 3 ploughs in lordship. Then 4 men's ploughs, now 1.

Meadow, 24 acres; woodland, 500 pigs; then 1 mill, now 2. Then 2 cattle, 7 pigs, 37 sheep; now 8 cattle, 21 pigs, 6 asses, 130 sheep, 13 beehives.

Value then £8; when acquired 40s. Value now £7.

5 He also holds from him CURLING TYE (Green), which Grim held before 1066 as a manor, for 1 hide.

Then 2 villagers, now 4; always 9 smallholders. Then 4 slaves, now none. Always 2 ploughs in lordship; 1 men's plough.

Meadow, 22 acres; woodland, 40 pigs; then 1 mill, now none.

Value then and later 40s; now £4.

Godric also has ½ hide from Ralph, which he has by exchange as he states; but the Hundred does not know. Always ½ plough.

Value 10s.

Hundred of DUNMOW

6 Ralph holds (Little) DUNMOW in lordship which Aethelgyth, a free woman, held as a manor for 4½ hides. Always 3 ploughs in lordship. Then 7 men's ploughs, now 6.

Always 15 villagers; 1 priest. Then 12 smallholders, now 16;

Sēp . x . ser . Silua . cl . porc . l . ac . pti . m . i . mol . Tc . iii . runc . xi . anim . xl . porc . xv . ou . xxiii . cap . m . xi . runc . xxi . an . xxx . porc . ciiii . ou . liii . cap . viii . uasa apū . Tc 7 p ual . viii . lib . m . x . Huic tre addita ē . i . hid . qm ten . i . lib hō . t . r . e . Sēp . i . car . 7 . i . uill . 7 . i . bord . 7 . i . ser . Silu . xxiiii . porc . x . ac . pti . Val . xx . sol . Et huic man . adjac& adhuc . dim hid quā tenuit . i . soc antecessoris baignardi . 7 . adhuc ten& Tc . i . car . 7 . dim in dnio . m . i . Sēp . i . uill . 7 . i . ser . 7 . silu . xx . porc . ix . ac . pti . Val sēp xx . sol .

Wimbeis ten& . R . in dnio qd tenuit Ailid t . r . e . p man . 7 . p . viii . hid . Sēp . iii . car . in dnio . Tc . xxi . car hom . m . xv . Sēp . xxvi . uill . 7 . i . pbr Tc . xviiii . bord . m . lv . Tc . vi . ser . m null . Tc silu . d . porc . m . cccc . xl . ac . pti . Tc . ii . runc . 7 . iiii . an . lx . porc . cxx . ou . iiii . uasa apū . m . ii . runc . iiii . anim . xxviii . porc . lxxx . ou . iiii . uasa apū . Tc ual . xii . lib . m . xx .

Hund de Wensistreu . Borooldituna ten& Modbt de . R . qd tenuit Aluric lib hō . t . r . e . p . Man . 7 . p . i . hid . Sēp . i . car . in dnio . tc . iii . bord . m . iiii . Silu . xx . porc . Tc . ii . runc . i . anim . i . porc . xv . ou . m . ii . runc . i . anim . ii . porc . xxxiii . ou . xxxiiii . cap . Val xxx . sol .

Metcinges ten& Bernard . de . R . qd ten . liba femina . p . Man . 7 p . d hid . t . r . e . m . i . bord . Silu . xii . porc . Tc ual . x . sol . m . iii .

always 10 slaves. 69 b

Woodland, 150 pigs; meadow, 50 acres; now 1 mill. Then 3 cobs, 11 cattle, 40 pigs, 15 sheep, 23 goats; now 11 cobs, 21 cattle, 30 pigs, 104 sheep, 53 goats, 8 beehives.

Value then and later £8; now [£] 10.

1 hide was added to this land, which 1 free man held before 1066. Always 1 plough;

1 villager; 1 smallholder; 1 slave.

Woodland, 24 pigs; meadow, 10 acres.

Value 20s.

A further ½ hide is attached to this manor, which 1 Freeman of Baynard's predecessor held and still holds. Then 1½ ploughs in lordship, now 1.

Always 1 villager; 1 slave.

Woodland, 20 pigs; meadow, 9 acres.

Value always 20s.

[Hundred of UTTLESFORD]

7 Ralph holds WIMBISH in lordship, which Aethelgyth held before 1066 as a manor, for 8 hides. Always 3 ploughs in lordship. Then 21 men's ploughs, now 15.

Always 26 villagers; 1 priest. Then 19 smallholders, now 55; then 6 slaves, now none.

Woodland, then 500 pigs, now 400; meadow, 40 acres. Then 2 cobs, 4 cattle, 60 pigs, 120 sheep, 4 beehives; now 2 cobs, 4 cattle, 28 pigs, 80 sheep, 4 beehives.

Value then £12; now [£] 20.

Hundred of WINSTREE

8 Modbert holds BARN HALL from Ralph which Aelfric, a free man, held before 1066 as a manor, for 1 hide. Always 1 plough in lordship.

Then 3 smallholders, now 4.

Woodland, 20 pigs. Then 2 cobs, 1 (head of) cattle, 1 pig, 15 sheep; now 2 cobs, 1 (head of) cattle, 2 pigs, 33 sheep, 34 goats.

Value 30s.

[Hundred of LEXDEN]

9 Bernard holds MESSING from Ralph, which a free woman held as a manor, for ½ hide before 1066.

Now 1 smallholder.

Woodland, 12 pigs.

Value then 10s; now 3[s].

Hund de Clauelinga . In Magellana tenuit . i . lib hō . t . r . e .
. xxx . ac . qđ ten& Amelfrid de . R . Sēp . i . car . Tc̄ . uał . v . sol . m̄ . x .

Hund de hidingforda . Pentelauuā tenuit liba femina . t . r . e
ꝓ Man . 7 . ꝓ . iiii . hid . 7 . iii . uirḡ . Sēp . iii . car in dn̄io . 7 . v . car

70 a

car hom . 7 . viii . uilł . tc̄ 7 p̄ . i . bord . m̄ . viii . Tc̄ . viii . ser . m̄ null .
Silu . cc . porc . xxx . ac . p̄ti . Sēp . i . mol . Tc̄ . ii . runc . xxii . anim . xlviii .
porc . x . ou . viii . uasa apū . m̄ . iii . runc . xxiiii . anim . xx . porc . lxxx .
ou . viii . uasa apū . Et . xviii . soc . de . ii . hid . 7 . xxx . ac . 7 hnt . v . car .
tc̄ . iiii . ser . m̄ . i . m̄ . iiii . bord . Silu . x . porc . x . ac . p̄ti . Hoc totū uał
t . r . e . x . lib . m̄ . xvi . De hoc manerio . ten& Galicer . xxx . ac . 7 uał
. x . sol in eod p̄tio .

Hund de Witbrictesherna . Burneham ten& . R . in dn̄io
qđ tenuit Aluuart lib hō . t . r . e . ꝓ . Man . 7 ꝓ . iiii . hid . 7 . xii . ac .
Sēp . i . uilł . tc̄ . vi . bor . m̄ . xii . tc̄ . iiii . ser . m̄ null . Sēp . ii . car in dn̄io
7 . i . car . hom . Past . ccc . ou . Tc̄ . ii . runc . iiii . anim . xii . porc .
. cc . ou . m̄ . vi . runc . xiii . anim . xvi . porc . cccxxxvi . ou . Tc
uał . iiii . lib . m̄ . c . sol . In Ead uilł . x . libi hoēs . t . r . e . hn̄tes . viii .
hid . 7 . xxviii . ac . qđ ten& . R . in dn̄io . Tc̄ . x . bord . m̄ . xvi . Sēp
. vii . ser . 7 . viii . car . m̄ . i . mol . Past . dc . ou . Tc̄ . 7 p̄ uał . vii . lib .
m̄ . viii . lib . hanc trā reclamat . R . baignard ꝓ escangio

Hund de Celmeresfort . Baduuen ten& Germund de . R .
qđ tenuit Leuuin ꝓ Man . 7 ꝓ . iiii . hid . Sēp . ii . uilł . 7 . ii . bord . Tc̄
. ix . ser . m̄ . vii . Sēp . iiii . car . in dn̄io . Tc̄ . int hoēs . i . car . m̄ nulł .

Hundred of CLAVERING

10 In MANUDEN 1 free man held 30 acres before 1066. Amalfrid holds it from Ralph. Always 1 plough.
Value then 5s; now 10[s].

Hundred of HINCKFORD

11 A free woman held PENTLOW before 1066 as a manor, for 4 hides and 3 virgates. Always 3 ploughs in lordship; 5 men's ploughs; 70 a
8 villagers. Then and later 1 smallholder, now 8; then 8 slaves, now none.
Woodland, 200 pigs; meadow, 30 acres; always 1 mill. Then 2 cobs, 22 cattle, 48 pigs, 10 sheep, 8 beehives; now 3 cobs, 24 cattle, 20 pigs, 80 sheep, 8 beehives.
18 Freemen with 2 hides and 30 acres have 5 ploughs.
Then 4 slaves, now 1; now 4 smallholders.
Woodland, 10 pigs; meadow, 10 acres.
Value of the whole of this before 1066 £10; now [£] 16.
Of this manor, Walchere holds 30 acres.
Value 10s in the same assessment.

Hundred of 'WIBERTSHERNE'

12 Ralph holds BURNHAM in lordship which Alfward, a free man, held before 1066 as a manor, for 4 hides and 12 acres.
Always 1 villager. Then 6 smallholders, now 12; then 4 slaves, now none. Always 2 ploughs in lordship; 1 men's plough.
Pasture, 300 sheep. Then 2 cobs, 4 cattle, 12 pigs, 200 sheep; now 6 cobs, 13 cattle, 16 pigs, 336 sheep.
Value then £4; now 100s.
In the same village 10 free men who had 8 hides and 28 acres before 1066. Ralph holds it in lordship.
Then 10 smallholders, now 16. Always 7 slaves; 8 ploughs.
Now 1 mill; pasture, 600 sheep.
Value then and later £7; now £8.
Ralph Baynard claims back this land by exchange.

Hundred of CHELMSFORD

13 Germund holds (Little) BADDOW from Ralph, which Leofwin held as a manor, for 4 hides.
Always 2 villagers; 2 smallholders. Then 9 slaves, now 7.
Always 4 ploughs in lordship. Then among the men 1 plough, now none.

Silu. c . porc . I . ac . p̃ti . Sep̃ . I . mol . Tc̃ . VII . runc . XLVII . an . CVIII.
porc . LXXX . ou . m̃ . X . runc . LIII . anim . CLXIII . ou . Tc̃ 7 post
ual . c . sol . m̃ . VI . lib . 7 . V . libi hões . tenuer̃ . II . hid . 7 . XXXI . ac.
q̃ possent ire q̃ uellent . M̊ ten& Idẽ Germ . 7 . IIII . franci.
Sep̃ . III . bord . 7 . I . ser . tc̃ . II . car . m̃ . I . Silu . XXVI . porc . XIII . ac . p̃ti.

70 b
Sep̃ ual . XX . sol.
Haningefeldã ten& Berengeri de . R . qd tenuit Normann p . M.
7 . p . III . hid . Tc̃ . III . uill . m̃ null . m̃ . IX . bord . Sep̃ . II . ser . tc̃ . II . car in dñio
m̃ . I . tc̃ . I . car hom . m̃ . d . Silu . CC . porc . M̊ . III . an . XXIII . porc . XLVII . ou.
. IIII . cap . Tc̃ 7 p ual . XL . X . sol . m̃ . IIII . lib.
Hund de Tendringa . Adem ten& . Germund de . R . qd tenuit
Ednod p Man . 7 p . V . hid . 7 . dim . tc̃ . VII . uill . m̃ . XVII . Sep̃ . IIII . bord.
7 . VIII . ser . 7 . III . car . in dñio . 7 . III . car . hom . Silu . XXXIII . porc.
. II . ac . p̃ti . I . pisc . Past . c . ou . tc̃ . II . runc . 7 . XIII . an . L . porc . L . ou . m̃.
. III . runc . IIII . an . XXVII . porc . CXVIII . ou . Tc̃ . 7 p ual . VII . lib . m̃ . IX.
Rameseiam ten& . Rog̃ . qd ten . Aluric cãp . p Man . 7 p . VII . hid . 7 . XXXV.
ac . Sep̃ . XVIII . uill . Tc̃ . VI . bord . m̃ . IX . Sep̃ . VI . ser . 7 . III . car . in dñio.
Tc̃ . int hões . VII . car . m̃ . V . Silu . LX . porc . VIII . ac . p̃ti . m̃ . I . mol . I . sal.
tc̃ ual . XII . lib . m̃ . XV . tc̃ . I . runc . 7 . XX . an . XXII . porc . CXV.
ou . m̃ . II . runc . XX . anim . XL 7 IX . porc . CCC . IX . ou . VIII . uasa apũ.
Michelestou ten& Bernard . de . R . qd tenuit Alric p . Man . 7 p
. II . hid . 7 . dim . Tc̃ . III . bor . m̃ . I . Tc̃ . III . ser . m̃ null . Sep̃ . II . car . ĩ dñio.
tc̃ int hões . dim . car . m̃ . ñ . IIII . ac . p̃ti . Tc̃ . II . runc . VI . an . XXVII . porc.
. CL . ou . m̃ . XXV . porc . LXXXIII . ou . Tc̃ ual LXX . sol . m̃ . IIII . lib.

Woodland, 100 pigs; meadow, 1 acre; always 1 mill. Then 7 cobs, 47 cattle, 108 pigs, 80 sheep; now 10 cobs, 53 cattle, 163 sheep.
Value then and later 100s; now £6.
5 free men held 2 hides and 31 acres; they could go whither they would. Now Germund also holds (it). 4 Frenchmen.
Always 3 smallholders; 1 slave. Then 2 ploughs, now 1.
Woodland, 26 pigs; meadow, 13 acres.
Value always 20s. 70 b

14 Berengar holds (East) HANNINGFIELD from Ralph, which Norman held as a manor, for 3 hides.
Then 3 villagers, now none; now 9 smallholders; always 2 slaves. Then 2 ploughs in lordship, now 1. Then 1 men's plough, now ½.
Woodland, 200 pigs. Now 3 cattle, 23 pigs, 47 sheep, 4 goats.
Value then and later ... s; now £4.

Hundred of TENDRING

15 Germund holds (Little) OAKLEY from Ralph, which Ednoth held as a manor, for 5½ hides.
Then 7 villagers, now 17. Always 4 smallholders; 8 slaves; 3 ploughs in lordship; 3 men's ploughs.
Woodland, 33 pigs; meadow, 2 acres; 1 fishery; pasture, 100 sheep. Then 2 cobs, 13 cattle, 50 pigs, 50 sheep; now 3 cobs, 4 cattle, 27 pigs, 118 sheep.
Value then and later £7; now [£] 9.

16 Roger holds RAMSEY, which Aelfric Kemp held as a manor, for 7 hides and 35 acres.
Always 18 villagers. Then 6 smallholders, now 9. Always 6 slaves; 3 ploughs in lordship. Then among the men 7 ploughs, now 5.
Woodland, 60 pigs; meadow, 8 acres; now 1 mill; 1 salt-house.
Value then £12; now [£] 15.
Then 1 cob, 20 cattle, 22 pigs, 115 sheep; now 2 cobs, 20 cattle, 49 pigs, 309 sheep, 8 beehives.

17 Bernard holds MICHAELSTOW from Ralph, which Alric held as a manor, for 2½ hides.
Then 3 smallholders, now 1; then 3 slaves, now none. Always 2 ploughs in lordship. Then among the men ½ plough, now none.
Meadow, 4 acres. Then 2 cobs, 6 cattle, 27 pigs, 150 sheep; now 25 pigs, 83 sheep.
Value then 70s; now £4.

7 . II . soc . ten& . R . in suo escang . sic sui hoes dict . sed alij n testant . nisi ipsi soli . de manerio qd uocat Laleforda : tenentes . dim hid . 7 . xxxv . ac . Tqd ten& Ide . B . de . R . tc . I . car . m . dim . tc . ual . VIII . sol . m . x . 7 in Witelebroc . ten& Rog . I . hid de . R . qd ten Aluric . p . Man . Sep . I . bord . 7 . I . car . 7 . I . ac . pti . val . x . sol . 7 hec

71 a

tra . n jacuit in alijs tris . hec . III . maner ual . xx . lib.

Hund de Vdelesfort . Wendena ten& Amelfrid qd tenuit . I . lib ho . Aluuin stille . p Man . 7 . p . I . hid . 7 dim . 7 . xxx . ac . 7 . R . ht i escangio. Sep . v . uill . 7 . III . bord . 7 . II . ser . 7 . II . car . in dnio . 7 . I . car . hom . Silu . LXXX . porc . III . ac . pti . Tc . ual . IIII . lib . m . v.

Dim Hund de Frosseuuella . Henham ten& . R . i dnio qd tenuit Ailid p Man . 7 . p . XIII . hid . 7 . d . x . ac . min . Tc 7 p . XVIII . uill . m . VIII . Tc 7 p . v . bord . m . XXXVIII . tc . 7 p . VIII . ser . m null . Sep . IIII . car . in dnio . 7 . VIII . car hom . Silu . cc . porc . XVI . ac . pti . Tc . III . runc . VIII . anim . LXXX . por . CLX . ou . XVI . uasa ap . m . VIII . runc . VII . anim . c . porc . LXXX . ou . x . uasa ap . Tc ual . XII . lib . m . xx.

Ascenduna ten& . R . in dnio qd tenuit . Ailid . p Man . 7 . p . II . hid . Tc XIIII . uill . m . xx . Tc . III . bord . m . IX . Tc . II . ser . m . null . Sep . II . car in dnio . 7 . IIII . car . hom . Silu . c . porc . VI . ac . pti . I . ac . uineæ . tc . II . runc . v . an . LX . porc . cc . ou . x . uasa ap . m . I . runc . VII . an . LX . porc . LXV . ou . III . uasa ap . Tc ual . VI . lib . m . VIII . 7 . II . soc tenentes . xv . ac . libæ . hos accep . R . in escang . val . III . sol.

Ralph holds 2 Freemen – in exchange so his men state; but others do not testify except for those alone from the manor which is called Lawford – who hold ½ hide and 35 acres, which Bernard also holds from Ralph.

Then 1 plough, now ½.

Value then 8s; now 10[s].

In *WITELEBROC* Roger holds 1 hide from Ralph, which Aelfric held as a manor.

Always 1 smallholder; 1 plough.

Meadow, 1 acre.

Value 10s.

This land did not lie in the other lands. 71 a

Value of these three manors £20.

Hundred of UTTLESFORD

18 Amalfrid holds WENDON (Lofts) which 1 free man, Alwin Still, held as a manor for 1½ hides and 30 acres. Ralph has it in exchange.

Always 5 villagers; 3 smallholders; 2 slaves; 2 ploughs in lordship; 1 men's plough.

Woodland, 80 pigs; meadow, 3 acres.

Value then £4; now [£] 5.

Half-Hundred of FRESHWELL

19 Ralph holds HENHAM in lordship, which Aethelgyth held as a manor, for 13½ hides less 10 acres.

Then and later 18 villagers, now 8; then and later 5 smallholders, now 38; then and later 8 slaves, now none. Always 4 ploughs in lordship; 8 men's ploughs.

Woodland, 200 pigs; meadow, 16 acres. Then 3 cobs, 8 cattle, 80 pigs, 160 sheep, 16 beehives; now 8 cobs, 7 cattle, 100 pigs, 80 sheep, 10 beehives.

Value then £12; now [£] 20.

20 Ralph holds ASHDON in lordship, which Aethelgyth held as a manor, for 2 hides.

Then 14 villagers, now 20; then 3 smallholders, now 9; then 2 slaves, now none. Always 2 ploughs in lordship; 4 men's ploughs.

Woodland, 100 pigs; meadow, 6 acres; 1 acre of vines. Then 2 cobs, 5 cattle, 60 pigs, 200 sheep, 10 beehives; now 1 cob, 7 cattle, 60 pigs, 65 sheep, 3 beehives.

Value then £6; now [£] 8.

2 Freemen who hold 15 acres freely. Ralph acquired them in exchange.

Value 3s.

Hund de Rochefort. In Pachesham ten& Tedric pointel. dim hid. 7. xv. qd tenuit. i. lib ho tc. ii. bord. m. v. Sep. i. car. Past. L. ou. Sep ual. xx. sol. hoc reclamat. R. p escangio.

Hund de Turestapla Langhefordā tenuit Gola. 7 Agelmar p Man. 7 p. iii. hid. 7. dim. 7 hanc dim hid tenuit Agelmar ad censū de sco paulo. s; R. inde ē saisit. 7 Goisfrid ten& totū de. R. Sep. i. uill. Tc. iiii. bor. m. ix. tc. iiii. ser. m. iii. Tc in dnio. iii. car. m. ii.

71 b

Silua. xx. porc. xxv. ac. pti. Sep. i. mol. Tc. iii. runc. v. anim. xxiiii. porc. xl. ou. m. ii. runc. iiii. anim. xl. porc. lxxx. ou. Tc ual. c. sol 7 qn rec simil. m. iiii. lib. Tc. ibi fuer. v. libi hoes de. i. hid. 7. dim. m. iiii. hoes. Tc. i. car. 7. dim. m. i. Tc. i. bor. m. iii. tc. i. ser. m. n. tc. ual. xxx. sol. m. xx.

Toleshuntā ten& Bernard de. R. qd ten Ailmar p. Man. 7. p. iii. hid 7. viii. ac. Tc. iiii. uill. m. viii. Sep. v. bord. Tc. iiii. ser. m. i. Sep. i. car 7. dim. in dnio. 7. ii. car hom. Silu. cc. porc. Past. xx. ou. v. salinæ. Tc. ii. runc. vi. anim. xx. porc. c. ou. M. ii. runc. v. an. xx. porc. c. ou. xxviii. cap. Sep ual. lx. sol. In Ead uill. viii. libi hoes. de. i. hid. 7. dim. 7. xiiii. ac. Sep. ii. bord. 7. ii. car. val. xx. sol. hanc tram ht. R. baignard p escangio.

.XXXIIII. TERRE RANulfi piperelli. Hund de bdestapla. In bura ten& Serlo de. Ranulfo. i. hid. i. car. 7. i. ser. qd tenuit Alestan lib homo. Past. cxx. ou. Tc. i. runc. c. ou. xiiii. porc. iiii. uitul. m. ii. runc. c. ou. xiiii. porc. iiii. uit. Tc ual. xx. sol. m. xl.

Hundred of ROCHFORD

21 In PAGLESHAM Theodoric Pointel holds ½ hide and 15 [acres], which 1 free man held.

Then 2 smallholders, now 5. Always 1 plough.

Pasture, 50 sheep.

Value always 20s.

Ralph claims this back by exchange.

Hundred of THURSTABLE

22 Cola and Aelmer held LANGFORD as a manor, for 3½ hides. Aelmer held this ½ hide from St. Paul's for the customary dues; but Ralph is in possession of it and Geoffrey holds the whole from Ralph.

Always 1 villager. Then 4 smallholders, now 9; then 4 slaves, now 3. Then 3 ploughs in lordship, now 2.

Woodland, 20 pigs, meadow, 25 acres; always 1 mill. Then 3 cobs, 5 cattle, 24 pigs, 40 sheep; now 2 cobs, 4 cattle, 40 pigs, 80 sheep. 71 b

Value then 100s; when acquired, the same; now £4.

Then 5 free men with 1½ hides were there; now 4 men. Then 1½ ploughs, now 1.

Then 1 smallholder, now 3; then 1 slave, now none.

Value then 30s; now 20[s].

23 Bernard holds TOLLESHUNT from Ralph, which Aelmer held as a manor, for 3 hides and 8 acres.

Then 4 villagers, now 8. Always 5 smallholders. Then 4 slaves, now 1. Always 1½ ploughs in lordship; 2 men's ploughs.

Woodland, 200 pigs; pasture, 20 sheep; 5 salt-houses. Then 2 cobs, 6 cattle, 20 pigs, 100 sheep; now 2 cobs, 5 cattle, 20 pigs, 100 sheep, 28 goats.

Value always 60s.

In the same village 8 free men with 1½ hides and 14 acres.

Always 2 smallholders; 2 ploughs.

Value 20s.

Ralph Baynard has this land by exchange.

34 LANDS OF RANULF PEVEREL

Hundred of BARSTABLE

1 In BOWERS (Gifford) Serlo holds from Ranulf 1 hide, 1 plough and 1 slave which Alstan, a free man, held.

Pasture, 120 sheep. Then 1 cob, 100 sheep, 14 pigs, 4 calves; now 2 cobs, 100 sheep, 14 pigs, 4 calves.

Value then 20s; now 40[s].

Phenge ten& Idē Serlo de . R . qđ tenuit lib̄ hō ꝓ man . 7 ꝓ . I . hid . q t . r . Willi effect ē hō antecessoris Ranulfi piperelli . ſ; trā suam sibi non dedit. Quando ů rex dedit trā Ranulfo saisiuit illam cū

72 a

cum alia . In q erat tc̄ . I . car . m̄ nulla . Past . xxx . ou . Tc̄ ual . xx . sol . m̄ . x . Ingā ten& Idē Serlo qđ tenuit Alsid t . r . e . ꝓ . Man . 7 ꝓ . I . hid . 7 xx . ac . Sēp . I . car . tc̄ . III . bord . m̄ . IIII . Silu . xxx . porc . Tc̄ ual . xx . sol m̄ . x.

Hund de Witham Hadfeldam ten& . R . in dn̄io . qđ ten Ailmar . t . r . e . ꝓ Man . 7 ꝓ . IX . hid . 7 LXXXII . ac . Sēp . v . car in dn̄io Tc̄ . XIII . car . hom . m̄ . XI . Tc̄ . XII . uilt . m̄ . XIII . Tc̄ . XII . bord . m̄ XXXVIII . Tc̄ . x . ser . m̄ . VII . Silu . DCC . porc . L . ac . p̄ti . Tc̄ . II . mol . m̄ . I . Tc̄ . VI . runc . 7 . IIII . pulli . 7 . VI . uac . 7 . VIII . uit . CL . ou . C . porc . m̄ . v . runc . IIII . pulli . v . uacæ . VII . uit . LVII . ou . XXXIX . porc . xx . cap . Tc̄ ual . XVI . lib̄ . m̄ . xx . 7 hoc maneriū recep̄ tantū ualens ut modo. De hoc manerio ten& Serlo . 7 Ernulf . 7 . Ricard . III . hid . 7 . xx . ac . 7 ual . IIII . lib̄ . in eod p̄tio . 7 . IIII . hid . tenent . v . milit . 7 . xv . ac . de . R . qđ tenuer . XIII . libi hōes . t . r . e . Sēp . VII . car . XVI . bord . II . uilt . 7 . II . ser . 7 . I . mol . val . IIII . lib̄.

Blundeshala . ten& Humfrid de . R . qđ tenuit brictmar t . r . e . ꝓ man . 7 ꝓ . II . hid . 7 . dim . Sēp . II . car . in dn̄io . Tc̄ . I . car hōū m̄ . I . 7 . dim . Sēp . II . uilt . Tc̄ . III . bor . m̄ . v . tc̄ . VI . ser . m̄ . IIII . XVIII . ac . p̄ti . 7 . I . mol . 7 . I . soc . de . xv . ac . Tc̄ . I . runc . IIII . an . 7 . IIII . uit . LX . ou . XVI . porc . m̄ . II . runc . IIII . uac . 7 . IIII . uit . LXXX . ou . XXXVI . porc . Sēp ual . IIII . lib̄.

2 Serlo also holds VANGE from Ranulf, which a free man, who after 1066 was made the man of Ranulf Peverel's predecessor, held as a manor for 1 hide; but he did not give his land to him. However when the King gave land to Ranulf he took possession of it with the other (land). On it there was then 1 plough, now none. 72 a

Pasture, 30 sheep.

Value then 20s; now 10[s].

3 Serlo also held INGRAVE, which Alfsi held before 1066 as a manor, for 1 hide and 20 acres. Always 1 plough.

Then 3 smallholders, now 4.

Woodland, 30 pigs.

Value then 20s; now 10[s].

Hundred of WITHAM

4 Ranulf holds HATFIELD (Peverel) in lordship, which Aelmer held before 1066 as a manor, for 9 hides and 82 acres. Always 5 ploughs in lordship. Then 13 men's ploughs, now 11.

Then 12 villagers, now 13; then 12 smallholders, now 38; then 10 slaves, now 7.

Woodland, 700 pigs; meadow, 50 acres; then 2 mills, now 1. Then 6 cobs, 4 foals, 6 cows, 8 calves, 150 sheep, 100 pigs; now 5 cobs, 4 foals, 5 cows, 7 calves, 57 sheep, 39 pigs, 20 goats.

Value then £16; now [£] 20.

He acquired this manor at as much value as now.

Of this manor, Serlo, Arnulf and Richard hold 3 hides and 20 acres.

Value £4 in the same assessment.

5 men-at-arms hold 4 hides and 15 acres from Ranulf, which 13 free men held before 1066. Always 7 ploughs;

16 smallholders; 2 villagers; 2 slaves.

1 mill.

Value £4.

5 Humphrey holds BLUNT'S HALL from Ranulf, which Brictmer held before 1066 as a manor, for 2½ hides. Always 2 ploughs in lordship. Then 1 men's plough, now 1½.

Always 2 villagers. Then 3 smallholders, now 5; then 6 slaves, now 4.

Meadow, 18 acres; 1 mill. 1 Freeman with 15 acres. Then 1 cob, 4 cattle, 4 calves, 60 sheep, 16 pigs; now 2 cobs, 4 cows, 4 calves, 80 sheep, 36 pigs.

Value always £4.

⁊ Terlingā ten& Ricard de . R . qđ tenuit Ailmar teinn reḡ . t . r . e.
p Man . 7 p . II . hiđ . 7 . dim . 7 . XXX . ac . Sēp . II . car . in dnio . 7 . III . car
hom . Tc . XI . uitt . m . V . m . XI . borđ . Tc . V . ser . m . null . Silu . CL . porc.

72 b
XX . ac . p̄ti . Past . C . ou . Tc . I . mol . m . II . 7 . II . dom in colecestra . unā
reddit . VI . đ . 7 . alta . XIIII . 7 . I . lib hō . de . V . ac . 7 reddebat antecessori
Ranulfi . X . đ . 7 . R . m simil . Tc . XII . anim . CLXXX . ou . L . cap . XL . porc.
m . II . runc . 7 . II . pult . VIII . an . LXXV . ou . XVI . cap . XXXIIII . porc . Tc ual
. VIII . lib . 7 qn rec simit . m . VI . lib.
⁊ Fairstedam ten& Turold qđ ten Brictmar . t . r . e . p . M . 7 p . LV . ac.
Sēp . II . car in dnio . 7 . II . car hom . 7 . IIII . uitt . Tc . VII . bor . m . X . Tc . IIII.
ser . m . III . Silu . C . porc . XL . ac . p̄ti . Past de . IIII . đ . m . I . mol . Tc . I . runc.
XIII . ou . VI . porc . m . II . runc . CXXIIII . ou . XXXII . porc . IIII . uac . c̄ uitul.
. III . uasa ap . 7 . XV . ac . ibi jacebāt t . r . e . de qbꝫ Sasuual desaisiuit
7 jacent ad feudū . G . de magna uitt . Tc ual . IIII . lib . m . C . sol.
⁊ Hunđ de beuentreu . Hame ten& . R . in dnio qđ tenuit Alestan
lib hō . t . r . e . p . man . 7 p . VIII . hiđ . 7 . XXX . ac . 7 hoc maneriū dedit
Witt rex . R . piper . 7 Robto grenoni . Tc . V . car in dnio m . IIII . tc.
. VIII . car hom . m . XII . Tc . XXXII . uitt . m XLVIII . Tc . XVI . borđ . m
LXXX . I . min . Sēp . III . ser . Silu . C . porc . LX . ac . p̄ti . Tc . IX . mol . m . VIII.
Tc . I . runc . I . uac . III . porc . M . II . runc . II . pult . II . uac cū uit . XX . por.
LX . ou . Tc ual . XVI . lib . 7 qn recepunt . XII . lib . m ual . XXIIII . lib.
7 de hoc manerio ht . R . ḡreno medietatē.
⁊ Hunđ de Dōmauua. Cicchenai ten& Garin de . R . qđ tenuit
Siuuard . I . tegn regis . ē . p Man . 7 p . II . hiđ . 7 . dim . Sēp . III . car ī dnio.
7 . II . car hom . tc . II . uitt . m null . Tc . VII . bor . m . I . pbr . 7 . XIIII.
borđ Silu . LX . porc . XX . ac . p̄ti . Tc . II . runc . III . uac c̄ uit . LX . oues
XX . porc . XXIIII . cap . m . III . runc . VI . uac . uitul . C . ou . XXX . por.

73 a
. XXX . cap . Tc ual . C . sol . m . VII . lib.

6 Richard holds TERLING from Ranulf which Aelmer, a King's thane, held before 1066 as a manor, for 2½ hides and 30 acres. Always 2 ploughs in lordship; 3 men's ploughs.

Then 11 villagers, now 5; now 11 smallholders; then 5 slaves, now none.

Woodland, 150 pigs; meadow, 20 acres; pasture, 100 sheep; 72 b
then 1 mill, now 2. 2 houses in Colchester, one pays 6d, the other 14[d]. 1 free man with 5 acres paid Ranulf's predecessor 10d and now [pays] Ranulf the same. Then 12 cattle, 180 sheep, 50 goats, 40 pigs; now 2 cobs, 2 foals, 8 cattle, 75 sheep, 16 goats, 34 pigs.

Value then £8; when acquired, the same; now £6.

7 Thorold holds FAIRSTEAD, which Brictmer held before 1066 as a manor, for 55 acres. Always 2 ploughs in lordship; 2 men's ploughs;

4 villagers. Then 7 smallholders, now 10; then 4 slaves, now 3.

Woodland, 100 pigs; meadow, 40 acres; pasture at 4d; now 1 mill. Then 1 cob, 13 sheep, 6 pigs; now 2 cobs, 124 sheep, 32 pigs, 4 cows with calves, 3 beehives.

15 acres lay there before 1066 of which Saswalo dispossessed (him) and they lie in G(eoffrey) de Mandeville's Holding.

Value then £4; now 100s.

Hundred of BECONTREE

8 Ranulf holds (West) HAM in lordship which Alstan, a free man, held before 1066 as a manor, for 8 hides and 30 acres. King William gave this manor to Ranulf Peverel and Robert Gernon. Then 5 ploughs in lordship, now 4. Then 8 men's ploughs, now 12.

Then 32 villagers, now 48; then 16 smallholders, now 80 less 1. Always 3 slaves.

Woodland, 100 pigs; meadow, 60 acres; then 9 mills, now 8. Then 1 cob, 1 cow, 3 pigs; now 2 cobs, 2 foals, 2 cows with calves, 20 pigs, 60 sheep.

Value then £16; when acquired £12. Value now £24.

Robert Gernon has half of this manor.

Hundred of DUNMOW

9 Warin holds CHICKNEY from Ranulf which Siward, 1 thane of King Edward's, held as a manor for 2½ hides. Always 3 ploughs in lordship; 2 men's ploughs.

Then 2 villagers, now none; then 7 smallholders, now 1 priest and 14 smallholders.

Woodland, 60 pigs; meadow, 20 acres. Then 2 cobs, 3 cows with calves, 60 sheep, 20 pigs, 24 goats; now 3 cobs, 6 cows
[with] calves, 100 sheep, 30 pigs, 30 goats. 73 a

Value then 100s; now £7.

¶ Willingehalam ten& Rauenot de . R . qđ ten . Siuuard . t . r . e . p Man
7 p . I . hid . 7 . I . uirg . 7 . dim . Sep . III . car in dnio . Tc . dim . car hom . m . I.
Tc . I . uill . m . III . Sep . VI . bord . tc . VI . ser . m . IIII . Silu . CXX . porc . XII . ac.
pti . Tc . III . runc . XVI . anim . XXX . porc . m . III . runc . IIII . pulli . XVI.
anim . C . ou . LXV . porc . V . uasa ap . Tc ual . C . sol . 7 qn rec . VI . lib . m . X.
¶ huic træ addit e . I . soc . que tenuit antec . R . piperelli 7 . Adhuc ten&
. R . 7 Rauenot de illo . 7 adhuc addite st huic træ . XXX . ac . t . r . Will.
qs ten lib ho t . r . e . val . X . sol.
¶ Hund de Wibrictesherna Odeham ten& . R . in dnio . qđ
ten Siuuard p Man . 7 p . V . hid . Sep . IIII . uill . Tc . IX . bord . m . VIII . Tc
. V . ser . m . II . Sep . II . car . in dnio tc . IIII . car . hom . m . I . 7 . dim . III.
ac . pti . Silu . CC . porc . Tc . II . runc . VI . uac . IIII . uit . LX . ou . XX . porc.
XLV . cap . m . III . runc . II . pull . IIII . uac . IIII . uit . CXXXV . ou . XLVI.
porc . C . cap . Sep ual . C . sol.
¶ Meldonam ten& . R . in dnio qđ ten . Siuuard . t . r . e . p . Man . 7 . p.
. V . hid . 7 . dim . 7 . X . ac . Tc . XVI . uill . m . IX . m . X . bor . Sep . III . ser.
7 . II . car in dnio . tc . X . hom . m . V . X . ac . pti . Silu . L . porc . I . mol.
Tc . II . runc . m similit . 7 m . III . uac . IIII . uit . CXL . poues . XXIX . porc.
Sep ual . XII . lib. ★
¶ Halesheiam ten& Serlo de . R . qđ ten . Ide . S . p man . 7 . p . IIII.
hid . 7 . dim . Sep . IIII . uill . tc . IIII . ser . m . III . Tc . II . car . m . I . Tc
. I . car . hom . m . dim . Silu . LX . porc . Tc . II . runc . II . uac . II . uit.
LX . ou . V . porc . m . II . runc . IIII . uac . C . ou . IX . porc . Val . IIII . lib.

73 b

¶ Halesleiam ten& Godric de . R . qđ tenuit Ailmar lib ho . t . r . e.
p Man . 7 . p dim hid . 7 . XX . ac . Sep . I . uill . Tc . II . bord . m . null . Sep . I . car
in dnio . Silu . LXXX . porc . Val . XX . sol.

10 Ravenot holds WILLINGALE (Doe) from Ranulf, which Siward held before 1066 as a manor, for 1 hide and 1½ virgates. Always 3 ploughs in lordship. Then ½ men's plough, now 1.
Then 1 villager, now 3. Always 6 smallholders. Then 6 slaves, now 4.
Woodland, 120 pigs; meadow, 12 acres. Then 3 cobs, 16 cattle, 30 pigs; now 3 cobs, 4 foals, 16 cattle, 100 sheep, 65 pigs, 5 beehives.
Value then 100s; when acquired £6; now [£] 10.
To this land has been added 1 Freeman whom Ranulf Peverel's predecessor held and (whom) Ranulf still holds and Ravenot from him.
Also added to this land after 1066 were 30 acres which a free man held before 1066.
Value 10s.

Hundred of 'WIBERTSHERNE'

11 Ranulf holds WOODHAM (Mortimer) in lordship, which Siward held as a manor, for 5 hides.
Always 4 villagers. Then 9 smallholders, now 8; then 5 slaves, now 2. Always 2 ploughs in lordship. Then 4 men's ploughs, now 1½.
Meadow, 3 acres; woodland, 200 pigs. Then 2 cobs, 6 cows, 4 calves, 60 sheep, 20 pigs, 45 goats; now 3 cobs, 2 foals, 4 cows, 4 calves, 135 sheep, 46 pigs, 100 goats.
Value always 100s.

12 Ranulf holds MALDON in lordship, which Siward held before 1066 as a manor, for 5½ hides and 10 acres.
Then 16 villagers, now 9; now 10 smallholders. Always 3 slaves; 2 ploughs in lordship. Then 10 men's [ploughs], now 5.
Meadow, 10 acres; woodland, 50 pigs; 1 mill. Then 2 cobs, now the same; now 3 cows, 4 calves, 140 sheep, 29 pigs.
Value always £12.

13 Serlo holds HAZELEIGH from Ranulf, which Siward also held as a manor, for 4½ hides.
Always 4 villagers. Then 4 slaves, now 3. Then 2 ploughs, now 1. Then 1 men's plough, now ½.
Woodland, 60 pigs. Then 2 cobs, 2 cows, 2 calves, 60 sheep, 5 pigs; now 2 cobs, 4 cows, 100 sheep, 9 pigs.
Value £4.

14 Godric holds HAZELEIGH from Ranulf which Aelmer, a free man, 73 b
held before 1066 as a manor for ½ hide and 20 acres.
Always 1 villager. Then 2 smallholders, now none. Always 1 plough in lordship.
Woodland, 80 pigs.
Value 20s.

Hund de Wensistreu. Legrā ten& Turold de. R. qđ ten. A. t. r. e. p man. 7. p. i. hid. xii. ac. 7. dim. min. Sēp. i. car. in dnio m dim. car hom. Tc. i. bord. m. iiii. tc. iiii. ser. m. i. Silu. xvi. porc. Tc. i. runc. v. uac. v. uit. c. ou. m. ii. runc. iiii. uac. v. uit. ciii. ou. Tc ual. xxx. sol. m. xx.

Edburgetunā ten&. R. in dnio qđ tenuit. i. lib hō. t. r. e. p Man. 7 p. i. hid. 7. dim. 7. i. uirg. Sēp. i. car. in dnio. 7. dim. car. hom. 7. iiii. bord. 7. i. ser. Silu. lx. porc. iiii. ac. pti. Tc ual. lx. sol. m. l.

Wighebgā ten& Algar de. R. qđ ten. i. lib hō. t. r. e. p. Man. 7 p dim. hid. Sēp. i. car. tc. i. bor. m. ii. Val. x. sol.

Hund de Wdelesfort. Deppedanā ten&. R. in dnio. qđ ten. Siuuard. p Man. 7. p. xvi. hid. 7. dim. Sēp. vi. car. in dnio. 7. xi. car. hom. 7. xxxvi. uilt. Tc 7 p. i. bord. m. xvii. sēp. xii. ser. Silu. m. porc. xl. ac. pti. Sēp. i. mol. m. ii. arpenni uineæ portantes. 7 alij. ii. n portantes. Tc. vi. runc. xxviii. anim. cl. ou. ccl. porc. vi. uasa ap. m. vii. runc. ii. pulli. x. anim. clxviii. ou. cx. porc. iii. uasa ap. Tc 7 p ual xxiiii. lib. m xxx. De hoc manerio ten& Vital de. R. xv. ac. 7. ual. x. sol in eod ptio.

Ambdanā ten&. R. in dnio. qđ ten. Siuuard p Man. 7. p. v. hid. Sēp. iii. car. in dnio. 7. vi. car. hom. Tc 7 p. xiii. uilt

74 a

. m. xviiii. Tc. i. bord. Post. ii. m. vii. Sēp. vi. ser. Tc 7 p silu. ccl. porc. m. cc. xxx. ac. pti. Tc. ii. runc. vi. anim. xl. ou. xl. porc. v. uasa apū m. iii. runc. i. pult. xiiii. anim. lxviii. ou. xxx. porc. i. uas. apū. Sēp ual. xii. lib. s; R. inde habuit p. iii. annos. unoqq; xviii. lib. hanc uillā calumpniat abbas de eli. 7 hund testat qđ jacuit ad ecclam

Hundred of WINSTREE

15 Thorold holds LAYER from Ranulf, which A. held before 1066 as a manor, for 1 hide less 12½ acres. Always 1 plough in lordship. Now ½ men's plough.

Then 1 smallholder, now 4; then 4 slaves, now 1.

Woodland, 16 pigs. Then 1 cob, 5 cows, 5 calves, 100 sheep; now 2 cobs, 4 cows, 5 calves, 103 sheep.

Value then 30s; now 20[s].

16 Ranulf holds ABBERTON in lordship, which 1 free man held before 1066 as a manor, for 1½ hides and 1 virgate. Always 1 plough in lordship; ½ men's plough.

4 smallholders; 1 slave.

Woodland, 60 pigs; meadow, 4 acres.

Value then 60s; now 50[s].

17 Algar holds WIGBOROUGH from Ranulf, which 1 free man held before 1066 as a manor, for ½ hide. Always 1 plough.

Then 1 smallholder, now 2.

Value 10s.

Hundred of UTTLESFORD

18 Ranulf holds DEBDEN in lordship, which Siward held as a manor, for 16½ hides. Always 6 ploughs in lordship; 11 men's ploughs;

36 villagers. Then and later 1 smallholder, now 17; always 12 slaves.

Woodland, 1000 pigs; meadow, 40 acres; always 1 mill. Now 2 *arpents* of vines bearing (fruit) and another two not bearing (fruit). Then 6 cobs, 28 cattle, 150 sheep, 250 pigs, 6 beehives; now 7 cobs, 2 foals, 10 cattle, 168 sheep, 110 pigs, 3 beehives.

Value then and later £24; now [£] 30.

Of this manor, Vitalis holds 15 acres from Ranulf.

Value 10s in the same assessment.

19 Ranulf holds AMBERDEN (Hall) in lordship, which Siward held as a manor, for 5 hides. Always 3 ploughs in lordship; 6 men's ploughs.

Then and later 13 villagers, now 19; then 1 smallholder, 74 a
later 2, now 7; always 6 slaves.

Woodland, then and later 250 pigs, now 200; meadow, 30 acres. Then 2 cobs, 6 cattle, 40 sheep, 40 pigs, 5 beehives; now 3 cobs, 1 foal, 14 cattle, 68 sheep, 30 pigs, 1 beehive.

Value always £12. But Ranulf has had from it £18 each (year) for three years.

The Abbot of Ely lays claim to this village and the Hundred testifies that it lay in (the lands of) the Church.

Hund de Hidingforda. Stabingā ten&. R. in dn̄io qđ tenuit
Siuuard t. r. e. ꝓ. man. 7 ꝓ. III. hid. 7. XXX. ac. Tc̄. car. in dn̄io. 7. qn̄
rec. VI. m̄. V. Sēp. XI. car. hom. Tc̄ 7 p̄ XVIII. uilt. m̄. XIX. Tc̄ 7 post.
XIIII. bor. m̄. XXXI. Tc̄ 7 p̄. XIII. ser. m̄. XI. Silu. CC. porc. XXIIII. ac
p̄ti. Tc̄. I. mol. 7 qn̄ rec. I. 7 dim. m̄. II. m̄. II. arpenni uineæ. 7. đ.
7. dimidi tantū portat. Tc̄. V. runc. V. uac. C. ou. L. porc. V. uasa
apū. Tc̄ ual. X. lib. P̄. XII. m̄. XVI. lib. De h Man. Vital XXXV. ac. 7. X. sol ual. in eođ. p̄tio.
Henies. ten& Turold de. R. qđ tenuit Vluuin lib hō t. r. e.
ꝓ man. 7 ꝓ. II. hid. 7. dim. 7. XLV. ac. sēp. II. car in dn̄io. 7. III. car
hom. 7. V. uilt. 7. XI. bord. Tc̄ 7 p̄. II. ser. m̄. null. Silu. LXXX. porc.
XII. ac. p̄ti. sēp. I. mol. Tc̄. II. runc. V. uac. cū uit. L. ou. XIIII.
porc. III. uasa apū. m̄. I. runc. IX. uac. c̄ uit. CXXXIIII. ou. XXXVI.
porc. 7 huic manerio ꝑtin& de Sudbia. XXII. đ. de consuetudine.
Tc̄. ual. XL. sol. m̄. IIII. lib.
Lamers ten& Turold de. R. qđ tenuit Algar. t. r. e. ꝓ. Man.
7 ꝓ. III. hid. 7. dim. Sēp. II. car. in dn̄io. Tc̄ 7 p̄. II. car. 7 dim. hoū.
m̄. II. Sēp. IIII. uilt. m̄. VIII. bord. Silu. LXX. porc. XIII. ac. p̄ti.
Tc̄. VI. uac. c̄ uit. LIIII. ou. XI. porc. m̄. VII. runc. V. pult. X. uac.
VIII. uit. XX. ou. LIIII. porc. LX. cap. VI. uasa ap̄. Tc̄ ual. IIII. lib

74 b
m̄. VI. In Lamers tenuit Aluuard. I. hid 7 dim ꝓ man. t. r. e. m̄ ten&
Idē. T. de Ranulfo. Sēp. I. car in dn̄io. 7. I. car hom. 7. II. uilt. Tc̄. III.
bord. m̄. IX. Silu. XXX. porc. VII. ac. p̄ti. Tc̄ ual. XL. sol. m̄. LX.
Hæe due tr̄e erant sic diuisæ duob; fratrib; t. r. e. Post ea date s̄t
Ranulfo ꝓ. I. manerio ut dict̄ sui hoēs.
Hund de Witbrictesherna. Dunā ten&. R. in dn̄io qđ
tenuit Siuuard ꝓ. Man. 7 ꝓ. XIIII. hid. Tc̄. II. uilt. m̄. IIII. Tc̄. III. bor.
m̄. XV. Tc̄. XII. ser. m̄. VI. Sēp. V. car in dn̄io. Tc̄. II. car hom. m̄. III.

Hundred of HINCKFORD

20 Ranulf holds STEBBING in lordship, which Siward held before 1066 as a manor, for 3 hides and 30 acres. Then ... ploughs in lordship; when acquired 6; now 5. Always 11 men's ploughs.

Then and later 18 villagers, now 19; then and later 14 smallholders, now 31; then and later 13 slaves, now 11.

Woodland, 200 pigs; meadow, 24 acres; then 1 mill, when acquired 1½, now 2; now 2½ *arpents* of vines and only the ½ bears (fruit).

Then 5 cobs, 5 cows, 100 sheep, 50 pigs, 5 beehives.

Value then £10; later [£] 12; now £16.

Of this manor, Vitalis [holds] 35 acres.

Value 10s in the same assessment.

21 Thorold holds (Great) HENNY from Ranulf which Wulfwin, a free man, held before 1066 as a manor for 2½ hides and 45 acres. Always 2 ploughs in lordship; 3 men's ploughs;

5 villagers; 11 smallholders. Then and later 2 slaves, now none.

Woodland, 80 pigs; meadow, 12 acres; always 1 mill. Then 2 cobs, 5 cows with calves, 50 sheep, 14 pigs, 3 beehives; now 1 cob, 9 cows with calves, 134 sheep, 36 pigs.

To this manor belongs 12d of the customary due from Sudbury.

Value then 40s; now £4.

22 Thorold holds LAMARSH from Ranulf, which Algar held before 1066 as a manor, for 3½ hides. Always 2 ploughs in lordship. Then and later 2½ men's ploughs, now 2.

Always 4 villagers. Now 8 smallholders.

Woodland, 70 pigs; meadow, 13 acres. Then 6 cows with calves, 54 sheep, 11 pigs; now 7 cobs, 5 foals, 10 cows, 8 calves, 20 sheep, 54 pigs, 60 goats, 6 beehives.

Value then £4; now [£] 6. 74 b

In LAMARSH Alfward held 1½ hides as a manor before 1066. Now Thorold also holds them from Ranulf. Always 1 plough in lordship; 1 men's plough;

2 villagers. Then 3 smallholders, now 9.

Woodland, 30 pigs; meadow, 7 acres.

Value then 40s; now 60[s].

These two lands were divided thus between two brothers before 1066; later on they were given to Ranulf as 1 manor as his men state.

Hundred of 'WIBERTSHERNE'

23 Ranulf holds DOWN (Hall) in lordship, which Siward held as a manor, for 14 hides.

Then 2 villagers, now 4; then 3 smallholders, now 15; then 12 slaves, now 6. Always 5 ploughs in lordship. Then 2 men's ploughs, now 3.

Silu̓ . L . porc̓ . Past̓ . L . ou̓ . Tc̄ 7 p̓ uał . x . lib̄ . m̊ . XIII . De hoc manerio ten& Afcelin̓ . I . hiđ . 7 . dim̓ . de . R . 7 uał . XX . foł in eođ p̄tio.

Lalinge ten& . R . in dn̄io qđ tenuit Brun . lib̄ hō . t̓ . r̓ . e̓ . ꝓ Man̓. 7 ꝓ . II . hiđ . 7 . dim̓ . 7 . XXXV . ac̓ . Sēp . II . fer̓ . 7 . II . car̓ . Silu̓ . XX . porc̓. Past̓ . L . ou̓ . m̊ . I . pifc̓ . Tc̄ 7 p̓ uał . IIII . lib̄ . m̊ . III . lib̄ . 7 . XV . foł.

In Duna tenuer̄ . VIII . lib̄i hōes . V . hiđ . VI . ac̓ min̓ . qđ ten& . R. in dn̄io . Sēp . VI . borđ . 7 . II . car̓ . 7 dim̓ . Tc̄ 7 p̓ uał . LX . foł . m̊ . IIII . lib̄ 7 . X . foł.

Stanefgatā ten& Rad fili̓ . brien qđ tenuit Siuuard̓ ꝓ Man̓. 7 ꝓ . VIIIJ . hiđ . 7 . dim̓ . t̓ . r̓ . e̓ . Sēp . II . uilł . Tc̄ . XXII . borđ . m̊ . XVIII. Tc̄ . VIII . fer̓ . m̊ . III . Tc̄ . IIII . car̓ 7 dim̓ in dn̄io . m̊ . IIII . Sēp . III. car̓ hom̓ . Silu̓ . LX . porc̓ . Past̓ . LX . ou̓ . Tc̄ 7 p̓ uał . X . lib̄ . m̊ . VIII.

Hunđ de Laffendena Pereftedā ten& Idē . R . qđ tenuit Bric̄tmar̓ . t̓ . r̓ . e̓ . ꝓ man̓ . 7 ꝓ . I . hiđ . 7 . dim̓ . Tc̄ . V . bor . m̊ . X . Tc̄ . IIII. fer̓ . m̊ . null̓ . Sēp . II . car̓ . in dn̄io . Silu̓ . C . porc̓ . VIII . ac̓ . p̄ti . Tc̄ . II. runc̓ . X . an̓ . LXXX . ou̓ . XV . porc̓ . XX . cap̓ . II . uafa apū . m̊ . I . eq.

75 a
7 . I . pull̓ . LX . ou̓ . XX . porc̓ . IX . cap̓ . II . uafa apū . Sēp uał . IIII . lib̄. 7 . I . lib̄ hō sēp ten& . V . ac̓ . 7 fuit c̄om̄dat̓ anteceffori . R . ſ; c̄ tr̄a fua poff& ire q̊ uell& . 7 m̊ . h̄t . R . Tc̄ . I . car̓ . m̊ . dim̓ . Tc̄ uał . XVI . foł m̊ . XII.

Hunđ de Angra . Plumtunā ten& Rauenot de . R . qđ ten̓ . Vluric̓ . pb̄r de heroldo ꝓ . XIIII . ac̓ . lib̄e . 7 m̊ h̄t . R . idō qđ anteceffor ej̓ fuit faifit̓ ſ; n̄ ꝑtinuit ad eū : fic̓ comitat̓ teftat̓. Sēp . I . uilł . 7 . đ . car̓ . Silu̓ . XX . porc̓ . I . ac̓ . 7 . dim̓ . p̄ti . uał . V . foł

Woodland, 50 pigs; pasture, 50 sheep.
Value then and later £10; now [£] 13.
Of this manor, Ascelin holds 1½ hides from Ranulf.
Value 20s in the same assessment.

24 Ranulf holds LAWLING in lordship which Brown, a free man, held before 1066 as a manor for 2½ hides and 35 acres.
Always 2 slaves; 2 ploughs.
Woodland, 20 pigs; pasture, 50 sheep; now 1 fishery.
Value then and later £4; now £3 15s.

25 In DOWN (Hall) 8 free men held 5 hides less 6 acres, which Ranulf holds in lordship.
Always 6 smallholders; 2½ ploughs.
Value then and later 60s; now £4 10s.

26 Ralph son of Brian holds STANSGATE, which Siward held as a manor, for 9½ hides before 1066.
Always 2 villagers. Then 22 smallholders, now 18; then 8 slaves, now 3. Then 4½ ploughs in lordship, now 4. Always 3 men's ploughs.
Woodland, 60 pigs; pasture, 60 sheep.
Value then and later £10; now [£] 8.

Hundred of LEXDEN

27 Ranulf also holds PRESTED, which Brictmer held before 1066 as a manor, for 1½ hides.
Then 5 smallholders, now 10; then 4 slaves, now none. Always 2 ploughs in lordship.
Woodland, 100 pigs; meadow, 8 acres. Then 2 cobs, 10 cattle,
80 sheep, 15 pigs, 20 goats, 2 beehives; now 1 mare and 1 75 a
foal, 60 sheep, 20 pigs, 9 goats, 2 beehives.
Value always £4.
1 free man has always held 5 acres and was under the patronage of Ranulf's predecessor, but he could go with his land whither he would. Now Ranulf has it. Then 1 plough, now ½.
Value then 16s, now 12[s].

Hundred of ONGAR

28 Ravenot holds PLUNKER'S (Green) from Ranulf, which Wulfric the priest held from Harold freely, for 14 acres. Now Ranulf has it because his predecessor was in possession of it; but it did not belong to him, so the Hundred testifies.
Always 1 villager; ½ plough.
Woodland, 20 pigs; meadow, 1½ acres.
Value 5s.

Hund de Celmeresfort. Springafeldā ten&. Rob. de. R.
qđ tenuit Alestan p man. 7 p. v. hid. 7. xx. ac. Tc. vi. uill. m
. IIII. Tc. III. borđ. m. x. Tc. VIII. bor. m. vi. Sep. III. car. in dnio.
Tc. 7. p. III. car. hom. m. II. Silu. xxx. porc. xxv. ac. pti. Sep. I.
mol. Tc. II. runc. XII. anim. c. ou. L. porc. M. IIII. runc. v. pull.
xxvi. an. xl. ou. xxv. porc. xii. cap. ii. asini. I. uas ap. Tc. uat. v.
lib. m. vi. 7. ii. libi hoes tenuer. xiii. ac. qđ ht. R. val. II. sol.
Radendunam ten&. Rađ fili brien qđ tenuit. Siuuard. p Man.
7 p. I. hid. 7. xxx. ac. Sep. I. bor. 7. I. car in dnio. Silu. vi. porc. Sep
ual. xxv. sol. 7 abbia de eli calumpniat.
Dimid Hund de Melduna. In Melduna ten&. R. in dnio
dim hid. 7 xxIIII. ac. qđ tenuit Siuuard. t. r. e. p. man. Tc. I. borđ.
m. III. val. v. sol. 7 hec tra apptiata e in. xII. lib de melduna
Hund de Tendringa. Tendringā ten&. R. in dnio
qđ tenuit Olui libe p man. 7 p dim hid. 7. xxx. ac. 7 R. ht in
escangio. Tc. II. ser. m. I. Tc. II. car. Post 7 m. I. Silu. xxx. porc.

75 b
. II. ac. pti. Tc 7 p ual. xx. sol. m LX.
Cice ten& Turold de. R. qđ tenuit Siuuard p man. 7 p. II. hid. 7. đ.
Tc. 7. p. IX. uill. m. vi. Tc. 7 p. xII. bor. m. xI. Sep. vII. ser. Tc. 7 p. IIII.

Hundred of CHELMSFORD

29 Robert holds SPRINGFIELD from Ranulf, which Alstan held as a manor, for 5 hides and 20 acres.

Then 6 villagers, now 4; then 3 smallholders, now 10; then 8 smallholders, now 6. Always 3 ploughs in lordship. Then and later 3 men's ploughs, now 2.

Woodland, 30 pigs; meadow, 25 acres; always 1 mill. Then 2 cobs, 12 cattle, 100 sheep, 50 pigs; now 4 cobs, 5 foals, 26 cattle, 40 sheep, 25 pigs, 12 goats, 2 asses, 1 beehive.

Value then £5; now [£] 6.

2 free men held 13 acres, which Ranulf has.

Value 2s.

30 Ralph son of Brian holds RETTENDON, which Siward held as a manor, for 1 hide and 30 acres.

Always 1 smallholder; 1 plough in lordship.

Woodland, 6 pigs.

Value always 25s.

The Abbey of Ely lays claim to it.

Half-Hundred of MALDON

31 In MALDON Ranulf holds ½ hide and 24 acres in lordship, which Siward held before 1066 as a manor.

Then 1 smallholder, now 3.

Value 5s.

This land is assessed in the £12 from Maldon.

Hundred of TENDRING

32 Ranulf holds TENDRING in lordship, which Wulfwy held freely as a manor, for ½ hide and 30 acres. Ranulf has (it) in exchange.

Then 2 slaves, now 1. Then 2 ploughs, later and now 1.

Woodland, 30 pigs; meadow, 2 acres. 75 b

Value then and later 20s; now 60[s].

33 Thorold holds ST. OSYTH from Ranulf, which Siward held as a manor, for 2½ hides.

Then and later 9 villagers, now 6; then and later 12 smallholders, now 11; always 7 slaves. Then and later 4

car in dnio . m . III . Tc . 7 p . VII . car hom . m . V . Silu . DCCC . porc . IIII . ac . pti . Past . CC . ou . sep . I . mol . Tc . VI . runc . L . anim . CCC . ou . XL . porc . VI . uasa apu . M . IIII . runc . IIII . an . LXVIII . ou . XXXVII . porc . XVIII . cap . Tc 7 p uat . IX . lib . m . VIII .

Fretinga ten& Ide . T . de . R . qd tenuit Ketel . p . man . 7 p . II . hid . Tc . II . bor . m . III . Tc . III . ser . m . II . Tc . in dnio . II . car . m . I . Sep . I . car hom . Silu . CL . porc . IIII . ac . pti . Tc . I . runc . IIII . an . IIII . uit . C . ou . XL . porc . M . I . runc . II . uac . II . uit . LXVI . ou . XX . porc . VI . uas apu . Tc uat . XL . sot . m . LX .

Hund de Rochefort Legra ten& . R . in dnio . qd tenuit . I . lib ho . p man . 7 p . I . hid . Sep . II . uilt . 7 . II . bor . 7 . I . car in dnio . 7 . dim car hom . 7 . V . bor . sup aqm . q n tenent tra . Past . C . ou . Tc . I . runc . V . uac . V . uit . C . ou . m . II . runc . IIII . uac . V . uit . CIII . ou . Tc uat . XL . sot . m . C .

Hund de Turestapla . Toleshunta ten& Humfrid de . R . qd tenuit Siuuard p man . 7 p . IIII . hid . 7 . dim . 7 . XXX . ac . Tc . IX . uilt . m . X . Tc . IIII . bord . m . XIII . tc . X . ser . m . VI . Sep . III . car in dnio . 7 . III . car hom . I . salina . V . ac . pti . Past . XXX . ou . Silu . CL . porc . Tc . III . runc . XX . anim LXXX . ou . LX . porc . m . III . runc . XX . an . CLX . ou . XXXVII . porc . XVIII . cap . Sep uat . C . sot . In hoc manerio tenuer . IIII . libi hoes . dim . hid . 7 . V . ac . s; Rad

76 a
baign ht ea 7 hugo de montfort.

Goldhangra ten& Ricard de . R . qd tenuit Leuuin 7 vluard pbr p man . 7 . p . II . hid . 7 dim . 7 . XXV . ac . Tc . III . bor . m . XIIII . Sep . II . ser . Tc . II . car in dnio . m . I . m . I . car hom Silu . LXXX . porc . Past . L . ou . III . ac . 7 dim . pti . Tc . LI . ou . VIII . porc . m . I . runc . I . uac . III . ou . III . porc . Sep uat . XL . sot . In Ead . II . libi hoes de . VII . ac . 7 . d . 7 uat . XX . d .

ploughs in lordship, now 3. Then and later 7 men's ploughs, now 5.

Woodland, 800 pigs; meadow, 4 acres, pasture, 200 sheep; always 1 mill. Then 6 cobs, 50 cattle, 300 sheep, 40 pigs, 6 beehives; now 4 cobs, 4 cattle, 68 sheep, 37 pigs, 18 goats.

Value then and later £9; now [£] 8.

34 Thorold also holds FRATING from Ranulf, which Ketel held as a manor, for 2 hides.

Then 2 smallholders, now 3; then 3 slaves, now 2. Then 2 ploughs in lordship, now 1. Always 1 men's plough.

Woodland, 150 pigs; meadow, 4 acres. Then 1 cob, 4 cattle, 4 calves, 100 sheep, 40 pigs; now 1 cob, 2 cows, 2 calves, 66 sheep, 20 pigs, 6 beehives.

Value then 40s; now 60[s].

Hundred of ROCHFORD

35 Ranulf holds LEIGH in lordship, which 1 free man held as a manor, for 1 hide.

Always 2 villagers; 2 smallholders; 1 plough in lordship; ½ men's plough; 5 smallholders above the water who do not hold land.

Pasture, 100 sheep. Then 1 cob, 5 cows, 5 calves, 100 sheep; now 2 cobs, 4 cows, 5 calves, 103 sheep.

Value then 40s; now 100[s].

Hundred of THURSTABLE

36 Humphrey holds TOLLESHUNT (D'Arcy) from Ranulf, which Siward held as a manor, for 4½ hides and 30 acres.

Then 9 villagers, now 10; then 4 smallholders, now 13; then 10 slaves, now 6. Always 3 ploughs in lordship; 3 men's ploughs.

1 salt-house; meadow, 5 acres; pasture, 30 sheep; woodland, 150 pigs. Then 3 cobs, 20 cattle, 80 sheep, 60 pigs; now 3 cobs, 20 cattle, 160 sheep, 37 pigs, 18 goats.

Value always 100s.

In this manor 4 free men held ½ hide and 5 acres. But Ralph Baynard has it, and Hugh de Montfort. 76 a

37 Richard holds GOLDHANGER from Ranulf, which Leofwin and Wulfward the priest held as a manor, for 2½ hides and 25 acres.

Then 3 smallholders, now 14; always 2 slaves. Then 2 ploughs in lordship, now 1. Now 1 men's plough.

Woodland, 80 pigs; pasture, 50 sheep; meadow, 3½ acres. Then 51 sheep, 8 pigs; now 1 cob, 1 cow, 3 sheep, 3 pigs.

Value always 40s.

In the same (Goldhanger) 2 free men with 7½ acres.

Value 20d.

TERRA Alberici de uer. Hund de Dommauua. .XXXV.

Canedfeldam ten& Albic in dnio. qd tenuit Vluuin. t. r. e. p. Man.
7. p. II. hid. Sep. II. car in dnio. Tc. IIII. car hom. m. III. Sep. x. uill.
Tc. IIII. bor. m. IX. Sep. IIII. ser. Silu. CLX. porc. LI. ac. pti. I. mol.
Tc. VII. an. II. runc. xx. porc. LXXX. ou. III. uasa ap. m. VIII. an.
. III. runc. xxx. porc. c. ou. III. uasa ap. Sep ual. VI. lib.

Vdecheshale ten&. A. in dnio qd tenuit Vluuin p. m. 7. p
. I. hid. Sep. II. car. in dnio. Tc. III. car hom. m. I. Tc. XI. uill. m. VI.
Tc. II. bor. m. IIII. Sep. IIII. ser. Silu. c. porc. XLVIII. ac. pti.
Tc. VI. an. II. runc. xx. porc. LX. ou. III. uasa ap. m. VIII. an.
. II. runc. xxx. porc. LXXX. ou. III. uasa ap. Sep ual. LX. sol.

76 b

Huic tre addita e. I. uirg. 7. VIII. ac. qs ten. lib ho. t. r. e. m ten&. Rad
de. A. Sep. I. car. in dnio. Tc. I. bor. m. III. Silu. xxx. porc. IX. ac. pti.
Tc. ual. XVI. sol. m. xxx.

Hund de Vdelesfort. Tunresleam ten& Rad de. A. qd tenuit
Ailmar lib ho. t. r. e. p Man. 7 p. v. hid. Tc. 7 p. II. car. in dnio. m. III.
Sep. III. car hom. 7. I. pbr. 7. XI. uill. 7. v. bord. Tc 7 p silu. c. porc.
m. LXXX. XII. ac. pti. Tc. CXX. ou. XL. porc. LX. cap. VIII. an. III. runc.
. v. uasa ap. M. CXL. ou. LX. porc. Aliud similit. Tc 7 p ual VI. lib. m. VII.

Dim. Hund de Clauelinga. Vggheleam ten&. Rad de. A. qd
tenuit Vluuin p man. 7 p. v. hid. Sep. III. car. in dnio. 7. IIII. car.
hom. Tc. x. uill. Post. 7. m. VII. Tc. 7 p. I. bor. m. x. tc 7 p. VI. ser. m. II.
Tc 7 p silu. cc. porc. m. CLX. XXV. ac. pti. tc. v. an. L. porc. CLX.
ou. II. runc. L. cap. II. uasa ap. m. III. an. XXII. porc. LXXX. ou. IIII.
runc. xx. cap. II. uasa ap. Tc ual. VI. lib. m. VIII.

35 LAND OF AUBREY DE VERE

Hundred of DUNMOW

1 Aubrey holds (Great) CANFIELD in lordship, which Wulfwin held as a manor, for 2 hides. Always 2 ploughs in lordship. Then 4 men's ploughs, now 3.

Always 10 villagers. Then 4 smallholders, now 9; always 4 slaves.

Woodland, 160 pigs; meadow, 51 acres; 1 mill. Then 7 cattle, 2 cobs, 20 pigs, 80 sheep, 3 beehives; now 8 cattle, 3 cobs, 30 pigs, 100 sheep, 3 beehives.

Value always £6.

2 Aubrey holds *UDECHESHALE* in lordship, which Wulfwin held before 1066 as a manor, for 1 hide. Always 2 ploughs in lordship. Then 3 men's ploughs, now 1.

Then 11 villagers, now 6; then 2 smallholders, now 4; always 4 slaves.

Woodland, 100 pigs; meadow, 48 acres. Then 6 cattle, 2 cobs, 20 pigs, 60 sheep, 3 beehives; now 8 cattle, 2 cobs, 30 pigs, 80 sheep, 3 beehives.

Value always 60s.

To this land has been added 1 virgate and 8 acres, which a free 76 b
man held before 1066. Now Ralph holds (it) from Aubrey. Always 1 plough in lordship.

Then 1 smallholder; now 3.

Woodland, 30 pigs; meadow, 9 acres.

Value then 16s; now 30[s].

Hundred of UTTLESFORD

3 Ralph holds THUNDERLEY (Hall) from Aubrey which Aelmer, a free man, held before 1066 as a manor for 5 hides. Then and later 2 ploughs in lordship; now 3. Always 3 men's ploughs;

1 priest; 11 villagers; 5 smallholders.

Woodland then and later, 100 pigs, now 80; meadow, 12 acres. Then 120 sheep, 40 pigs, 60 goats, 8 cattle, 3 cobs, 5 beehives; now 140 sheep, 60 pigs, otherwise the same.

Value then and later £6; now [£] 7.

Half-Hundred of CLAVERING

4 Ralph holds UGLEY from Aubrey, which Wulfwin held as a manor, for 5 hides. Always 3 ploughs in lordship; 4 men's ploughs.

Then 10 villagers, later and now 7; then and later 1 smallholder, now 10; then and later 6 slaves, now 2.

Woodland then and later, 200 pigs, now 160; meadow, 25 acres. Then 5 cattle, 50 pigs, 160 sheep, 2 cobs, 50 goats, 2 beehives; now 3 cattle, 22 pigs, 80 sheep, 4 cobs, 20 goats, 2 beehives.

Value then £6; now [£] 8.

Hund de Hidingforda. Haingheham ten&. A. in dnio. qd ten.
Vluuin p man. 7 p. II. hid. Sep. IIII. car. in dnio. 7. VI. car. hom. 7. XV
uill. 7. VII. bor. 7. VIII. ser. Silu. CC. porc. XXX. ac. pti. Tc. I. mol. m. II.
m. VI. arpenni. uineæ. Tc. XI. an. CXL. ou. LXXX. porc. IIII. runc.
M. CLX. ou. C. porc. I. runc. C. cap. 7. XIII. soc. q n potant recede
tenentes. I. hid. 7. X. ac. Sep. V. car. Tc. XV. uill. m. XVIII. m. XXII.
bor. Tc. VI. ser. m. II. hntes. III. car. Silu. LX. porc. XLIII. ac. pti. Sep
. I. mol. Tc ual. XIII. lib. m. XX. Huic manerio jacent. XV. burg
in sudbia 7 appt in ill. XX. lib. De hoc manerio ten&. Rob blund
XXXV. ac. Garin. XXV. ac. Pincun. XV. ac. Godun. XV. ac. hntes

77 a

. V. car. 7. ual. VII. lib in eod ptio.

Dim Hund de Thunrestau. Belcamp ten&. A. in dnio qd
tenuit Vluuin. t. r. e. p Man. 7. p. II. hid. 7. dim. Sep. IIII. car hom.
7. VII. car. hom. Tc. 7 p. XIII. uill. m. XV. Tc. 7 p. IX. bor. m. XIIII.
Tc. 7 p. VI. ser. m. VIII. Silu. XX. porc. LX. ac. pti. M. XI. arpenni uineæ.
. I. portat. Tc XXIIII. an. CLX. ou. LXXX. porc. II. runc. m. XXVIII. an.
. CC. ou. C. porc. II. runc. Huic man adjacent. sep. VII. soc. de. I.
hid. 7. dim. 7. XV. ac. Sep. III. car. 7. dim. m. IIII. bor. X. ac. 7. dim. pti.
Tc. 7 p ual. XIIII. lib. m. XVIII. De hoc man. ten&. Enisant de. A.
dim. hid. 7. XXX. ac. Will peccatu. dim. hid. Suad. XXX. ac. 7. ual
. IIII. lib. in eod. ptio.

Hund de Hidingaforda. Hersam ten&. Adelelmus de. A.
qd tenuer. II. sochemani de antecessore. Albici. ita qd non potant
recede sine licentia ej. sep. I. car. 7. dim. Tc. V. bor. m. X. Tc. silu.
XL. porc. m. XXX. VII. ac. pti. Val. XX. sol

Hundred of HINCKFORD

5 Aubrey holds (Castle) HEDINGHAM in lordship, which Wulfwin held as a manor, for 2 hides. Always 4 ploughs in lordship; 6 men's ploughs;

15 villagers, 7 smallholders; 8 slaves.

Woodland, 200 pigs; meadow, 30 acres; then 1 mill, now none; now 6 *arpents* of vines. Then 11 cattle, 140 sheep, 80 pigs, 4 cobs; now 160 sheep, 100 pigs, 1 cob, 100 goats.

13 Freeman who could not withdraw (and) who held 1 hide and 10 acres. Always 7 ploughs.

Then 15 villagers, now 18; now 22 smallholders; then 6 slaves, now 2; who have 3 ploughs.

Woodland, 60 pigs; meadow, 43 acres; always 1 mill.

Value then £13; now [£] 20.

To this manor are attached 15 burgesses in Sudbury; they are assessed in the £20.

Of this manor, Robert Blunt holds 35 acres, Warin 25 acres, Pinson 15 acres, Godwin 15 acres; who have 5 ploughs. 77 a

Value £7 in the same assessment.

Half-Hundred of 'THUNDERLOW'

6 Aubrey holds BELCHAMP (Walter) in lordship, which Wulfwin held before 1066 as a manor, for 2½ hides. Always 4 men's ploughs; 7 men's ploughs.

Then and later 13 villagers, now 15; then and later 9 smallholders, now 14; then and later 6 slaves, now 8.

Woodland, 20 pigs; meadow, 60 acres; now 11 *arpents* of vines, 1 bears (fruit). Then 24 cattle, 160 sheep, 80 pigs, 2 cobs; now 28 cattle, 200 sheep, 100 pigs, 2 cobs.

To this manor have always been attached 7 Freemen with 1½ hides and 15 acres. Always 3½ ploughs.

Now 4 smallholders.

Meadow, 10½ acres.

Value then and later £14; now [£] 18.

Of this manor, Enisant holds from Aubrey ½ hide and 30 acres, William Peche ½ hide, Suadus 30 acres.

Value £4 in this assessment.

Hundred of HINCKFORD

7 Aethelhelm holds HORSEHAM (Hall) from Aubrey, which 2 Freemen held from Aubrey's predecessor on condition that they could not withdraw without his permission. 45 acres. Always 1½ ploughs.

Then 5 smallholders, now 10.

Woodland then 40 pigs, now 30; meadow, 7 acres.

Value 20s.

⁊ Hund de Lexendana. Coles ten&. A. in dn̄io qđ tenuit Vluuin. ꝑ Man. 7. ꝑ. v. hid. Sep̄. uill. 7. xiii. bor. 7. vi. ser. Tc. iii. car. in dn̄io. m̄. v. Tc. int hoes. iii. car. m̄. iiii. Silu. cccc. porc. xl. ac. p̄ti. ii. mol. Tc. xx. uac. 7 xix. an. cxx. ou. lx. por. lx. cap. iii. runc. m̄. xlv. an. clx. ou. lxxx. porc. lxxx. cap. iiii. runc. 7 vi. asini. 7. xx. equæ. 7. iiii. soc manser in his. v. hid. 7. x. bor. 7. iiii. ser. Tc. 7 p uat. x. lib. m̄. xii. De hoc manerio ten& Dimidi blanc. i. hid. 7. vii. bor. 7. ii. car. in dn̄io. 7. i. car. hom. 7. uat. xlv. sol. in eod p̄tio.

77 b

⁊ Hund de Tendringa Benetleiam ten&. A. in dn̄io qđ tenuit Vluuin ꝑ. Man. 7 ꝑ. iii. hid. Tc 7 p. vii. uill. m̄. vi. Tc. v. bor. m̄. x. Sep. iiii. ser. Tc. iiii. car. in dn̄io. m̄. iii. Tc int. v. car. m̄. iiii. Silua. cl. porc. vi. ac. p̄ti. Past. cl. ou. i. salina. Tc. iii. runc. c. ou. xx. an. xl. porc. m̄. c. ou. &. iii. runc. xxvi. an. xl. porc. Tc. uat. vi. lib. m̄. x.

⁊ Druurecurt ten&. A. in dn̄io. qđ tenuit Vluuin ꝑ man. 7. ꝑ. vi. hid. Tc. viii. uill. m̄. vi. Tc. vi. bor. m̄. xii. Sep. vi. ser. 7. iii. car. in dn̄io 7. vi. car hom. iii. ac. p̄ti. Past. cc. ou. Tc. iii. runc. xii. an. cc. ou. xl. por. 7 m̄ similit Tc uat. vi. lib. m̄. xii.

⁊ Fulepet ten& Eduuard de. A. qđ tenuit Vluuin ꝑ Man. 7. ꝑ. ii. hid. Sep. xvii. uill. Tc. iii. bor. m̄. i. Tc. iii. ser. m̄ null. Tc. in dn̄io. ii. car. m̄. i. Sep. v. car. hom. Silu. xv. porc. x. ac. p̄ti. ii. sal. Tc. xii.

Hundred of LEXDEN

8 Aubrey holds (Earls) COLNE in lordship, which Wulfwin held as a manor, for 5 hides.

Always ... villagers; 13 smallholders; 6 slaves.

Then 3 ploughs in lordship, now 5. Then among the men 3 ploughs, now 4.

Woodland, 400 pigs; meadow, 40 acres; 2 mills. Then 20 cows, 19 cattle, 120 sheep, 60 pigs, 60 goats, 3 cobs; now 45 cattle, 160 sheep, 80 pigs, 80 goats, 4 cobs, 6 asses and 20 mares.

4 Freemen dwelt on these 5 hides; 10 smallholders; 4 slaves.

Value then and later £10; now [£] 12.

Of this manor, Demiblanc holds 1 hide. 7 smallholders. 2 ploughs in lordship. 1 men's plough.

Value 45s in the same assessment.

Hundred of TENDRING 77 b

9 Aubrey holds (Great) BENTLEY in lordship, which Wulfwin held as a manor, for 3 hides.

Then and later 7 villagers, now 6; then 5 smallholders, now 10; always 4 slaves.

Then 4 ploughs in lordship, now 3. Then among [the men] 5 ploughs, now 4.

Woodland, 150 pigs; meadow, 6 acres; pasture, 150 sheep; 1 salt-house. Then 3 cobs, 100 sheep, 20 cattle, 40 pigs; now 100 sheep, 3 cobs, 26 cattle, 40 pigs.

Value then £6; now [£] 10.

10 Aubrey holds DOVERCOURT in lordship, which Wulfwin held as a manor, for 6 hides.

Then 8 villagers, now 6; then 6 smallholders, now 12. Always 6 slaves;

3 ploughs in lordship; 6 men's ploughs.

Meadow, 3 acres; pasture, 200 sheep. Then 3 cobs, 12 cattle, 200 sheep, 40 pigs; now the same.

Value then £6; now [£] 12.

11 Edward holds BEAUMONT from Aubrey, which Wulfwin held as a manor, for 2 hides.

Always 17 villagers. Then 3 smallholders, now 1; then 3 slaves, now none.

T Then 2 ploughs in lordship, now 1. Always 5 men's ploughs.

Woodland, 15 pigs; meadow, 10 acres; 2 salt-houses. Then 12

an . cl . ou . xxx . porc . ii . runc . M . iiii . an . c . ou . xxx . por . i . runc . iii . uasa ap . Tc̄ ual . c . sol . m̄ . viii . lib̄ . huic manerio ptin& . i . soc . q̄ n̄ potat recede a tr̄a sine licentia antecessoris Albici . tenens . ii . hid xv . ac . min . Tc̄ . ii . uill . m̄ . null . Tc̄ . ii . bor . m̄ . iii . Tc̄ . i . ser . m̄ null . Sēp . i . car in dn̄io . Tc̄ . int hōes . i . car . m̄ . n̄ . Silu . l . porc . ii . ac . p̄ti . Tc̄ ual . xx . sol . m̄ . xl .

Dimid Hund de Frossenuella . Bumesteda ten& Adelelm . de . A . qd tenuit Vluuin p . man . 7 p . ii . hid . Sēp . vii . uill . 7 . iii . bor . 7 . iiii . ser . Tc̄ . 7 p . ii . car . in dn̄io . m̄ . ii . 7 . dim . Tc̄ . 7 p . ii . car . hōu m̄ . i . 7 . dim . Silu . xx . porc . v . ac . p̄ti . Tc̄ . vii . anim . viii . porc . i . runc . v . ou . xv . cap . iii . uasa apū . m̄ . xii . an . xl . porc . v . runc . lxxx . ou . xl . cap . v . uasa apū . Tc̄ ual . v . lib̄ . m̄ . viii .

78 a

Redeuuintram ten& Dim blanc . de . A . qd tenuit Aluric sochem . p Man . 7 p dim hid . 7 . xv . ac . 7 potat uende tr̄a s; soca 7 saca rema nebat antecessori . Albici . Tc̄ . iiii . uill . m̄ . ii . Tc̄ . i . bor . m̄ . v . Tc̄ . i . ser . m̄ . ii . Tc̄ . i . car . in dn̄io . m̄ . ii . Tc̄ . ii . car . hom . m̄ . i . Silu . xxx . porc . ix . ac . p̄ti . Tc̄ ual . xx . sol . m̄ . lx .

In Stauintuna ten& Renold de . A . xxx . ac . qd tenuit Aluuin . 7 . Ordric . tenuit . xv . ac . 7 . isti . ii . fuer in soca regis . s; eos dedit Albico . Sēp . iii . uill . 7 . ii . bor . 7 . i . car . Silu . x . por . iii . ac . p̄ti . Tc̄ ual . xx . sol . m̄ . xxx . In Ead ten& q̄da anglic . de . A . xl . ac . qs tenuit Aluric . soc . potens uende tr̄a . s; soca 7 saca remanebat . Sēp . ii . bor . 7 . i . car . val . x . sol .

cattle, 150 sheep, 30 pigs, 2 cobs; now 4 cattle, 100 sheep, 30 pigs, 1 cob, 3 beehives.
Value then 100s; now £8.

To this manor belongs 1 Freeman who could not withdraw from the land without the permission of Aubrey's predecessor (and) who holds 2 hides less 15 acres.

Then 2 villagers, now none; then 2 smallholders, now 3; then 1 slave, now none.

Always 1 plough in lordship. Then among the men 1 plough, now none.

Woodland, 50 pigs; meadow, 2 acres.
Value then 20s; now 40[s].

Half-Hundred of FRESHWELL

12 Aethelhelm holds (Helions) BUMPSTEAD from Aubrey, which Wulfwin held as a manor, for 2 hides.

Always 7 villagers; 3 smallholders; 4 slaves. Then and later 2 ploughs in lordship, now 2½. Then and later 2 men's ploughs, now 1½.

Woodland, 20 pigs; meadow, 5 acres. Then 7 cattle, 8 pigs, 1 cob, 5 sheep, 15 goats, 3 beehives; now 12 cattle, 40 pigs, 5 cobs, 80 sheep, 40 goats, 5 beehives.
Value then £5; now [£] 8.

13 Demiblanc holds RADWINTER from Aubrey, which Aelfric, a Freeman, held as a manor, for ½ hide and 15 acres; he could sell his land but the full jurisdiction remained with Aubrey's predecessor. 78 a

Then 4 villagers, now 2; then 1 smallholder, now 5; then 1 slave, now 2. Then 1 plough in lordship, now 2. Then 2 men's ploughs, now 1.

Woodland, 30 pigs; meadow, 9 acres.
Value then 20s; now 60[s].

14 In STEVINGTON (End) Reginald holds 30 acres from Aubrey, which Alwin held; and Ordric held 15 acres. These two were in the King's jurisdiction but he gave them to Aubrey.

Always 3 villagers; 2 smallholders; 1 plough.

Woodland, 10 pigs; meadow, 3 acres.
Value then 20s; now 30[s].

In the same (Stevington End) an Englishman holds from Aubrey 40 acres which Aelfric, a Freeman, held; he could sell his land but the full jurisdiction remained.

Always 2 smallholders; 1 plough.
Value 10s.

TERRA Petri ualoniensis. Hund de HERlaua. .XXXVI.

Sceringā ten& Petr̄ in dn̄io qđ tenuer̄ .III .lib̄i hōes .t̄.r̄.ē
ꝑ man̄ . 7 ꝑ. v . hiđ . 7 . xxx . ac̄ . Sēp . v . car̄ in dn̄io . 7 . I . car̄ . homin̄.
7 . III . uilł . Tc̄ . III . bor . m̊ . VI . Sēp . VIII . ser̄ . Silu̇ . c . por . XXXII.
ac̄ . p̊ti . Sēp . I . mol . Tc̄ . VIII . uac̄ . c̄ uit̄ . 7 . I . runc̄ . XXXV . ou̇ . XVI.
porc̄ . m̊ . II . runc̄ . 7 . I . mul̄ . 7 . I . asin̄ . LXXXIIII . ou̇ . LVI . por . III . uasa
apū Tc̄ 7 p̄ uał . c . sol . m̊ . VI . lib̄.

Lattunā ten& Turgis̄ de . P . qđ tenuit lib̄ hō . t̄ . r̄ . ē . ꝑ Man̄.

78 b

7 . ꝑ . II . hiđ . 7 . dim̄ . 7 . xxx . ac̄ . Tc̄ . II . car̄ in dn̄io m̊ . I . dim̄ . car̄ . hominū.
Sēp . I . uilł . 7 . I . pb̄r . m̊ . IIII . bor . Tc̄ . IIII . ser̄ . m̊ null̄ . Silu̇ . ccc . L . porc̄.
xxxv . ac̄ . p̊ti . Sēp uał . LX . sol.

Perindunā ten& . Rog̃ . de . P . qđ tenuit . I . lib̄ hō . t̄ . r̄ . ē . ꝑ . man̄ . 7 . ꝑ.
. III . hiđ . Tc̄ . II . car̄ . in dn̄io . m̊ . I . 7 . dim̄ . m̊ dim̄ car̄ hom̄ . Tc̄ . I . bor.
m̊ . v . Sēp . III . ser̄ . Silu̇ . c . porc̄ . XLV . ac̄ . int̄ p̊tū 7 maresc . Sēp . I . mol
7 . v . ac̄ t̄ræ additæ st̄ . q̄s ten̄ lib̄ hō . t̄ . r̄ . ē . Tc̄ . VIII . an̄ . 7 . XLI . ou̇ . M̊
. XIIII . an̄ . 7 . I . runc̄ . 7 . LXXVI . ou̇ . 7 . XXVI . porc̄ . 7 . III . uasa ap̄ . Tc̄ 7 p̄
uał . XL . sol . m̊ LX.

In Walda ten& . Rađ . xxx . ac̄ . de . P . qđ tenuit lib̄ hō . t̄ . r̄ . ē . ꝑ . m̄.
Sēp . I . car̄ . 7 . II . ser̄ . 7 . I . bor . Silu̇ . c . por . II . ac̄ . p̊ti . vał . xx . sol.

Hunđ de beuentreu . Leintunā ten& P . in dn̄io qđ tenuit Suen̄
suart . ꝑ Man̄ . 7 . ꝑ . III . hiđ . Sēp . I . car̄ . in dn̄io . 7 . I . car̄ . hom̄ . tc̄ . m̊ . II.

36 LAND OF PETER OF VALOGNES

Hundred of HARLOW

1 Peter holds SHEERING in lordship, which 3 free men held before 1066 as a manor, for 5 hides and 30 acres. Always 5 ploughs in lordship; 1 men's plough;

3 villagers. Then 3 smallholders, now 6; always 8 slaves.

Woodland, 100 pigs; meadow, 32 acres; always 1 mill. Then 8 cows with calves, 1 cob, 35 sheep, 16 pigs; now 2 cobs, 1 mule, 1 ass, 84 sheep, 56 pigs, 3 beehives.

Value then and later 100s; now £6.

2 Thorgils holds LATTON from Peter, which a free man held before 1066 as a manor, for 2½ hides and 30 acres. Then 2 ploughs in 78 b
lordship, now 1. ½ men's plough.

Always 1 villager; 1 priest. Now 4 smallholders; then 4 slaves, now none.

Woodland, 350 pigs; meadow, 35 acres.

Value always 60s.

3 Roger holds (Little) PARNDON from Peter, which 1 free man held before 1066 as a manor, for 3 hides. Then 2 ploughs in lordship, now 1½. Now ½ men's plough.

Then 1 smallholder, now 5; always 3 slaves.

Woodland, 100 pigs; 45 acres of meadow and marsh; always 1 mill. 5 acres of land have been added, which a free man held before 1066. Then 8 cattle and 41 sheep; now 14 cattle, 1 cob, 76 sheep, 26 pigs and 3 beehives.

Value then and later 40s; now 60[s].

4 In (NORTH) WEALD (BASSETT) Ralph holds 30 acres from Peter, which a free man held before 1066 as a manor.

Always 1 plough; 2 slaves; 1 smallholder.

Woodland, 100 pigs; meadow, 2 acres.

Value 20s.

Hundred of BECONTREE

5 Peter holds LEYTON in lordship, which Swein Swart held as a manor, for 3 hides. Always 1 plough in lordship. Then 1 men's plough, now 2.

Tc̄ . vii . uilt . m̊ . x . Sēp . ii . bor . Silu . xxx . porc . xxiiii . ac . p̄ti . Tc̄ . i . mol
m̊ null . q . t . r . Willi . inde ablatus ē . Tc̄ . ii . pisc . m̊ null . m̊ . i . runc .
7 . xi . porc . Tc̄ ual . xx . sol . 7 qn̄ rec n̄ erat ibi p̄t sola tr̄a . 7 m̊ ual
xl . sol .

Hecham ten& . P . in dn̄io qđ tenuit haldan lib hō . t . r . e .
p . man . 7 p . v . hiđ . Sēp . ii . car . in dn̄io . 7 . iiii . car . hom . Tc̄ . viii .
uilt . m̊ . x . Tc̄ . ii . bor . m̊ . iii . Sēp . iiii . ser . Silu . ccc . porc . xviii . ac .
p̄ti . tc̄ . iii . pisc . 7 . đ . m̊ null . Tc̄ . i . bou . m̊ . xv . anim . 7 . i . runc .
7 . xxxvii . porc . 7 . ii . uasa ap . Tc̄ . ual . lx . sol . m̊ . iiii . lib . 7 . x . sol .
7 qn̄ rec hoc maneriū n̄ inuenit p̄t unū bouē . 7 unā ac . seminatā
7 . de his . v . hiđ . qs supi dixi : unā tenuer̄ . ii . libi hōes . t . r . e .

79 a

quæ huic manerio addita ē t . r . Willi . 7 ualebat t . r . e . x . sol . m̊
xx . 7 hoc ten& Witt de Petro ualoniensi .

Lochetunā ten& . Rađ . de . P . qđ tenuit vluric lib hō . t . r . e . p . m̊ . 7 p . i . hiđ .
7 . xxx . ac . Sēp . i . car in dn̄io . m̊ . v . bor . Silu . lxxx . porc . vi . ac . p̄ti . Tc̄ ual
x . sol . m̊ . xx .

Dim Hunđ de Thunreslau Belindune ten& Rađ fatat . de . P .
qđ tenuit Aluric lib homo . t . r . e . p man . 7 . p . iii . hiđ . 7 . dim . Sēp . ii .
car . in dn̄io . 7 . i . car . hom . Tc̄ . 7 p . iii . bor . m̊ . ix . Sēp . iiii . ser . xxxiii .
ac . p̄ti . Tc̄ . v . uac . c̄ uit . 7 . xxx . porc . m̊ . xxxiii . anim . 7 . xxviii . porc .
Tc̄ ual . xl . sol . m̊ . c .

Binesleam ten& . P . in dn̄io qđ tenuit Vluuin t . r . e . p . i . hiđ . Sēp
. i . car . in dn̄io . 7 . dim . car . hom . 7 xiii . bor . Tc̄ 7 p . ii . ser . m̊ . i . Silu .
xx . porc . iiii . ac . p̄ti . Val . xx . sol . hanc tr̄am . P . in uadimonio jussu
regis . ne tam̄ pđ& suā consuetudinē . teste ep̄o baiocensi .

Then 7 villagers, now 10; always 2 smallholders.
Woodland, 30 pigs; meadow, 24 acres; then 1 mill, now none, it was taken away from there after 1066; then 2 fisheries, now none. Now 1 cob and 11 pigs.
Value then 20s; when acquired, there was nothing there except the land. Value now 40s.

6 Peter holds HIGHAM (Hill) in lordship which Haldane, a free man, held before 1066 as a manor, for 5 hides. Always 2 ploughs in lordship; 4 men's ploughs.
Then 8 villagers, now 10; then 2 smallholders, now 3; always 4 slaves.
Woodland, 300 pigs; meadow, 18 acres; then 3½ fisheries, now none. Then 1 ox; now 15 cattle, 1 cob, 37 pigs and 2 beehives.
Value then 60s; now £4 10s; when he acquired this manor he found nothing except 1 ox and 1 sown acre.
Of these 5 hides which I have mentioned above, 2 free men held 1 before 1066 which was added to this manor after 1066. 79 a
Value before 1066, 10s; now 20[s].
William holds this from Peter of Valognes.

7 Ralph holds LOUGHTON from Peter which Wulfric, a free man, held before 1066 as a manor, for 1 hide and 30 acres. Always 1 plough in lordship.
Now 5 smallholders.
Woodland, 80 pigs; meadow, 6 acres.
Value then 10s; now 20[s].

Half-Hundred of 'THUNDERLOW'

8 Ralph the Haunted holds BALLINGDON from Peter which Aelfric, a free man, held before 1066 as a manor for 3½ hides. Always 2 ploughs in lordship; 1 men's plough.
Then and later 3 smallholders, now 9; always 4 slaves.
Meadow, 33 acres. Then 5 cows with calves and 30 pigs; now 33 cattle and 28 pigs.
Value then 40s; now 100[s].

[Hundred of HINCKFORD]

9 Peter holds 'BINSLEY' in lordship, which Wulfwin held before 1066, for 1 hide. Always 1 plough in lordship; ½ men's plough.
13 smallholders. Then and later 2 slaves, now 1.
Woodland, 20 pigs; meadow, 4 acres.
Value 20s.
Peter (has) this land in pledge by the King's order, provided that he does not lose his customary due; (to which) the Bishop of Bayeux is witness.

Lochintunā ten& . P . in dn̄io qđ tenuit Leofcild . ꝑ . man . 7 ꝑ . I . hid. tc̄ . III . bor . m̊ . II . Tc̄ . II . ser . m̊ null . Sēp . I . car . Silu . XXX . porc . IIII . ac . p̄ti . Sēp . I . mol Tc̄ ual . Tc̄ ual . XX . sol 7 qn̄ rec . XXX . m̊ ual . XX . sol.

Taindenā ten& . P . in dn̄io . qđ tenuit Hacun ꝑ man . 7 ꝑ . III . hid . 7 . đ . 7 . LXXX . ac . Tc̄ . VII . uilt . m̊ . XII . tc̄ . III . bor . m̊ . IIII . Sēp . V . ser . Silu . CCCC . porc . XVI . ac . p̄ti . I . mol . Tc̄ . II . uac . 7 . III . runc . 7 . LIIII . porc . 7 . XLVII . ou . m̊ . II . runc . 7 . LXXXXII . porc . 7 CLVII . ou . 7 . XII . uasa apū . Tc̄ ual . LX . sol . m̊ . C . 7 . VII . libi hōes tenuer̄ . II . hid . 7 . I . uirg . 7 . dim . qđ m̊ ten& Petr . Sēp . II . ser . 7 . I . bor . Tc̄ 7 p̄ . VI . car.

79 b

m̊ . IIII . Silu . CXL . porc . XX . ac . p̄ti . Sēp ual XLVI . sol . 7 hoc est ꝑ escangio ut ipse . P . dic . 7 . dim . hid . 7 . XL . ac . ten& Galt̄ . de . P . qđ tenuit Vluuin . 7 petr ht̄ in uadimonio sic̄ ipse dicit concessu reḡ Tc̄ . I . uilt . m̊ null . m̊ . III . bor . Tc̄ . I . ser . m̊ null . Tc̄ . II . car . Post 7 m̊ . I . Silu . C . porc . VII . ac . p̄ti . tc̄ ual . XVI . sol . m̊ . XX.

Wallam ten& . Rađ . fatat de . P . qđ tenuer̄ . II . libi hōes . t . r . e . ꝑ . II . man . 7 ꝑ . II . hid . 7 . XL . ac . 7 Petr ħt in escangio . Tc̄ 7 p̄ . VII . uilt . m̊ . XIII . Tc̄ . 7 p̄ . III . bor . m̊ . VIII . Tc̄ . 7 p̄ . IX . ser . m̊ . VII . Tc̄ . V . car in dn̄io . Post . III . m̊ . II . Tc̄ 7 p̄ . II . car . 7 dim hom . m̊ . V . Silu . ↀD . porc XL . ac . p̄ti . Tc̄ . III . uac . 7 . I . runc . 7 . XXXV . porc . 7 . V . ou . 7 . III . cap . m̊ . XVII . an . 7 . I . runc . 7 . XXVIII . porc . 7 . LXX . ou . 7 . V . uasa apū . Tc̄ ual . VII . lib . 7 qn̄ rec . VI . lib . m̊ ual . XII . lib . 7 qdā hō libe tenuit XL . ac . quē ħt . P . in escangio . Sēp . IIII . uilt . m̊ . II . bor . Silu . LX . porc . V . ac . p̄ti . Sēp . I . car . 7 ual . XX . sol.

[Hundred of BECONTREE]

10 Peter holds LOUGHTON in lordship, which Leofcild held as a manor, for 1 hide.

Then 3 smallholders, now 2; then 2 slaves, now none. Always 1 plough.

Woodland, 30 pigs; meadow, 4 acres; always 1 mill.

Value then 20s; when acquired 30[s]. Value now 20s.

[Hundred of ONGAR]

11 Peter holds THEYDON (Bois) in lordship, which Hakon held as a manor, for 3½ hides and 80 acres.

Then 7 villagers, now 12; then 3 smallholders, now 4; always 5 slaves.

Woodland, 400 pigs; meadow, 16 acres; 1 mill. Then 2 cows, 3 cobs, 54 pigs and 47 sheep; now 2 cobs, 92 pigs, 157 sheep and 12 beehives.

Value then 60s; now 100[s].

7 free men held 2 hides and 1½ virgates, which Peter now holds.

Always 2 slaves; 1 smallholder. Then and later 6 ploughs, now 4. 79 b

Woodland, 140 pigs; meadow, 20 acres.

Value always 46s.

This is by exchange, as Peter himself states.

Walter holds from Peter ½ hide and 40 acres, which Wulfwin held. Peter holds (it) in pledge, so he states, by the King's grant.

Then 1 villager, now none; now 3 smallholders; then 1 slave, now none. Then 2 ploughs, later and now 1.

Woodland, 100 pigs; meadow, 7 acres.

Value then 16s; now 20[s].

[Hundred of HARLOW]

12 Ralph the Haunted holds (NORTH) WEALD (BASSETT) from Peter, which 2 free men held before 1066 as 2 manors, for 2 hides and 40 acres. Peter has (it) in exchange.

Then and later 7 villagers, now 13; then and later 3 smallholders, now 8; then and later 9 slaves, now 7. Then 5 ploughs in lordship, later 3, now 2. Then and later 2½ men's ploughs, now 5.

Woodland, 1500 pigs; meadow, 40 acres. Then 3 cows, 1 cob, 35 pigs, 5 sheep and 3 goats; now 17 cattle, 1 cob, 28 pigs, 70 sheep and 5 beehives.

Value then £7; when acquired £6. Value now £12.

A man held 40 acres freely, which Peter has in exchange.

Always 4 villagers. Now 2 smallholders.

Woodland, 60 pigs; meadow, 5 acres. Always 1 plough.

Value 20s.

.XXXVII. TERRA Ranulfi fr̃is Ilgerí. Hund̃ de ƀdestapla

Ingam ten&. W. de. R. qđ tenuit Osſac. t. r. e. | p man'. 7. II. hid. Sẽp. I. car̃ in dñio. 7. I. car. hom. tc̃. v. bor. m̃. IX. tc̃. II. ser. m̃. null. Silua. . c. porc. Tc̃. XIIII. anim. LX. ou. LX. porc. m̃. VIII. an. c. ou. XX. porc. III. uasa ap. Tc̃. ual. XL. sol. m̃. XXX.

Ramesdanã. ten& Humfrid de. R. qđ tenuit Siric libe ꝓ. II. hid.

80 a

7. XXX. ac. Tc̃. II. car. in dñio. m̃. I. 7. dim. m̃. dim. car. hom. 7. I. lib hõ. Sẽp. III. ser. 7. I. bor Silu. c. porc. II. ac. p̃ti. Nichil inuenit. m̃. IIII. an. . II. runc. LVIII. ou. XXI. porc. Tc̃ ual. LX. sol. m̃. XL.

Hund̃ de Herlaua. Ruindune. ten&. R. in dñio qđ tenuit Inguar lib hõ. t. r. e. ꝓ Man. 7 ꝓ. VI. hid. Sẽp. III. car. in dñio. 7. IIII. car. hom. tc̃. XII. uilt. m̃. VIII. Tc̃. II. bor. m̃. XII. Tc̃. VIII. ser. m̃. III. Silu. CXX. porc. LX. ac. p̃ti. Past. de. II. sol. I. mol. Tc̃. VI. an. LX. ou. XXX. porc. m̃. . X. anim. LX. ou. XXX. porc. X. eq. Tc̃ ual. VI. lib. m̃. IX. huic mancrio adjac&. I. ƀiuuita herlaua. qđ ten& Ricard de. R. ꝓ. I. hid. 7. I. uirg. Sẽp. I. car. Tc̃. II. uilt. m̃. I. Silu. L. porc. VII. ac. p̃ti. Tc̃. 7 p ual. XXV. sol. m̃. XXX. huic tr̃e addite sť. IIII. hid. tr̃æ. qas tenuer. V. libi hões. t. r. e. Sẽp. IIII. car. tc̃. III. uilt. m̃. II. Tc̃. V. bor. m̃. VII. Tc̃. I. ser m̃ null. Silu. LX. porc. XXV. ac. p̃ti. Sẽp ual. IIII. lib.

Perendunã ten& Rog de. R. qđ tenuit Alsi bolla lib hõ. t. r. e. ꝓ. man. 7 ꝓ. II. hid. Tc̃. I. car. in dñio. m̃. I. 7. dim. Tc̃. I. uilt. m̃. V. bor. Sẽp. I. ser. Silu. CXL. por. XVIII. ac. p̃ti. Tc̃. XII. an. m̃. VIII. XXXIIII. porc. LXXX. ou. Tc̃ ual. XXX. sol. m̃. XL.

37 LAND OF RANULF BROTHER OF ILGER

Hundred of BARSTABLE

1 W. holds INGRAVE from Ranulf, which Oslac held before 1066 as a manor, for 2 hides. Always 1 plough in lordship; 1 men's plough.
Then 5 smallholders, now 9; then 2 slaves, now none.
Woodland, 100 pigs. Then 14 cattle, 60 sheep, 60 pigs; now 8 cattle, 100 sheep, 20 pigs, 3 beehives.
Value then 40s; now 30[s].

2 Humphrey holds RAMSDEN from Ranulf, which Siric held freely, for 2 hides and 30 acres. Then 2 ploughs in lordship, now 1½. 80 a
Now ½ men's plough; 1 free man. Always 3 slaves; 1 smallholder.
Woodland, 100 pigs; meadow, 2 acres. He found nothing; now 4 cattle, 2 cobs, 58 sheep, 21 pigs.
Value then 60s; now 40[s].

Hundred of HARLOW

3 Ranulf holds ROYDON in lordship which Ingvar, a free man, held before 1066 as a manor for 6 hides. Always 3 ploughs in lordship; 4 men's ploughs. Then 12 villagers, now 8; then 2 smallholders, now 12; then 8 slaves, now 3.
Woodland, 120 pigs; meadow, 60 acres; pasture at 2s; 1 mill. Then 6 cattle, 60 sheep, 30 pigs; now 10 cattle, 60 sheep, 30 pigs, 10 horses.
Value then £6; now [£] 9.

To this manor is attached 1 outlier (called) HARLOW, which Richard holds from Ranulf for 1 hide and 1 virgate. Always 1 plough.
Then 2 villagers, now 1.
Woodland, 50 pigs; meadow, 7 acres.
Value then and later 25s; now 30[s].

To this land have been added 4 hides of land which 5 free men held before 1066. Always 4 ploughs.
Then 3 villagers, now 2; then 5 smallholders, now 7; then 1 slave, now none.
Woodland, 60 pigs; meadow, 25 acres.
Value always £4.

4 Roger holds PARNDON from Ranulf which Alfsi Bowl, a free man, held before 1066 as a manor for 2 hides. Then 1 plough in lordship, now 1½.
Then 1 villager; now 5 smallholders; always 1 slave.
Woodland, 140 pigs; meadow, 18 acres. Then 12 cattle; now 8 (cattle), 34 pigs, 80 sheep.
Value then 30s; now 40[s].

Perendunā ten& Alured . de . R . qđ tenuit Alueua liƀa femina
p Man 7 . p . dim . hid . Sēp . dim . car . 7 . I . bor . Silu . xxx . porc.
. v . ac . pti . ual . xI . sol.

In Perenduna ten& Rog de . R . xxxv . ac . qs tenuit Tstin lib hō
t . r . e . Sēp . dim . car . Silu . xx . porc . II . ac . pti . ual . vI . sol.

Waldā ten& . Ricard . de . R . qđ tenuit Goduin lib hō . t . r . e.
p . m . 7 . p . dim . hid . 7 . xv . ac . Sēp . I . car . in dn̄io . 7 . dim . car hom.

80 b

Tc̄ . I . uill . m̄ . II . Sēp . I . bord . Tc̄ . II . ser . m̄ . I . Silu . cc . porc . II . ac . pti . Tc̄ . xx.
porc . m̄ . LX . xvII . anim . LXV . ou . 7 . III . runc . Tc̄ ual . xx . sol . m̄ . xxx.

In Nasinga ten& . Odo de . R . I . hid . 7 . I . uill . 7 . IIII . bor . 7 . I . car . 7 . ual.
xx . sol.

Hund de Waltham . Nasingā . 7 Epingā tenuer . II . libi hoes . t . r . e.
p . Man . 7 p . IIII . hid . 7 . dim . xv . ac . min . Tc̄ . III . car . in dn̄io . m̄ . II . Sēp.
. III . car . hom . Tc̄ . xI . uill . m̄ . vII . m̄ . Ix . bord . tc̄ . III . ser . m̄ null . Silu . c . por.
. LIIII . ac . pti . Past . de . xxxII . đ . Tc̄ . I . mol . m̄ . n̄ . Tc̄ . vII . anim . 7 xxx . porc.
m̄ . II . an . 7 . xvIII . por . hoc est in Nasinga . 7 In Eppinges . II . anim.
7 . xxvI . ou . 7 . vI . porc . Sēp ualent . IIII . lib . Nasinga . LX . sol 7 Epping
xx . sol . 7 Pt hoc addita ē huic tr̄e . I . hid . quā tenuit lib hō . t . r . e.
7 adhuc ten& . Tc̄ . I . car . m̄ . dim . Tc̄ . II . bor . m̄ . III . Silu . xx . porc.
xII . ac . pti . Tc̄ ual . x . sol . m̄ . xx . 7 adhuc . I . uirg tr̄æ . que addita ē
t . r . Willi . 7 ptinebat in Waltham . t . r . e . quā inde tulit . R . fr̄ ilgeri.
ut hund testat . 7 ual . III . sol . Hoc totū ten& . R . in dn̄io.

5 Alfred holds PARNDON from Ranulf which Aelfeva, a free woman, held as a manor for ½ hide. Always ½ plough;

1 smallholder.

Woodland, 30 pigs; meadow, 5 acres.

Value 11s.

6 In PARNDON Roger holds 35 acres from Ranulf which Thurstan, a free man, held before 1066. Always ½ plough.

Woodland, 20 pigs; meadow, 2 acres.

Value 6s.

7 Richard holds (NORTH) WEALD (BASSETT) from Ranulf which Godwin, a free man, held before 1066 as a manor for ½ hide and 15 acres. Always 1 plough in lordship; ½ men's plough.

Then 1 villager, now 2; always 1 smallholder. 80 b

Then 2 slaves, now 1.

Woodland, 200 pigs; meadow, 2 acres. Then 20 pigs; now 60 pigs, 17 cattle, 65 sheep and 3 cobs.

Value then 20s; now 30[s].

[Hundred of WALTHAM]

8 In NAZEING Odo holds 1 hide from Ranulf.

1 villager; 3 smallholders. 1 plough.

Value 20s.

Hundred of WALTHAM

9 2 free men held NAZEING and EPPING before 1066 as a manor, for 4½ hides less 15 acres. Then 3 ploughs in lordship, now 2. Always 3 men's ploughs.

Then 11 villagers, now 7; now 9 smallholders; then 3 slaves, now none.

Woodland, 100 pigs; meadow, 54 acres; pasture at 32d; then 1 mill, now none. Then 7 cattle and 30 pigs; now 2 cattle and 18 pigs: this is in Nazeing. In Epping, 2 cattle, 26 sheep and 6 pigs.

Value always £4: Nazeing 60s; Epping 20s.

Besides this, 1 hide has been added to this land, which a free man held before 1066 and still holds. Then 1 plough, now ½.

Then 2 smallholders, now 3.

Woodland, 20 pigs; meadow, 12 acres.

Value then 10s; now 20[s].

A further 1 virgate of land, which was added after 1066 and belonged to Waltham [Holy Cross] before 1066, which Ranulf brother of Ilger took from there, as the Hundred testifies.

Value 3s.

Ranulf holds all this in lordship.

Hund de . Rochefort . Thorp . ten& Odo de . R . qđ tenuit . t . r . e.
Inguar p Man . 7 . p . II . hiđ . 7 . dim . Sep . IIII . uilt . 7 . IIII . bor . 7 . IIII . ser.
7 . II . car . in dnio . 7 . III . car . hom . Silu . LX . porc . Past . c . ou . Tc . II.
an . 7 . II . runc . 7 . c . ou . 7 . XXX . porc . M . II . anim . 7 . I . runc . 7 . c . ou.
7 . VII . porc . 7 . XVIII . cap . 7 . IIII . uasa ap . Tc 7 p uat . IIII . lib . m . VI.

Hund de Hidingforda Bridebroc ten& . R . in dno . qđ ten.
. I . lib hō . t . r . e . p . man . 7 . p . II . hiđ . Tc . III . car . in dnio . Post . II.
m . III . Sep . III . car . hom . Tc . 7 p . VII . uilt . m . VI . Tc 7 . p . I . bor.
m . IX . Sep . IIII . ser . Silu . XVI . porc . XXII . ac . pti . Tc . XV . animal

81 a

7 . L . porc . 7 . LXXX . ou . 7 . XIII ; 7 . XXV . cap . m . IIII . an . 7 . X . porc.
7 . LV . ou . 7 . II . runc . Tc . 7 p uat . VIII . lib . m . IX.

Babitna ten& . R . in dnio . qđ tenuit Inguar . p . Man . 7 p . II . hiđ.
t . r . e . Sep . II . car . in dnio . 7 . IIII . car . hom . 7 . VI . uilt . m . VII . bor . Tc . 7 p.
. II . ser . m . III . XXXI . ac . pti . sep . I . mot . Tc 7 p uat . VII . lib . m . VIII.
his . II . manerijs . adjacent . sep . II . soc . de . V . ac.

Geldham ten& Galt de . R . qđ tenuit lib hō . t . r . e . p man . 7 . p . dim.
hiđ . Tc . I . car . Post nulla . m . I . IX . ac . pti . Tc . nich . M . II . an . 7 . I . runc.
7 . XXX . ou . 7 . II . porc . uat . XX . sol.

Hund de Witbrictesherna . Niuuelanda ten& . W . de . R . qđ
tenuit Inguuar . t . r . e . p man . 7 . p . I . hiđ . 7 . dim . 7 . XXXV . ac . m . IIII.
bor . sep . I . ser . 7 . I . car . in dnio . Tc uat . XX . sol . Post 7 . m . XXX . 7 . VII.
ac . 7 . dim . qs ten& . I . lib hō . 7 uat . VII . đ.

Hundred of ROCHFORD

10 Odo holds THORPE(HALL) from Ranulf, which Ingvar held before 1066 as a manor, for 2½ hides.

Always 4 villagers; 4 smallholders; 4 slaves; 2 ploughs in lordship; 3 men's ploughs.

Woodland, 60 pigs; pasture, 100 sheep. Then 2 cattle, 2 cobs, 100 sheep and 30 pigs; now 2 cattle, 1 cob, 100 sheep, 7 pigs, 18 goats and 4 beehives.

Value then and later £4; now [£] 6.

Hundred of HINCKFORD

11 Ranulf holds BIRDBROOK in lordship, which 1 free man held before 1066 as a manor, for 2 hides. Then 3 ploughs in lordship, later 2, now 3. Always 3 men's ploughs.

Then and later 7 villagers, now 6; then and later 1 smallholder, now 9; always 4 slaves.

Woodland, 16 pigs; meadow, 22 acres. Then 15 cattle, 50 pigs, 81 a
80 sheep, 13 ... and 25 goats; now 4 cattle, 10 pigs, 55 sheep and 2 cobs.

Value then and later £8; now [£] 9.

12 Ranulf holds BAYTHORN (End) in lordship, which Ingvar held as a manor, for 2 hides before 1066. Always 2 ploughs in lordship; 4 men's ploughs;

6 villagers. Now 7 smallholders; then and later 2 slaves, now 3.

Meadow, 31 acres; always 1 mill.

Value then and later £7; now [£] 8.

2 sokemen with 5 acres have always been attached to these 2 manors.

13 Walter holds YELDHAM from Ranulf, which a free man held before 1066 as a manor, for ½ hide. Then 1 plough, later none, now 1.

Meadow, 9 acres. Then nothing; now 2 cattle, 1 cob, 30 sheep and 2 pigs.

Value 20s.

Hundred of 'WIBERTSHERNE'

14 W. holds ST. LAWRENCE from Ranulf, which Ingvar held before 1066 as a manor, for 1½ hides and 35 acres.

Now 4 smallholders. Always 1 slave; 1 plough in lordship.

Value then 20s; later and now 30[s].

7½ acres which 1 free man holds. Value 7d.

Bubingeordā. ten& Ricard de. R. qđ tenuer. II. libi hões. t. r. e. p. I. hid. 7. XXX. ac. Tc. I. bor. m. II. Tc. IIII. ser. m. II. Tc. II. car. in dnio p 7 m. I. Silu. LXXX. porc. IIII. ac. pti. sep. I. uac. 7. III. porc. 7. CVII. ou. Tc uat. XL. sol. m. LX.

Hund de Celmeresfort Gingā ten&. R. in dnio. qđ tenuit Inguuara p Man. 7. p. IX. hid. Tc. XVIII. uilt. m. XVI. tc. VIII. bor. m. XX. tc. V. ser. m. VII. Tc. in dnio. II. car. m. I. Tc. int hões. XII. car. M. IX. Silu. DCC. porc. m. VII. anim. 7. LX. ou. Tc. uat. VIII. lib. m. X. 7. I. lib hō. ten. XX. ac. 7. uat. III. sol. In Ead ten& Witt. de bosc. II. hid. 7. XXVI. ac. de. R. 7 ht in suo escangio. qđ tenuit Alfega. 7 Algar. t. r. e. m. III. bor. Tc. II. ser. m. I.

81 b

Tc. II. car. in dnio. m. I. Silu. LX. porc. Past. C. ou. uat. XL. sol.

Cubrigeam ten& Witts. de. R. qđ tenuit Aluuin. p man. 7. p dim. hid. 7. VI. ac. 7. dim. 7. dim. car potest esse. I. ac. pti. Silu. XX. porc. uat. X. sol.

Gingā tenuer. II. puellæ. libæ p LXXX. ac. m. R. in suo escangio. 7. W. de eo. Sep. I. car. Vat. XV. sol.

Hund de Tendringa. In Derleiā tenuit Edric de Estorp. I. man. de. II. hid. 7. dim. m ten&. R. p. I. hid. 7. dim. 7. Rog de illo. Tc. II. uilt. m. I. Tc. I. ser. m null. Tc 7 p. I. car in dnio. m. dim. Tc. 7. p. I. car hom. m nult. 7. III. car posst esse. Silu. XX. porc. IIII. ac. pti. Tc 7 p uat. XXX. sol. m. X. hanc trā ht. R. p escangio. ht &iā in soca de Laleforda. XV. ac. 7. ibi man&. I. hō. q reddit. VII. sol. 7. VIII. đ.

[Hundred of ONGAR]

15 Richard holds BOBBINGWORTH from Ranulf, which 2 free men held before 1066, for 1 hide and 30 acres.

Then 1 smallholder, now 2; then 4 slaves, now 2. Then 2 ploughs in lordship, later and now 1.

Woodland, 80 pigs; meadow, 4 acres. Always 1 cow, 3 pigs and 107 sheep.

Value then 40s; now 60[s].

Hundred of CHELMSFORD

16 Ranulf holds MOUNTNESSING in lordship, which Ingvar held as a manor, for 9 hides.

Then 18 villagers, now 16; then 8 smallholders, now 20; then 5 slaves, now 7. Then 2 ploughs in lordship, now 1. Then among the men 12 ploughs, now 9.

Woodland, 700 pigs. Now 7 cattle and 60 sheep.

Value then £8; now [£] 10.

1 free man holds 20 acres. Value 3s.

17 In the same (Mountnessing) William of Bosc holds 2 hides and 26 acres from Ranulf, and he has (it) in exchange, which Alfheah and Algar held before 1066.

Now 3 smallholders; then 2 slaves, now 1. Then 2 ploughs in lordship, now 1. 81 b

Woodland, 60 pigs; pasture, 100 sheep.

Value 40s.

18 William holds COWBRIDGE from Ranulf, which Alwin held as a manor, for ½ hide and 6½ acres. ½ plough possible.

Meadow, 1 acre; woodland, 20 pigs.

Value 10s.

19 2 girls held FOUCHERS freely for 80 acres. Now Ranulf (holds it) in exchange, and W. from him. Always 1 plough.

Value 15s.

Hundred of TENDRING

20 In 'DERLEIGH' Edric of Easthorpe held 1 manor at 2½ hides. Now Ranulf holds (it) for 1½ hides, and Roger from him.

Then 2 villagers, now 1; then 1 slave, now none. Then and later 1 plough in lordship, now ½. Then and later 1 men's plough, now none. 3 ploughs possible.

Woodland, 20 pigs; meadow, 4 acres.

Value then and later 30s; now 10[s].

Ranulf has this land by exchange. He also has 15 acres in the jurisdiction of Lawford. 1 man dwells there, who pays 7s 8d.

XXXVIII. TERRA Tihelli brittonis. Hund de Vdelesforda.

Gerdelai . tenuer . II . libi hões . t . r . e . p Man . 7 . p . I . hid . Sep . I . car
in dnio . 7 . II . bor . m . VII . Tc . silu . XL . porc . P 7 m . XXX . X . ac.
pti Tc . V . anim . XIIII . ou 7 . XXVI . porc . 7 . XXXII . cap . 7 . I . runc
7 . I . uas apu . m . IIII . an . 7 . XIIII . porc . 7 . XXXVIII . ou.
7 . III . uasa ap . 7 . I . runc . Hoc ten& Serlo de . tihello
hanc tra reclamat Tihell de dono regis . Tc . ual . XVI.
sol . m . XX.

82 a

Hund de Frosseuuella. Steintuna . ten& Tihell in dnio . qd
tenuit Oslac lib ho . t . r . e . p . man . 7 p . XLII . ac . 7 . dim . Sep . II . car.
in dnio . Tc p p . I . bor . m . III . Sep . IIII . ser . V . ac . pti . Tc . V . an . 7 . V . porc. ★
7 . X . ou . 7 . II . uasa apu . M . V . uac . 7 . I . runc . 7 . XXX . porc . 7 . L . ou . 7.
. I . uas . apu . Tc . 7 p ual . LX . sol . m . C . sol . 7 . I . uncia auri.

Redeuuintra ten& Goderet de . T . qd . tenuit Lefsiu . t . r . e . p
man . 7 . p dim . hid . 7 . dim . uirg . Sep . II . car in dnio . 7 . I . car hom . 7.
. IIII . uilli . Tc . V . bor . m . VII . Silu . LX . porc . VIII . ac . pti . tc . VI . an.
m . IIII . 7 . XVIII . porc . 7 m simil . tc XLIX . ou . m . XXXII . IIII . uasa
apu . tc XX . cap . m null . Tc ual . XX . sol . m LX . hoc reclamat
Tihell de dono regis.

Bunsteda . ten& . T . in dnio qd tenuit Leuuin cilt . t . r . e . p
man . 7 . p . IIII . hid . Sep . IIII . car in dnio . tc . IIII . car . hom . m . II.
tc . IX . uill . m . VII . Sep . VIII . bor . 7 . VIII . ser . Silu . C . porc . VII.
ac . pti . Sep . VI . anim . tc . XXIIII . porc . m . XL . tc . XL . ou . M . CXV.
Tc . I . runc . m . I . 7 . I . pull . tc . uasa ap . m . III . Tc ual . VI . lib . m . IX.

Hund de Hindingaforda. Bumesteda . ten& . T . in dnio
qd tenuit . lib ho . t . r . e . p man ; 7 . p . I . hid 7 . p . I . uirg . Sep . III . car in dnio ★
7 . II . car . hom . 7 . V . uill . 7 . XIII . bor . 7 . VI . ser . Silu . XX . por.
XV . ac . pti . Sep . I . mol . Tc 7 p ual . LX . sol . m . VI . lib.

38 LAND OF TIHEL THE BRETON

Hundred of UTTLESFORD

1 2 free men held YARDLEY before 1066 as a manor, for 1 hide. Always 1 plough in lordship.

[Then] 2 smallholders, now 7.

Woodland, then 40 pigs, later and now 30; meadow, 10 acres. Then 5 cattle, 14 sheep, 26 pigs, 32 goats, 1 cob and 1 beehive; now 4 cattle, 14 pigs, 38 sheep, 3 beehives and 1 cob.

Serlo holds this from Tihel. Tihel claims this land as the King's gift.

Value then 16s; now 20[s].

Hundred of FRESHWELL 82 a

2 Tihel holds STEVINGTON (End) in lordship which Oslac, a free man, held before 1066 as a manor for 42½ acres. Always 2 ploughs in lordship.

Then [and] later 1 smallholder, now 3; always 4 slaves.

Meadow, 5 acres. Then 5 cattle, 5 pigs, 10 sheep and 2 beehives; now 5 cows, 1 cob, 30 pigs, 50 sheep and 1 beehive.

Value then and later 60s; now 100s and 1 ounce of gold.

3 Guthred holds RADWINTER from Tihel, which Leofsi held before 1066 as a manor, for ½ hide and ½ virgate. Always 2 ploughs in lordship; 1 men's plough;

4 villagers. Then 5 smallholders, now 7.

Woodland, 60 pigs; meadow, 8 acres. Then 6 cattle, now 4; 18 pigs, now the same; then 49 sheep, now 32; 4 beehives; then 20 goats, now none.

Value then 20s; now 60[s].

Tihel claims this as the King's gift.

4 Tihel holds (Helions) BUMPSTEAD in lordship, which Young Leofwin held before 1066 as a manor, for 4 hides. Always 4 ploughs in lordship. Then 4 men's ploughs, now 2.

Then 9 villagers, now 7. Always 8 smallholders; 8 slaves.

Woodland, 100 pigs; meadow, 7 acres. Always 6 cattle. Then 24 pigs, now 40; then 40 sheep, now 115; then 1 cob, now 1 (cob) and 1 foal; then ... beehives, now 3.

Value then £6; now [£] 9.

Hundred of HINCKFORD

5 Tihel holds (Steeple) BUMPSTEAD in lordship, which a free man held before 1066 as a manor, for 1 hide and 1 virgate. Always 3 ploughs in lordship; 2 men's ploughs;

5 villagers; 13 smallholders; 6 slaves.

Woodland, 20 pigs; meadow, 15 acres; always 1 mill.

Value then and later 60s; now £6.

Sturmere ten&. T. in dnio qđ tenuit liba femina t. r. e.
p man. 7 p. I. hid. 7. dim. 7. xv. ac. Sep. II. car. in dnio. 7. I. car.
hom. 7. II. uill. III. bor. Tc. 7. p. I. ser. m. II. XVI. ac. pti. Tc. uac.
7. II. runc. 7. LX. porc. 7. III. uasa apu. m. IIII. anim. 7. I. runc.

82 b

7. I. pull. 7. XLIIII. porc. 7. LXXII. ou. 7. III. uasa apu. Tc uat. XL. sol.
m. LX.
Sturmere ten&. T. in dnio qđ tenuit. lib. ho. t. r. e. p. m. 7. p. I. hid.
7. dim. Sep. II. car. in dnio. 7. I. uill. 7. VI. ser. XX. ac. pti. I. mol.
Tc. VI. an. 7. I. runc. 7. XII. porc. 7. LX. ou. m. XII. an. 7. XXX. porc.
7. C. ou. II. min. 7. I. runc. 7. III. pull. Tc 7 p. uat. XL. sol. m. LX.
Tilibiam ten&. T. in dnio qđ tenuit lib ho. t. r. e. p man. 7. p. I. hid.
7. XXXVIII. ac. Sep. III. car. in dnio. 7. I. car. hom. 7. V. uill. 7. I. bord.
7. VI. ser. Silu. XX. porc. XVIIII. ac. pti. Tc. XV. an. 7. XL. porc. 7
LXXX. ou. 7. VI. uasa ap. m. V. an. 7. I. runc. 7. XXXVI. porc. 7. LXIII.
ou. Tc 7 p uat. LX. sol. m. C.

.XXXIX. TERRA Rogeri de Ramis. Hund de Hidingforda.

Raines ten& Rog in dnio. qđ tenuit Aluuin lib ho. t. r. e.
p manerio. 7. p. I. hid. 7. XX. ac. Sep. II. car. in dnio. Tc. 7. p. IIII.
car hom. m. III. Tc. 7 p. IX. uill. m. VIII. Sep. V. bord. tc. 7 p. IIII.
ser. m. III. Silu. C. porc. I. mol. Tc. VIII. uac. m. III. tc. (c 7. XI. ac. pti.)
. I. runc. m null. Sep. C. ou. tc. XXX. porc. m. XL. Sep uat. IIII. lib.
De hoc manerio ten&. Rog. de. R. XXX. ac. 7 Wibga. XXX. ac.
7 uat. XX. sol in eod ptio.

83 a

Raines ten&. R. in dnio. qđ tenuit Edric lib ho. t. r. e. p Man.
7. p. I. hid. tc. II. car. in dnio. P 7 m. I. m dim. car. hom. 7. III. bor. tc 7 p
. VI. ser. m. III. Silu. XL. porc. XIII. ac. pti. Sep uat. LX. sol.

6 Tihel holds STURMER in lordship, which a free woman held before 1066 as a manor, for 1½ hides and 15 acres. Always 2 ploughs in lordship; 1 men's plough.
2 villagers; 3 smallholders. Then and later 1 slave, now 2.
Meadow, 16 acres. Then a cow, 2 cobs, 60 pigs and 3 beehives; now 4 cattle, 1 cob, 1 foal, 44 pigs, 72 sheep and 3 beehives. 82 b
Value then 40s; now 60[s].

7 Tihel holds STURMER in lordship, which a free man held before 1066 as a manor, for 1½ hides. Always 2 ploughs in lordship;
1 villager; 6 slaves.
Meadow, 20 acres; 1 mill. Then 6 cattle, 1 cob, 12 pigs and 60 sheep; now 12 cattle, 30 pigs, 100 sheep less 2, 1 cob and 3 foals.
Value then and later 40s; now 60[s].

8 Tihel holds TILBURY (-JUXTA-CLARE) in lordship, which a free man held before 1066 as a manor, for 1 hide and 38 acres. Always 3 ploughs in lordship; 1 men's plough;
5 villagers; 1 smallholder; 6 slaves.
Woodland, 20 pigs; meadow, 19 acres. Then 15 cattle, 40 pigs, 80 sheep and 6 beehives; now 5 cattle, 1 cob, 36 pigs and 63 sheep.
Value then and later 60s; now 100[s].

39 LAND OF ROGER OF RAISMES

Hundred of HINCKFORD

1 Roger holds RAYNE in lordship which Alwin, a free man, held before 1066 as a manor for 1 hide and 20 acres. Always 2 ploughs in lordship. Then and later 4 men's ploughs, now 3.
Then and later 9 villagers, now 8; always 5 smallholders. Then and later 4 slaves, now 3.
Woodland, 100 pigs; meadow, 11 acres; 1 mill. Then 8 cows, now 3; then 1 cob, now none; always 100 sheep. Then 30 pigs, now 40.
Value always £4.
Of this manor, Roger holds 30 acres from Roger, and Wiberga (holds) 30 acres.
Value 20s in the same assessment.

2 Roger holds RAYNE in lordship which Edric, a free man, held before 1066 as a manor for 1 hide. Then 2 ploughs in lordship; later and now 1. Now ½ men's plough; 83 a
3 smallholders. Then and later 6 slaves, now 3.
Woodland, 40 pigs; meadow, 13 acres.
Value always 60s.

¶ Hedingham ten& Garenger de . R . qđ tenuit Goduin lib hō . t . r . e .
p . man . 7 p . dim . hiđ . Sēp . II . car in dn̄io . 7 . III . car . hom . 7 . VIII . uilł .
Tc̄ . 7 p̄ . I . bor . m̊ . III . Tc̄ . IIII . ser . Post 7 m̊ . II . Tc̄ . 7 p̄ . filu . ꝺc . por . m̊ . ꝺ .
XVIII . ac . p̄ti . Huic manerio sēp adjacent . II . soc . de . III . ac . Tc̄ 7 p̄ . uał
. IIII . lib . m̊ . c . soł .

¶ Hunđ de Lassendana . Metcinges ten& . R . in dn̄io qđ tenuit
Ormar lib hō . t . r . e . p man . 7 p dim . hiđ . Tc̄ . VI . uilł . m̊ . III . Tc̄ . XII .
bor . m̊ . XVIII . Tc̄ . VI . ser . m̊ . IIII . Sēp . II . car in dn̄io . Tc̄ . int̄ hōes . V . car
m̊ . III . Silu . XL . por . XX . ac . p̄ti . m̊ . I . mol . Sēp . II . runc . 7 . II . uac .
cū uit . 7 . c . ou . tc̄ . XXX . por . m̊ . XX . Sēp . XXXV . cap . Sēp uał . c . soł .
de hoc manerio ten& Anschetill de . R . XVI . ac . 7 . uał . V . soł in eođ
p̄tio . 7 . III . soc tenentes libe . XVIII . ac . ptinent huic manerio qs ten&
Gerold de . R . 7 . Rog dic̄ se eos habe in escangio . Sēp . dim . car . Tc̄ . 7 p̄ .
uał . X . soł . m̊ . III .

¶ Delham . ten& . R . in dn̄io . qđ tenuit Aluric . cāp . p man . 7 . p .
. II . hiđ . 7 . dim . tc̄ . VII . uilł . m̊ . V . Sēp . XXIIII . bor . tc̄ . IIII . ser . m̊ . III .
Tc̄ . II . car . in dn̄io . m̊ . III . tc̄ . int̄ hōes . X . car . m̊ . V . Silu . CCL . porc .
XL . ac . p̄ti . Tc̄ . I . mol . m̊ . II . Tc̄ . II . runc . m̊ . X . Tc̄ . V . uac . m̊ . III .
Tc̄ . XL . ou . m̊ . c . Tc̄ . XXV . por . m̊ . XXX . Sēp uał . XII . lib .
De hoc manerio ten& Gerold . XXX . ac . 7 . uał . X . soł . in eođ p̄tio .
In bura hť . R . XXV . ac . Sēp . III . bor . 7 . dim . car . Silu . XV . porc .

83 b
. I . ac . p̄ti . Vał . VII . soł .

3 Warengar holds (Sible) HEDINGHAM from Roger which Godwin, a free man, held before 1066 as a manor for ½ hide. Always 2 ploughs in lordship; 3 men's ploughs;

8 villagers. Then and later 1 smallholder, now 3; then 4 slaves, later and now 2.

Woodland, then and later 600 pigs, now 500; meadow, 18 acres.

To this manor have always been attached 2 Freemen with 3 acres.

Value then and later £4; now 100s.

Hundred of LEXDEN

4 Roger holds MESSING in lordship which Ordmer, a free man, held before 1066 as a manor for ½ hide.

Then 6 villagers, now 3; then 12 smallholders, now 18; then 6 slaves, now 3. Always 2 ploughs in lordship. Then among the men 6 ploughs, now 3.

Woodland, 40 pigs; meadow, 20 acres; now 1 mill. Always 2 cobs, 2 cows with calves, and 100 sheep. Then 30 pigs, now 20; always 35 goats.

Value always 100s.

Of this manor, Ansketel holds 16 acres from Roger.

Value 5s in the same assessment.

3 Freemen belong to this manor, who hold 18 acres freely (and) whom Gerald holds from Roger. Roger states he has them in exchange. Always ½ plough.

Value then and later 10s; now 3[s].

5 Roger holds DEDHAM in lordship, which Aelfric Kemp held as a manor, for 2½ hides.

Then 7 villagers, now 5; always 24 smallholders. Then 4 slaves, now 3. Then 2 ploughs in lordship, now 3. Then among the men 10 ploughs, now 5.

Woodland, 250 pigs; meadow, 40 acres; then 1 mill, now 2. Then 2 cobs, now 10; then 5 cows, now 3; then 40 sheep, now 100; then 25 pigs, now 30.

Value always £12.

Of this manor, Gerald holds 30 acres. Value 10s in the same assessment.

6 In (Mount) BURES Roger has 25 acres.

Always 3 smallholders; ½ plough.

Woodland, 15 pigs; meadow, 1 acre. 83 b

Value 7s.

Hund de Tendringa. Bradefeldã ten&. R. in dñio. qđ tenuit Aluric camp. p man. 7. p. IIII. hiđ. 7. dim. Tc. VII. uilł. Post 7. m. IIII Sep. x. bor. 7. II. ser. 7. II. car. in dñio. tc. 7 p. VII. car. hom. m. III. Silu. xxx. porc. I. sal. Tc. IIII. uac. c uit. m nulł. Sep. c. ou. Tc. xx. porc. m. xxxIII. Tc. 7. p uał. VII. lib. m. LX. sol. De hoc manerio ten& quedã uxor sui militis. Dimiđ. hiđ. 7. uał. x. sol in eođ ptio.

Erlegam ten&. R. in dñio qđ tenuit Bond p. man. 7. p. I. hiđ. Sep. I. uilł. Tc. XI. bor. m. x. tc. I. ser. m. ñ. Sep. II. car. in dñio. tc. 7 p. IX. car. hom. m. I. Silu. XL. por. IIII. ac. 7. dim. pti. Tc. XL. ou. m. c. Tc. II. uac. 7. III. runc. m nulł. Tc. 7. p uał. IIII. lib. m. xxx. sol. De hoc manerio ten& Rađ de hastinges. xxx. ac. 7 uał. x. sol in eođ. ptio.

Manestunã ten&. R. in dñio qđ tenuit Alselm t. r. e. p. man. 7. p. I. hiđ. 7. xxv. ac. Sep. I. uilł. Tc. 7. p. IIII. bor. m. III. Sep. I. ser. tc. 7 p. II. car in dñio. m. I. tc. int hões. I. car. m nulł. Silu. xv. porc. . I. ac. 7. dim. pti. Past. xv. ou. m. I. sal. Tc. 7 p uał. IIII. lib. m. xx. sol.

Mittesleam ten& uxor ~~Albici~~ Henrici. de. R. qđ tenuit Alric p. man. 7. p. I. hiđ. Sep. I. borđ. tc. II. car. m. nulł. Tc uał. xx. sol. m. II. sol.

In Cliua ten&. R. in dñio. VIII. libos hões. de. xxx. ac. 7. I. car. 7. uał. v. sol.

In herlegã ten&. R. i dñio. VI. libos hões. de. I. hiđ. 7. II. car. 7 uał. XL. sol. De hoc ten&. Rađ. x. ac. 7. Restolt. XL. ac. 7 uał. xx. sol in eođ ptio. hoc est p escangio.

Hundred of TENDRING

7 Roger holds BRADFIELD in lordship, which Aelfric Kemp held as a manor, for 4½ hides.

Then 7 villagers, later and now 4. Always 10 smallholders; 2 slaves; 2 ploughs in lordship. Then and later 7 men's ploughs, now 3.

Woodland, 30 pigs; 1 salt-house. Then 4 cows with calves, now none; always 100 sheep. Then 20 pigs, now 33.

Value then and later £7; now 60s.

Of this manor, the wife of his man-at-arms holds ½ hide.

Value 10s in the same assessment.

8 Roger holds ARDLEIGH in lordship, which Bondi held as a manor, for 1 hide.

Always 1 villager. Then 11 smallholders, now 10; then 1 slave, now none. Always 2 ploughs in lordship. Then and later 9 men's ploughs, now 1.

Woodland, 40 pigs; meadow, 4½ acres. Then 40 sheep, now 100; then 2 cows and 3 cobs, now none.

Value then and later £4; now 30s.

Of this manor, Ralph of Hastings holds 30 acres.

Value 10s in the same assessment.

9 Roger holds JACQUES HALL in lordship, which Alfhelm held before 1066 as a manor, for 1 hide and 25 acres.

Always 1 villager. Then and later 4 smallholders, now 3; always 1 slave. Then and later 2 ploughs in lordship, now 1. Then among the men 1 plough, now none.

Woodland, 15 pigs; meadow, 1½ acres; pasture, 15 sheep; now 1 salt-house.

Value then and later £4; now 20s.

10 Henry's wife holds MISTLEY from Roger, which Alric held as a manor, for 1 hide.

Always 1 smallholder. Then 2 ploughs, now none.

Value then 20s; now 2s.

11 In CLIFF Roger holds in lordship 8 free men with 30 acres. 1 plough.
Value 5s.

12 In ARDLEIGH Roger holds in lordship 6 free men with 1 hide. 2 ploughs.
Value 40s.

Of this, Ralph holds 10 acres, Restald (holds) 40 acres.

Value 20s in the same assessment. This is by exchange.

84 a

Hund de Withā

TERRA Johis filij Walerami. Nutleam ten& Johs fili ernucūn .XL.
de Johe. qđ tenuit Harold. t. r. e. p. man. 7. p. IIII. hid. 7. XXX. ac.
tc. v. car. in dnio. m. III. tc. IIII. car. hominū. m. II. Tc. VII. uill. m. v.
Tc. XIII. bor. m. XI. tc. IIII. ser. m. null. Tc. silu. CCCXXX. por. m.
CC. XXIIII. ac. pti. Sep. I. mol. Past. de. VI. đ. Tc. I. runc. 7. II. uac.
m nichil. Tc. ual. VII. lib. m. VI.

Hund de Hidingforda. Salinges ten& Turstin de. Johe.
qđ tenuit. I. lib hō t. r. e. p maner. 7. p. dim. hid. Tc. II. car. in dnio.
Post null. m. I. Tc. I. car. 7. dim. hom. Post nulla. m. dim. Tc. III. uill.
7. I. pbr. Post. I. m. II. uill. 7. I. pbr. Tc. 7. p. III. bor. m. v. Tc. IIII. ser.
P 7. m. III. Tc. 7 p silu. CCL. porc. m. CC. X. ac. pti. Vat. LX. sol.

Mapledestedam ten& Osmund de Johe. qđ. Grim lib hō. t. r. e. p
man. 7. p. dim. hid. Tc. II. car. in dnio. Post nulla. m. I. Tc. II. bor.
Post. I. m. v. 7. I. pbr. Sep. II. ser. Tc. silu. LX. por. Post 7. m. XVI.
. III. ac. pti. Tc. I. mol. quē m ten& Will de garenda. p uadimonio.
Tc. nichil rec. m. II. uac. 7. XIIII. porc. 7. LVII. ou. Tc. ual. XL.
sol. Post 7. m. XXX.

Heni. ten& Rog de. Johe qđ tenuit lib hō. t. r. e. p. maner.
7. p. II. hid. 7. dim. Tc. II. car. in dnio. Post. I. m. II. Sep. I. car.
hom. tc. 7 p. I. uill. m null. Sep. III. bor. 7. II. ser. Tc. silu. LX. porc.

84 b

post. 7. m. XXX. XII. ac. pti. Tc. VI. anim. 7. XV. porc. 7. XI. ou. m. V. runc.
7. VIII. an. 7. XXX. porc. 7. LXVI. ou. 7. XV. cap. huic manerio jac&
una consuetudo. de. XXII. đ. 7. ob. quæ ē de Sutbia. Tc ual. XL. sol.
Post. 7 m. L.

In Bura ten& hugo de. I. XV. ac. qs tenuit Tosti lib hō. Sep. dim.
car. 7. II. uill. 7. II. bor. Silu. IIII. porc. I. ac. pti. val. VI. sol. hec tra
ē in comitatu de Sudfolc.

40 LAND OF JOHN SON OF WALERAN 84 a

Hundred of WITHAM

1 John son of Ernucion holds NOTLEY from John, which Harold held before 1066 as a manor, for 4 hides and 30 acres. Then 5 ploughs in lordship, now 3. Then 4 men's ploughs, now 2.

Then 7 villagers, now 5; then 13 smallholders, now 11; then 4 slaves, now none.

Woodland, then 330 pigs, now 200; meadow, 24 acres; always 1 mill. Pasture at 6d. Then 1 cob and 2 cows; now nothing.

Value then £7; now [£] 6.

Hundred of HINCKFORD

2 Thurstan holds (Great) SALING from John, which 1 free man held before 1066 as a manor, for ½ hide. Then 2 ploughs in lordship, later none, now 1. Then 1½ men's ploughs, later none, now ½.

Then 3 villagers and 1 priest, later 1, now 2 villagers and 1 priest; then and later 3 smallholders, now 5; then 4 slaves, later and now 3.

Woodland, then and later 250 pigs, now 200; meadow, 10 acres.

Value 60s.

3 Osmund holds (Little) MAPLESTEAD from John which Grim, a free man, [held] before 1066 as a manor for ½ hide. Then 2 ploughs in lordship, later none, now 1.

Then 2 smallholders, later 1, now 5 and 1 priest; always 2 slaves.

Woodland, then 60 pigs, later and now 16; meadow, 3 acres; then 1 mill, which William of Warenne now holds as a pledge. Then he acquired nothing; now 2 cows, 14 pigs and 57 sheep.

Value then 40s; later and now 30[s].

4 Roger holds HENNY from John, which a free man held before 1066 as a manor, for 2½ hides. Then 2 ploughs in lordship, later 1, now 2. Always 1 men's plough.

Then and later 1 villager, now none. Always 3 smallholders; 2 slaves.

Woodland, then 60 pigs, later and now 30; meadow, 12 acres. 84 b
Then 6 cattle, 15 pigs and 11 sheep; now 5 cobs, 8 cattle, 30 pigs, 66 sheep and 15 goats.

To this manor belongs a customary due of 22½d which is from Sudbury.

Value then 40s; later and now 50[s].

5 In BURES Hugh holds from John 15 acres which Tosti, a free man, held. Always ½ plough;

2 villagers; 2 smallholders.

Woodland, 4 pigs; meadow, 1 acre.

Value 6s.

This land is in the County of Suffolk.

Hund de Angra Fifhidam ten& Rog̃ de Johe qđ tenuit Leuric.t.r.e.ꝑ man.7.ꝑ.I.hid.7.dim.7.xxx.ac.Tc̃.xii.uitt.m̃.vii. tc̃.7.p.ii.bor.m̃.x.sep̃.iiii.ser.7.ii.car.in dn̄io.tc̃.7.p.iiii.car hom.m̃.iii.Silu.cccc.porc.x.ac.p̃ti.m̃.i.mol.m̃.xi.uac.7.xi. porc.7.lx.ou.7.i.uas ap.Tc̃.7.p.ual.v.lib.m̃.vii.

Altam Fifhidā ten& Idē de eod.qđ tenuit Alestan ꝑ man.7.ꝑ xxx.ac.Sep̃.iii.bor.Tc̃.i.car.m̃ nutt.Silu.xl.porc.vi.ac.p̃ti.Sep̃ ual.xx.sol.

Angrā.ten& Idē de eod qđ tenuit Leuric.ꝑ man.7.ꝑ.iii.uirg̃. Sep̃.vi.bor.7.i.ser.7.i.car.in dn̄io.Silu.cc.porc.viii.ac.p̃ti.m̃. xxx.porc.7.xl.ou.Tc̃.ual.xl.sol.7.qn̄ rec.xx.sol.m̃ ual.xl.sol.

Hund de Cefforda.Auileiam tenuit libe suan t.r.e.ꝑ.man. 7.ꝑ.iii.hid.7.dim.m̃ ten& Johs in dn̄io.ꝑ tantudē.Tc̃.viii.uitt.m̃.vi. tc̃.iii.bor.m̃.v.tc̃.iiii.ser.m̃.i.tc̃.ii.car.in dn̄io.m̃.i.tc̃.int̃ hōes .iii.car.m̃.ii.lx.ac.p̃ti.Tc̃ 7 p ual.viii.lib.m̃.c.sol.7 qdā lib hō vlsi tenuit.dim.hid.qm posset uende.s; uualeram pat̃ ihōis addidit eū huic manerio.Sep̃.i.uitt.7.i.bor.tc̃.dim.car.m̃ nichil.Tc̃.ual

85 a

.x.sol.7.qn̄ rec.similit̃.m̃ ual.vii.sol.

Hundred of ONGAR

6 Roger holds FYFIELD from John, which Leofric held before 1066 as a manor, for 1½ hides and 30 acres.

Then 12 villagers, now 7; then and later 2 smallholders, now 10. Always 4 slaves; 2 ploughs in lordship. Then and later 4 men's ploughs, now 3.

Woodland, 400 pigs; meadow, 10 acres; now 1 mill. Now 11 cows, 11 pigs, 60 sheep and 1 beehive.

Value then and later £5; now [£] 7.

7 He also holds the other FYFIELD from the same (John), which Alstan held as a manor, for 30 acres.

Always 3 smallholders. Then 1 plough, now none.

Woodland, 40 pigs; meadow, 6 acres.

Value always 20s.

8 He also holds (High) ONGAR from the same (John), which Leofric held as a manor, for 3 virgates.

Always 6 smallholders; 1 slave; 1 plough in lordship.

Woodland, 200 pigs; meadow, 8 acres. Now 30 pigs and 40 sheep.

Value then 40s; when acquired, 20s. Value now 40s.

Hundred of CHAFFORD

9 Swein held AVELEY freely before 1066 as a manor, for 3½ hides. Now John holds (it) in lordship, for as much.

Then 8 villagers, now 6; then 3 smallholders, now 5; then 4 slaves, now 1. Then 2 ploughs in lordship, now 1. Then among the men 3 ploughs, now 2.

Meadow, 60 acres.

Value then and later £8; now 100s.

A free man, Wulfsi, held ½ hide which he could sell; but Waleran, John's father, added him to this manor.

Always 1 villager; 1 smallholder. Then ½ plough, now nothing.

Value then 10s; when acquired, the same. Value now 7s. 85 a

TERRA. Robti filij Corbutionis. Hund de bdestapla. Doddenhenc .XLI.
ten& Girard de. R. qd tenuit Aluric libe. t. r. e. p man. 7. p. I. hid. 7. XVII. ac.
Sep. I. car. Silu. XX. por. Val. XX. sol.

Hund de Witham Smalelant ten& Nigell de. R. qd tenuit comes
Algar. p man. 7. p. II. hid. Sep. I. car. 7. I. bor. 7. I. ser. IX. ac. pti. m. II.
partes piscinæ. Tc. II. anim. m. IIII. Tc. I. por. m. XXV. m. II. pull.
tc. VI. ou. m. XXXV. Tc. VI. cap. m null Sep ual. XX. sol.

Hund de beuentreu. Leintunā ten&. R. in dnio. qd tenuit
Harold. t. r. e. p man. 7. p. IIII. hid. 7. dim. Tc. II. car. in dnio. m null.
Sep. I. car. hom. Tc. III. uill. m. V. 7. I. pbr. Tc. IIII. bor. m. VI. tc. IIII. ser.
m null. Silu. CCC. porc. XL. ac. pti. Tc. VII. pisc. m null. Tc. I. mol. m. n.
7. adhuc posst restaurari. II. car. Tc. ual. IIII. lib. m. XX. sol.
In Leintuna. ten&. R. III. hid. qs tenebat. VIII. soc. t. r. e.
tc. IIII. car. m null. m. VI. uill. 7. I. bor. Silu. X. por.
XXX. ac. pti. Dim. pisc. tc. m. n. Tc ual. LX. sol
m. XX. 7 isti soc reddebant. t. r. e. consuet
ad hauelingas. maneriu reg. 7. m reddt.

41 LAND OF ROBERT SON OF CORBUCION

Hundred of BARSTABLE

1 Gerard holds DODDINGHURST from Robert, which Aelfric held freely before 1066 as a manor, for 1 hide and 17 acres. Always 1 plough.

Woodland, 20 pigs.

Value 20s.

Hundred of WITHAM

2 Nigel holds SMALLANDS from Robert, which Earl Algar held as a manor, for 2 hides. Always 1 plough;

1 smallholder; 1 slave.

Meadow, 9 acres; now 2 parts of a fishery. Then 2 cattle, now 4; then 1 pig, now 25; now 2 foals; then 6 sheep, now 35; then 6 goats, now none.

Value always 20s.

Hundred of BECONTREE

3 Robert holds LEYTON in lordship, which Harold held before 1066 as a manor, for 4½ hides. Then 2 ploughs in lordship, now none. Always 1 men's plough.

Then 3 villagers, now 5 and 1 priest; then 4 smallholders, now 6; then 4 slaves, now none.

Woodland, 300 pigs; meadow, 40 acres; then 7 fisheries, now none; then 1 mill, now none. A further 2 ploughs can be restored.

Value then £4; now 20s.

4 In LEYTON Robert holds 3 hides, which 8 Freemen held before 1066. Then 4 ploughs, now none.

Now 6 villagers; 1 smallholder.

Woodland, 10 pigs; meadow, 30 acres; then ½ fishery, now none.

Value then 60s; now 20[s].

These Freemen paid a customary due before 1066 to the King's manor of Havering (-atte-Bower); they pay it now.

⁋ Lalinge . ten& . W . de . R . qđ tenuit
Leuinc lib hō . t . r . e . ꝑ . manerio

85 b

7 ꝑ . IIII . hid . 7 . dim . tc . III . bor . m . v . Sep . IIII . ser . 7 . II . car . Pastura
XL . ou . Tc . II . runc . m . III . Tc . VII . an . m . IX . Tc . CVII . ou . m . CXXIIII .
Tc . VI . cap . m . null . Tc uat . III . lib . m . IIII . ⁋ Hund de Celme . . . fort. ★
⁋ Haningefeldā ten& Ranulf de . R . qđ tenuit Alestan . lib hō . t . r . e
ꝑ man . 7 . ꝑ . I . hid . 7 . dim . m . I . bor . 7 . I . ser . 7 sep . I . car . II . ac . pti . Silu
. XII . porc . Sep uat . XXX . sol.
⁋ Waltham ten& . W . de . R . qđ . tenuit Vlsi ꝑ maner . 7 . ꝑ . I . hid . 7 . XXX . ac.
tc . I . uill . m null . tc . IX . bor . m . XI . Sep . I . ser . 7 . I . car . Silu . XXX . por.
. VIII . ac . pti . Sep . I . mol . Tc uat . XXX . sol . m . XL.
⁋ In Ead ten& Ranulf . de . R . I . libm hōem . de . XXX . ac . quē inuasit
. R . Sep . dim . car . vat . IIII . sol.
⁋ Bedenestedam ten& Nigell de . R . qđ tenuit Stercher . ꝑ man.
7 . ꝑ . III . hid . 7 . dim . Tc . II . uill . m . null . Sep . VII . bor . 7 . II . ser . 7 . I . car
in dnio . 7 . I . car . hom . Silu . C . porc . I . ac . 7 . dim . pti . Tc . I . runc . 7 . IIII .
uac . cū uit . m null . Tc . XL . ou . m . XXX . tc . XVI . por . m . VII . Tc uat.
XL . sol . m . L . 7 qdā lib hō tenuit dim hid . quē inuasit . R . m ten&
Godefrid de eo . tc . 7 . p . dim . car . m null . Silu . x . porc.
vat . x . sol.
Hund de Tendringa . Fuletunā ten&
Girard de . R . qđ tenuit Ednod lib hō . t . r . e
ꝑ man . 7 . ꝑ . II . hid . 7 . dim . 7 . XX . ac.
tc . I . uill . m . IIII . Sep . II . bor . 7 . II . ser.
7 . II . car . in dnio . tc . I . car hom.
m . null . III . ac . pti . Past . LX . ou.

86 a

Tc . IIII . anim . m . III . Tc . I . runc . m . null . Tc . x . por . m . XX . Tc . XL .
ou . m . XX . Tc . uat . L . sol . 7 qn rec . XX . sol . m uat . L . sol.

[Hundred of 'WIBERTSHERNE']

5 W. holds LAWLING from Robert which Leofing, a free man, held before 1066 as a manor for 4½ hides. 85 b
Then 3 smallholders, now 5. Always 4 slaves; 2 ploughs.
Pasture, 40 sheep. Then 2 cobs, now 3; then 7 cattle, now 9; then 107 sheep, now 124; then 6 goats, now none.
Value then £3; now [£] 4.

Hundred of CHELMSFORD

6 Ranulf holds HANNINGFIELD from Robert which Alstan, a free man, held before 1066 as a manor for 1½ hides.
Now 1 smallholder; 1 slave. Always 1 plough.
Meadow, 2 acres; woodland, 12 pigs.
Value always 30s.

7 W. holds WALTHAM from Robert which Wulfsi held as manor, for 1 hide and 30 acres.
Then 1 villager, now none; then 9 smallholders, now 11. Always 1 slave; 1 plough.
Woodland, 30 pigs; meadow, 8 acres; always 1 mill.
Value then 30s; now 40[s].

8 In the same (Waltham) Ranulf holds from Robert 1 free man with 30 acres whom Robert annexed. Always ½ plough.
Value 4s.

9 Nigel holds 'BENSTED' from Robert, which Starker held as a manor, for 3½ hides.
Then 2 villagers, now none. Always 7 smallholders; 2 slaves; 1 plough in lordship; 1 men's plough.
Woodland, 100 pigs; meadow, 1½ acres. Then 1 cob and 4 cows with calves, now none; then 40 sheep, now 30; then 16 pigs, now 7.
Value then 40s, now 50[s].

A free man, whom Robert annexed, held ½ hide. Now Godfrey holds (it) from him. Then and later ½ plough, now none.
Woodland, 10 pigs.
Value 10s.

Hundred of TENDRING

10 Gerard holds FOULTON from Robert which Ednoth, a free man, held before 1066 as a manor for 2½ hides and 20 acres.
Then 1 villager, now 4. Always 2 smallholders; 2 slaves; 2 ploughs in lordship. Then 1 men's plough, now none.
Meadow, 3 acres; pasture, 60 sheep. Then 4 cattle, now 3; 86 a
then 1 cob, now none; then 10 pigs, now 20; then 40 sheep, now 20.
Value then 50s; when acquired, 20s. Value now 50s.

Hund de. Rochefort. Pachesham ten& Idē. G. de. R. qđ tenuit
lib hō. p. manerio. 7. p. dim. hid. 7. xxx. ac. Sēp. II. bor. 7. I. car. in dnio
Tc uat. XL. sol. m. v. ★

Hund de Turestapla. Toleshuntā ten& Malger de. R. qđ
tenuit Sercar. p man. 7. p. I. hid. Tc. v. uill. m. IIII. Tc. I. bor. m. VI.
Tc. v. ser. m. II. Tc. 7. p. II. car. m. I. in dnio. Tc. 7. p. II. car. hom.
m. I. Silu. c. por. I. ac. pti. Past. LX. ou. Tc. XV. an. m. II. uac.
7. I. uit. Tc. L. ou. m. XXV. Tc. I. runc. m null. Tc. II. uasa ap. m. n.
Tc. uat. IIII. lib. Post. III. m. XL. sol.
7 VIII. libi hões tenuer. IIII. hid. 7. II. ac. 7. possent ire q uellent.
qs. Rob. inuasit. 7. m tenent. IIII. milites de. R. tc. IIII. ser. m. II.
sēp. II. car. silu. CXX. porc. Past. LX. ou. I. sal. Val. L. sol.

TERRA Galteri diaconi. Hund de bdestapla. In bura ten& .XLII.
Galt. II. hid. de tra Teddrici fris sui. 7 qdam miles ten& de eo. Sēp. I.
car. 7. I. bor. 7. I. ser. 7. XXX. ac uastatæ siluæ. Past. LX. ou. huic manerio
addite st. XL. ac. t. regis Willi. qs tenuit lib hō. t. r. e. 7 illas
habuit Tedric. 7. tc ualebant. pdictæ hidæ. XL. sol. 7. m. similit. 7
XL. ac. uat. VIII. sol. 7. IIII. đ. In dnio recepit Galt. IIII. animal.

86 b
m. similit. Tc. II. runc. m. I. Tc. c. ou. II. min. m. LV. Tc. X.... porc.
m. XI.

Hund de Witbrictesherna. Purlai ten& Galt in dnio qđ tenuit
Leuuin. t. r. e. p man. 7. p. III. hid. 7. dim. Sēp. II. uill. m. I. bor. Tc.
. III. ser. m. I. Tc. II. car in dnio. m. I. 7. dim. Sēp. dim. car. hom. silu.
. LX. porc. Sēp. VIII. anim. Tc. V. runc. m. IIII. Tc. CLII. ou. m. LXXX.
tc. LXII. por. m. XLVII. m. XXIII. cap. Sēp uat. LX. sol.

Hundred of ROCHFORD

11 Gerard also holds PAGLESHAM from Robert, which a free man held as a manor, for ½ hide and 30 acres.

Always 1 smallholder; 1 plough in lordship.

Value then 40s; now 5[s].

Hundred of THURSTABLE

12 Mauger holds TOLLESHUNT (Major) from Robert, which Starker held as a manor, for 1 hide.

Then 5 villagers, now 4; then 1 smallholder, now 6; then 5 slaves, now 2. Then and later 2 ploughs in lordship, now 1. Then and later 2 men's ploughs, now 1.

Woodland, 100 pigs; meadow, 1 acre; pasture, 60 sheep. Then 15 cattle, now 2 cows and 1 calf; then 50 sheep, now 25; then 1 cob, now none; then 2 beehives, now none.

Value then £4; later [£] 3; now 40s.

8 free men, whom Robert annexed, held 4 hides and 2 acres and could go whither they would. Now 4 men-at-arms hold (them) from Robert.

Then 4 slaves, now 2. Always 2 ploughs.

Woodland, 120 pigs; pasture, 60 sheep; 1 salt-house.

Value 50s.

42 LAND OF WALTER THE DEACON

Hundred of BARSTABLE

1 In BOWERS (Gifford) Walter holds 2 hides of his brother Theodoric's land. A man-at-arms holds from him.

Always 1 plough; 1 smallholder; 1 slave.

Woodland, 30 acres, laid waste; pasture, 60 sheep.

To this manor 40 acres were added after 1066, which a free man held before 1066. Theodoric had them.

Value of the said hides, then 40s; now the same.

Value of the 40 acres, 8s 4d.

Walter acquired in lordship 4 cattle, now the same; then 2 cobs, 86 b
now 1; then 100 sheep less 2, now 55; then 1 ... pigs, now 11.

Hundred of 'WIBERTSHERNE'

2 Walter holds PURLEIGH in lordship, which Leofwin held before 1066 as a manor, for 3½ hides.

Always 2 villagers. Now 1 smallholder; then 3 slaves, now 1. Then 2 ploughs in lordship, now 1½. Always ½ men's plough.

Woodland, 60 pigs. Always 8 cattle. Then 5 cobs, now 4; then 152 sheep, now 80; then 62 pigs, now 47; now 23 goats.

Value always 60s.

Eistanes ten& Galt in dnio . qd . tenuit Dodinc . t . r . e . p . maner
7 . p . II . hid . Tc . VI . car . in dnio . m . IIII . Tc . V . uill . 7 . I . pbr . M . I . pbr
7 . III . uill . Tc . II . bor . m . XXV . Tc . VII . ser . m . I . Tc . silu . DCCC . por.
m . CCCC . XXVI . ac . pti . I . mol . Sep . VI . uac . IIII . uit m . XV . an . tc.
. II . runc . m . VI . Tc . LXXX . ou . m . CXX . Tc . LXXIIII . porc . m LXII.
Tc . XXIIII . cap . m . XXXIIII . II . uasa apu . Tc uat . VII . lib . m . VIII.

Purlai ten& Galt in dnio . qd tenuit Leuuin cilt . p man . 7 . p . V.
. hid . t . r . e . Tc . X . uill . m . V . Tc . I . bor . m . VI . Sep . IIII . ser 7 . III . car.
in dnio . 7 . IIII . car . hom . silu . C . porc . Past . C . ou . Tc uat . VII . lib . m.
uat . VI . lib.

Fenna ten& . I . miles de . G . qd tenuit lib ho . p man . 7 . p . II . hid . sep.
. II . bor . 7 . I . ser . 7 . I . car . 7 . uat . L . sol . H de Lassendena.

Colun . ten& . I . miles de . G . qd tenuit Leuuin . p man . 7 . p . d.
hid . 7 . XIII . ac . Sep . XII . bord . 7 . II . ser . 7 . II . car . in dnio . 7 . I . car.
hom . silu . C . porc . XIII . ac . pti . Sep . I . mol . Tc . VI . anim . m . II.
tc . II . runc . m null . tc . XII . ou . m . XXIIII . Tc . XVI . porc . m . XIIII.
m XIII . cap . 7 . III . uasa . ap . Sep uat . XL . sol.

87 a

Hund de Tendringa . Wica ten& Galt in dnio qd tenuit
Edeua regina p man . 7 . p . IIII . hid . Sep . XIIII . uill . Tc . XVIII . bord . m
XXVIII . Tc . IIII . ser . m . III . Sep . IIII . car . in dnio . Tc . 7 p . XII . car . hom.
m . VIII . Silu . C . porc . VIII . ac . pti . Tc . XII . an . m . XIIII . Sep . II . runc.
Tc . C . ou . m . LXXXIIII . Tc . XL . porc . m LXXI . Tc . XXX . cap . m . XXXIIII.
tc . VII . uasa ap . m . X . Tc . 7 p uat . VI . lib . 7 . X . sol . m . vat . X . lib.
7 hanc tra dedit . E . regina Walto post aduentu reg Willi.

[Hundred of DUNMOW]

3 Walter holds (Little) EASTON in lordship, which Doding held as a manor, for 2 hides. Then 6 ploughs in lordship, now 4.
Then 5 villagers and 1 priest, now 1 priest and 3 villagers; then 2 smallholders, now 25; then 7 slaves, now 1.
Woodland, then 800 pigs, now 400; meadow, 26 acres; 1 mill. Always 6 cows; 4 calves. Now 15 cattle; then 2 cobs, now 6; then 80 sheep, now 120; then 74 pigs, now 62; then 24 goats, now 34; 2 beehives.
Value then £7; now [£] 8.

[Hundred of 'WIBERTSHERNE']

4 Walter holds PURLEIGH in lordship, which Young Leofwin held as a manor, for 5 hides before 1066.
Then 10 villagers, now 5; then 1 smallholder, now 6. Always 4 slaves; 3 ploughs in lordship; 4 men's ploughs.
Woodland, 100 pigs; pasture, 100 sheep.
Value then £7. Value now £6.

5 1 man-at-arms holds STOW MARIES from Walter, which a free man held as a manor, for 2 hides.
Always 2 smallholders; 1 slave; 1 plough.
Value 50s.

Hundred of LEXDEN

6 1 man-at-arms holds COLNE (Engaine) from Walter, which Leofwin held as a manor, for ½ hide and 13 acres.
Always 12 smallholders; 2 slaves; 2 ploughs in lordship; 1 men's plough.
Woodland, 100 pigs; meadow, 13 acres; always 1 mill. Then 6 cattle, now 2; then 2 cobs, now none; then 12 sheep, now 24; then 16 pigs, now 14; now 13 goats and 3 beehives.
Value always 40s.

Hundred of TENDRING 87 a

7 Walter holds WIX in lordship, which Queen Edith held as a manor, for 4 hides.
Always 14 villagers. Then 18 smallholders, now 28; then 4 slaves, now 3. Always 4 ploughs in lordship. Then and later 12 men's ploughs, now 8.
Woodland, 100 pigs; meadow, 8 acres. Then 12 cattle, now 14; always 2 cobs. Then 100 sheep, now 84; then 40 pigs, now 71; then 30 goats, now 34; then 7 beehives, now 10.
Value then and later £6 10s. Value now £10.
Queen Edith gave this land to Walter after King William's arrival.

Brumleiam ten& . I . miles de Galt̃o qđ ten̉ . E . regina . ꝓ maner̉
7 . ꝓ . II . hid . xx . ac̉ . min̉ . Sep̃ . I . uilł . tc̃ . xvII . bor . m̊ . xv . Tc̃ . IIII . ser̉.
m̊ . III . Sep̃ . II . car̉ . in dn̄io . tc̃ . int̃ hões . VI . car̉ . m̊ . IIII . Silủ . XL . porc.
. IIII . ac̉ . p̃ti . tc̃ . IX . anim̉ . m̊ . VII . tc̃ . II . runc̉ . m̊ . IIII . Tc̃ . c . oủ . m̊ . cc.
tc̃ . XII . por . m̊ . xxx . m̊ . II . uasa apũ . Tc̃ ual . v . lib̃ . m̊ . IIII.

Hund de Vdelesforda . Cestrefort . ten& . I . mil de Galt̃o qđ tenuit
. E . regina . ꝓ man̉ . 7 . ꝓ . v . hid . Sep̃ . x . uilł . tc̃ . IIII . bor . m̊ . XVI . tc̃.
. IIII . ser̉ . m̊ . I . Sep̃ . II . car̉ . in dn̄io . 7 . III . car̉ . hom̉ . Silủ . xx . porc̉ . VIII . ac̉.
p̊ti . Sep̃ . I . mol . Tc̃ . II . anim̉ . m̊ . IIII . Tc̃ . I . runc̉ . m̊ . null . Tc̃ . XXXVI.
oủ . m̊ . XLIII . tc̃ . XVI . porc̉ . m̊ . XXXIIII . m̊ . XXIII . cap̉ . Tc̃ . ual . c.
sol . m̊ . VI . lib̃.

★

87 b

XLIII TERRA Rogeri bigoti Hund de Hidingfort.

Hidingham ten& Garenger̉ de . R . ꝓ . xxv . ac̉ . q̊s tenuer̃t
. xv . libi hões . t̉ . r̉ . ẻ . Sep̃ . v . car̉ . 7 dim̉ . 7 . I . uilł . 7 . II . ser̉ . Silủ . LXX . porc̉.
. XI . ac̉ . p̃ti . tc̃ ual . XL . sol m̊ . IIII . lib̃ . In Ead uilla tenuer̃ . III . libi hões
. t̉ . r̉ . ẻ . XLVIII . ac̉ . tr̃æ . 7 . dim̉ . M̊ ten& Idẽ . G . de . R . Sep̃ . II . car̉ in dn̄io
7 . II . car̉ hom̉ . 7 . v . uilł . Tc̃ . VI . ser̉ . m̊ . IIII . Tc̃ . silủ . cc . porc̉ . m̊ . CLX.
XXIIII . ac̉ . p̃ti . m̊ . I . mol . Tc̃ ual . XL . sol . m̊ . LX . De his XLVIII . ac̉.
ñ testat̉ Hund . R . qđ inde de parte regis ess& saisit̉ . Has . II . tr̃as
ten& . Garenger̉ . 7 Rog̃ de Ramis calũpniat̉ eas . s; nec hund ei
testatur.

8 1 man-at-arms holds (Little) BROMLEY from Walter, which Queen Edith held as a manor, for 2 hides less 20 acres.

Always 1 villager. Then 17 smallholders, now 15; then 4 slaves, now 3. Always 2 ploughs in lordship. Then among the men 6 ploughs, now 4.

Woodland, 40 pigs; meadow, 4 acres. Then 9 cattle, now 7; then 2 cobs, now 4; then 100 sheep, now 200; then 12 pigs, now 30; now 2 beehives.

Value then £5; now [£] 4.

Hundred of UTTLESFORD

9 1 man-at-arms holds (Little) CHESTERFORD from Walter, which Queen Edith held as a manor, for 5 hides.

Always 10 villagers. Then 4 smallholders, now 16; then 4 slaves, now 1. Always 2 ploughs in lordship; 3 men's ploughs.

Woodland, 20 pigs; meadow, 8 acres; always 1 mill. Then 2 cattle, now 4; then 1 cob, now none; then 36 sheep, now 43; then 16 pigs, now 34; now 23 goats.

Value then 100s; now £6.

43 LAND OF ROGER BIGOT 87 b

Hundred of HINCKFORD

1 Warengar holds (Sible) HEDINGHAM from Roger for 25 acres, which 15 free men held before 1066. Always 5½ ploughs;

1 villager; 2 slaves.

Woodland, 70 pigs; meadow, 11 acres.

Value then 40s; now £4.

In the same village 3 free men held 48½ acres of land before 1066. Now Warengar also holds (them) from Roger. Always 2 ploughs in lordship; 2 men's ploughs;

5 villagers. Then 6 slaves, now 4.

Woodland, then 200 pigs, now 160; meadow, 24 acres; now 1 mill.

Value then 40s; now 60[s].

Concerning these 48 acres, the Hundred does not testify for Roger that he was put in possession of them on the King's behalf.

Warengar holds these 2 lands. Roger of Raismes claims them, but the Hundred does not testify for him either.

Pebeners. ten& Idē. G. de. R. qđ tenueř. III. libi hões. t. r. e. sēp. I. car 7. dim. 7. I. borđ. silu. VIII. porc. III. ac. 7. dim. pti. Tc uat. XL. sot. m. IIII. lib

Ouitunam ten&. R. in dnio. qđ tenuit lib hō. t. r. e. p man. 7 p. I. hid. 7. XXX. ac. sēp. II. car in dnio. 7. II. car. hom. Tc. IIII. uitt. Post 7. m. III. Tc. VI. bor. Post 7 m. V. sēp. II. ser. XXIIII. ac. pti. Tc uat. XL. sot. m. IIII. lib.

Belcham ten& Rob de uals de. R. qđ ten. VI. libi hões. t. r. e. p. I. hid. 7. XXXVIII. ac. 7. dim. Sēp. III. car. in dnio. tc. 7 p. I. car. hom. m. dim. Tc. III. uitt. Post 7. m. II. Tc. 7 p. IX. bor. m. XII. Tc. IIII. ser. Post 7. m. I. Silu. XXX. porc. XV. ac. pti. Tc uat. LX. sot. m. C.

Heni. ten& Idē. R. de. R. qđ tenueř. V. libi hões

88 a

. t. r. e. p. I. hid. 7 dim. IIII. ac. min. Sēp. IIII. car. in dnio. Tc. IIII. uitt. Post 7. m. I. Tc. 7. p. II. bor. m. III. Sēp. II. ser. tc. 7 p silu. XXX. porc. m. XX. XVIII. ac. pti. Tc. 7 p uat. XL. sot. m. LXIIII.

Westunā ten& hugo de hosdenc qđ tenueř. IIII. libi hões. t. r. e. q fueř de soca Algari. p. I. hid. 7. L. ac. Sēp. V. car. in dnio. tc. 7. p. V. bor. m. X. tc. 7 p. IX. ser. m. IIII. Silu. VI. porc. XXIIII. ac. pti. m. I. mot. Tc. 7 p uat. LX. sot. m. IIII. lib.

2 Warengar also holds PEBMARSH from Roger, which 3 free men held before 1066. Always 1½ ploughs;
1 smallholder.
Woodland, 8 pigs; meadow, 3½ acres.
Value then 40s; now £4.

3 Roger holds OVINGTON in lordship, which a free man held before 1066 as a manor, for 1 hide and 30 acres. Always 2 ploughs in lordship; 2 men's ploughs.
Then 4 villagers, later and now 3; then 6 smallholders, later and now 5; always 2 slaves.
Meadow, 24 acres.
Value then 40s; now £4.

4 Robert of Vaux holds BELCHAMP (Otten) from Roger, which 6 free men held before 1066, for 1 hide and 38½ acres. Always 3 ploughs in lordship. Then and later 1 men's plough, now ½.
Then 3 villagers, later and now 2; then and later 9 smallholders, now 12; then 4 slaves, later and now 1.
Woodland, 30 pigs; meadow, 15 acres.
Value then 60s; now 100[s].

5 Robert also holds HENNY from Roger, which 5 free men held
before 1066, for 1½ hides less 4 acres. Always 4 ploughs in lordship. 88 a
Then 4 villagers, later and now 1; then and later 2 smallholders, now 3; always 2 slaves.
Woodland, then and later 30 pigs, now 20; meadow, 18 acres.
Value then and later 40s; now 64[s].

6 Hugh of Houdain holds WESTON (Hall) which 4 free men, who were of Algar's jurisdiction, held before 1066 for 1 hide and 50 acres. Always 5 ploughs in lordship.
Then and later 5 smallholders, now 10; then and later 9 slaves, now 4.
Woodland, 6 pigs; meadow, 24 acres; now 1 mill.
Value then and later 60s; now £4.

TERRA Robti malet. Hund de hedingfort. Stanestedā.
ten& Hub de. Robto. qd tenuit Goduin lib hō. t. r. e. p man.
7 p. I. hid. sēp. II. car. in dnio. Tc. 7 p. v. car. hom. m. IIII. Tc. x. uilt.
Post. VIII. m. IIII. Sēp. VII. bor. tc. VII. ser. m. VI. Tc. silu. D. porc.
m. CCCC. x. ac. pti. tc. I. mol. m. II. Huic manerio adjac&. I. hid.
7. dim. 7. LII. ac. qs tenuer. sochemani. t. r. e. tc. IIII. car. m
. IIII. 7. dim. tc. 7 p. VI. bor. m. XXIIII. tc. IIII. ser. m. I. Silua.
XXX. porc. XVI. ac. pti. Tc XVI. an. v. runc. LX. ou. L. cap. XL.
por. x. uasa. apū. m. x. an. L. ou. XXVI. cap. XL. porc. VIII. uasa
apū. tc. ual. VI. lib. m. IX. 7. I. soc. q n potat recede a tra
tenens. XX. ac. 7. ual. II. sol.
Goldingham ten& Idē hub. de. R. qd tenuit lib hō Goduin.
t. r. e. p man. 7 p. II. hid. Tc. III. car. in dnio. Post 7. m. II. Sēp.

88 b
VI. uilt. 7. v. bor. Tc. 7 p. VI. ser. m. II. Sēp. XVI. ac. pti. huic maner.
adjacebant. IIII. soc. de. XVII. ac. 7. I. ac. pti. Tc. x. an. 7. II. runc.
. L. ou. XL. caporc. m. XII. an. I. runc. CCLX. ou. LXV. por. v. uasa apū
tc ual. LX. sol. m. VI. lib. Hund de Lassendena.
Colun. ten&. R. in dnio. qd tenuit Assorin. p man. 7. p. I. hid. 7. XXX. ac.
Sēp. VII. uilt. 7. XV. bor. tc. IIII. ser. m. III. 7 sēp. III. car. in dnio.
tc. int hōes. v. car. m. IIII. Silu. CCCC. porc. sēp. I. mol. XIII. ac pti.
Tc. XII. anim. III. runc. LX. por. XL. cap. XX. ou. m. VI. an. XX. porc.
. XXX. ou. III. uasa ap. Sēp. ual. VI. lib. 7. tc. fuit. I. soc. q libe tenuit
. I. uirg. m. ht. R. sēp. dim. car. Tc. ual. VIII. sol. m. VII.

44 LAND OF ROBERT MALET

Hundred of HINCKFORD

1 Hubert holds STANSTEAD (Hall) from Robert which Godwin, a free man, held before 1066 as a manor for 1 hide. Always 2 ploughs in lordship. Then and later 5 men's ploughs; now 4.

Then 10 villagers, later 8, now 4; always 7 smallholders. Then 7 slaves, now 6.

Woodland, then 500 pigs, now 400; meadow, 10 acres; then 1 mill, now 2.

To this manor are attached 1½ hides and 52 acres, which Freemen held before 1066. Then 4 ploughs; now 3½.

Then and later 6 smallholders, now 24; then 4 slaves, now 1.

Woodland, 30 pigs; meadow, 16 acres. Then 16 cattle, 5 cobs, 60 sheep, 50 goats, 40 pigs, 10 beehives; now 10 cattle, 50 sheep, 26 goats, 40 pigs, 8 beehives.

Value then £6; now [£] 9.

1 Freeman, who could not withdraw from the land, who holds 20 acres.

Value 2s.

2 Hubert also holds GOLDINGHAM (Hall) from Robert which Godwin, a free man, held before 1066 as a manor for 2 hides. Then 3 ploughs in lordship, later and now 2.

Always 6 villagers; 5 smallholders. Then and later 6 slaves, 88 b
now 2.

Meadow, always 16 acres.

To this manor were attached 4 Freemen with 17 acres and 1 acre of meadow.

Then 10 cattle, 2 cobs, 50 sheep, 40 pigs; now 12 cattle, 1 cob, 260 sheep, 65 pigs, 5 beehives.

Value then 60s; now £6.

Hundred of LEXDEN

3 Robert holds (Wakes) COLNE in lordship, which Azorin held as a manor, for 1 hide and 30 acres.

Always 7 villagers; 15 smallholders. Then 4 slaves, now 3. Always 3 ploughs in lordship. Then among the men 5 ploughs, now 4.

Woodland, 400 pigs; always 1 mill. Meadow, 13 acres. Then 12 cattle, 3 cobs, 60 pigs, 40 goats, 20 sheep; now 6 cattle, 20 pigs, 30 sheep, 3 beehives.

Value always £6.

Then there was 1 Freeman who held 1 virgate freely. Now Robert has (it). Always ½ plough.

Value then 8s; now 7[s].

⁋ Paruā colun ten& Galt̃ de . R . qđ tenuit Goduin⁹ . ꝓ man̄ . 7 ꝓ . I .
hiđ . 7 . I . uirḡ . Tc̄ . VIII . bor . m̊ . XVII . tc̄ . IIII . ser . m̊ . I . Silū . xxx . porc̄ .
. XI . ac̄ . p̄ti . I . mol . Tc̄ . uat . XL . sol . m̊ . LX . 7 ē in p̄tio de Stanesteda .
in . IX . lib .

⁋ Hunđ de Angra

XLV ⁋ Terra Witti de Scohies . Mortunā ten& Witts in dn̄io .
qđ tenuit Sexi⁹ . ꝓ manerio . 7 . ꝓ . I . hiđ . 7 . XX . ac̄ . Tc̄ . IIII . uitt . m̊ .
. III . Sēp . XVI . bor . Tc̄ . VI . ser . m̊ . IIII . tc̄ . 7 . p⁹ . III . car . in dn̄io . m̊ . II .
tc̄ . 7 p⁹ . II . car . hom̄ . m̊ . I . 7 . dim̄ . Silū . cccc . porc̄ . XX . ac̄ . p̄ti .
Tc̄ . runc̄ . m̊ . IIII . tc̄ . VIII uac̄ . 7 . VI . uit . m̊ . XI . an̄ . m̊ . XXXVI . ou̇ .
Tc̄ . LX . por . m̊ . XIIII . tc̄ . XXX . cap̄ . m̊ . LX . Tc̄ uat . VIII . lib . m̊ . X .
7 . I . lib hō tenuit . XLIII . ac̄ . 7 . dim̄ . m̊ . W . inuasit . 7 . n̄ ꝑtinebat
isti manerio qđ ten& Rađ de . eo . Sēp . I . uitt . 7 . II . bor . 7 . I . ser .

89 a
7 . I . car . in dn̄io . 7 . dim̄ . car . hom̄ . Sēp uat . XX . sol . s; hucusq; habuit
xxx . sol .

TERRA Rogeri . Pictauensis . Hunđ de Lessendena . Burā : XLVI :
tenuit Vlmer⁹ ꝓ man̄ . 7 . ꝓ . I . hiđ . m̊ . R . ꝓ tantundē . Tc̄ . VI . uitt . 7 . qn̄
rec̄ similit̃ . m̊ . V . Sēp . IX . bor . Tc̄ . 7 p⁹ . VI . ser . m̊ . IIII . Tc̄ . 7 p⁹ . III . car . in dn̄io .
m̊ . II . Tc̄ . 7 p⁹ . III . car . hom̄ . m̊ . I . 7 . dim̄ . Silū . ccc . porc̄ . XII . ac̄ . p̄ti . sēp .
. I . mol . 7 adhuc sēp ꝑtinent . III . uitt . 7 . II . bor . h̄ntes . I . car . Tc̄ . II . runc̄ .
XIIII . anim̄ . LXXX . ou̇ . XXVIII . porc̄ . XXVI . cap̄ . m̊ . VII . anim̄ . LIIII . ou̇ .
. VI . por . Tc̄ . ~~7 post~~ uat . VII . lib . m̊ . XI . 7 . qn̄ rec̄ similit̃ . 7 . VIII . libi hōes
tenuer̄ . dim̄ . hiđ . 7 . XXX . ac̄ . sēp . III . car . 7 . III . ac̄ . p̄ti . Silū . XXX . porc̄ .
hoc app̄tiatū ē supi⁹ .

4 Walter holds COLNE (Engaine) from Robert, which Godwin held as a manor, for 1 hide and 1 virgate.
Then 8 smallholders, now 17; then 4 slaves, now 1.
Woodland, 30 pigs; meadow, 11 acres; 1 mill.
Value then 40s; now 60[s].
It is in the £9 assessment of Stanstead (Hall).

45 LAND OF WILLIAM OF ÉCOUIS

Hundred of ONGAR

1 William holds MORETON in lordship, which Saxi held as a manor, for 1 hide and 20 acres.
Then 4 villagers, now 3; always 16 smallholders. Then 6 slaves, now 4. Then and later 3 ploughs in lordship, now 2. Then and later 2 men's ploughs, now 1½.
Woodland, 400 pigs; meadow, 20 acres. Then ... cobs, now 4; then 8 cows and 6 calves, now 11 cattle; now 36 sheep; then 60 pigs, now 14; then 30 goats, now 60.
Value then £8; now [£] 10.
1 free man held 43½ acres. Now William has annexed him. He did not belong to this manor which Ralph holds from him.
Always 1 villager; 2 smallholders; 1 slave; 89 a
1 plough in lordship; ½ men's plough.
Value always 20s, but up to now he has had 30s.

46 LAND OF ROGER OF POITOU

Hundred of LEXDEN

1 Wulfmer held (Mount) BURES as a manor, for 1 hide. Now Roger (holds it) for as much.
Then 6 villagers, when acquired the same, now 5; always 9 smallholders. Then and later 6 slaves, now 4. Then and later 3 ploughs in lordship, now 2. Then and later 3 men's ploughs, now 1½.
Woodland, 300 pigs; meadow, 12 acres; always 1 mill.
A further 3 villagers and 2 smallholders have always belonged, who have 1 plough.
Then 2 cobs, 14 cattle, 80 sheep, 28 pigs, 26 goats; now 7 cattle, 54 sheep, 6 pigs.
Value then £7; now [£] 11; when acquired, the same.
8 free men held ½ hide and 30 acres. Always 3 ploughs.
Meadow, 3 acres; woodland, 30 pigs.
This is assessed above.

⁊ Bercolt tenuit Leuuin᷒ Croc . ꝑ man̄ . 7 . ꝑ . i . hid̄ . 7 . xxv . ac̄ . m̄ . Rog̃.
similit̃ . Tc̄ . vii . uill̄ . P᷒ 7 . m̄ . v . Tc̄ . v . bor . 7 . qn̄ recep̄ . vii . m̄ . v . Sēp
. ii . ser̄ . Tc̄ . 7 . p᷒ . ii . car̄ . . dn̄io . m̄ . i . tc̄ . 7 . p᷒ . ii . car̄ . hom̄ . m̄ . i . Silu̅ . ccc . porc̄ . ★
. viii . ac̄ . p̄ti . Sēp . i . mol̄ . huic man̄ ptin& . i . biuuita quæ uocat̄ . Bradefelda.
ꝑ . dim̄ . hid̄ . 7 . xxx . ac̄ . Tc̄ . 7 . p᷒ . i . car̄ . m̄ . null̄ Tc̄ . rec̄ . R . in dn̄io.
. i . runc̄ . 7 . xiiii . anim̄ . 7 . xlviii . ou̅ . 7 . c . ou̅ . 7 . vi . porc̄ . xxxii . cap̄.
m̄ . iiii . anim̄ . lxxx . ou̅ . xi . porc̄ . Tc̄ . ual . vi . lib̄ . 7 . qn̄ recepit . vii.
m̄ ual . lx . sol̄ . 7 . vii . libi hões tenuer̄ . dim̄ hid̄ . 7 . xi . ac̄ . 7 . dim̄ . tc̄.
7 . p᷒ . ii . car̄ . m̄ . i . ii . ac̄ . p̄ti . 7 . app̄tiatū ē in sup̄dictis lib̄.
⁊ Hund̄ de Tendringa . In Bradefelda tenuit Leuuin᷒ . dim̄ . hid̄.
7 . xv . ac̄ . tc̄ . i . bor . 7 . i . ser̄ . m̄ . n̄ . Tc̄ . 7 p᷒ . i . car̄ . m̄ . n̄ . Tc̄ ual . xl . sol̄.

89 b
7 . qn̄ recepit . xxx . sol̄ . m̄ . ual . v . sol̄.

. XLVII . TERRA Hugonis de Gurnai . Hund̄ de Hidingaforda.
Listunā ten& . Goisfrid᷒ . talebot qd̄ tenuit lib̄ homo ꝑ man̄ . 7 . ꝑ dim̄ . hid̄.
7 . xxx . ac̄ . Sēp . ii . car̄ . in dn̄io . 7 . i . car̄ . hom̄ . Tc̄ . 7 . p᷒ . vi . bor . m̄ . v . tc̄ . 7 p᷒.
. iii . ser̄ . m̄ null̄ . xxx . ac̄ . p̄ti . dim̄ . mol̄ . Tc̄ . iii . uac̄ . c̄ uit̄ . xii . ou̅.
. vii . porc̄ . M̊ . iii . uac̄ . c̄ uit̄ . xxii . ou̅ . viii . uasa ap̄ . Sēp ual . lxviii . sol̄.
⁊ Hund̄ de Tendringa . Erleiam tenuit Osb̄t᷒ . ꝑ . man̄ . 7 . ꝑ . ii . hid̄.
7 . dim̄ . m̄ . ten& Agnes . Tc̄ . xvi . uill̄ . Post 7 . m̄ . vii . tc̄ . iiii . bor.
m̄ null̄ . tc̄ . iiii . ser̄ . m̄ null̄ . Sēp . ii . car̄ . in dn̄io . Tc̄ . int̄ hões . viii . car̄.
7 . qn̄ rec̄ . vi . m̄ . iii . Silu̅ . xl . porc̄ . iii . ac̄ . p̄ti . m̄ . ii . mol̄ . Tc̄ . xxx.
ou̅ . v . porc̄ . m̊ . xliiii . ou̅ . viii . porc̄ . vii . an̄ . x . cap̄ . iii . uasa apū.
Tc̄ ual . vi . lib̄ . Post 7 . m̄ . iiii.

2 Leofwin Croc held (West) BERGHOLT as a manor, for 1 hide and 25 acres. Now Roger (holds it) for the same.

Then 7 villagers, later and now 5; then 5 smallholders, when acquired 7, now 5; always 2 slaves. Then and later 2 ploughs [in] lordship, now 1. Then and later 2 men's ploughs, now 1.

Woodland, 300 pigs; meadow, 8 acres; always 1 mill.

To this manor belongs 1 outlier which is called BRADFIELD, for ½ hide and 30 acres. Then and later 1 plough, now none.

Then Roger acquired in lordship 1 cob, 14 cattle, 48 sheep, 100 sheep, 6 pigs, 32 goats; now 4 cattle, 80 sheep, 11 pigs.

Value then £6; when acquired [£]7. Value now 60s.

7 free men held ½ hide and 11½ acres. Then and later 2 ploughs, now 1.

Meadow, 2 acres.

It is assessed in the above pounds.

Hundred of TENDRING

3 In BRADFIELD Leofwin held ½ hide and 15 acres.

Then 1 smallholder and 1 slave, now none. Then and later 1 plough, now none.

Value then 40s; when acquired 30s. Value now 5s. 89 b

47 LAND OF HUGH OF GOURNAI

Hundred of HINCKFORD

1 Geoffrey Talbot holds LISTON, which a free man held as a manor, for ½ hide and 30 acres. Always 2 ploughs in lordship; 1 men's plough.

Then and later 6 smallholders, now 5; then and later 3 slaves, now none.

Meadow, 30 acres; ½ mill. Then 3 cows with calves, 12 sheep, 7 pigs; now 3 cows with calves, 22 sheep, 8 beehives.

Value always 68s.

Hundred of TENDRING

2 Osbert held ARDLEIGH as a manor, for 2½ hides. Now Agnes holds (it).

Then 16 villagers, later and now 7; then 4 smallholders, now none; then 4 slaves, now none. Always 2 ploughs in lordship. Then among the men 8 ploughs, when acquired 6, now 3.

Woodland, 40 pigs; meadow, 3 acres; now 2 mills. Then 30 sheep, 5 pigs; now 44 sheep, 8 pigs, 7 cattle, 10 goats, 3 beehives.

Value then £6; later and now [£] 4.

Hund de Lassendena . Forham ten& Goisfrid de . Hugone.
qd tenuit Esbern p man . 7 . p . II . hid . Tc . x . uilt . m . VII . tc . v . bor.
m . XI . Tc . v . ser . m . IIII . Sep . III . car . in dnio . Tc . v . car . hom . m . III.
Silu . c . porc . XII . ac . pti . Sep . I . mot . Tc . II . runc . 7 . III . uac . cu
uit . LX . ou . XII . cap . VIII . porc . x . uasa . ap . m . II . runc . VIII . an.
LXXX . ou . XXV . cap . x . porc . VI . uasa ap . 7 . III . libi hoes . tenent
. XIII . ac . Sep . dim . car . Sep . val . VII . lib . 7 . x . ac . abstulit
Rog Pictauensis . de isto manerio . sic hund testat.

90 a

TERRA Willi Piperelli. .XLVIII.

Torindunam ten& Drogo de Willo . qd tenuit . Ailmar lib ho
t . r . e . p man . 7 p . I . hid . 7 . dim . m st . III . hid . 7 . dim . 7 . XXI . ac.
Sep . II . car . in dnio . Tc . II . car . hom . m . III . Tc . I . uilt . m . non.
Tc . IIII . bor . m . XI . Tc . III . ser . m . II . Tc . I . uac . LX . ou . XI . por.
m . v . uac . XV . porc . LX . ou . Tc . IIII . soc . 7 . modo simili tenentes
. II . hid . 7 . dim . 7 . XXI . ac . de ead tra . 7 . inde ablate st . LVI . ac.
Sep ibi e . silua . c . porc . Past . LX . ou . Tc ual . LX . sol . m . c.

Hund de Cesseurda . Turruc . ten& . W . in dnio . qd ten.
Ailmar . t . r . e . p man . 7 . p . III . hid . 7 . XLII . ac . Tc . II . uilt . m . III.
tc . XI . bor . m . XVIII . Sep . II . ser . 7 . II . car . in dnio . tc . IIII . car . hou
. m . v . Past . c . ou . sep . I . pisc . Te . II . uilt . LVIII . ou . I . runc . m.
. v . uac . IIII . uit . LXXXV . ou . VIII . porc . Tc . ual . VI . lib . 7 qn rec.
m . XII . lib . 7 . uncia auri . In hoc manerio jacebant . IX . soc . t . r . e.
tenentes . III . hid . m . st . v . soc . 7 . tenent . I . hid . 7 . dim . 7 . Gislebt
ho epi baiocensis tenet . I . hid . 7 . dim . x . ac . min . 7 . hund nesc
qm . XX . ac . Etiam ten& Anschetill . ho epi . Londoniæ . que
jacebant in hoc manerio . t . r . e . 7 similit nescit hund.

Hundred of LEXDEN

3 Geoffrey holds FORDHAM from Hugh, which Esbern held as a manor, for 2 hides.

Then 10 villagers, now 7; then 5 smallholders, now 11; then 5 slaves, now 4. Always 3 ploughs in lordship. Then 5 men's ploughs, now 3.

Woodland, 100 pigs; meadow, 12 acres; always 1 mill. Then 2 cobs, 3 cows with calves, 60 sheep, 12 goats, 8 pigs, 10 beehives; now 2 cobs, 8 cattle, 80 sheep, 25 goats, 10 pigs, 6 beehives.

3 free men hold 13 acres. Always ½ plough.

Value always £7.

Roger of Poitou took away 10 acres from this manor; so the Hundred testifies.

48 LAND OF WILLIAM PEVEREL 90 a

[Hundred of BARSTABLE]

1 Drogo holds (East) HORNDON from William which Aelmer, a free man, held before 1066 as a manor for 1½ hides. Now there are 3½ hides and 21 acres. Always 2 ploughs in lordship. Then 2 men's ploughs, now 3.

Then 1 villager, now none; then 4 smallholders, now 11; then 3 slaves, now 2.

Then 1 cow, 60 sheep, 11 pigs; now 5 cows, 15 pigs, 60 sheep.

Then 4 Freemen and now the same, who hold 2½ hides and 21 acres of this land. 56 acres have been taken away from it.

There has always been woodland, 100 pigs. Pasture, 60 sheep.

Value then 60s; now 100[s].

Hundred of CHAFFORD

2 William holds (Grays) THURROCK in lordship, which Aelmer held before 1066 as a manor, for 3 hides and 42 acres.

Then 2 villagers, now 3; then 11 smallholders, now 18. Always 2 slaves; 2 ploughs in lordship. Then 4 men's ploughs, now 5.

Pasture, 100 sheep; always 1 fishery. Then 2 villagers, 58 sheep, 1 cob; now 5 cows, 4 calves, 85 sheep, 8 pigs.

Value then and when acquired £6; now £12 and an ounce of gold.

9 Freemen belonged in this manor before 1066, who held 3 hides. Now there are 5 Freemen and they hold 1½ hides. Gilbert, a man of the Bishop of Bayeux, holds 1½ hides less 10 acres; the Hundred does not know how. Also Ansketel, a man of the Bishop of London, holds 20 acres which lay in (the lands of) this manor; likewise the Hundred does not know (how).

Terra Radulfi de Limeseio. Brandunā ten&. Rad̄ in dn̄io. qđ tenuit lib̄ hō. t. r. e. p man. 7. p. II. hid̄. 7. dim. XV. ac. min. Sēp. II. car. in dn̄io. 7. III. car. hom. 7. VII. uill

90 b

7. VII. bor. 7. IIII. ser. Silu. X. porc. XXXII. ac. pti. I. molt. Tc ual. IIII. lib. P 7 m. VI. Huic manerio addidit Harduin t. r. Willi. XX. ac. Sēp. dim. car. m. I. bor. Tc. silu. XX. por. m. VI. Apptiatū ē supi.

In Niuetuna. jacet. I. soc. hn̄s. dim. car. sēp; 7. ual. III. sol

Hund̄ de Angra. Cinghe uuellā ten&. R. in dn̄io qđ tenuit Harold de Rege. E. p man. 7. p. VII. hid̄. Sēp. XIX. uill. 7. II. bor. 7. II. car. in dn̄io. Tc. XVI. car. hom. m. XI. Silu. DCCC. porc. XXXI. ac. pti. sēp. I. mol. Tc ual. VIII. lib̄. m. X. 7. VI. libi. hōes. manser in. II. hid̄. 7. XV. ac. qs m ht. Rob̄ greno. ex dono regis sic ipse. dic. 7 Tc. habebant. III. car. m II. Silu. XL. porc. VIII. ac. pti. Tc. I. mol. m. null. Sēp ual. XL. sol. 7. qdā lib̄ hō ten& 7. tenuit. XXX. ac. quē m ht petr uicecomes. Tc. I. car. m. dim. Silu. XXX. porc. II. ac. pti. ual. V. sol. De ista trā habuit. P. libatorē c suo feudo.

In supdicto manerio de Brumduna rec. R. III. anim. XV. ou. XV. por. I. runc. m. VI. anim. XXIIII. ou. XVIII. porc. I. runc. 7 In Cingheuuella. rec. VI. an. 7. XVII. ou. 7. XI. porc. m. X. an. LX. ou. XX. porc. Rad̄ de Limeseio. ten&. VI. ac. de soca reg. s; antecessor ej inuasit.

49 LAND OF RALPH OF LIMÉSY

[Hundred of HINCKFORD]

1 Ralph holds BRUNDON in lordship, which a free man held before 1066 as a manor, for 2½ hides less 15 acres. Always 2 ploughs in lordship; 3 men's ploughs;

7 villagers; 7 smallholders; 4 slaves. 90 b

Woodland, 10 pigs; meadow, 32 acres; 1 mill.

Value then £4; later and now [£] 6.

To this manor Hardwin added 20 acres after 1066. Always ½ plough.

Now 1 smallholder.

Woodland, then 20 pigs, now 6.

It is assessed above.

2 In *NIUETUNA* lies 1 Freeman who has always had ½ plough.
Value 3s.

Hundred of ONGAR

3 Ralph holds CHIGWELL in lordship, which Harold held from King Edward as a manor, for 7 hides.

Always 19 villagers; 2 smallholders; 2 ploughs in lordship.

Then 16 men's ploughs, now 11.

Woodland, 800 pigs; meadow, 31 acres; always 1 mill.

Value then £8; now [£] 10.

6 free men dwelt on 2 hides and 15 acres, whom Robert Gernon has by the King's gift, so he states.

Then they had 3 ploughs, now 2.

Woodland, 40 pigs; meadow, 8 acres; then 1 mill, now none.

Value always 40s.

A free man, whom Peter the Sheriff now has, holds and held 30 acres. Then 1 plough, now ½.

Woodland, 30 pigs; meadow, 2 acres.

Value 5s.

Peter had delivery of this land with his own Holding.

[Hundred of HINCKFORD]

4 In the above-mentioned manor of BRUNDON Ralph acquired
3 cattle, 15 sheep, 15 pigs, 1 cob; now 6 cattle, 24 sheep, 18 pigs, 1 cob.

[Hundred of ONGAR]

5 In CHIGWELL he acquired
6 cattle, 17 sheep and 11 pigs; now 10 cattle, 60 sheep, 20 pigs.

6 Ralph of Limésy holds 6 acres of the King's jurisdiction, but his predecessor annexed it.

.L. TRRA . Robti de todeneio . Hund de Vdelesfort . Ceseuuic tenuit . I . lib hō . t . r . e . p . m . 7 . p . I . hid . 7 . dim . Sēp . I . car . ī dn̄io. 7 . II . car . hom . Tc . 7 p . IIII . uill . m̄ . III . m̄ . II . bor . Silu . c . porc . IIII . ac . p̄ti . Val . XL . sol.

91 a

TERRA Radulfi de Todeneio . Hund de Herlaua . In Ouesham ten& Rog de . R . dim hid q̄m tenuit Etmar . Sēp . I . car . Silu . XII . porc . Tc . ual . x . sol . m̄ . xv. .LI.

Laghefarā ten& . Rog de . R . qd tenuit Sexi p man . 7 . p . I . hid. tc . IIII . uill . m̄ . III . m̄ . VII . bor . Tc . IIII . ser . m̄ . III . Tc . II . car . in dn̄io m̄ . I . Silu . xxx . porc . XVI . ac . p̄ti . Sēp . XIII . porc . 7 . LX . ou . 7 . IIII . uac. Sēp ual . LXX . sol.

TERRA Walti de doai . Hund de Ceffeurda . Vpmunstre ten& Walt in dn̄io . qd tenuit Suen suart p . man . 7 p . VI . hid . 7 . d 7 . xxx . ac . Sēp . VIII . uill . tc . v . bor . m̄ . VII . Sēp . IIII . ser . 7 . II . car in dn̄io . Tc . v . car . hom . m̄ . IIII . Silu . cc . porc . VIII . ac . p̄ti . Tc . I . pull . m̄ . n̄ . M . LXXXV . ou . 7 . XXV . ou . Tc . ual . VII . lib . m̄ . VIII. 7 . x . ac . jacuer in hoc manerio q̄s ten& . G . de magna uill . in suo escangio ut dicit. .LII.

Reineham ten& . Galt in dn̄io . qd tenuit Lefstan p̄posit . t . r . e. p man . 7 . p . VIII . hid . Tc . III . car . in dn̄io . m̄ . II . tc . VI . car . hom. m̄ . v . Sēp . XII . uill . Tc . II . bor . m̄ . IX . Tc . v . ser . m̄ . IIII . cv . ou. . xx . por . I . runc . Sēp . ual . x . lib . huic manerio addita est . dim. hid . q̄m tenebant . III . libi hōes . t . r . e . ~~7 . p .~~ W . rex uenit Galt ★

50 LAND OF ROBERT OF TOSNY

Hundred of UTTLESFORD

1 1 free man held CHISWICK before 1066 as a manor, for 1½ hides. Always 1 plough in lordship; 2 men's ploughs.

Then and later 4 villagers, now 3; now 2 smallholders.

Woodland, 100 pigs; meadow, 4 acres.

Value 40s.

51 LAND OF RALPH OF TOSNY

91 a

Hundred of HARLOW

1 In HOUSHAM (Hall) Roger holds ½ hide from Ralph, which Edmer held. Always 1 plough.

Woodland, 12 pigs.

Value then 10s; now 15[s].

[Hundred of ONGAR]

2 Roger holds LAVER from Ralph, which Saxi held as a manor, for 1 hide.

Then 4 villagers, now 3; now 7 smallholders; then 4 slaves, now 3. Then 2 ploughs in lordship, now 1.

Woodland, 30 pigs; meadow, 16 acres. Always 13 pigs, 60 sheep and 4 cows.

Value always 70s.

52 LAND OF WALTER OF DOUAI

Hundred of CHAFFORD

1 Walter holds UPMINSTER in lordship, which Swein Swart held as a manor, for 6½ hides and 30 acres.

Always 8 villagers. Then 5 smallholders, now 7. Always 4 slaves; 2 ploughs in lordship. Then 5 men's ploughs, now 4.

Woodland, 200 pigs; meadow, 8 acres. Then 1 foal, now none; now 85 sheep and 25 sheep.

Value then £7; now [£] 8.

10 acres lay in (the lands of) this manor, which G(eoffrey) de Mandeville holds in exchange, as he states.

2 Walter holds RAINHAM in lordship, which Leofstan the reeve held before 1066 as a manor, for 8 hides. Then 3 ploughs in lordship, now 2. Then 6 men's ploughs, now 5.

Always 12 villagers. Then 2 smallholders, now 9; then 5 slaves, now 4.

105 sheep, 20 pigs, 1 cob.

Value always £10.

To this manor has been added ½ hide, which 3 free men held before 1066. [And after] King William came, Walter

eos addidit suo manerio . cui . n̄ adjacebant . t . r . e . ut consulat
testat . 7 . tc̄ . habebant . i . car . m̊ . dim . 7 . qn̄ rec . dim . val . xx . sol.
Hund de Tendringe . Holandā ten Lestan p . vi . hid . 7 . d . Sēp . xvii . uilt . Tc̄ . 7 p . x . bor.
m̊ . xi ;

91 b
Tc̄ . 7 p . v . ser . m̊ . iii . tc̄ . 7 p . iiii . car in dn̄io . m̊ . iii . Tc̄ . 7 p . xi . car hom . m̊ . viii.
Silu . c . porc . xiiii . ac . p̄ti . Sēp ual . xiiii . lib.

.LIII. TERRA Mathei mauritaniensiS . Hund de Dōmauua.

Estanes ten& . M . in dn̄io qd tenuit . Achi lib hō . t . r . e . p . man.
7 p . v . hid . Tc̄ . v . car . in dn̄io . 7 . qn̄ rec . iiii . m̊ . iii . tc̄ . x . car . hom.
m̊ . vii . Tc̄ . xi . uilt . 7 . i . p̄br . m̊ . xv . uilt . 7 . i . p̄br . Tc̄ . x . bor . m̊.
. xvi . Tc̄ . x . ser . m̊ . ix . Silu . cc . porc . tc̄ . m̊ . cl . lxvii . ac . p̄ti . Sēp
. i . mol . 7 . i . runc . 7 . viii . an . . xxx . por . 7 . lx . ou . 7 . x . cap.
7 . iii . uasa ap . Tc̄ . ual . x . lib . 7 . qn̄ rec similit . m̊ ual . xv . lib. ★

Hund de Celmeresfort . Gingā ten& . M . qd tenuit Ansehill.
p . man . 7 . p . v . hid . Sēp . vii . uilt . 7 . viii . bor . 7 . iiii . ser . 7 . ii . car.
in . dn̄io . 7 . iii . car . hom . Silu . ccc . porc . 7 . i . runc . v . anim.
. xx . porc . xxx . ou . Tc̄ . ual . sol . m̊ . vi . lib.

LIIII Terra Comitisse de Albamarla . Hund de Hidingfort.

Barleā . ten& . in dn̄io . qd tenuit Leuuin lib hō . t . r . e . p man.
7 . p . ii . hid . 7 . xxx . ac . Tc̄ . iii . car . in dn̄io . Post 7 . m̊ . ii . Sēp . v.
car . hom . 7 . x . uilt . 7 . v . bor . Silu . xxx . porc . xl . ac . p̄ti.
7 . vii . anim . 7 . xxv . ou . 7 . xxiiii . cap . xxviii . porc . ii . uasa
apu . Tc̄ . 7 p ual . viii . lib . m̊ . xii.

added them to his manor, to which they were not attached before 1066, as the County testifies. Then they had 1 plough, now ½, when acquired ½.
Value 20s.

Hundred of TENDRING

3 Leofstan holds HOLLAND for 6½ hides.
Always 17 villagers. Then and later 10 smallholders, now 11; then and later 5 slaves, now 3. Then and later 4 ploughs in lordship, now 3. Then and later 11 men's ploughs, now 8. 91 b
Woodland, 100 pigs; meadow, 14 acres.
Value always £14.

53 LAND OF MATTHEW OF MORTAGNE

Hundred of DUNMOW

1 Matthew holds (Great) EASTON in lordship which Aki, a free man, held before 1066 as a manor for 5 hides. Then 5 ploughs in lordship, when acquired 4, now 3. Then 10 men's ploughs, now 7.
Then 11 villagers and 1 priest, now 15 villagers and 1 priest; then 10 smallholders, now 16; then 10 slaves, now 9.
Woodland, then 200 pigs, now 150; meadow, 67 acres. Always 1 mill; 1 cob, 8 cattle, 30 pigs, 60 sheep, 10 goats and 3 beehives.
Value then £10; when acquired the same; value now £15.

Hundred of CHELMSFORD

2 Matthew holds MARGARETTING, which Askell held as a manor, for 5 hides.
Always 7 villagers; 8 smallholders; 4 slaves; 2 ploughs in lordship; 3 men's ploughs.
Woodland, 300 pigs. 1 cob, 5 cattle, 20 pigs, 30 sheep.
Value then ... s; now £6.

54 LAND OF THE COUNTESS OF AUMÂLE

Hundred of HINCKFORD

1 She holds BORLEY in lordship which Leofwin, a free man, held before 1066 as a manor for 2 hides and 30 acres. Then 3 ploughs in lordship, later and now 2. Always 5 men's ploughs;
10 villagers; 5 smallholders.
Woodland, 30 pigs; meadow, 40 acres. 7 cattle, 25 sheep, 24 goats, 28 pigs, 2 beehives.
Value then and later £8; now [£] 12.

Hund de Tendringa. Sciddinchov. ten& in dnio qd tenuit Aluric p maner. 7. p. II. hid. Sep. xv. bor. tc. IIII. ser.

92 a

post 7. modo. I. Tc. II. car. in dnio p 7. m. I. Tc. IIII. car. hom. Post. 7. m. II. Silu. XL. porc. VI. ac. pti. Tc. I. mol. 7. I. pisc. m. n. past. XL. ou. Tc. III. uac. III. uit. XL. ou. II. runc. XXX. porc. m. I. runc. III. an. XLVIII. ou. Sep. ual. LX. sol.

TERRA Judith comitissæ. Hund de beuentreu. Wilcumestou tenuit Wallef comes t. r. e. p. man. 7. p. x. hid. 7. dim. Sep. II. car. in dnio. Tc. xv. car. hominu. m. XXII. Tc. xxv. uill m. XXXVI. Tc. I. bor. m. XXV. Sep. IIII. ser. Silu. CCC. porc. LXXX. ac. pti. Past. de. VIII. sol. Sep. I. mol. Tc. VI. piscinæ. m. I. m. VIII. anim. I. runc. XXXV. por. LX. ou. XX. cap. Tc ual. XV. lib. m. XXVIII. lib. 7. II. uncias auri. .LV.

TERRA Frodonis. fris abbis. Redeuuintra ten&. F. in dnio qd tenuit Orgar p man. 7. p. I. hid. 7. I. uirg. Sep. xv. uill. 7. VI. bor. 7. III. 7. III. car. in dnio. 7. VI. car. hom. Silu. c. porc. XXX. ac. pti. Tc. x. anim. LX. ou. L. porc. XXV. cap. I. uas ap. m. XVIII. an CXL. ou. XXXVII. porc. XXX. cap. IIII. uasa ap. Tc ual. VIII. lib. m. XV. De hoc manerio ten& Alger. de Frodone. XXX. ac. 7. ual. x. sol. in eod. ptio. LVI.

92 b

.LVII. TERRA Saffelini. Hund de bdestapla.
Stantmere. 7 Winthelle. qs tenet. S. tenuer. Alric. 7. Vluuin. p man. 7 p. II. hid. 7. XXX. ac. Sep. II. car. in dnio. 7. II. bou hom. Silu. XL. porc. Tc. I. runc. 7. VII. porc. 7. XV. ou. m. I. runc. LXX. ou. XVIII. por. XX. cap. Sep ual. L. sol.

Hundred of TENDRING

2 She holds OLD HALL in lordship, which Aelfric held as a manor, for 2 hides.

Always 15 smallholders. Then 4 slaves, later and now 1. Then 2 ploughs in lordship, later and now 1. Then 4 men's ploughs, later and now 2. 92 a

Woodland, 40 pigs; meadow, 6 acres; then 1 mill and 1 fishery, now none; pasture, 40 sheep. Then 3 cows, 3 calves, 40 sheep, 2 cobs, 30 pigs; now 1 cob, 3 cattle, 48 sheep.

Value always 60s.

55 LAND OF COUNTESS JUDITH

Hundred of BECONTREE

1 Earl Waltheof held WALTHAMSTOW before 1066 as a manor, for 10½ hides. Always 2 ploughs in lordship. Then 15 men's ploughs, now 22.

Then 25 villagers, now 36; then 1 smallholder, now 25; always 4 slaves.

Woodland, 300 pigs; meadow, 80 acres; pasture at 8s; always 1 mill. Then 6 fisheries, now 1. Now 8 cattle, 1 cob, 35 pigs, 60 sheep, 20 goats.

Value then £15; now £28 and 2 ounces of gold.

56 LAND OF FRODO THE ABBOT'S BROTHER

[Half-Hundred of FRESHWELL]

1 Frodo holds RADWINTER in lordship, which Ordgar held as a manor, for 1 hide and 1 virgate.

Always 15 villagers; 6 smallholders; 3 ...; 3 ploughs in lordship; 6 men's ploughs.

Woodland, 100 pigs; meadow, 30 acres. Then 10 cattle, 60 sheep, 50 pigs, 25 goats, 1 beehive; now 18 cattle, 140 sheep, 37 pigs, 30 goats, 4 beehives.

Value then £8; now [£] 15.

Of this manor, Algar holds 30 acres from Frodo.

Value 10s in the same assessment.

57 LAND OF SASSELIN 92 b

Hundred of BARSTABLE

1 Alric and Wulfwin held STANMER and CRAYS HILL, which Sasselin holds as a manor, for 2 hides and 30 acres. Always 2 ploughs in lordship; 2 men's oxen.

Woodland, 40 pigs. Then 1 cob, 7 pigs and 15 sheep; now 1 cob, 70 sheep, 18 pigs, 20 goats.

Value always 50s.

Hund de Witham . In Nutlea ten& . S . dim . hid . 7 . xxii . ac .
qđ tenuit Leuecild . t . r . e . Tc̄ . i . car . m̊ . dim . tc̄ . i . an . m̊ . iiii . 7 . xii .
ou . vi . porc . i . runc . Vał . x . soł .

Hund de Wensistreu Legrā ten& . S . qđ tenueř . ii . libi hoēs
t . r . e . p maner . 7 . p . viii . hid . Tc̄ . iiii . car . in dn̄io . m̊ . ii . Sēp . ii . car .
hom . 7 . i . uilt . 7 . xvii . bor . tc̄ . viii . ser . m̊ . iii . Tc̄ . silu . c . porc . m̊ . lx .
. vii . ac . pti . Tc̄ . xxiiii . anim . cc . ou . xxiii . porc . iii . runc . iiii .
uasa ap . m̊ . vii . an . cxxv . ou . ix . porc . iii . runc . iiii . uasa apū .
Sēp . uał . vii . lib .

Dim Hund de Clauelinga . Pincepo ten& . S . qđ tenuit lib hō
p . man . 7 . p . i . hid . Sēp . i . car . m̊ . iii . bor . 7 . i . ser 7 . iiii . ac . pti . 7
xviii . ou . 7 . xviii . porc . Vał . xx . soł .

Hund de Cessfeurda . In Cikedic ten& . S . i . maner . de . i . hid .
7 . dim . 7 . xxx . ac . qđ tenuit Orgar lib hō . t . r . e . Tc̄ . i . car . in dn̄io
m̊ . i . 7 . dim . Sēp . ii . car . hom . Tc̄ . iii . uilt . m̊ . iiii . Sēp . vi . bor . Tc̄
. ii . ser . m̊ . null . Silu . c . porc . Past . lx . ou . Tc̄ . l . ou . xxiiii . por
. iiii . runc . xii . anim . m̊ . iiii . an . xii . ou . vi . por . i . runc . Tc̄
uał . lx . soł . m̊ . iiii . lib . 7 . i . soc . fuit in hac trā de . xv . ac . qs potāt
uende . s; soca jacebat in Warleia . trā sc̄i pauli . Sēp . dim . car . 7

93 a

uał . iii . soł .
Hund de Vdelesfort . Banhuntā ten& . S . p maner . qđ . ten .
Aluric lib hō . t . r . e . p . man . 7 p . ii . hid . Quando recep . iiii . bor .
7 . m̊ . Sēp . i . car . in dn̄io . m̊ . dim . car . hom . x . ac . pti . Tc̄ . i .
an . 7 . i . porc . m̊ . xxx . ou . ii . an . i . runc . Tc̄ . 7 p uał . xl . soł . m̄ . lv .

Hundred of WITHAM

2 In NOTLEY, Sasselin holds ½ hide and 22 acres, which Leofcild held before 1066. Then 1 plough, now ½.

Then 1 (head of) cattle, now 4; 12 sheep, 6 pigs, 1 cob.

Value 10s.

Hundred of WINSTREE

3 Sasselin holds LAYER, which 2 free men held before 1066 as a manor, for 8 hides. Then 4 ploughs in lordship, now 2. Always 2 men's ploughs;

1 villager; 17 smallholders. Then 8 slaves, now 3.

Woodland, then 100 pigs, now 60; meadow, 7 acres. Then 24 cattle, 200 sheep, 23 pigs, 3 cobs, 4 beehives; now 7 cattle, 125 sheep, 9 pigs, 3 cobs, 4 beehives.

Value always £7.

Half-Hundred of CLAVERING

4 Sasselin holds PINCHPOOLS, which a free man held as a manor, for 1 hide. Always 1 plough.

Now 3 smallholders; 1 slave.

Meadow, 4 acres. 18 sheep and 18 pigs.

Value 20s.

Hundred of CHAFFORD

5 In CHILDERDITCH, Sasselin holds 1 manor of 1½ hides and 30 acres, which Ordgar, a free man, held before 1066. Then 1 plough in lordship, now 1½. Always 2 men's ploughs.

Then 3 villagers, now 4; always 6 smallholders. Then 2 slaves, now none.

Woodland, 100 pigs; pasture, 60 sheep. Then 50 sheep, 24 pigs, 4 cobs, 12 cattle; now 4 cattle, 12 sheep, 6 pigs, 1 cob.

Value then 60s; now £4.

1 Freeman was in this land with 15 acres, which he could sell, but the jurisdiction lay in St. Paul's land of (Little) Warley. Always ½ plough.

Value 3s. 93 a

Hundred of UTTLESFORD

6 Sasselin holds BONHUNT as a manor which Aelfric, a free man, held before 1066 as a manor, for 2 hides.

When acquired and now, 4 smallholders. Always 1 plough in lordship. Now ½ men's plough.

Meadow, 10 acres. Then 1 (head of) cattle and 1 pig; now 30 sheep, 2 cattle, 1 cob.

Value then and later 40s; now 55[s].

TRa Gisleḃti filij Turoldi. Hunđ de Vdelesfort. Wicam tenuit Sexi. t. R. e. liḃ hō. ꝑ. man. 7. ꝑ. III. hiđ. 7. XIII. ac. tc 7. p̄. VIII. uilł. m̄. IX. Tc̄. 7 p̄. VIII. bor. m̄. XI. Sēp. III. ser. 7. II. car. in dn̄io. 7. III. car. hom. Tc̄. 7. p̄. silu. c. por. m̄. LX. x. ac. p̄ti. Sēp ual. VII. liḃ. Tc̄. I. runc. L. ou. XXX. por. XXXVI. cap. m̄. I. runc. XL. ou. XXX. cap. XXVI. porc. II. an. .LVIII.

Terra Willi Leuric. Scilcheham tenuit Ansgot liḃ hō t. r. e. ꝑ man. 7. ꝑ. VIII. hiđ. Sēp. VI. uilł. Tc̄. VIII. bor. m̄. X. Sēp. III. ser. 7. II. car. in dn̄io. 7. III. car. hom. Past. c. ou. Sēp ual. VI. liḃ. .LIX.

Tra Hugonis de sc̄o q̄ntino. Hornindunā tenuit Winge t. r. e. ꝑ man. 7. ꝑ. I. hiđ. 7. dim. sēp. I. car. in dn̄io. Tc̄. III. bor. m̄. IIII. Silu. x. porc. VIII. pars piscinæ. Sēp. I. runc. I. an. XXX. ou. I. porc. ual. XX. sol. De hac tr̄a abstulit Goduin. II. mansiones. .LX.

Hunđ de Wensistreu. Wigheḃgā. tenuit Aluric. liḃ hō

93 b

ꝑ man. 7. ꝑ. II. hiđ. Sēp. I. car. in dn̄io. tc̄. I. bor. m̄. II. tc̄. II. ser. m̄. III. Tc̄. I. mol. m̄. n̄. Sēp. I. runc. 7. VII. an. 7. I. porc. Tc̄. LV. ou. m̄. XLV. Sēp ual. XXX. sol.

Hunđ de Laxendena. Paruā bricceiam. tenuit Wluard t. r. e. ꝑ man. 7. ꝑ. dim. hiđ. 7. XV. ac. m̄ ten& Hugo de dono reginæ. ꝑ tantundē. silu. x. porc. IIII. ac. p̄ti. tc̄. I. bor. 7. I. ser. 7. m̄. simil. Sēp. I. runc. VII. anim. XXV. por. LIII. ou. Tc̄. 7 p̄ ual. XX. sol. m̄. XVI.

58 LAND OF GILBERT SON OF THOROLD

Hundred of UTTLESFORD

1 Saxi, a free man, held WICKEN (Bonhunt) before 1066 as a manor, for 3 hides and 13 acres.

Then and later 8 villagers, now 9; then and later 8 smallholders, now 11. Always 3 slaves; 2 ploughs in lordship; 3 men's ploughs.

Woodland, then and later 100 pigs, now 60; meadow, 10 acres.

Value always £7.

Then 1 cob, 50 sheep, 30 pigs, 36 goats; now 1 cob, 40 sheep, 30 goats, 26 pigs, 2 cattle.

59 LAND OF WILLIAM LEOFRIC

[ ]

1 Ansgot, a free man, held *SCILCHEHAM* before 1066 as a manor, for 7 hides.

Always 6 villagers. Then 8 smallholders, now 10. Always 3 slaves; 2 ploughs in lordship; 3 men's ploughs.

Pasture, 100 sheep.

Value always £6.

60 LAND OF HUGH OF ST. QUENTIN

[Hundred of BARSTABLE]

1 Winge held HORNDON (-on-the-Hill) before 1066 as a manor, for 1½ hides. Always 1 plough in lordship.

Then 3 smallholders, now 4.

Woodland, 10 pigs; the eighth part of a fishery. Always 1 cob, 1 (head of) cattle, 30 sheep, 1 pig.

Value 20s.

From this land Godwin took away 2 places.

Hundred of WINSTREE

2 Aelfric, a free man, held WIGBOROUGH as a manor, for 2 hides. 93 b

Always 1 plough in lordship.

Then 1 smallholder, now 2; then 2 slaves, now 3.

Then 1 mill, now none. Always 1 cob, 7 cattle and 1 pig. Then 55 sheep, now 45.

Value always 30s.

Hundred of LEXDEN

3 Wulfward held LITTLE BIRCH before 1066 as a manor, for ½ hide and 15 acres. Now Hugh holds it by the Queen's gift, for as much.

Woodland, 10 pigs; meadow, 4 acres.

Then 1 smallholder and 1 slave; now the same.

Always 1 cob, 7 cattle, 25 pigs, 53 sheep.

Value then and later 20s; now 16[s].

Hund de bdestapla

.LXI. TERRA Edmundi filij Algoti. Hornindunā. tenuer̄
.II. libi hōes. t. r. e. ꝑ man. 7. ꝑ. II. hid. 7. dim. 7. XV. ac. tc̄.
.III. car. in dn̄io. m̄. II. tc̄. II. car. hom. m̄. I. Sēp. I. uill. tc̄. XIIII.
bor. m̄. XVI. Tc̄. III. ser. m̄. null. Past. L. ou. XII. ac. p̄ti. Tc̄. v.
anim. I. runc. XX. por. C. L. ou. m̄. XXXV. ou. Val. L. sol.
In Ead uill. ē q̄dā diacon habens. XXX. ac. 7. q̄rtā partē eccliæ
7. jac& ad elemosinā regis.
Matcinge ten&. E. qd tenuit Almar Holefest. t. r. e. 7 ꝑ. I.
hid. 7. dim. 7. ꝑ man. Tc̄. II. car. in dn̄io. m̄. I. tc̄. III. car. 7. d.
hom. m̄. III. Tc̄. VII. uill. m̄. IX. m̄. IIII. bor. tc̄. IIII. ser. m̄.
null. Silu. L. porc. VIII. ac. p̄ti. Tc̄. VII. uac. I. porc. C. ou. v. min.
XL. cap. I. runc. VI. uasa ap. m̄. IIII. an. IX. por. XXIIII. ou.

94 a
.II. uasa. apū. Sēp uał. C. sol.
T

TERRA. Rōgi Marescalchi. Hund de bdestapla. .LXII.
Nezendenā. tenuit Aluuard dore. t. r. e. ꝑ man. 7. ꝑ. XL. ac.
m̄ ten&. R. Tc̄. dim. car. m̄. null. Sēp uał. IIII. sol. 7. In Nutlea.
.v. ac. qs tenuit. Cola lib hō. 7. uał. IIII. sol.
Bertunā tenuit Vluuin hapra. ꝑ man. 7. ꝑ. dim. hid. m̄. R.
tc̄. I. car. m̄. dim. I. ac. p̄ti. tc̄. uał. X. sol. m̄. v.
Lohou tenuit Aluuin. ꝑ man. 7. ꝑ. XL. ac. m̄. R. Sēp. dim. car.
silu. III. por. vał. v. sol.

61 LAND OF EDMUND SON OF ALGOT

Hundred of BARSTABLE

1 2 free men held HORNDON (-on-the-Hill) before 1066 as a manor, for 2½ hides and 15 acres. Then 3 ploughs in lordship, now 2. Then 2 men's ploughs, now 1.

Always 1 villager. Then 14 smallholders, now 16; then 3 slaves, now none.

Pasture, 50 sheep; meadow, 12 acres. Then 5 cattle, 1 cob, 20 pigs, 150 sheep; now 35 sheep.

Value 50s.

In the same village is a deacon who has 30 acres and ¼ of a church. He lies in the King's alms.

[Hundred of HARLOW]

2 Edmund holds MATCHING, which Aelmer Holdfast held before 1066 for 1½ hides, as a manor. Then 2 ploughs in lordship, now 1. Then 3½ men's ploughs, now 3.

Then 7 villagers, now 9; now 4 smallholders; then 4 slaves, now none.

Woodland, 50 pigs; meadow, 8 acres. Then 7 cows, 1 pig, 100 sheep less 5, 40 goats, 1 cob, 6 beehives; now 4 cattle, 9 pigs, 24 sheep, 2 beehives. 94 a

Value always 100s.

62 LAND OF ROGER MARSHAL

Hundred of BARSTABLE

1 Alfward Dore held NEVENDON before 1066 as a manor, for 40 acres. Now Roger holds it. Then ½ plough, now none.

Value always 4s.

[Hundred of WITHAM]

2 In NOTLEY, 5 acres which Cola, a free man, held.

Value 4s.

[Hundred of LEXDEN]

3 Wulfwin Hapra held 'BYRTON' as a manor, for ½ hide. Now Roger (holds it). Then 1 plough, now ½.

Meadow, 1 acre.

Value then 10s, now 5[s].

4 Alwin held *LOHOU* as a manor, for 40 acres. Now Roger (holds it). Always ½ plough.

Woodland, 3 pigs.

Value 5s.

Terra Adami Filij durandi malis op̄ib; Hund de Dōmauua. LXIII.
Willinghehalā tenuer̄. v. libi hōes. t. r. e. p̄ maner̄. 7. p̄. dim̄.
hid. tc̄. II. car. m̄. I. m̄. VI. bor. val. x. sol.

Hund de Hidingfort. Horstedafort. tenuit Godric. lib hō
p̄. xv. ac. t. r. e. m̄. ten&. A. Tc̄ 7. p̄. I. car. m̄. dim. Sep̄. v. bor.
Silu. xi. porc. III. ac. p̄ti. Tc̄ ual. x. sol. m̄. XIII.

Tra Goscelmi Loremarij. Hund de beuentreu Ilefort LXIIII.
tenuer̄. II. libi hōes. t. r. e. p̄ man. 7. p̄. III. hid. xxx. ac. min. tc̄
. II. car. in dn̄io. m̄. I. tc̄. II. car. 7. dim. hom. m̄. I. Tc̄. VII. uill. m̄. IIII.

94 b
Tc̄. IIII. bor. m̄. VI. Tc̄. I. ser. m̄. n̄. Silu. xx. porc. xx. ac. p̄ti.
m̄. I. mol. 7. I. pisc. Sep̄. ual. IIII. lib.

.LXV. Tra Johis nepotis Walerami. Hund de Wdelesfort.
Alsenham ten̄ Meruena liba fem. t. r. e. p̄ man. 7. p̄. IIII. hid.
Sep̄. II. car. in dn̄io. Tc̄. 7. p̄. VII. car. hom. m̄. VI. Sep̄. VIII. uill.
Tc̄. 7 p̄. I. bor. m̄. XII. Sep̄. v. ser. Tc̄ silu. ̄M ccc. por. 7. qn̄ rec.
. ̄M c. m̄. ̄M. XII. ac. p̄ti. sep̄. I. mol. 7. ccxx. ou. 7. VIII. uac.
7. LX. porc. 7. I. runc. 7. I. pull. Tc̄. 7 p̄ ual. VI. lib. m̄. VIII.

.LXVI. Tra Willi diaconi. Hund de Wensistreu. Peltendunā.
tenuit Turchill lib hō. t. r. e. p̄ man. 7. p̄. v. hid. Sep̄. II. car. in
dn̄io. 7. II. car. hom. Tc̄. IIII. uilli. m̄. III. tc̄. IX. bor. m̄. x. Tc̄. II. ser. m̄. IIII.

63 LAND OF ADAM SON OF DURAND MALZOR

Hundred of DUNMOW

1 5 free men held WILLINGALE before 1066 as a manor, for ½ hide. Then 2 ploughs, now 1.
Now 6 smallholders.
Value 10s.

Hundred of HINCKFORD

2 Godric, a free man, held STEBBINGFORD (House) for 15 acres before 1066. Now Adam holds it. Then and later 1 plough, now ½.
Always 5 smallholders.
Woodland, 11 pigs; meadow, 3 acres.
Value then 10s; now 13[s].

64 LAND OF JOCELYN LORIMER

Hundred of BECONTREE

1 2 free men held ILFORD before 1066 as a manor, for 3 hides less 30 acres. Then 2 ploughs in lordship, now 1. Then 2½ men's ploughs, now 1.
Then 7 villagers, now 4; then 4 smallholders, now 6; then 1 slave, now none. 94 b
Woodland, 20 pigs; meadow, 20 acres; now 1 mill and 1 fishery.
Value always £4.

65 LAND OF JOHN NEPHEW OF WALERAN

Hundred of UTTLESFORD

1 Merwen, a free woman, held ELSENHAM before 1066 as a manor, for 4 hides. Always 2 ploughs in lordship. Then and later 7 men's ploughs, now 6.
Always 8 villagers. Then and later 1 smallholder, now 12; always 5 slaves.
Woodland, then 1300 pigs, when acquired 1100, now 1000; meadow, 12 acres. Always 1 mill; 220 sheep, 8 cows, 60 pigs, 1 cob and 1 foal.
Value then and later £6; now [£] 8.

66 LAND OF WILLIAM THE DEACON

Hundred of WINSTREE

1 Thorkell, a free man, held PELDON before 1066 as a manor, for 5 hides. Always 2 ploughs in lordship; 2 men's ploughs.
Then 4 villagers, now 3; then 9 smallholders, now 10; then 2 slaves, now 4.

Silū. LX. porc̄. I. fat. 7. I. ecclia. de. XXX. ac̄. Sēp. dim̄. car̄. 7. I. soc̄. de XVII.
ac̄. De his. V. hid. tulit Hamo dapifer. LXXX. ac̄. de arabili tra. 7.
. CC. ac̄. de maresc. qd totū adjacebat huic manerio. t. r. e. 7 post
aduentū regis Willi. sic hund testat. 7 hanc occupationē pcepimus
in manu regis. Tc. supdictū maneriū cū hoc toto 7 qn rec. ual. VI. lib.
7. m̄. ual. C. sol. 7 qd inde ablatū ē ual. XX. sol.

Hund de hidngfort. Scaldefort tenuit Godere lib hō. p man.
7. p dim̄. hid. t. r. e. Tc. 7 p̄. I. car. m̄. I. 7. dim̄. tc. III. ser. m̄. I. bor.

95 a
silū. XII. porc̄. VII. ac̄. p̄ti. Tc ual. XL. sol. m̄. L.

Tra Galti coci. Hund de Hidingfort. Scaldefort tenuit LXVII.
lib hō. t. r. e. p man. 7. p. dim̄. hid. tc. 7 p̄. I. car̄. 7. dim̄. m̄. I. Sēp. I.
uill. 7. III. bor. tc. 7 p̄. II. ser. m̄. I. Silū. VIII. porc̄. XI. ac̄. p̄ti. Tc. II.
runc̄. 7. XII. anim̄. 7. LX. porc̄. 7. LIII. ou. 7. III. cap̄. m̄. X. anim̄. 7
. VIII. porc̄. 7. LIII. ou. 7. XX. cap̄. 7. V. uasa. ap̄. Tc ual. XL. sol. m̄. L.

In Asseuuella. tenuit Felaga. dim̄. hid. p man. m̄. Galt. Tc. III.
bor. m̄. VII. Tc. I. car̄. 7. dim̄. m̄. I. Silū. LX. por. XI. ac̄. p̄ti. tc. I. uac̄. 7.
. XXX. porc̄. 7. V. ou. m̄. IIII. an. 7. VIII. porc̄. 7. LIII. ou. Tc. ual. XL.
sol. m̄. LX.

Hund de bdestapla

TRA Moduini Wicfort tenuit Eduin grut libe. p maner̄ .LXVIII.
7. p. dim̄. hid. Sēp. I. car̄. 7. I. bor. IIII. ac̄. pti. Val. X. sol.

Woodland, 60 pigs; 1 salt-house; 1 church with 30 acres.
Always ½ plough; 1 sokeman with 17 acres.

From these 5 hides, Hamo the Steward took 80 acres of arable land and 200 acres of marsh, which were all attached to this manor before 1066 and after King William's arrival, as the Hundred testifies. We have received this appropriation (to be placed) in the King's hand.
Value of the said manor with all this, then and when acquired, £6.
Value now 100s. Value of what was taken from it, 20s.

Hundred of HINCKFORD

2 Godhere, a free man, held SHALFORD as a manor, for ½ hide before 1066. Then and later 1 plough, now 1½.
Then 3 slaves; now 1 smallholder.
Woodland, 12 pigs; meadow, 7 acres. 95 a
Value then 40s; now 50[s].

67 LAND OF WALTER COOK

Hundred of HINCKFORD

1 A free man held SHALFORD before 1066 as a manor, for ½ hide. Then and later 1½ ploughs, now 1.
Always 1 villager; 3 smallholders. Then and later 2 slaves, now 1.
Woodland, 8 pigs; meadow, 11 acres. Then 2 cobs, 12 cattle, 60 pigs, 53 sheep and 3 goats; now 10 cattle, 8 pigs, 53 sheep, 20 goats and 5 beehives.
Value then 40s; now 50[s].

2 In ASHWELL (Hall) Fellow held ½ hide as a manor. Now Walter (holds it).
Then 3 smallholders, now 7. Then 1½ ploughs, now 1.
Woodland, 60 pigs; meadow, 11 acres. Then 1 cow, 30 pigs and 5 sheep; now 4 cattle, 8 pigs and 53 sheep.
Value then 40s; now 60[s].

68 LAND OF MODWIN

Hundred of BARSTABLE

1 Edwin Groat held WICKFORD freely as a manor, for ½ hide. Always 1 plough;
1 smallholder.
Meadow, 4 acres.
Value 10s.

Hund de Witham. In Witham. ten&. M. I. hid. qm tenuit Harold. Sep. I. car. Tc. I. bor. m. II. Silu. XII. porc. tc. VIII. ac. pti. m. IIII. 7 alias tulit. Goisfrid baignard. Tc. IIII. por. m. VII. Tc. XX. ou. m. XL. Tc. IIII. an. m. X. m. II. runc. val. XX. sol.

Hund de Witbrictesherna. Cricchesciam tenuit Aluuard t. r. e. p. man. 7. p. I. hid. Tc. II. bor. m. I. Sep. I. car. past. XL. ou. m LXXXV. ou. Sep ual. XXX. sol.

Hund de Wensistreu. Legrā tenuit lib hō. t. r. e. p. man.

95 b

7. p. II. hid. Sep. II. car. in dnio. tc. V. bor. m. IIII. Sep. II. ser. Silu. XX. porc. Tc. XXXII. ou. m. C. Tc. I. uac. cū uit. m. X. anim. m XL. cap. 7. II. runc. Tc. VII. por. m. X. Sep ual. LX. sol.

Hund de Lassendena Crepinges. tenuit Aluuard p. I. uirg trae. m ten&. moduin. Tc. I. car. m. dim. II. ac. pti. Silu. XL. porc. val. X. sol. hoc tenuit. I. lib hō.

In Dunilanda tenuit Laghemann. I. uirg. m ten& Moduin. Sep. I. bor. tc. 7 p. dim. car. m null. Tc ual. X. sol. m. VI.

Hund de Tendringa. Tendringā tenuit Aluric p. XV. ac. m. Mod. p. man. 7 p tant. Tc. II. ser. m. I. Sep. I. car. val. XX. sol Sep. I. runc. m. IIII. por. 7. IIII. cap. 7. X. ou. 7. VI. an. hoc ē in dnio.

Dereleiam tenuit Goduin pbr. p. man. 7 p. I. hid. 7. V. ac. M ten& M. Tc. I. car. m. null. Tc ual. X. sol. m. XXX. d.

Hundred of WITHAM

2 In WITHAM Modwin holds 1 hide, which Harold held. Always 1 plough.

Then 1 smallholder, now 2.

Woodland, 12 pigs. Meadow, then 8 acres, now 4; Geoffrey Baynard took the others. Then 4 pigs, now 7; then 20 sheep, now 40; then 4 cattle, now 10; now 2 cobs.

Value 20s.

Hundred of 'WIBERTSHERNE'

3 Alfward held CREEKSEA before 1066 as a manor, for 1 hide.

Then 2 smallholders, now 1.

Always 1 plough. Pasture, 40 sheep. Now 85 sheep.

Value always 30s.

Hundred of WINSTREE

4 A free man held LAYER before 1066 as a manor, for 2 hides. 95 b

Always 2 ploughs in lordship.

Then 5 smallholders, now 4; always 2 slaves.

Woodland, 20 pigs. Then 32 sheep, now 100; then 1 cow with a calf, now 10 cattle; now 40 goats and 2 cobs; then 7 pigs, now 10.

Value always 60s.

Hundred of LEXDEN

5 Alfward held CREPPING for 1 virgate of land. Now Modwin holds it.

Then 1 plough, now ½.

Meadow, 2 acres; woodland, 40 pigs.

Value 10s.

1 free man held this.

6 In (East) DONYLAND Lawman held 1 virgate. Now Modwin holds it.

Always 1 smallholder. Then and later ½ plough, now none.

Value then 10s; now 6[s].

Hundred of TENDRING

7 Aelfric held TENDRING for 15 acres. Now Modwin (holds it) as a manor, for as much.

Then 2 slaves, now 1. Always 1 plough.

Value 20s.

Always 1 cob. Now 4 pigs, 4 goats, 10 sheep and 6 cattle.

This is in lordship.

8 Godwin the priest held 'DERLEIGH' as a manor, for 1 hide and 5 acres. Now Modwin holds it. Then 1 plough, now none.

Value then 10s; now 30d.

Hund de bdestapla

.LXIX. TRRA Ilbodonis. Wicfort tenuer. II. libi hões. t. r. e. p. XL. ac. &. m̊ ten& Ilbodo simil. Sep. dim. car. 7. II. libi hões. val. XL. đ.

Hund de Hidingfort. Listunā ten& Ilbodo. qđ tenuit lib hõ t. r. e. p. man. 7. p. dim. hid. 7. I. uirg. Sep. II. car. in dnio. 7. I. car. hom. 7. V. bor. 7. IIII. ser. 7. XXX. ac. pti. 7. dim. mol. Sep. V. an. 7. I. runc. 7. XLIII. ou. 7. XV. porc. 7 Val. LX. sol. 7 VII. libos hões ten& Ilbodo. tenentes. dim. hid. t. r. e. Tc. 7 qn rec. II. car. m̊. dim. 7. IIII. bor. Tc uat. XX. sol. m̊. XV. sol. 7. VI. đ.

96 a

Dunilandam tenuer. IIII. libi hões. p. I. hid. 7. dim. 7. VIII. ac. m̊ ten&. I. tc. II. car. int eos. m̊. I. car. m̊. III. bor. II. ac. pti. tc. uat. x. sol. m̊. VII.

Tra Hghebni Hund de bdestapla. Nezendenā tenuit Toui. lib hõ. t. r. e. p. LIIII. ac. Tc. I. car. m̊. null. Tc uat. x. sol. m̊. III. sol. 7. IIII. đ. .LXX.

Dunilandā tenuit Moduin. p dim. hid. 7. XII. ac. m̊ ten& haghebt p tant. Sep. II. bor. Tc. I. car. m̊ null. Tc uat. XIIII. sol. m̊. X. Raineham tenuit. I. pbr libe p. dim. hid. m̊. ten&. hag. tc. dim. car. m̊. n̄. Vat. x. sol.

69 LAND OF ILBOD

Hundred of BARSTABLE

1 2 free men held WICKFORD before 1066, for 40 acres. Now Ilbod holds it for the same. Always ½ plough;

2 free men.

Value 40d.

Hundred of HINCKFORD

2 Ilbod holds LISTON, which a free man held before 1066 as a manor, for ½ hide and 1 virgate. Always 2 ploughs in lordship; 1 men's plough;

5 smallholders; 4 slaves.

Meadow, 30 acres; ½ mill. Always 5 cattle, 1 cob, 43 sheep and 15 pigs.

Value 60s.

Ilbod holds 7 free men who held ½ hide before 1066. Then and when acquired, 2 ploughs, now ½.

4 smallholders.

Value then 20s; now 15s 6d.

[Hundred of LEXDEN] 96 a

3 4 free men held (East) DONYLAND for 1½ hides and 8 acres. Now Ilbod holds it. Then 2 ploughs among them, now 1 plough.

Now 3 smallholders.

Meadow, 2 acres.

Value then 10s; now 7[s].

70 LAND OF HAGEBERN

Hundred of BARSTABLE

1 Tovi, a free man, held NEVENDON before 1066, for 54 acres. Then 1 plough, now none.

Value then 10s; now 3s 4d.

[Hundred of LEXDEN]

2 Modwin held (East) DONYLAND for ½ hide and 12 acres. Now Hagebert holds it for as much.

Always 2 smallholders. Then 1 plough, now none.

Value then 14s; now 10[s].

[Hundred of CHAFFORD]

3 1 priest held RAINHAM freely, for ½ hide. Now Hagebern holds it. Then ½ plough, now none.

Value 10s.

TRa Tedrici pointel. Tilibiam ten& Hunald de. Tedrico.
qd tenuit lib ho. t. r. e. p man. 7. XLV. ac. Sep. dim. car. 7. I. bor.
. 7. IIII. ac. p̃ti. Past. L. ou. Tc uat. VII. sol. m. VIII.

Hund de Witbrictesherna. Fanbruge tenuit Godric
lib ho. t. r. e. p. man. 7 p. VIII. hid. m. T. in dnio. Tc. XII. uill
m. II. m. X. bor. tc. X. ser. m. V. Sep. II. car. in dnio. tc. IIII. car.
hom. m. II. Silu. CC. porc. hic fuer. II. libi. hoes hntes. L. ac.
pt supdictas hid. Tc. II. runc. X. anim. X. porc. CL. ou. m
. II. runc. V. asini. VIII. anim. XX. por. CC. ou. Sep uat. VII. lib.

Tedric. ten&. I. hid. 7. dim. p escangio de Coghesbala qd tenuit
Tiselin. Tc. II. car. m nult. Tc. III. bor. m nult. Silu. III. por.
XII. ac. p̃ti. Tc uat. XX. sol. m. X.

96 b

Hund de. Rochefort. Suttunam ten&. T. in dnio. qd tenuit
lib ho. t. r. e. p man. 7. p. II. hid. 7. XXX. ac. Sep. II. car. in dnio. 7.
. VI. ser. Tc. I. bor. m. IX. Silu. L. porc. Past. C. ou. IIII. ac. p̃ti. huic
manerio jacebant. III. libi hoes. un tenebat. d. hid. 7 potat abire
sine licentia dni ipsi mansionis. 7. ali tenebat. XXX. ac. qs ten&.
Grimbold | 7 uat. x. sol. de. T. 7 tci. XXX. ac. qs ten& hunold. | 7 uat. x. sol. 7 potant abire
In dnio. rec. T. II. runc. 7. VII. an. VI. por. C. ou. VI. uasa apu.
m. II. runc. VII. an. XXI. porc. CVI. ou. Tc int totu uat. IIII.
lib. m. VII. De hoc manerio ten&. Rob. de. T. dim. hid. 7.
. II. bor. 7. II. car. 7 uat. X. sol. in eod p̃tio. 7 huic manerio ad
jacebat. I. soc. q n potat recede;

71 LAND OF THEODORIC POINTEL

1 Hunald holds TILBURY from Theodoric, which a free man held before 1066 as a manor, for 45 acres. Always ½ plough;
1 smallholder.
Meadow, 4 acres; pasture, 50 sheep.
Value then 7s; now 8[s].

Hundred of 'WIBERTSHERNE'

2 Godric, a free man, held (North) FAMBRIDGE before 1066 as a manor, for 8 hides. Now Theodoric (holds it) in lordship.
Then 12 villagers, now 2; now 10 smallholders; then 10 slaves, now 5. Always 2 ploughs in lordship. Then 4 men's ploughs, now 2.
Woodland, 200 pigs.
2 free men were here, who had 50 acres separate from the above-mentioned hides.
Then 2 cobs, 10 cattle, 10 pigs, 150 sheep; now 2 cobs, 5 asses, 8 cattle, 20 pigs, 200 sheep.
Value always £7.

3 Theodoric holds 1½ hides, by exchange for Coggeshall, which Tesselin held. Then 2 ploughs, now none.
Then 3 smallholders, now none.
Woodland, 3 pigs; meadow, 12 acres.
Value then 20s; now 10[s].

Hundred of ROCHFORD 96 b

4 Theodoric holds SUTTON in lordship, which a free man held before 1066 as a manor, for 2 hides and 30 acres. Always 2 ploughs in lordship;
6 slaves.
Then 1 smallholder, now 9.
Woodland, 50 pigs; pasture, 100 sheep; meadow, 4 acres.
To this manor belonged 3 free men. One held ½ hide; he could go away without the permission of the lord of this place. The second held 30 acres which Grimbald holds from Theodoric, value 10s; the third (held) 30 acres which Hunold holds, value 10s; they could go away.
In lordship Theodoric acquired 2 cobs, 7 cattle, 6 pigs, 100 sheep, 6 beehives; now 2 cobs, 7 cattle, 21 pigs, 106 sheep.
Value then in total £4; now [£] 7.
Of this manor, Robert holds ½ hide from Theodoric.
2 smallholders; 2 ploughs.
Value 10s in the same assessment.
To this manor was attached 1 Freeman, who could not withdraw.

.LXXII. TRA. Rogeri. dš salu& dñas. Hund de Witham Ruenhale
tenuit Vlsi lib hō ꝓ. man. 7. ꝓ. xxx. ac. t. r. e. sep. i. car. val. xx. sol.
Hund de hidingfort. Felstede. tenuit. vlsi sub comite. Algaro.
ꝓ. man. 7. ꝓ dim hid. 7. xxx. ac. Sep. ii. car. in dnio. 7. iii. ser.
silu. xx. porc. x. ac. pti. Tc. ual. xxx. sol. m. xl.
Baduuen. tenuit Vlsi lib hō ꝓ. man. 7. ꝓ. i. hid. 7. dim. Tc. i. bor
p 7. m. iii. Sep. iiii. ser. 7. ii. car. in dnio. Silu. xl. porc. viii. ac. pti.
Sep. ual. xl. sol.

.LXXIII. Tra Gislebti filij. salomonis. Hund de. Hidingfort. In

97 a
Felesteda tenuit lib hō. xxx. ac. quas ten&. G. sep. i. car. val. xx. sol.

TRA Willi filij constantini. Taindenā tenuit. Suen. ꝓ. man. ★ .LXXIIII.
7. ꝓ. ii. hid. t. r. e. 7. xl. ac. m ten&. W. simil. Tc. v. uill. p 7. m. iiii.
tc. 7. p. vii. bor. m. x. tc. iiii. ser. m null. Sep. ii. car. in dnio. tc. int
hoēs. iiii. car. P 7. m. iii. Silu. ꝺ. porc. xx. ac. pti. sep. i. mol. Tc. 7 p
ual. lx. sol. m. c.

Tra Ansgeri coci. Aluielea tenuit Godeman libæ ꝓ. l. ac. Sep .LXXV.
dim. car. 7 In Stifort tenuit lib hō. xxv. ac. 7. int istā trā 7. supdictā
ē sep. dim. car. 7. ual. x. sol.

72 LAND OF ROGER GOD-SAVE-LADIES

Hundred of WITHAM

1 Wulfsi, a free man, held RIVENHALL as a manor, for 30 acres before 1066. Always 1 plough.
Value 20s.

Hundred of HINCKFORD

2 Wulfsi held FELSTED under Earl Algar as a manor, for ½ hide and 30 acres. Always 2 ploughs in lordship;
3 slaves.
Woodland, 20 pigs; meadow, 10 acres.
Value then 30s; now 40[s].

[Hundred of CHELMSFORD]

3 Wulfsi, a free man, held (Great) BADDOW as a manor, for 1½ hides.
Then 1 smallholder, later and now 3. Always 4 slaves; 2 ploughs in lordship.
Woodland, 40 pigs; meadow, 8 acres.
Value always 40s.

73 LAND OF GILBERT SON OF SOLOMON

Hundred of HINCKFORD

1 In FELSTED a free man held 30 acres, which Gilbert holds. 97 a
Always 1 plough.
Value 20s.

74 LAND OF WILLIAM SON OF CONSTANTINE

[Hundred of ONGAR]

1 Swein held THEYDON as a manor, for 2 hides and 40 acres before 1066. Now William holds it for the same.
Then 5 villagers, later and now 4; then and later 7 smallholders, now 10; then 4 slaves, now none. Always 2 ploughs in lordship. Then among the men 4 ploughs, later and now 3.
Woodland, 500 pigs; meadow, 20 acres; always 1 mill.
Value then and later 60s; now 100[s].

75 LAND OF ANSGER COOK

[Hundred of CHAFFORD]

1 Godman held AVELEY freely, for 50 acres. Always ½ plough.

2 In STIFFORD a free man held 25 acres. There has always been ½ plough between this land and the above-mentioned (land).
Value 10s.

/ Tra Robti filij Roscelini. Hund de Vdelesfort. Haidenam. .LXXVI.
tenuit Aluuin lib homo. t. r. e. p man. 7. p. v. hid. 7. xv. ac.
sep. xviii. uill. Tc. iii. bor. Post 7. m. vii. sep. v. ser. 7. iii. car. in
dnio. 7. viii. car. hom. 7. viii. ac. pti. Silu. viii. porc. ii. runc.
. cc. vi. ou. xl. porc. xiii. uasa ap. m. i. runc. ccvi. ou. xx. por.
. x. uasa ap. Tc 7 p uat. x. lib. m. xii. 7 qda anglic Goduin ten&
sep. xii. ac. sep. i. bor. 7. Leuuin similit. v. ac. 7. uat. xii. d.

/ TRA Radulfi Pinel. Hund de Tendringa. Brubeleiam. LXXVII.
7 Westnanetuna. tenuit. Brictmar. p man. 7. p. iiii. hid. 7. d.
7 fuer. ibi. ii. hallæ. m ten&. R. Sep. v. uill tc. 7. p. xxv. bor

97 b
m. xxiii. Tc. vi. ser. m. ix. Tc. iii. car. in dnio. m. ii. Tc. 7 p.
. x. car. hom. m. vi. Silu. dc. porc. xvi. ac. pti Sep uat. vii. lib.
hanc tra deseruiuit. R. erga. G. de magnauilla p hoc qd ipse
. G. dixit ei. qtin rex sibi dederat seRuitiu illi træ. s; p duas uices ★
dedit de suo censu ministris regis. qn rex misit legatos suos in hanc
tra.

.LXXVIII. / Tra Robti filij Gobti. Belestedam tenuer. iii. libi hoes p. man.
7. p. i. hid. 7. d. 7. xl. ac. Sep. iii. bor. 7. i. ser. 7. ii. car. in dnio. Silu.
. x. porc. xv. ac. pti. Tc. uat. xxx. sol. m. l.

. LXXIX. / Tra Rainaldi balistarij. Phenbruge ten&. R. de rege.
p. man. 7. p. iii. hid. 7. dim. sep. i. uill. 7. vii. bor. 7. ii. car. in dnio.

76 LAND OF ROBERT SON OF ROZELIN

Hundred of UTTLESFORD

1 Alwin, a free man, held HEYDON before 1066 as a manor, for 5 hides and 15 acres.

Always 18 villagers. Then 3 smallholders, later and now 7. Always 5 slaves; 3 ploughs in lordship; 8 men's ploughs.

Meadow, 8 acres; woodland, 8 pigs. [Then] 2 cobs, 206 sheep, 40 pigs, 13 beehives; now 1 cob, 206 sheep, 20 pigs, 10 beehives.

Value then and later £10; now [£] 12.

Godwin, an Englishman, has always held 12 acres.

Always 1 smallholder.

Leofwin likewise has always held 5 acres.

Value 12d.

77 LAND OF RALPH PINEL

Hundred of TENDRING

1 Brictmer held (Great) BROMLEY and *WESTNANETUNA* as a manor, for 4½ hides. There were 2 halls there. Now Ralph holds (them).

Always 5 villagers. Then and later 25 smallholders, now 23; 97 b
then 6 slaves, now 9. Then 3 ploughs in lordship, now 2. Then and later 10 men's ploughs, now 6.

Woodland, 600 pigs; meadow, 16 acres.

Value always £7.

Ralph gave service for this land to G(eoffrey) de Mandeville, because the same G(eoffrey) stated to him how the King had given him the service of that land; but on two occasions he gave of his dues to the King's officers when the King sent his Commissioners into this land.

78 LAND OF ROBERT SON OF GOBERT

[Hundred of CHELMSFORD]

1 3 free men held BELSTEAD (Hall) as a manor, for 1½ hides and 40 acres.

Always 3 smallholders; 1 slave; 2 ploughs in lordship.

Woodland, 10 pigs; meadow, 15 acres.

Value then 30s; now 50[s].

79 LAND OF REGINALD GUNNER

[Hundred of ROCHFORD]

1 Reginald holds (South) FAMBRIDGE from the King as a manor, for 3½ hides.

Always 1 villager; 7 smallholders; 2 ploughs in lordship;

7 . II . car . hom . Past . c . ou . Sēp uat . c . sot . sed monachi de eli calumpniāt & hundret eis testat . & dimidiā hidā saisiuit juxta illam trā p aduentū regis Witti que p annum uat . xxx . sot.

.LXXX. Terra Gonduini Hund de Turestapla . Toleshuntam tenuit Alric . p man . 7 p . I . hid . m ten& . G . Sēp . II . bor . tc . IIII . ser . m . v . Tc . I . car . m . dim . tc uat . xxx . sot . 7 . qn recepit ualebat xx . sot . m uat . x . sot

LXXXI TERRA Ottonis aurifabri . Hund de hidingfort.

98 a

Glestingethorp . tenuit Comes Algar p dim . hid . m ten& Otto . simil . Sēp . III . car . in dnio . 7 . III . car hom . Tc . XIII . bor . m . XVI . Sēp . VI . ser . Silu . LX . porc . XXV . ac . pti . LXXX . ou . XXXII . anim . LXXXVIII . por . 7 . III . runc . 7 . XII . soc fuer . t . r . e . m . st . XI . manentes in hoc man . 7 . tenent . dim . hid . 7 . XXX . ac . Sēp . IIII . bor . 7 . I . car . 7 . I . ser . Tc . uat . . x . lib . m . XII . 7 . qn . R . dedit . xv.

Tra Gisiebti pbri . Hund de Hidincfort . Mildeltunā tenuer . .IX . soc . comitis Algari . p . I . hid . 7 . dim . 7 . XXVIII . ac . Sēp . I . car . 7 . d . in dnio . IIII . ac . 7 . dim . pti . vat . xx . sot . hanc trā reclamat ex dono reginæ. .LXXXII.

Hund de bdestapla

Tra Grimi Pposit . In bura ht . Grim . II . hid . In qbz erat . I . car . .LXXXIII.
7 . II . serui . t . r . e . m ū st . II . car . in dnio . 7 . dim . car . hom . III . uitt .
. VI . bor . III . ser . Pastura . c . ou . [7 d . hid . 7 . x . ac uastatæ siluæ.] 7 de istis . II . hid ē una de hominibz forisfactis.

2 men's ploughs.
Pasture, 100 sheep.
Value always 100s, but the monks of Ely lay claim to it and the Hundred testifies for them. He took possession of ½ hide next to that land after King William's arrival, which (land's) value is 30s a year.

80 LAND OF GUNDWIN

Hundred of THURSTABLE

1 Alric held TOLLESHUNT as a manor, for 1 hide. Now Gundwin holds it.
Always 2 smallholders. Then 4 slaves, now 5. Then 1 plough, now ½.
Value then 30s. Value when acquired 20s. Value now 10s.

81 LAND OF OTTO THE GOLDSMITH

Hundred of HINCKFORD

1 Earl Algar held GESTINGTHORPE for ½ hide. Now Otto holds it for the same. Always 3 ploughs in lordship; 3 men's ploughs. 98 a
Then 13 smallholders, now 16; always 6 slaves.
Woodland, 60 pigs; meadow, 25 acres. 80 sheep, 32 cattle, 88 pigs and 3 cobs.
12 Freemen were there before 1066; now there are 11 dwelling in this manor. They hold ½ hide and 30 acres.
Always 4 smallholders; 1 plough; 1 slave.
Value then £10; now [£] 12; when the King gave it [£] 15.

82 LAND OF GILBERT THE PRIEST

Hundred of HINCKFORD

1 9 Freemen of Earl Algar held MIDDLETON for 1½ hides and 28 acres. Always 1½ ploughs in lordship.
Meadow, 4½ acres.
Value 20s.
He claims this land by the Queen's gift.

83 LAND OF GRIM THE REEVE

Hundred of BARSTABLE

1 In BOWERS (Gifford) Grim has 2 hides in which there were 1 plough and 2 slaves before 1066, but now there are 2 ploughs in lordship and ½ men's plough.
3 villagers; 6 smallholders; 3 slaves.
Pasture, 100 sheep; woodland, ½ hide and 10 acres, laid waste.
One of these 2 hides is from men who committed offences

erga regē . quā post aduentū . reg addidit . G . ad suā aliā trā . p . R.
filiū Wimarc . uicecomitē . sic ipse . G . dicit . 7 hoc totū ual . t . r . e.
xl . sol . m̄ . l. In Celdeuuella tenuit Godman lib hō . xx . ac . 7 . foris
fact : non potuit emdare . Dedit aut . Grim regi p . eo : xxx . sol.
7 . p licentiā hubti de portu ten& trā . 7 ual . xx . đ.

Tra Vlueue uxoris Phin . Hund de bdestapla In Pice
seia erant . t . r . e . iii . hid . qs ten& Vlueua . Tc . ii . car . in dnio . 7 .LXXXIIII.

98 b
7 . i . uilt de dim . car . 7 . iiii . ser . 7 . i . mol . Past . lx . ou . Dim . hid siluæ . m.
. ii . car . in dnio . iii . bor . v . ser . Val . lx . sol . M his hid . addite st aliæ . iii.
hid . 7 . xxx . ac . siluæ . in qbz manent . viii . libi hōes . c . ii . car . Past . cxxx . ou.
Int totū ual . lx . sol . 7 . istæ . iii . hid . remanent regi.
Hund de Wibrictesherna . Lacendunā tenuit . Phin . lib hō . t . r . e.
p . man . 7 . p . v . hid . 7 . xv . ac . m ten& . v . Tc . vi . uilt . m . iii . bor.
Tc . iiii . ser . m . v . Sēp . iii . car . in dnio . vii . runc . xiii . an . xxxi . porc.
. ccxlv . ou . Sēp ual . iiii . lib.

.LXXXV. In Hund de Ceffeurda . tenuit Eduuard fili Suani . dim . hid.
m ten& Edeua uxor ej . Tc . i . car . m . dim . Past . xxx . ou . ual . x . sol.

.LXXXVI. Tra Turchilli pposti Hund de Celmeresfort In Walfarā
ten& . T . i . hid . x . ac . min . Sēp . iii . bor . 7 . i . ser . 7 . i . car . in dnio . tc

against the King, which after the King's arrival Grim added to his other land through Robert son of Wymarc, the Sheriff, so Grim himself states.
Value of all this before 1066, 40s; now 50[s].

2 In CHADWELL Godman, a free man, held 20 acres. He committed an offence and could not pay compensation. But Grim gave 30s to the King on his behalf and holds the land by permission of Hubert of Port.
Value 20d.

84 LAND OF WULFEVA WIFE OF FINN

Hundred of BARSTABLE

1 In PITSEA there were 3 hides before 1066, which Wulfeva holds.
Then 2 ploughs in lordship; 1 villager with ½ plough; 4 slaves. 98 b
1 mill; pasture, 60 sheep; woodland, ½ hide.
Now 2 ploughs in lordship. 3 smallholders; 5 slaves.
Value 60s.
Now there have been added to these hides 3 other hides and 30 acres of woodland in which dwell 8 free men with 2 ploughs.
Pasture, 130 sheep.
In total value 60s. These 3 hides still belong to the King.

Hundred of 'WIBERTSHERNE'

2 Finn, a free man, held LATCHINGDON before 1066 as a manor, for 5 hides and 15 acres. Now Wulfeva holds it.
Then 6 villagers; now 3 smallholders; then 4 slaves, now 5.
Always 3 ploughs in lordship.
7 cobs, 13 cattle, 31 pigs, 245 sheep.
Value always £4.

85 [LAND OF EDWARD SON OF SWEIN]

In the Hundred of CHAFFORD

1 Edward son of Swein held ½ hide. Now Edeva his wife holds it.
Then 1 plough, now ½.
Pasture, 30 sheep.
Value 10s.

86 LAND OF THORKELL THE REEVE

Hundred of CHELMSFORD

1 In WALTER (Hall) Thorkell holds 1 hide less 10 acres.
Always 3 smallholders; 1 slave; 1 plough in lordship. Then

int̃ hões . dim̃ . car̃ . Silu̇ . xl . porc̃ . vi . ac̃ . p̃ti . Tc̃ ual . xx . sol . m̃ . xxx.

7 q̃dã famul9 regis ten& . viii . ac̃ . 7 . ual . ii . sol.

.LXXXVII. 7 q̃dã lib hõ noẽ Stanard9 tenuit 7 . ten& de rege . xxx . ac̃ . 7
ptinent ad Witheresfelda . Sẽp . iii . bor . Tc̃ . i . car̃ . m̃ . dim̃ . Silu̇.
. viii . porc̃ . vii . ac̃ . p̃ti . sẽp . i . mol . val . viii . sol.

.LXXXVIII. 7 Goduin9 diacon9 tenuit 7 . ten& . ix . ac̃ . 7 . ual . xvi . đ.
7 . i . hõ Willi . filij grossæ ten& . ii . ac̃ . de soca regis . 7 reddit con
suetudinẽ reg̃.

99 a

Libi homines regis. In Hundret de Laxendena hẽ rex . vii . libos homines . 7 hos p̃po .LXXXIX.
sit9 hund hab& . tenentes dim̃ hid . 7 ual . viii . sol . 7 . i . lib homo tenuit . iii . ac̃ . 7 . đ.
7 in his ẽ pasta . c . ouib; 7 . tr̃a . ad . ii . boues . Tc̃ ual . x . sol . 7 q̃ndo . Rob de monte
begonis inuasit: ualebat . x . sol . m̃ nichil.
7 . i . lib hõ tenuit . xiii . ac̃ . ibi ẽ sẽp . i . car̃ . 7 silu̇ . xx . porc̃ . 7 . i . ac̃ . p̃ti . Tc̃ ual . x . sol . m̃ reddit
. xx . sol . 7 Ricard9 hõ hamonis inuasit istã tr̃am . 7 hẽ hucusq; ej9 spolia

INVASIONES SVp regẽ in Exsessa . In Hornínduna inuasit Goduin9 .XC.
gudhen . ii . mansiones . quæ st̃ de tr̃a quã hug de sc̃o quintino de rege tenet.
7 inde dedit uadem

among the men ½ plough.
Woodland, 40 pigs; meadow, 6 acres.
Value then 20s; now 30[s].

2 A servant of the King holds 8 acres, value 2s.

87 [LAND OF STANHARD]

[Hundred of HINCKFORD]

1 A free man, Stanhard by name, held and holds from the King 30 acres. They belong to Wethersfield.
Always 3 smallholders. Then 1 plough, now ½.
Woodland, 8 pigs; meadow, 7 acres; always 1 mill.
Value 8s.

88 [LAND OF GODWIN THE DEACON]

1 Godwin the deacon held and holds 9 acres.
Value 16d.

2 1 man of William son of Gross holds 2 acres of the King's jurisdiction and pays the King's customary due.

89 [LAND OF] THE KING'S FREE MEN 99 a

In the Hundred of LEXDEN

1 The King has 7 free men. The Hundred-reeve has these, who hold ½ hide.
Value 8s.

2 1 free man held 3½ acres. In these there is pasture for 100 sheep; land for 2 oxen.
Value then 10s. Value when Robert of Montbegon annexed it, 10s; now nothing.

3 1 free man held 13 acres. Always 1 plough there.
Woodland, 20 pigs; meadow, 1 acre.
Value then 10s; now it pays 20s.
Richard, a man of Hamo, annexed that land. He still has the booty from it.

90 ANNEXATIONS IN THE KING'S DESPITE IN ESSEX [GODWIN WOODHEN'S ANNEXATIONS]

[Hundred of BARSTABLE]

1 In HORNDON (-on-the-Hill) Godwin Woodhen annexed 2 places which belong to the land which Hugh of St. Quintin holds from the King. He has given a pledge for them.

In eadē uilla idē Goduin[9].inuasit.III.uirgatas terræ sup regē de tr̄a cujdā[9] libi.hōis que remanet regi p judiciū hundret 7 iterū dedit uadē. In dantuna.xv.ac̄ tr̄e q̄s tenuit uluuinus.& remanent regi q̄etæ: INvasio tedrici.puintel

In thurrucca quā.t.r.e.ten.xi.libi.hōes.i.h̄.7 dimidia.7.XLII. ac̄.tr̄e.7.m̊.III.car.in dn̄io.tc̄.m̊.II.Past.ad.xxx.o.Tc̄ ual.xl.I s. m̊.xx.& hanc.tr̄a.inuasit.t.pointel 7 ē in manu regis.

99 b

Hund de Wensistreu.Legram tenuit.Vluric[9] lib hō.t.r.e.p.man.7.p.II.hid. 7.hoc inuasit.Idē.T.tc̄.II.car.m̊.nulla.neç qn̄ rec.m̊.II.bor.Tc̄.silu.XL.por.m̊ xxx. Tc̄ ual.LX.sol.7 qn̄ rec.XL.m̊.xx.7 In burnham inuasit.T.xv.ac.7.dim. 7.tm̄ erant in manu regis pquā hec placita fierent.

Hund de Rochefort.Stanbruge inuasit.T.qđ.tenuit.lib hō.t.r.e.p man.7.p .I.hid.7.dim.7.xx.ac.7 hoc man tenent.III.milit.de.T.Tc̄.III.uill.m̊.II. Tc̄.I.ser.m̊.null.Tc̄.II.bor.m̊.v.Sēp.I.car.in dn̄io.Tc̄.II.car.hom.m̊.I.Tc̄ ual.XL. sol.m̊.c.Pachesham inuasit.T.qđ tenuer.II.libi.hōes.p.dim.hid.7.xv.ac.Sēp. .I.car.[: Rob. ten& de eo.] ual.xx.sol. Hec.II.maneria tenuit.T.pointel p escangio de coghes-hala.7 m̊ st̄ in manu reg. *

2 In the same village Godwin also annexed 3 virgates of land in the King's despite from the land of a free man, which still belong to the King by the judgement of the Hundred. Again he has given a pledge.

3 In DUNTON 15 acres of land which Wulfwin held and (which) still belong to the King undisputed.

THEODORIC POINTEL'S ANNEXATION(S)

4 In (Little) THURROCK, which 11 free men held before 1066 and (hold) now, 1½ hides and 42 acres of land. Then 3 ploughs in lordship, now 2.

Pasture for 30 sheep.

Value then 41s; now 20[s].

Theodoric Pointel annexed this land. It is in the King's hand.

Hundred of WINSTREE 99 b

5 Wulfric, a free man, held LAYER before 1066 as a manor, for 2 hides. Theodoric also annexed this. Then 2 ploughs, now none, nor when acquired.

Now 2 smallholders.

Woodland, then 40 pigs, now 30.

Value then 60s; when acquired 40[s]; now 20[s].

[Hundred of 'WIBERTSHERNE']

6 In BURNHAM Theodoric annexed 15½ acres. However, they were in the King's hand before these pleas were brought about.

Hundred of ROCHFORD

7 Theodoric annexed (Little) STAMBRIDGE, which a free man held before 1066 as a manor, for 1½ hides and 20 acres. 3 men-at-arms hold this manor from Theodoric.

Then 3 villagers, now 2; then 1 slave, now none; then 2 smallholders, now 5. Always 1 plough in lordship. Then 2 men's ploughs, now 1.

Value then 40s; now 100[s].

8 Theodoric annexed PAGLESHAM, which 2 free men held for ½ hide and 15 acres. Always 1 plough.

Value 20s.

Robert holds from him.

Theodoric Pointel held these 2 manors by exchange for Coggeshall. Now they are in the King's hand.

7 In Midebroc inuasit . xx . ac̃ . Sep̃ . I . uill . 7 uał
. IIII . sol . 7 soca jac& in ecclia sc̃æ trinitatis de cantorbury . ut hund testatur.
hoc &iam tenuit . T . pointel p̄ escangio . 7 ẽ in manu regis.

Inuasio Ranulfi piperelli . In Terlinga inuasit . R . v . libos . hões . tenentes . III.
hid . xv . ac̃ . min̄ . t . r . e . de hoc manerio ten& . Rog̃ . de . R . II . hid . 7 . LXXX . ac̃.
7 . Ranulf . xxx . ac̃ . Tc̃ . III . car̃ . 7 . dim̃ . m̃ . VI . tc̃ . II . uill . m̃ . v . m̃ . v . bor . Silũ.
. xx . porc̃ . XXII . ac̃ . p̃ti . Tc̃ uał LXXV . sol . m̃ . IIII . lib . 7 . xv . sol.
7 in . Widituna . inuasit . R . xxx . ac̃ q̃s ten& in dñio . 7 uał . v . sol
7 In Stanesgata . inuasit . R . I . hid . 7 . xxx . ac̃ . qd ten& . Rad fili brien de eo . qd
tenuer̃ . II . libi . hões . t . r . e . Sep̃ . II . bor . 7 . I . car̃ . Past̃ . xx . ou̇ . Tc̃ uał . xv . sol
m̃ . x . 7 in Henies xx . ac̃ . 7 . đ . q̃s tenuer̃ . XII . libi hões . t . r . e . m̃ ten& Turold.
7 uał . III . sol . 7 in Lamers . II . ac̃ . libe træ 7 . uał . IIII . đ

100 a

Inuasio hugonis de monteforti in Exsessa.
Hugo de montf̃ . inuasit . I . libm hominẽ sup regẽ . 7 . W . fili grossæ . x . libos . hões . hij
oms tenebant . III . hid . 7 . IX . ac̃ . t . r . e . In qbz erant tc̃ . VIII . car̃ . 7 . dim̃ . m̃ VII . 7 . dim̃.
Sep̃ . XIII . bor . 7 . v . ser̃ . Tc̃ . II . mol . m̃ . I . Silũ . CLVII . porc̃ . xxx . ac̃ . p̃ti . Sep uał . VI.
lib . 7 . II . sol.

9 In *MIDEBROC* he annexed 20 acres.
Always 1 villager.
Value 4s.
The jurisdiction lies in (the lands of) the Church of Holy Trinity, Canterbury, as the Hundred testifies.
Theodoric Pointel also held this by exchange. It is in the King's hand.

RANULF PEVEREL'S ANNEXATION(S)

[Hundred of WITHAM]

10 In TERLING Ranulf annexed 5 free men who held 3 hides less 15 acres before 1066. Of this manor, Roger holds 2 hides and 80 acres from Ranulf and Ranulf (holds) 30 acres. Then 3½ ploughs, now 6.
Then 2 villagers, now 5; now 5 smallholders.
Woodland, 20 pigs; meadow, 22 acres.
Value then 75s; now £4 15s.

[Hundred of UTTLESFORD]

11 In WIDDINGTON Ranulf annexed 30 acres, which he holds in lordship.
Value 5s.

[Hundred of 'WIBERTSHERNE']

12 In STANSGATE Ranulf annexed 1 hide and 30 acres, which Ralph son of Brian holds from him (and) which 2 free men held before 1066.
Always 2 smallholders; 1 plough.
Pasture, 20 sheep.
Value then 15s; now 10[s].

[Hundred of HINCKFORD]

13 In (Great) HENNY 20½ acres which 12 free men held before 1066. Now Thorold holds (them).
Value 3s.

14 In LAMARSH 2 acres of free land. Value 4d.

HUGH DE MONTFORT'S ANNEXATION(S) IN ESSEX 100 a

15 Hugh de Montfort annexed 1 free man in the King's despite and William son of Gross (annexed) 10 free men. All these held 3 hides and 9 acres before 1066, in which there were then 8½ ploughs, now 7½.
Always 13 smallholders; 5 slaves.
Then 2 mills, now 1; woodland, 157 pigs; meadow, 30 acres.
Value always £6 2s.

7 adhuc . IIII . libos hoes inuasit . de . II . hid . 7 . XX . ac . quæ uat XXX . sol. 7 . erant ibi . tc . II . car . 7 . dim . m null . 7 in hund de Laxendena inuasit . III . libos . hoes . tenentes . I . hid . 7 . XXX . ac . in qbz erant . III . car . m . II . 7 . dim . Tc . I . bor . m . VI. Silu . c . porc . XII . ac . pti . Tc uat . XXX . sol . m . L . 7 . un ex his . tribz jac& ad feudu sci petri de . Westmonstio ad feringas . 7 hoc e testimonio hundreti . set fuit libat hugoni . in numero suoz maerioz . ut dicunt sui homines.
7 In Botingham . XV . ac . træ . qs tenuit lib ho . 7 m ten& . W . fili grossæ 7 uat XXXII . d

In Hund de Cesseorda e . I . lib ho de . XL . ac . q ptinebat ad hauelingas . t . r . e . que m ht . Scs Petr . de uuestmonastio . qa sua sponte uenit ad abbiam . 7 n reddit consuetudine ad hauelingas.

Inuasio . G . de magna uill . Mascebiam tenuit Alueua liba femina . t . r . e . qua m ten& . Vluric . ex dono regis . 7 . G . eam inuasit sup rege . in q tra e . I . hid . 7 sep . I . car . 7 . I . ser . 7 . VIII . ac . pti . Tc uat . X . sol . m . XXX . 7 in Canefelda . VIII . ac . træ qs . G . inuasit sup rege . 7 . Ricard ten& . de . eo.

. Wigghepet tenuit . Boso . lib ho . t . r . e . p . man . 7 p . II . hid . 7 . dim . tc 7 p . II . car . in dnio . m . I . 7 . dim . tc . IIII . car . hom . Post 7 . m . VI . Tc . 7 p . VII . uill . m . VIII . tc . V . ser . post 7 m . VII . Silu . XXX . porc . XXIIII . ac . pti . Sep . I . mol tc . 7 p uat . c . sol . m . VI . lib.

16 He annexed a further 4 free men with 2 hides and 20 acres. Value 30s. Then there were 2½ ploughs, now none.

In the Hundred of LEXDEN

17 He annexed 3 free men who held 1 hide and 30 acres, in which there were 3 ploughs, now 2½.

Then 1 smallholder, now 6.

Woodland, 100 pigs; meadow, 12 acres.

Value then 30s; now 50[s].

One of these three (free men) belongs to the Holding of St. Peter's, Westminster, at Feering; this is with the witness of the Hundred. But he was delivered to Hugh in the numeration of his manors, as his men state.

18 In BOCKINGHAM 15 acres of land, which a free man held. William son of Gross now holds (them). Value 32d.

[ANNEXATION OF ST. PETER'S, WESTMINSTER]

In the Hundred of CHAFFORD

19 There is 1 free man with 40 acres, who belonged to Havering (-atte-Bower) before 1066, whom St. Peter's, Westminster, now has because he came of his own accord to the Abbey; he does not pay customary dues to Havering (-atte-Bower).

GEOFFREY DE MANDEVILLE'S ANNEXATION(S)

[Hundred of DUNMOW]

20 Aelfeva, a free woman, held MASHBURY before 1066, which Wulfric now holds by the King's gift. G(eoffrey) annexed it in the King's despite. In which land there is 1 hide. Always 1 plough;

1 slave.

Meadow, 8 acres.

Value then 10s; now 30[s].

21 In CANFIELD 8 acres of land which G(eoffrey) annexed in the King's despite. Richard holds (them) from him.

[Hundred of UTTLESFORD]

22 Boso, a free man, held ROCKELL'S FARM before 1066 as a manor, for 2½ hides. Then and later 2 ploughs in lordship, now 1½. Then 4 men's ploughs, later and now 6.

Then and later 7 villagers, now 8; then 5 slaves, later and now 7.

Woodland, 30 pigs; meadow, 24 acres; always 1 mill.

Value then and later 100s; now £6.

Wicgepet.tenuit.liƀ hō.t.r.e.ꝑ man.7 ꝑ.III.hid.tc̄.7 p.II.car.in dn̄io.m̄
.I.7.dim.m̄.I.car.hom.7.I.uilt.Sēp.v.bor.tc̄.I.ser.m̄.null.Sēp uał.XL.
sol.7 In Wendena.ten.liƀ hō.VI.ac.7.dim.7.uał.II.sol.

In pherneham ten.IIII.liƀi.hōes.t.r.e.III.hid.7.III.uirg.7 m̄ tenent.IIII
milit de.G.Tc̄.7 p.VIII.car.m̄.v.tc̄.7 p.VI.uilt.m̄.III.tc̄.7 p.IIII.bor.m̄.XV.
tc̄.7 p.VII.ser.m̄.III.tc̄.7 p.silu.LX.por.m̄.L.XIIII.ac.pti.Sēp uał.VI.liƀ.

In Stanburna.dim.hid.ten.liƀ hō.t.r.e.tc̄.7 p.II.car.in dn̄io.m̄ null.
Sēp.dim.car.hom.7.III.bor.7.I.ser.XII.ac.pti.Tc̄.7 p.uał.XL.sol.m̄.L.

In Wesuunic.VI.liƀi hōes.t.r.e.de.I.hid.7.XLVI.ac.tc̄.I.car.m̄.null.tc̄.7 p
.XV.sol.m̄.X.

In Archesdana tenuit Goduin sech.I.hid.VIII.ac.min.modo ē in manu reg
Tc̄.I.bor.7.I.car.m̄.nich.II.ac.pti.Tc̄.uał.XX.sol.m̄.X.7 istā trā.tenuit.G.
de magna uilt.7.XV.ac.tenuit.Vlmar.ad feudū Ansgari sub.G.7.co
mitat non testat.

Hugo de ƀnerijs.tenebat.XXXVII.ac.de rege.qđ negauit 7.postea
fuit derationata ad opus reg.7.dedit uadē.Sēp.I.car.in dn̄io.7.I.bor.Silu.
XL.porc.IIII.ac.pti.tc̄.uał.X.sol.m̄.XX.

23 A free man held ROCKELL'S FARM before 1066 as a manor, for 3 hides. Then and later 2 ploughs in lordship, now 1½. Now 1 men's plough; 100 b

1 villager. Always 5 smallholders. Then 1 slave, now none.

Value always 40s.

24 In WENDENS a free man holds 6½ acres. Value 2s.

[Half-Hundred of CLAVERING]

25 In FARNHAM 4 free men held 3 hides and 3 villagers before 1066. Now 4 men-at-arms hold (them) from G(eoffrey). Then and later 8 ploughs, now 5.

Then and later 6 villagers, now 3; then and later 4 smallholders, now 15; then and later 7 slaves, now 3.

Woodland, then and later 60 pigs, now 50; meadow, 14 acres.

Value always £6.

[Hundred of HINCKFORD]

26 In STAMBOURNE a free man held ½ hide before 1066. Then and later 2 ploughs in lordship, now none. Always ½ men's plough;

3 smallholders; 1 slave.

Meadow, 12 acres.

Value then and later 40s; now 50[s].

[Hundred of 'WIBERTSHERNE']

27 In *WESUUNIC* 6 free men before 1066 with 1 hide and 46 acres. Then 1 plough, now none.

Value then and later 15s; now 10[s].

[Hundred of UTTLESFORD]

28 In ARKESDEN Godwin Sech held 1 hide less 8 acres. Now it is in the King's hand.

Then 1 smallholder and 1 plough; now nothing.

Meadow, 2 acres.

Value then 20s; now 10[s].

Geoffrey de Mandeville held that land. Wulfmer held 15 acres in Asgar's Holding under Geoffrey; the County does not testify.

[HUGH OF BERNIÈRES'S ANNEXATION]

29 Hugh of Bernières used to hold 37 acres from the King, which he denied; later on it was adjudged to the King's use and he gave a pledge. Always 1 plough in lordship;

1 smallholder.

Woodland, 40 pigs; meadow, 4 acres.

Value then 10s; now 20[s].

In Plesinchov . tenut lib̄ hō . I . hid . trǣ . q̊m humfrid aurei testiculi . inuasit sup . regē . Sēp . I . car . in dn̄io . 7 . VII . bor . 7 . II . ser . Silu . XXX . porc . VII . ac . p̄ti . tc̄ . I . mol . tc̄ uat . XVI . sol . m̊ . XXIII.

In Wighebga addidit Hamo dapifer . II . soc . reḡ . q̊s inuasit sup regē . de . XXX . ac . 7 uat . IIII . sol . 7 In Caresfeia . VIII . ac . 7 uat . VIII . đ . 7 in Stanburna . ✕

✝ . xl . ac . q̊s ten . Alestan lib̄ hō . 7 XXI . libi hōes . t . r . e . 7 adhuc . hn̄t Sēp . II . car . 7 . XII . bor . 7 uat . xl . sol.

In Hund de Odelesfort . occupauit . W . cardun . I . soc . de . VIII . ac . 7 . jac& ad Cishelle . de feudo . G . de magna uill . 7 . uat . II . sol.

101 a

Dim . Hund de . Clauelinga . Inuasio Suani . Bolitunā 7 . Bertunā . ten Goduin lib̄ hō . de Heroldo . t . r . e . p man . 7 . p . IIII . hid . 7 . dim . m̄ ten& Alured de . eo . Sēp . II . car . in dn̄io . 7 . v . car . hom . 7 . VII . uill . 7 . XIII . bor . 7 . v . ser . Silu . . XX . porc . II . ac . p̄ti . Tc̄ . 7 p uat . IIII . lib̄ . m̊ . VI . hanc trā inuasit Rob fili uuimarc t . r . Willi . 7 . adhuc ten& . Suen.

[HUMPHREY GOLDENBOLLOCKS'S ANNEXATION]

[Hundred of DUNMOW]

30 In 'PLESINGHO' a free man held 1 hide of land, which Humphrey Goldenbollocks annexed in the King's despite. Always 1 plough in lordship;
7 smallholders; 2 slaves.
Woodland, 30 pigs; meadow, 7 acres; then 1 mill.
Value then 16s; now 23[s].

[HAMO THE STEWARD'S ANNEXATION]

[Hundred of WINSTREE]

31 In (Little) WIGBOROUGH Hamo the Steward added 2 Freemen of the King's with 30 acres, whom he annexed in the King's despite. Value 4s.

[Hundred of 'WIBERTSHERNE']

32 In NORTHEY ISLAND 8 acres. Value 8d.

[Hundred of HINCKFORD]

33 In STAMBOURNE 40 acres, which Alstan, a free man, and 12 free men held before 1066 and still have. Always 2 ploughs;
3 smallholders.
Value 40s.

[WILLIAM CARDON'S ANNEXATION]

In the Hundred of UTTLESFORD

34 William Cardon appropriated 1 Freeman with 8 acres. He belongs to (Great) Chishill, of Geoffrey de Mandeville's Holding. Value 2s.

Half-Hundred of CLAVERING 101 a

SWEIN'S ANNEXATION

35 Godwin, a free man, held BOLLINGTON (Hall) and *BERTUNA* from Harold before 1066 as a manor, for 4½ hides. Now Alfred holds (them) from him. Always 2 ploughs in lordship; 5 men's ploughs;
7 villagers; 13 smallholders; 5 slaves.
Woodland, 20 pigs; meadow, 2 acres.
Value then and later £4; now [£] 6.
Robert son of Wymarc annexed this land after 1066. Swein still holds (it).

In Magghedana . Inuasit Albic de uer̃ . I . hid . 7 . dim . 7 . xv . ac . qd ten . III . libi hões . t . r . e . Tc . v . car . Post 7 m . IIII . Sep . VI . uill . 7 . VI . bor . 7 . III . ser . Silu . xxx . porc . 7 . IX . ac . pti . tc 7 p uat . LX . sol . m . IIII . lib .
7 In Smaltuna . xv . ac . træ . qs ten lib hõ . t . r . e . Tc . I . car . Post . dim . m null . 7 . uat . III . sol . In Mappesteda 7 In Pebeners . inuasit uxor albici . de uer . + × . v . libos hões . de . I . ac . 7 . IIII . parte al : r . qd tenuit Tidbald sub ea . 7 uat . III . sol .
. Rad . baignard inuasit in . henhã . dim . hid . 7 . x . ac . qd tenuer . II . libi hões . t . r . e . Sep . I . car . uat . XII . sol . 7 In Celuestuna . I . hid . 7 . XLIII . ac . qs tenuer . VI . libi . hões . t . r . e . Tc . 7 p . IIII . car . m . III . xv . ac . pti . uat . XL . sol .

In bolintuna tenuit . I . lib . hõ . xx . ac . t . r . e . 7 . adhuc ten& . s; celauit 7 idõ dedit uadẽ 7 uat . x . sol . (.III.)

In Pherneham tenuit lib hõ . xxx . ac . m ten& . Rad Latimar . s; celauit . 7 idõ dedit uad . 7 uat . x . sol .

[AUBREY DE VERE'S ANNEXATIONS]

36 In MANUDEN Aubrey de Vere annexed 1½ hides and 15 acres, which 3 free men held before 1066. Then 5 ploughs, later and now 4.

Always 6 villagers; 6 smallholders; 3 slaves.

Woodland, 30 pigs; meadow, 9 acres.

Value then and later 60s; now £4.

[Hundred of HINCKFORD]

37 In SMALTON 15 acres of land, which a free man held before 1066. Then 1 plough, later ½, now none.

Value 3s.

[AUBREY DE VERE'S WIFE'S ANNEXATION]

38 In (Little) MAPLESTEAD and in PEBMARSH Aubrey de Vere's wife annexed 5 free men with 1 acre and the fourth part of another which Theobald held under her. Value 3s.

[RALPH BAYNARD'S ANNEXATIONS]

[Hundred of FRESHWELL]

39 Ralph Baynard annexed ½ hide and 10 acres in HENHAM, which 2 free men held before 1066. Always 1 plough. Value 12s.

[Hundred of HINCKFORD]

40 In COUPALS FARM 1 hide and 43 acres, which 6 free men held before 1066. Then and later 4 ploughs, now 3.

Meadow, 15 acres.

Value 40s.

[1 FREE MAN'S ANNEXATION]

[Half-Hundred of CLAVERING]

41 In BOLLINGTON (Hall) 1 free man held 20 acres before 1066. He still holds (them), but he concealed (the fact) and so he has given a pledge. Value 3s.

[RALPH LATIMER'S ANNEXATION]

42 In FARNHAM a free man held 30 acres. Now Ralph Latimer holds (them), but he concealed (the fact) and so he has given a pledge. Value 10s.

In Lissildeuuella . tenuit . ten& sēp . I . lib hō . xxx . ac . 7 . uał . vi . sol . 7 . viii . đ.
Inuasio Turoldi In Hanies tenuer . IIII . libi hões . t . r . e . xviii . ac.
7 . adhuc tenent . Sēp . dim . car int eos . 7 . uał . III . sol.

101 b
In Lamers inuasit . Turold . xLvII . ac . qs tenuer . vIII . libi hões . t . r . e . 7 adhuc tenent.
Sēp . dim . car . 7 uał . v . sol.

In vasio Walerami . In Heni . dim . hid . 7 . x . ac . 7 . & . dim . qđ tenuer
. vII . libi . hões . t . r . e . 7 hnt sēp . I . car . 7 . IIII . ac . pti . 7 . uał . x . sol . hoc ten&
Rog de . Iohe . In halsteda ten . Vluuin . x . ac . qs inuasit Waler . Sēp . I . car . tc.
. I . bor . m . xL . tc . III . ser . m . null . Silu . xvI . por . v . ac . pti . tc uał . xx . sol . m . xxx.
In branchetreu . xxx . ac . trǽ tenuer . III . libi hões . t . r . e . 7 . uał . III . sol . hanc
trā inuasit Ledmar de hamesteda . 7 . tenuit ad feudū Ricardi . 7 . R . n̄ ē inde
sibi tutor.
Invasio . Ricardi filij . Comitis Gislebti . Almar de blea . Golstan.
Aluric de Alreforda . Vluric de branduna . Isti tenent . dim hid . 7 . vI . ac.
7 tenuerunt . t . r . e . m tenet eos . Goismer . de . R . Sēp . I . car . 7 . I . bor . 7
. v . ac . Sēp uał . xxvIII . sol.

[1 FREE MAN'S ANNEXATION]

43 In *LIFFILDEUUELLA* 1 free man held (and) has always held 30 acres. Value 6s 8d.

THOROLD'S ANNEXATION(S)

[Hundred of HINCKFORD]

44 In (Great) HENNY 4 free men held 18 acres before 1066 and still hold (them). Always ½ plough among them. Value 3s.

45 In LAMARSH Thorold annexed 47 acres which 8 free men held 101 b
before 1066 and still hold. Always ½ plough. Value 5s.

WALERAN'S ANNEXATION(S)

46 In HENNY ½ hide and 10½ acres, which 7 free men held before 1066. They have always had 1 plough.

Meadow, 4 acres.

Value 10s.

Roger holds this from John.

47 In HALSTEAD Wulfwin held 10 acres which Waleran annexed. Always 1 plough.

Then 1 smallholder, now 40; then 3 slaves, now none.

Woodland, 16 pigs; meadow, 5 acres.

Value then 20s; now 30[s].

[LEDMER OF HEMPSTEAD'S ANNEXATION]

48 In BRAINTREE 3 free men held 30 acres of land before 1066. Value 3s. Ledmer of Hempstead annexed this land and held it of Richard's Holding. Richard is not his protector for it.

ANNEXATION(S) OF RICHARD SON OF COUNT GILBERT

49 Aelmer of Borley, Goldstan, Aelfric of Alderford, Wulfric of Brundon. These men hold ½ hide and 6 acres and held (them) before 1066. Now Goismer holds them from Richard. Always 1 plough;

1 smallholder.

5 acres.

Value always 28s.

In Phincinghefelda ten& Ernald de . R . LXXX . ac . qđ tenuit brictic . lib
hō . t . r . e . Sēp . II . car . in dn̄io . Tc̄ . 7 p . I . uilt . m̊ . nult . Tc̄ . 7 p . III . bor . m̊ . VIII .
Sēp . III . ser . Tc̄ silu . XL . porc . m̊ . XXX . Tc̄ . 7 p uat . XL . sot . m̊ . LX .
Ad Laceleam tenuit Grim . lib hō . dim hid . q̄m ten& Ernald . Sēp . II . car . tc̄ . 7 p
. IIII . bor . m̊ . VIII . Tc̄ . II . ser . m̊ . null . tc̄ 7 p silu . LXXX . por . m̊ . LX . X . ac .
p̄ti . tc̄ . 7 p uat . XL . sot . m̊ . LX .
Ad Ersham tenuit brictmar lib hō . I . hid . t . r . e . m̊ ten& Wielard .
Tc̄ . 7 p . I . car . m̊ . I . 7 . dim . tc̄ . II . bor . Post 7 . m̊ . VII . IX . ac . p̄ti . Tc̄ uat . XXX . sot
post 7 m̊ . XL .

In Weninghou ten& Germund XXXVII . ac . 7 . dim . qđ .

102 a

qđ tenuit Coleman lib hō . t . r . e . Sēp . III . car . in dn̄io . . Tc̄ . 7 . p . II . car . hom . m̊ . III .
. I . ser . Silu . IIII . porc . X . ac . p̄ti . tc̄ . uat . LX . sot . m̊ . IIII . lib . 7 . X . sot .
In Geldeham ten& burnart . XL . ac . q̄s tenuit . Goduin lib hō . t . r . e . Sēp . I . car .
7 . II . bor . Silu . X . porc . V . ac . p̄ti . Tc̄ uat . XX . sot . Post 7 m̊ . XXX .
In barlea ten& Anschetill . dim . hid . 7 . XXIII . ac . qđ ten . Grim . 7 . Godeua . libi
hōes . t . r . e . Tc̄ . I . car . m̊ . I . 7 . dim . Tc̄ . 7 p . III . bor . m̊ . V . IX . ac . p̄ti . Tc̄ . uat . XX . sot
post . XXX . m̊ . XL .
In Topesfelda ten& . Rađ . XV . ac . qđ tenuit Alestan lib hō . t . r . e . Sēp . I . car .
tc̄ . 7 p . IIII . bor . m̊ . VII . tc̄ . 7 p . IIII . ser . m̊ . null . Silu . XX . por . VI . ac . p̄ti . Tc̄ .
7 p uat . XX . sot . m̊ . XXX .

50 In FINCHINGFIELD Arnold holds 80 acres from Richard which Brictric, a free man, held before 1066. Always 2 ploughs in lordship.
Then and later 1 villager, now none; then and later 3 smallholders, now 8; always 3 slaves.
Woodland, then 40 pigs, now 30.
Value then and later 40s; now 60[s].

[Hundred of DUNMOW]

51 At LASHLEY (Hall) Grim, a free man, held ½ hide which Arnold holds. Always 2 ploughs.
Then and later 4 smallholders, now 8; then 2 slaves, now none.
Woodland, then and later 80 pigs, now 60; meadow, 10 acres.
Value then and later 40s; now 60[s].

[Hundred of HINCKFORD]

52 At HORSEHAM (Hall) Brictmer, a free man, held 1 hide before 1066. Now Widelard holds (it). Then and later 1 plough, now 1½.
Then 2 smallholders, later and now 7.
Meadow, 9 acres.
Value then 30s; later and now 40[s].

53 In HOWE Germund holds 37½ acres which Colman, a free man, 102 a
held before 1066. Always 3 ploughs in lordship. Then and later 2 men's ploughs, now 3.
1 slave.
Woodland, 4 pigs; meadow, 10 acres.
Value 60s; now £4 10s.

54 In YELDHAM Bernard holds 40 acres which Godwin, a free man, held before 1066. Always 1 plough;
2 smallholders.
Woodland, 10 pigs; meadow, 5 acres.
Value then 20s; later and now 30[s].

55 In BORLEY Ansketel holds ½ hide and 23 acres, which Grim and Godiva, free men, held before 1066. Then 1 plough, now 1½.
Then and later 3 smallholders, now 5.
Meadow, 9 acres.
Value then 20s; later 30[s]; now 40[s].

56 In TOPPESFIELD Ralph holds 1·5 acres which Alstan, a free man, held before 1066. Always 1 plough.
Then and later 4 smallholders, now 7; then and later 4 slaves, now none.
Woodland, 20 pigs; meadow, 6 acres.
Value then and later 20s; now 30[s].

In Topesfelda . ten& . G . xv . ac . qđ tenuit . duua . Sep . i . car . in dnio . 7 . i . car hominū . 7 . iii . uill . 7 . ii . bor . 7 . ii . ser . Silu . xxx . porc . viii . ac . p̃ti . Tc 7 p uat . l . sol . m̃ . lx.

In Nortuna ten& Mascherell . lv . ac . qđ tenuit . brictric lib hō . t . r . e. tc . i . car . in dnio . post . 7 . m̃ . ii . Sep . i . car . hom . 7 . v . uill . Tc . 7 post . v . bor . m̃ . viii . Tc . 7 p . iii . ser . m̃ . ii . Silu . xl . por . x . ac . p̃ti . Tc uat . xl. sol . post 7 . m̃ . lx.

In bebenhers tenuit Leuecilt . lib hō . iii . ac . 7 . adhuc ten& . 7 . Derolf in Alfelmestuna . iiii . ac . 7 . holt . lib hō . i . ac . 7 In bumesteda Leuuin 7 Lemar . v . ac . 7 In Salinges Algar . xx . ac . 7 In Oluituna . brictolf xxx . ac . Isti oñs habebant . t . r . e . iii . car . Tc . 7 p . iii . bor . m̃ . viii. tc . 7 p . ii . ser . m̃ null . Silu . xii . por . viii . ac . 7 . dim . p̃ti . Tc 7 p uat . xxx . sol m̃ . xlv . 7 . ii . đ.

De istis sup̃dictis hōibȝ habuit Wisgar comdationē tantū.

102 b

In benedisc . inuasit Wisgar antec . R . xxx . ac . pquā rex uenit in hanc trā. 7 post ea habuit Ingelric illā . 7 hunđ testat qđ ptinebat ad feudū Ingelrici . s; huc usq; tenuit illā . R.

In byrdefelda . tenuit Felaga . i . hiđ . 7 . xxx . ac . de comite . Algaro . 7 postq rex uenit in hanc patriā inuasit . R . istā terrā qm ñ tenuit antecessor ej ut hunđ testat . Sep . iii . uill . m̃ . vii . bor . tc . iii . ser . m̃ . i . tc . i . car . 7 . dim in dnio . m̃ . i . Sep . i . car . hom . Silu . c . por . xxvii ac . p̃ti . m̃ . i . mol . tc uat . iiii . lib . m̃ . lx . sol.

In hocsenga tenuit Felaga dim . hiđ . m̃ ten& . Ric . sic istā sup̃dictā . 7 . Galt de eo . Sep . ii . uill . 7 . i . car . Silu . ii . porc . iiii . ac . p̃ti . vat . xii . sol. ★

57 In TOPPESFIELD G. holds 15 acres, which Dove held. Always 1 plough in lordship; 1 men's plough;
3 villagers; 2 smallholders; 2 slaves.
Woodland, 30 pigs; meadow, 8 acres.
Value then and later 50s; now 60[s].

58 In CORNISH HALL Mascerel holds 55 acres which Brictric, a free man, held before 1066. Then 1 plough in lordship, later and now 2. Always 1 men's plough;
5 villagers. Then and later 5 smallholders, now 8; then and later 3 slaves, now 2.
Woodland, 40 pigs; meadow, 10 acres.
Value then 40s; later and now 60[s].

59 In PEBMARSH Leofcild, a free man, held 3 acres and still holds (them).

60 In ALPHAMSTONE Derwulf (holds) 3 acres and Hold, a free man, 1 acre.

61 In (Steeple) BUMPSTEAD Leofwin and Leofmer (hold) 5 acres.

62 In (Great) SALING Algar (holds) 20 acres.

63 In OVINGTON Brictwulf (holds) 30 acres.
All these had 3 ploughs before 1066.
Then and later 3 smallholders, now 8; then and later 2 slaves, now none.
Woodland, 12 pigs; meadow, 8½ acres.
Value then and later 30s; now 45[s] 2d.
Of the above-mentioned men Withgar had only the patronage.

64 In BENDYSH (Hall) Withgar, Richard's predecessor, annexed 30 acres after the King came to this land. Later on Engelric had it. The Hundred testifies that it belonged to Engelric's Holding, but up to now Richard has held it. 102 b

65 In (Great) BARDFIELD Fellow held 1 hide and 30 acres from Earl Algar. After the King came to this land, Richard annexed that land which his predecessor did not hold, as the Hundred testifies.
Always 3 villagers. Now 7 smallholders; then 3 slaves, now 1.
Then 1½ ploughs in lordship, now 1. Always 1 men's plough.
Woodland, 100 pigs; meadow, 27 acres; now 1 mill.
Value then £4; now 60s.

66 In *HOCSENGA* Fellow held ½ hide. Now Richard holds (it) as (he holds) the above-mentioned land. Walter (holds) from him.
Always 2 villagers; 1 plough.
Woodland, 2 pigs; meadow, 4 acres.
Value 12s.

In Hasinghā tenuit lib̄ hō . II . ac . 7 . dim . in hunđ de Laxedana . m̊ ten& . R.
7 . ibi ē m̊ . I . mot . reddens . xv . sot . 7 tn̄ erat c̄mdat antec Ricardi.
In Hunđ de Laxendena tenuit Luttin in Colun . XL . ac . m̊ ten& . R.
7 in hac tr̄a antec ej nullā habuit consuetudinē . n cōmdationē . Tc̄ . IIII.
bor . m̊ . VI . Sēp . I . car . Silu . xx . por . IIII . ac p̄ti . m̊ . I . mot . vat . xx . sot.
In Crepinga . ten& Aluuard . LX . ac . 7 . IIII . ac . 7 . IIII . ac . 7 . dim . lib̄e . qđ . m̊
ten& . R . sicuti aliā . tc̄ . sub ipso . IIII . bor . m̊ . VI . Sēp . I . car . Silu . xx . porc.
. II . ac . p̄ti . vat . xx . sot.
7 Aluui uenator tenuit lib̄e . dim hiđ . 7 . XXVI . ac . 7 . dim . m̊ ten& . R.
in b̄colt sic aliā . tc̄ . II . bor . m̊ . VI . Sēp . I . car . Silu . xv . por . II . ac . p̄ti.
Tc̄ . dim mot . m̊ n̄ . tc̄ uat . xx . sot . m̊ . XXXVI.
In Colun tenuit vluric lib̄e . v . ac . m̊ . R . sic alios . vat . II . sot.
In Forhā tenuit Touillda . III . ac . m̊ . R . sic alios . 7 uat . VII . đ.
In b̄colt ten . Goding . VI . ac . m̊ . R . tc̄ . đ . car . m̊ . II . bou . I . ac . p̄ti . tc̄ uat . XXXII . đ.
m̊ . v . sot.

103 a

In Halsteda tenuit lib̄ hō . t . r . e . II . ac . 7 . dim . 7 uat . xxx . đ . Istos denarios
recepit Aluret p̄posit . R . 7 inde dedit uadē.
In Hersham tenuit lib̄a femina . xxx . ac . m̊ ten& Wielard de rege ut dic̄.
s; hunđ non testat . 7 . R . fili comitis . G . habuit seruitiū . Tc̄ . dim . car . m̊ . n̄.
m̊ . II . bor . Vat . x . sot.
In branchetreu . III . lib̄i hōes . t . r . e . xxx . ac . qs Letmar p̄posit reclamauit ad
feudū . Ricardi . s; hōes illi n̄ testant . 7 inde dedit uadē . 7 uat . III . sot.

67 In *HASINGHAM* a free man held 2½ acres in the Hundred of LEXDEN. Now Richard holds (them).
Now 1 mill there, which pays 15s.
However, he was under the patronage of Richard's predecessor.

In the Hundred of LEXDEN

68 Lutting held 40 acres in COLNE. Now Richard holds (them). In this land his predecessor had no customary due nor patronage.
Then 4 smallholders, now 6. Always 1 plough.
Woodland, 20 pigs; meadow, 4 acres; now 1 mill.
Value 20s.

69 In CREPPING Alfward holds freely 60 acres and 4 acres and 4½ acres, which Richard now holds (on the same terms) as the other land.
Then under him 4 smallholders, now 6. Always 1 plough.
Woodland, 20 pigs; meadow, 2 acres.
Value 20s.

70 Alfwy Hunter held ½ hide and 26½ acres freely. Now Richard holds (them), in (West) BERGHOLT, (on the same terms) as the other land.
Then 2 smallholders, now 6. Always 1 plough.
Woodland, 15 pigs; meadow, 2 acres; then ½ mill, now none.
Value then 20s; now 36[s].

71 In COLNE Wulfric held 5 acres freely. Now Richard (holds them on the same terms) as the others. Value 2s.

72 In FORDHAM Tovild held 3 acres. Now Richard (holds them on the same terms) as the others. Value 7d.

73 In (West) BERGHOLT Goding held 6 acres. Now Richard (holds them). Then ½ plough, now 2 oxen. Meadow, 1 acre. Value then 32d; now 5s.

[Hundred of HINCKFORD] 103 a

74 In HALSTEAD a free man held 2½ acres before 1066. Value 30d. Alfred, Richard's reeve, has acquired those pence and has given a pledge for them.

75 In HORSEHAM (Hall) a free woman held 30 acres. Now Widelard holds (them) from the King, as he states; but the Hundred does not testify. Richard son of Count Gilbert has had the service. Then ½ plough, now none.
Now 2 smallholders.
Value 10s.

76 In BRAINTREE 3 free men (held) 30 acres before 1066, which Ledmer the reeve has claimed for Richard's Holding; but the latter's men do not testify. He has given a pledge for them.
Value 3s.

In Ceauride . xxx . ac . qs ten Vluric lib hō . t . r . e . m ten& Garner hō . Ricardi . 7 uocauit Ilbodonē ad tutorē . 7 p ea n̄ adduxit tutorē 7 . uał . viii . sol.
In Eađ uilł ten . ii . libi hōes . dim . hiđ . t . r . e . hanc trā inuasit Ailmar ppośit . R . 7 reuocauit eū ad tutorē . s; ipse sibi defuit . 7 . ex hoc dedit ille uadē . 7 uał . xvi . sol.

Monachi de cantorbia tenent in Lalinga . i . hiđ . qm tenebant . iii . libi hōes t . r . e . Sēp . i . car . uał . xx . sol . hec trā addita ē illi manerio t . r . Willi.

In Colun ten& Turbn . xxii . ac . sine dono reg 7 . nullā reddit consuet.

Henric de Ferrerijs inuasit . i . libm hominē . de . xvi . ac . in Stepla . 7 uał . ii . sol.

. W . Leuric inuasit in Sciddehā . i . libm hom . de . vi . ac . uał . xii . đ. ★

In bumesteda inuasit Rob blund . x . ac . qs tenuit Edui lib hō Sēp . i . car . uał . xx . sol.

103 b

In Mildetuna Inuasit . R . malet . xv . ac . qs ten lib hō . t . r . e . Sēp . dim car . uał . v . sol.

[Hundred of DUNMOW]

77 In CHAURETH 30 acres which Wulfric, a free man, held before 1066. Now Warner, a man of Richard's, holds (them). He called Ilbod as a protector. Later on he did not produce a protector. Value 8s.

78 In the same village 2 free men held ½ hide before 1066. Aelmer, Richard's reeve, annexed this land and called him as a protector but he failed him. Because of this he has given a pledge. Value 16s.

[ANNEXATION OF THE MONKS OF CANTERBURY]

[Hundred of 'WIBERTSHERNE']

79 The monks of Canterbury hold 1 hide in LAWLING, which 3 free men used to hold before 1066. Always 1 plough. Value 20s.
This land was added to the manor after 1066.

[THORBERN'S ANNEXATION]

[Hundred of LEXDEN]

80 In COLNE Thorbern holds 22 acres without the King's gift. He has paid no customary due.

[HENRY OF FERRERS'S ANNEXATION]

[Hundred of 'WIBERTSHERNE']

81 Henry of Ferrers annexed 1 free man with 16 acres in STEEPLE. Value 2s.

[WILLIAM LEOFRIC'S ANNEXATION]

82 W(illiam) Leofric annexed 1 free man with 6 acres in *SCIDDEHAM*. Value 12d.

[ROBERT BLUNT'S ANNEXATION]

[Hundred of FRESHWELL]

83 In (Helions) BUMPSTEAD Robert Blunt annexed 10 acres which Edwy, a free man, held. Always 1 plough. Value 20s.

[ROBERT MALET'S ANNEXATION]

[Hundred of HINCKFORD] 103 b

84 In MIDDLETON R(obert) Malet annexed 15 acres, which a free man held before 1066. Always ½ plough. Value 5s.

Frodo fr̄ abb̄is tenuit ^h^ucusq̧ II . lib̄os hōes . In Staumtuna q̄s Orgar̄ ante
cessor ej inuasit . manentes in soca reḡ . 7 . h̄nt . xx . ac̄ . Sēp . dim̄ . car̄ . 7
uał . IIII . soł.

In Cishella tenuit Leuuin̄ . v . ac̄ . 7 m̄ ten& . Roḡ de otburuilł.
i dō qđ antecessor ej fuit saisit.

In Hunđ de Rochefort jacent . xv . ac̄ . de angra . qđ ten& Berengari
hō comitis . E . tunc uał . xv . đ . m̄ . xx.

104 a

Hundret de colecesTRA . In eadē colecestra tenuit.
Godric . I . lib̄ hō tēpr̄ regis eaduuardi . IIII . mansiones . tr̄æ.
7 unā ecclam . & . IIII . hidas in Grenesteda . Quo mortuo filij ej.
terrā inquat dimiserunt . partes . Quarū rex habet duas . in
quibus ptinent due dom̄ in burgo . quæ sēp regi reddiderunt.
consuetudinem . 7 adhuc reddt̄ . In duabus hidis . tc̄ . II . car̄.
in dn̄io . 7 m̄ . Tc̄ . III . uilł 7 m̄ . Tc̄ . II . s . 7 m̄ . Tc̄ XXIIII . ac̄ p̄ti.
7 maresc 7 m̄ . Tc̄ . I . moł . m̄ . dim̄ . Tc̄ uał XL . soł . 7 m̄ . Et
de duab̧ alijs partib̧ h̄t comes eustachi . I . h̄ . Et ioh̄s
fili Walerami . alterā . h̄ . Et in qrta Comitis euastachij . ē.
tota eccła . 7 qrta pars molendini . 7 . qrta pars p̄ti . tc̄ . I . car̄.
m̄ . nulla . 7 ualit in̄ totū . xxx . soł . Et in qrta parte
ioh̄s fuit . I . car̄ tēpr̄ . r̄ . æ . m̄ . nulla . Et quarta pars molendini.
q̄rta pars p̄ti . ; 7 uał int̄ totū . xxx . s . Et de his duab̧ partib̧
nullā habet rex consuetudinē.

Et burgenses calumpniant̄ . v . hidas de lex sendena
ad consuetudinē . 7 Cootū ciuitatis . quæ jacuert̄ ad p̄dictā
tr̄ā quā tenebat Godric.

[ANNEXATION OF FRODO THE ABBOT'S BROTHER]

[Hundred of FRESHWELL]

85 Frodo the Abbot's brother has held up to now 2 free men in STEVINGTON (End), whom Ordgar his predecessor annexed (and) who dwelt in the King's jurisdiction. They have 20 acres. Always ½ plough. Value 4s.

[ROGER OF AUBERVILLE'S ANNEXATION]

[Hundred of UTTLESFORD]

86 In CHISHILL Leofwin held 5 acres. Now Roger of Auberville holds (them) because his predecessor was in possession.

[BERENGAR'S ANNEXATION]

In the Hundred of ROCHFORD

87 lie 15 acres of ONGAR, which Berengar, a man of Count Eustace's, holds. Value then 15d; now 20[d].

B Hundred of COLCHESTER 104 a

1 In the same COLCHESTER before 1066, 1 free man, Godric, held 4 pieces of land and a church, and 4 hides in GREENSTEAD. On his death his sons separated the land into four parts. The King has two of these, in which belong two houses in the Borough which have always paid a customary due to the King and still pay (it). In 2 hides, then and now 2 ploughs in lordship.

Then and now 3 villagers; then and now 2 slaves.

Then and now meadow and marsh, 24 acres; then 1 mill, now ½.

Value then and now 40s.

From the two other parts Count Eustace has 1 hide and John son of Waleran (has) the other hide. In Count Eustace's fourth,

a whole church, ¼ mill, and ¼ of the meadow. Then 1 plough, now none.

Value in total 30s.

In John's fourth was 1 plough before 1066, now none.

¼ mill and ¼ of the meadow.

Value in total 30s.

From these two parts the King has no customary due.

2 The burgesses claim 5 hides of LEXDEN, which belonged to the said land which Godric used to hold, (to be liable) to the customary due and the city's levy.

Isti st̃ burgenses regis . q̃ reddunt ꝯsuetudinẽ
Colemanꝰ . habet . i . domũ de colecestra . tenʾ . 7 . v . ac̃ . tr̃æ.
& sep̃ . reddit regi consuetudinẽ . Leuuinꝰ . ii . domꝰ . 7 . xxv.
ac̃ . tr̃æ . Vluricꝰ . i . domꝰ . Eduinꝰ pr̃ . i . domꝰ . 7 . xx . ac̃.
Tchillꝰ . i . đ . 7 nouẽ . ac̃ . Ulstanꝰ eudlac . iiii . domꝰ . 7 xx.
ac̃ . Leuuinꝰ . crist. i . domꝰ . 7 . x . ac̃ . Manuuinꝰ . iiii . domꝰ . 7 . xxx . acʾ.

104 b
Aluricꝰ . i . domꝰ . 7 . v . acʾ . Herdedunꝰ . x . đ . 7 dimʾ . xx . ac̃. ★
Alfeihc pr̃ . i . domꝰ . 7 . xxv . acʾ . Leuot . i . domꝰ . 7 . xv . acʾ.
Vluricꝰ . i . domꝰ . 7 . vii . acʾ . Suertlincꝰ . i . domꝰ . 7 . x . ac̃.
Aluuart . i . domꝰ . 7 . ii . ac̃ . Eduinꝰ . i . domꝰ . Goda . xiii . domꝰ.
7 . xx . ac̃ . Sprot . ii . đ . 7 . iii . ac̃ . Edricꝰ . iiii . domꝰ . 7 . xv . ac̃.
Goduuinꝰ . i . đ . 7 . xv . ac̃ . Goduuinꝰ uuachefet . 7 filij ejꝰ . v . đ.
7 . xii . ac̃ . Blancꝰ . vi . domꝰ . 7 . xx . ac̃ . Aluricꝰ . ii . domꝰ.
7 . xiiii . ac̃ . Stanart . ii . đ . 7 . dimʾ . 7 . x . ac̃ . Goduinꝰ . i . đ.
7 . ix . ac̃ . Vluricꝰ . ii . đ . 7 . i . ac̃ . Alsiꝰ . i . đ . 7 . iii . ac̃ . 7 . dimʾ.
Aluuardus . ii . đ . 7 . xxiii . ac̃ . Manuuinꝰ . ii . đ . 7 . vii . ac̃.
Lesfesse . i . đ . 7 . ii . ac̃ 7 dimʾ . Leuuinꝰ . x . ac̃ . Vluuinꝰ . i . đ.
7 . ii . ac̃ . 7 dimʾ . Godincꝰ . ii . đ . 7 . x . ac̃ . Goda . i . đ . 7 . vii . ac̃.
Vluuinꝰ . monitor . i . đ . 7 . vii . acʾ . Alfgarꝰ . i . đ . Vluart.
. ii . đ . 7 . i . ac̃ . Aluuinꝰ . i . đ . 7 . x . ac̃ . Alfgarꝰ . pr̃ . i . đ . 7 . i . ac̃.
Frent . i . đ . 7 . ii . ac̃ . Osgot . ii . đ . 7 . i . ac̃ . Vluricꝰ . ii . đ.
Arturꝰ . i . đ . 7 . iiii . ac̃ . Eduinꝰ . i . đ . 7 . iiii . ac̃ . Saluare . i . đ.
7 . vii . ac̃ . Leflet . iii . đ . 7 . xxv . ac̃ . 7 . i . mol . Aluricꝰ . i . đ.
Goduuinꝰ . i . đ . Sprot . i . đ . 7 . iii . ac̃ . Grimolf . ii . đ . 7 . ix . ac̃.
Sagarꝰ . i . đ . 7 . x . ac̃ . Aluricꝰ . i . đ . Aluuinꝰ . iii . đ . 7 . ix . ac̃.
Vluricꝰ . i . đ . 7 . vi . ac̃ . Sprot . i . đ . 7 . iii . ac̃ . Vluuart . i . đ.
7 . viii . ac̃ . Leuuinꝰ . i . đ . 7 . x . ac̃ . consilio . Goduinꝰ . i . domꝰ.
Golstanꝰ . i . đ . 7 . v . ac̃ . Vluuinꝰ . i . đ 7 . iiii . ac̃ . Vluuart.
i . đ . 7 . iii . ac̃ . Vluuinꝰ . ii . đ . 7 . vii . ac̃ . Goduuinꝰ . ii . domꝰ.
7 . vi . ac̃ . consilio . Alfsiꝰ . ii . đ . Lefstanꝰ . i . đ . 7 . i . ac̃ . Godricꝰ . i . đ.

105 a
Alricꝰ . i . đ . Not . i . đ . Brictuuinꝰ . i . đ . 7 . v . ac̃ . Lefflet . i . đ.
Alricꝰ . i . đ . 7 . iiii . ac̃ . 7 . dimʾ . Eduuinꝰ . i . đ . 7 . ii . ac̃ . 7 dimʾ.
Scadebutre . i . đ . Manuuinꝰ . iiii . ac̃ . Golduuinꝰ . i . đ . Vluricꝰ.
i . đ . 7 . ii . ac̃ . Osiet . i . đ . Eduuinꝰ . i . đ . 7 . x . ac̃ . Vluricꝰ . ii . đ.
7 . v . ac̃ . Aluuinꝰ . ii . đ . Eduuinꝰ . i . đ . 7 . iii . ac̃ . Vluuinꝰ . i . đ.
Blacstan . ii . đ . Manstan . ii . đ . 7 . x . ac̃ . Aluricꝰ . i . đ . 7 . i . ac̃.
Leuuinꝰ . i . đ . Aluuinꝰ . ii . đ . 7 . xxii . ac̃ . Leuuinꝰ . ii . đ . Edricꝰ.

3a These are the King's burgesses who pay the customary due: Colman has 1 house in COLCHESTER; and he holds 5 acres of land and has always paid the customary due to the King. Leofwin (holds) 2 houses and 25 acres of land; Wulfric, 1 house; Edwin the priest, 1 house and 20 acres; Thorkell, 1 house and nine acres; Wulfstan Eadlac, 4 houses and 20 acres; Leofwin Crist, 1 house
and 10 acres; Manwin, 4 houses and 30 acres; Aelfric, 1 house 104 b
and 5 acres; Hardekin, 10½ houses (and) 20 acres; Alfheah the priest, 1 house and 25 acres; Leofwold, 1 house and 15 acres; Wulfric, 1 house and 7 acres; Swartling, 1 house and 10 acres; Alfward, 1 house and 2 acres; Edwin, 1 house; Goda, 13 houses and 20 acres; Sprot, 2 houses and 3 acres; Edric, 4 houses and 15 acres; Godwin, 1 house and 15 acres; Godwin Weakfeet and his son, 5 houses and 12 acres; Blanc, 6 houses and 20 acres; Aelfric, 2 houses and 14 acres; Stanhard, 2½ houses and 10 acres; Godwin, 1 house and 9 acres; Wulfric, 2 houses and 1 acre; Alfsi, 1 house and 3½ acres; Alfward, 2 houses and 23 acres; Manwin, 2 houses and 7 acres; Leofsexe, 1 house and 2½ acres; Leofwin, 10 acres; Wulfwin, 1 house and 2½ acres; Goding, 2 houses and 10 acres; Goda, 1 house and 7 acres; Wulfwin the summoner, 1 house and 7 acres; Alfgar, 1 house; Wulfward, 2 houses and 1 acre; Alwin, 1 house and 10 acres; Alfgar the priest, 1 house and 1 acre; Freond, 1 house and 2 acres; Osgot, 2 houses and 1 acre; Wulfric, 2 houses; Arthur, 1 house and 4 acres; Edwin, 1 house and 4 acres; Saeware, 1 house and 7 acres; Leofled, 3 houses, 25 acres and 1 mill; Aelfric, 1 house; Godwin, 1 house; Sprot, 1 house and 3 acres; Grimwulf, 2 houses and 9 acres; Saegar, 1 house and 10 acres; Aelfric, 1 house; Alwin, 3 houses and 9 acres; Wulfric, 1 house and 6 acres; Sprot, 1 house and 3 acres; Wulfward, 1 house and 8 acres; Leofwin, 1 house and 10 acres by agreement; Godwin, 1 house; Goldstan, 1 house and 5 acres; Wulfwin, 1 house and 4 acres; Wulfward, 1 house and 3 acres; Wulfwin, 2 houses and 7 acres; Godwin, 2 houses and 6 acres by agreement; Alfsi, 2 houses;
Leofstan, 1 house and 1 acre; Godric, 1 house; Alric, 1 house; 105 a
Not, 1 house; Brictwin, 1 house and 5 acres; Leofled, 1 house; Alric, 1 house and 4½ acres; Edwin, 1 house and 2½ acres; Shed-butter, 1 house; Manwin, 4 acres; Goldwin, 1 house; Wulfric, 1 house and 2 acres; Osgeat, 1 house; Edwin, 1 house and 10 acres; Wulfric, 2 houses and 5 acres; Alwin, 2 houses; Edwin, 1 house and 3 acres; Wulfwin, 1 house; Blackstan, 2 houses; Manstan, 2 houses and 10 acres; Aelfric, 1 house and 1 acre; Leofwin, 1 house; Alwin, 2 houses and 22 acres; Leofwin, 2 houses; Edric,

I. đ. Leuuin. I. đ. Vued. I. đ. Vlsi. I. đ. Goldric. II. đ. 7. XXII. ac. Goda. XXII. ac. Calebot. VII. ac. Manstan. II. đ. 7. I. ac. Ulfeih. I. đ. Manuuin. I. đ. Winemer. I. đ. Sacrim. III. đ. 7. IIII. ac. Leuric. I. đ. Vluuart. I. đ. 7. IIII. ac. Vl uuin. I. đ. 7. X. ac. Lesflet. I. đ. 7. XXV. ac. Godric. I. đ. Dereman. I. đ. Tstan. I. đ. DuHel. I. đ. 7. dim. ac. Goddæ. II. đ. Got citt. I. đ. 7. I. ac. Stan. I. đ. Oriet. I. đ. Alfstan. I. đ. Toui. I. đ. Goldinc. I. đ. Leuiet. I. đ. 7. II. ac. Blacstan. I. đ. Manuuin. I. đ. Aluuin. I. đ. Lefsun. II. đ. Aluric. I. đ. 7. II. ac. Brumman. I. đ. Aluuin. I. đ. Saulf. II. đ. 7. dim. 7. X. ac. Leuuin. III. ac. Vluric. I. đ. Alfstan. I. đ. Goduuin. III. ac. Golduin. I. đ. Goduuin. I. đ. 7. I. ac. Wicga. I. đ. Ledmar. I. đ. Vlstan. II. đ. Godesun. I. đ. 7. III. ac. Elebolt. II. đ. 7. I. ac. Goduuin. I. đ. Godeua. I. đ. Lefstan. I. đ. Eduardus pr. I. đ. Hacon. I. đ. Ailbriest. I. đ. Tate. I. đ. Sauuart. I. đ. Berda. I. đ. 7. V. ac. Vluuart. pr. I. đ. 7. I. ac. Cullinc. II. đ. 7. VII. ac. Aluuolt. I. đ. Filieman. I. đ. 7. V. ac. Godeua. I. đ.

105 b

Siuuardus. pr. I. đ. 7. IIII. ac. Pic. I. đ. Vluuin. III. đ. 7. IIII. ac. Leueua. I. đ. 7. IIII. ac. 7. dim. Aluric. XV. ac. Aluuen. II. đ. Vluric. I. đ. 7. I. ac. 7. dim. Witt. peccatu. I. đ. Best. I đ. Roseli. I. đ. 7. IIII. ac. Leuuin. I. đ. 7. II. ac. Goda. I. đ. Vluuin. I. đ. Leuesun. I. đ. Golman. I. đ. Pote. IIII. ac. Godric. I. đ. Siricus. I. đ. 7. II. ac. Alric. I. đ. 7. II. ac. Liuidi. I. đ. Brictric. I. đ. 7. IX. ac. 7. dim. Lefstan. I. đ. Vudebil. I. đ. Blacstan. I. đ. Alflet. I. đ. Vlueua. I. đ. 7. XX. ac. Goda. I. đ. 7. XX. ac. Ascere. I. đ. 7 XIX. ac. Godric. I. đ. Brunloc. I. đ. Alnod. II. đ. 7. IIII. ac. Goduuin. I. đ. 7. X. ac. Leuuin. I. đ. 7. X. ac. Aluric. pr. III. đ. 7. II. ac. Rogerius. I. đ. 7. IIII. ac. Godric. I. đ. Aluric. I. đ. 7. II. ac. Suertinc. I. đ. 7. X. ac. Godid. II. đ. 7. XIIII. ac. Brunuin. I. đ. 7. III. ac. Vluuin. I. đ. Brungar. II. đ. 7. XVIII. ac. Sunegot. I. đ. Siuuard. I. đ. 7. VI. ac. 7. dim. Vlstan. XI. ac. Leffiuf. II. đ. 7. VIII. ac. Sagrim. I. đ. Vluuin. I. đ. Leuuin. I. đ. Leuric. I. đ. Godinc. I. đ. 7. I. ac. Westan. II. đ. 7. XXX. ac. Ainolf. I. đ. 7. XV. ac. Tunric. I. đ. Alstan. V. ac. Alffius. I. đ. Goldere. I. ac. Godsune. I. ac. 7. dim. Vluuin. I. đ. Aluric. I. đ. Goduuin. I. đ. Pecoc. I. đ. Aluuin. I. đ. Brictric. I. đ. Manuuin. I. đ. Vluric. I. đ. Godsune. 7. dim. 7. VI. ac. Brunuin. I. đ. Manuuin. I. đ. Edric. I. đ. Leueua.

1 house; Leofwin, 1 house; Wulfgith, 1 house; Wulfsi, 1 house; Goldric, 2 houses and 22 acres; Goda, 22 acres; Calebot, 7 acres; Manstan, 2 houses and 1 acre; Wulfheah, 1 house; Manwin, 1 house; Winemer, 1 house; Saegrim, 3 houses and 4 acres; Leofric, 1 house; Wulfward, 1 house and 4 acres; Wulfwin, 1 house and 10 acres; Leofled, 1 house and 25 acres; Godric, 1 house; Derman, 1 house; Thurstan, 1 house; Dublel, 1 house and ½ acre; Godday, 2 houses; Got Chill, 1 house and 1 acre; Stan, 1 house; Ordgeat, 1 house; Alfstan, 1 house; Tovi, 1 house; Golding, 1 house; Leofgeat, 1 house and 2 acres; Blackstan, 1 house; Manwin, 1 house; Alwin, 1 house; Leofson, 2 houses; Aelfric, 1 house and 2 acres; Bruman, 1 house; Alwin, 1 house; Saewulf, 2½ houses and 10 acres; Leofwin, 3 acres; Wulfric, 1 house; Alfstan, 1 house; Godwin, 3 acres; Goldwin, 1 house; Godwin, 1 house and 1 acre; Wicga, 1 house; Ledmer, 1 house; Wulfstan, 2 houses; Godson, 1 house and 3 acres; Aethelbald, 2 houses and 1 acre; Godwin, 1 house; Godiva, 1 house; Leofstan, 1 house; Edward the priest, 1 house; Hakon, 1 house; Aethelbrict, 1 house; Tate, 1 house; Saeward, 1 house; Beard, 1 house and 5 acres; Wulfward the priest, 1 house and 1 acre; Culling, 2 houses and 7 acres; Alfwold, 1 house;
Filiman, 1 house and 5 acres; Godiva, 1 house; Siward the priest, 105 b
1 house and 4 acres; Pic, 1 house; Wulfwin, 3 houses and 4 acres; Leofeva, 1 house and 4½ acres; Aelfric, 15 acres; Alwen, 2 houses; Wulfric, 1 house and 1½ acres; William Peche, 1 house; Best, 1 house; Rosell, 1 house and 4 acres; Leofwin, 1 house and 2 acres; Goda, 1 house; Wulfwin, 1 house; Leofson, 1 house; Goldman, 1 house; Pote, 4 acres; Godric, 1 house; Siric, 1 house and 2 acres; Alric, 1 house and 2 acres; Lundi, 1 house; Brictric, 1 house and 9½ acres; Leofstan, 1 house; Woodbill, 1 house; Blackstan, 1 house; Aelfled, 1 house; Wulfeva, 1 house and 20 acres; Goda, 1 house and 20 acres; Aeschere, 1 house and 19 acres; Godric, 1 house; Brunloc, 1 house; Alnoth, 2 houses and 4 acres; Godwin, 1 house and 10 acres; Leofwin, 1 house and 10 acres; Aelfric the priest, 3 houses and 2 acres; Roger, 1 house and 4 acres; Godric, 1 house; Aelfric, 1 house and 2 acres; Swarting, 1 house and 10 acres; Godith, 2 houses and 14 acres; Brunwin, 1 house and 3 acres; Wulfwin, 1 house; Brungar, 2 houses and 18 acres; Sunegod, 1 house; Siward, 1 house and 6½ acres; Wulfstan, 11 acres; Leofswith, 2 houses and 8 acres; Saegrim, 1 house; Wulfwin, 1 house; Leofwin, 1 house; Leofric, 1 house; Goding, 1 house and 1 acre; Wigstan, 2 houses and 30 acres; Ainulf, 1 house and 15 acres; Tunric, 1 house; Alstan, 5 acres; Alfsi, 1 house; Godhere, 1 acre; Godson, 1½ acres; Wulfwin, 1 house; Aelfric, 1 house; Godwin, 1 house; Peacock, 1 house; Alwin, 1 house; Brictric, 1 house; Manwin, 1 house; Wulfric, 1 house; Godson, 6½ acres; Brunwin, 1 house; Manwin, 1 house; Edric, 1 house; Leofeva,

I.đ. Ouuiñ. I.đ. Alstan. II.đ. Aluolt. VI. ac̄. 7 dim̄. Manuiñ. I.đ. 7. V. ac̄. aluuart. I.đ. 7. XV. ac̄. Lemerus. X. ac̄. Abbas sc̄i Eadmundi. II.đ. 7. XXX. ac̄. Stanhert. I. dom̄.

106 a

Vluuin. I.đ. Sæuuele. I.đ. Leuret. I.đ. 7 VI. ac̄. Alueua. X. ac̄. Vlstan. I.đ. 7. XIII. ac̄. Leuuin. II.đ. Leueua. I.đ. Aluric. I.đ. Godric. I.đ. 7. IX. ac̄. Vlric. I.đ. 7. IIII. ac̄. Vluuin. I.đ Aluuen. I.đ. Tescho. II.đ. 7. XX. ac̄. tr̄æ. 7 debet consuetudines regi 7 numquā reddit. Vluricus. III. ac̄. Stotinc. I.đ. Herstan. . I.đ. Leuric. I.đ. 7. XLII. ac̄. Edric. I.đ. Dela. I.đ. Hunec. II.đ. Manuuin. II.đ. Aluric. II.đ. Got hugo. VI. ac̄. Leuuinus. I.đ. 7. XXV. ac̄. Dimidi. blanc. IIII.đ. Lefsune. I. ac̄. Alueua. I.đ. Leueua. III. ac̄. Sueno. I.đ. Vlsi. I.đ. Alflet. I.đ. Rađ pinel. IIII.đ. infra muros. 7. V. ac̄. 7 non reddidit. consuetudinē 7 indedit uadē. Orlaf. III. ac̄. 7. dim̄. Galt̄. II.đ. Horrap. I.đ. Aluuin. I.đ. Stamburc. I.đ. Vlstan. II.đ. 7. V. ac̄. Chentinc. I.đ. Sprot. I.đ. 7. V. ac̄. Eduuin. I.đ. 7. III. ac̄. Got flet. XX. ac̄. Mansune. X. ac̄. Godinc. I.đ. 7. V. ac̄. Vlueua. V. ac̄. Vluric. I.đ. 7. I. ac̄. 7. dim̄. Lorchebret. I.đ. 7. X. ac̄. Goldere. I.đ. P̄t suam tr̄am habent. isti burgenses. LI. ac̄. p̄ti. Amo Hamo dapifer. I.đ. 7. I. curiā. 7. I. hidā. tr̄æ. 7. XV. burgenses. 7 hoc tenūit ante cessor suus. Thurb̄n. tēpr̄. r. e. Et hoc totū p̄t suam aulā reddebat consuetudinē tēpr̄ regis. e. 7 adhuc reddt̄ burgenses. de suis capitibus. Set de tr̄a sua. & de hida quā tenent de hamone n̄ c̄ reddita consuetudo. In hida. I. car̄. tc̄. m̄ nulla. Tc̄. VI. ac̄. p̄ti. 7. m̄. & hoc totū ual. tēpr̄. r. e. IIII. lib̄. 7. q̄do simil. recep̄. & m̄. XL. sol. / Mansune. II.đ. 7. IIII. ac̄. Goda. I.đ. / Eudo dapif̄. V.đ. 7 XL. ac̄. tr̄æ. quas tenebant.

106 b

burgenses tēpr̄. r. e. 7 reddebant. omnē consuetudinē burgensiū. M̊ ů n̄ reddt̄ 9suedinē. n̄ de suis capitibus. Hoc totū c̄ quarte parte æcclæ sc̄i petri. reddit XXX. sol. / Hug̃. de monte forti. I.đ. quam ten̄ tēpr̄. e. Godric. suus ante cessor 7 reddebat tc̄ consuetudinē regis. M̊ n̄ reddit nec postea reddidit. ex quo Hugo habuit.

1 house; Owin, 1 house; Alstan, 2 houses; Alfwold, 6½ acres; Manwin, 1 house and 5 acres; Alfward, 1 house and 15 acres; Ledmer, 10 acres; the Abbot of St. Edmund's, 2 houses and 30
acres; Stanhard, 1 house; Wulfwin, 1 house; Seafowl, 1 house; 106 a
Leofred, 1 house and 6 acres; Aelfeva, 10 acres; Wulfstan, 1 house and 13 acres; Leofwin 2 houses; Leofeva, 1 house; Aelfric, 1 house; Godric, 1 house and 9 acres; Wulfric, 1 house and 4 acres; Wulfwin, 1 house; Alwen, 1 house; Tesco, 2 houses and 20 acres of land, and he owes customary dues to the King and never pays; Wulfric, 3 acres; Stoting, 1 house; Herstan, 1 house; Leofric, 1 house and 42 acres; Edric, 1 house; Dela, 1 house; Hunning, 2 houses; Manwin, 2 houses; Aelfric, 2 houses; Got Hugh, 6 acres; Leofwin, 1 house and 25 acres; Demiblanc, 4 houses; Leofson, 1 acre; Aelfeva, 1 house; Leofeva, 3 acres; Swein, 1 house; Wulfsi, 1 house; Aelfled, 1 house; Ralph Pinel, 4 houses below the walls, and 5 acres, and he has not paid the customary due and has given in a pledge; Ordlaf, 3½ acres; Walter, 2 houses; Horrap, 1 house; Alwin, 1 house; Stanburg, 1 house; Wulfstan, 2 houses and 5 acres; Kenting, 1 house; Sprot, 1 house and 5 acres; Edwin, 1 house and 3 acres; Got Fleet, 20 acres; Manson, 10 acres; Goding, 1 house and 5 acres; Wulfeva, 5 acres; Wulfric, 1 house and 1½ acres; Lorce Bret, 1 house and 10 acres; Goldhere, 1 house;

Apart from their land, those burgesses have 51 acres of meadow.

b Hamo the Steward (has) 1 house, 1 court, 1 hide of land and 15 burgesses; his predecessor Thorbern held this before 1066. All this, apart from his hall, paid the customary due before 1066; the burgesses still pay (a tax assessed) on their heads, but a customary due has not been paid from their land and from the hide which they hold from Hamo. In the hide, 1 plough then, now none.

Meadow, then and now 6 acres.

Value of all this before 1066 £4; when acquired, the same; now 40s.

c Manson (has) 2 houses and 4 acres; Goda, 1 house.

d Eudo the Steward (has) 5 houses and 40 acres of land, which the
burgesses used to hold before 1066. They paid all the customary 106 b
due of burgesses; but now they do not pay the customary due, apart from (a tax assessed) on their heads. The whole of this, with ¼ of St. Peter's Church pays 30s.

e Hugh de Montfort (has) 1 house, which Godric his predecessor held before 1066. Then it used to pay the King's customary due; now it does not pay, nor did it pay later on, since Hugh has had it.

Rḡ pictauienſis . I . đ . quam tenuit . alſlet ſua ante ceſſor.
tēpr̄ . r . e . 7 reddebat conſuetudinē regis; m̊ n̄ reddit nec reddit
ex quo Roḡ habuit . Euſtachi⁹ . comes XII . đ 7 unā quā occupauit
engelric⁹ . 7 reddebant conſuetudinē regis tēpr̄ . r . e . M̊ n̄ reddt̄
nec reddiderunt ex quo euſtachi⁹ habuit . 7 ualent . XII . ſol.
Wilt nepos ep̄i . II . đ . quam ten̄ thurchill⁹ 7 reddit conſuetudinē
Otto . aurifab̄ . III . đ . que jacent ad eſceldeforde quas tenebat.
Alueua . comitiſſa . 7 reddebant conſuetudinē regis . 7 . m̊ n̄ reddt̄;
& hoc . ē . de tr̄a regina . Abbas de uueſtmonaſtio . IIII . đ
quas tēpr̄ . r . e . tenuit comes haroldus ad ferigens . & tc̄ reddebant
conſuetudinem . m̊ n̄ reddt̄ . Goisfridus de magna uilla . II . đ.
quas ten̄ . Geni⁹ tēpr̄ . r . e . ad erligam . 7 reddebant conſuetudinē
m̊ non reddt̄ . Sueno . I . đ . quā tenuit . Goda . tēpr̄ . r . e . ad elmeſteda.
7 tc̄ reddebant conſuetudinē regis . m̊ reddt̄ . n̄ caput hōis.
Wilt de uuateuilla . I . đ . de ſue none quā ten̄ . Rob̄ uuimarc.
tēpr̄ . regis . e . 7 reddebat conſuetudinē . m̊ n̄ reddit . Turſtinus
uuiſcart . III . đ . de iohanne filio uualerā 7 dim̄ hidā . tr̄e . qđ
tēpr̄ . r . e . tenuer̄ duo burgenſes 7 reddebant conſuetudinē.
regis . m̊ n̄ reddt̄ conſuedo . Illa dim̄ hida ual . tc̄ x . ſol . 7 . qdo.

107 a

recep̄ . VI . ſol . m̊ . v . s . Ran̄ piperell⁹ . v . đ . quas tenuit . Ailmar⁹
tēpr̄ . regis . e . ad terlingas . 7 reddebant conſuet . m̊ n̄ reddunt.
Quarū una extra muras . ē . Rađ baignart . I . đ . quā tenet.
Ailmar⁹ . melc . tēpr̄ . r . e . ad collenſum te . 7 reddebant conſuet̄ . m̊ . n̄.

f Roger of Poitou (has) 1 house, which Aelfled his predecessor held before 1066. It used to pay the King's customary due; now it does not pay and has not paid since Roger has had it.

g Count Eustace (has) 12 houses and one which Engelric has annexed. They paid the King's customary due before 1066; now they do not pay, and have not paid since Eustace has had them. Value 12s.

h William the Bishop's nephew (has) 2 houses, which Thorkell held. He pays the customary due.

j Otto the Goldsmith (has) 3 houses which belong to Shalford, which Countess Aelfeva used to hold. They used to pay the King's customary due; now they do not pay. This is of the Queen's land.

k The Abbot of Westminster (has) 4 houses, which Earl Harold held before 1066 (belonging) to Feering. Then they used to pay the customary due; now they do not pay.

l Geoffrey de Mandeville (has) 2 houses, which Ginni held before 1066 (belonging) to Ardleigh. They used to pay the customary due; now they do not pay.

m Swein (has) 1 house, which Goda held before 1066 (belonging) to Elmstead. Then they used to pay the King's customary due; now they only pay (a tax assessed) on a man's head.

n William of Vatteville (holds) 1 house from Swein, which Robert Wymarc held before 1066. It used to pay the customary due; now it does not pay.

p Thurstan Wishart (holds) 3 houses from John son of Waleran, and ½ hide of land, which 2 burgesses held before 1066. They used to pay the King's customary due; now they do not pay the customary due.
Value of the ½ hide, then 10s; when acquired, 6s; now 5s. 107 a

q Ranulf Peverel (has) 5 houses, which Aelmer held before 1066 (belonging) to Terling. They used to pay the customary due; now they do not pay. One of these is outside the walls.

r Ralph Baynard (has) 1 house, which Aelmer Milk held before 1066 (belonging) to Tolleshunt. They used to pay the customary due; now they do not.

Abbatiſſa de ſchingis . III . đ . tēpr̄ . r . e . & tc̄ reddebat . conſuetudinē ; m̄ . n̄ Albic⁹ . de 'uer . II . đ . 7 . III . ac̄ tr̄æ . qªs tenuit . Vluuin⁹ . ſuus ante ceſſor . tēpr̄ . r . e . Tc̄ reddebant conſuetudinem.

Dominium regis in colecestra . CII . ac̄ tr̄æ . de q̇bꝫ st̄ . x . prati. in quibꝫ st̄ . x . borđ . Et . CC . 7 . XL . ac̄ inter paſt⁹ . 7 fructectam & hoc totū jacet ad firmā regis. In cōmune burgenſum . IIII . XX . ac̄ tr̄æ ; & circa murum . VIII . percæ . de q̊ toto ꝑ annū habent burgenſes . LX . ſol . ad ſeruicium regis ſi op⁹ fuerit . ſin autē : in cōmune diuidt̄ ;

Eſt autē conſuetudo ut uno q̊qꝫ anno quinto decimo die poſt paſcha reddant burgenſes regij duas marcas argenti 7 hoc ꝑtinent ad firmā regis . Pt̄ ea de una quaqꝫ domo. ꝑ annum . VI . denarios quæ reddē poteſt ad uictū ſolda-riorum regis . vł . ad expetitionē tr̄æ ł maris ; & hoc n̄ ē ad firmā. Et hoc ſit ſi rex ſoldarios habuerit ł expetitionē fecerit. Et propt̄ hos . VI . denarios tota ciuitas ex omnib; debitis reddebat tēpr̄ . r . e . XV . lib̄ . 7 . V . ſol . 7 . III . đ in uno quoqꝫ anno ; De quibꝫ reddebant monetarij . IIII . lib̄ . tēpr̄ . regis . e . M̊ reddit . IIII . XX . lib̄ . 7 . IIII . ſextarios mellis uł . XL . ſol . IIII . Et p̄ter hoc . C . ſol . uice comiti de gerſuma . Et . X . ſol . 7 . VIII . đ ad p̄bendarios

107 b

paſcendos . Et p̄ter hoc reddunt burgenſes de colecestra & de mel-duna . XX . lib̄ . ꝓ moneta . 7 hoc conſtituit . Waleram⁹ . & aduocaꝰ regē adturtorē . qđ condonauit illis . X . lib̄ . & ten̄ . Walchelin⁹. epc . querit ab illis . XL . lib̄.

In colecestra ē quedā eccłe ſc̄i Petri quā . tenuit . II . p̄ri . tēpr̄ . r . e. in elemaſina regis . cui adjacent . II . ħ . terræ . in quibus erant . II . car̄. ★

7 . m̊ . Tc̄ . III . b . m̊ . IIII . Tc̄ . III . s . m̊ . II . Tc̄ . XII . ac̄ . p̊ti . 7 m̊ . Tc̄ . I . mol. 7 m̊ . Tc̄ . II . domus in burgo . 7 m̊ . Tc̄ totū uał . XXX . ſol . m̊ . XLVIII . ſol. De hac elemoſina reclamat . Rob̄ . f . rađ . de hatingis . III . partes. 7 eudo dapifer tenet q̄uartā . & tēpr̄ . r . e . reddebant conſue- ★ -tudinē . 7 . m̊ non reddit.

s The Abbess of Barking (had) 3 houses before 1066. Then it used to pay the customary due; now it does not.

t Aubrey de Vere (has) 2 houses and 3 acres of land, which Wulfwin his predecessor held before 1066. Then they used to pay the customary due.

4 The King's lordship in Colchester (is) 102 acres of land, of which 10 are of meadow, in which are 10 smallholders. Also 240 acres of pasture and scrubland. All this lies in the King's revenue.

5 In the burgesses' common property (are) 24 acres of land, and 8 perches round the wall, from the whole of which the burgesses have 60s a year for the King's service, if it should be needed, but if not, it is divided in common.

6 There is, moreover, a custom that every year, on the fifteenth day after Easter, the royal burgesses should pay 2 marks of silver. This belongs to the King's revenue.

Apart from this, from each house that can pay, 6d a year for the supplies of the King's mercenaries for a (military) expedition either on land or on sea; this does not belong to the (King's) revenue. This is to be whether the King has mercenaries or makes a (military) expedition. For these 6 pence, the whole city used to pay £15 5s 3d before 1066, in each year, out of all things owed (to it).

Of this (sum) the moneyers used to pay £4 before 1066; now it pays £80 and 4 sesters of honey or 40s 4[d].

Apart from this, 100s to the Sheriff in gifts; and 10s 8d for feeding the prebendaries. 107 b

Apart from this, the burgesses of Colchester and of Maldon pay £20 for the mint. Waleran arranged this. They summon the King as protector (to the fact) that he pardoned them £10. Bishop Walkelin holds (it); he demands £40 from them.

7 In Colchester is St. Peter's Church which 2 priests held before 1066 in the King's alms (and) to which are attached 2 hides of land, in which were, and (are) now, 2 ploughs.

Then 3 smallholders, now 4; then 3 slaves, now 2.

Meadow, then and now 12 acres; then and now 1 mill; then and now 2 houses in the Borough.

Total value then 30s; now 48s.

Of this alms, Robert son of Ralph of Hastings claims 3 parts, and Eudo the Steward holds the fourth. Before 1066 they used to pay the customary due; now it does not pay.

ESSEX HOLDINGS
ENTERED ELSEWHERE IN THE SURVEY

The Latin text of these entries is given in the county volumes concerned

In HUNTINGDONSHIRE

D **DECLARATIONS OF THE SWORN MEN** DB 208 a

EHu

7 They testify that the lands of Aelfric of Yelling and Hemingford were St. Benedict's; and that they had been granted to Aelfric for his life-time on the condition that after his death they should revert to the church, and BOXTED with them. However Aelfric was killed in the battle at Hastings, and the Abbot recovered his lands, until Aubrey de Vere dispossessed him.

In KENT

5 **LAND OF THE BISHOP OF ROCHESTER** DB 8 d

EKt

(In WROTHAM Hundred)

104 Adam holds Chalk from the Bishop . . .
In Essex there is 1 hide which rightly belongs to this manor. Godwin son of Dudeman held it; now Ranulf Peverel holds it. 9 a

In NORFOLK

38 **LAND OF ROBERT OF VERLY** LDB 262 a

ENf

The Hundred of (North) GREENOE

3 In (Field) Dalling G(odwin), the uncle of Ralph, held 11 Free men before 1066; 1c. of land. Now R(obert) of Verly holds them, saying that he holds it by exchange for RODING, in another county . . .
In this he vouches Robert Blunt as the deliverer.

In **SUFFOLK**

1
ESf 1

96 LAND OF THE KING, of which Peter of Valognes has charge. LDB 286 b

SAMFORD Hundred and a Half.

Harold held Harkstead before 1066; as an outlier in BRIGHTLINGSEA in the county of Essex; 5 acres of land.

Then 21 villagers, later and now 8; always 13 smallholders; then 4 slaves.

Always 2 ploughs in lordship; then 8 men's ploughs, later 2, now 1;

Meadow, 4 acres. A church; always 1 cob; 3 cattle; 7 pigs; 12 sheep.

Value then and later £6 at face value, now £6 by weight and 30s at face value.

It has 12½ furlongs in length and 12 in width; 30d in tax.

ESf 2
32 **LAND OF GEOFFREY DE MANDEVILLE** LDB 411 b

7 In Ipswich 1 dwelling: it belongs to MOZE.

NOTES

ABBREVIATIONS used in the Notes:

AN ... Anglo-Norman.
Appx ... Appendix.
arr ... *arrondissement*.
Battle 1980 ... *Proceedings of the Battle Conference on Anglo-Norman Studies III, 1980*, ed. R. Allen Brown (Boydell Press, Woodbridge, Suffolk, 1981).
DB ... Domesday Book.
DBE ... H. C. Darby, *Domesday England* (Cambridge 1977).
DG ... H. C. Darby and G. R. Versey, *Domesday Gazetteer* (Cambridge 1975).
ECE ... C. R. Hart, *The Early Charters of Essex* (revised edn., Leicester University Press, 1971).
Ellis ... Sir H. Ellis, *A General Introduction to Domesday Book* (2 vols. 1833, reprinted 1971).
EPNS ... *The Place-Names of Essex*, ed. P. H. Reaney (*English Place-Name Society* xii, Cambridge 1935).
von Feilitzen 1945 ... O. von Feilitzen, 'Some unrecorded Old and Middle English personal names', *Namn och Bygd* xxxiii (1945), 69-98.
von Feilitzen 1968 ... idem, 'Some Old English uncompounded personal names and bynames', *Studia Neophilologica* xl (1968), 5-16.
von Feilitzen 1976 ... idem, 'The personal names and bynames of the Winton Domesday', *Winchester in the Early Middle Ages*, ed. M. Biddle (*Winchester Studies* i, Oxford 1976), 143-229.
Fellows Jensen ... G. Fellows Jensen, *Scandinavian Personal-Names in Lincolnshire and Yorkshire* (Copenhagen 1968).
Forssner ... T. Forssner, *Continental-Germanic Personal-Names in England in Old and Middle English Times* (Uppsala 1916).
Förstemann ... E. Förstemann, *Altdeutsches Namenbuch*, Band 1, *Personennamen* (2nd edn., Bonn 1900).
Gt ... Great.
Harmer, *AS Writs* ... F. E. Harmer, *Anglo-Saxon Writs* (Manchester University Press, 1952).
ICC ... The Cambridgeshire Inquiry, *Inquisitio Comitatus Cantabrigiensis*, quoted from the same edition as IE, below; on it see further, Cambridgeshire, Introduction.
IE, IEAL, IEBrev, IENV ... For these texts see Appx, The Ely Inquiry; references are to pages in *Inquisitio Comitatus Cantabrigiensis*, ed. N. E. S. A. Hamilton (1876); in the notes below, page numbers are not repeated when they are the same as for the preceding note within each LDB section.
Kökeritz ... H. Kökeritz, 'Notes on the pre-conquest personal names of Domesday Book', *Namn och Bygd* xxvi (1938), 25-41.
Latham ... R. E. Latham (ed.), *Revised Medieval Latin Word-List from British and Irish Sources* (*British Academy*, 1965).
LDB ... Little Domesday Book.
LibEl ... *Liber Eliensis*, ed. E. O. Blake (*Camden Society*, 3rd series, xcii, 1962).
Lt ... Little.
ME ... Middle English.
MLat ... Medieval Latin.
ModE ... Modern English.
MS ... Manuscript.
NED ... *A New English Dictionary* (Oxford 1888-1933).
NFr ... Norman French.
OBret ... Old Breton.
ODan ... Old Danish.
OE ... Old English.
OEB ... G. Tengvik, *Old English Bynames* (*Nomina Germanica* iv, Uppsala 1938).
OFr ... Old French.
OG ... Old German.
OIr ... Old Irish.
ON ... Old Norse.
ONFr ... Old Norman French.
OScand ... Old Scandinavian.
OSw ... Old Swedish.
OW ... Old Welsh.
OWScand ... Old West Scandinavian.
PNDB ... O. von Feilitzen, *The Pre-Conquest Personal Names of Domesday Book* (*Nomina Germanica* iii, Uppsala 1937).

Reaney ... P. H. Reaney, *A Dictionary of British Surnames* (2nd edn. by R. M. Wilson, 1977).
Redin ... M. Redin, *Studies on Uncompounded Personal Names in Old English* (Uppsala 1919).
Rom ... Romance.
Sawyer ... P. H. Sawyer, *Anglo-Saxon Charters, an Annotated List and Bibliography* (*Royal Historical Society*, 1968).
Seltén ... B. Seltén, *The Anglo-Saxon Heritage in Middle English Personal Names, Part II* (Lund 1979).
VCH ... *The Victoria History of the County of Essex*, i, edd. H. A. Doubleday, W. Page (1903), with Domesday section by J. H. Round.

The Editor is grateful to Mr. John McN. Dodgson for his advice on the more obscure place- and personal-names.

The text of the DB Survey for Essex is contained in Little Domesday Book (now preserved, with the larger volume, at the Public Record Office, London). The manuscript was written, by more than one scribe, on either side of leaves, or folios, of parchment (sheep-skin) measuring about 11 by 8 inches (28 by 20 cms). On each side, or page, is a single column, making two to each folio. The folios were numbered in the 17th century, and the two columns of each are here lettered a, b. Red ink was used to distinguish chapter and Hundred headings. Deletion was marked by putting a line (in the ink of the text) through incorrect words. The running title on the recto of folios was usually an abbreviated form of the name of the Landholder whom the chapter concerned; the running title on the verso was an abbreviation of the county name.

ESSEX. *EXSESSA*, *EXSAESSA*, abbreviated as *ESS̄*, *EŜS* or *ESS*. At the top of the page, to the left of centre.

References to other DB counties are to the Chapter and Section of the editions in this series.

L LANDHOLDERS. LDB does not give a heading to the list and does not list B (Colchester). Farley omits the Chapter-numbers 2–4, 19–21, 23–24, 29, 72, and 89–90, all of which are present, but faded, in the MS and facsimile. See also folios 9a and 17a for partial lists of landholders which were subsequently deleted.

L6 WESTMINSTER. Farley supplies the overline abbreviation for *er*, omitted in error in the MS.

L9 [BARK]ING. The three dots in Farley represent a mark in the MS, obscuring the first part of the place-name, but cf. Chapter 9, heading (folio 17b).

L15 CAEN. Farley misreads initial *k* in the MS name-form *kadomo* as a paragraph-mark followed by initial *c*.

L41 CORBUCION. Farley *corbucionis*, MS *corbutionis*.

L54 AUMÂLE. LDB *albamarla*; facsimile (in error) *albamarl*.

L64 JOCELYN. LDB *Goscelm(us)*, see 1,2 note.

L75 ANSGER. Farley *Añs*, MS *Ansḡ*.

L80 GUNDWIN. Facsimile (in error) *Gonduin*, omitting the final abbreviation-mark.

L89 FREE. Farley omits the otiose abbreviation-mark (standing for *er*) on the letter *b*, given in the MS.

1,1-4 HAROLD. Earl of Wessex (1053–), King 1066. For his landholding, see Ann Williams, 'Land and power in the eleventh-century: the estates of Harold Godwineson', *Battle 1980*, 171–187.
RANULF BROTHER OF ILGER. See *37*.

1,1 BENFLEET. Probably North Benfleet, see VCH 428, n.1.
THEN. *T(un)c*, before 1066.
NOW. *M(odo)*, in 1086.
ALWAYS. *Se(m)p(er)*; before 1066 and still in 1086.
THEN 3 SLAVES, NOW 3. There is perhaps a statistical error in LDB here, as this situation would have been better expressed as 'Always 3 slaves'.
FREE MAN ... ONE OF THE VILLAGERS. He may have held the ½ hide mentioned in the next sentence and have suffered a loss of status when his land was given to the church.
CHURCH OF ANOTHER MANOR. Probably St. Mary's Church mentioned in 6,1.
49 ACRES. Farley and facsimile show the otiose abbreviation-mark over the letter *c* as in the MS.

1,2 PETER THE SHERIFF. See *36*.

SWEIN AND BAYNARD. See *24* and *33*. The patronym 'Baynard' is used on its own here in relation to Ralph Baynard, being qualified by the title 'Sheriff'. Cf. 1,27 note.
THROUGH ... CATTLE PLAGUE. *p(er) mortem bestiaru(m)*. This occurred at some time between 1066 and 1086 and affected the number of ploughs through the death of the oxen which drew them.
4 ... The category of livestock has been omitted in LDB.
ILBOD. See *69*.
THEODORIC POINTEL. See *71*.
RANULF PEVEREL. See *34*.
VALUE 15s. The gap in Farley before *xv* represents an erasure in the MS.
WILLIAM SON OF GROSS. See 11,1 note.
RALPH BAYNARD. See *33*.
HAMO THE STEWARD. See *28*.
JOCELYN LORIMER. See *64*. LDB *Goscelm(us)* is in error for *Goscelin(us)*. ECE 44, note, identifies this hide with land at Terling said in the Ely land pleas of 1071 x 1075 to be held by one *Gotselm* but which formerly belonged to Ely; see *Inquisitio Comitatus Cantabrigiensis*, ed. N. E. S. A. Hamilton (1876), 193.
MONKS OF ... ELY. This hide is not mentioned in Chapter 10, but see IE 128.

1,3 PLOUGHS, NOW 31½. The ½ plough represents ½ a plough-team, 4 oxen.
ALL OF THE SHERIFFS. That is, it was a cumulative loss due to a disease which had continued since 1066, during which time there was a succession of Sheriffs in Essex.
SWEIN ... SHERIFFDOM. He had been replaced as Sheriff first by Ralph Baynard (*33*) and then by Peter of Valognes (*36*) before 1086.
GEOFFREY DE MANDEVILLE. See *30*.
COUNT EUSTACE. See *20*.
OSMUND OF ANJOU. LDB *angeuin(us)* from OFr *angeuin*, OEB 132.
ROBERT GERNON. See *32*.
HERTFORD, AMWELL, HODDESDON ... RALPH OF LIMESY. Ralph is recorded as holding 14½ hides at Amwell in 1086 (Hertfordshire 23,4), held by Earl Harold in 1066 and presumably including the outlier at Amwell mentioned here. The Hoddesdon and Hertford outliers are probably the woodland at Hailey belonging 'to 3 hides of Amwell' and the 24 acres of Hertford, respectively, which Ralph claimed from Geoffrey of Bec in 1086 (Hertfordshire 34,13 and 23,4 note). *Hodesduna* has been altered in the MS from *Hodestuna*.
LATER ON WE RECOVERED ½ HIDE. The use of the first person plural here reflects the compilation of the chapter on the King's lands by his own officials who had taken action to recover this ½ hide between 1066 and 1086, cf. 66,1. The ½ hide was at Ryes (see 28,6), and had been granted out again by the King in 1086.
RALPH OF MARCY. From Marcy (La Manche: arr. Avranches), OEB 97. See 28,6. Cf. also 20,6 for another annexation by him from Earl Harold's land.

1,4 HAVERING. VCH p. 429, n.6 takes *Haueringas* to be a plural Latin accusative form but it is in fact an OE plural nominative. Cf. 6,6 note on Feering.
ROBERT SON OF CORBUCION ... 3 HIDES. These were at Leyton (41,4), although 8 Freemen are recorded there. MS has an erasure after *M(odo)*, whence the gap in the facsimile, not shown by Farley.
HUGH DE MONTFORT ... FOURTH HIDE. At Leyton. See 27,3.
4½ HIDES. Presumably referring to those at Leyton in 41,3 although Havering is not mentioned there.
30 ACRES. Probably at Fyfield, see 40,7 note.

1,6 THEODORIC POINTEL. See *71*.
'STUDLY'. Lost, in Woodham Ferrers, EPNS 276.
ANOTHER VILLAGER. Farley *7.ali(us) uill(anus)* is in error for *7.i.ali(us) uill(anus)* of the MS.

1,9 EARL 'EDGAR'. In error for Earl Algar (he of 1,11 note), see Cambridgeshire 1,10; 15; 22 where he is correctly named. Cf. LibEl 166 where he is called *Elgarus*; the LDB error was probably caused by the misreading of a similar spelling. There may however have been some confusion with Earl Algar's son Earl Edwin (d.1071).
PICOT THE SHERIFF. Of Cambridgeshire in 1086.
1½ HIDES ... IN CAMBRIDGESHIRE. At Hinxton (Cambridgeshire 1,10; 22. EE1).
A MILL. Farley *7. mol(endinum)* is in error for *7.i.mol(endinum)* of the MS.
LATER. *P(ost)*; between 1066 and 1086.
1½ HIDES WHICH HARDWIN ... HOLDS. Probably at Babraham and Hinxton (Cambridgeshire 26,11; 14. EE1).

PAID SUIT. *reddebat soca(m)*, attended court or paid a fine in lieu.
PICOT HOLDS ½ HIDE. At Babraham (Cambridgeshire 1,15. EE1).

1,10 HORWULF. LDB *Horolf(us)*; OE *Heoruwulf*, PNDB 289.
TASCELIN THE PRIEST. See also 3,11.

1,11-12 EARL ALGAR. Of East Anglia 1051–52, 1053–57; of Mercia 1057–62. He was probably dead by 1066, see Harmer, *ASWrits*, 546–547. See also 1,9 note. For his wife Aelfeva, see B3j.
THE QUEEN. Probably Matilda, consort to William I, who appears to have been given the lands formerly belonging to Earl Algar, VCH 337. Cf. B3j.
OTTO THE GOLDSMITH. See *81*, and B3j.
AS DUES. *Ad censu(m)*; Otto was enjoying its revenue as a payment from the King.

1,11 LATER ON. *post ea*, with incorrect word division; so in MS.
RICHARD SON OF COUNT GILBERT. See *23*.
WALTER SON OF GILBERT. He was probably the same as Walter Cook, see *67* note.

1,13 LESS 15 ACRES. *min(us)* is written overline in the MS preceded by an insertion-sign in the form of a colon, repeated at the point of insertion in the text after *ac(re)*.
7 PIGS. In the MS *por(ci)* has been altered to *bor(darii)*. Farley is in error here and the correct reading is 'smallholders'.
COUNT ALAN. LDB *Alam(us)*, probably for *Alain(us)*. See *21*.
45 ACRES. See 23,28.

1,13a APART ... KING'S SERVICE. Perhaps referring to the general liability to help with the '3 burdens' of military service and the upkeep of bridges and fortifications.

1,14 'WIBERTSHERNE'. The Hundred rubric is in error for Barstable, being placed one entry too soon.
FISHERY. In the present edition *piscina* has in most counties been translated as 'fishpond' in distinction to *piscaria* 'fishery', but since in Essex only *piscina* occurs, it has been translated as 'fishery' throughout. Cf. DBE 279.

1,16 *ULWINESCHERHAM*. Unidentified; 'Wulfwine's *Cherham* or *Scherham'*. The primary place-name here is either OE *c(i)err* 'a turn, bend' or OE *scir* 'bright' with either OE *hām* 'estate' or *hamm* 'an enclosure'.

1,17 RANULF PEVEREL. He held 5½ hides and 10 acres in that part of Maldon which was in this Hundred, see 34,12. He also had another ½ hide and 24 acres in the Half-Hundred of Maldon, see 34,31.

1,17a BAYNARD. Probably Ralph Baynard (*33*).

1,18 GRIM THE REEVE. See *83*.
HAS ALWAYS HELD. Translating *ten& se(m)p(er)*.

1,19 LAYER. The boundary of Stanway partly overlaps with that of Layer de la Haye in Winstree Hundred.
LEXDEN. See also B2.
PETER. The Sheriff. Cf. 1,2.
RAYMOND GERALD. LDB *Reimund(us) girald(us)*, the second name probably being a patronym (OG *Gerald*, Forssner 103–104) although *filius* is omitted. Cf. 32,24 where it is stated that Raymond took away another villager in this Hundred.
ROGER OF POITOU. Cf. 32,24 where Roger is recorded in possession of the villager mentioned in preceding note. In 47,3 he is said to have appropriated another 10 acres in this Hundred.
32 PENNIES. That is two *ora* of 16 pence, see S. Harvey, 'Royal revenue and Domesday terminology', *Economic History Review* 2nd series xx (1967), 221–228.

1,20 3[s]. LDB omits *sol(idos)*.

1,21 HUNDRED OF CHAFFORD. In error for Chelmsford Hundred, in which Fingrith Hall lay, cf. EPNS 236. There is some scribal confusion between the two Hundreds in this and the following four entries. *cesfeworda* is a LDB error for *ceffeworda*.

1,22 FRIDEBERT. LDB *Frieb(er)t(us)*; either OG *Fridebert, Frithebert* or possibly OE *Frithubeorht*; see PNDB 254. Cf. *70* note *sub* Hagebern.
MARGARETTING. Identified by VCH 433, n.4.

1,23 THE QUEEN. Probably Matilda (as in 1,11–12 note).
SHERIFF OF SURREY. Named as Ranulf in Surrey 1c and 5,28.
[VALUE]. LDB omits *ual(uit)*.

1,24 16 HIDES ... 14. Engelric had taken 2 hides, see below.
BY WEIGHT. *ad pond(us)*, that is the coins were weighed (although apparently not assayed) rather than being accepted at face value. This was to counteract any payment in coins which had been clipped.

ENGELRIC ... OF IT. Cf. 20,51. Engelric was Count Eustace's predecessor.
ROBERT GERNON ... WOODLAND. Robert himself was probably the King's Forester in Essex, see VCH 347.
FREE. *lib(er)ae*, for *lib(er)e* and describing the intended tenure rather than the act of giving.
R(OBERT) BISHOP OF HEREFORD. Robert Losinga 1079-95.
IN WRITTLE ... 50s. Most of this information is repeated at 19,1.

1,25-27 PETER. The Sheriff.

1,25 SWEIN'S LAND. See 24,63 where however the King is said to have only 3s from customary dues.
RANULF PEVEREL. See 34,31 for his Maldon land in this Half-Hundred.
FOR 3s. *p(er).iii.sol(idos)*, that is 'to the value of 3s'.
BEFORE 1066 ... BY WEIGHT. Cf. 34,31 note.

1,26 HUNDRED OF TENDRING. *Tendering &* in Farley is in error for *Tenderingae* of MS.
HARKSTEAD. A Suffolk outlier of Brightlingsea, see ESf1.
P(ETER). Farley *p̄*, MS *P̄*.
4 CATTLE AND 5 PIGS. Apparently additional to the previous total. These figures do not tally with those for Harkstead in ESf1.

1,27 BAYNARD. Ralph Baynard (*33*), cf. 1,2 note. Here the context again allows the forename to be omitted.
WOODLAND. Farley *Silua*, MS *Silú*.
1 OUTLIER ... IT. Cf. 20,69.
ROGER OF RAISMES. See *39*.
CALLS ... DELIVERER. That is, to bear witness that he had delivered ownership, as Sheriff, on the King's behalf to Roger.
RICHARD SON OF COUNT GILBERT. He held Alresford (23,33) which came within the jurisdiction of Lawford.
WALERAN. The father of John (*40*).
HAGEBERT. Apparently OG *Hagabert, Hagibert* (Forssner 138) but cf. *70* note.
COUNT E(USTACE). Cf. 20,69 for his holding at Lawford.
BISHOP OF BAYEUX ... HIM. See 18,44 note.
RANULF ... 15 ACRES. See 37,20.
RALPH BAYNARD ... 35 ACRES. See 33,17.
ROGER ... LONDON. Probably he of 4,5.

1,28 SHELFORD. Cambridgeshire EE2.
THIS OUTLIER WAS. *Hec berewita erat*, altered from *Hec berewita e(st)*; so in MS. For *berewica*, OE *bere-wīc*.
ROBERT GERNON. See *32*.

1,30 EDEVA. The Fair, some of whose land in Suffolk (1,61; 63-64; 67; 73) was later held by Earl Ralph and then by Godric the Steward. See also 21,2-5 note.
EARL RALPH. As 21,9 note.

2 HOLY TRINITY, CANTERBURY. That is Christ Church, Canterbury. The lands in this chapter were later subject to the Dean of Bocking, see VCH 340.

2,2 2 HIDES IN (WEST) MERSEA. Bocking Hall (in Winstree Hundred, EPNS 320-321), an estate in West Mersea granted with Bocking to Christ Church, Canterbury between 995 and 999 by AEthelric and Leofwynn (ECE, no. 30; Sawyer no. 1218).

2,4 HOLY TRINITY HOLDS. Repeated before 2,5-8.
LAWLING. For the annexation by the monks of 1 hide there, see 90,79.

2,6 ST. LAWRENCE. Formerly 'Newland', EPNS 224.

Folio 8a, foot. In the bottom margin (not shown by Farley, but in facsimile) is written *iii. v(irgate). iiii. 7 d(imidia).̇.ii.' 7 d(imidia).xiiii.ii.iii.vii.* This is a list of the hidages in this chapter, the last figure being the sum of the hidages of 2,7-9 on folio 8b. Cf. notes on folios 20a,87a.

Folio 9a. A partial list of landholders (*3-8*) has been crossed through on this folio, the remainder of which is blank. A similar list occurs at folio 17a. These folios are the first leaves of quires 2 and 3 respectively of LDB and each list contains only those landholders whose Holdings form chapters in that particular quire which the list introduces. The presence of these lists in the MS reflects the fact that LDB was originally intended to be no more than a circuit return.

3,1 AELFTHRYTH. LDB *Alftred queda(m) femina*; PNDB 181.

3,2 BISHOP WILLIAM. Of London, 1051-75. See *4*, note.
COUNT EUSTACE ... 100 MANORS. See 20,4.
WOODLAND, 1000 [PIGS]. LDB omits *porci*.

3,5 ST. PAUL'S HELD. Literally 'St. Paul held'. Referring to St. Paul's Cathedral, London.

BRIAN. Farley *brieu*, MS *brien*.
FROM THE BISHOP. LDB *depo* is in error for *de ep(iscop)o*.
3,9 IN SOUTHMINSTER. The preposition *in* was added as an afterthought and is squeezed into the space before *Sudmunstrā*. Although the addition of *in* made the abbreviation-mark on the place-name incorrect, the scribe forgot to erase it.
BISHOP HOLDS IN LORDSHIP. The words *ep(is)c(opus) in d(omi)nio* are interlined in the MS and replace *xiiii.milites de ep(iscop)o* '14 men-at-arms from the Bishop', which is deleted; the plural verb *tenent* 'hold' is altered to the singular *tenet* by placing points above and below the letter *n*.
14 MEN. Probably the '14 men-at-arms' referred to in previous note.
KING CANUTE. 1016–35.
3,10 WERE 17 ACRES. LDB *fuere*, a short form for *fuerunt*. Also at 9,10 etc.
1 VIRGATE. ECE, no. 27, note, suggests that this is both the woodland in 32,5 and Glazenwood (EPNS 283).
3,11 TASCELIN THE PRIEST. See also 1,10.
AFTER HE CROSSED THE SEA. After 1066.
3,14 NOW ... The number in Farley is damaged but should read *ii*.
3,16 COLCHESTER. The Bishop's land is not referred to in *B*. The 14 houses and 4 acres may have been the land which in 1206 was referred to as a Soke, while the whole of 3,16 may be represented by the parish of St. Mary's-at-the-Walls; see VCH 424.
APART FROM THE LEVY. *p(re)t(er) Scotu(m)*. See B2 note.
4 It is suggested by VCH 339 that the lands in the present chapter represent those acquired by Bishop William (1051–75). Cf. the references in Hertfordshire (4,1;22) to lands bought by Bishop William.
4,1 CRANHAM. Formerly 'Bishop's Ockendon', EPNS 124–125.
4,2-3 TOTHAM. Rok Hall in Little Totham, VCH 440; Rook Hall, EPNS 312.
4,3 WILLIAM BOLD. LDB *Will(elmus) balt*; perhaps OFr *balt* rather than OE *beald* in this particular instance, OEB 340–341.
4,5 ROGER. Cf. 1,27 note.
TENDRING. New Hall in Tendring, VCH 440.
4,6 ANSKETEL. See 48,2 note.
4,10 HORNDON (-ON-THE-HILL). The estate of Cantis there, VCH 441, n.2 and 398–399.
4,16 HARLOW. Farley and MS *herlaua*; facsimile (in error) *herlauan*.
EDEVA. The Fair, who had also held Bishop's Stortford (Hertfordshire 4,22) from Bishop William of London. See 21,2-5 note.
4,18 BASSETTS. In Woodham Walter EPNS 232 (6"). The manorial name also survives in Bassett's Farm in Little Baddow, but that is in Chelmsford Hundred. The LDB spelling *Mildemet* is metathesized, as later forms of this (superseded) name show it to have meant 'middle meadowland', possibly because of its location between the water meadow along the R. Chelmer to the north and higher woodland to the south.
5 CANONS OF ST. PAUL'S. That is, of St. Paul's Cathedral, London.
5,1 LEE (CHAPEL). For this identification, see EPNS 163.
5,2-5 ST. PAUL'S HELD/HOLDS ... Literally, 'St. Paul held/holds'.
5,6 GODITH. Probably the woman called Gotild in 28,16.
A WRIT. *breue(m)*, apparently here referring to the written record of Godith's grant rather than to a writ of the King.
5,8 THURSTAN THE RED. LDB *Turstin(us) ruff(us)*; OEB 330–331.
THE OTHER NAVESTOCK. A different manor, but within the present parish.
5,10 HEYBRIDGE. Formerly 'Tidwoldington', EPNS 303–304.
½ HIDE. Recorded under Langford, see 33,22.
5,11 THE NAZE. LDB *AEduluesnasa(m)*, 'Eadwulf's or Ealdwulf's promontory', EPNS 354–355.
MARK OF SILVER. Later in the medieval period a 'mark' was an accounting term equal to 13s 4d. Here it is probably a term denoting weight.
6 ST. PETER'S WESTMINSTER. The abbey refounded by Edward the Confessor. See also 90,19 for an annexation by St. Peter's.
6,1 ST. PETER'S HAS. Literally, 'St. Peter has'.
ST. MARY'S CHURCH. Apparently a reference to a church at South Benfleet before 1066, rather than to St. Mary's Barking (*9*). See also 1,1 note.
WESTMINSTER. Farley *Westmonasterio*; MS *Westmonsterio*.
50 SHEEP ... PIGS. Farley omits an insertion mark in the form of a colon before *L* and after *mot*.
ST. MARTIN'S. See *12* note.

COUNTY. LDB *consulat(us)*.

6,4 ALSTAN STRIC. The byname may be a variant of the OE name *Stric(c)a* (Redin 79), here used as a patronym. The OWScand nickname *Strikr* 'boy', is also possible, see OEB 337.

6,6 BECONTREE. Farley *Beuentreu*, MS *Beuentrev*.

6,8 FEERING. See also 90,17. VCH, p. 444 and n.8 mistakes the OE nominative plural form *Pheringas* for a Latin accusative plural. Cf. 1,4 note on Havering and 9,7 note on Barking. See also 6,11 note.

2 HOUSES IN COLCHESTER. According to B3k the Abbot had 4 houses there belonging to Feering.

ROGER OF RAISMES. He held land adjacent at Messing, see 39,4.

MAUGER ... ARCHBISHOP. He held land at Orpington (Kent, 2,30) from the Archbishop of Canterbury.

HE IS ... KING'S HAND. Or 'it is'; *est* here could refer to either the ½ virgate or the free man.

6,9 ALRIC ... NAVAL BATTLE AGAINST KING WILLIAM. Alric was called Aethelric the Chamberlain in Harmer, *ASWrits*, no. 74 (Sawyer, No. 118). The location of the battle is not known.

FELL. Farley *cecidet*, MS *cecidit*.

WRIT. Harmer, *ASWrits*, p. 494, prints a spurious writ, claiming to be issued by King William I, confirming Kelvedon Hatch to Westminster Abbey. ECE, no. 82 note, suggests that it was fabricated to make good the lack of documentary evidence reported here.

6,10 [HUNDRED OF CHAFFORD]. LDB puts the Hundred heading one entry late, before 6,11.

6,11 EXCHANGE. Together with Feering (cf. 6,8), North Ockendon had been granted by King William between 1066 and 1075 to Westminster Abbey in exchange for Windsor, Berks., ECE, no. 73.

6,12 WENNINGTON. Farley *Wemtuna(m)*, MS *Wenituna(m)*.

ROBERT THE PERVERTED. LDB *Inuesiat(us)* may be derived from Latin *invertere*, 'to pervert'. OEB 348 refers to MLat *invasatus* 'invaded by a devil'. He was identical with Robert the Lascivious (*lasciuus*) in 32,28, see VCH 518, n.7.

6,13 *GEDDESDUNA*. Unidentified, OE *Gieddesdūne* 'at Gieddi's upland'. Between 1066 and 1075 it (*Gyddesdúne*) had been granted by King William to Deorman, ECE, no. 72.

6,15 TO BATTLE IN YORK(SHIRE) WITH HAROLD. A reference to the Battle of Stamford Bridge in 1066. Cf. 30,16 note.

7,1 HAROLD HELD WALTHAM (HOLY CROSS). Earl (later King) Harold, who greatly extended the landholding of the Canons of Waltham (*8*).

WOODLAND, 202 PIGS. So in MS but *ii.7.cc.* is probably a scribal error for *m̄.7.cc.*, that is 1200.

TRIBUTARIES. *Censarii, cens(it)ores*, chiefly in north-east Mercia, Yorkshire, Essex and Dorset, paid tribute in money, not work.

1 PLOUGH CAN BE RESTORED. The one plough in lordship lacking in 1086, see above.

HOLY CROSS. The Canons of Waltham (*8*).

RANULF BROTHER OF ILGER ... 30 ACRES. See 37,9 note.

A GATE. Aldgate in the City of London. In 1108 the Priory of Holy Trinity Aldgate was freed from its subjection to the Canons of Waltham. See W. Page, *London: its origin and early development* (London, 1929), 153–154 and *The cartulary of Holy Trinity Aldgate*, ed. G. A. J. Hodgett (*London Record Society* 7, 1971), nos. 1-11. (*Ex inf*. Dr. D. J. Keene).

BISHOP'S PREDECESSOR. Altered in MS from 'his predecessor', *suo antecessori*. Probably referring to Bishop Walchere, 1071–80.

8 CANONS OF WALTHAM. The college of secular canons, favoured by King Harold. The latter's heart is buried at Waltham.

8,3 WOODFORD. The gap in Farley after the place-name represents an erasure in the MS.

WOODLAND ... NOW NONE. Added in the margin of the MS and here placed in the translation in its proper place.

8,4 1 PLOUGH ... RESTORED. That is, in lordship.

8,9 IN THIS MANOR. LDB *In ho manerio*, in error for *In hoc manerio*.

1 CARUCATE. LDB *.i.carr̄.t̄rae*. Probably the land described at 32,29.

Folio 17a. A partial list of landholders (*9–18*) has been crossed through on this folio, the remainder of which is blank. See note to folio 9a.

9 ST. MARY'S BARKING. The Benedictine nunnery, founded in the mid-7th century and refounded in the mid-10th.

9,1 ST. MARY'S HOLDS. Literally, 'St. Mary holds'.

THOROLD OF ROCHESTER ... 30 ACRES. The 30 acres entered under the adjacent Chadwell in 18,11.

VILLAGERS' PLOUGHS. *car(uce) uill(an)is*, with dative of possession. An alternative to the more usual 'men's ploughs', *caruce hominum*.

9,2 RAVENGAR. LDB *Rauengari(us)*; OG *Hrabangar*, Forssner 212.

9,5 WOODHEN. LDB *cudhen* (here), *gudhen* (90,1). Unexplained OEB 390, but probably a byname **Wudhen* from OE *wude-henn* 'a female wood-cock'.

3 VIRGATES. See 90,2 where they are recorded as an annexation.

9,7 BARKING. VCH, p. 448 again mistakes the OE nominative plural form *Berchingas* for a Latin accusative plural. Cf. 6,8 note on Feering.

24 GOATS. So in MS, facsimile (in error) *xviiii*.

LONDON ... ½ CHURCH. A reference to All Hallows, Barking-by-the-Tower. The three dots in Farley at the foot of folio 17b represent an erasure (of *xiii*) in the MS.

ENGLISHMEN ... FRENCHMEN. The men of the Hundred jury, four French and four English.

JOCELYN LORIMER. He held land adjacent at Ilford (64,1).

9,8 WIGBOROUGH. The manor of Abbot's (formerly Abbess) Hall in Great Wigborough, EPNS 324.

3 HOUSES IN COLCHESTER. See B3s.

9,10 THERE WERE. *Fuere*; as in 3,10 note.

9,11 INGATESTONE. Owned by Barking Abbey until the Dissolution, EPNS 253-254.

9 CATTLE. LDB repeats *.ix.an(imales)* in error.

9,12 The gap before this entry in Farley represents a tear (repaired) in the MS. Cf. 10,1 note.

9,13 WILLIAM OF BOURSIGNY. Probably from Boursigny (Calvados); OEB 78.

10 ST. ETHELDREDA'S, ELY. Ely Abbey. For possessions alienated by 1086, not mentioned in this chapter, see 1,2. 18,36. 22,7. 25,3. 27,14. 30,27;41. 34,19. 79,1.

10,1 BROXTED. The same information is given in IE 125, IEBrev 172, IENV 175.

70 SHEEP ... MANOR. The gap in Farley at the two line-ends represents the reverse of the same tear referred to in 9,12 note.

9 ACRES ... £4. The last two lines on folio 18b are written in the MS over an erasure.

9 ACRES. See 25,12.

ALSO. Farley replaces the ampersand of the MS with the tironian *nota*.

10,2 RODING. See also IE 126. The information in 22,7-8 and IEAL 184 suggests that LDB is defective here as it appears that 22,7 was also alienated from Ely while the statistics in 10,2 include elements from both 22,7-8.

THIRD HIDE. See 22,8.

23 PIGS. LDB *xvviii*; IE *xviii*.

10,3 RETTENDON. See also IE 126, IEBrev 172, IENV 175.

3 PLOUGHS IN LORDSHIP. IEBrev lists 4.

SIWARD HOLDS. LDB *ten&* is an LDB error for *tenuit* 'held'.

1 HIDE AND 30 ACRES. See 34,30.

2 HIDES AND 30 ACRES; EUDO. See 25,20. Farley uses the same symbol for *q(ue)* in *q(ue) tenuit* as for *q(uia)* in *q(uia) antecessor*; in the MS and facsimile these symbols differ.

10,4 HADSTOCK. For this entry, see also IE 126. For the name represented by LDB *Cadenhou*, see EPNS 510-511.

10,5 LITTLEBURY. See also IE 126-127, IEBrev 172, IENV 175.

19 SMALLHOLDERS. IEBrev lists 16.

7 SLAVES. IEBrev lists 6.

CALLED STRETHALL. Farley *vocat(ur)*, MS *uocat(ur)*.

ALWIN LDB *Eluui(us)*; IE *Alwinus* (MSS B,C), *alfpinus* (MS A).

HUGH. IE 127, IEAL 182, Hugh of Bernières. Also in Cambridgeshire (27, etc).

HEYDON. According to IEAL 182 this was also appropriated by Hugh of Bernières. Farley *hamdena*, MS *haindena*.

ALWIN [HELD]. LDB omits *tenuit*.

WILLIAM CARDON. The byname is OFr *cardon* 'thistle'; OEB 368-369. The byname survives in Cardon's Hall in Chishall, VCH 356.

WRONGFULLY. *i(n)i(us)te(m)* Farley, in error for *i(n)i(us)te* of MS.

11 ST. EDMUND'S. Literally, 'St. Edmund'. The Abbey of Bury St. Edmunds, Suffolk.

11,1 WILLIAM SON OF GROSS. An undertenant of Hugh de Montfort (27,2. 90,15;18). See also 1,2 and 88,2.

11,3 FOR 4½ HIDES. So in MS, facsimile has '3½ hides'.

11,5 HUNDRED OF LEXDEN. LDB *Laxefelda*; this spelling would appear to be in error. The scribe of LDB has substituted the OE element *feld* for *denu* contained in Lexden, see EPNS 359,376.

11,7 (LITTLE) WALTHAM. The manor of Channels there, VCH 451, n.8.

Folio 20a, foot. Farley does not show the summary of hidages in Chapter 11 given in the bottom margin of the MS and facsimile. This reads *i.i.d(imidia) . iii. d(imidia) . iii. d(imidia) . iii. d(imidia).ii.v.* Cf. notes on folios 8a,87a.

12 ST. MARTIN'S, LONDON. St. Martin le Grand, founded by Engelric the predecessor of Count Eustace (*20*).

12,1 OUTLIER. According to ECE, no. 84, dated 1068, this was at Mashbury.

13 ST. MARTIN'S, BATTLE. Battle Abbey, founded by King William on the battlefield of Hastings.

13,1 GOTI. See 28,1 note.

HUTTON. LDB *Atahov*, OE *aet* and *hōh*, 'at the hill', with later addition of *tūn* 'estate', EPNS 160.

FREE LAND. *lib(er)ae t(er)rae* (genitive singular). VCH 452, n.4, suggests it was free from geld.

13,2 HORSEHAM (HALL). Later in Freshwell Hundred, EPNS 509, VCH 452, n.5.

33 SHEEP. So in MS; facsimile '28'.

14 ST. VALÉRY'S. King William granted 12½ hides in Essex to the Abbey in 1068 (ECE, no. 85) to repay St. Valéry for having sent a favourable wind to enable him to cross the Channel before the Battle of Hastings.

14,1 MATCHING. VCH 452, n.8 identified this as Matching Barns in Hatfield Broad Oak but this was not confirmed by EPNS 43,45.

14,2 LINDSELL. The manor of Prior's Hall there, EPNS 487.

Folio 21a, lines 2-7. Farley omits to show an oblique gap caused by a (repaired) tear in the MS.

14,3 TAKELEY. The manor later called Warish Hall in Takeley, EPNS 535-536, whose name commemorates ownership by St. Valéry's.

14,5 WIDDINGTON. The manor of Prior's Hall there, EPNS 546.

20 SHEEP. LDB *.xx.ou(es)* is in error, probably for *.xx.bor(darii)*, '20 smallholders'.

14,6 ST. PETER'S CHAPEL. The estate was one of those near St. Peter's Chapel (*Ythancaestir* *c.* 735) on the site of the Roman fort of Othona (see EPNS 210-211). Identified by VCH 453,392 as the manor of East Hall in Bradwell.

14,7 HE ALSO HELD. LDB *teñ*, here for *tenuit*, governed as in 14,6 by 'Thorkell'.

15 HOLY TRINITY, CAEN. The Nunnery there, founded by Queen Matilda.

15,1 FELSTED. Granted to Holy Trinity in 1082 by King William and Queen Matilda, ECE, no. 92.

3 VIRGATES. Recorded at 72,2.

THE FOURTH. Recorded at 73,1.

16 ST. STEPHEN'S, CAEN. The Monastery there, founded by William the Conqueror.

16,1 PANFIELD. See ECE, no. 88, for King William's confirmation of Panfield to St. Stephen's between 1071 and 1077. It had been granted by Waleran son of Ranulf between 1069 and 1076, ECE, no. 86.

17 ST. OUEN'S. The Abbey at Rouen, dedicated to St. Audoenus.

17,1 ST. OUEN'S HELD. Literally, 'St. Ouen held'.

(WEST) MERSEA. The estate appears to have been granted to St. Ouen's by Edward the Confessor in 1046 (Sawyer, no. 1015; ECE, no. 63).

WALERAN TOOK IT AWAY. See B6 for Waleran's connection with Colchester.

17,2 KING'S MANOR AT LAYER. For the King's land there (said to be an outlier of Stanway manor) see 1,19.

FORFEITURES OF THE HUNDRED. The profits of jurisdiction in the Hundred court, see further Harmer, *ASWrits*, 73-85.

18 BISHOP OF BAYEUX. Odo, King William's half-brother. Although he was imprisoned from 1082-87, his lands were maintained as a unit.

18,1 THOROLD'S SON. As elsewhere in this chapter, this no doubt refers to Ralph son of Thorold of Rochester.

30 ACRES ... 1066. See 20,1.

18,2 WOODLAND, ½ HIDE. The measurement of woodland in hides, here, in 18,5 and in several entries in Chapter 24, is unusual in the DB Survey.

18,5 INGRAVE. The second part of the modern name preserves the name of the Domesday tenant, (Ralph) son of Thorold; EPNS 161.

WOODLAND. See 18,2 note.

3 HIDES. *v* deleted, *iii* interlined.

11 SMALLHOLDERS. Misplaced among the resources.

18,7 WHEATLEY. Later in Rochford Hundred, EPNS 195.

POINTEL. Probably Theodoric Pointel (*71*).
18,9 TEHER. A NFr form of OG *Theothere*, Forssner 228.
18,11 30 ACRES. At Mucking, see 9,1.
18,16 BARLING. The manor of Mucking Hall there, VCH 456, n.7.
18,17 2 OXEN. That is, ¼ plough-team.
18,18 23s. *xiii* with another *x* interlined.
18,19 POINTEL. As 18,7 note.
18,20 35 ACRES. *xxx* with *v* interlined.
18,21 AUBREY'S WIFE. That is, of Aubrey de Vere (*35*). Cf. 18,24.
'NAPSTED'. Lost in Lt. Maplestead, EPNS 447. Cf. also 90,38 for Aubrey's wife's annexation at Lt. Maplestead.
18,21a TIHEL OF HELLÉAN. See *38*, note.
18,23-24 Farley does not show two oblique tears (repaired) which affect the writing of these entries and 18,30-32 (on the reverse) in the MS.
18,23 BRADWELL QUAY. Formerly 'Hackfleet', EPNS 209-210.
18,24 AUBREY'S WIFE. As 18,21 note.
18,25 HERBERT'S NEPHEW. Or possibly his grandson (*nepos*). He was probably Hugh, who held Screveton (Nottinghamshire 7,6) from the Bishop.
18,26-27 MAUGER. As 6,8 note.
18,29 MANNING. LDB *Mannic(us)*; PNDB 324.
18,30-32 See 18,23-24 note.
18,30 RAINHAM. The manor of Southall there, VCH 458, n.3; South Hall, EPNS 128.
18,32 WILLIAM PEVEREL ... THURROCK. See 48,2.
18,33 CRANHAM. LDB *Craohv*; for the identification, see EPNS 124-125.
18,34 GILBERT ... 10 ACRES. See 48,2.
18,35 *LIMPWELLA*. Unidentified, a place named from a spring of some sort (OE *wella*). The first element looks like OE *(ge)limp*, 'an event, happening, accident'.
BISHOP. LDB *comite*, 'Count', deleted.
18,36 ELY ABBEY. See IE 128, IEAL 188.
2 MEN. IE, 'free men', *liberi homines*.
18,37 DANE. *dac(us)*; see OEB 135.
BEREWIC. Unidentified, OE *bere-wīc*, 'outlier'.
THOROLD. Perhaps in error for (Ralph) son of Thorold of Rochester.
18,38-43 R(ALPH); RALPH. Son of Thorold of Rochester.
18,39 ANAND THE DANE. ODan *Anund*, PNDB 161. For *dac(us)* see OEB 135.
AS A MANOR. *iii* at first written, *m(anerio)* added overline as a correction.
18,40 SAEGAR. LDB *Segar(us)*; PNDB 352, s.n. **Sǣgār*.
PATCHING (HALL). VCH 459, n.9 misinterprets *Pacingas* as Latin accusative plural rather than as OE nominative plural.
18,41 This entry would appear to have been originally begun in LDB on the previous line, where the paragraph-mark and an initial *M* have been left in suspension.
18,42 THE OTHER MOULSHAM (HALL). Another manor, also within the area now called Moulsham Hall.
18,43 AETHELSTAN. LDB *Adstan(us)*; PNDB 188.
18,44 OTHER LAND. Possibly a reference to the ½ hide belonging to Lawford (in the same Hundred) mentioned in 1,27 as being held by Ralph son of Thorold under the Bishop of Bayeux.
19,1 [HUNDRED OF CHELMSFORD]. LDB omits the Hundred rubric.
WRITTLE. See 1,24 for an almost duplicate entry.
HAROLD'S HOLDING. Referring to Earl Harold; in 1,24 the same information is given in reference to 'the King's Holding'.
20 COUNT EUSTACE. Of Boulogne, brother-in-law of King Edward.
20,1 30 ACRES ... HOLDING. Entered under Vange (18,1), adjacent to Fobbing.
ENGELRIC. Count Eustace's predecessor in many of his lands. The founder of St. Martin le Grand (*12*).
20,2 WARNER. The LDB form *Garner(us)* is an OFr form of OG *Warinhari*; Forssner 247-248.
20,3 THEN 2 PLOUGHS. In the MS, *ii* has been altered from *i*.
20,4 ORSETT. The manor of Loft Hall there, VCH 461, n.2.
BISHOP OF LONDON. Bishop William, see 3,2.
20,4-5 100 MANORS. These are also mentioned in 3,2. They may refer to a total number of manors promised to Count Eustace by King William.
20,5 'GRAVESEND'. LDB *Grauesanda(m)*. Probably a detached part of Gravesend, Kent,

which lies on the opposite bank of the Thames to Barstable Hundred. Cf. the Chalk entry (EKt) for another connection between estates in Kent and Essex.

20,6 AELFRIC ... HOLDS. *Tenuit* 'held' altered to *Tenet* 'holds'.
30 ACRES. See 28,3. Cf. 1,3 note.

20,7 ALWAYS ... 1 PLOUGH. *Se(m)p(er)* in this instance means 'then and now', since a different figure is given for 'when acquired'.
HIRED MAN. Translating *mercennari(us)*.

20,8 QUEEN EDITH. The consort of Edward the Confessor and daughter of Earl Godwin of Wessex.
300 AND A HALF. That is, 350; unless *dim* has been entered in error through confusion with the line below.
COLCHESTER. See B3g for Count Eustace's houses there.
RICHARD OF SACKVILLE ... ½ MILL. See 25,1 note. He probably took his name from Sacquenville (Eure: arr. Evreux), OEB 111-112.

20,12 IWAIN. LDB *Iunain(us)* here, *Iunan(us)* 20,50. The first *n* in both spellings is in error for *u*. *Iwain* is OBret or OW.

20,13 ADELULF. Of Marck, see 20,15 note.
LATTON. The manor of Mark Hall there (EPNS 44), named from the byname of the 1086 subtenant. Cf. 20,15 note.
ERNULF. Probably OE *Earnwulf*, but possibly ODan *Arnulf*; PNDB 244.
AT A CHURCH. Translating *ad una(m) eccl(es)iam*. A possible alternative is '(belonging) to a church'.

20,14 BRICTMER. LDB *Brictnar(us)*.
;½ HIDE. *7 dim(idia) hid(a)* in Farley is in error for *p(ro) dim(idia) hid(a)* of MS.

20,15 ADELULF OF MARCK. From Marck (Pas-de-Calais), OEB 98. His first name is OG, Forssner 10. For his family and estates, see VCH 344.
DUNMOW. The manor of Marks there (EPNS 477), named from the family of the 1086 subtenant. Cf. 20,13 note.

20,17 THERE. LDB *.i.bi.* in error for *ibi*.

20,18 'PLESINGHO'. Lost, in Willingale Doe, EPNS 500-501. See also 90,30.

20,19 7 HIDES. NOW. Farley omits to show a gap, caused by an erasure, in the MS between *hid(is)* and *M(odo)*.
½ HIDE. See 28,9 note.

20,21 THEN 38 SHEEP. 'Then' (*tunc*) is interlined.

20,22;24 ADELULF. As 20,13 note.

20,27 (STEEPLE) BUMPSTEAD. The manor of Garnons there, VCH 464, n.6; EPNS 420, s.n. Garland's Farm.
CATTLE. Farley adds an otiose abbreviation-mark above *n* of *anim(ales)*, not in MS.

20,28 VCH 464, n.9, identifies this as Belchamp St. Ethelbert in Ovington (see EPNS 448, s.n. Allbrights), but this is not supported by EPNS 408-409 or by DG 131.
WHICH ... HELD. Deleted thus in MS.

20,29 ADELULF. As 20,13 note.
HOLDS. Deleted thus in MS.

20,30 20 ... LESS 1. LDB omits the category of livestock. Probably pigs or sheep.

20,32 VILLAGERS, NOW 3. *ii* altered to *iii* in MS.
14 SMALLHOLDERS. *xiiii*, the *x* has been altered from *i* in the MS.
ENGELRIC ... MANORS. Presumably those of Finchingfield (20,30) and Smeetham Hall (20,32).

20,34 ST. MARTIN'S. See *12* note.
VALUE ... 100s. Deleted thus in MS.

20,36-37 BLANCHED. Both the adjectives *candidus* and *blancus* are used here to describe pounds of pennies which have been assayed.

20,36 COLCHESTER. As 20,8 note.

20,37 AELFRIC ... BOXTED. See EHu.
2 COBS. MS *iii* with last minim erased; facsimile *iii*.

20,39 COLCHESTER. As 20,8 note.

20,40 EDRIC. Called Edric of Easthorpe in 37,20 from his holding here.

20,41 COLNE. VCH 466, n.2 identifies this as Colne Engaine but this is not supported by EPNS 379 or by DG 134.
AELFRIC BIG. The byname *biga* is probably identical with ME *bigge* 'of large, bulky size', OEB 290-292.

20,42 GODRIC OF COLCHESTER. See B1-2.
20,43 AS MUCH. LDB has an otiose abbreviation-mark above *u* of *tantunde(m)*.
ACQUIRED 7, NOW 5. Farley does not show the gap in the text in MS, caused by an erasure between *vii* and *m(odo)*.
VALUE ALWAYS 5s. Corrected thus in MS.
20,44 AELFRIC'S FATHER HELD. There is a deletion of about two letters in the MS after *teñ*; *ten&* has probably been altered to *teñ* standing here for *ten(uit)*.
(AS) OF ENGELRIC'S HOLDING. Translating *de feudo ingelrici*, meaning that it had *formerly* been held by Engelric.
20,46 ONGAR. For an annexation there by a man of Count Eustace's, see 90,87.
20,49 (HIM). Alternatively '(them)', referring to the 10 acres.
20,50 IWAIN. See 20,12 note.
20,51 ENGELRIC ... 1066. See 1,24.
20,54 ADELULF. As 20,13 note.
20,56 UNDER THEM. That is, under Lambert before 1066 and under Engelric after 1066.
WHO ... DEFENDER. *unde reuocat ea(m)* [Farley error for *eu(m)* of MS] *ad defensore(m)*.
AS. LDB *u* is in error for *ut*.
20,57 TOLLESHUNT. VCH 468, n.6 identifies this as the manor of Tolleshunt Guines in Tollesbury. EPNS 305, s.n. Guines Court, does not quote the LDB form however.
THORBERN. Cf. *70* note *sub* Hagebern.
20,57-58 ADELULF. As 20,13 note.
20,60 ST. MARTIN'S. See *12* note.
20,61 'BLATCHAMS'. Lost, in Great Totham; EPNS 310-311.
VALUE 10s. LDB has omitted *Tunc* before *Val(uit)*.
20,62 AMALFRID. The LDB form *Alm̅frid(us)* is corrupt. The name is OG, Forssner 26.
FREE MAN. LDB repeats *lib(er)* in error.
20,63 ST. OSYTH. LDB *Cita(m)* is in error for *Cica(m)*. The place-name commemorates St. Osyth who is said to have founded a nunnery at *Cicc* in the 7th century, see EPNS 347-348. The present holding is identified by VCH 469, n.5, as the manor of Earl's Hall in St. Osyth.
BURNA. Unidentified, OE *burna* '(place at) the stream'.
30 ACRES. In the MS there is a deletion (?of *quas*) after *.xxx.ac(re)*.
20,64 TENDRING. The manor of Old Hall there, VCH 469, n.9.
AS MUCH. LDB *tantude(m)* is in error for *tantu(n)de(m)*.
20,65 HATO. OG *Hado, Hatto*, see Förstemann PN 790, s.n. *Hatho*.
20,67 ST. PAUL'S, LONDON. See *5*.
20,68-69 ADELULF. As 20,13 note.
20,69 LAWFORD. The manor of Dale Hall there, VCH 470, n.5. Cf. in 1,27 the reference to an outlier of 4 hides annexed by Engelric and held by Count Eustace.
THEM. Referring to the 3 Freemen.
20,70 TENDRING. VCH 470, n.7; as 20,64 note.
20,71 (AS) OF ENGELRIC'S HOLDING. See 20,44 note.
APPROPRIATED AFTER 1066. *t(empore) r(egis) Will(elm)i* has been altered, by deletion in MS, from *t(empore) r(egis) e(dwardi)*.
THESE 8 ACRES. Presumably those belonging to the 2 Freemen who had not been appropriated by Engelric.
HE PAID. The Freeman.
20,72 SIRED. Corrected from Siward; *Siuuard(us), -uuard(us)* underlined for deletion, *-red(us)* interlined.
3 PLOUGHS IN LORDSHIP. Farley does not show a gap caused by an erasure in MS between *car(uce)* and *in*. There are also deletions and alterations in the following line in MS.
20,74 200 SHEEP; 88 SHEEP. Thus in MS. The second lot of sheep may be in error for goats however.
20,75-76 BRICTWULF. According to ECE, no. 83, a writ of King William dated between 1066 and 1087, Brictwulf's lands were to be held by the Abbey of Bury St. Edmunds. This writ does not appear to have taken effect by the time of Domesday.
20,77 ENGELRIC. See 90,64 where Engelric is said to have also held an annexation of 30 acres at Bendysh (Hall).
20,79 ADELULF. As 20,13 note.
Folio 35 is a half-sheet in the MS, containing the whole of Chapter 21.
21 COUNT ALAN. Of Brittany, son-in-law of King William. His name is OBret *Alan*.
21,2-5 EDEVA. Probably Edeva the Fair, one of Count Alan's predecessors, see Cambridgeshire (Chapter 14) and Hertfordshire (Chapter 16). See also 1,30 note; 4,16 note; and 21,11-12.

21,3 AMONG MEADOW AND MARSH. Translating *int(er) p(ra)tu(m) 7 maresc.*
21,4 FINCHINGFIELD. The manor of Spain's Hall there (EPNS 427).
21,9 EARL R(ALPH). Of East Anglia. Called Ralph 'Wader' in Cambridgeshire 19,4. With Earl Waltheof (see 55,1 note) and Earl Roger of Hereford, he rebelled against King William in 1075 and ended his life in exile. The byname 'Wader', DB *Waders*, may be a place-name, see OEB 119.
THIS LAND. *han* is a LDB error for *hanc*.
21,10 EMANUEL (WOOD). Between 1089 and 1093 this was granted by Count Alan to the Abbey of Bury St. Edmunds, ECE, no. 104.
21,11-12 EDEVA. As 21,2-5 note.
21,12 HERVEY. *Herueu(us)* is a LDB error for *Herue(us)*.
22 WILLIAM OF WARENNE. Later created Earl of Surrey by King William II.
22,1 *UPHAM*. Unidentified, OE *up-hām*, or *up-hamm*, 'upper estate' or 'upper enclosure'.
22,3 HOLDFAST. Probably identical with Aelmer Holdfast, see 61,2 note.
22,4 ALWIN GOTTON. The rest of his land had lain in Herts. On his byname, probably deriving from a lost place in that county, see Hertfordshire 10,6 note.
22,5 DOVE. LDB *Duua*. Either OE **dūfe* or ON *dúfa* 'a dove'; PNDB 227, Redin 116.
(GREAT) EASTON. The manor of Blamsters there, according to VCH 474, n.3.
22,6 MEN HELD. LDB *tenuit* has been corrected to *tenuerunt*, but rather untidily.
THEN 1 PRIEST. In the MS the *p* of *p(res)b(ite)r* has been altered from *b*.
VILLAGERS. In LDB the number of villagers 'then' has been altered from 7 to 9 and that 'now' from 9 to 7.
22,7 VATTEVILLE. Either the place in Eure or that in Seine-Inf., OEB 120. Cf. Robert in 23,41.
ABBOT OF ELY. See 10,2 note. Cf. IEAL 184.
22,8 NOW ... 3½ HIDES. See following note.
HIDE ... ADDED TO THIS MANOR. See 10,2 and IE 126, IEAL 184.
22,9 WULFBERT. LDB *Guib(er)t(us)* is probably in error for *Gulb(er)t(us)* a Rom form for OG *Wulfbert*, PNDB 418; cf. Forssner 259. See also 22,12 note.
DUNMOW. The manor of Southall there, VCH 474, n.8.
22,10 SIMOND. OG *Sigemund*, with Rom *o* < *u*; cf. Forssner 225.
22,11 HALSTEAD. The manor of Hipworth Hall there, VCH 475, n.2.
22,12 (STEEPLE) BUMPSTEAD. The manor of Moyns there, VCH 475, n.4.
WULFBERT. LDB *Gulb(er)t(us)*, see 22,9 note.
22,13 HUNT'S HALL. Formerly 'Pooley', EPNS 450.
GLADIOU. It is uncertain whether the person named was a man or a woman. If a woman, the form *Gladiou* might be from **Glaedgeofa* a variant of OE **Glaedgifu*. If a man, the final element of the name has been obscured but could possibly have been originally *-uin* from *-wine*, and thus the full name might be **Glaedwine* (PNDB 261–262).
SLAVES, NOW 5. *null(us)*, 'none', deleted before '5'. Thus in MS, but not shown in facsimile.
[THEN]. LDB omits *Tunc*.
22,14-15 WULFBERT LDB *Wlb(er)t(us)*. See 22,9 note.
22,14 VALUE ... S. LDB omits the numeral.
22,16 GODRIC SKIPPER. LDB *scipri*, probably an Anglicized form of OWScand *skipari* 'sailor'; OEB 267.
22,18 GODRIC POINC. OEB 328–329 derives the byname from OFr *poign(e)* 'fist'; since his first name is OE, this would appear to be an Englishman with a French byname and the French word might be a translation of an English byname such as *Hand* or *Fyst*.
22,19 WENDENS (AMBO). Little Wendon therein, VCH 476.
22,20 CHARDWELL. Formerly 'Ainsworth' see EPNS 517, VCH 476, n.2.
THEN 4. *T(un)c* has been altered in MS from *7c̄*.
THEN ... LDB omits the numeral.
22,21 (GREAT) CHISHILL. The manor of Tewes or Lisles there, VCH 476, n.4.
22,22 PAGLESHAM. The manors of East Hall and South Hall there, VCH 476, n.6.
SLAVES, NOW 3. In the MS *iii* was originally written at the end of the same line as *m(odo)*, but was then erased and transferred to the following line.
22,23 [VALUE]. LDB omits *valuit*.
EXCHANGE IN NORMANDY. That is, in exchange for land in Normandy.
22,24 SAME EXCHANGE. That mentioned in 22,23.
OF THE KING'S JURISDICTION. Translating *e(st) de socna regis*.
23 RICHARD, SON OF COUNT GILBERT. In Kent Ch. 11 (col. 14b) he is also called Richard of Tonbridge, while in Suffolk Ch. 76 (col. 448a) he appears to have been known as Richard

of Clare, which names referred to his important residences in these two counties. For his annexations in Essex, see 90,49-78. For the origin and distribution of his Holding, see R. Mortimer, 'The beginnings of the Honour of Clare', *Battle 1980*, 119-141.

23,1 MEADOW. LDB *ap(ra)ti* is in error for *p(ra)ti*.

23,2-3 WITHGAR. Richard's predecessor in most of his East Anglian estates, see Mortimer, 'Honour of Clare', 128-129.

23,2 16 PLOUGHS ... RESTORED. That is, the difference in number between the former 34 men's ploughs and the present 18.
AS ... FRENCH AND ENGLISH SAY. A reference to the Hundred jury. Farley *dic̄* is in error for *dicŧ* of MS and facsimile.
WARNER. Probably he of 90,77.

23,4 W(ILLIAM) PECHE. See 35,6 note.
LEDMER THE PRIEST. Head of the collegiate church at Clare, Suffolk, founded *c.* 1045 by Aelfric the father of Richard's predecessor Withgar, see VCH 348.

23,5 ELINANT. The name is OG, Forssner 66-67.

23,6 2 PLOUGHS ... RESTORED. That is, to the lordship.

23,7 (GREAT) YELDHAM. For Richard's annexation at Yeldham, see 90,54.
GOISMER. Probably he of 90,49. The name is OG *Gausmar*, Forssner 127.

23,9 FINCHINGFIELD. For Richard's annexation here, also held from him by Arnold, see 90,50.

23,10 'BINSLEY'. Lost, in Bulmer; EPNS 418. See 35,6 note.
WIDELARD. LDB *Wielardus* is a NFr form of OG *Widelardus*, Forssner 253-254. Probably he of 23,42 and 90,52;75.

23,11 ALDERFORD. Cf. Aelfric of Alderford, associated with an annexation by Richard in 90,49.
12 [PIGS]. LDB omits *porc(i)*.

23,13 4 SMALLHOLDERS. In the MS, *iiii* has been altered from *iii*.
3 SLAVES. This is a Farley error of *iii* for the *iiii* of MS.

23,14 BULMER. Later the manor of Butler's Hall there, VCH 479, n.1.
MASCEREL. LDB *Mascerel* here, *Mascherell(us)* 90,58. Apparently an OFr byname from the verb *mascher*, 'to mix, chew up, grind, mash'; perhaps related to ModE *mash-roll*, *mash-rule*, 'a paddle or staff used by a brewer for stirring and mixing his mash', NED.

23,15 HOWE. In Finchingfield. LDB *Weninchou*; identified by VCH 479 n.2 and DG, although EPNS 427 is less certain. For Richard's annexation here, held from him by Germund, see 90,53.

23,16 BURES. An Essex hamlet of Bures St. Mary (Suffolk), see EPNS 420, VCH 408,479 n.4. Cf. 23,29 and 40,5.

23,18-19 PEBMARSH; ALPHAMSTONE. For Richard's annexations here, see 90,59-60.

23,19 5 ACRES. MS *xv* altered by deletion to *v*; facsimile *xv*.

23,21 (STEEPLE) BUMPSTEAD. See 90,61 for Richard's annexation here.

23,23 COUPALS FARM. Formerly Chelveston, EPNS 462.

23,24 TWINSTEAD. LDB *Tumesteda* is in error for *Tuinesteda*. Cf. *Bumesteda*, 3 lines above, which may have caused the error.

23,25 *CHENEBOLTUNA*. Unidentified, OE *Cynebeald-tūn*, 'Cynebeald's estate'.

23,26 HALSTEAD. For Richard's annexation there, see 90,74.

23,27 SUDBURY. In Suffolk (1,97).
THE WHOLE. That is, 23,16-27.

23,28 COLSEGE. LDB *Colsege*; possibly a corrupt form of *Colswegen* < ON *Kol(l)sveinn*, PNDB 218.
VALUE THEN 40s. The tironian *nota* in LDB after *T(un)c* is otiose.
45 ACRES. See 1,13.

23,29 BURES. As 23,16 note; see VCH 480, n.4.

23,30 [HUNDRED OF ONGAR]. LDB omits the Hundred rubric in error.
('MORRELL') RODING. A detached part of Ongar Hundred, now lost, in White Roding (EPNS 494-495). Identified by VCH 480, n.5.

23,31 (LITTLE) BENTLEY. LDB *Menetleam* is a sport form; one would have expected *Benetleam*, see EPNS 328.

23,32 (LITTLE) BROMLEY. The manor of Braham Hall there, VCH 480, n.7.
R(OGER). Cf. 23,31.

23,33 HE ALSO HOLDS. *Ide(m)* is taken here to refer to Algar; alternatively it could perhaps refer to R(oger) of 23,32.
KING'S JURISDICTION ... LAWFORD. Cf. 1,27.

23,34 COLNE. According to VCH 481, n.1, this was probably Berwick Hall in White Colne. For Richard's annexations there, see 90,68;71.

WHO HOLD. *tenentes* at the foot of folio 40b is deleted thus in MS.

23,35 FORDHAM. For Richard's annexation there, see 90,72. Farley *Sordeha(m)* is in error for *fordeha(m)* of MS.

23,36 (WEST) BERGHOLT. For Richard's annexations there, see 90,70;73.

23,37 *WITESUUORDA*. Unidentified, perhaps OE *Wihtesweorð*, 'Wiht's enclosure'.
COULD NOT. LDB *potat* is in error for *poterat*.

23,38 WALTER TIREL. LDB *Walt̄ t̄irelde.R* standing for *Walt(erus) tirel de. R(icardo)* with an erroneous repetition of the abbreviation-mark above *t* and a wrong word-division of *tirel* and *de*. For the byname Tirel, perhaps from OF *tirer* 'to draw', see OEB 226, Reaney 350. Walter was the son-in-law of Richard and the slayer of King William Rufus in 1100; A. L. Poole, *From Domesday Book to Magna Carta* (Oxford, 1951), 113–114.
FINN THE DANE. On him, see Mortimer, 'Honour of Clare', 128–129. For his wife, see *84*.

23,39 [MEN'S] PLOUGHS. LDB omits *hominum*.

23,41 VATTEVILLE. As 22,7 note.
[MEN'S] PLOUGHS. As 23,39 note.

23,42 BARDFIELD. Possibly Bardfield Saling, cf. VCH 481, n.8.
WIDELARD. See 23,10 note.

24 SWEIN OF ESSEX. Sheriff of Essex at a date between 1066 and 1086 in succession to his father Robert son of Wymarc and before Ralph Baynard (*33*); see VCH 345–346. For Swein's newly-built castle, see 24,17. For an annexation by him, see 90,35.

24,1 ROBERT. Son of Wymarc, formerly Sheriff of Essex, see preceding note.

24,1-3 WOODLAND ... HIDES. See 18,2 note.

24,4 ALWEN. LDB *Aluuen*; see PNDB 160–161 s.n. *Al-wynn*, a late OE form of *AElfwynn* or of *AEthelwynn*.
ROBERT SON OF WYMARC. See 24,1 note.
1 HIDE THERE. LDB has *.i.bi* in error for *ibi*.

24,5 HORNDON (-ON-THE-HILL). The manor of Wythefeld there, VCH 482, n.14; Wyfields, EPNS 157.

24,7 AS A MANOR ... 15 ACRES. The order of the Latin is 'for 1 hide as a manor and 15 acres'.

24,8 GODITH, A FREE MAN. Here, as on other occasions, the DB Inquiry uses the term *liber homo* to describe status irrespective of gender. LDB *God&* stands for *Godet* from OE *Godgyth*, PNDB 264.

Folio 43a A line of writing has been erased in the MS above the present first line.

24,10 2 SMALLHOLDERS. MS *ii*, so in Farley but the ink has blotted on the second minim.

24,11 BEFORE 1066. Farley *t̄. r. E.*, interpreting an unusually-large *e* in MS as a capital. Its irregularity was in fact caused by its having been altered from *V*, probably the first two strokes of initial *W* of *Will(elm)i*.

24,13 NOW 1;1. Farley has substituted the tironian *nota* for the ampersand of MS.

24,14-15 WHEATLEY. In Rayleigh, EPNS 195. Swein gave land at Wheatley to St. Paul's before his death *c.* 1087, see ECE, no. 99.

24,16 3 COBS AND 1 COB. So in MS.

24,17 CASTLE. For a brief description and plan of Rayleigh Castle, see VCH 299–300.

24,18 WHO ... HAD. LDB *hntes*, omitting the abbreviation-mark from *h*.

24,20 HIS FATHER. Robert son of Wymarc.
NOW 2 COBS. In the MS a letter (?*c*) has been erased before *runc(ini)*.

24,22 PRITTLEWELL. The manor of Prior's Hall there, VCH 485, n.3.
PASTURE, 12 PIGS. *Past(ura)* here is an error in LDB for *Silua*.
GRAPINEL. Apparently a byname derived from OFr *grapon*, 'grapnel; grappling hook'.

24,23 SHOEBURY. Probably the manor of South Shoebury, see VCH 485, n.8.

24,24 THEN 3 COBS. *iii* in Farley is an error for *iiii* of MS.

24,26 160 SHEEP ... 23 SHEEP. So in MS.

24,27 WICARD. DB *Wiard(us)* from OG *Wichard*, Forssner 252–253. Cf. 24,56 note.
(GREAT) STAMBRIDGE. The manor of Barton Hall there, VCH 486, n.3.

24,28 SHOEBURY. Probably the manor of North Shoebury, cf. VCH 485, n.8.

24,30-32 ASCELIN. OFr *Ascelin*, from OG *Azelin*; Forssner 38–39.

24,30 50 PIGS. *.&.L.* is a Farley error for *.x.l.* of MS, the number of pigs should thus be 40.

24,35 ALFITH. LDB *Aluid*; probably from OE *AElfgyth*, cf. PNDB 174.

24,36-39 ROBERT. As 24,1 note.

24,41a SAID HUNDRED. That of Rochford, see rubric before 24,17.

24,43 Cf. 24,55, another entry concerning a holding here, with several identical statistics, suggesting the division of an earlier unit into equal parts.
ASHELDHAM. LDB *Hainctuna(m)*. Identified by VCH, 392–393. See also EPNS 208; and below 24,55.

THEN NOTHING. That is, no livestock.
NOW 3 CATTLE. *iiii* altered by erasure to *iii* in the MS.

24,46 HALLINGBURY. LDB *Halingebiam*, omitting the abbreviation-mark on *b*.

24,48 NOW 5 CATTLE. The first letter of *anim(ales)* has been altered, ?from *v*, in the MS.

24,49 [MEN'S] PLOUGHS. LDB omits *hominum*.

24,51 ABBERTON. The manor of Badcocks there, VCH 489, n.1.

24,53 1 PLOUGH ... RESTORED. This statement perhaps suggests that the figures for the lordship ploughs (then and later 4, now 5) have been reversed in error; or alternatively, that they have been misconstrued.

24,54 ROBERT. As 24,1 note.

24,55 See 24,43 note.
ASHELDHAM. LDB *Haintuna(m)*. See 24,43 note.

24,56 WICARD. LDB *Wicard(us)*, from the same name as in 24,27 note.

24,57 R(OBERT). As 24,1 note.
NAYLAND. The Essex part of the estate of Nayland (Suffolk), now represented by Gt. and Lt. Horkesley, VCH 408, 489, n.11.
4 [PLOUGHS]. LDB omits *caruce*.

24,59 FREE MEN. The facsimile adds an otiose abbreviation-mark to the ascender of *b* in *hominib(us)*.
WERE NO SMALLHOLDERS. Literally, 'was no smallholder', *null(us) bordari(us) erat*.

24,61 WARLEY. The manor of Franks in Great Warley, VCH 490, n.8; EPNS 134.
17 PIGS. Farley omits the abbreviation-mark above *c* of *porc(i)*.
VALUE THEN £4. Farley does not show the gap in the MS, caused by a repair, between *ual(uit)* and *.iiii.* See also 24,66 note.

24,62 KENNINGTONS. In Aveley, EPNS 122. According to VCH 490, n.10, it was later known as the manor of Bretts.
WULFSTAN. LDB *Vstan(us)* is probably a palaeographical error for *Vlstan(us)*, due to confusion between *l* and caroline minuscule *s*.

24,63 ROBERT. As 24,1 note.
MALDON. Probably the manor of Southouse and Sayers there, VCH 491, n.1.
THE KING ... DUES. See 1,25 note.
HE AIDS. That is, Gunner aids.
HORSE ... SHIP. This obligation is not mentioned in the other entries concerning Maldon. A ship levy was imposed in 1008 at the rate of one ship per 310 hides. For the 1008 levy and earlier references to ships owed to the King, see Harmer, *ASWrits*, 266-267.

24,64 ELMSTEAD. For a house in Colchester belonging to Elmstead, see B3m.

24,65-66 ROBERT. As 24,1 note.

24,65 ODARD. The Rom form of OG *Authart*; Forssner 194.
LESS 10 ACRES. *x* has been altered from *7* in the MS.
ACQUIRED NOTHING. That is, no livestock.

24,66 4 SMALLHOLDERS THERE. Farley does not show the gap in the MS between *s(un)t* and *.iiii.* caused by the reverse of the repair at 24,61.

25 EUDO THE STEWARD. The King's Steward, called Eudo son of Hubert in Cambridgeshire *25* and Hertfordshire *31*.

25,1 RICHARD. Of Sackville, cf. 20,8 (Rivenhall) whence the ½ mill was acquired; VCH 379.

25,2 75 [SHEEP]. LDB omits *oues*.
LEOFSI. LDB *Lefsi(us)*. VCH 492, note 3, suggests that this is a bad spelling for *Lisois(us)*, that is Lisois of Moutiers, who is mentioned in 25,5.

25,3 See also IE 130, IEAL 187; and below 30,41.
('MORRELL') RODING. Tentatively identified by VCH 492, n.4. See above 23,30 note.
SAEMER. Also at 30,41.
45 ACRES. See 28,8 note.
NOW £6. IE (?in error), £5.

25,4 1 COB ... LDB may have omitted some livestock here.
WORTH THAT MUCH. Presumably £6.

25,5 LISOIS. Of Moutiers (probably Moutiers-Hubert, Calvados; OEB 102). He was also mentioned in connection with manors of Eudo in Bedfordshire (21,13) and Cambridgeshire (25,9). See also 25,2 note.
WAS OUTLAWED. LDB *utllagauit*.
250 [SHEEP]. LDB omits *oues*.
WRINGEHALA. Unidentified, perhaps OE **Wringehale*, 'at the nook of land at the place with a bend', cf. A. H. Smith, *English Place-Name Elements*, ii, EPNSoc 26, Cambridge 1956, s.v. **wrēo, *wrīo*.

25,6 WULFRIC CAVE. LDB *cassa* is a scribal error for *caffa*, cf. *cauuā* 30,28. The byname is from OE *cāf*, 'quick, bold', OEB 343. Leofwin Cave occurs in Bucks. 57,8.
25,9 *LANDUNA*. Unidentified, OE **lang-dūne* 'at the long upland'.
25,10 *ACLETA*. Unidentified, OE *āc-hliðe*, 'at the oak-hillside'.
1½ [HIDES]. LDB omits *hidis*.
25,11 Duplicated at 25,25 but there said to be in lordship.
PIROT. LDB *Pirot* is almost certainly a palaeographical error for *Picot*, as in Cambridgeshire (25,1-2; see note there) and Bedfordshire (21,14-15. 24,18;24). Picot was Sheriff of Cambridge.
25,12 RICHARD. ECE, no. 91, note, identifies him as Richard son of Count Gilbert (*23*).
9 ACRES. See also 10,1 and IE 128-129, IEAL 187.
25,15 TAKELEY. The manor of Colchester Hall there, VCH 494, n.3.
25,19 (ABBESS) RODING. For the identification, see VCH 492, n.4.
25,20 CHURCH OF ELY. See also 10,3 and IE 126, IEAL 187.
25,23 ... COBS. LDB omits the numeral.
25,24 AELFRIC WAND. The byname is from OE *wand* 'mole', OEB 367.
25,25 EUDO ... LORDSHIP; FOR 3½ HIDES. Deleted thus in MS. Farley omits a large marginal cross which occurs in the MS at this point and which may be a contemporary indication of the duplication of text with that of 25,11 above. Cf. 30,50 note.
25,26 AELFRIC WAND. LDB *uuants* is an AN form of the byname discussed in 25,24 note.
26 ROGER OF AUBERVILLE. He possibly came from Auberville-la-Renaut (Seine Inf: arr. Le Hâvre); OEB 104-105.
26,1 ONE OF THESE MANORS. *unu(m) maneriu(m) ex istis*; LDB treats each of the 2 free men's property as a separate manor here, although at the beginning of the entry it refers to only one manor.
26,2 THEN ... [PLOUGHS]. LDB omits *caruce* and the numeral.
WHO HAVE 1 PLOUGH. *h(abe)ntes .i. car(ucam)* is probably to be taken to refer to all the population rather than just the 3 slaves.
26,5 CHISHILL. Probably the manor of 'Lisles' in Gt. Chishill, VCH 496, n.11. For Roger's annexation there, see 90,86.
27 HUGH DE MONTFORT. He came from Montfort-sur-Risle (Eure: arr. Bernai); OEB 100-101. See 90,15-18 for his annexations.
27,1 RAMSDEN. This entry is said by VCH 497, n.1, to refer to Downham, adjacent to Ramsden Bellhouse and Crays.
27,2 KELVEDON. The manor there later known as Felix Hall, VCH 497, n.2.
27,3 HAVERING (-ATTE-BOWER). See 1,4.
27,7 VALUE OF THE WHOLE OF THE ABOVE. That is, of 27,1-7.
27,8 *HALESDUNA*. Unidentified, OE *Haegelesdūn*, 'Haegel's upland'; see EPNS 215, s.n. Hazeleigh.
27,9 'STUDLY'. As 1,6 note.
WHICH ... HELD. *tenuit* is a Farley error for *tenent* of MS.
[THEN] 1½ PLOUGHS. LDB omits *Tunc*.
27,12 'WIBERTSHERNE'. Farley *Witbricteshema* is in error for *Wibricteshema* of the MS.
ST. PETER'S CHAPEL. This entry is said by VCH 499, n.1, to refer to the manor of Battails in Bradwell-on-Sea; EPNS 211, s.n. Buckles Grove.
27,14 See also IE 129, IEAL 186.
'BENSTED'. Bensted Green (lost) in Sandon, see EPNS 266-267. Cf. VCH 389-390.
GUTHMUND. LDB *Gudmund(us)*, IE *Godmundus*. He was the brother of Abbot Wulfric of Ely, through whom, in order to make a good marriage, he obtained leases on several estates in East Anglia (including 'Bensted') belonging to the monks. After 1066 Hugh de Montfort took possession of Guthmund's holding, including the Ely lands. See LibEl 166-167, 424-425. Cf. 27,2;4-5;11;13.
27,15 QUEEN EDITH. As 20,8 note.
27,16 48 GOATS. LDB *cap(re)* may be in error for *oues*, 'sheep' here, since the following category is also goats.
27,17 HAGER. OG *Hager, Hagero*; Förstemann 717. Farley has modernised the word-division from *posthagra* of the MS.
DELIVERER. Someone with the authority or right to transfer possession.
27,18 HUMPHREY HOLDS TOLLESHUNT (D'ARCY). He is probably the Humphrey of 34,36.
28 HAMO THE STEWARD. For his annexations, see 90,31-33.
28,1 *ATELEIA*. Unidentified, OE *ātan-lēage*, 'at the clearing where oats are grown'.
GOTI. Probably he of 13,1, in the same Hundred.

28,3 30 ACRES. See 20,6.
28,5 (GREAT) BRAXTED. Westhall there, VCH 500, n.13; EPNS 284, s.n. West Hall Wood.
28,6 HARLOW. *herlaua* altered from *heru-* in the MS.
RALPH of Marcy. See 1,3 note.
RYES. In Hatfield Broad Oak, EPNS 41. See 1,3 note.
28,8 RODING. The manor of Marks Hall in Margaret Roding, EPNS 494, see VCH 501, n.4.
45 ACRES. The difference between the 1½ hides of before 1066 and the 1 hide and 15 acres of 1086. Perhaps the same as the 45 acres mentioned in 25,3 ('Morrell' Roding).
28,9 (LITTLE) WIGBOROUGH. See 90,31 for Hamo's annexation here.
BERNARD ... BAYNARD'S HOLDING. This hide of woodland may be the woodland for 200 pigs recorded in 33,23 (Tolleshunt, held in 1086 by Bernard from Ralph Baynard).
ENGELRIC ... HOLDS. Probably the ½ hide mentioned in 20,19 (Langenhoe).
28,11 STAMBOURNE. See 90,33 for Hamo's annexation here. LDB *Scanburne* is in error for *St-*.
28,12 NORTHEY ISLAND. For the identification, see VCH 502, n.5. This is the traditional site of the Battle of Maldon in 991. See 90,32 for Hamo's annexation here.
28,13-14 GOTILD. From OG *Gothild*, PNDB 264-265, Forssner 120. See 28,16 note.
28,14 NAVESTOCK. For the identification, see VCH 502, n.7.
28,16 GOTILD. Probably the person (called Godith in 5,6) who gave ½ hide at Norton Mandeville to St. Paul's after 1066. See also 28,13-14 note.
28,17-18 THORBERT. Cf. *70* note *sub* Hagebern.
29 HENRY OF FERRERS. From Ferrières-Saint-Hilaire (Eure: arr. Bernay): OEB 88.
29,2 60 PIGS. Farley omits to show a gap in the text, caused by an erasure in the MS between *Lx* and *.porc(i)*.
29,3 STEEPLE. For Henry's annexation there, see 90,81.
29,5 BUTTSBURY. Formerly one of the Essex names in *Ginge, Inge*, EPNS 242-244 and 258-259.
30 GEOFFREY DE MANDEVILLE. Ancestor of the de Mandevilles, Earls of Essex. The place from which he was named has not been positively identified, see OEB 96. For Geoffrey's annexations, see 90,20-28.
30,1 (MARKS) TEY. The modern name preserves that of the family descended from Adam *de Merck*, undertenants of the de Mandeville family; EPNS 400.
30,2 ASGAR. The Constable, Geoffrey de Mandeville's predecessor in a number of counties. On him, see Harmer, *ASWrits*, 560-561 (s.n. Esgar, the staller); Ellis ii 43.
HE ... MAN. Leofday had been under the jurisdiction of Asgar but did not hold this land from him. Nevertheless Geoffrey de Mandeville had taken it, as Asgar's successor in many other places. Cf. following note.
30,3 BARKING ABBEY. Leofhild had been under Asgar's jurisdiction but only held Abbess Roding as leasehold. Nevertheless, as in the previous note, Geoffrey de Mandeville had seized it.
30,4 THOROLD. Geoffrey de Mandeville's steward, see ECE, no. 93.
OCKENDON. According to VCH 505, this is South Ockendon.
EXCHANGE. See also 52,1 note.
30,5 20 BEEHIVES. Farley omits to show a gap in the text, caused by the erasure in the MS of two letters (*ac*), between *xx.* and *uasa*.
WALTER (HOLDS) 30 ACRES ... HUBERT 30 ACRES. This sentence repeats information already given above, 30 acres being equal to 1 virgate.
30,10 PLOUGHS IN LORDSHIP. Farley *car(uce) . hom d(omi)nio* stands for *car(uce) . hoin d(omi)nio* of the MS, where a correction has been made from 'men's ploughs' to 'ploughs in lordship' but incompletely since *ho* should have been erased.
30,11 LESS 5 ACRES. Farley omits to show a gap in the text, caused by an erasure in the MS, before *.v.*
RICHARD GARNET. LDB *gernet*, from OFr *gernat, grenat* 'garnet', OEB 369.
30,13 MASHBURY. See 90,20 for Geoffrey's annexation here.
30,16 GUARDS. LDB *huscarlo* (Latin dative singular). The term *huscarl* in Domesday Book probably denoted a trained soldier. In Cambridgeshire (14,64) it is however also used as a byname.
SCALPI. LDB *Scalpin(us)*; ON *Skálpi*, here with the Latin and OFr suffix *-in(us)* (PNDB 365 and § 148) but in Suffolk (16,35. 36,1-2;8;15) the same man is simply called *Scalpi(us), Scalp(us), Scapi(us)*. The latter form also occurs at 32,40 below.
YORK(SHIRE). LDB *ebroica*. The reference is probably to the northern rebellion against King William in 1069-70, see Ann Williams (article cited in 1,1-4 note), 178-179.
J. H. Round (VCH 507) quoted the erroneous facsimile spelling *ehroica* and identified it

as Evreux. Although LDB *ebroica* is similar to later spellings for Evreux (*Ebricae* 1212, *Ebroyce* 1258) given by OEB 87, it is less likely to be that place here, on historical grounds, than York(shire). Also, the LDB form is comparable to the French form *Euroic* for York, referred to in Wace's *Brut*, see A. H. Smith, *The Place-Names of the East Riding of Yorkshire and York* (EPNSoc xiv, Cambridge 1937), 276, n.2. Cf. 6,15 (*Eurewic*).

30,18 MOZE. See also ESf 2.
WHEN ... LONDON. LDB *q(ua)n(do) remansit Londoniae*. It is unclear to whom this phrase refers, to King William or to Geoffrey.

30,19 RAINALM. LDB *Renelm(us)* from *Rainalm* the Rom form of OG *Raginhelm*, Forssner 210. Cf. 30,39 note.

30,20 ARDLEIGH. The manor of Martells Hall there, VCH 508, n.3. For 2 houses in Colchester belonging to Ardleigh, see B31.

30,21 12 HIDES. According to VCH 374, these were at East Tilbury.
(WEST) TILBURY. See 24,3.

30,22 (BLACK) NOTLEY. Identified by VCH 508.
CLAIMS ... THEM. That is, in relation to his ownership of them.

30,24 MARTEL. Here (as in 30,31-32;35;43) 'Martel' may refer to Geoffrey Martel of 30,3.
(LITTLE) HALLINGBURY. The manor of Monkbury there, VCH 508, n.11; Monksbury, EPNS 36.

30,25 MATCHING. The manor of Stock Hall there, VCH 509, n.2.

30,27 See also IE 127, IEAL 186.
(HIGH) EASTER. Identified by VCH 509. Pleshey Castle later stood on part of this land.
GUTBERT. Probably OG *Gutbert* (Förstemann PN 661) but possibly from OE *Cuthbeorht* with NFr *G* for *C-*.

30,28-30 HUGH OF BERNIÈRES. Named from one of the places called Bernières (-d'Ailly; -le Patry; -sur la Mer) in Calvados, see OEB 72. For an annexation by him, see 90,29.

30,28 WULFRIC CAVE. See 25,6 note.

30,30 (BERNERS) RODING. The modern name preserves that of the Domesday undertenant; EPNS 492. See 30,28-30 note.
THESE 3 MANORS. Those in 30,28-30.

30,31 BIGODS. Formerly called Alfriston, EPNS 475-476.

30,32 (LITTLE) DUNMOW. Probably the manor of South Hall there, VCH 510, n.7.

30,33 3 CATTLE ... SHEEP. Presumably 'now', but perhaps 'then and now'.

30,35 (WHITE) RODING. The manor of Maskelsbury there, VCH 511, n.1; EPNS 495, s.n. Mascallsbury.

30,36 DUNMOW. Possibly Shingle Hall in Gt. Dunmow, VCH 511, n.2.

30,38 (LITTLE) CANFIELD. The manor of Langthorns there, VCH 511, n.6. See 90,21 for Geoffrey's annexation of 8 acres at Canfield, also held of him by Richard.

30,39 RAINALM. LDB *Rainalm(us)*; as 30,19 note.

30,41 See also IE 129, IEAL 186.
1 FREE MAN. Named by IE as Saemer (*Samarus*). See also 25,3.
35 ACRES. IE, 30; IEAL, 34.
('MORRELL') RODING. See 25,3.

30,42 ASGAR. LDB *angari* is in error for *ansgari*.

30,43 (WHITE) RODING. Identified by VCH 512.
LEOFITH. LDB *Leuid*; from OE *Lēofgȳth*, PNDB 312.

30,44 Cf. 30,50 which repeats much of this information, with minor differences.
STOW MARIES. The second element of the modern name is from the medieval family name *de Marisco*, 'of the marsh', possibly referring to the same feature as the 'fen' in the name of the place in LDB *Fenne*. See EPNS 228-229.
FRIDEBERN. LDB *Frieb(er)n(us)*; OG *Fridebern, Frithu- Frethubern*; see PNDB 253-254. Cf. *70* note *sub* Hagebern.

30,45 6½ HIDES. LDB repeats 'hides', adding it above *.vi.* in order to avoid confusion with the preceding numerals describing Freemen.
11 CATTLE. The number of cattle may in fact be 12, but the MS has been erased and blotted here.

30,46 WILLIAM CARDON. See 10,5 note.
(GREAT) CHISHILL. The manor of Cardons there, VCH 512, n.5. See also 90,34.

30,49 ANSGAR'S ... LDB has probably omitted *tenuit pro* after *Angari*.

30,50 Farley omits to show a marginal cross which occurs in the MS, probably indicating the partial duplication of text between this entry and 30,44. Cf. 25,25 note.

30,51 *WENESUUIC*. Unidentified; the second element is OE *wīc*, 'an industrial or trading settlement' with the genitive singular of either the OE personal-name *Wine* or of *wenn* 'a wen, blister; tumulus, hill'. Cf. 90,27 (*Wesuunic*), which may be a corrupt form of the same name.

THEY ALSO HOLD. That is, Godfrey and Evrard.

31 THE COUNT OF EU. From Eu (Seine Inf: arr. Dieppe), OEB 105.

31,1 (WEST) THURROCK. Identified by VCH 388.

32 ROBERT GERNON. The byname is from OFr *grenon* 'moustache', OEB 314-315.

32,3 WITHAM. Identified as Powers Hall therein, VCH 514, n.2.

32,5 RIVENHALL. Identified as the manor of Archers there, VCH 514, n.5.
WOODLAND. See 3,10 note.

32,7 CHINGFORD. Identified as the manor of Earl's Chingford, VCH 514, n.6.

32,8 (WEST) HAM. Identified by VCH 515, n.2. Cf. 34,8 which duplicates parts of this entry.
KING WILLIAM [GAVE]. LDB omits *dedit* but cf. 34,8.
MEADOW 60 ACRES. In the MS *lx.ac(re)* has been altered, ?from *lx.v.*
RANULF PEVEREL ... MANOR. See 34,8.

32,9 (EAST) HAM. Identified by VCH 515.

32,11 W. CORBUN. Perhaps from Corbon (Calvados), OEB 83-84, 127.

32,14 *LEGA*. Unidentified, OE *lege*, '(place at) the woodland clearing'.
GOTRE. From ON *Gautarr*, ODan, OSw *Gøtar*, PNDB 258. Cf. 32,45 note.

32,15 VIRLEY. LDB *Salcota(m)*; by 1291 the surname of the 1086 tenant Robert of Verly had been added to make *Salcote Verly*, but the modern form consists only of the affix. See EPNS 323.

32,17 TAKELEY. The manor of Bassingborns there, VCH 516, n.4.
CATTLE, NOW 3. In the MS *iii* has been altered from *ii*.
1 SMALLHOLDER. LDB *.i.b.* for *.i.bordarius*.

32,18 WENDENS (AMBO). Identified by VCH 516 as Great Wendon therein.

32,21 FARNHAM. The manor of Hertisho-bury there, VCH 517, n.2; EPNS 550, s.n. Hassobury.

32,23 (GREAT) MAPLESTEAD. Identified by VCH 517.

32,24 RAYMOND GERALD ... ROGER OF POITOU. See 1,19 notes.

32,25 WHICH THE HUNDRED-REEVE HAS. LDB *q(ua)s h(abe)t custos hundret*. At 89,1 the same man is described as *prepositus hundredi*.

32,26 ROBERT. Of Verly, see VCH 389.
(LITTLE) BIRCH. Identified by VCH 389.

32,27 STAPLEFORD (ABBOTTS). The manor of Batayles there, VCH 518, n.5; EPNS 79, s.n. Battles Hall.
AMONG THEM. It is unclear whether *int(er) eos* refers to the 5 free men or to the smallholders.

32,28 RAINHAM. Possibly the manor of Berwick there, VCH 518, n.6.
ROBERT THE LASCIVIOUS. LDB *Lasciuus*; OEB 348. The same as Robert the Perverted, see 6,12 note.

32,29 (SOUTH) WEALD. The manor of Caldecots there, VCH 518, n.8; EPNS 138, s.n. Calcott Hall. Cf. 8,9.
HUBERT OF PORT. Although his main holding was at Mapledurwell (Hampshire 24,1), he appears to have had jurisdiction over a group of men in Essex (cf. 83,2 below) and Suffolk (16,34). He took his name from Port-en-Bessin (Calvados: arr. Bayeux), OEB 108.

32,32 CHIGNALL. The manor of Chignall Zoyn in Chignall St. James, VCH 519, n.2.

32,33 CORP. Farley *C̄orp*, MS *Córp*. Redin 28, unexplained. The significance of the mark above *o* is not apparent and the form appears to be scribally corrupt; it might possibly be for *C̄osp*, an abbreviated form for OG *Gosbert* (Forssner 124, Förstemann PN 615), or, in insular minuscule, might be from *Cofsi* (< ON *Kofsi*, PNDB 306).

32,34 SELVA. LDB *Selua*; probably from ODan *Sylvi*, PNDB 382.
THEN 10 CATTLE. In the MS, *x* has been altered from *v*.

32,34-35 BORDA. LDB *borda*, from OE *Brorda*, PNDB 208. The LDB spelling was not given a capital initial and was perhaps confused with *bord(arius)* 'smallholder'.

32,36 AZO. LDB *Asso*. Cf. PNDB 170-171 s.n. *Azur*, and below, 44,3 note on AZORIN.
CULVERT'S FARM. Identified by VCH 519, n.8. LDB *Richeham*. See EPNS 238-239.

32,37 TOLLESHUNT (D'ARCY). Identified EPNS 307. See also below, 32,45.

32,38 AELFRIC KEMP. The byname is either OE *cempa* 'warrior' or a derivative of OWScand *kampr* 'moustache'. He also occurs in Cambridgeshire (21,2-3. 25,1-3).

32,38a TENDRING. The manor of Gernons there, VCH 520, n.3; EPNS 352, s.n. Grove Farm.

32,40 WILLIAM. Called William de Alno in Suffolk (36,1;15). It is uncertain to which place his byname refers, see OEB 67-68.

A MANOR IN SUFFOLK. William held several manors after Scalpi in Suffolk (Chapter 36, *passim*) but it is not possible to identify any with the one here referred to.
32,43 ARKESDEN. The manor of Mynchens there, VCH 521, n.2.
32,45 TOLLESHUNT (D'ARCY). The manors of Gernons and Verli there, VCH 521, n.5. See also 32,37.
GOTRE. LDB *Gotra*. The same name as is discussed 32,14 note.
33 RALPH BAYNARD. He had been Sheriff of Essex between Swein (*24*) and Peter of Valognes (*36*) at a date between 1066 and 1086. For his annexations, see 90,39-40. Castle Baynard in London was named after him.
33,1 PART OF THE CUSTOMARY DUE. Translating *s(un)t de sua consuetudine*, where *sua* refers to King William, who however is not mentioned in the present translation's rendering of *t(empore) . r(egis) . Will(elm)i* as 'after 1066'.
[BEE]HIVES. LDB omits *apium*.
33,2 3 ACRES. Probably of meadow, although LDB omits *prati*.
33,4 POINTEL. Probably to be identified as Theodoric Pointel (*71*).
WOODHAM (WALTER). Identified by VCH 522.
33,5 CURLING TYE (GREEN). Identified by EPNS 232. Cf. VCH 522, n.5.
33,6 (LITTLE) DUNMOW. Identified by VCH 522.
33,6-7 AETHELGYTH. Also Ralph's predecessor at 33,19-20. She was the widow of Thurstan son of Wine, whose will had included bequests of several of the estates later held in DB by Ralph Baynard, see ECE, no. 59 (Sawyer, no. 1531). See also 33,11 note.
33,11 A FREE WOMAN. Perhaps Aethelgyth (see 33,6-7 note), to whom Pentlow was bequeathed by her husband Thurstan.
MEN'S PLOUGHS. LDB repeats *car(uce)* in error, where the text starts a new page.
33,13 (LITTLE) BADDOW. Identified by VCH 524.
33,14 (EAST) HANNINGFIELD. The manor of Claydons there, VCH 524, n.3.
VALUE ... S. LDB *.xl.x.*, altered from *.xl.*, perhaps in error for *lxx*.
33,15 (LITTLE) OAKLEY. Identified by VCH 524. LDB *Adem* is in error for *Aclem*.
13 CATTLE. *xiii* has been altered in the MS from *viii*.
33,16 THEN 1 COB ... BEEHIVES. The livestock has been placed, unusually, after the value.
33,17 WHO HOLD ... 35 ACRES. That is, the 2 Freemen.
WHICH BERNARD. LDB *Tqd*, where the scribe has anticipated the *t* of *t(un)c* six words later, and has not erased it.
WITELEBROC. Unidentified; OE *hwītlēa-brōc*, 'brook at the place called the white wood or clearing'.
IN THE OTHER LANDS. *Witelebroc* had been held as a separate manor before 1066 but appears to have been counted as part of Michaelstow in 1086.
THESE THREE MANORS £20. Presumably Ramsey (£15), Michaelstow (£4 + 10s) and *Witelebroc* (10s).
33,18 WENDON (LOFTS). Identified by VCH 525, n.3.
ALWIN STILL. The byname is OE *stille* 'still, quiet', OEB 355.
33,19 HENHAM. For Ralph's annexation here, see 90,39. Henham was later in Uttlesford Hundred (EPNS 528). The Hundred rubric in LDB immediately before Henham may have been inserted one entry too soon (since Ashdon was later in Freshwell Hundred); however, both Henham and Ashwell were held by Ralph in lordship in 1086 and had been held by Aethelgyth in 1066 and thus there may have been a tenurial reason for regarding Henham as in Freshwell Hundred, where it has been left in the present translation.
33,19-20 AETHELGYTH. See 33,6-7 note.
33,20 1 ACRE OF VINES. The usual Domesday measure for vineyards is *arpent*.
33,21 [ACRES]. LDB omits *acre*.
33,22 ½ HIDE ... ST. PAUL'S. See 5,10.
33,23 TOLLESHUNT. This manor adjoined Tolleshunt D'Arcy, see VCH 532, n.6. Cf. 34,36.
AELMER. Called Aelmer Milk in B3r, which mentions a house in Colchester belonging to Tolleshunt.
WOODLAND. See 28,9 note.
34 RANULF PEVEREL. His lands later became part of the Honour of Peverel of London, having a distinct history from the Peverel lands in Chapter 48, see VCH 346. For Ranulf's annexations, see 90,10-14.
34,1 VALUE THEN. The facsimile omits the abbreviation-mark from *T(un)c*.
34,2 HE TOOK POSSESSION. Referring to Ranulf.
IT. Referring to the free man's land.
WITH THE OTHER. LDB repeats *cum* where the text begins a new page.

34,3 INGRAVE. Identified EPNS 161.
34,6 TERLING. See also 90,10 for Ranulf's annexations there.
2 HOUSES IN COLCHESTER. 5 are recorded in B3q.
34,7 15 ACRES ... SASWALO ... HOLDING. The personal name is Rom *Saxwalo*, Forssner 223. He was an undertenant of Geoffrey de Mandeville in Berkshire (38,1-2) and Oxfordshire (39,1-2) but neither he nor the 15 acres are mentioned in Chapter 30 describing Geoffrey's Essex lands.
34,8 (WEST) HAM. See 32,8 note.
WHEN ACQUIRED. *q(ua)n(do) recep(er)unt*, 'when they (i.e. Ranulf Peverel and Robert Gernon) acquired it'.
ROBERT GERNON ... MANOR. See 32,8.
34,9 WARIN. LDB *Garin(us)*; an OFr form of OG *Warin*, Forssner 246-247.
SIWARD. Probably he who was Ranulf Peverel's predecessor in other places in this Chapter and also in Suffolk where (34,1-2) he was called Siward of Maldon from his tenure of 34,12 below.
[WITH] CALVES. LDB omits *c(um)* before *vitul(is)*, perhaps indicating misassociation with *c(entum)* following.
34,10 RAVENOT. An Anglo-French or NFr diminutive from ON *Hrafn* and the OFr suffix *-ot*. Also at 34,28.
WILLINGALE (DOE). Identified by VCH 528, n.1.
34,11 WOODHAM (MORTIMER). Identified by VCH 528.
100 GOATS. This is a Farley error for '5 goats'; MS *.v. cap(re)*.
34,12 MALDON. Called Little Maldon by VCH 528.
MEN'S [PLOUGHS]. LDB omits *caruce*.
SHEEP. Farley *poues*, MS *por-* altered to *pou-*; the *p* was meant to be erased in the MS but was not.
34,13-14 HAZELEIGH. Respectively, the manors of Great and Little Hazeleigh, VCH 528, nn.4-5.
34,15 A. Perhaps, but not necessarily, an abbreviation for *Ailmar(us)* of 34,14.
34,16 ABBERTON. Ranulf Peverel subsequently granted it to St. Paul's, ECE, no. 96.
34,19 13 VILLAGERS, NOW 19. IE adds, 'and 1 Freeman', *sochemann(us)*.
ABBOT OF ELY. See IE 129, IEAL 189.
34,20 ... PLOUGHS. LDB omits the numeral.
VITALIS [HOLDS]. Probably he of 34,18.
34,21 (GREAT) HENNY. Identified by VCH 529. See 90,13 for Ranulf's annexation here, and 90,44 for Thorold's.
SUDBURY. Suffolk (1,97), to the north of Gt. Henny.
34,22 LAMARSH. See 90,14 for Ranulf's annexation here, and 90,45 for Thorold's.
TWO BROTHERS. Presumably Algar and Alfward.
34,24 LAWLING. The manor of Peverells there, VCH 530, n.5.
34,26 STANSGATE. See 90,12 for Ranulf Peverel's annexation here.
34,27 HAS IT. Alternatively, 'has him'.
34,28 RAVENOT. As 34,10 note.
PLUNKER'S (GREEN). For this identification, see EPNS 153.
½ PLOUGH. In the MS *.7. d(imidia) . car(uca)* has been altered from *.7.i.car(uca)*.
34,29 SPRINGFIELD. The manor of Springfield Hall, VCH 531, n.3.
SMALLHOLDERS. LDB repeats the *bordarius* category of population. Possibly the second group is in error for *serui*, 'slaves'.
34,30 ABBEY OF ELY. See 10,3 and IE 126.
34,31 £12 FROM MALDON. This does not tally with the values given in 1,25.
34,33 ST. OSYTH. The manor of St. Clere's Hall there, VCH 531, n.8; EPNS 350, s.n. St. Clairs Hall.
50 CATTLE. An unusually high number of cattle.
34,35 SMALLHOLDERS ABOVE THE WATER. They were probably fishermen dwelling on the shore of the Thames Estuary here. In the MS *sup(er)* has been altered from *sub*!
34,36 TOLLESHUNT (D'ARCY). Identified by VCH 532, n.5.
RALPH BAYNARD. Cf. 33,23.
HUGH DE MONTFORT. Cf. 27,18.
35 AUBREY DE VERE. Named from Ver (La Manche: arr. Coutances) or Ver (Calvados), see OEB 118. For his annexations, see 90,36-37.
35,1 (GREAT) CANFIELD. Identified by VCH 532.
WULFWIN. He was also Aubrey's predecessor in Cambridgeshire (29,1 note etc.).
35,2 *UDECHESHALE*. Unidentified, OE **Udeceshale*, 'at Udec's nook of land'; **Udec* may be a

diminutive of the recorded personal-name *Uda* (cf. *Udel* in Uttlesford, EPNS 516) but could be from a place-name **Wuda-hecc* 'Woodhatch', if the LDB spelling *ch* here represents [*tʃ*].

35,5 (CASTLE) HEDINGHAM. Identified by VCH 533. For Aubrey's annexation of 15 acres at Smalton here, see 90,37.

WHO ... PLOUGHS. *h(abe)ntes* probably refers to all the village population listed here, rather than to the slaves. The clause is another way of expressing the number of 'men's ploughs'. A similar construction is used below in relation to the ploughs belonging to Robert Blunt, etc.

SUDBURY. Suffolk (1,97).

ROBERT BLUNT. A landholder in Suffolk (*66*) and Middlesex (*17*), etc. See also 90,83. The byname is from OFr *blund, blond*, 'blonde, fair', OEB 294. In Wiltshire (*60*) he has the Latin byname *flavus* (OEB 313), 'yellow, blonde'; in Northamptonshire (*33*) the Latin byname *albus* 'white' (OEB 293); and in Norfolk (LDB folios 140,243) the OFr byname *blanchart* 'whitish' (OEB 293).

PINSON. LDB *Pincūn̄*, for *Pinc(io)un* from OFr *pinçon* 'finch', a nickname; see Reaney 274 s.n. Pinchen, Pinson.

GODWIN. LDB *Godun*.

35,6 HALF-HUNDRED OF 'THUNDERLOW'. This unit occurs only here and before 36,8. It was later subsumed into Hinkford Hundred. The meeting-place was in Bulmer parish, see EPNS 418. The inclusion of 'Binsley' in it (VCH 405–406) is not so in LDB, see 23,10 and 36,9.

BELCHAMP (WALTER). Identified by VCH 534.

4 MEN'S PLOUGHS. The first instance of LDB *car(uce) hom(inum)* is here in error for *car(uce) in dominio*.

ARPENT. The normal unit of extent for vineyards in the Domesday Survey, of unknown extent.

WILLIAM PECHE. LDB *peccatu(m)*, equivalent to OFr *peche* 'sin', OEB 353.

SUADUS. Perhaps a nickname from Latin *suadus* 'persuasive', but possibly it is OE *swaeth* 'bandage, wrapping' used as a byname, see von Feilitzen 1968, 14–15 in relation to *Osferth Swade beard*.

35,7 PREDECESSOR. LDB *antec̉essore*, with an otiose abbreviation-mark above *c*.

35,8 (EARLS) COLNE. The modern form commemorates the rank, as Earls of Oxford, of the DB tenant's descendants; EPNS 381.

... VILLAGERS. LDB omits the numeral.

DEMIBLANC ... 1 HIDE. The manor of Ingledethorp in White Colne; VCH 534, n.11, EPNS 384. White Colne was named from Demiblanc's byname 'half-white' (*dimidius blancus*), possibly referring to the colour of his hair. He also occurs in Colchester (B3a), where also cf. Blanc. J. H. Round (VCH 534, n.11) related the name Demiblanc to 'the name of a certain coin in Old French' but the source of his statement is unknown and the word has not been found in any dictionary.

35,9 (GREAT) BENTLEY. Identified by VCH 535, n.1.

AMONG [THE MEN]. LDB omits *homines*.

35,11 BEAUMONT. LDB *Fulepet*. The first OE name 'foul hollow' is the direct opposite of the later (by 1175–80) OFr one 'fair hill', EPNS 327–328.

35,12 (HELIONS) BUMPSTEAD. The manor of Bumpstead Hall there, VCH 535, n.8.

35,14 STEVINGTON (END). Identified by VCH 536, n.2, as the manor of Waltons in Ashdon.

36 PETER OF VALOGNES. The Sheriff of Essex and Hertfordshire in 1086, see VCH 349. He was named from Valognes (La Manche), OEB 117.

36,3 (LITTLE) PARNDON. Identified by VCH 536.

36,4 (NORTH) WEALD (BASSETT). For this identification, see VCH 397.

36,6 HIGHAM (HILL). In Walthamstow, EPNS 106–107.

I HAVE MENTIONED ABOVE. *sup(er)i(us) dixi*, a rare use of the first person in the Domesday texts. The subject of the verb may have been the Sheriff of Essex, whose Holding this was, rather than the compiler of LDB.

WILLIAM ... VALOGNES. *hoc*, if it agrees with any other word here, ought grammatically, to refer to the whole manor (*manerium*), rather than to just the 1 hide (*hida*), but it should probably be taken here as standing on its own and meaning 'that just described', i.e. the 1 hide.

36,8 HALF-HUNDRED OF 'THUNDERLOW'. See 35,6 note.

RALPH THE HAUNTED. LDB *fatat(us)*, unexplained OEB 389, but see Latham 186 s.v. *fatatus* 'haunted' *c*. 1212.

36,9 'BINSLEY'. See 23,10 note. VCH 405–406 puts it in 'Thunderlow' Half-Hundred but above at 23,10 it appears to be in Hinckford Hundred. Hundred-rubrics appear to have been omitted in this part of the present Chapter.

36,10 VALUE THEN. LDB repeats *T(un)c ual(uit)*.

36,11 THEYDON (BOIS). Identified by VCH 537, n.11.

36,12 RALPH THE HAUNTED. As 36,8 note.
(NORTH) WEALD (BASSETT). As 36,4 note.

37 RANULF BROTHER OF ILGER. Ranulf appears consistently in the DB Survey as 'the brother of Ilger', although in IE (149) he is called 'the son of Ilger'. Ilger is from OG *Hilger*, see OEB 187.

37,1 INGRAVE. Identified by VCH 161.

37,2 FOUND NOTHING. No livestock, when acquired.

37,3 INGVAR. Ranulf brother of Ilger also took possession of Everton (Huntingdonshire 24,1) which had previously been held by Ingvar. The name *Ingvar* is ON (PNDB 298) and hence the spelling 'Ingward' used in the Hunts. translation is incorrect and should be altered to 'Ingvar'.

37,4-6 PARNDON. Probably Great Parndon, VCH 539.

37,4 ALFSI BOWL. LDB *bolla*, from the OE for 'bowl, cup'; OEB 294-295.

37,7 (NORTH) WEALD (BASSETT). As 36,4 note.

37,9 1 VIRGATE ... FROM THERE. The 30 acres mentioned in 7,1 as being held by Ranulf brother of Ilger.

37,11 13 ... LDB *.7.xiii;* Probably the missing category is 'cobs', *runcini*.

37,12 THESE 2 MANORS. Referring to 37,11-12.

37,13 THEN NOTHING. That is, no livestock before 1066.

37,14 ST. LAWRENCE. As 2,6 note. Identified as East Newland by VCH 540, n.5.

37,17 The text demands a new section here, although LDB has not supplied a paragraph mark.
AND ... EXCHANGE. Perhaps the subject of this clause is Ranulf brother of Ilger, not William of Bosc; cf. 37,19.

37,19 FOUCHERS. Called *Gynge Puelle* in 1373, from the tenants before 1066, EPNS 159. Not Mountnessing as VCH 541.
FREELY. LDB *lib(er)ae* is probably for *libere*, being influenced by the previous word *puellae*. The alternative translation, 'free girls', is less likely since it should have been written in the order *liberae puellae*.
EXCHANGE. Cf. 37,16 note.

37,20 'DERLEIGH'. Lost, in Little Bromley; EPNS 333. Not, as VCH 541, Ardleigh.
EDRIC OF EASTHORPE. He of 20,40.
LAWFORD. Adjoining Little Bromley. See 1,27.

38 TIHEL THE BRETON. The forename is Breton *Tihellus*. In 18,21a he is called 'of Helléan' (Morbihan: arr. Pontivy; OEB 91), which byname has been fossilized in Helions Bumpstead, held by Tihel (38,4).

38,1 [THEN]. LDB has *7* in error for *T(un)c*.

38,2 STEVINGTON (END). As 35,14 note (VCH 541, n.9). Farley *Steintuna(m)* is in error for *Steuituna(m)* of the MS.
THEN [AND] LATER. *T(un)c p(ro) p(ost)* is a Farley error for *T(un)c 7 p(ost)* of the MS.
SMALLHOLDER, NOW 3. In the MS *iii* has been altered from *ii*.

38,3 GUTHRED. LDB *Goderet*; ON *Guthrøðr* PNDB 279-280, Fellows Jensen 111.

38,4 (HELIONS) BUMPSTEAD. The manor of Helions there, VCH 541, n.11. See *38* note.
... BEEHIVES. LDB omits the numeral.

38,5 MANOR, FOR 1 HIDE. The semi-colon in Farley is a misreading of the MS where a full point after *man(erio)* has been misassociated with an insertion-mark below the line in the form of a comma. The insertion-mark is repeated in the MS, but not in Farley, before the interlineation of *7 p(ro) .i. hid(a)*.

38,6 44 PIGS. In the MS, *porc(i)* has been altered from *ou-*.

38,7 LDB omits the paragraph-mark before this entry.

39 ROGER OF RAISMES. LDB *de Ramis*; from Raismes (Nord), OEB 109.

39,1-2 RAYNE. The manor of Old Hall there, VCH 542, n.7.

39,1 MEADOW, 11 ACRES. The LDB interlineation reads *c 7 .xi. ac(re) p(ra)ti*. The *c* is most probably a repetition of the number of pigs, already given. '111 acres of meadow' is a very unlikely alternative.
OF THIS MANOR. The paragraph-mark here does not distinguish a separate manor.
WIBERGA. OG, Forssner 252.

39,3 WARENGAR. OG *Weringer*, Forssner 246. The LDB form has OFr *G-* for *W-*. Warengar also held lands in Sible Hedingham from Roger Bigot which Roger of Raismes claimed, see 43,1.

(SIBLE) HEDINGHAM. The manor of Greys there, VCH 543, n.2.
SLAVES, LATER AND NOW 2. In the MS *ii* has been altered from *i*.

39,7 WIFE. Cf. 39,10 note.

39,8 ARDLEIGH. The manor of Picotts there, VCH 543, n.6.
RALPH OF HASTINGS. Presumably named from Hastings, Sussex, although he is not identifiable in the DB Survey of that county. See also B7 note.

39,9 JACQUES HALL. Formerly 'Manston', EPNS 329.
ALFHELM. LDB *Alselm(us)* is in error for *Alfelm(us)*.
4 SMALLHOLDERS, NOW 3. In the MS *iii* has been altered from *ii*.

39,10 HENRY'S WIFE. 'Henry's' *Henrici* has been substituted for 'Aubrey's' *Alb(er)ici*. Possibly the 'wife of a man-at-arms' in 39,7.

39,11 CLIFF. In Mistley, EPNS 344.

40 JOHN SON OF WALERAN. For his father's annexations, see 90,46–47.

40,1 ERNUCION. Perhaps an extended form of OG *Ernust*, see OEB 181.
NOTLEY. Perhaps Black Notley, VCH 544.

40,2 THURSTAN. Probably Thurstan Wishart of B3p, who held 3 houses and ½ hide of land in Colchester from John son of Waleran.
(GREAT) SALING. Identified by VCH 544.

40,3 (LITTLE) MAPLESTEAD. Identified by VCH 544.
[HELD]. LDB omits *tenuit*.
AS A PLEDGE. Translating *p(ro) uadimonio*.
NOTHING. That is, no livestock.

40,4 HENNY. Roger also held from John an annexation here, see 90,46.
SUDBURY. Suffolk (1,97).

40,5 BURES. See 23,16 note.

40,7-8 HE ALSO HOLDS. That is, Roger of 40,6.

40,7 THE OTHER FYFIELD. A different manor, but within the present parish. VCH 545, n.5, suggests that this is the 30 acres mentioned under Havering-atte-Bower in 1,4.

40,8 (HIGH) ONGAR. Identified by VCH 545.

41 ROBERT SON OF CORBUCION. His patronym is perhaps OFr **Corbucion*, from Vulgar Latin **Corbutio*, an extended form of Latin *corvus*, 'raven'; OEB 178–179.

41,3 4½ HIDES. See 1,4 note.

Folio 85a, foot. Farley imitates the irregular shape of the bottom corner of the leaf in the MS here and on the reverse (85b).

41,4 8 FREEMEN HELD. In the MS *uiii* has apparently been altered by elongating the second minim below the line; since the verb *tenebat* is wrongly in the singular here, the scribe may have at first misread *uiii soc(hemanni)* in his exemplar as *unus soc(hemannus)*, before altering it to *uiii* but forgetting to correct the verb to *tenebant*.
FREEMEN ... HAVERING (-ATTE-BOWER). See 1,4 and note.

41,6 HUNDRED OF CHELMSFORD. Farley indicates an erasure in the MS by means of three dots, *Celme ... fort*; MS reads *Celme[.]sfort*, with only one letter erased.

41,9 'BENSTED'. As 27,14 note.

Folio 85b, foot. See note on folio 85a, foot.

41,11 VALUE ... NOW 5[s]. Farley omits to show a gap in the text, caused by an erasure in the MS, between *m(odo)*. and *.v*.

41,12 TOLLESHUNT (MAJOR). The modern form of the place-name commemorates Mauger, the DB undertenant; EPNS 307.

42 WALTER THE DEACON. The head of his Holding was at Little Easton (42,3), see VCH 349.

42,1 1 ... PIGS. Farley *.x....porc(i)* indicates a gall-stain in the MS obscuring the text here.

42,2 PURLEIGH. With 42,4 below, the manors of Frerne and Jakelets in Purleigh, VCH 548, n.3.
LEOFWIN. Probably Young Leofwin of 42,4 (see VCH 351). Cf. 42,6 note.

42,3 (LITTLE) EASTON. Identified by VCH 548.

42,4 PURLEIGH. As 42,2 note.
YOUNG LEOFWIN. See 42,2;6 notes.

42,5 STOW MARIES. See 30,44 note.

42,6 COLNE (ENGAINE). The manor of Overhall there, VCH 548, n.6.
LEOFWIN. Probably Young Leofwin of 42,4 (see VCH 351). Cf. 42,2 note.

42,7-9 QUEEN EDITH. As 20,8 note.

42,8 (LITTLE) BROMLEY. Identified by VCH 548.

42,9 (LITTLE) CHESTERFORD. Identified by VCH 549.

Folio 87a, foot. Farley omits to show a summary (?of hidages) which occurs in the bottom margin of the MS. It reads: *.v.ii.iiii.ii.7 d(imidia) .iii.iii.7 d(imidia)ii.v*. It does not fit the hidages of Chapter 42, however. Cf. notes on folios 8a,20a.

43 ROGER BIGOT. The ancestor of the Bigots, Earls of Norfolk. His byname was OFr and meant 'bigot', OEB 342.
43,1-2 WARENGAR. See 39,3 note.
43,1 (SIBLE) HEDINGHAM. Identified by VCH 549.
THESE 48 ACRES. LDB has '48' in error for '48½' here.
THESE 2 LANDS. The 25 acres and the 48½ acres.
43,4 VAUX. Unidentified; OEB 117.
BELCHAMP (OTTEN). The manor of Vaux there, named from the 1086 subtenant, VCH 549, n.6.
43,5 HENNY. Probably Little Henny, VCH 549, n.7.
43,6 HUGH OF HOUDAIN. Probably from Houdain (Pas-de-Calais: arr. Béthune), but cf. also Houdeng-au-Bosc (Seine-Inf.) and Houdain (Nord); OEB 92-93.
44 ROBERT MALET. His Holding, mainly in Suffolk, was later known as the Honour of Eye. His byname was OFr *malet*, a diminutive of *mal* 'evil', OEB 350-351. For his annexation of 15 acres at Middleton, see 90,84.
44,1 HUBERT. Called Hubert of Montchesny in Suffolk (*57*); VCH 550, n.4.
44,2 40 PIGS. LDB *caporc*, where the scribe began to write *cap(ri)*, 'goats', but changed to *porc(i)* without erasing either *ca* or the abbreviation-mark above *p*.
44,3 (WAKES) COLNE. Identified by VCH 550, n.10; EPNS 383.
AZORIN. LDB *Assorin(us)*. PNDB 170-171 s.n. ODan, OSw *Azur*. Cf. 32,36 note on Azo.
44,4 WALTER. In Suffolk (6,5;7) he is named as Walter of Caen.
COLNE (ENGAINE). LDB *Parua colun*. For this identification, see EPNS 379-380.
45 WILLIAM OF ÉCOUIS. From Écouis (Eure); OEB 114.
45,1 MORETON. According to ECE, no. 75, William of Écouis had granted the estate to St. Stephen's, Caen, between 1066 and 1077. It was later confirmed to St. Stephen's by King Henry II.
THEN ... COBS. LDB omits the numeral.
HOLDS FROM HIM. That is, from William.
46 ROGER OF POITOU. A younger son of Roger of Montgomery, Earl of Shrewsbury. He appears to have forfeited lands in Lancashire, Derbyshire, Nottinghamshire and Norfolk by 1086, possibly for supporting King William's rebellious son, Robert of Normandy.
46,1 WHO HAVE 1 PLOUGH. In the MS the *h* of *h(abe)ntes* has been altered from *7*.
VALUE THEN. LDB *7 post*, 'and later' deleted after *T(un)c*.
46,2 LEOFWIN CROC. The byname is ON *krókr*, 'hook'; OEB 179. See also Reaney, s.n. Crook.
[IN] LORDSHIP. Farley indicates a blot in the MS by the use of three dots; however, the implication of loss of text is not warranted since *in* is clearly visible in the MS.
48 SHEEP, 100 SHEEP. Thus in MS.
ABOVE POUNDS. In the 60s (= £3), above.
46,3 LEOFWIN. Perhaps he of 46,2.
47 HUGH OF GOURNAI. From Gournai-en-Brai (Seine-Inf.: arr. Neufchâtel); OEB 90-91.
47,1 GEOFFREY TALBOT. The byname may be OFr *talebot*, 'pillager', but see further OEB 225 and Reaney 315. Cf. Calebot in B3a.
47,3 10 ACRES. Roger of Poitou held adjacent at both Mount Bures and West Bergholt. Cf. 1,19 note for another annexation by him in this Hundred.
48 WILLIAM PEVEREL. His lands later became part of the Honour of Peverel of Nottingham, see VCH 346; cf. *34* note.
48,1 (EAST) HORNDON. The manor of Abbots there (later held by Waltham Abbey), VCH 399.
48,2 (GRAYS) THURROCK. Identified by VCH 388.
THEN 11 SMALLHOLDERS. In the MS *xi* has been altered from *vi*.
2 VILLAGERS, 58 SHEEP. Thus in MS. LDB *uill'* is probably for *uit(uli)*, 'calves'.
GILBERT ... 10 ACRES. At Stifford, see 18,34.
ANSKETEL ... MANOR. Ansketel was the Bishop of London's tenant at Little Thurrock (4,6).
49 RALPH OF LIMÉSY. From Limésy (Seine-Inf.: arr. Rouen); OEB 95.
49,1 BRUNDON. In Suffolk since 1835, see EPNS 407, n.1. See also 49,4.
HARDWIN. On him, see VCH 553, n.7, and Suffolk (21,16).
49,2 *NIUETUNA*. Unidentified, OE *nīwe-tūn*, 'the new estate'.
49,3 CHIGWELL. The manor of Chigwell Hall there, VCH 553, n.10. See also 49.5.
PETER THE SHERIFF. See *36*.
HAD DELIVERY. Literally, 'had the deliverer', *habuit ... lib(er)atore(m)*.
49,4 This entry belongs with 49,1.
49,5 This entry belongs with 49,3.

49,6 6 ACRES. Unlocated, perhaps in Ongar Hundred.
50 ROBERT OF TOSNY. Named from Tosny (Eure), see OEB 116.
51 RALPH OF TOSNY. As *50* note.
51,2 LAVER. Perhaps Magdalen Laver, VCH 554, n.6.
SAXI. Probably the Guard (*huscarl*) of this name who was Ralph of Tosny's predecessor at Westmill, Hertfordshire 22,2.
52 WALTER OF DOUAI. From Douai (Nord); OEB 87.
52,1 UPMINSTER. The manor of Gaines there, VCH 554, n.9.
85 SHEEP AND 25 SHEEP. Thus in MS.
10 ACRES ... EXCHANGE. Perhaps part of the exchange mentioned in relation to the adjacent Ockendon in 30,4.
52,2 [AND AFTER]. Farley shows *7 . p(ost)* as deleted and there is a line through it in the MS but it is uncertain whether this is more than a smudge since the text makes more sense here without a deletion.
53 MATTHEW OF MORTAGNE. From Mortagne (La Manche); OEB 101.
53,1 (GREAT) EASTON. Identified by VCH 555.
30 PIGS. Farley *.xxx* is in error for *cxx* (120) of the MS, where the text is affected by an ink smudge.
53,2 MARGARETTING. Identified by VCH 555, n.4.
VALUE THEN ... S. LDB omits the numeral.
54 COUNTESS OF AUMÂLE. King William's half-sister, Ellis i, 366-367.
54,2 OLD HALL. LDB *Sciddinchov*; formerly Sheddon or Sharing Hall in Mistley, EPNS 344. VCH 555, n.7 identifies as Manningtree, adjacent to Mistley.
55 COUNTESS JUDITH. Niece of King William and widow of Earl Waltheof (see following).
55,1 EARL WALTHEOF. Of Huntingdon and Northumbria, executed for treason in 1076 . (having joined two of his fellow Earls in rebellion, one of them Earl Ralph of 21,9 note).
56 FRODO THE ABBOT'S BROTHER. Brother of Abbot Baldwin of Bury St. Edmund's. See also 90,85.
ORDGAR. Frodo's predecessor, who had made the annexation recorded in 90,85.
56,1 3 ... LDB omits the category, probably *servi*, 'slaves'.
57 SASSELIN. A diminutive of OG *Saxo*; Forssner 223.
57,1 STANMER. In Ramsden Bellhouse, EPNS 168.
CRAY'S HILL. LDB *Winthelle*. In Ramsden Crays, EPNS 168-169.
2 MEN'S OXEN. That is, ¼ plough belonging to the men.
57,3 LAYER. Probably Layer Breton, VCH 556, n.7.
57,5 (LITTLE) WARLEY. See 3,11.
59,1 *SCILCHEHAM*. The same place as *Sciddeham* (90,82) where William annexed a free man. The name may be related to that of Sheddon or Sharing Hall, the former name of Old Hall (54,2) in Tendring Hundred, EPNS 344. The spelling is here scribally corrupt.
60 HUGH OF ST. QUENTIN. Probably from Saint-Quentin (La Manche: arr. Avranches); OEB 113.
60,1 WINGE. Probably from ODan, OSw *vinge* 'wing', PNDB 416, Redin 128.
GODWIN. Called Godwin Woodhen in 90,1 which records the same annexation.
60,3 THE QUEEN'S GIFT. Cf. the same phrase in 82,1 where Matilda is meant.
61 EDMUND SON OF ALGOT. The patronym is either ODan, OSw *Algot, Algut* or OG *Adalgot, Alfgot, Altgot*; OEB 170. He also held a mill from the Bishop of London in Stepney, Middlesex (3,10).
61,2 AELMER HOLDFAST. The byname is probably OE **Holdfaest* 'hold fast', OEB 221-222. Probably the same man as Holdfast in 22,3 who also held land in Harlow Half-Hundred before 1066.
Folio 94a, line 2. LDB began the *T* of *TERRA* and the paragraph-mark in the heading to Chapter 62 two lines too early and abandoned them, wishing to leave space between chapters.
62,1 ALFWARD DORE. The byname is probably OE *dora* 'humble-bee', but see further OEB 361-362.
62,3 WULFWIN HAPRA. OEB 347 suggests a byname derived from OE *(ge)haep* 'fit' with an AN suffix. A name such as OE **Haepp, *Haeppa* is also possible (cf. OG *Heppo*, etc., Förstemann 748; see Reaney s.v. *Happe*). Alternatively, *Hapra* might be a misreading of *Hafra*, an Anglicized form of OScand *Hafri*, a byname derived from ON *hafr* 'he-goat', see *Hafr, Hafri* in Fellows Jensen, 121.
'BYRTON'. Lost, in Stanway; EPNS 399.
62,4 *LOHOU*. Unidentified, probably OE **Lōh-hōe*; the second element is *hōh* 'a promontory, hill', and the first *lōg, lōh*, 'place', perhaps also 'hollow, camp, lair'.

63 ADAM SON OF DURAND MALZOR. The Latin byname *malis operibus* 'associated with bad works or evil deeds' corresponds to OFr *malesouvres*; OEB 349.
66 WILLIAM THE DEACON. Probably the same as William the Bishop's nephew in B3h, see note there.
66,1 WE HAVE RECEIVED ... HAND. Another instance of the use of the first person in LDB, here in the plural and reporting the work of the Domesday Commissioners. Cf. 1,3.
66,2 HUNDRED OF HINCKFORD. LDB *hidngfort* is in error for *hidingfort*.
67 WALTER COOK. The ½ hide at Shalford described in 67,1 is probably that mentioned in 1,11 as being held by Walter son of Gilbert, which suggests that these two Walters were identical. See also 90,66 note.
67,2 FELLOW. He of 90,65-66.
68 MODWIN. According to PNDB 328 this name is OG *Modwin* rather than an unrecorded OE **Mōdwine*; however, he appears to have been the former tenant in 70,2, which entry, like 68,6, relates to East Donyland, and this may lend weight to the OE derivation of his name.
68,1 EDWIN GROAT. The byname is from OE *grūt*, 'groats, coarse meal', OEB 376-377.
68,5 ALFWARD. Probably he of 90,69.
68,8 'DERLEIGH'. As 37,20 note.
69 ILBOD. The name is probably OG *Hildebodo, Hilbod*; Forssner 162.
69,2 LISTON. Either the manor of Over Hall or that of Netherhall there, VCH 561, n.7.
VALUE THEN. In the MS the *T* of *T(un)c* appears to have been altered from *S* (?of *Semper*).
70 HAGEBERN. Here LDB has *Hgheb(er)ni*, below in 70,2 *hagheb(er)t(us)*. OG **Hagabern*; Forssner 138. Cf. also Hagebert in 1,27. There is persistent confusion in post-Conquest records between similar endings in the names Osbern (ON *Ásbiorn*) and Osbert (OG *Ósbert*). Cf. also in Domesday Essex the pairs of names Fridebern/Fridebert and Thorbern/Thorbert which may also have been confused; see references in Index of Persons.
70,2 MODWIN. See *68* note.
HAGEBERT. See *70* note.
71 THEODORIC POINTEL. His byname is OFr *pointel*, 'point, sharp instrument', OEB 328-329. At 18,7;19 and 33,4 he is referred to by his byname alone. For his annexations, see 90,4-9.
71,3 COGGESHALL. See 90,7-8 for 2 manors obtained by Theodoric by a similar exchange.
WHICH TESSELIN HELD. Referring to the 1½ hides.
72,2 ½ HIDE AND 30 ACRES. The 3 virgates recorded at 15,1.
72,3 (GREAT) BADDOW. Identified by VCH 562.
73,1 30 ACRES. Also mentioned in 15,1.
74 CONSTANTINE. Farley *constantini* is in error for *costantini* of the MS.
76,1 ALWIN. Probably Alwin Stickhare, Robert son of Rozelin's predecessor at Stepney, Middlesex (16,1).
[THEN]. LDB omits *Tunc*.
77,1 (GREAT) BROMLEY. Identified by VCH 563.
WESTNANETUNA. Unidentified; probably OE **Westmannatune*, 'at the estate of the men who live to the west', cf. Westmancote, Worcs., DEPN 508.
SERVICE. LDB *seRuitiu(m)*, with *R* altered from *p*. The initial misreading was probably due to the similarity of *r* and *p* in insular minuscule.
79,1 MONKS OF ELY ... THEM. In the Ely land pleas of 1071 x 1075, Reginald *milis* is stated to hold 6½ hides in (South) Fambridge rightfully belonging to Ely; see *Inquisitio Comitatus Cantabrigiensis*, ed. N. E. S. A. Hamilton (1876), 193. See also IE 128.
80 GUNDWIN. Perhaps the same as Gundwin the Chamberlain (Suffolk *58*) and Gundwin the keeper of the granaries (Wiltshire 68,29). The name is OG *Gund(e)win*; Forssner 135.
81 OTTO THE GOLDSMITH. The craftsman who constructed the bejewelled tomb of King William at Caen, VCH 350-351. See also B3j note and 1,11-12.
81,1 GESTINGTHORPE. The manor of Overhall there, VCH 564, n.8.
82,1 THE QUEEN'S GIFT. Probably Matilda, see 1,11-12 note.
83 GRIM THE REEVE. See also 1,18.
83,1 ONE ... KING. 1 hide had been forfeited to the King for felony and Grim had been in a position, as Reeve, to acquire it for himself. Cf. 83,2.
83,2 HUBERT OF PORT. See 32,29 note.
84 WULFEVA WIFE OF FINN. Wife of Finn the Dane (23,38;43), see VCH 348-349. Her lands were granted to Eudo the Steward by King William II in 1099 or 1100, ECE, no. 124.
84,1 LORDSHIP; 1 VILLAGER. LDB repeats 7 where the text goes from recto to verso of the folio.

THESE HIDES. In the MS *hid(is)* has been altered from *his*. The scribe had here repeated the previous word by mistake.

88,2 THE KING'S CUSTOMARY DUE. Alternatively, 'the customary due to the King'.

89,1 HUNDRED-REEVE. See 32,25 note.

89,3 RICHARD. Probably he at 28,12;17-18.

HAMO. The Steward (*28*).

90 ANNEXATIONS. This Chapter records instances of unlawful occupation of lands in Essex, brought to light by the Domesday Survey. The entries fall into groups associated with particular institutions and individuals almost all of which are named as Landholders or undertenants in preceding Chapters.

90,1-4 These entries are by a different scribe to the one who wrote most of the rest of the county. He also wrote *B*, below.

90,1 WOODHEN. See 9,5 note.

2 PLACES. See 60,1.

90,2 3 VIRGATES. See 9,5.

90,3 DUNTON. This place is adjacent to Horndon-on-the-Hill.

90,4-9 THEODORIC POINTEL. See *71*.

90,4 (LITTLE) THURROCK. Identified by DG.

VALUE THEN 41s. LDB *.xl.i s(olidos).*; it is not absolutely certain however that the stroke before *s(olidos)* should be taken as the number *i*, rather than an anticipation of *s* of *s(olidos)*. 40s would be more to be expected as a value than 41s.

90,6 BEFORE THESE PLEAS. LDB *p(rius)qua(m) hec placita fierent*; that is, before the Domesday Survey.

90,7 (LITTLE) STAMBRIDGE. Identified by VCH 566, n.18.

90,8 ROBERT ... HIM. Interlined, preceded by an insertion-mark in the form of a colon. In the MS this mark is repeated after *sol(idos)* but is not shown by Farley.

EXCHANGE ... COGGESHALL. See 71,3 for another 1½ hides obtained by Theodoric by a similar exchange.

90,9 *MIDEBROC*. Unidentified; either OE **Midelbrōc* 'marsh-meadow in the middle' or OE **Myðe-* or **Myðan-brōc* 'marsh-meadow at a confluence'.

HOLY TRINITY, CANTERBURY. See *2*.

90,10-14 RANULF PEVEREL. See *34*.

90,10 3 HIDES LESS 15 ACRES. That is, 2 hides and 105 acres. This had apparently become 2 hides and 110 acres by 1086 (2 hides and 80 acres + 30 acres), unless there is an error of computation here. Ranulf also held another 2 hides and 90 acres (2½ hides and 30 acres) there, see 34,6.

90,12 STANSGATE. See 34,26 for other land here held by Ralph son of Brian from Ranulf.

90,13 (GREAT) HENNY. Identified by VCH 567. See 34,21 for other land here held by Thorold from Ranulf. Cf. 90,44.

90,14 LAMARSH. See 34,22 for land as in preceding note. Cf. 90,45.

FREE LAND. Taking *lib(er)e* of LDB to stand for *lib(er)ae*, agreeing with *t(er)rae*.

90,15-18 HUGH DE MONTFORT. See *27*.

90,15 WILLIAM SON OF GROSS. Hugh's tenant at Kelvedon in 27,2 above.

90,17 HUNDRED OF LEXDEN. Hugh held Markshall (27,13) in this Hundred, adjacent to Feering.

FEERING. 6,8 above.

90,19 ST. PETER'S, WESTMINSTER. See *6*.

HAVERING-ATTE-BOWER. The King's manor, see 1,4.

90,20-28 GEOFFREY DE MANDEVILLE. See *30*.

90,20 MASHBURY. See 30,13 for Geoffrey's other land here.

90,21 CANFIELD. Richard held land from Geoffrey at Little Canfield (30,38).

90,22-23 ROCKELL'S FARM. Formerly '*Wyggepet*', EPNS 526-527.

90,25 FARNHAM. The manor of Earlsbury there, VCH 568, n.10; EPNS 550-551.

90,26 STAMBOURNE. The manor of Moone Hall there, VCH 568, n.11.

90,27 *WESUUNIC*. Perhaps the same place as that called *Wenesuuic* in 30,51, although the 6 free men are not necessarily the same in both entries, there being a different amount of land and a different 1066 value. However, it may be a different place and a different name; perhaps OE **Wesu-wīc* 'farm, etc. at a wet place', from *wese* 'soaked' and *wīc*, or OE **Wēsung-wīc* 'factory where soaking (e.g. of flax, dyeing, etc.) is carried on', from *wēsung* the gerund of OE *wēsan* 'to soak' and *wīc*.

90,28 GODWIN SECH. The byname is probably from OE *saec* 'sack', rather than OFr *sec* 'dry, withered'; cf. OEB 333-334 and Alwin Sack, Bedfordshire 4,5.

90,29 HUGH OF BERNIÈRES. See 30,28-30.
90,30 'PLESINGHO'. As 20,18 note.
HELD. LDB *tenut* is in error for *tenuit*.
HUMPHREY GOLDENBOLLOCKS. LDB *humfrid(us) aurei testiculi*; OEB 285. Perhaps a nickname for a man who had sired many children.
90,31-33 HAMO THE STEWARD. See *28*.
90,31 (LITTLE) WIGBOROUGH. Identified by VCH 569, n.3. For Hamo's land here see 28,9.
90,32 NORTHEY ISLAND. As 28,12 note.
90,33 STAMBOURNE. See 28,11 for Hamo's land here.
40 ACRES ... 40s. Interlined in the MS.
90,34 WILLIAM CARDON. LDB *Cardun*, see 10,5 note.
(GREAT) CHISHILL. Held by William from Geoffrey de Mandeville (30,46).
90,35 SWEIN. See *24*.
BERTUNA. Unidentified, OE *bere-tūn*, 'outlier'.
ROBERT SON OF WYMARC. See 24,1 note.
90,36-37 AUBREY DE VERE. See *35*.
90,37 SMALTON. In Castle Hedingham (cf. 35,5); EPNS 440.
90,38 AUBREY DE VERE'S WIFE. See also 18,21;24.
90,38 (LITTLE) MAPLESTEAD. Identified by VCH 569. Aubrey's wife held 'Napsted' here from Odo of Bayeux (18,21).
5 FREE MEN ... 3s. Interlined in the MS.
90,39-40 RALPH BAYNARD. See *33*.
90,39 HENHAM. For Ralph Baynard's land here (13½ hides less 10 acres) see 33,19. Ralph's two holdings here would amount to 14 hides.
90,40 COUPALS FARM. As 23,23 note.
After this entry the MS has a gap of about two lines. This gap is introduced in the facsimile by a paragraph-mark, not shown by Farley since in the MS it has been erased.
90,41 3s. *x* corrected to *iii*; so in MS.
90,42 RALPH LATIMER. He is named in ICC as Ely Abbey's tenant at Hardwick in 1086 (Cambridgeshire 5,37 note), and may be identical with the Ralph who held Albury (Hertfordshire 4,11; adjacent to Farnham) from the Bishop of London in 1086.
90,43 *LIFFILDEUUELLA*. OE *Leofhildewella*, 'Lēofhild's spring'. Unidentified, but possibly associated with Levit's Corner in Pebmarsh, see EPNS 447.
Folio 101a, foot. Farley's tapering of the right-hand margin in the last three lines of this page reflects a repair in the MS, also affecting the left-hand margin at the foot of folio 101b.
90,44-45 THOROLD. Ranulf Peverel's undertenant at Great Henny and Lamarsh, 34,21-22. Cf. also 90,13-14.
90,46-47 WALERAN. Father of John (*40*).
90,46 10½ ACRES. LDB repeats 'and', using both the tironian *nota* and the ampersand.
JOHN. Son of Waleran, see *40*. For his land at HENNY held from him by Roger, see 40,4.
90,47 HELD. LDB *ten'*, probably for *ten(uit)*.
NOW 40. LDB *xl* is almost certainly an error.
90,48 LEDMER OF HEMPSTEAD ... RICHARD. Ledmer is called Ledmer the reeve in 90,76 which refers to the same annexation. He was the reeve of Richard son of Count Gilbert, who held Hempstead (23,41) in 1086.
BRAINTREE. Probably Sandpit Leet, VCH 570, n.19.
90,49-78 RICHARD SON OF COUNT GILBERT. See *23*.
90,49 AELMER OF BORLEY. Cf. 90,55.
AELFRIÇ OF ALDERFORD. Richard held 36 acres at Alderford (23,11).
GOISMER. See 23,7 note.
5 ACRES. Probably of meadow, if LDB has omitted *prati*.
90,50-51 ARNOLD. Probably he of 23,3;8-9.
90,50 FINCHINGFIELD. See 23,9 for 38 acres here, held by Arnold from Richard.
90,52 HORSEHAM (HALL). See also 90,75.
WIDELARD. Probably he of 23,10;42 and 90,75.
90,53 HOWE. See 23,15 note.
GERMUND. Richard's tenant in 23,15.
WHICH COLMAN. LDB repeats *q(uo)d* where the text begins a new folio.
Folio 101b, foot. See note to folio 101a.
90,54 YELDHAM. Richard held Great Yeldham (23,7).
90,55 BORLEY. Cf. Aelmer of Borley in 90,49.

FREE MEN. Although Godiva was a woman, she could still technically be termed a *liber homo* in relation to her status.
90,56-57 TOPPESFIELD. Probably the manor of Scoteneys there, VCH 571, n.11; EPNS 464, s.n. Scotney's Farm.
90,58 CORNISH HALL. Formerly 'Norton', EPNS 426–427.
MASCEREL. See 23,14 note.
90,59-60 PEBMARSH; ALPHAMSTONE. See 23,18–19 for Richard's lands here.
90,61 (STEEPLE) BUMPSTEAD. See 23,21 for Richard's land here.
90,63 ALL THESE. The men named in 90,59–63. *ōns* is a LDB error for *ōms, om(ne)s*.
THE ABOVE MEN. Either those in 90,59–63 or all the pre-1066 free men in 90,49–63.
WITHGAR. The predecessor of Richard son of Count Gilbert, see 90,64.
90,64 ENGELRIC. See 20,77 where he is said to have held 4½ hides at Bendysh (Hall) before Count Eustace.
90,65 (GREAT) BARDFIELD. Identified by VCH 572. For Richard's land there, see 23,39.
90,65-66 FELLOW. He of 67,2.
90,66 *HOCSENGA*. This is a Farley error for *hoosenga* of the MS. Unidentified, perhaps OE **hōsinge* 'place having to do with an association or company of people', from OE *hōs* (Beowulf 924).
WALTER. Possibly Walter Cook (*67*) who succeeded Fellow at Ashwell (67,2).
90,67 *HASINGHAM*. Unidentified, OE *Hasing-hām* or *Hasing-hamm*, 'Hasu's estate or Hasu's enclosure', cf. DEPN 224, s.n. Hassingham, Norfolk.
90,68 LUTTING. LDB *Luttin(us)*; PNDB 322.
COLNE. For Richard's holding there, see 23,34.
90,69 ALFWARD HOLDS. LDB *ten&* is in error for *tenuit*. Alfward is probably the pre-1066 tenant named in 68,5.
90,69-70 THE OTHER LAND. That in 90,68.
90,70 (WEST) BERGHOLT. For Richard's holding there, see 23,36.
90,71-72 THE OTHERS. LDB *alios*, probably agreeing with *locos* 'places' (understood); those in 90,69–70.
90,71 COLNE. As 90,68 note.
90,72 FORDHAM. For Richard's holding there, see 23,35.
TOVILD. LDB *Touillda*; ON **Tófa-Hildr*, 'Hildr the daughter of Tófi', PNDB 384.
90,73 (WEST) BERGHOLT. As 90,70 note.
2 OXEN. That is, ¼ plough.
90,74 HALSTEAD. For Richard's holding there, see 23,26.
90,75 HORSEHAM (HALL); WIDELARD. See also 90,52.
90,76 BRAINTREE ... LEDMER. See 90,48 note.
90,77 WARNER. Probably he of 23,2. He had given the tithes of this land to the Abbey of Bec by 1086, see ECE, no. 78.
ILBOD. See *69*.
90,79 MONKS OF CANTERBURY. See *2*.
LAWLING. For the monks' manor there, see 2,4.
90,80 THORBERN WITHOUT ... GIFT. The King had not granted them to him.
90,81 HENRY OF FERRERS. See *29*.
STEEPLE. For Henry's holding there, see 29,3.
90,82 WILLIAM LEOFRIC. See *59*.
SCIDDEHAM. The same place as *Scilcheham* in 59,1.
VALUE 12d. Farley omits to show a gap in the text, caused by an erasure in the MS, between *val(et)* and *.xii.d(enarios)*. The text erased is *ii.sol(idi)*.
90,83 ROBERT BLUNT. See 35,5 note.
90,84 ROBERT MALET. See *44*.
90,85 FRODO THE ABBOT'S BROTHER. See *56*.
STEVINGTON (END). LDB *Staumtuna* is in error for *Stauintuna*.
90,86 ROGER OF AUBERVILLE. See *26*.
CHISHILL. For Roger's holding there, see 26,5.
90,87 ONGAR. For Count Eustace's holding here (in Ongar Hundred), see 20,46. The 15 acres were presumably a detached part of the manor of Ongar, perhaps for sheep-rearing.
B This section is written by the same scribe as 90,1–4.
B1-2 GODRIC. Probably Godric of Colchester (20,42).
B1 4 PIECES OF LAND. LDB *.iiii.mansiones.t(er)rae*.
VALUE ... 30s. LDB *ualit* is in error for *ualet*.
B2 LEXDEN. See also 1,19.

CITY'S LEVY. LDB *Cootu(m) ciuitatis* is almost certainly a misreading of *scotu(m) ciuitatis*, cf. 3,16. VCH 574, note 15, emends to *compotum civitatis*, 'account of the city'.

B3a WULFSTAN EADLAC. LDB *eudlac*, OEB 217 takes the byname to be a side-form of OE *Ēadlāc*, resting on a derivation from an archaic form **eud-* which is unlikely at this date; a palaeographical confusion of *ea/eu* is more probable.

LEOFWIN CRIST. OEB 308 interprets the byname as OWScand **krist* 'cheep, peep', possibly applying to someone with a squeaky voice.

HARDEKIN. Farley *Herdedun(us)* is in error for *Herdechin(us)* of the MS, from OG **Hardekin* (PNDB 286).

LEOFWOLD. LDB *Leuot*, from OE *Lēofwald* (PNDB 316).

GODWIN WEAKFEET. LDB *uuachefet*, probably an original OE byname **Wācfēt*, 'weak feet'; OEB 339-340.

BLANC. LDB *Blanc(us)*. Cf. Demiblanc 35,8 etc.

LEOFSEXE. LDB *Leffesse* standing for *Lefsesse* from OE *Lēofsexe*, an Anglo-Scandinavian hybrid of OE *Lēof* and OScand *Saxi* (PNDB 352).

FREOND. LDB *Frent*, see von Feilitzen 1945, 80.

SAEWARE. LDB *Saluare*, from OE (feminine) *Sǣwaru* (PNDB 353).

BY AGREEMENT. LDB *consilio*, perhaps meaning here 'by mutual estimation'.

NOT. From OE *hnott*, 'bald-headed', see von Feilitzen 1945, 83.

SHED-BUTTER. LDB *Scadebutre*, an OE nickname from *butere* 'butter' and *sceadan* 'to separate, divide, give off' etc. Cf. ME *Sparebutter* in P. H. Reaney, *The Origin of English Surnames* (1967), 288.

WULFGITH. LDB *Vued*, from OE (feminine) *Wulfgyth*, cf. PNDB 420,280.

CALEBOT. This may be in error for OFr *Talebot* (see Geoffrey Talbot, 47,1 note), but may be a hitherto unrecorded OG name **Galabod, *Calabod* (cf. Förstemann 590-591).

DUBLEL. LDB *DuHel* is very probably an error for *Dublel*, an OFr byname meaning 'the double, the twin' (OEB 375).

GODDAY. LDB *Goddae*; this may be an OE byname from *gōd* + *dǣge* meaning 'good maidservant' or one from *gōd-daeg* 'good day' (someone who gives a cheery greeting), Reaney 150 s.n. *Goodday*. Alternatively an OE masculine personal-name **Gōd-daeg* is also possible.

GOT CHILL. LDB *Got cill'*. Got is from ON *Gautr*, ODan *Gøt*, see von Feilitzen 1976, 160; *cill'* is from OE *cielle* 'chill', as a byname meaning 'the cold one' (cf. OEB 300). There were three Colchester burgesses with the forename *Got*, each distinguished by a byname; the other two were Got Hugh and Got Fleet, below.

ORDGEAT. LDB *Oriet(ur)* probably in error for *Oriet(us)*. See von Feilitzen 1945, 86.

AETHELBALD. LDB *Elebolt*; OE *AEthelbeald, Ethelbald, -bold*, cf. Seltén 25.

AETHELBRICT. LDB *Ailbriest*; OE *AEthelbriht, -beorht* (PNDB 182).

TATE. Either OE *Tat(a)*, masculine, or *Taete*, feminine; Redin 54,114.

BEARD. LDB *Berda*, from the OE personal-name *Bearda* (von Feilitzen 1945, 74 and 1976, 208; cf. Reaney, s.n. *Beard*).

FILIMAN. LDB *Filieman*; OG *Filiman*, a rather rare personal-name (Förstemann 505).

PIC. From *pīc* 'point', Redin 22. Cf. also OEB 326-327, where one possible significance of the corresponding byname given is of 'a man armed with a pick-axe', another being to describe 'a tall, thin person'.

BEST. Probably an OE nickname from either *baest* 'bast, inner bark of a tree' or *bēost* 'beestings'; but possibly an early instance of the ME surname *Best(e)* from OFr *beste* 'beast', see Reaney s.n. *Best* and von Feilitzen 1968, 7.

ROSELL. From OFr *rossel*, 'red-faced, ruddy', see von Feilitzen 1976, 215; Reaney, s.n. *Russel*.

POTE. An OE personal-name and byname **Pota*, related to the verb OE *potian*, ME *pote* 'to push, poke, thrust' and the ME, ModE noun *pote* 'a poker, a plough-staff', see NED.

LUNDI. LDB *Liuidi*, probably from the OScand personal-name and byname *Lundi* (well-attested, e.g. Fellows Jensen 191).

WOODBILL. LDB *Vudebil*, an original byname from OE *wudubill* 'hatchet'; Kökeritz NOB 26, p. 36, von Feilitzen 1945, 92. The etymology suggested PNDB 417 is incorrect.

AESCHERE. An OE personal-name *AEschere*, see von Feilitzen 1945, 72 and 73 n.1.

SUNEGOD. LDB *Sunegot*; OG, see Forssner 226.

LEOFSWITH. LDB *Leffiuf*, OE (feminine) *Lēofswith*.

WIGSTAN. LDB *Westan*; OE *Wīgstān*, PNDB 413.

AINULF. LDB *Ainolf*; OG *Aginulf*, Forssner 15.

TUNRIC. OE *Tūnrīc*, so far recorded only here, von Feilitzen 1945, 90.

PEACOCK. LDB *Pecoc*, von Feilitzen 1945, 86.
6½ ACRES. *.7.dim'.7.vi.ac(ras)*. LDB *.7.dim'* may be in error for *.i. dom'*, '1 house'.
SEAFOWL. LDB *Saeuuele*; OE (Anglo-Scandinavian) *Saefugel*; OEB 162, Reaney s.n. *Saffel* (a ME surname in East Anglia and Essex).
TESCO. LDB *Tescho*; OG *Thieziko, Tizeko*, Förstemann 1417.
HERSTAN. OE *Herestān*, which occurs in D. Whitelock, *Anglo-Saxon Wills* (Cambridge, 1930), 3 (p. 14, 1.4), Sawyer 1539, of ?*c*. 950.
DELA. OE *Dela*, Redin 75, s.n. *Dealla*.
HUNNING. LDB *Hunec*; OE *Hunning*, PNDB 296.
GOT HUGH. LDB *Got hugo*, for the forename, see Got Chill, above. The byname here is a patronym from OG *Hugo* (Forssner 157–158) or OScand *Hughi*. Reaney, s.n. *Hugh*, overlooks this instance.
DEMIBLANC. See 35,8 note and cf. Blanc, above.
RALPH PINEL. See 77.
HORRAP. In its present form this resembles no known personal-name. It may possibly be a misreading of OE *Hofw(e)ard* (PNDB 291); alternatively a compound byname whose final element is OE *rāp* 'rope' might be suggested.
STANBURG. LDB *Stamburc*; OE (feminine) *Stanburg* (from ON *Steinbiǫrg*), PNDB 371, n.4.
GOT FLEET. LDB *Got flet*; for the forename, see Got Chill, above. The byname here probably represents the ON adjective *fljotr*, ME *flete* 'fleet, swift'; cf. OE *flēotig* 'swift', see Reaney, s.n. *Fleet*.
MANSON. LDB *Mansune*; probably OE **Mansuna*, PNDB 325.
LORCE BRET. LDB *Lorchebret*, 'Lorce the Breton'. For the byname, see OEB 133 (*Brito*), 130 (*Bryt*); Reaney, s.n. *Bret*. The forename is probably OBret, cognate with OIr *lorc* 'fierce', rather than OScand *Lurkr* (PNDB 322).

B3b HAMO THE STEWARD. LDB *Amo Hamo*, where the scribe has misspelt the name Hamo and has then written it correctly but has not erased his error.
COURT. Translating *curia*. The meaning is probably that of a group of houses built around a courtyard.
HELD THIS. LDB *tenūit* has an otiose abbreviation-mark above *u*.
A TAX ... HEADS. Translating *de suis capitibus*. Cf. *caput ho(min)is* in B3m. The burgesses paid a tax levied on individuals, rather than on households.
HAS NOT BEEN PAID. LDB *c̄ reddita* is in error for *e(st) reddita*.

B3c The paragraph-mark indicates this to be a separate section, although no value is given.

B3d THE CUSTOMARY DUE. LDB *(con)suedine(m)* is in error for *(con)suetudine(m)*.
ST. PETER'S CHURCH. See B7.

B3e BEFORE 1066. LDB *tēpr̄.e.* is in error for *tēp̄.r.e.*, that is *te(m)p(ore) . r(egis).e(dwardi)*.

B3g COUNT EUSTACE. See 20,8 for a burgess of Colchester belonging to the Count's holding at Rivenhall; 20,36 for a house in Colchester belonging to his manor of Tey; and 20,39 for 2 houses belonging to his manor of Great Birch.
ENGELRIC. He had held the Count's manor of Great Birch (20,39) at a date between 1066 and 1086.

B3h WILLIAM THE BISHOP'S NEPHEW. Identical with William the deacon, see *66* note. VCH 418 suggests that he was the nephew of Bishop William of London, 1051–75, a suggestion supported by ECE, no. 94.
WHICH. *quam* (accusative singular) in error for *quas* (accusative plural), referring to '2 houses'.

B3j OTTO THE GOLDSMITH ... SHALFORD ... AELFEVA. Aelfeva was the wife of Earl Algar who held Shalford before 1066. Otto the Goldsmith (*81*) was in possession of it in 1086, see 1,11. In Cambridgeshire (1,18) he also held part of Litlington at a revenue in 1086 which Earl Algar had held.
THE QUEEN'S LAND. Probably Queen Matilda's, see 1,11–12 note.

B3k ABBOT OF WESTMINSTER; FEERING. See 6,8 where only 2 houses are recorded.

B3l GINNI. LDB *Geni(us)*; ODan *Ginni*, PNDB 261.
ARDLEIGH. For Geoffrey de Mandeville's holding there, see 30,20.

B3m ELMSTEAD. For Swein's holding there, see 24,64.
A TAX ... HEAD. See B3b note.

B3p THURSTAN WISHART. LDB *Turstinus uuiscart*; the byname is a patronym from ONFr *Wischard, Guisc(h)ard, -art*, see Reaney, s.n. *Wishart*. Probably he of 40,2.
THE CUSTOMARY DUE. LDB *consuedo* is in error for *consuetudinem*.

B3q TERLING. For Ranulf's holding there, also previously held by Aelmer, see 34,6. That entry records only 2 houses in Colchester however.

B3r TOLLESHUNT. For Ralph's holding there, see 33,23. The LDB form *collensum te* is corrupt.
THEY USED TO PAY. LDB *reddebant*, in error for *reddebat*, 'it used to pay'. Cf. B3s note.

B3s 3 HOUSES. Recorded under Barking Abbey's manor of Wigborough (9,8).
IT USED TO PAY. LDB *reddebat*, in error for *reddebant*, 'they used to pay'. Cf. B3r note.

B4 SCRUBLAND. Translating *fructecta*.

B6 THIS BELONGS. LDB *hoc p(er)tinent* is in error for *hoc p(er)tinet*. The custom in this sentence is being contrasted to that in the next which is *not* part of the King's revenue: *hoc n(on) e(st) ad firma(m)*.
THIS ... EXPEDITION. The King still had mercenaries to support while not actually on campaign.
FOR THESE 6 PENCE. Translating *propt(er) hos .vi. denarios*, but note that *propt(er)* is probably in error for *pret(er)* 'apart from', cf. following sentences beginning *p(re)ter hoc*.
NOW IT PAYS. If *reddit* is not in error for *reddunt*, then the subject of this clause is the mint.
£80. Expressed as *.iiii.xx. lib(ras)*.
SESTERS OF HONEY. A sester was usually 4, but sometimes 5 to 6, gallons, see R. E. Zupko, *A dictionary of English weights and measures from Anglo-Saxon times to the nineteenth century* (Univ. of Wisconsin Press, 1968), 155.
PREBENDARIES. A similar charge was put on the Boroughs of Norwich and Thetford (Norfolk 1,61;70).
WALERAN ... THIS. Waleran was the father of John (*40*) and is mentioned in 17,1 as having taken 1 house in Colchester away from St. Ouen's Abbey's land at West Mersea. He had apparently administered Colchester for the King at some time between 1066 and 1086 and may perhaps have done the same with Norwich (Norfolk, 1,63).
AS PROTECTOR. LDB *adturtore(m)* is in error for *ad tutore(m)*.
BISHOP WALKELIN. Of Winchester, 1070–98.

B7 ST. PETER'S CHURCH. See also B3d. LDB *eccl(esi)e* is in error for *eccl(esi)a*.
KING'S ALMS. Farley *elemasina* corrects the MS reading *clemasina*.
RALPH OF HASTINGS. LDB *hatingis* is in error for *hastingis*, cf. *hastinges*, folio 83b, (39,8). Ralph held 30 acres at Ardleigh, adjoining Colchester.
THE FOURTH. LDB has an otiose abbreviation-mark on *quarta(m)*, Farley places it above the *u*, the MS has it above the first *a*.

EKt Cf. note on 'Gravesend' at 20,5.

ESf 1 HARKSTEAD. See also 1,26.

The Hundreds and Half-Hundreds

Most of the twenty-one DB Hundreds and Half-Hundreds survived without much change into the 19th century. Some are termed alternately 'Hundred' or 'Half-Hundred' in DB and later medieval records and there appears to have been little actual difference in status between the two terms in the post-Conquest period – a small Hundred might occasionally be called a Half-Hundred, that was all. The tiny 'Thunderlow' Half-Hundred, in the north of the county, was later subsumed into Hinckford Hundred. 'Wibertsherne' Hundred was known as Dengie Hundred from the late 12th century onwards. The Royal Liberty of Havering-atte-Bower was created in 1465 out of the eastern part of Becontree Hundred.

Maldon appears from DB to have been in 1086 partly in its own (urban) Half-Hundred and partly in 'Wibertsherne' Hundred. Epping appears to have been partly in the Half-Hundred of Harlow and partly in that of Waltham.

There are a few changes in the Hundredal ascription of places between DB and later records. Gt. Coggeshall was placed in the DB Hundred of Witham, but was later in Lexden Hundred. Henham was placed in Freshwell Hundred but was later in that of Uttlesford. Horseham Hall was put in Hinckford Hundred but was later in Freshwell Hundred. Wheatley was put in Barstable Hundred but was later in that of Rochford.

The Hundredal units usually occur within chapters in more or less the order given in VCH, 409. This (excluding 'Thunderlow' Half-Hundred, which occurs only twice) is as follows: Barstable, Witham, Harlow, Waltham, Becontree, Dunmow, 'Wibertsherne', Winstree, Uttlesford, Clavering, Hinckford, 'Wibertsherne' (again), Lexden, Ongar, Chafford, Chelmsford, Maldon, Tendring, Uttlesford (again), Freshwell, Rochford, and Thurstable. This order does not represent any one geographical progression as it crosses and re-crosses the county several times.

The County Boundary

The county has its origin in the Kingdom of the East Saxons. Its inland boundary is mainly marked by major rivers – the Stour in the north, the Thames in the south and the Lea and the Stort in the west. There is however a small area in the north-west, adjacent to Hertfordshire and Cambridgeshire, which does not follow a watercourse and may have been fixed relatively late in the Anglo-Saxon period. Both along the Stour and the Thames there is evidence of some cross-river tenurial association with estates in Suffolk (Bures St. Mary and Nayland) and Kent (Chalk and Gravesend) before 1086.

The parish of Ballingdon cum Brundon was transferred to the Borough of Sudbury, Suffolk in 1832 and 1835 (EPNS 407, n.). Gt. and Lt. Chishill and Heydon were transferred to Cambridgeshire in 1895 (EPNS 520,529).

APPENDIX

THE ELY INQUIRY
Inquisitio Eliensis (IE)

The Ely Inquiry, usually referred to as IE, is a collection of material relating to holdings of Ely Abbey in Cambridgeshire, Essex, Hertfordshire, Huntingdonshire, Norfolk and Suffolk whose source appears to have been drafts (now lost) of the returns for three different circuits of the DB Survey. It was put together, for the benefit of Ely Abbey, very soon after 1086, but survives only in three manuscripts written in the second half of the 12th century – British Library, Cotton Tiberius A.vi, folios 38–70 (MS A); Trinity College Cambridge 0.2.41, pages 161–274 (MS B) and 0.2.1, folios 177v–213 (MS C) – of these, B and C are derived from a common source, while A is a copy of B. Although B is now thought to be the most reliable of the three manuscripts, IE was reproduced in record type in 1816 by Sir Henry Ellis from A (see DB4, 495–528). N. E. S. A. Hamilton also used A as the base text for his edition of IE in 1876 (*Inquisitio Comitatus Cantabrigiensis*, 97–168), but also gave variant readings from B and C in footnotes.[1]

For Essex, IE (Hamilton 125–130; and summaries at 122) supplies details of the Ely Abbey lordship holdings in the county (cf. above, Chapter *10*) and of other pieces of land claimed by the Abbey. The information given in IE is identical in type to that in DB Essex, differing only in a few small details. Hamilton also edited some other documents, subsidiary to IE, which are dependent upon, or relevant to, the DB Survey. The *Inquisitio Eliensis* Breviate (IEBrev; Hamilton 168–173) gives summaries of the numbers of ploughs and people in each of the Abbey's holdings, and the *Nomina Villarum* (IENV; Hamilton 174–175) lists the number of ploughs held by the villagers therein. These are followed by lists of holdings alienated from the Abbey's possession (IEAL; Hamilton 175–189) and an account of an inquiry into the Abbey's losses held between 1071 and 1075 (Hamilton 192–195). In the present volume, quotations from IE and its related documents have only been given where information occurs which is different or extra to that in LDB.

For further comments on IE, see R. Welldon Finn, 'The Inquisitio Eliensis reconsidered', *English Historical Review* lxxv (1960), 385–409. For the Ely Abbey claims, see E. Miller, 'The Ely land pleas in the reign of William I', *English Historical Review* lxii (1947), 438–456 and *Liber Eliensis*, ed. E. O. Blake, 426–432. See also the Introduction to the Cambridgeshire volume for a sample of text from IE.

1. Note that in the Cambridgeshire volume, Introduction, The Ely Inquiry, it is wrongly stated that Ellis and Hamilton edited IE from MS C and that Hamilton collated it to MSS A and B. The true situation is as stated in the present Appendix.

INDEX OF PERSONS

Familiar modern spellings are given where they exist. Unfamiliar names are usually given in an approximate late 11th century form, avoiding variants that were already obsolescent or pedantic. Spellings that mislead the modern eye are avoided where possible. Two, however, cannot be avoided; they are combined in the name 'Leofgeat', pronounced 'Leffyet', or 'Levyet'. The definite article is used before bynames where there is a probability that they described the individual, rather than one of his ancestors. While an attempt has been made to differentiate individuals with the same name, there remain several individuals who cannot be so differentiated. Readers are therefore advised that a group of references given under a single name (e.g. Aelmer) do not necessarily refer to the same individual; where the same name occurs more than once in a single entry (e.g. in B3a) and could refer to different individuals, the number of occurrences of the name is shown in brackets after the entry reference. *The chapter-numbers of listed landholders are printed in italics, as are the names of persons referred to in the text, but not named there, who have been identified in footnotes.*

A.	34,15
Adam son of Durand Malzor	*63*
Adam	EKt
Adelulf of Marck	20,15;27
Adelulf (of Marck)	20,13;22;24;29;54;57-58;68-69;79
Countess Aelfeva	B3j
Aelfeva	90,20. B3a(×2)
Aelfled	B3a(×2);f
Young Aelfric	32,6
Aelfric Big	20,41
Aelfric Kemp	32,38. 33,16. 39,5;7
Aelfric of Alderford	90,49
Aelfric the priest	24,3;5. B3a
Aelfric Wand	25,24;26
Aelfric	1,15. 4,1;3;11;14. 18,32. 20,6;37;44;69. 22,24. 28,3. 32,2;25. 33,8;17. 35,13-14. 36,8. 41,1. 54,2. 57,6. 60,2. 68,7. B3a(×11). EHu
Aelfric's father	20,44
Aelfthryth	3,1
Aelmer Holdfast	61,2
Aelmer Milk	B3r
Aelmer (Milk)	33,23
Aelmer of Borley	90,49
Aelmer, reeve of Richard son of Count Gilbert	90,78
Aelmer	12,1. 20,59;74. 24,36. 33,22. 34,4;6;14. 35,3. 48,1-2. B3q
Aeschere	B3a
Aethelbald	B3a
Aethelbrict	B3a
Aethelgyth	20,46. 33,6-7;19-20
Aethelhelm	35,7;12
Aethelstan	18,43
Agnes	47,2
Ainulf	B3a
Aki	24,45. 53,1
Count Alan	*21*. 1,13
Countess of Aumâle	*54*
Albert	11,7
Alchere	27,11
Aldred	25,23
Alfeva	37,5
Alfgar the priest	B3a
Alfgar	B3a
Alfheah the priest	B3a

Alfheah	37,17
Alfhelm	39,9
Alfith	24,35
Alfred, reeve of Richard son of Count Gilbert	90,74
Alfred	24,26;54. 37,5. 90,69.
Alfsi Bowl	37,4
Alfsi	18,30. 20,78. 27,3. 34,3. B3a(×3)
Alfstan	B3a(×2)
Alfward, ?Algar's brother	34,22
Alfward Dore	62,1
Alfward	4,5. 18,23;28. 32,28. 33,12. 68,3;5; 90,69. B3a(×3)
Alfwold	B3a(×2)
Alfwy Hunter	90,70
Earl Algar, 'Edgar'	1,9;11-13. 15,1-2. 22,9. 41,2. 72,2. 81,1. 82,1. 90,65
Algar, ?Alfward's brother	34,22
Algar	18,25. 23,33;37. 30,20. 32,12. 34,17. 37,17. 43,6. 56,1. 90,62
Algot, see Edmund	
Alnoth	B3a
Alric, Bondi's brother	30,20
Alric	6,9. 20,21;58. 24,2. 33,17. 39,10. 57,1. 80,1. B3a(×3)
Alstan Stric	6,4
Alstan	28,3. 30,12. 32,5;8;39. 34,1;8;29. 40,7. 41,6. 90,33;56. B3a(×2)
Alwen	24,4. B3a(×2)
Alwin Gotton	22,4
Alwin (Stickhare)	76,1
Alwin Still	33,18
Alwin	1,6. 4,15;18. 10,5. 18,33. 20,45;50. 21,9. 23,32. 24,1;13. 27,8. 35,14. 37,18. 39,1. 62,4. B3a(×8)
Amalfrid	20,62. 33,10;18
Anand the Dane	18,39
Anselm	20,73
Ansger Cook	*75*
Ansgot	24,56. 59,1
Ansketel	3,2. 4,6. 18,29. 22,17. 32,2;13;32. 39,4. 48,2. 90,55
Arnold	23,3;8-9. 90,50-51
Arnulf	34,4
Arthur	25,17. B3a
Ascelin	24,30-32. 32,5. 34,23
Asgar (the Constable)	30,2;5;16;22-25;27;31-33;35-36;38-40;42-43; 45;48-49;51. 90,28
Askell	53,2
Aubrey de Vere	*35*. 21,3;8. 90,36;B3t. EHu
Aubrey de Vere's wife	90,38
Aubrey (de Vere)'s wife	18,21;24
Azo	32,36
Azorin	44,3
Baynard, see Geoffrey, Ralph	
Beard	B3a
Berengar	33,14. 90,87
Bernard	20,18;28;33;70. 28,9. 33,9;17;23. 90,54
Best	B3a
Big, see Aelfric	
Bigot, see Roger	
Blackstan	B3a(×3)
Blanc	B3a

Blunt, see Robert
Bold, see William
Bondi, Alric's brother 30,20
Bondi 29,3-5. 39,8
Borda 32,34-35
Boso 90,22
Bowl, see Alfsi
Brian, see Ralph, William
Bricteva 1,19. 24,9
Brictmer 20,1;14;47;49. 32,4. 34,5;7;27. 77,1. 90,52
Brictric 90,50;58. B3a(×2)
Brictsi 24,65
Brictwin 20,43. B3a
Brictwulf 20,75-76. 90,63
Brown 24,66. 34,24
Bruman B3a
Brungar B3a
Brunloc B3a
Brunwin B3a(×2)
Budd 20,3
Burghard 32,3
Calebot B3a
King Canute 3,9
Cardon, see William
Cave, see Wulfric
Chill, see Got
Clarenbold 24,44
Cola 20,7. 27,16. 33,22. 62,2
Colman 23,30. 90,53. B3a
Colsege 23,28
Constantine, see William
Corbucion, see Robert
Corbun, see W.
Corp 32,33
Crist, see Leofwin
Croc, see Leofwin
Culling B3a
David 20,48
Dela B3a
Demiblanc 35,8;13. B3a
Derman B3a
Derwulf 90,60
Doding 29,1. 42,3
Dore, see Alfward
Dot 24,11. 32,32
Dove 22,5. 90,57
Drogo 48,1
Dublel B3a
Dudeman, see Godwin
Durand Malzor, see Adam
Eadlac, see Wulfstan
Edeva (the Fair) 1,30. 4,16. 21,2-5;11-12
Edeva, wife of Edward son of Swein 85,1
Edeva 5,1. 20,17;54. 22,1
Earl 'Edgar', see Earl Algar
Queen Edith 20,8. 27,15. 42,7-9
Edmer 20,15. 24,48. 51,1
Edmund son of Algot *61*
Ednoth 20,28;70. 33,15. 41,10
Edric of Easthorpe 37,20
Edric (of Easthorpe) 20,40
Edric 18,18;35. 20,38-39. 24,14. 25,21. 26,5. 39,2. B3a(×4)

Edsi 21,8. 30,15
Edward son of Swein *85*
Edward son of Swein, see Edeva
Edward the priest B3a
Edward 18,27. 20,63;65. 30,7-8. 35,11
Edwin Groat 32,31. 68,1
Edwin, a free priest 32,9
Edwin the priest B3a
Edwin 30,13. B3a(×6)
Edwold, King Edward's reeve 18,11
Edwold 4,2;4
Edwy 90,83
Elinant 23,5
Engelric 1,19;24;27. 6,1. 17,2. 20,1;4-5;16-17;19;22; 25-27;32;34-35;38-39;41;43-45;49;51-56; 62-63;66-71;73-80. 28,9. 90,64. B3g
Enisant 35,6
Erling 30,14
Ernucion, see John
Ernulf 20,13
Esbern 47,3
Count of Eu *31*
Eudo the Steward *25*. 1,25;27. 10,1. 28,8. 30,41. B3d;7
Eudo (the Steward) 10,3
Count Eustace *20*. 1,3;24;27. 3,2. 12,1. 17,2. 28,9. B1;3g
Count Eustace's cleric 1,28
Evrard 30,51
Fair, see Edeva
Fellow 67,2. 90,65-66
Filiman B3a
Finn the Dane 23,38;43
Finn (the Dane) 84,2
Finn (the Dane), see Wulfeva
Fleet, see Got
Freond B3a
Frewin 20,64
Fridebern 30,44;50
Fridebert 1,22. 18,36. 30,4
Frodo, the Abbot (of Ely)'s brother *56*. 90,85
G. 90,57
Garnet, see Richard
Geoffrey Baynard 68,2
Geoffrey de Mandeville *30*. 1,3. 5,2. 8,9. 10,5. 20,71. 25,16. 34,7. 52,1. 77,1. 90,20-28. B31. ESf2
Geoffrey Martel 30,3
(Geoffrey) Martel 30,24;31-32;35;43
Geoffrey Talbot 47,1
Geoffrey 20,14. 24,20. 33,2;22. 47,3
Gerald 24,24. 39,4-5
Gerald, see Raymond
Gerard 33,1. 41,1;10-11
Germund 23,15. 30,48. 33,13;15. 90,53
Gernon, see Robert
Count Gilbert, see Richard
Gilbert son of Solomon *73*. 15,1
Gilbert son of Thorold *58*
Gilbert son of Warin 1,13
Gilbert the priest *82*
Gilbert 3,2. 18,34. 48,2
Gilbert, see Walter Cook
Ginni B31'
Gladiou 22,13

Gobert, see Robert
Goda B3a(×6),m
Godbold 24,19;45;57
Godday B3a
Godfrey 24,40. 30,51. 41,9
Godhere 4,17. 66,2
Goding 23,36. 28,4. 90,73. B3a(×3)
Godith 5,6. 24,8. 30,26. B3a
Godiva 90,55. B3a(×2)
Godman 24,54. 75,1. 83,2
Godmund 20,62
Godric of Colchester 20,42
Godric (of Colchester) B1-2
Godric Poinc 22,18
Godric Skipper 22,16
Godric the Steward 1,30
Godric 4,12. 14,1. 18,9;41. 20,73. 24,12;16;25;29;43; 46;59-61. 32,33. 33,5. 34,14. 63,2. 71,2. B3a(×6),e
God-save-ladies, see Roger
Godson B3a(×3)
Godwin Sech 90,28
Godwin son of Dudeman EKt
Godwin the deacon *88*. 30,11
Godwin the priest 68,8
Godwin the uncle of Ralph ENf
Godwin Weakfeet B3a
Godwin Weakfeet's son B3a
Godwin Woodhen 9,5. 90,1-3
Godwin (Woodhen) 60,1
Godwin 4,8;10. 20,23. 24,10. 25,2;5;22. 32,24;36. 35,5. 37,7. 39,3. 44,1-2;4. 76,1. 90,35;54. B3a(×10)
Goismer 23,7. 90,49
Goldenbollocks, see Humphrey
Goldhere B3a(×2)
Golding B3a
Goldman B3a
Goldric B3a
Goldstan 1,8. 90,49. B3a
Goldwin B3a(×2)
Got Chill B3a
Got Fleet B3a
Got Hugh B3a
Goti 13,1. 28,1;9;11
Gotild 28,13-14;16
Gotre 32,14;45
Grapinel 24,22
Grim the reeve *83*. 1,18
Grim 25,17. 35,5. 40,3. 90,51;55
Grimbald 71,4
Grimkel 32,42-43
Grimwulf B3a
Groat, see Edwin
Gross, see William
Gundwin *80*
Gunner 24,63;67
Gutbert 30,27
Guthmund 20,62. 27,2;4-5;11;13-14
another Guthmund 28,5
Guthred 38,3
Guy 20,30-31;72-73

Gyrth	3,11
Hagebern/Hagebert	*70*. 1,27
Hager	27,17
Hakon	33,1. 36,11. B3a
Haldane	36,6
Hamo the Steward	*28*. 1,2. 66,1. 90,31. B3b
Hamo (the Steward)	1,3. 89,3
Hamo (the Steward)'s son	20,6
Hapra, see Wulfwin	
Hardekin	B3a
Hardwin of Scales	1,9
Hardwin	49,1
Earl Harold	B3k
(Earl) Harold	1,1-4;19-21;23-24;26-29. 6,8;11;15. 7,1. 19,1. 20,5-6;9;11;51;66. 28,1;6;8. 30,16;34. 31,1. 34,28. 40,1. 41,3. 49,3. 68,2. 90,35. ESf1
(Earl) Harold's priest	1,24
(Earl) Harold's reeve	1,24
Hato	20,65
Haunted, see Ralph	
Henry of Ferrers	*29*. 90,81
Henry of Ferrers's steward	29,5
Henry's wife	39,10
Herbert's nephew, see Hugh	
Herstan	B3a
Hervey of 'Spain'	21,9-11
Hervey (of 'Spain')	21,2;4;12
Hold	90,60
Holdfast	22,3
Holdfast, see Aelmer	
Horrap	B3a
Horwulf	1,10. 14,2
Howard	5,7
Hubert of Port	32,29. 83,2
Hubert	30,5. 44,1-2
Hugh de Montfort	*27*. 1,4;17;27. 24,24. 34,36. 90,15-18. B3e
Hugh nephew of Herbert	18,25
Hugh of Bernières	30,28-30. 90,29
Hugh of Gournai	*47*
Hugh of Houdain	43,6
Hugh of St. Quentin	*60*. 90,1
Hugh of Verly	30,50
Hugh son of Mauger	27,16-17
Hugh	3,16. 4,1;17. 10,5. 18,28;30-33;35. 20,39-40. 24,37. 30,26;44. 32,3;6;18. 40,5
Hugh, see Got	
Hugolin	4,11;14
Humphrey Goldenbollocks	90,30
Humphrey	3,11. 4,4. 27,5;18. 34,5;36. 37,2
Hunald	71,1;4
Hunning	B3a
Ilbod	*69*. 1,2. 90,77
Ilger	32,9;23-24;31
Ilger, see Ranulf	
Ingulf	27,12. 32,41
Ingvar	18,2. 20,71. 37,3;10;12;14;16
Iwain	20,12;50
Jocelyn Lorimer	*64*. 1,2. 9,7
John nephew of Waleran	*65*
John son of Ernucion	40,1
John son of Waleran	*40*. 1,4. B1;3p
John (son of Waleran)	90,46

John	24,24;34
John, see Waleran	
Countess Judith	*55*
Kemp, see Aelfric	
Kenting	B3a
Ketel	34,34
Lambert	20,52-53;55-56. 30,33
Lascivious, see Robert	
Lawman	68,6
Ledmer of Hempstead, the reeve	90,48;76
Ledmer the priest	20,77. 23,4
Ledmer the reeve, see Ledmer of Hempstead	
Ledmer	20,25-26. B3a(×2)
Leofcild	23,36. 24,15. 36,10. 57,2. 90,59
Leofday	30,2
Leofeva	18,24. 23,29. 28,15. 33,4. B3a(×4)
Leofgeat	B3a
Leofhard	1,14
Leofhild	30,3
Leofing	27,10. 41,5
Leofith	30,43
Leofled	B3a(×3)
Leofmer	90,61
Leofred	32,9. B3a
Leofric	18,19. 23,34. 30,12. 40,6;8. B3a(×3)
Leofric, see William	
Leofsexe	B3a
Leofsi	20,48;76. 25,2. 38,3
Leofson	10,3. 25,20. 30,12;18-19. B3a(×3)
Leofstan the reeve	52,2
Leofstan	20,53;55;68. 24,6-7;9;42;44. 32,13;44. 52,3. B3a(×3)
Leofswith	B3a
Young Leofwin	38,4. 42,4
(Young) Leofwin	42,2;6
Leofwin Crist	B3a
Leofwin Croc	46,2
Leofwin	1,7. 20,43;45;52. 21,8. 24,62. 26,3. 27,17. 30,12. 33,13. 34,37. 46,3. 54,1. 76,1. 90,61; 86. B3a(×12)
Leofwold	B3a
Lisois (of Moutiers)	25,2 note;5
Lorce Bret	B3a
Lundi	B3a
Lutting	90,68
Malet, see Robert	
Malzor, see Adam	
Manning	18,29
Manson	B3a,c
Manstan	B3a(×2)
Manwin	B3a(×9)
Martel	30,24;31-32;35;43
Martel, see Geoffrey	
Mascerel	23,14. 90,58
Queen Matilda	1,11-12;23. 60,3. 82,1. B3h
Matthew of Mortagne	*53*
Mauger	6,8. 18,26-27. 20,51. 41,12
Mauger, see Hugh	
Maynard	24,12
Merwen	65,1
Milk, see Aelmer	
Modbert	33,8

Moding 25,8;10
Modwin *68*. 70,2
Nigel 27,13. 32,25;27;39. 41,2;9
Norman 1,19. 20,30;79. 25,7. 33,14
Not B3a
Odard 24,65
Odin the Dane 18,37
Odo 9,14. 24,19;25;50-51;66. 30,45. 37,8;10
Odo, see William
Ordgar 13,2. 32,7. 56,1. 57,5. 90,85
Ordgeat B3a
Ordlaf B3a
Ordmer 39,4
Ordric 35,14
Osbern 18,7. 21,1. 24,3-4. 27,1. 32,8
Osbert 24,58. 30,17. 47,2
Osgeat B3a
Osgot B3a
Oslac 18,45. 37,1. 38,2
Osmund of Anjou 1,3
Osmund 40,3
Osward 18,14
Otto the Goldsmith *81*. 1,11-12. B3j
Owin B3a
Payne 24,5;33
Peacock B3a
Peche, see William
Perverted, see Robert
Peter of Valognes, the Sheriff (of Essex) *36*. 1,2;4. 5,2. 49,3. ESf1
Peter (of Valognes, the Sheriff of Essex) 1,19;25-27
Peter 32,17;44
Peverel, see Ranulf, William
Pic B3a
Picot the Sheriff (of Cambridge) 1,9
Picot (the Sheriff of Cambridge)/Pirot 1,13. 25,11. 32,35;43
Pinel, see Ralph
Pinson 35,5
Pirot, see Picot
Poinc, see Godric
Pointel, see Theodoric
Pote B3a
Rainalm 30,19;39
Rainer 20,32
Earl Ralph (Wader) 1,30. 21,9
Ralph Baynard *33*. 1,2;27. 2,9. 5,10. 6,7. 20,46. 34,36. 90,39. B3r
(Ralph) Baynard 1,2;17a. 28,9
Ralph Latimer 90,42
Ralph of Hastings 39,8
Ralph of Hastings, see Robert
Ralph of Limésy *49*. 1,3
Ralph of Marcy 1,3. 20,6;20;66
Ralph (of Marcy) 28,6
Ralph of Tosny *51*
Ralph Pinel *77*. B3a
Ralph son of Brian 3,5. 4,15;18. 34,26;30. 90,12
Ralph son of Thorold (of Rochester) 1,27. 18,20;36
Ralph (son of Thorold of Rochester) 18,38-43
(Ralph) son of Thorold (of Rochester) 18,1;4-5;8;10-11;34
Ralph the Haunted 36,8;12
Ralph 3,1. 4,7;13. 20,45. 24,3;42;55-56. 25,14. 28,2-4;13-15. 30,12. 32,29. 35,2-4. 36,4;7. 39,12. 45,1. 90,56

Ralph, see Godwin
Ranulf brother of Ilger *37*. 1,1;27. 7,1
Ranulf Peverel *34*. 1,2;17;25. 9,14. 10,3. 20,56. 32,8. 90,10-14. B3q. EKt
Ranulf the Sheriff of Surrey 1,23
Ranulf 22,2;14;16;23. 41,6;8
Ravengar 9,2. 18,6-7;15. 30,21
Ravenot 34,10;28
Raymond Gerald 1,19. 32,24
Red, see Thurstan
Reginald the Gunner *79*
Reginald 30,2;45. 35,14
Restald 39,12
Richard Garnet 30,11
Richard of Sackville 20,8
Richard (of Sackville) 25,1
Richard son of Count Gilbert *23*. 1,11;13;27. 25,12 note. 30,23. 90,49-78
Richard son of Count Gilbert, see Aelmer, Alfred
Richard 20,11;47;49. 22,3-4;11;13;18-21. 25,6-10;12;16;20-21;23-24. 27,16. 28,12;17-18. 30,10;15;37-38;49. 32,4;12. 34,4;6;37. 37,3;7;15. 89,3. 90,21;48
Bishop Robert of Hereford 1,24
Robert Blunt 35,5. 90,83. ENf
Robert d'Oilly 30,30
Robert father of Swein, see Robert son of Wymarc
Robert Gernon *32*. 1,3;24;28. 3,10. 6,12. 8,9. 9,5. 34,8. 49,3
Robert Malet *44*. 90,84
Robert of Montbegon 89,2
Roger of Sommery 20,74
Robert of Tosny *50*
Robert of Vatteville 23,41
Robert of Vaux 43,4-5
Robert of Verly 32,14-15;37;45. ENf
Robert (of Verly) 32,26
Robert son of Corbucion *41*. 1,4
Robert son of Gobert *78*
Robert son of Ralph of Hastings B7
Robert son of Rozelin *76*
Robert son of Wymarc, the Sheriff (of Essex), father of Swein (the Sheriff of Essex), Robert Wymarc 18,6. 24,4;23;25;29;31;35;43;49;53;55;64. 83,1. 90,35. B3n
Robert (son of Wymarc, as above) 24,1;36-39;54;57;59-60;63;65-66
Robert son of Wymarc, as above 24,20
Robert the Lascivious, the Perverted 6,12. 32,28
Robert 20,35;41-42;67. 23,6. 24,29;41;56;60. 27,14. 32,20;28;41-42. 34,29. 71,4. 90,8
Roger Bigot *43*
Roger God-save-ladies *72*. 15,1
Roger Marshal *62*. 30,16
Roger of Auberville *26*. 90,86
Roger of Poitou *46*. 1,19. 32,24. 47,3. B3f
Roger of Raismes *39*. 1,27. 6,8. 43,1
Roger 1,19;27. 3,4;6-8;10. 4,5. 20,3;75. 23,31-32. 24,38. 27,15. 30,6. 33,16-17. 36,3. 37,4;6;20. 39,2. 40,4;6-8. 51,1-2. 90,10;46. B3a
Rosell B3a
Rozelin, see Robert
Saegar 18,40. B3a
Saegrim B3a(×2)
Saemer 25,3
(Saemer) 30,41

Saeward B3a
Saeware B3a
Saewin the priest 30,15
Saewulf 30,9. B3a
Sasselin *57*
Saswalo 34,7
Saxi 45,1. 51,2. 58,1
Scalpi 30,16. 32,40
Scalpi's wife 30,16
Saefowl B3a
Sech, see Godwin
Selva 32,34
Serlo 28,1;7-8;10;13. 34,1-4;13. 38,1
Shed-butter B3a
Sigar 4,9
Simond 22,10
Sired 20,72
Siric 18,22. 24,1;59;64. 37,2. B3a
Siward (of Maldon) 34,9-12;18-20;23;26;30-31;33;36
Siward the priest B3a
Siward 9,14. 10,3. 20,20. 21,10. 29,2. 32,30. B3a
Skipper, see Godric
Solomon, see Gilbert
Sprot 32,29. B3a(×4)
Stan B3a
Stanburg B3a
Stanhard *87*. 11,7. B3a(×2)
Starker 41,9;12
Stickhare, see Alwin
Still, see Alwin
Stoting B3a
Stric, see Alstan
Suadus 35,6
Sunegod B3a
Swart, see Swein
Swarting B3a
Swartling B3a
Sweeting 22,2
Swein the Sheriff, of Essex *24*. 1,2-3;27-28. 10,5
Swein (the Sheriff, of Essex) 1,13;25. 9,14. 18,14;18;23. 30,21. 90,35. B3m,n
Swein (the Sheriff, of Essex), see Robert son of Wymarc
Swein Swart 36,5. 52,1
Swein 40,9. 74,1. B3a
Swein, see Edward, Robert
Talbot, see Geoffrey
Tascelin the priest 1,10. 3,11
Tate B3a
Teher 18,9
Tesco B3a
Tesselin 71,3
Theobald 90,38
Theodoric brother of Walter the deacon 42,1
Theodoric Pointel *71*. 1,2;6;14;16;27. 33,21. 90,4-9
(Theodoric) Pointel 18,7;19. 34,4-5
Thorbern 20,57. 28,2;5;12. 90,80. B3b
Thorbert 28,17-18
Thorgils 25,2-3. 36,2
Thorgot 11,3
Thorkell the reeve *86*

Thorkell 14,3-7. 18,38. 24,9;58. 26,2. 30,5. 66,1. B3a,h
Thorold of Rochester 9,1. 18,36;43-44
Thorold (of Rochester) 20,1
Thorold (of Rochester), see Ralph
Thorold 4,7. 18,37. 24,6-7. 30,4. 34,7;15;21-22;33-34. 90,13;44-45
Thorold, see Gilbert
Thurstan the Red 5,8
Thurstan Wishart B3p
Thurstan (Wishart) 40,2
Thurstan 37,6. B3a
Tidbald 3,2
Tihel of Helléan, the Breton *38*. 18,21a
Tirel, see Walter
Toli 30,17
Topi 32,34
Tosti 6,7. 40,5
Toti 23,1
Tovi 70,1. B3a
Tovild 90,72
Tunric B3a
Ulf 20,12
Vitalis 23,3. 28,9. 34,18;20
W. 24,8;21. 30,16. 37,1;14;19. 41,5;7
W. Corbun 32,11
Wader, see Earl Ralph
Bishop Walchere of Durham 7,1
Walchere 33,3;11
Waleran father of John 40,9
Waleran (father of John) 90,46-47
Waleran 1,27. 17,1. B6
Waleran, see John nephew of, John son of
Bishop Walkelin (of Winchester) B6
Walter Cook, son of Gilbert *67*. 1,11
Walter (of Caen) 44,4
Walter of Douai *52*
Walter son of Gilbert, see Walter Cook
Walter the deacon *42*. 1,27
Walter the deacon, see Theodoric
Walter Tirel 23,38
Walter 4,8. 22,8. 24,2;14;28;46. 30,5;7-9;22-23. 32,38a. 36,11. 37,13. 90,66. B3a
Earl Waltheof 55,1
Wand, see Aelfric
Warengar 39,3. 43,1-2
Warin 34,9. 35,5
Warin, see Gilbert
Warner 20,2. 23,2. 24,21;43;47. 90,77
Weakfeet, see Godwin
Wiberga 39,1
Wicard 24,27;56
Wicga B3a
Widelard 23,10;42. 90,52;75
Wigstan B3a
Bishop William (of London) 3,2;7-9;11-13. See also B3h note
William Bold 4,3
William Cardon 10,5. 20,71. 30,46. 90,34
William (de Alno) 32,40
William Leofric *59*. 90,82
William of Bosc 37,17
William of Boursigny 9,13
William of Écouis *45*

William of Vatteville 22,7. B3n
William of Warenne *22*. 7,1. 9,10. 10,2. 40,3
William Peche 23,4. 35,6. B3a
William Peverel *48*. 18,32;34
William son of Brian 4,2
William son of Constantine *74*
William son of Gross 1,2. 11,1. 27,2. 88,2. 90,15;18
William son of Odo 24,11
William the Bishop's nephew, see William the deacon
William the Chamberlain 6,10
William the deacon, the Bishop's nephew *66*. B3h
William 3,1-3. 4,9-10;12. 9,4. 10,5. 30,14;20;36;40-41. 32,34. 36,7. 37,18
Wimund 28,16
Winemer B3a
Winge 60,1
Wishart, see Thurstan
Withgar 21,1. 23,2-3;6-15;30-32;34-35;37;39-42. 90,63-64
Withi 28,8
Woodbill B3a
Woodhen, see Godwin
Wulfa 26,4
Wulfbert 22,9;12;14-15
Wulfeva wife of Finn (the Dane) *84*
Wulfeva B3a(×2)
Wulfgith B3a
Wulfheah 30,46. B3a
Wulfmer 4,13. 18,42. 20,26. 22,19-20. 23,35. 25,4;11. 27,5;12-13;15;18-19;25. 46,1. 90,28
Wulfric Cave 25,6. 30,28
Wulfric of Brundon 90,49
Wulfric the priest 34,28
Wulfric 20,2;31;60. 22,3. 30,1;30;34. 33,3. 36,7. 90,5; 20;71;77. B3a(×13)
Wulfsi 5,7. 27,18. 40,9. 41,7. 72,1-3. B3a(×2)
Wulfstan Eadlac B3a
Wulfstan 24,62. B3a(×4)
Wulfward the priest 34,37. B3a
Wulfward 60,3. B3a(×4),t
Wulfwin Hapra 62,3
Wulfwin the summoner B3a
Wulfwin 4,6-7. 18,26;31. 22,14. 23,34. 30,6;12;29. 32,23;26;42. 34,21. 35,1-2;4-6;8-12. 36,9;11. 57,1. 90,3;47. B3a(×12)
Wulfwin's two sisters 23,34
Wulfwy 34,32
Wymarc, see Robert

CHURCHES AND CLERGY

Barking (St. Mary's)	*9*. 30,3
Abbess	9,14. B3s
Battle (St. Martin's)	*13*
Bayeux, Bishop	*18*. 1,27. 4,9-10. 9,1. 20,1. 36,9. 48,2
[**Bury**] **St. Edmund's**	*11*
Abbot	11,1;7. B3a
Caen (Holy Trinity)	*15*
(St. Stephen's)	*16*
Canterbury (Holy Trinity)	*2*. 90,9
monks	90,79
Colchester (St. Peter's)	B3d;7
Durham, Bishop	*7*. See also Walchere
Ely (St. Etheldreda's)	*10*. 18,36. 22,8. 25,12;20. 34,30. EHu
Abbot	10,3;5. 18,36. 22,7. 25,3. 30,27;41. 34,19. EHu. See also Frodo
monks	1,2. 27,14. 79,1
Hereford, Bishop	*19*. See also Robert
London, Bishop	*3-4*. 20,4. 48,2. See also William
(St. Martin's)	*12*. 6,1. 20,34;60
(St. Paul's)	3,5;11. 20,67. 33,22. 57,5
canons	*5*
Rochester, Bishop	EKt
[**Rouen**] (St. Ouen's)	*17*
St. Mary's, ?	1,1 note. 6,1
St. Valéry	*14*
Waltham (Holy Cross)	7,1
canons	*8*
Westminster (St. Peter's)	*6*. 90,17;19
Abbot	6,7;10. B3k
Winchester, Bishop	See Walkelin
deacons	Godwin, Walter, William
free priest	Edwin
priests	Aelfric, Aelfgar, Aelfheah, Edward, Edwin, Gilbert, Godwin, Ledmer, Leofstan, Saewin, Siward, Tascelin, Thorkell, Wulfric, Wulfward

SECULAR TITLES AND OCCUPATIONAL NAMES

Burgess (*burgensis*) ... of Colchester B2;3a,b,d,p;5-6. Of Maldon B6. **Chamberlain** (*camerarius*) ... William. [**Constable** (*stalre*, but not used in the text of DB Essex)] ... Asgar. **Cook** (*cocus*) ... Ansger, Walter. **Count** (*comes*) ... Alan, of Eu, Eustace, Gilbert; (*consul*) ... Eustace. **Countess** (*comitissa*) ... Aelfeva, of Aumâle, Judith. **Earl** (*comes*) ... Algar, 'Edgar', Harold, Waltheof. **Forester of the King's woodland** (*foristarius de silva regis*) ... 1,24. **Goldsmith** (*aurifaber*) ... Otto. **Gunner** (*balistarius*) ... Reginald. **Hundred-reeve** (*custos hundredi, prepositus hundredi*) ... 32,25. 89,1. **Hunter** (*venator*) ... Alfwy. **King's free men** (*liberi homines regis*) ... *89*. **King's servant** (*famulus regis*) ... 1,16a. **King Edward's reeve** (*prepositus regis Edwardi*) ... Edwold, and 1,3. [**King**] **Harold's reeve** (*prepositus Haroldi*) ... 1,4;24. **Latimer** (*latimarus*) ... Ralph. **Lorimer** (*loremarius*) ... Jocelyn. **Marshal** (*marescalcus*) ... Roger. **Queen** (*regina*) ... Edith, Matilda. **Reeve** (*prepositus*) ... Aelmer, Alfred, Grim, Ledmer. **Sheriff** (*vicecomes*) ... Baynard, Peter of Valognes, Picot, Robert son of Wymarc, Swein. **Sheriff of Surrey** (*vicecomes de Surreia*) ... Ranulf. **Steward** (*dapifer*) ... Godric, Hamo, and 29,5. **Summoner** (*monitor*) ... Wulfwin. **Young** (*cild, cilt*) ... Aelfric, Leofwin.

INDEX OF PLACES

The name of each place is followed by (i) the abbreviated name of its Hundred and its location on the Map in this volume; (ii) its National Grid reference; (iii) chapter and section references in LDB. Bracketed chapter and section references denote mention in sections dealing with a different place. Unless otherwise stated, the identifications of EPNS and the spellings of the Ordnance Survey are followed for places in England; of OEB for places abroad. Inverted commas indicate lost places with known modern spelling; unidentifiable places are given in LDB spelling, in italic print. Places whose names have changed since 1086 are entered under their present name. The National Grid reference system is explained on all Ordnance Survey maps, and in the Automobile Association Handbooks; the figures reading from left to right are given before those reading from bottom to top of the map. All places which have been given grid references in the present index are in the 100 km grid square lettered TL, apart from those marked with a (*) which are in square TQ, and those marked with a (†) which are in square TM. Places with bracketed Grid references do not appear on 1 inch or 1:50,000 maps. Where LDB does not differentiate between what are now two distinct settlements (e.g. Great and Little Bardfield), both sets of Grid references are given. The Essex Hundreds and Half-Hundreds are Barstable (Ba), Becontree (Be), Chafford (Cha), Chelmsford (Che), Clavering (Cl), Dunmow (D), Freshwell (F), Harlow (Ha), Hinckford (Hi), Lexden (L), Maldon (M), Ongar (O), Rochford (R), Tendring (Te), 'Thunderlow' (Tl), Thurstable (Ts), Uttlesford (U), Waltham (Wa), 'Wibertsherne' (Wb), Winstree (Wn), Witham (Wt); the places in each Hundred are listed after the index, immediately before the Map. Ballingdon cum Brundon has been in Suffolk since 1832 and 1835. [Great and Little] Chishill and Heydon have been in Cambridgeshire since 1895.

	Map	*Grid*	*Text*
Abberton	Wn 2	99 19	20,20. 24,51. 34,16
Acleta	–	–	25,10
Alderford	Hi 42	(76 33)	23,11
Alderford, see Aelfric			
Alderton Hall	O 20	(*42 96)	8,7
Aldham	L 14	91 25	18,24
Alphamstone	Hi 34	87 35	11,4. 23,19. 90,60
Alresford	Te 30	†06 20	4,4. 18,44. 20,65. 23,33
Amberden Hall	U 29	55 30	34,19
Amwell (Herts)	–	37 12	1,3
Ardleigh	Te 10	†05 29	30,20. 32,40. 39,8;12. 47,2. B31
Arkesden	U 20	48 34	25,26. 26,3-4. 32,43. 90,28
Ashdon	F 4	58 41	33,20
Asheldham	Wb 18	97 01	24,43;55
Ashen	Hi 11	74 42	23,12
Ashingdon	R 7	*86 93	24,38
Ashwell Hall	Hi 48	70 30	67,2
Ateleia	–	–	28,1
Aveley	Cha 10	*56 80	18,27. 40,9. 75,1
Great Baddow	Che 20	72 04	15,2. 72,3
Little Baddow	Che 16	77 07	20,52. 33,13
Ballingdon (Suffolk)	Tl 2	86 40	36,8
[Great and Little] Bardfield	F 12	67 30 65 30	20,79. 23,39;42. 90,65
Barking	Be 11	*44 83	9,7. (9,5)
Barling	R 15	*93 89	5,12. 18,16
Barn Hall	Wn 5	92 14	33,8
Barnston	D 13	64 19	30,29
Barrow Hall	R 18	*92 88	23,43
Barstable Hall	Ba 18	(*70 89)	18,4
Basildon	Ba 19	*71 89	24,7-8
Bassetts	Wb 1	79 08	4,18

	Map	Grid	Text
Baythorn End	Hi 10	72 42	37,12
Beaumont	Te 24	†17 24	35,11
Beckney	R 1	*84 95	18,15
Belchamp [Otten, St. Paul, and Walter]	Hi 13	80 41 79 42 82 40	5,3. 20,26;28. 43,4
Belchamp Walter	Tl 1	82 40	35,6
Belstead Hall	Che 9	72 10	22,18. 78,1
Bendysh Hall	F 7	60 39	20,77. 90,64
[North and South] Benfleet	Ba 14	*76 90 *77 86	1,1;14. 6,1. 24,13
'Bensted'	Che 23	(74 03)	27,14. 41,9
Bentfield Bury	Cl 9	49 26	32,19
Great Bentley	Te 28	†10 21	35,9
Little Bentley	Te 22	†12 24	21,9. 23,31
Benton Hall	Wt 15	82 13	11,1
Berden	Cl 2	46 29	24,54
Berewic	—	—	18,37
West Bergholt	L 11	95 28	23,36. 46,2. 90,70;73
Bertuna	—	—	90,35
Bigods	D 9	62 24	30,31
'Binsley'	Hi 25	(84 38)	23,10. 36,9
Great Birch	L 27	94 19	20,39
Little Birch	L 23	94 20	32,26. 60,3
Birchanger	U 32	50 22	1,10. 14,4. 30,48
Birch Hall	Te 26	†21 22	20,67
Birdbrook	Hi 17	70 41	37,11
'Blatchams'	Ts 4	(86 10)	20,61
Blunt's Hall	Wt 10	80 14	20,10. 34,5
Bobbingworth	O 7	53 05	37,15
Bocking	Hi 55	75 23	2,2
Bockingham	L 21	93 21	90,18
Bollington Hall	Cl 5	50 27	32,20. 90,35;41
Bonhunt	U 23	51 33	57,6
Boreham	Che 14	75 09	20,56. 22,17. 24,58
Borley	Hi 9	84 43	54,1. 90,55
Borley, see Aelmer			
Bowers Gifford	Ba 25	*75 87	6,3. 34,1. 42,1. 83,1
Boxted	L 4	99 33	20,37. 25,17. EHu
Boyton Hall	Hi 35	(71 33)	23,28. (23,29)
Bradfield	Te 9	†14 30	39,7. 46,2-3
Bradwell Quay	Wb 6	99 07	18,23
Braintree	Hi 59	75 23	90,48;76
Great Braxted	Wt 13	85 15	25,1
Little Braxted	Wt 12	83 14	4,14. 28,5
Brightlingsea	Te 33	†07 18	1,26. ESf1
Great Bromley	Te 20	†08 26	77,1
Little Bromley	Te 18	†09 27	23,32. 42,8
Broomfield	Che 8	70 10	30,9
Broxted	D 5	57 26	10,1. 25,12
Brundon (Suffolk)	Hi 15	86 42	49,1;4
Brundon, see Wulfric			
Bulmer	Hi 21	84 40	23,14
Bulphan	Ba 26	*63 85	9,2
Helions Bumpstead	F 5	65 41	35,12. 38,4. 90,83
Steeple Bumpstead	Hi 16	67 41	20,27. 21,5. 22,12. 23,21. 38,5. 90,61
Bures	Hi 40	90 34	23,16;29. 40,5
Mount Bures	L 2	90 32	39,6. 46,1
Burna	Te	—	20,63
Burnham	Wb 28	*94 96	33,12. 90,6

	Map	Grid	Text
Great Burstead	Ba 8	*68 92	18,2
Little Burstead	Ba 10	*66 91	4,8
Buttsbury	Che 32	(*66 98)	29,5
'Byrton'	L 15	(93 24)	62,3
Canewdon	R 4	*89 94	24,24
[Great and Little] Canfield	D 12	59 18 58 21	21,3. 22,6. 30,38. 35,1. 90,21
Chadwell	Ba 35	*64 78	4,11. 18,11. 83,2
Chalk (Kent)	—	67 72	EKt
Chardwell	U 19	47 34	22,20
Chatham	Che 5	70 13	30,7
Chaureth	D 3	58 28	90,77-78
Chelmsford	Che 18	70 06	3,12
Ceneboltuna	—	—	23,25
Great Chesterford	U 1	50 42	1,9
Little Chesterford	U 2	51 41	42,9
Chickney	D 2	57 28	34,9
Chignall	Che 7	66 10	30,10-12;15. 32,32
Chigwell	O 24	*44 93	49,3;5
Childerditch	Cha 3	*60 89	1,23. 24,4. 57,5
Chingford	Wa 3	*38 94	5,2. 32,7
[Great and Little] Chishill (Cambs.)	U 9	42 38 41 37	20,72-73. 22,21. 26,5. 30,46. 90,34;86
Chiswick	U 14	44 37	50,1
Chrishall	U 10	45 38	20,71
[Great and Little] Clacton	Te 35	†17 16 †16 18	3,15
Claret Hall	Hi 8	76 43	20,25
Clavering	Cl 1	47 31	24,52-53;56
Cliff	Te 8	(†11 30)	39,11
[Great and Little] Coggeshall	Wt 1	85 22 85 21	2,1. 20,7. (71,3. 90,8)
Colchester	C	99 25	*B*. 3,16. (6,8. 9,8. 17,1. 20,8;36;39. 34,6)
Colchester, see Godric			
[Earls, Wakes, and White] Colne	L 8	86 28 88 28 87 29	11,5. 20,41. 23,34. 35,8. 42,6. 44,3. 90,68; 71;80
Colne Engaine	L 7	85 30	44,4
Copford	L 19	93 22	3,10
Cornish Hall	Hi 32	68 35	90,58
Corringham	Ba 30	*70 83	4,9
Coupals Farm	Hi 3	(68 44)	23,23. 90,40
Cowbridge	Che 34	*65 95	37,18
Cranham	Cha 5	*57 86	4,1. 18,33
Crawleybury	U 5	(44 39)	20,76
Crays Hill	Ba 9	*71 92	57,1
Creeksea	Wb 25	*93 96	18,18;19. 68,3
Crepping	L 9	90 28	68,5. 90,69
Culvert's Farm	Che 15	76 09	32,36
Curling Tye Green	Wb 2	81 07	33,5
Cuton Hall	Che 13	73 08	30,17
Field Dalling (Norf.)	—	—	ENf
Danbury	Che 21	77 05	30,14
Debden Green	O 14	*43 98	8,8
Debden	U 24	55 33	34,18
Dedham	L 6	†05 33	39,5
Dengie	Wb 19	98 01	14,7. 18,22
'Derleigh'	Te 14	(†07 28)	37,20. 68,8
Dickley	Te 11	†11 29	32,39
Doddinghurst	Ba 1	*58 99	41,1

	Map	*Grid*	*Text*
East Donyland	L 24	†01 20	20,38;42. 68,6. 69,3. 70,2
Dovercourt	Te 7	†23 31	35,10
Down Hall	Wb 8	†00 06	25,8. 34,23;25
[Great and Little] Dunmow	D 11	62 22 65 21	20,15. 22,9. 23,3. 24,48. 25,14. 28,7. 30,32;36;42. 33,6
Dunton	Ba 20	*65 88	18,3. 90,3
Good Easter	D 16	62 12	12,1
High Easter	D 15	62 14	30,27
[Great and Little] Easton	D 8	60 25 60 23	22,5. 30,37. 42,3. 53,1
Easthorpe	L 20	91 21	20,40
Easthorpe, see Edric			
Eastwood	R 16	*84 88	24,20;41
Elmdon	U 6	46 39	20,74
Elmstead	Te 19	†06 26	24,64. B3m
Elsenham	U 30	54 25	32,44. 65,1
Emanuel Wood	U 3	53 41	21,10. 30,47
Epping	Ha 14	45 02	21,1
Epping	Wa 2	45 02	8,1. 37,9
Fairstead	Wt 6	76 16	34,7
North Fambridge	Wb 26	*85 97	71,2
South Fambridge	R 2	*86 95	79,1
Fanton Hall	Ba 13	*76 91	6,2;4. 9,3
Farnham	Cl 10	48 24	28,10. 32,21. 90,25;42
Faulkbourne	Wt 7	80 16	28,2
Feering	L 22	87 20	6,8. (90,17. B3k)
Felsted	Hi 60	67 20	15,1. 72,2. 73,1
Finchingfield	Hi 44	68 32	1,12. 20,30-31. 21,4;7. 23,5;9;13;22. 90,50
Fingrith Hall	Che 22	60 03	1,21. (1,22)
Fobbing	Ba 31	*71 83	20,1
Fordham	L 10	92 28	22,24. 23,35. 47,3. 90,72
Fouchers	Che 36	(*63 91)	37,19
Foulton	Te 13	†22 29	24,65. 41,10
Foxearth	Hi 4	83 44	23,17
Frating	Te 27	†08 22	20,63. 34,34
Frinton	Te 32	†23 19	20,66. 30,19
Fristling	Che 27	67 00	9,12
Frowick Hall	Te 34	†12 18	20,63
Fryerning	Che 24	63 00	32,30-31;34
Fyfield	O 6	57 06	20,49-50. 40,6-7
Geddesduna	—	—	6,13
Gestingthorpe	Hi 24	81 38	23,4. 81,1
Goldhanger	Ts 8	90 08	20,58. 27,17. 34,37
Goldingham Hall	Hi 20	83 40	44,2
Gravesend (Kent)	G	*64 74	20,5 note
'Gravesend'	Ba 37	(*67 77)	20,5
Greenstead	C 1	†01 24	B1
Greensted	O 10	53 02	28,13
Hadstock	F 1	55 44	10,4
Halesduna	—	—	27,8
[Great and Little] Hallingbury	Ha 1	51 19 50 17	4,16. 24,46. 26,1. 30,24;26
Halstead	Hi 49	81 30	22,11. 23,26. 90,47;74
East Ham	Be 10	*42 83	6,6. 32,9
West Ham	Be 9	*39 83	32,8. 34,8
[East, South, and West] Hanningfield	Che 28	77 01 *74 98 *73 99	18,36. 22,15-16. 33,14. 41,6

	Map	*Grid*	*Text*
Harkstead (Suff.)	H	†18 34	ESf1. (1,26)
Harlow	Ha 8	47 11	11,2. 20,14. 25,2. (37,3)
Hasingham	—	—	90,67
Hassenbrook Hall	Ba 29	(*68 83)	18,10. 24,6
Hastings (Sussex)	—	—	EHu
Hatfield Broad Oak	Ha 4	54 16	1,3. (28,6)
Hatfield Peverel	Wt 16	78 11	18,13. 34,4
Havering-atte-Bower	Be 2	*51 93	1,4. (27,3. 41,4. 90,19)
Hawkwell	R 9	*86 91	24,40. 25,11;25
Hazeleigh	Wb 12	83 03	34,13-14
Castle Hedingham	Hi 33	78 35	35,5
Sible Hedingham	Hi 36	77 34	39,3. 43,1
Hemingford (Hunts.)	—	—	EHu
Hempstead	F 9	63 37	23,41
Hempstead, see Ledmer			
Henham	F 13	54 28	33,19. 90,39
[Great and Little] Henny	Hi 26	86 37 86 38	34,21. 40,4. 43,5. 90,13;44;46
Hertford (Herts.)	—	32 12	1,3
Heybridge	Ts 7	85 07	5,10
Heydon (Cambs.)	U 4	43 39	10,5. 76,1
Higham Hill	Be 4	*35 90	36,6
Hockley	R 5	*82 93	9,13. 24,19;33
Hocsenga	—	—	90,66
Hoddesdon (Herts.)	—	37 08	1,3
[Great and Little] Holland	Te 36	†21 19 †20 16	20,68. 52,3
[East and West] Horndon	Ba 16	*63 89 *62 88	18,12. 24,1. 48,1
Horndon-on-the-Hill	Ba 28	*66 83	4,10. 20,2. 24,5. 60,1. 61,1. 90,1-2
Horseham Hall	Hi 6	66 43	13,2. 35,7. 90,52;75
Housham Hall	Ha 9	50 11	22,3. 51,1
Howbridge	Wt 14	(81 13)	4,15. 32,4
Howe	Hi 41	69 33	23,15. 90,53
Hunt's Hall	Hi 46	84 32	22,13
Hutton	Ba 3	*63 94	13,1
Ilford	Be 8	*44 86	64,1
Iltney Farm	Wb 10	88 04	20,16. 24,42
Ingatestone	Che 25	*65 99	9,11
Ingrave	Ba 7	*62 92	18,5. 34,3. 37,1
Ipswich (Suff.)	I	†15 44	ESf2
Jacques Hall	Te 4	†15 31	39,9
Kelvedon	Wt 5	85 18	6,5. 27,2
Kelvedon Hatch	O 18	*56 98	6,9. 18,25. 28,15
Kenningtons	Cha 8	*56 81	22,14. 24,62
Laindon	Ba 17	*68 89	3,1. 4,13
Lamarsh	Hi 31	88 36	34,22. 90,14;45
Lambourne	O 22	47 96	20,48
Landuna	—	—	25,9
Langdon	Ba 27	*67 86	24,2
Langenhoe	Wn 4	†01 17	20,19
Langford	Ts 6	83 09	33,2;22
Langham	L 5	†03 33	23,38
Lashley Hall	D 7	64 26	90,51
Latchingdon	Wb 21	88 00	1,6-7. 2,5. 27,5. 84,2
Latton	Ha 12	(46 10)	11,3. 20,13. 36,2
[High, Little, and Magdalen] Laver	O 3	52 08 54 09 51 08	20,45;47. 51,2

	Map	Grid	Text
Lawford	Te 2	†08 31	1,27. 20,69. (23,33. 33,17. 37,20)
Lawling	Wb 17	90 01	2,4. 25,6. 34,24. 41,5. 90,79
Lawn Hall	Che 2	65 17	18,38
Layer [Breton, de la Haye, and Marney]	Wn 1	94 18 96 19 92 17	1,19. 3,6-7. 20,21. 27,10. 34,15. 57,3. 68,4. 90,5. (17,2)
Lee Chapel	Ba 21	*69 88	5,1
Elmdon Lee	U 12	48 38	20,75
Lega	—	—	32,14
Leigh	R 22	*84 86	34,35
[Great and Little] Leighs	Che 3	73 17 71 16	25,21. 30,16
Lexden	L 16	97 25	1,19. B2
Leyton	Be 7	*37 86	6,7. 27,3. 32,10. 36,5. 41,3-4
Liffildeuuella	—	—	90,43
Limpwella	—	—	18,35
Lindsell	D 4	64 27	14,2. 25,4
Liston	Hi 5	85 44	47,1. 69,2
Littlebury	U 8	51 39	10,5
Littlethorpe	R 20	(*91 87)	24,25
Lohou	—	—	62,4
London	—	—	(7,1. 9,7. 30,18. 31,1)
Loughton	Be 1	*42 96	8,4-5. 32,11. 36,7;10. (1,4)
Maldon	M	85 07	1,25. 24,63. 34,31. (B6)
Maldon	Wb M	85 07	1,17. 20,34. 34,12. See also Siward.
Manuden	Cl 8	49 26	32,16;22. 33,10. 90,36
Great Maplestead	Hi 38	80 34	32,23
Little Maplestead	Hi 39	82 33	40,3. 90,38
Margaretting	Che 26	66 00	1,22. 53,2
Markshall	L 12	84 25	27,13
Mashbury	D 17	65 11	12,1 note. 30,13. 90,20
Matching	Ha 7	52 12	14,1. 30,25. 32,6. 61,2
East Mersea	Wn 10	†05 14	24,49
West Mersea	Wn 9	†10 31	2,2. 17,1
Messing	L 28	89 18	33,9. 39,4
Michaelstow	Te 6	(†21 31)	33,17
Middleton	Hi 27	87 39	23,20. 82,1. 90,84
Midebroc	—	—	90,9
Milton	R 26	(*87 85)	2,7
Mistley	Te 3	†01 31	39,10
Moreton	O 5	53 07	45,1
Moulsham Hall	Che 1	72 18	18,41-42
Moulsham Lodge	Che 19	71 05	6,14
Mountnessing	Che 33	*64 96	37,16-17
Moze	Te 21	†20 26	30,18. ESf2
Mucking	Ba 33	*68 81	9,1;4
Mundon	Wb 16	87 02	25,5
'Napsted'	Hi 45	(81 32)	18,21
Navestock	O 17	*54 98	5,7-8. 28,14
Nayland	L 1	97 34	24,57
The Naze	Te 25	†23 23 etc.	5,11
Nazeing	Wa 1	41 06	8,2. 37,8-9
Nevendon	Ba 12	*73 91	62,1. 70,1
Newland Hall	Che 6	63 09	20,51
Newnham Hall	F 2	58 42	20,78
Newport	U 21	52 34	1,28
Newton Hall	D 10	61 22	30,28

	Map	*Grid*	*Text*
Niuetuna	—	—	49,2
Northey Island	Wb 4	87 06	28,12. 90,32
Norton Mandeville	O 9	58 04	5,6. 28,16
Cold Norton	Wb 23	*85 99	33,3
[Black and White] Notley	Wt 3	76 20 78 18	20,6. 24,45. 28,3. 30,22. 40,1. 57,2. 62,2
Great Oakley	Te 16	†20 28	32,38
Little Oakley	Te 17	†21 28	33,15
[North and South] Ockendon	Cha 6	*58 84 *60 83	1,21-21a. 6,10-11. 30,4
Old Hall	Te 1	(†10 32)	54,2
[Chipping and High] Ongar	O 11	55 03 56 03	20,46. 40,8. (90,87)
Orsett	Ba 32	*64 81	3,2. 20,4
Osea Island	Ts 9	91 06	28,18
Ovington	Hi 12	76 42	43,3. 90,63
Paglesham	R 8	*92 93	6,15. 22,22. 33,21. 41,11. 90,8
Panfield	Hi 53	73 25	16,1. 23,6
[Great and Little] Parndon	Ha 11	43 08 44 11	9,6. 20,12. 36,3. 37,4-6
Paslow Hall	O 12	57 03	8,6
Patching Hall	Che 11	69 08	18,40. 30,8. 32,35
Pebmarsh	Hi 43	85 33	23,18. 43,2. 90,38;59
Peldon	Wn 3	98 16	24,50. 66,1
Pentlow	Hi 1	81 46	33,11
Peyton Hall	Cl 3	48 28	22,10
Pinchpools	Cl 4	49 27	57,4
Pitsea	Ba 24	*73 87	84,1
Pledgdon Hall	Cl 7	55 27	25,16. 30,49
'Plesingho'	D 18	(59 08)	20,18. 90,30
Plumberow	R 6	*83 93	22,23. 24,31
Plunker's Green	O 19	(*58 97)	34,28
Prested	L 26	88 19	34,27
Prittlewell	R 23	*87 86	24,22
Pudsey Hall	R 3	*88 95	24,32;34;36-37
Purleigh	Wb 15	84 02	20,17. 27,4;6-7. 32,12. 42,2;4
Quendon	U 27	51 31	25,23
Quicksbury Farm	Ha 5	49 14	22,4
Radwinter	F 8	60 37	25,24. 35,13. 38,3. 56,1
Rainham	Cha 7	*52 82	18,30. 32,28. 52,2. 70,3
Ramsden [Bellhouse and Crays]	Ba 4	*71 94 *70 93	3,3. 4,12. 18,6. 27,1. 32,1-2. 37,2
Ramsey	Te 12	†18 29	33,16
Rayleigh	R 11	*80 90	24,17-18
Rayne	Hi 58	73 22	3,8. 27,11. 28,4. 39,1-2
Rettendon	Che 29	*76 98	10,3. 25,20. 34,30
Rickling	U 26	49 31	1,29
Ridgewell	Hi 18	73 40	20,23
Ridley Hall	Wt 8	75 15	30,23
Rivenhall	Wt 4	82 17	20,8-9. 24,44. 32,5. 72,1
Rochford	R 12	*87 90	24,26
Rockell's Farm	U 15	46 36	90,22-23
Abbess Roding	O 2	57 11	25,19. 30,3
Beauchamp Roding	O 4	57 09	21,8
'Morrell' Roding	O 1	(56 15)	23,30. 25,3. (30,41)
[Aythorpe, Berners, High, Leaden, Margaret, and White] Roding	D 14	58 15 60 09 60 17 59 13 59 12 56 13	1,8. 10,2. 22,7-8. 26,2. 28,8. 30,30;35;39-40; 43. ENf

	Map	*Grid*	*Text*
Rothend	F 6	(59 39)	21,11
Roydon	Ha 10	40 10	37,3
Runwell	Che 35	*75 94	5,9. 20,53-54
Ryes	Ha 3	52 16	28,6
St. Lawrence	Wb 11	96 04	2,6. 37,14
St. Osyth	Te 37	†12 15	3,14. 20,63. 34,33
St. Peter's Chapel	Wb 5	†03 08	14,6. 27,12
Great Saling	Hi 52	70 25	40,2. 90,62
Great Sampford	F 10	64 35	1,30
Little Sampford	F 11	65 33	23,40
Sampson's Farm	Wn 7	99 15	18,20
Sciddeham, Scilcheham	—	—	59,1. 90,82
Shalford	Hi 50	72 29	1,11. 66,2. 67,1 (B3j)
Sheering	Ha 6	50 13	36,1
Shelford (Cambs.)	—	45 51	(1,28)
Shelley	O 8	55 05	30,2
Shellow Bowells	D 20	60 07	1,5. 25,13. 30,33-34;41
Shenfield	Ba 2	*60 95	20,3
[North and South] Shoebury	R 25	*92 86 (*93 84)	18,17. 24,23;28
Shopland	R 17	*89 88	20,80
Shortgrove	U 18	52 35	20,22;24. 32,42
Slampseys	Wt 2	73 19	3,4
Smallands	Wt 17	(81 10)	41,2
Smalton	Hi 37	(78 34)	90,37
Smeetham Hall	Hi 14	84 41	20,32
Southchurch	R 24	*90 86	2,8
Southminster	Wb 24	*96 99	3,9
Springfield	Che 12	71 08	32,33. 34,29
Stambourne	Hi 22	72 38	28,11. 90,26;33
Great Stambridge	R 13	*89 90	18,14. 24,27
Little Stambridge	R 10	*88 91	2,9. 90,7
Stanford Rivers	O 13	53 00	20,43-44
Stanmer	Ba 5	(*72 93)	57,1
Stansgate	Wb 7	93 05	34,26. 90,12
Stanstead Hall	Hi 51	82 28	44,1. (44,4)
Stansted Mountfitchet	U 31	51 24	32,16
Stanway	L 18	93 24	1,19
Stapleford Abbotts	O 23	*50 95	11,6. 32,27
Stapleford Tawney	O 16	*50 99	24,59
Stebbing	Hi 54	66 24	29,2. 34,20
Stebbingford House	Hi 57	67 22	63,2
Steeple	Wb 13	93 03	1,15. 25,7. 29,3. 90,81
Stevington End	F 3	59 42	21,12. 35,14. 38,2. 90,85
Stifford	Cha 11	*60 80	9,10. 18,32;34. 75,2
Stisted	Hi 56	79 24	2,3
Stow Maries	Wb 22	*83 99	30,44;50. 42,5
Strethall	U 7	48 39	10,5
'Studly'	Che 31	(81 00)	1,6. 27,9
Sturmer	Hi 7	69 43	38,6-7
Sudbury (Suff.)	—	87 41	23,27. (34,21. 35,5. 40,4)
Sutton	R 14	*88 89	24,30;35;39. 71,4
Takeley	U 33	55 21	14,3. 25,15. 32,17
Tendring	Te 23	†14 24	4,5. 20,64;70. 32,38a. 34,32. 68,7
Terling	Wt 9	77 14	1,2 note. 34,6. 90,10. B3q
[Great and Little] Tey	L 13	89 25 89 23	20,36

	Map	Grid	Text
Marks Tey	L 17	91 23	30,1
Thaxted	D 1	61 31	23,2
Theydon [Bois, Garnon, and Mount]	O 15	*44 99 *47 99 *49 99	24,60. 25,18. 36,11. 74,1
Thorpehall	R 27	(*91 85)	37,10
Thorrington	Te 31	†09 19	18,43
Thunderley Hall	U 16	55 36	35,3
Thundersley	Ba 22	*78 88	24,16
[Grays and West] Thurrock	Cha 12	*61 77 *59 77	18,28-29;31. 31,1. 48,2. (18,34)
Little Thurrock	Ba 34	*62 77	4,6. 90,4
Tilbury-juxta-Clare	Hi 19	75 40	38,8
[East and West] Tilbury	Ba 36	*68 77 *66 77	22,2. 24,3. 71,1. (30,21)
Tillingham	Wb 14	99 03	5,5
Tilty	D 6	59 26	29,1
Tollesbury	Ts 5	95 10	9,14. 20,62
Tolleshunt [D'Arcy, Knights, and Major]	Ts 1	92 11 92 14 90 11	18,45. 20,57;59-60. 24,66. 27,18. 32,37;45. 33,23. 34,36. 41,12. 80,1. B3r
Toppesfield	Hi 28	73 37	20,33. 28,11. 90,56-57
[Great and Little] Totham	Ts 2	86 13 88 11	4,2-3. 24,67. 27,16. 28,17
Twinstead	Hi 30	86 36	23,24
Udecheshale	–	–	35,2
Ugley	Cl 6	51 28	35,4
Uleham's Farm	Wb 25	*87 98	4,17. 20,35
Ulting	Wt 18	80 08	33,1
Uluuinescherham	–	–	1,16
Upham	–	–	22,1
Upminster	Cha 4	*56 87	8,10. 18,26. 52,1
Vange	Ba 23	*72 87	18,1. 34,2
Virley	Wn 8	94 13	32,15
Great Wakering	R 21	*94 87	24,21
Little Wakering	R 19	*93 88	24,29
Saffron Walden	U 13	53 38	30,45
Wallbury	Ha 2	49 17	23,1
Walter Hall	Che 10	73 10	8,11. 18,39. 86,1
Waltham Holy Cross	Wa 4	38 00	7,1. (32,7. 37,9)
[Great and Little] Waltham	Che 4	69 13 71 12	11,7. 20,55. 30,5-6. 41,7-8
Walthamstow	Be 5	*37 89	55,1
Wanstead	Be 6	*40 88	3,5
[Great and Little] Warley	Cha 2	*59 88 *60 90	3,11. 9,9. 24,61. (57,5)
North Weald Bassett	Ha 13	49 05	36,4;12. 37,7
South Weald	Cha 1	*57 93	8,9. 32,29
Weeley	Te 29	†15 21	25,22
Well Farm	Ba 11	(*67 91)	4,7
Wendens Ambo, Wendon Lofts	U 11	51 36 46 38	22,19. 32,18. 33,18. 90,24
Wenesuuic	–	–	30,51
Wennington	Cha 9	*53 80	6,12
Weston Hall	Hi 2	83 45	20,29. 43,6
Westnanetuna	–	–	77,1
Wesuunic	–	–	90,27
Wethersfield	Hi 47	71 31	1,13. 87,1. (23,28)
Wheatley	Ba 15	*79 90	18,7. 24,14-15
Great Whitmans	Wb 20	83 00	32,13

	Map	Grid	Text
Wicken Bonhunt	U 22	49 33	58,1
Wickford	Ba 6	*74 93	18,7-9. 24,9-12. 68,1. 69,1
Wickham Bishops	Ts 3	83 12	3,13
Wickham St. Paul's	Hi 29	82 37	5,4. 23,8
Widdington	U 28	53 31	14,5. 32,41. 90,11
[Great and Little] Wigborough	Wn 6	96 15 / 98 14	9,8. 28,9. 34,17. 60,2. 90,31
Willingale [Doe and Spain]	D 19	59 07 / (58 06)	21,2. 24,47. 34,10. 63,1
Wimbish	U 17	58 36	33,7
Witelebroc	–	–	33,17
Witesuuorda	–	–	23,37
Witham	Wt 11	81 14	1,2. 20,11. 32,3. 68,2
Wivenhoe	L 25	†03 21	32,25
Wix	Te 15	†16 28	27,15. 42,7
Woodford	Be 3	*40 92	8,3
Woodham Ferrers	Che 30	*79 99	29,4
Woodham Mortimer	Wb 9	81 04	34,11
Woodham Walter	Wb 3	80 06	33,4
Woolston Hall	O 21	*44 95	1,20
Wormingford	L 3	93 32	32,24
Wrabness	Te 5	†17 31	11,8
Wringehala	–	–	(25,5)
Writtle	Che 17	67 06	1,24. 19,1. (20,51)
Yardley	U 25	59 32	38,1
[Great and Little] Yeldham	Hi 23	75 38 / 77 39	20,25. 21,6. 23,7. 37,13. 90,54
Yelling (Hunts.)	–	–	EHu
York(shire)	–	–	(6,15. 30,16)

Places not named

1,13a. 1,16a. 1,17a. 1,18. 1,31. 9,5. 12,1. 17,2. 18,21a. 30,21. 85,1. 86,2. 88,1. 88,2. 89,1. 89,2. 90,15. 90,16. 90,17. 90,19. 90,29. 90,49. 90,87. EKt.

Unnamed in Suffolk: (32,40)

Places not in Essex

Names starred are in the Index of Churches and Clergy. Apart from the SURREY entry, the rest are in the Indices of Persons and Places.

Elsewhere in Britain

CAMBRIDGESHIRE ... Ely*. Picot the Sheriff. Shelford. Co. DURHAM ... Durham*. HAMPSHIRE ... Winchester*. HEREFORDSHIRE ... Hereford*. HERTFORDSHIRE ... Amwell. Hertford. Hoddesdon. HUNTINGDONSHIRE ... Hemingford. Yelling. KENT ... Canterbury*. Chalk. Rochester, see Thorold. LONDON* ... see also Places Index. MIDDLESEX ... Westminster*. NORFOLK ... Field Dalling. SUFFOLK ... Bury St. Edmund's*. Harkstead. Ipswich. Sudbury. See also Unnamed Places. SURREY ... Sheriff, see Secular Titles. SUSSEX ... Battle*. Hastings, and see Ralph. YORKSHIRE. UNIDENTIFIED ... Gotton, see Alwin.

Outside Britain

More precise details as to location are given in the General Notes.

Alno ... William. Anjou ... Osmund. Auberville ... Roger. Aumâle ... Countess. Bayeux*. Bernières ... Hugh. Bosc ... William. Boursigny ... William. Brittany ... see Lorce Bret, Tihel the Breton. Caen* ... Walter. Corbon (?) ... W. Corbun. Denmark ... see Anand, Finn, and Odin the Danes. Douai ... Walter. Écouis ... William. Eu ... Count. Ferrers ... Henry. Gournai ... Hugh. Helléan ... Tihel. Houdain ... Hugh. Limésy ... Ralph. Mandeville ... Geoffrey. Marck ... Adelulf. Marcy ... Ralph. Montbegon ... Robert. Montfort ... Hugh. Mortagne ... Matthew.

Outside Britain (cont'd.)

Moutiers ... Lisois. Oilly ... Robert. Poitou ... Roger. Port ... Hubert. Raismes ... Roger. Rouen*. Sackville ... Richard. St. Quentin ... Hugh. St. Valéry*. Scales ... Hardwin. Sommery ... Robert. 'Spain' (Épaignes) ... Hervey. Tosny ... Ralph, Robert. Valognes ... Peter. Vatteville ... Robert, William. Vaux ... Robert. Vere ... Aubrey. Verly ... Hugh, Robert. Wader (?) ... Ralph. Warenne ... William.

MAPS AND MAP KEYS

The County Boundary is marked by thick lines, dotted for the modern boundary; Hundred boundaries by thin lines, broken where uncertain.

An open circle denotes a place in another county but referred to in this text, or in the Notes.

The letters of National Grid 10-kilometre squares are shown on the map border. Each four-figure square covers one square kilometre (5/8ths of a square mile).

Unidentified Places Not Mapped

Acleta
Ateleia
Berewic
Bertuna
Burna
Cheneboltuna
Geddesduna
Halesduna
Hasingham
Hocsenga
Landuna
Lega
Liffildeuuella
Limpwella
Lohou
Midebroc
Niuetuna
Sciddeham, Scilcheham
Udecheshale
Uluuinescherham
Upham
Wenesuuic
Wesuunic
Westnanetuna
Witelebroc
Witesuuorda
Wringehala

Barstable (Ba)

18 Barstable Hall
19 Basildon
14 North and South Benfleet
25 Bowers Gifford
26 Bulphan
8 Great Burstead
10 Little Burstead
35 Chadwell
30 Corringham
9 Crays Hill
1 Doddinghurst
20 Dunton
13 Fanton Hall
31 Fobbing
37 'Gravesend'
29 Hassenbrook Hall
16 East and West Horndon
28 Horndon-on-the-Hill
3 Hutton
7 Ingrave
17 Laindon
27 Langdon
21 Lee Chapel
33 Mucking
12 Nevendon
32 Orsett
24 Pitsea
4 Ramsden Bellhouse and Crays
2 Shenfield
5 Stanmer
22 Thundersley
34 Little Thurrock
36 East and West Tilbury
23 Vange
11 Well Farm
15 Wheatley
6 Wickford

Becontree (Be)

11 Barking
10 East Ham
9 West Ham
2 Havering-atte-Bower
4 Higham Hill
8 Ilford
7 Leyton
1 Loughton
5 Walthamstow
6 Wanstead
3 Woodford

Chafford (Cha)

10 Aveley
3 Childerditch
5 Cranham
8 Kenningtons
6 North and South Ockendon
7 Rainham
11 Stifford
12 Grays and West Thurrock
4 Upminster
2 Great and Little Warley
1 South Weald
9 Wennington

Chelmsford (Che)

20 Great Baddow
16 Little Baddow
9 Belstead Hall
23 'Bensted'
14 Boreham
8 Broomfield
32 Buttsbury
5 Chatham
18 Chelmsford
7 Chignall
34 Cowbridge
15 Culvert's Farm
13 Cuton Hall
21 Danbury
22 Fingrith Hall
36 Fouchers
27 Fristling
24 Fryerning
28 East, South and West Hanningfield

Chelmsford (Che) *cont'd.*
25 Ingatestone
2 Lawn Hall
3 Great and Little Leighs
26 Margaretting
1 Moulsham Hall
19 Moulsham Lodge
33 Mountnessing
6 Newland Hall
11 Patching Hall
29 Rettendon
35 Runwell
12 Springfield
31 'Studly'
10 Walter Hall
4 Great and Little Waltham
30 Woodham Ferrers
17 Writtle

Clavering (Cl)
9 Bentfield Bury
2 Berden
5 Bollington Hall
1 Clavering
10 Farnham
8 Manuden
3 Peyton Hall
4 Pinchpools
7 Pledgdon Hall
6 Ugley

Dunmow (D)
13 Barnston
9 Bigods
5 Broxted
12 Great and Little Canfield
3 Chaureth
2 Chickney
11 Great and Little Dunmow
16 Good Easter
15 High Easter
8 Great and Little Easton
7 Lashley Hall
4 Lindsell
17 Mashbury
10 Newton Hall
18 'Plesingho'
14 Aythorpe Roding
Berners Roding
High Roding
Leaden Roding
Margaret Roding
White Roding
20 Shellow Bowells
1 Thaxted
6 Tilty
19 Willingale Doe and Spain

Freshwell (F)
4 Ashdon
12 Great and Little Bardfield
7 Bendysh Hall
5 Helions Bumpstead
1 Hadstock
9 Hempstead
13 Henham
2 Newnham Hall
8 Radwinter
6 Rothend
10 Great Sampford
11 Little Sampford
3 Stevington End

Harlow (Ha)
14 Epping
1 Great and Little Hallingbury
8 Harlow
4 Hatfield Broad Oak
9 Housham Hall
12 Latton
7 Matching
11 Great and Little Parndon
5 Quicksbury Farm
10 Roydon
3 Ryes
6 Sheering
2 Wallbury
13 North Weald Bassett

Ongar (O)
20 Alderton Hall
7 Bobbingworth
24 Chigwell
14 Debden Green
6 Fyfield
10 Greensted
18 Kelvedon Hatch
22 Lambourne
3 High, Little and Magdalen Laver
5 Moreton
17 Navestock
9 Norton Mandeville
11 Chipping and High Ongar
12 Paslow Hall
19 Plunker's Green
2 Abbess Roding
4 Beauchamp Roding
1 'Morrell Roding'
8 Shelley
13 Stanford Rivers
23 Stapleford Abbotts
16 Stapleford Tawney
15 Theydon Bois, Garnon and Mount
21 Woolston Hall

Uttlesford (U)
29 Amberden Hall
20 Arkesden
32 Birchanger
23 Bonhunt
19 Chardwell
1 Great Chesterford
2 Little Chesterford
9 Great and Little Chishill
14 Chiswick
10 Chrishall
5 Crawleybury
24 Debden
6 Elmdon
30 Elsenham
3 Emanuel Wood
4 Heydon
12 Elmdon Lee
8 Littlebury
21 Newport
27 Quendon
26 Rickling
15 Rockell's Farm
18 Shortgrove
31 Stansted Mountfitchet
7 Strethall
33 Takeley
16 Thunderley Hall
13 Saffron Walden
11 Wendens Ambo and Wendon Lofts
22 Wicken Bonhunt
28 Widdington
17 Wimbish
25 Yardley

Waltham (Wa)
3 Chingford
2 Epping
1 Nazeing
4 Waltham Holy Cross

In Other Counties
In Kent
G Gravesend

Colchester
C Colchester
1 Greenstead

Hinckford (Hi)
42 Alderford
34 Alphamstone
11 Ashen
48 Ashwell Hall
10 Baythorn End
13 Belchamp Otten, St. Paul and Walter
25 'Binsley'
17 Birdbrook
55 Bocking
9 Borley
35 Boyton Hall
59 Braintree
15 Brundon
21 Bulmer
16 Steeple Bumpstead
40 Bures
8 Claret Hall
32 Cornish Hall
3 Coupals Farm
60 Felsted
44 Finchingfield
4 Foxearth
24 Gestingthorpe
20 Goldingham Hall
49 Halstead
33 Castle Hedingham
36 Sible Hedingham
26 Great and Little Henny
6 Horseham Hall
41 Howe
46 Hunt's Hall
31 Lamarsh
5 Liston
38 Great Maplestead
39 Little Maplestead
27 Middleton
45 'Napsted'
12 Ovington
53 Panfield
43 Pebmarsh
1 Pentlow
58 Rayne
18 Ridgewell
52 Great Saling
50 Shalford
37 Smalton
14 Smeetham Hall
22 Stambourne
51 Stanstead Hall
54 Stebbing
57 Stebbingford House
56 Stisted
7 Sturmer
19 Tilbury-juxta-Clare
28 Toppesfield
30 Twinstead
2 Weston Hall
47 Wethersfield
29 Wickham St. Paul's
23 Great and Little Yeldham

Lexden (L)
14 Aldham
11 West Bergholt
27 Great Birch
23 Little Birch
21 Bockingham
4 Boxted
2 Mount Bures
15 'Byrton'
8 Earls, Wakes and White Colne
7 Colne Engaine
19 Copford
9 Crepping
6 Dedham
24 East Donyland
20 Easthorpe
22 Feering
10 Fordham
5 Langham
16 Lexden
12 Markshall
28 Messing
1 Nayland
26 Prested
18 Stanway
13 Great and Little Tey
17 Marks Tey
25 Wivenhoe
3 Wormingford

Maldon (M)
M Maldon

Rochford (R)
7 Ashingdon
15 Barling
18 Barrow Hall
1 Beckney
4 Canewdon
16 Eastwood
2 South Fambridge
9 Hawkwell
5 Hockley
22 Leigh
20 Littlethorpe
26 Milton
8 Paglesham
6 Plumberow
23 Prittlewell
3 Pudsey Hall
11 Rayleigh
12 Rochford
25 North and South Shoebury
17 Shopland
24 Southchurch
13 Great Stambridge
10 Little Stambridge
14 Sutton
27 Thorpehall
21 Great Wakering
19 Little Wakering

Tendring (Te)
30 Alresford
10 Ardleigh
24 Beaumont
28 Great Bentley
22 Little Bentley
26 Birch Hall
9 Bradfield
33 Brightlingsea
20 Great Bromley
18 Little Bromley
35 Great and Little Clacton
8 Cliff
14 'Derleigh'
11 Dickley
7 Dovercourt
19 Elmstead
13 Foulton
27 Frating
32 Frinton
34 Frowick Hall
36 Great and Little Holland
4 Jacques Hall
2 Lawford
6 Michaelstow
3 Mistley
21 Moze
25 The Naze
16 Great Oakley
17 Little Oakley
1 Old Hall
12 Ramsey

Tendring (Te) *cont'd.*
37 St. Osyth
23 Tendring
31 Thorrington
29 Weeley
15 Wix
5 Wrabness

'Thunderlow' (Tl)
2 Ballingdon
1 Belchamp Walter

Thurstable (Ts)
4 'Blatchams'
8 Goldhanger
7 Heybridge
6 Langford
9 Osea Island
5 Tollesbury
1 Tolleshunt D'Arcy, Knights and Major
2 Great and Little Totham
3 Wickham Bishops

'Wibertsherne' (Wb)
18 Asheldham
1 Bassetts
6 Bradwell Quay
28 Burnham
25 Creeksea
2 Curling Tye Green
19 Dengie
8 Down Hall
26 North Fambridge
12 Hazeleigh
10 Iltney Farm
21 Latchingdon
17 Lawling
M Maldon
16 Mundon
4 Northey Island
23 Cold Norton
15 Purleigh
11 St. Lawrence
5 St. Peter's Chapel
24 Southminster
7 Stansgate
13 Steeple
22 Stow Maries
14 Tillingham
25 Uleham's Farm
20 Great Whitmans
9 Woodham Mortimer
3 Woodham Walter

Winstree (Wn)
2 Abberton
5 Barn Hall
4 Langenhoe
1 Layer Breton, de la Haye and Marney
10 East Mersea
9 West Mersea
3 Peldon
7 Sampson's Farm
8 Virley
6 Great and Little Wigborough

Witham (Wt)
15 Benton Hall
10 Blunt's Hall
13 Great Braxted
12 Little Braxted
1 Great and Little Coggeshall
6 Fairstead
7 Faulkbourne
16 Hatfield Peverel
14 Howbridge
5 Kelvedon
3 Black and White Notley
8 Ridley Hall
4 Rivenhall
2 Slampseys
17 Smallands
9 Terling
18 Ulting
11 Witham

In Other Counties
In Suffolk
H Harkstead
I Ipswich
S Sudbury

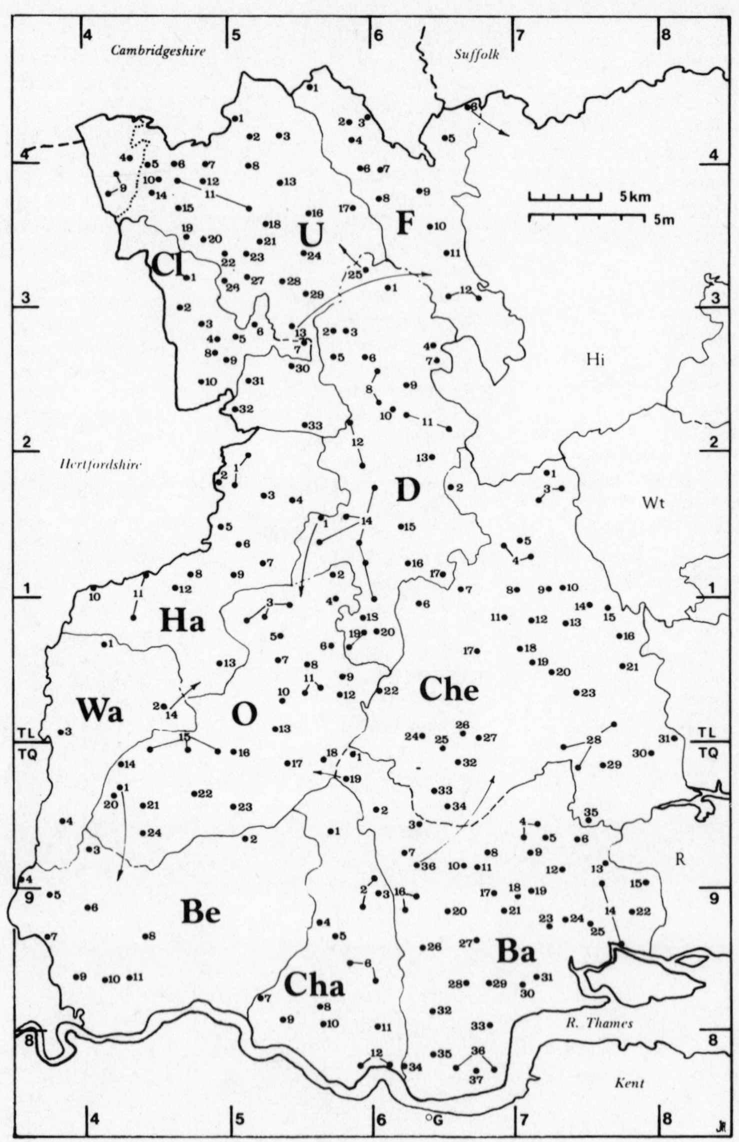

ESSEX HUNDREDS AND HALF-HUNDREDS (WEST)

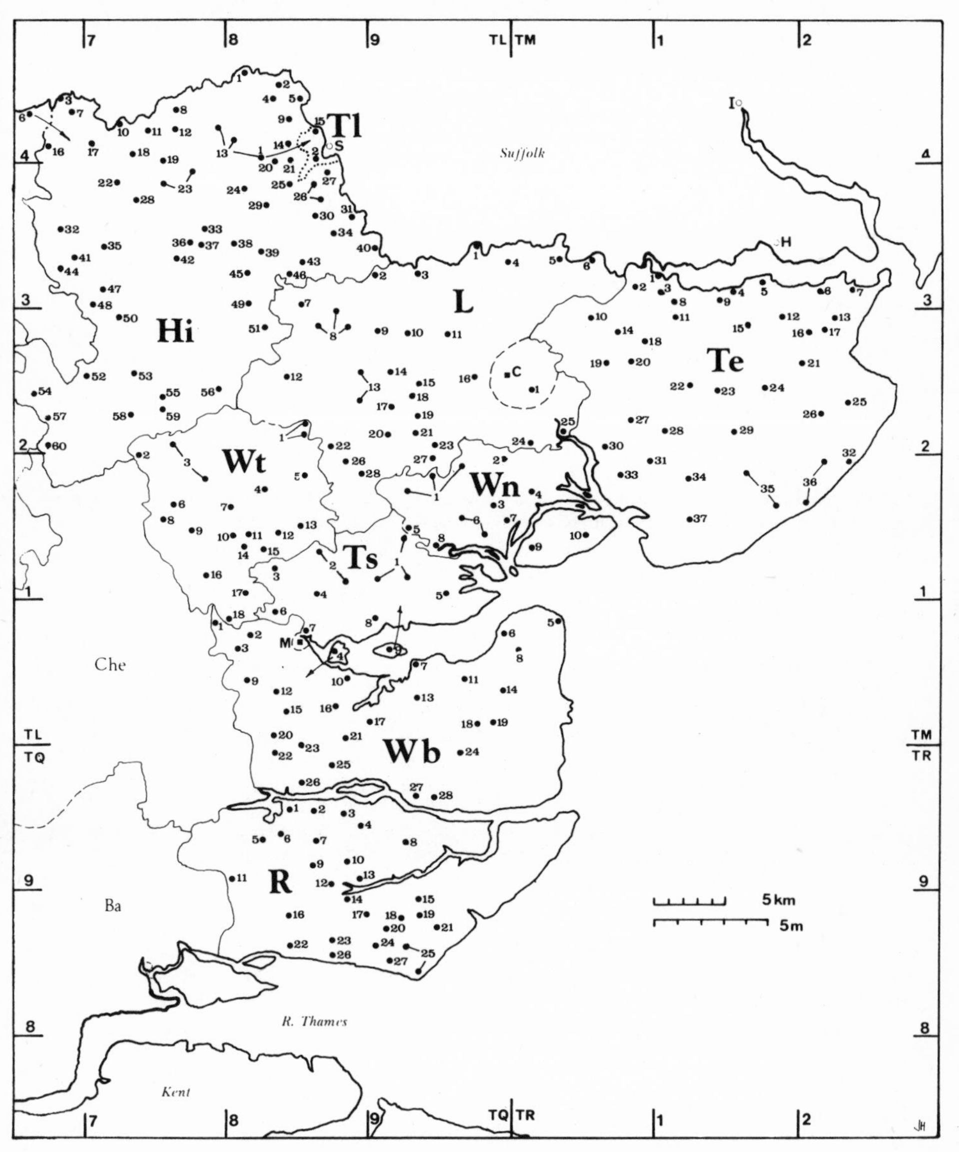

ESSEX HUNDREDS AND HALF-HUNDREDS (EAST)

SYSTEMS OF REFERENCE TO THE TWO VOLUMES OF DOMESDAY BOOK

The manuscript of the larger volume (here referred to as DB) is divided into numbered chapters, and the chapters into sections, usually marked by large initials and red ink. Farley did not number the sections and later historians, using his edition, have referred to the text of DB by folio numbers, which cannot be closer than an entire page or column. Moreover, several different ways of referring to the same column have been devised. In 1816 Ellis used three separate systems in his indices: (i) on pages i–cvii, 435--518, 537–570; (ii) on pages 1–144; (iii) on pages 145–433 and 519–535. Other systems have since come into use, notably that used by Vinogradoff, here followed. The present edition numbers the sections, the normal practicable form of close reference; but since all discussion of DB for two hundred years has been obliged to refer to folio or column, a comparative table will help to locate references given. The five columns below give Vinogradoff's notation, Ellis's three systems, and that used by Welldon Finn and others. Maitland, Stenton, Darby, and others have usually followed Ellis (i).

Vinogradoff	*Ellis (i)*	*Ellis (ii)*	*Ellis (iii)*	*Finn*
152a	152	152a	152	152ai
152b	152	152a	152.2	152a2
152c	152b	152b	152b	152bi
152d	152b	152b	152b2	152b2

The manuscript of Little Domesday Book (here referred to as LDB), in which the text of the Essex survey is preserved, has one column per page but is again divided into numbered chapters and the chapters into sections, usually distinguished by paragraph-marks. Modern users of LDB have referred to its text by folio number, e.g. 152(a) 152b. Farley's edition presents both *recto* and *verso* of a folio on one printed page. In Essex, the relation between the column notation and the chapters and sections is:

1a	Landholders	26a,b	18,45 – 20, 7	53a,b	27, 3 – 27,13	81a,b	37,11 – 38, 1
b	1, 1 – 1, 2	27a,b	20, 7 – 20,19	54a,b	27,13 – 28, 2	82a,b	38, 2 – 39, 1
2a,b	1, 2 – 1, 4	28a,b	20,19 – 20,27	55a,b	28, 3 – 28,12	83a,b	39, 2 – 39,12
3a,b	1, 4 – 1,11	29a,b	20,28 – 20,37	56a,b	28,13 – 29, 2	84a,b	40, 1 – 40, 9
4a,b	1,12 – 1,19	30a,b	20,37 – 20,46	57a,b	29, 2 – 30, 4	85a,b	40, 9 – 41,10
5a,b	1,19 – 1,25	31a,b	20,46 – 20,56	58a,b	30, 4 – 30,13	86a,b	41,10 – 42, 6
6a,b	1,25 – 1,27	32a,b	20,56 – 20,67	59a,b	30,14 – 30,22	87a,b	42, 7 – 43, 5
7a,b	1,28 – 1,31	33a,b	20,67 – 20,75	60a,b	30,22 – 30,30	88a,b	43, 5 – 45, 1
8a,b	2, 1 – 2, 9	34a,b	20,75 – 20,80	61a,b	30,30 – 30,40	89a,b	45, 1 – 47, 3
9a	Landholders	35a,b	21, 1 – 21,12	62a,b	30,40 – 30,49	90a,b	48, 1 – 50, 1
b	3, 1 – 3, 5	36a,b	22, 1 – 22, 9	63a,b	30,49 – 32, 5	91a,b	51, 1 – 54, 2
10a,b	3, 6 – 3,13	37a,b	22,10 – 22,18	64a,b	32, 6 – 32,14	92a,b	54, 2 – 57, 5
11a,b	3,13 – 4, 9	38a,b	22,19 – 23, 3	65a,b	32,14 – 32,23	93a,b	57, 5 – 61, 2
12a,b	4, 9 – 5, 3	39a,b	23, 3 – 23,16	66a,b	32,23 – 32,30	94a,b	61, 2 – 66, 2
13a,b	5, 3 – 5,12	40a,b	23,16 – 23,34	67a,b	32,30 – 32,40	95a,b	66, 2 – 69, 2
14a,b	5,12 – 6, 9	41a,b	23,34 – 23,43	68a,b	32,40 – 33, 2	96a,b	69, 3 – 73, 1
15a,b	6, 9 – 8, 1	42a,b	24, 1 – 24,10	69a,b	33, 2 – 33,11	97a,b	73, 1 – 81, 1
16a,b	8, 1 – 8,11	43a,b	24,10 – 24,20	70a,b	33,11 – 33,17	98a,b	81, 1 – 88, 2
17a	Landholders	44a,b	24,20 – 24,28	71a,b	33,17 – 34, 2	99a,b	89, 1 – 90,14
b	9, 1 – 9, 7	45a,b	24,28 – 24,42	72a,b	34, 2 – 34, 9	100a,b	90,15 – 90,34
18a,b	9, 7 – 10, 1	46a,b	24,42 – 24,53	73a,b	34, 9 – 34,19	101a,b	90,35 – 90,53
19a,b	10, 2 – 11, 3	47a,b	24,53 – 24,61	74a,b	34,19 – 34,27	102a,b	90,53 – 90,73
20a,b	11, 3 – 14, 2	48a,b	24,61 – 24,67	75a,b	34,27 – 34,36	103a,b	90,74 – 90,87
21a,b	14, 2 – 15, 2	49a,b	25, 1 – 25,10	76a,b	34,36 – 35, 5	104a,b	B1 – B3a
22a,b	15, 2 – 18, 5	50a,b	25,10 – 25,19	77a,b	35, 5 – 35,12	105a,b	B3a
23a,b	18, 5 – 18,19	51a,b	25,19 – 25,26	78a,b	35,13 – 36, 6	106a,b	B3a – B3p
24a,b	18,20 – 18,34	52a,b	26, 1 – 27, 3	79a,b	36, 6 – 37, 2	107a,b	B3p – B7
25a,b	18,34 – 18,45			80a,b	37, 2 – 37,11		

TECHNICAL TERMS

Most of the words expressing measurements have to be translitterated. Translation may not, however, dodge other problems by the use of obsolete or made-up words which do not exist in modern English. The translations here used are given below in italics. They cannot be exact; they aim at the nearest modern equivalent.

ANTECESSOR. Person whom a tenant had followed in the rightful possession of his holding; also the previous holder of an office. *predecessor*

BORDARIUS. Cultivator of inferior status, usually with a little land. *smallholder*

CARUCA. A plough, with the oxen which pulled it, usually reckoned as 8. *plough*

CARUCATA. See 8,9 note. *carucate*

CENSARIUS. See 7,1 note. *tributary*

COMMENDATUS (adj.). Relating to the situation in which a free man gave up rights over his land to someone who could guarantee his protection. *under the patronage of*

CONSUETUDO. A fixed rent or service payable at regular intervals. *customary due*

DOMINIUM. The mastery or dominion of a lord (*dominus*); including ploughs, land, men, villages, etc., reserved for the lord's use; often concentrated in a home farm or demesne. *lordship*

FEUDUM. Continental variant, not used in England before 1066, of *feuum* (the Latin form of Old English *feoh*, cattle, money, possessions in general); either a landholder's holding, or land held under the terms of a specific grant. *Holding*

FIRMA. Old English *feorm*, provisions due to the King or lord; a fixed sum paid in place of these and of other miscellaneous dues. *revenue*

HIDA. A unit of land measurement, reckoned in DB at 120 fiscal acres; 4 *virgates*; see Sussex, Appendix. *hide*

HUNDREDUM and DIMIDIUM HUNDREDUM. Administrative districts within a shire, each of whose assemblies of notables and village representatives usually met once a month. *hundred* and *half-hundred*

MANERIUM. A territorial and jurisdictional holding. *manor*

PREPOSITUS. Old English *gerefa*, a local official of the King or lord. *reeve*

SOCA. 'Soke', from Old English *socn*, seeking, comparable with Latin *quaestio*. Jurisdiction, with the right to receive fines and other dues from those who paid suit to the court of the district in which such *soca* was exercised; jurisdiction included the right to settle a dispute or *saca*, from Old English *sāc*, and sometimes the terms *soca* and *saca* are used in combination to show that the jurisdiction is of the fullest sort. *jurisdiction* and (payment of) *suit*

SOCHEMANNUS. '*Soke man*', liable to attend the court of a *soca* and serve its lords; before 1066 often with more land and higher status than villagers; bracketed in the Commissioners' brief with the *liber homo* (free man); see Bedfordshire, Appendix. *Freeman*

TEIGNUS. Person of superior status; originally one of the King's military companions, later often in his service in an administrative capacity. *thane*

T.R.E. *tempore regis Edwardi*, in King Edward's time. *before 1066*

VILLA. Translating Old English *tūn*, estate, town, village. The later distinction between a small *village* and a large *town* was not yet in use in 1066. *village* or *town*

VILLANUS. Member of a *villa*, usually with more land than a *bordarius*. *villager*

VIRGATA. A quarter of a hide; 30 fiscal acres in DB. *virgate*